The eighteenth-century Chu[illegible]
has been unduly neglected by[illegible]
Despite the pioneering work of Norman Sykes the century and a half before the Tractarian revival is widely regarded as a dark age, a time of clerical sloth and negligence. Religion is seen as peripheral to the main trends in Georgian society. In the last decade, however, there has been a resurgence of interest in this subject, as historians have examined how the Church responded to the challenges and problems that resulted from the ending of its legal monopoly over the religious life of the nation in 1689 and from the social, economic and demographic developments of the period. Political, social and cultural historians have joined with ecclesiastical historians in this process. The diversity of approaches is reflected in the contents of this volume, which range from the intellectual debates over toleration in the 1690s and the ecclesiastical policy of Lord North to the character of pre-Tractarian High Churchmanship and the pastoral problems caused by industrialization in Saddleworth. The full-length introduction provides an overview of the fruits of recent scholarship. Whilst this collection does not constitute a comprehensive history of the Anglican Church between 1689 and 1833, it demonstrates that our understanding of eighteenth-century England will remain incomplete until we have fully integrated religion into its history. As such this volume will be of interest not only to ecclesiastical historians but also to all students of the 'long' eighteenth century.

JOHN WALSH is a Senior Research Fellow of Jesus College, Oxford. He was Birkbeck Lecturer at Cambridge University in 1987, and has held visiting appointments at Brown University, the University of South Carolina and the Huntington Library. He edited (with G.V. Bennett) *Essays in Modern English Church History* (1966), and has published widely on eighteenth-century religious history.

COLIN HAYDON is Senior Lecturer in History at King Alfred's College, Winchester. He was Visiting Professor at the University of Wisconsin – Eau Claire, and is the author of *Anti-Catholicism in Eighteenth-Century England c. 1714–1780: A Political and Social Study* (Manchester, 1993).

STEPHEN TAYLOR is a Lecturer in History at the University of Reading. He has held visiting appointments at Yale University, and has published several articles on aspects of Anglican history.

The eighteenth-century Church of England has been unduly neglected by historians. Despite the pioneering work of Norman Sykes the century and a half before the Tractarian revival is widely regarded as a dark age, a time of clerical sloth and negligence. Religion is seen as peripheral to the main trends in Georgian society. In the last decade, however, there has been a resurgence of interest in this subject, as historians have examined how the Church responded to the challenges and problems that resulted from the ending of its legal monopoly over the religious life of the nation in 1689 and from the social, economic and demographic developments of the period. Political, social and cultural historians have joined with ecclesiastical historians in this process. The diversity of approaches is reflected in the contents of this volume, which range from the intellectual debates over toleration in the 1690s and the ecclesiastical policy of Lord North to the character of pre-Tractarian High Churchmanship and the pastoral problems caused by industrialization in Saddleworth. The full-length introduction provides an overview of the fruits of recent scholarship. Whilst this collection does not constitute a comprehensive history of the Anglican Church between 1689 and 1833, it demonstrates that our understanding of eighteenth-century England will remain incomplete until we have fully integrated religion into its history. As such this volume will be of interest not only to ecclesiastical historians but also to all students of the 'long' eighteenth century.

The Church of England, *c*. 1689 – *c*. 1833

The Church of England c.1689 – c.1833

From Toleration to Tractarianism

Edited by

JOHN WALSH
Jesus College, Oxford

COLIN HAYDON
King Alfred's College, Winchester

and

STEPHEN TAYLOR
University of Reading

CAMBRIDGE
UNIVERSITY PRESS

Published by the Press Syndicate of the University of Cambridge
The Pitt Building, Trumpington Street, Cambridge CB2 1RP
40 West 20th Street, New York, NY 10011-4211, USA
10 Stamford Road, Oakleigh, Melbourne 3166, Australia

First published 1993

Printed in Great Britain at the University Press, Cambridge

A catalogue record for this book is available from the British Library

Library of Congress cataloguing in publication data

The Church of England *c.* 1689 – *c.* 1833: from toleration to Tractarianism
/ edited by John Walsh, Colin Haydon, and Stephen Taylor.
p. cm.
ISBN 0 521 41732 5 (hard)
1. Church of England – History – 18th century. 2. Anglican Communion – England – History – 18th century. 3. England – Church history – 18th century. I. Walsh, John, 1927– . II. Haydon, Colin, 1955– . III. Taylor, Stephen, 1960– .
BX5088.C48 1993
283′.42′09033—dc20 92-42707 CIP

ISBN 0 521 41732 5 hardback

SE

Contents

Preface

The starting-point for any research into the eighteenth-century Church remains Norman Sykes's *Church and State in England in the Eighteenth Century*, published over half a century ago. This is a testimony to Sykes's scholarship, but it is also indicative of the relative neglect of the subject by subsequent historians. Recently, however, eighteenth-century church history has experienced a renaissance. It has attracted attention not just from practitioners of traditional ecclesiastical history, but also from others who have become aware of the significance of religion in a period still often treated as indifferentist, rationalist and secular. Some of these are political historians who recognize how religious affiliations continued to fashion political identity, not merely in the 'Church in danger' conflicts of Anne's reign, but long afterwards. Others are social historians, increasingly aware of the importance of religion in the formation of social and cultural identities.

The aim of this volume is to bring together some of the fruits of this research and thus, we hope, to make it more accessible to those who would not regard themselves as 'church historians'. The volume does not claim to be a collective history of the Church of England in the 'long' eighteenth century. Indeed, it would be difficult at present to write a new, comprehensive survey of the Georgian Church. These essays are intended quite consciously as an interim statement. It is hoped that they will give the reader some idea of the ways in which our understanding of the subject has been refashioned since Sykes, provide an introduction to research which is opening up new themes in the history of eighteenth-century religion and perhaps stimulate further work. Inevitably, there are gaps. The main focus of recent studies has been the institutional life of the Church of England, often within a broad political, social or cultural context. Remarkably little attention, on the other hand, has been given to theological issues, despite the need for research into a field in which the most obvious authority is still Leslie Stephen's *English Thought in the Eighteenth Century*, first published in 1876.

The essays collected in this volume began life as some of the papers presented to a conference on 'The Functioning of the Church of England 1662–1833' held at King Alfred's College, Winchester, in July 1990. We would like to thank all the participants at that conference for providing a critical and stimulating environment and King Alfred's College for their support in organizing the event. The contributors have subsequently made the editorial task much easier by their promptness in keeping to deadlines and dealing with queries. We are grateful to Derek Beales, Arthur Burns, Grayson Ditchfield, Martin Fitzpatrick, David Hempton, Paul Langford, John Stephens and Christopher Zealley for reading the Introduction and for their advice and comments on it. The History Department at Reading has been generous with secretarial assistance and we are grateful to Mrs Carol Mackay and, especially, Mrs Elizabeth Berry for their work in typing the manuscript. Finally, we would like to thank Richard Sharp for his assistance with the cover illustration.

J. D. W.
C. M. H.
S. J. C. T.

Abbreviations

Alum. Cantab.	John and J.A. Venn, *Alumni Cantabrigienses. A Biographical List of All Known Students, Graduates and Holders of Offices at the University of Cambridge, from the Earliest Times to 1900. Part I. From the Earliest Time to 1751* (4 vols., Cambridge, 1922–7) Idem, *Alumni Cantabrigienses. A Biographical List of All Known Students, Graduates and Holders of Offices at the University of Cambridge, from the Earliest Times to 1900. Part II. From 1752 to 1900* (6 vols., Cambridge, 1940–54)
Alum. Oxon.	Joseph Foster, *Alumni Oxonienses: The Members of the University of Oxford, 1500–1714: Their Parentage, Birthplace, and Year of Birth, with a Record of their Degrees* (4 vols., Oxford, 1891–2) Idem, *Alumni Oxonienses: The Members of the University of Oxford, 1715–1886: Their Parentage, Birthplace, and Year of Birth, with a Record of their Degrees* (4 vols., Oxford, 1888)
BL	British Library
Bodl.	Bodleian Library, Oxford
Clark, *English Society*	J.C.D. Clark, *English Society 1688–1832. Ideology, Social Structure and Political Practice during the Ancien Regime* (Cambridge, 1985)
DNB	*Dictionary of National Biography*
EHR	*English Historical Review*
ESRO	East Sussex Record Office

HJ	*Historical Journal*
HMC	*Historical Manuscripts Commission*
JBS	*Journal of British Studies*
JEH	*Journal of Ecclesiastical History*
JRL	John Rylands University Library of Manchester
LPL	Lambeth Palace Library, London
Parl. Hist.	*The Parliamentary History of England from the Earliest Period to the Year 1803* (36 vols., 1806–20)
PP	*Past and Present*
PRO	Public Record Office, London
RO	Record Office
SCH	*Studies in Church History*
SPCK	Society for the Promotion of Christian Knowledge, Archives, London
Sykes, *Church and State*	Norman Sykes, *Church and State in England in the Eighteenth Century* (Cambridge, 1934)
VCH	*Victoria County History*

Place of publication is London unless otherwise stated.

1 Introduction: the Church and Anglicanism in the 'long' eighteenth century

John Walsh and Stephen Taylor

Despite some valuable recent studies, most notably Jonathan Clark's influential *English Society 1688–1832* (1985),[1] the history of the eighteenth-century Church of England has long been neglected. In 1860 Mark Pattison wrote that 'the genuine Anglican omits that period from the history of the Church altogether. In constructing his *Catena Patrum* he closes his list with Waterland or Brett, and leaps at once to 1833, when the *Tracts for the Times* commenced – as Charles II dated his reign from his father's death.'[2] The same holds good for church history in many university and college syllabuses today, in which the eighteenth century is quietly omitted.

Since Victorian times the historiography of the eighteenth-century Church has often had a strongly judgemental slant. High Churchmen who revered the Caroline divines have found it hard to forgive the expulsion of the Nonjurors, 'the candlestick of the Church'; Evangelicals have censured it for its rejection of the Methodist movement of Wesley and Whitefield. Victorian Churchmen saw it as an era of decline, a period 'of lethargy instead of activity, of worldliness instead of spirituality, of self-seeking instead of self-denial, of grossness instead of refinement'.[3] This was the case not only with clerical partisans but even with the most accomplished and fair-minded of church historians: the tone of Abbey and Overton's Victorian classic, *The English Church in the Eighteenth Century*, was gloomy. They held that the state of the Church at Anne's accession in 1702 was flourishing and that the green shoots of revival were visible by 1800, but in the decades which lay between 'the Church partook of the general sordidness of the age; it was an age of great material prosperity, but of moral and spiritual poverty, such as hardly finds a parallel in our history'.[4] The violent party battles which gave rise to 'the Sacheverell "phrensy"' and the bitter

1 See also the important debates in *PP*, 115 and 117 (1987), and *Albion*, 21, 3 (1989).

2 M. Pattison, 'Tendencies of Religious Thought in England, 1688–1750', in *Essays*, ed. H. Nettleship (2 vols., Oxford, 1889), II, 43.

3 J. H. Overton and F. Relton, *The English Church from the Accession of George I to the End of the Eighteenth Century (1714–1800)* (1906), p. 1.

4 C. J. Abbey and J. H. Overton, *The English Church in the Eighteenth Century* (2 vols., 1878), II, 4.

Bangorian controversy were replaced under George I by 'spiritual lethargy', a 'sluggish calm'. From time to time Abbey and Overton attempted to qualify their depressing picture. They conceded that the eighteenth-century Church produced extremely able defenders of the faith – men of the calibre of Law, Butler and Berkeley. They shifted some of the blame for the low standards of clerical behaviour on to the corrupting influences of secular society in the age of Walpole. They derived some consolation from the comforting conviction that, if things were bad in the English Church, they were even worse in Catholic France.[5]

It was not until the appearance of Norman Sykes's *Church and State in England in the Eighteenth Century* in 1934 – a landmark in Anglican historiography – that the reputation of the eighteenth-century Church began to be seriously rehabilitated. Sykes's tone was one of qualified approval. He insisted that the Georgian Church should not be judged by anachronistic nineteenth-century standards. Many of its alleged abuses were age-old problems. The pluralism and non-residence which so many critics adduced were familiar in the middle ages and, indeed, among the Caroline clergy so admired by the Tractarians: Lancelot Andrewes was a pluralist on a grand scale, as was the devout Sancroft. If Hanoverian prelates were regularly absent from their sees for part of the year while attending Parliament, so too were medieval bishops, dragged away for protracted periods of service in the royal household. Moreover, Hanoverian Churchmen had to face new and unprecedented difficulties. In the post-Revolutionary world they had to learn to live with the pastoral problems caused by religious toleration and, later in the century, with those of increasing urbanization and industrialization. As an overall judgement on the eighteenth-century clergy, Sykes cited with approval the verdict of Ollard and Walker on those of the diocese of York in 1743: 'a body of dutiful and conscientious men, trying to do their work according to the standards of their day'.[6]

The analytical force and descriptive detail of Sykes's *Church and State* have ensured that it still remains the starting-point for anyone interested in the condition of the Hanoverian Church. Its conclusions, however, have not commanded universal acceptance and the debate between optimists and pessimists has continued to dominate the writings of historians. Judgements identical to those of the nineteenth century can be found today in simple-minded denominational histories. Highly pejorative verdicts are still visible in the work of sophisticated secular historians. In the tone of J. H. Plumb we can detect the detached, Enlightenment irony of a latter-day

[5] Ibid., I, 29, 2–3; II, 54. [6] Quoted Sykes, *Church and State*, p. 6.

Gibbon, as he talks of the 'worldliness, almost ... venality' of eighteenth-century prelates and of parish clergy so underemployed that 'time hung heavily on their hands'.[7] Historians further to the left see the Church as a central part of 'Old Corruption', parasitic on the labour and wealth of the working community – an angle of attack which carries on the tradition of early nineteenth-century radicals such as Cobbett, or John Wade in his *Extraordinary Black Book*. A similar judgement informs Roy Porter's damning conclusion that 'the year 1800 dawned with the Anglican Church ill-equipped to serve the nation ... But who missed it?'[8] Among specialist church historians roseate views of the eighteenth-century Church have by no means swept the field. Both favourable and adverse verdicts are still being delivered. Against the cautious optimism of Jeremy Gregory in his essay, 'The eighteenth-century Reformation' (below), must be set the cautious pessimism of Peter Virgin's important recent book, *The Church in an Age of Negligence*, which criticizes the established Church for a repeated failure to reform itself until forced to do so in the 1830s.[9]

In some respects, therefore, the debate about the Georgian Church has moved on little since the 1930s. The arguments of optimists and pessimists have a judgemental character that would be familiar to Sykes. Nonetheless, this debate has been highly productive, in that we now know much more about the condition of the Georgian Church. Where Sykes relied on memoirs, we now have figures. The last twenty-five years in particular have witnessed a proliferation of local studies of church life at every level, from the diocese to the deanery, from the county to the city. Some have concentrated on a single episcopate; others have looked at continuity and change through the whole century. A striking omission in all this work has been the capital. This has been partly remedied by Viviane Barrie-Curien's contribution to this volume and her new book:[10] her essay here exemplifies both the evidential basis and the conclusions of much recent work. The records of Queen Anne's Bounty, of visitation returns, of Parliamentary inquiries and of the Ecclesiastical Commissioners have all been scrutinized. As a result a considerable corpus of hard, quantified evidence is now available for many parts of the country on the wealth of the clergy, the frequency of church services, pluralism, non-residence, church building, the activities of the bishops and proceedings in the ecclesiastical courts. What, then, do we know?

[7] J. H. Plumb, *England in the Eighteenth Century* (Harmondsworth, 1950), pp. 43–4.

[8] R. Porter, *English Society in the Eighteenth Century* (Harmondsworth, 1982), p. 191.

[9] P. Virgin, *The Church in an Age of Negligence 1700–1840* (Cambridge, 1989).

[10] V. Barrie-Curien, *Clergé et pastorale en Angleterre au XVIIIe siècle. Le diocèse de Londres* (Paris, 1992).

The state of the Church

At the top of the ecclesiastical hierarchy stood the twenty-seven English and Welsh bishops. Even if we exclude the bishop of Sodor and Man, who had no seat in the House of Lords and whose diocese consisted of only seventeen parishes, there were marked differences between them, in both duties and emoluments. Their dioceses varied considerably in size, from Rochester, with fewer than 150 parishes, to Lincoln, with over 1,500. In 1762 the archbishop of Canterbury was receiving £7,000 per annum, the bishop of Lincoln £1,500 and the bishop of Bristol only £450. Sykes's verdict on these men, the governors of the clergy, as deserving 'a greater proportion of credit than of censure', has failed to command widespread assent.[11] Eighteenth-century bishops are commonly presented as undeserving younger sons of the aristocracy or political hacks, neglectful of their pastoral responsibilities. There is certainly no doubt that the episcopate was an increasingly aristocratic body. The fathers of over one fifth of the bishops appointed by George III were peers or close relatives of peers; none of Anne's creations fall into this category.[12] But the episcopal bench rarely provided sinecure posts for the well connected, despite George Grenville's statement that there was a group of 'bishoprics of ease for men of family and fashion'. On the contrary, the aristocrats included men of significant pastoral zeal and energy, including James Beauclerk and Robert Drummond.[13] And the Church remained a career open to the talent of the humbly born, as the careers of Potter, Gibson, Warburton and Hurd proved. As far as politics is concerned, it was as difficult for eighteenth-century bishops to balance the duties of 'prelate' and 'pastor' as it had been for their predecessors. In some respects it was more difficult, as annual Parliamentary sessions, the norm after the Revolution, increased the demands made on bishops and kept many of them in London for a considerable time each year. It must be recognized, however, that they were not merely ministerial voting fodder, but the representatives in Parliament of both Church and clergy, a role doubly important in the absence of a sitting Convocation after 1717. On occasions, and especially during debates concerning the Church or religion, they demonstrated a striking degree of independence. Moreover, there is considerable evidence that they were

[11] Sykes, *Church and State*, p. 187.

[12] N. Ravitch, *Sword and Mitre. Government and Episcopate in France and England in the Age of Aristocracy* (The Hague, 1966), p. 120.

[13] Quoted Sykes, *Church and State*, p. 157. For Beauclerk see W. Marshall, 'Episcopal Activity in the Hereford and Oxford Dioceses, 1660–1760', *Midland History*, 8 (1983), 106–20. For Drummond see S. Taylor, 'Church and State in England in the Mid-Eighteenth Century: The Newcastle Years 1742–62', PhD dissertation, University of Cambridge, 1987, p. 128.

competent administrators, who discharged diligently the episcopal tasks of visitation, confirmation and ordination. In 1718 Archbishop Wake wrote that 'the confirmations had never been so regular throughout this kingdom as within the last thirty years, nor the episcopal visitations and that by the bishops in person, so constant'.[14] In general, visitations, usually combined with confirmations, occurred every three or four years. Bishops turned visitations into more effective tools of pastoral oversight and tried to make confirmation more orderly, and thus more spiritually edifying. Even Benjamin Hoadly and Lancelot Blackburne, whose careers are so often used to illustrate the 'notorious' failings of the episcopate, are revealed to have been diligent, if not outstanding, Churchmen.

With the bishops absent in London for at least part of the year, much depended on the effectiveness of the diocesan administration, and especially the archdeacons. Examples of good and bad archdeacons are easy to find, but the history of diocesan administration in the Georgian Church remains to be written, as does that of the cathedral chapters.[15] Only one aspect of the administrative structure has received even limited attention: the ecclesiastical courts. Here too, much work remains to be done, but it is possible to provide an outline sketch. The church courts continued to have an important role in hearing testamentary and marriage cases throughout the century, but their disciplinary power had been in decline since the Reformation. They were revived at the Restoration along with the rest of the structure of the established Church, though they appear to have found increasing problems in securing compliance, and it has often been assumed that their disciplinary power was finally broken by the Revolution. Indeed, while anti-clerical Whigs continued to condemn the courts as a relic of popery, the weakness of church discipline in the eighteenth century was generally recognized and deplored by the clergy, and sneered at by the Dissenters. The Isle of Man under Bishop Thomas Wilson, though praised as a model by High Churchmen, is widely seen as an exception: not many diocesans would have sanctioned the punishment meted out by his correction court to a fallen woman in 1715 – 'to be dragged from a boat on such a day as the vicar will appoint'.[16] But recent research suggests that the picture of decay must be qualified. The diocese of Ely, where the courts appear to have collapsed within two decades of the Revolution, may well have been untypical. The ability of the ecclesiastical courts to enforce attendance at church was undoubtedly undermined by James II's Declarations of

[14] Quoted Sykes, *Church and State*, p. 120.

[15] But see J. Shuler, 'The Pastoral and Ecclesiastical Administration of the Diocese of Durham 1721–71', PhD dissertation, University of Durham, 1975, esp. chs. 3 and 4, and the forthcoming histories of Lincoln and Canterbury Cathedrals.

[16] Quoted M. Kinnear, 'The Correction Court in the Diocese of Carlisle, 1704–56', *Church History*, 59 (1990), 205.

Indulgence and by the Toleration Act. In the diocese of Hereford presentments for non-attendance were almost unknown after 1687. Elsewhere they were rare, although in Oxford they formed an important element in the courts' business until the 1730s. However, in many areas the courts continued to act as guardians of the nation's morality, kept alive not only by clerical zeal from above, but also by pressure from within the community itself. From the standpoint of the early nineteenth century decay is undeniable, but the chronology is different for each diocese. In the diocese of Carlisle the courts heard an increasing number of cases through the early eighteenth century, and were most active in the later 1730s, before declining. Jan Albers shows that the deanery courts in Lancashire were prosecuting sexual offences more vigorously, and more effectively, in the mid-eighteenth century than earlier; the number of cases peaked in north Lancashire in the 1770s, though it declined rapidly in the industrializing south of the county a little before that, and entered into a precipitate decline in the last two decades of the century. Individuals could still be found performing public penance in the mid-nineteenth century. The pertinacity of the church courts through the eighteenth century may say something about the resilience of the Church's administrative system; it certainly offers evidence of continued respect for the policing authority of the Church and its role as a focus for community values.[17]

The greatest advance since Sykes has come in our knowledge of the lower clergy, Addison's 'clerical subalterns'. Simple generalizations are impossible – the rector of Stanhope, County Durham, a living worth more than many bishoprics, had little in common with an impoverished Welsh curate. The records of Queen Anne's Bounty have ensured that we know much more about poorer benefices than richer ones. In 1736, 5,638 were classified as poor, that is, worth £50 per annum or under. In some respects the picture was bleaker than this statistic might suggest; almost 20 per cent of these were worth less than £10 and neither of these figures reflects the plight of the unbeneficed curates. Regional variations were marked, the north and the west in general containing more poor livings than the south and east – 18 per cent of Winchester benefices were poor compared with 79 per cent in Llandaff.[18] Overall, incomes increased dramatically in the course of the

[17] M. Cross, 'The Church and Local Society in the Diocese of Ely, *c.*1630–*c.*1730', PhD dissertation, University of Cambridge, 1991, pp. 302–3; W. M. Marshall, 'The Administration of the Dioceses of Hereford and Oxford 1660–1760', PhD dissertation, University of Bristol, 1978, pp. 78–9; Kinnear, 'Correction Court', pp. 191–206; J. Albers, 'Seeds of Contention: Society, Politics and the Church of England in Lancashire, 1689–1790', PhD dissertation, Yale University, 1988, 222–7; O. Chadwick, *The Victorian Church* (2 vols., 1966–70), I, 487; P. Rycroft, 'Church, Chapel and Community in Craven, 1764–1851', DPhil dissertation, University of Oxford, 1988, pp. 133–4.

[18] Durham and Norwich were exceptions. I. Green, 'The First Five Years of Queen Anne's Bounty', in *Princes and Paupers in the English Church 1500–1800*, ed. R. O'Day and F. Heal (Leicester, 1981), pp. 231–54; Taylor, 'Church and State', p. 39.

eighteenth and early nineteenth centuries, helped by the general rise in incomes from the land and by favourable tithe commutation during enclosure. Surprisingly, perhaps, it was the poorest clergy who benefited most from this process.[19] By the early nineteenth century only one third of livings fell below the clerical poverty line, now estimated at £150, compared with half in 1736. As Virgin points out, however, pluralism and private wealth meant that clerical incomes were often significantly higher than benefice incomes. Even so, 'extravagantly wealthy incumbents were few and far between'. Only seventy-six English and Welsh clergy received over £2,000 a year from ecclesiastical sources. In England the typical income was £275 per annum; in Wales only £172.[20]

The growing wealth of the clergy was probably accompanied by a rise in their social status. From the beginning of the eighteenth century the great majority were university educated, a fact which set even the poorest of them apart from their parishioners. But the eighteenth century witnessed their growing integration into local landed society. Tithe commutation at enclosure made more of them substantial landowners and from the 1740s clerical JPs were increasingly common. While the Church drew a high proportion of its clergy from clerical families throughout the eighteenth century, the regional studies of Paul Langford and Viviane Barrie-Curien have shown that the latter part of the century in particular saw an increase in recruitment from gentry families. Nonetheless, some caution must be expressed about the gentrification of the clergy. Overall, it seems unlikely that more than 20 per cent of clergymen came from the landed gentry in the late Georgian period, though the figure was significantly higher in the richer parts of England, and Langford has recently suggested that 'the trend towards a body of clergy whose background and upbringing were in essence those of laymen, seems to have been peculiarly a late eighteenth-century one'.[21]

What provision did the clergy make for public worship? This question, above all, has been used in recent research to assess the vitality of the Hanoverian Church. Three areas of church life have received particular attention – pluralism and non-residence by the clergy; the maintenance and building of churches; and the frequency of services. Here a considerable amount of evidence has been accumulated which allows us to reassess some common generalizations about the eighteenth-century Church.

One of the greatest failings of the Georgian Church is often seen as its inability to attain its self-imposed objective of a resident minister in every

[19] Virgin, *Age of Negligence*, p. 73.
[20] Ibid., p. 90; Green, 'Queen Anne's Bounty', p. 249.
[21] Virgin, *Age of Negligence*, pp. 94, 110; P. Langford, 'The English Clergy and the American Revolution', in *The Transformation of Political Culture*, ed. E. Hellmuth (Oxford, 1990), p. 304n; ch. 3 below.

parish in England and Wales who maintained the standard of double-duty; that is, of two services each Sunday. The non-residence of the clergy was a complaint frequently levelled against the Church of England by reformers before the Reformation and in the reigns of Elizabeth and James I, but the situation in the Georgian age was worse than in earlier periods. Immediately before the Reformation about three-quarters of all parishes were in the hands of resident incumbents; by the 1820s this had fallen to four out of every ten.[22] Moreover, the eighteenth century had witnessed not improvement, but deterioration. In Devon the proportion of non-residents rose from 34 per cent in 1744 to 41 per cent in 1779. In the diocese of Oxford 51 per cent of incumbents had been resident at the time of Thomas Secker's primary visitation in 1738, but only 39 per cent were forty years later.[23] There was, however, considerable regional variation. The dioceses of the north and west appear to have been less badly affected than those of the south and east. And within dioceses there was a contrast between town and country. The larger towns, in particular, were often well supplied with clergy, and London was so well endowed with preacherships that the vast majority of its parishes were served by two or more ministers.[24]

At first sight the figures for non-residence do much to support the claim that the parochial system was severely weakened in the eighteenth century, in a way which undermined the monopolistic claims of the Church of England and its influence in the localities. Alan Gilbert has calculated, on the basis of the Parliamentary returns of 1810, that over 1,000 parishes were 'simply unattended by ministers of the Established Church'.[25] But, as Mark Smith's essay on Saddleworth reveals, a non-resident incumbent was not necessarily incompatible with a high standard of pastoral care. Indeed, various strategies were available for dealing with non-residence and at a local level there is remarkably little evidence of total neglect. In 33 out of 100 cases of non-residence in the diocese of Oxford in 1778, for example, the incumbent lived nearby and performed the duty himself, a resident stipendiary curate was employed in 27 parishes, and the remaining 40 were served by neighbouring clergy.[26]

Reasons for non-residence were varied. Ill-health and the absence of a parsonage are among the most obvious. But the single most important cause of non-residence was pluralism – in 1705, 16 per cent of the beneficed clergy were pluralists, but by 1775, 36 per cent were.[27] Some contemporar-

[22] P. Heath, *The English Parish Clergy on the Eve of the Reformation* (1969), p. 57; Virgin, *Age of Negligence*, p. 200.

[23] A. Warne, *Church and Society in Eighteenth-Century Devon* (Newton Abbot, 1969), pp. 39–40; Marshall, 'Administration of Hereford and Oxford', p. 105; D. McClatchey, *Oxfordshire Clergy 1777–1869* (Oxford, 1960), p. 31.

[24] In 1812. See p. 105 below.

[25] A. Gilbert, *Religion and Society in Industrial England* (1976), pp. 6–7.

[26] McClatchey, *Oxfordshire Clergy*, pp. 31–3.

[27] Virgin, *Age of Negligence*, pp. 192–3. These figures may admit of some qualification and refinement, but the basic trend is clear.

ies claimed, with plausibility, that pluralism was necessitated by clerical poverty. Of fifteen pluralists in Northumberland in 1721 only four had a lucrative salary, and only two of these held parochial livings in plurality. But this argument must be qualified. The poor Welsh clergy were no more pluralistic than the richer English. Indeed, pluralism was sometimes least widely practised where it could have been most easily justified – it was remarkably infrequent among the starveling hill clergy of the Lake District, for example. The reasons for the increase in pluralism, however, are obscure. Poverty is hard to adduce as an explanation here – the clergy were, after all, getting wealthier. Moreover, it has generally been assumed that the Georgian Church was overstocked with clergy. But Peter Virgin has recently pointed to a decline in the number of ordinands in the eighteenth century, a trend which raises the intriguing possibility that a failure to recruit may have been partly responsible for the increase in pluralism.[28]

Pluralism was an open invitation to Dissenters and anti-clericals to attack the Church, but Churchmen could be equally vehement in their criticisms of the practice and their failure to reform the abuse was not due merely to lethargy and weakness of will. The hierarchy, however, often stood condemned by its own actions. In the cases of the patronage dispensed by both the bishops of Ely and the deans and chapter of Durham, pluralism appears mostly to have made wealthy clergymen more comfortable.[29] And, while the poverty of the see of Bristol may have justified Bishop Butler in holding the deanery of St Paul's as a commendam, there was surely no justification for James Cornwallis to enjoy the revenue of both the bishopric of Lichfield and the deanery of Durham for almost thirty years. The Church's failure to reform what it recognized as an evil must be admitted. On the other hand, the impact of pluralism and non-residence on standards of pastoral care should not be exaggerated.

Another frequent criticism of the eighteenth-century Church is that it failed to take adequate care of its places of worship. Visitations certainly revealed many examples of the neglect of church fabrics. Secker's charge to the clergy of Oxford in 1750 complained that 'too frequently the floors are meanly paved, or the walls dirty or patched, or the windows ill glazed, and it may be stopt up, or the roof not ceiled'.[30] Local records suggest, however, that these problems were less a result of the failure of rectors and churchwardens to act, than of the continual struggle necessary to keep medieval fabrics in decent repair. More seriously, the Georgian Church has been charged with failing to build new churches to accommodate the rising population. Even Sykes was unimpressed by its record in this respect,

[28] Shuler, 'Diocese of Durham', p. 27; Virgin, *Age of Negligence*, pp. 202, 288, 136.

[29] R. Mitchison, 'Pluralities and the Poorer Benefices in Eighteenth-Century England', *HJ*, 5 (1962), 188–90; W. B. Maynard, 'Pluralism and Non-Residence in the Archdeaconry of Durham, 1774–1856', *Northern History*, 26 (1990), 103–30.

[30] *The Works of Thomas Secker* (new edn, 6 vols., 1811), V, 395.

stating categorically that 'the Hanoverian age was not a period of church-building'.[31] Recent research is proving him wrong. The seating capacity of hundreds of churches was increased by the erection of galleries. More significantly, Basil Clarke has listed 224 churches which were either built or rebuilt by individual benefactions between 1700 and 1800. At the end of the eighteenth century in Lancashire almost three-quarters of the churches were either new or at least larger than they had been 100 years earlier. In Saddleworth five new chapels were built between 1743 and 1788, and, even more remarkably, the period between 1700 and 1790 saw an increase in the proportion of the local population which could be accommodated in church.[32]

A more telling criticism of eighteenth-century church building is its absence where it was most needed. Even in London, where money was voted by Parliament in 1711 for fifty new churches, the Commissioners decided not to provide as many cheap, functional buildings as possible, but to create architectural glories, 'monuments to her [Queen Anne's] piety & grandure'. In the end only ten were erected.[33] Outside London the Church was entirely dependent on local efforts; there was no state aid for church building until the Church Buildings Act of 1818. Individual benefactions by the wealthy were not unknown, but for the most part the Church was dependent on the commitment and money of the middling sort. New churches were least likely to be built in the working-class districts of the industrializing towns. But there were exceptions. In some industrial villages church building was the product of communal labour, as humble parishioners got to work with spade and trowel. The eleven churches rebuilt or substantially restored between 1748 and 1825 in the deanery of Craven were cheerfully paid for by rate.[34] Indeed, given that the Church's administrative structures were essentially medieval, overall it seems to have coped well with the demands of a growing population, especially, perhaps, in the industrializing north, until it was swamped by the dramatic urban expansion of the 1790s and beyond. If bricks, mortar and plasterwork can be adduced as proof of religious zeal, the Georgian Church compares remarkably favourably with that of the Tudor period or the seventeenth century.

More important than the provision of churches was the frequency of services within them. The form of public worship in the eighteenth-century Church was more or less uniform throughout England and Wales. The

[31] Sykes, *Church and State*, p. 232.

[32] B. F. L. Clarke, *The Building of the Eighteenth-Century Church* (1963), pp. 50–89; Albers, 'Seeds of Contention', pp. 48–56. For Saddleworth see ch. 4 below.

[33] E. de Waal, 'New Churches in East London in the Early Eighteenth Century', *Renaissance and Modern Studies*, 9 (1965), 98–114. The phrase is Vanbrugh's.

[34] Rycroft, 'Craven', pp. 103, 134; M. Smith, 'Religion in Industrial Society. The Case of Oldham and Saddleworth, 1780–1865', DPhil dissertation, University of Oxford, 1987, p. 63.

morning service on Sundays consisted of matins, ante-communion, that is, the communion service to the end of the prayer for the Church, and a sermon. Evening prayer was said in the afternoons, usually without a sermon if one had been preached in the morning, though sometimes the catechism was expounded. On those Sundays and festivals when communion was celebrated, non-communicants generally left after the ante-communion and the ideal envisaged was that those receiving the sacrament should move into the chancel for the rest of the service. Some ministers omitted the Athanasian Creed, variations occurred in vestments and ritual, and in Wales services were often conducted in Welsh, but the striking differences in liturgy and practice that have been a feature of Anglican worship since the later nineteenth century were absent.

Generalization about the regularity of services is much more difficult. The most striking feature of the fragmentary evidence available is that there was great regional diversity. The ideal performance of 'double-duty' – both matins and evensong – on Sundays was more common in the 'highland' north and Wales than in the lowlands of the south and east, surprisingly, perhaps, in view of the Church's alleged failure in those areas in the eighteenth and nineteenth centuries. A similar pattern emerges when we look at the frequency of communion services. Very few parish churches fell below the canonical minimum of three celebrations a year. Sykes suggested that the normal practice was four, at the three great festivals and around Michaelmas.[35] His statement is supported by the evidence of the dioceses of Oxford and Worcester, but in Wales monthly communion was the norm. Less surprisingly, services appear to have been more frequent in the towns than in the countryside. Almost all churches in the towns of Essex and Hertfordshire had two Sunday services at the time of the 1778 visitation, and nearly half of them also had monthly communion.[36] Generalizations about eighteenth-century public worship are further complicated when we ask whether the situation was improving or deteriorating. In the dioceses of London and Oxford the proportion of parishes offering 'double-duty' declined in the course of the century. In Devon a decline in the number of parishes offering week-day prayers was accompanied, curiously, by an increase in the frequency of communion. In the Wirral, on the other hand, the century saw an increase in the frequency of all forms of public worship.[37]

[35] Sykes, *Church and State*, p. 250.

[36] See F. Mather's seminal article, 'Georgian Churchmanship Reconsidered: Some Variations in Anglican Public Worship 1714–1830', *JEH*, 36 (1985), 255–83, and Taylor, 'Church and State', pp. 30–3, for further analysis of the evidence.

[37] Ch. 3 below; Marshall, 'Administration of Hereford and Oxford', p. 112; McClatchey, *Oxfordshire Clergy*, pp. 80–2; Warne, *Church and Society*, pp. 43–5; R. Pope, 'The Eighteenth-Century Church in Wirral', MA dissertation, University of Wales (Lampeter), 1971, pp. 49–56.

What emerges most clearly here is the regional variation in this as in other areas of church life. Two broad conclusions are justified by the available evidence: that the public worship of the Church was performed more frequently in the north and in Wales than in the south and east; and that within each region the towns and more populous parishes were best served. But a number of qualifications need to be made. First, as F. C. Mather has pointed out, significant variations can be seen within dioceses: 'To pass in 1772, within the single diocese of Lichfield, from the archdeaconry of Salop through Staffordshire into the archdeaconry of Derby was to move from a region where 63.3 per cent of churches celebrated communion more than four times a year, through one where the figure was 52.7 per cent, into one of 26.4 per cent.'[38] Second, the broad division between north and south must admit of exceptions. In 1738 the diocese of Oxford reflected 'northern' practice in its provision of Sunday services, 85 per cent of parishes having 'double-duty'. Finally, the simple diversity of practice must be emphasized. In Oxford, Hereford and York a 'northern' level of Sunday services was accompanied by a 'southern' pattern in the celebration of communion.[39] What the Church was providing varied from place to place, and it is clear that the 'normal' pattern of worship for a member of the established Church depended very much on where he lived.

We are still very far from possessing a complete picture of any of the issues that have been used as indexes of the vitality of the Georgian Church. Much material still lies unexplored in diocesan and county record offices and much work remains to be done. But the broad outlines are clear, and, even when we have a more complete picture, it is still unlikely that it will be any easier to interpret. All the signs are that the record of the eighteenth-century Church will continue to provide evidence to support the claims of both optimists and pessimists. This should not surprise us. The Church was very different in the north of England compared to the south, and in the towns compared to the countryside. Answers also depend on the questions asked, on whether historians view the eighteenth century from the perspective of the seventeenth or the nineteenth. But, however productive the arguments of optimists and pessimists may have been, this debate has lost some of its interest, dominated as it is by the agenda of nineteenth-century Churchmen. It has managed to obscure, rather than to reveal, the role of the Church in eighteenth-century society, diverting attention away from the ways in which eighteenth-century clergymen and laymen viewed their Church, what they expected from it and what they wanted of it. Much of the

[38] Mather, 'Georgian Churchmanship', pp. 273–4.

[39] Marshall, 'Administration of Hereford and Oxford', pp. 112, 119, 120–1; *Archbishop Herring's Visitation Returns 1743*, ed. S. Ollard and P. Walker (5 vols., Yorkshire Archaeological Society, 1927–31), I, xvii.

debate has been governed – like that on other areas of eighteenth-century institutional life, such as the law – by what has been called 'the reform perspective'; that is, by assessing the working of an institution in the light of subsequent legislative changes.[40] Historians are now creating a new agenda for the study of the Church and religion in the eighteenth century. What are its concerns?

Pastoralia

The past decade or so has witnessed a shift in attention from the quantifiable aspects of church life, such as those discussed above, to the unquantifiable. What did the clergy think their role to be? What was the quality of the pastoral care they provided? It is, above all, in its pastoral work that the eighteenth-century Church has been decried as lethargic and somnolent. To a remarkable degree our images of the clergy are still derived from satirists like Hogarth, with his 'Sleeping Congregation', and from picaresque novels in which the clergy 'did the duty' and no more. The persistence of such stereotypes and of the anti-clericalism that often informed them shows that the eighteenth century can plausibly be depicted as a period of pastoral failure. The apathy and negligence of the Georgian clergy, it is argued, were responsible for the decline of the Church from a position of near monopoly over the nation's worship to one where, according to the religious census of 1851, little over one quarter of the population attended services in Anglican churches. But is this view correct?

It is, of course, easy to find examples of clerical complacency, of ministers content merely with 'doing the duty', even of incumbents not seen in their parishes from one Sunday to the next. Some clergy undoubtedly revealed an unbecoming avarice in their pursuit of preferment and all too often clerical diaries, such as that of James Woodforde, seem to reveal men more concerned with the dinner menu than with the souls of their parishioners. More elevated figures also give credence to the contention that the Georgian clergy had only a limited conception of their duties. As late as 1837 Bishop Samuel Butler told an evangelically inclined curate that 'if the inhabitants will not take the trouble to come . . . far to hear your sermons, and much more the beautiful prayers of our Liturgy . . . I am sure they do not deserve to have them brought to their doors'. Such attitudes contrasted sharply with the practice of clergy such as Grimshaw of Howarth, who believed that if the people refused to come to church, then the Church had to go to them.[41] It is clear that the pastoral zeal of Grimshaw was

[40] J. Innes and J. Styles, 'The Crime Wave: Recent Writing on Crime and Criminal Justice in Eighteenth-Century England', *JBS*, 25 (1986), 383.

[41] Quoted R. Soloway, *Prelates and People. Ecclesiastical Social Thought in England 1783–1852* (1969), p. 341; E. Middleton, *Biographia Evangelica* (4 vols., 1786), IV, 404.

exceptional in the mid-eighteenth-century Church. However, it is also important to recognize that a respectable ecclesiastical principle underlay Butler's statement: the minister's primary responsibility was to his congregation, those who responded to the word of God. The laity had spiritual duties, as well as spiritual rights, and in a Christian society they were under a particular obligation to attend the public worship of the Church. Moreover, the idea that the clergyman's duties began and ended with the performance of the Sunday services received general condemnation. Non-residence may have been condoned, because in too many cases it appeared unavoidable, but it was never defended on principle. The 'private Labours of a Clergyman' were an integral part of his duty. In the words of Thomas Secker, whose charges became a pastoral manual recommended to ordinands well into the nineteenth century, parishioners had a right to expect that their minister would be 'always at hand, to order the disorderly, and countenance the well-behaved, to advise and comfort the diseased and afflicted, to relieve or procure relief for the necessitous, to compose little differences, and discourage wrong customs in the beginning, to promote friendly offices, and to keep up an edifying and entertaining conversation in the neighbourhood'.[42]

It is likely that most eighteenth-century clergy saw themselves first and foremost not as priestly mediators between God and man, dispensing the sacraments, but as pastoral educators, spiritual and moral teachers and guides – hence the need, emphasized by the Church since the Reformation, for a university-educated clergy. The education of the English nation in the Protestant religion is one of the most important themes linking the eighteenth-century Church with that of the sixteenth and seventeenth centuries. Even two centuries after the Reformation, as Gregory shows, the clergy were still all too conscious of the ignorance and apathy of their parishioners. Great efforts were put into combating this ignorance, into the gradual work of Christianizing the people, through catechizing, through charity and Sunday schools, through private exhortation and, above all, through regular preaching – the sermon, it should be remembered, was still one of the most popular and important of all literary forms. In this respect there was little difference between Evangelicals and their brethren. What distinguished the self-consciously 'serious' Evangelical clergy towards the end of the century was less their definition of pastoral duties than their conception of what it was to be a Christian.

The Evangelicals, however, did bring to the early nineteenth-century Church a missionary impulse notably lacking during the previous hundred years. Professor Ward reveals below how the writings of English Prot-

[42] I. Maddox, *The Charge of Isaac, Lord Bishop of Worcester ... at his Primary-Visitation ... 1745* (n.d.), p. 341; *Works of Secker*, V, 425.

estants were highly regarded on the Continent in the eighteenth century. By contrast, the attitudes of English Churchmen were remarkably insular. Despite the rapid growth of the empire, the Church of England showed little interest in the conversion of the heathen or even, after the overtures of Jablonski and Wake in the first quarter of the century, in developing closer relations with the continental churches. Many clergymen agreed with Ralph Blomer that they had more than enough work at home without looking abroad.[43] Gregory suggests that even parts of Kent were still regarded as *pays de mission*. Wales was certainly held to merit this description, being, as Bishop Herring put it, much further from 'ye Sun', and in the late seventeenth and early eighteenth centuries the Church launched a vigorous campaign to spread the basic doctrines of Protestantism in the Principality through more frequent and effective preaching, the distribution of the Scriptures in the vernacular and the dissemination of pious literature directed at all levels of understanding.[44] At first sight Ireland would also appear to have been an obvious target for Anglicans in their efforts to consolidate the Reformation. But, as David Hayton has remarked, the problem of the failure of the Reformation in eighteenth-century Ireland is '*une question jamais posée*'. In fact, the conversion of the Catholic majority received little attention; for much of the period the Church of Ireland was more concerned with providing adequate pastoral care for Protestants already there and with combating vibrant Presbyterianism in Ulster.[45] The insularity of Anglicanism becomes still more apparent when the history of the Society for the Propagation of the Gospel in Foreign Parts (SPG) is considered. Thomas Bray, the leading figure in the Society's formation, envisaged it as an Anglican *de propaganda fide*, but this comparison with the vigour of the missionary activity of the Counter-Reformation Church merely highlights the shortcomings of the Church of England. The Society showed very little interest in the conversion of the American Indians, but, much to the irritation of New England Dissenters, concentrated its energies on supporting 'missions' for colonial settlers. Even less attention was given to the opportunities offered in India. As Elizabeth Elbourne shows, it took a remarkably long time for a 'missionary culture' to develop within the Church of England, even under Evangelical

[43] N. Sykes, 'Ecumenical Movements in Great Britain in the Seventeenth and Eighteenth Centuries', in *A History of the Ecumenical Movement 1517–1948*, ed. R. Rouse and S. Neill (2nd edn, 1967), pp. 152–62. See below p. 69.

[44] Nottingham University Library, PWV/120/20; M. Clement, *The SPCK and Wales 1699–1740* (1954); G. H. Jenkins, *Literature, Religion and Society in Wales 1660–1730* (Cardiff, 1978).

[45] D. Hayton, 'Did Protestantism Fail in Early Eighteenth-Century Ireland?' (forthcoming); D. Hempton and M. Hill, *Evangelical Protestantism in Ulster Society 1740–1890* (1992), ch. 1.

influence in the early nineteenth century. Sydney Smith ridiculed missions, implying that Anglicanism was not for export.[46] Such views, possibly mildly eccentric when Smith wrote, may well have been typical of mainstream clerical opinion in the mid-eighteenth century. It is, therefore, hardly surprising that the established Church was so slow to apply missionary techniques to the problems of apathy and unbelief in England itself.

Fresh light is being cast on the pastoral activities of the eighteenth-century clergy in recent studies of the crises which gripped the Church in the aftermath of the Revolution of 1688 and in the 1790s. The response to these crises certainly does not suggest an apathetic or somnolent clergy, but one which was alarmed and challenged.

The Glorious Revolution – in particular, the Toleration Act of 1689 – transformed church-state relations. Many Churchmen construed it to be an extremely limited measure, no more than an 'Act of Indulgence'. The Corporation and Test Acts remained in force and full participation in civil life was restricted to the communicant members of the Church of England.[47] Crucially, however, Dissenting ministers and chapels now enjoyed the protection of the law. The resulting *crise de conscience* faced by the clergy has been delineated by G. V. Bennett in *The Tory Crisis in Church and State 1688–1730*. 'Were [the clergy] ready to accept the place in English society of a basically voluntary body working within the legal conditions of the establishment or were they going to agitate for a return to the past when Church and State had conjoined in a single authoritarian regime?'[48]

This was a pastoral as well as a political problem. In many parishes the clergy were now in open competition with rival Dissenting ministers for the hearts and minds of their parishioners. Unable to coerce, they now had to persuade. For many the experience was traumatic. Assumptions about the weakness of Dissent were shattered when meeting-houses were licensed in surprising numbers. The stagnation of Old Dissent in the eighteenth century should not obscure the fact that in the years after the Revolution it was widely perceived as posing a serious threat to the Church. Nor was Nonconformist encroachment the only cause of alarm: many clergymen were aghast when they saw their parishioners absenting themselves on

[46] C. Bridenbaugh, *Mitre and Sceptre. Transatlantic Faiths, Ideas, Personalities, and Politics 1689–1775* (New York, 1962), pp. 59, 225–6; S. Smith, 'Indian Missions', *Edinburgh Review*, 12 (1808), 151–81. For the SPCK's involvement in the Lutheran mission to India, see D. Brunner, 'The Role of the Halle Pietists in England (*c*.1700–*c*.1740)', DPhil dissertation, University of Oxford, 1988, ch. 4.

[47] The importance of the Test and Corporation Acts must not be exaggerated. They did not prevent Dissenters from sitting in Parliament or from controlling some borough corporations, such as Coventry. Moreover, the new agencies of local government, statutory bodies like turnpike trusts and improvement commissions, imposed no religious tests. P. Langford, *Public Life and the Propertied Englishman 1689–1798* (Oxford, 1991), ch. 4.

[48] G. V. Bennett, *The Tory Crisis in Church and State 1688–1730* (Oxford, 1975), p. 22.

Sunday not in order to worship in a conventicle but to relax in an alehouse. Though attendance at church remained a statutory obligation for all members of the established Church, it was widely assumed that the Toleration Act had in fact made churchgoing voluntary, and parish constables and churchwardens were reluctant to present absentees.[49] The diminution of clerical control intensified fears, strong since the Restoration, that a tide of profaneness and immorality was sweeping the nation, a theme which John Spurr explores below.

Yet a sense of crisis and of the 'Church in danger' had some positive results. It stimulated new pastoral initiatives. As Mark Goldie's essay shows, Gilbert Burnet's *Discourse of the Pastoral Care* (1692) was intended as a handbook for the post-Revolutionary Church, urging vigorous pastoral work and catechetical instruction rather than compulsion as the best way to counter the Dissenting challenge. High Churchmen fiercely denounced Burnet and the Latitudinarian coterie from which the *Discourse* had emerged; they still yearned nostalgically for an authoritarian regime in both church and state which would restore religious uniformity. But they too recognized the need for pastoral zeal. Even before the Revolution persuasion had been regarded as a necessary complement to compulsion in the High Church theory of intolerance.[50] High Churchmen and Latitudinarians could agree on the desirability of converting Dissenters – even Stillingfleet and Hoadly argued that Protestant Nonconformists were guilty of schism – their difference was over methods. Co-operation between clergy of opposite schools was even easier to secure in the fight against immorality and irreligion. Clergy of all parties could agree that a tide of profaneness and immorality was sweeping the nation.[51] Some striking alliances ensued. In the diocese of Exeter, for instance, the Sancroftian Bishop Trelawny secured the support of Atterbury, Blackburne and Wake – the former a High Tory, the latter both Whigs – in his campaign to improve discipline and order among the clergy and laity.

A remarkable development of this period, the subject of much recent research, is the willingness of some Churchmen to countenance, even to encourage, more voluntaristic approaches to pastoral problems.[52] The devotional groups known as the religious societies, which first appeared in London around 1678, aimed to stimulate reformation from within by providing voluntaristic models of piety and virtue for others to emulate. By

[49] Ibid., p. 12.

[50] M. Goldie, 'The Theory of Religious Intolerance in Restoration England', in *From Persecution to Toleration*, ed. O. Grell, J. Israel and N. Tyacke (Oxford, 1991), pp. 331–68.

[51] See below pp. 51–2. For an analysis of the clerical response in the Restoration, see J. Spurr, *The Restoration Church of England 1646–89* (New Haven, 1991), chs. 5 and 6.

[52] On voluntarism, and the fierce opposition it provoked from other clergy, see the essays by Spurr and Rose and the works cited therein.

contrast, the Societies for the Reformation of Manners (SRM), the first of which was formed in 1691, tried to combat the rising tide of vice and immorality directly, through a vigorous campaign of private prosecution against prostitution, profane swearing and cursing, and Sabbath-day trading. Where the SRM sought to reform people's behaviour, the Society for Promoting Christian Knowledge (SPCK), founded in 1699 and probably the most significant of all voluntaristic initiatives in this period, was concerned to educate their minds. Its response to the challenge to Christianity and the Church was consciously evangelistic, and in the first decades of its existence the Society put most of its effort into the distribution of godly tracts, the encouragement of catechetical education and the promotion of charity schools.

These voluntaristic endeavours faltered in the mid-eighteenth century. By 1740 subscriptions to the SPCK were declining, the SRM had disappeared and many of the religious societies were dead or dormant. The Evangelical Revival, it is true, represented a new wave of voluntarism. Religious societies were revived by the 'regular' Evangelical clergy who consciously perpetuated the Horneck–Woodwardian model of the 1680s and 1690s. Meanwhile, John Wesley, not content with cannibalizing many of the surviving societies, transformed and radicalized the Anglican model, linking his societies together in a new organizational form, the connexion.[53] However, it was only when the Church was faced with a new pastoral crisis in the last two decades of the eighteenth century that it again wholeheartedly embraced voluntarism.

In many ways this new 'Church in danger' crisis seemed to replicate that of the years after 1688. In part the crisis was political, as it had been in Anne's reign. The welcome given by some Dissenters – particularly Unitarians – to events in France in the early 1790s once more elevated Nonconformity into an apparent threat to the establishment. But the crisis began before the French Revolution and the most serious problems were pastoral. Defeat in America provoked a multi-faceted crisis of confidence in Britain which not only stimulated a movement for political reform but also provoked widespread calls for spiritual and moral renewal and focused attention on the inadequacies of the established Church. For the Church seemed to be losing its hold on the people. Industrialization and, in particular, urbanization were placing great burdens on its medieval structures. The rapid growth of the new industrial towns threatened to overwhelm the parochial system; as the Archbishop of Canterbury himself admitted in 1809, 'the fact was, that our population had, particularly in

[53] S. O'Brien, 'Transatlantic Communication and Influence during the Great Awakening, 1730–60', PhD dissertation, University of Hull, 1978, ch. 2; J. Walsh, 'Religious Societies: Methodist and Evangelical 1738–1800', *SCH*, 23 (1986), 279–302.

some large towns, far exceeded the machinery by which the beneficial effects of our church establishment could be universally communicated'.[54] This problem was not confined to urban areas – a survey of the diocese of Lincoln published in 1800 suggested that only one third of the population had anything to do with the Church.[55] The consequences were frightening. In 1815 Richard Yates, one of the most influential advocates of church reform in the early nineteenth century, warned that the great urban areas of England, including London itself, were becoming a 'Mine of Heathenism'.[56] Yates's phrase is revealing; the spread of popular Deism in the 1790s, and especially the success of Paine's *Age of Reason* (1795), made lower-class irreligion even more threatening to the cause of orthodox Christianity. At the same time, Nonconformity, revitalized by evangelicalism, was being transformed from a comparatively static, declining interest into an aggressive, proselytizing movement in open competition with the established Church. The spread of Dissent and, indeed, of Methodism, ever more clearly a separatist movement, was so rapid that by the first decades of the nineteenth century many clergy felt that they were in danger of being swamped. In a jeremiad preached in 1811 William Goddard warned 'that the Church of England would soon find itself outnumbered by "Sectaries"'.[57]

Faced with these threats Churchmen – both clergy and laity – re-embraced voluntarism, often consciously turning for inspiration to the precedents of the post-Revolutionary era. Beginning with the Sunday school movement in the 1780s, which, it was hoped, would instil principles of piety and true religion into the lower orders, there was a surge of voluntary activity, in which Churchmen were sometimes prepared to co-operate with Dissenters. The Proclamation Society (1787) and the Vice Society (1802) both campaigned against vice and immorality, and sought in particular to enforce Sunday observance and to suppress blasphemous literature. The purpose of the interdenominational British and Foreign Bible Society (1804) was to distribute the Bible to the poor and ignorant, while the Church Missionary Society (1799) hoped to spread the Gospel abroad, especially in India and Africa. The National Society was founded in 1811 to promote primary education for the poor on a sound Christian basis, while the establishment of the Church Building Society in 1817 was followed by the formation of numerous diocesan building societies. Moreover, the assistance of the legislature was enlisted, in marked contrast to the

[54] Quoted G. Best, *Temporal Pillars. Queen Anne's Bounty, the Ecclesiastical Commissioners and the Church of England* (Cambridge, 1964), pp. 148–9.

[55] *Report from the Clergy of a District in the Diocese of Lincoln* (1800).

[56] Quoted E. Norman, *Church and Society in England 1770–1970* (Oxford, 1976), p. 52.

[57] D. Lovegrove, *Established Church, Sectarian People. Itinerancy and the Transformation of English Dissent 1780–1830* (Cambridge, 1988), p. 124.

reigns of William and Anne, when party conflict had ensured the failure of so many attempts at reform in both Parliament and Convocation. Through the eighteenth century fear of clerical power informed a powerful opposition to church reform, but the French Revolution helped to convince clergymen and politicians of all parties that the Church needed strengthening to preserve the social fabric. Legislation was passed aiming at curbing non-residence, augmenting poor livings and encouraging church building. Much of this activity had little impact. A string of measures, beginning with Sir William Scott's Act of 1803, failed to make much impression on the problem of non-residence, and at least until the 1830s Parliamentary intervention appears to have been most successful when, as with the Church Buildings Act of 1818, it complemented voluntary endeavour.

The parish lay at the heart of the reforming initiatives of these years. Both voluntary and legislative action was premised on the assumption that the most important figure in the fight against immorality and infidelity was the parish minister. Non-residence had to be combated to ensure the presence of a minister in every parish. The church building programme was necessary to make it possible for all parishioners to attend the public worship of the Church. Both Sunday schools and, later, National Society schools were organized on parochial lines. Most important of all were the ministrations of the clergyman himself. It is well known that the Evangelicals set more demanding standards for the parochial clergy. But the attention lavished on the Evangelicals by historians has tended to obscure the contribution of other groups of Churchmen to improving the parochial ministry. As Arthur Burns shows below, the movement for diocesan reform, which began in the early years of the nineteenth century and utilized traditional episcopal authority in an attempt to raise clerical morale and improve pastoral oversight, was inspired, not by Evangelicals, but by Orthodox High Churchmen. The Evangelical response to the crisis facing the Church was distinctive, but not unique; they shared with others the conviction that higher standards of pastoral care had to be demanded of the clergy. Neither Evangelicals nor High Churchmen were reacting *against* the eighteenth-century Church. The outlook of both was firmly grounded in eighteenth-century attitudes and practices. These efforts to reinvigorate the Church thus provide strong evidence for what Peter Virgin has called the 'gradualistic' interpretation of the movement for church reform, which argues that the Georgian Church began to reform itself long before the 1830s.[58] Moreover, as Burns makes clear, older traditions of reform played an important part in the creation of what we know as the Victorian Church alongside the work of the Ecclesiastical Commissioners.

[58] Virgin, *Age of Negligence*, p. 264. See esp. Best, *Temporal Pillars*, chs. 4–6.

Critics of Georgian churchmanship, however, have tended to focus not on these periods of crisis, but on the middle decades of the eighteenth century. Indeed, the attention that has been given to clerical responses to the pastoral crises at the beginning and end of the century might even be thought to reinforce assumptions about the quiescence and laxity of the mid-Georgian Church. There is no doubt that the Church entered a period of greater stability in the years after 1730 as religious issues faded from the political agenda.[59] But stability is not the same thing as tranquillity, and it is certainly not to be equated with somnolence. Even in the middle of the eighteenth century much remained to induce pastoral anxiety in the clerical mind. Recent historians have generally focused on political causes of disturbance in the Church, but this is to ignore the capacity of clergymen, as a highly specialized profession, to worry about issues of morality and theology which did not concern the laity to the same degree. The 1730s were a particularly nervy decade for the clergy. Deism seemed to have become dangerously fashionable in the *haut monde* and contributed to an outbreak of anti-clericalism in Parliament unparalleled, in the opinion of Norman Sykes, since Henry VIII's Reformation Parliament.[60] At the same time, the gin craze and a crime wave suggested that the lower orders were glissading into immorality and religious indifference. The church leaders of the period sounded shrill notes of alarm. In 1734 Joseph Trapp wrote gloomily: 'all manner of wickedness, both in principle and practice, abounds among us to a degree unheard of since Christianity was in being ... I have lived in six reigns: but for about twenty years past, the English nation has been ... so prodigiously debauched that I am almost a foreigner in my own country'.[61] This was an over-reaction. By the late 1740s the deist movement ran out of steam and orthodoxy regained much of its influence. Yet the sermon literature of the period reveals a continuous flow of jeremiads on the moral and spiritual state of the nation, epitomized by John Brown's *Estimate of the Manners and Principles of the Time* (1757). The spread of 'luxury' and immorality was a constant source of anxiety to the clergy; they warned about the spread of heterodoxy and unbelief; they were highly sensitive to perceived deterioration in the nation's moral health, for whose well-being, as pastors, they felt directly responsible. As men with a professed duty to interpret the ways of God's providence for the guidance of their flocks, they studied the alarming 'signs of the times' – such as wars, political crises and epidemics – which unfolded continually in the life of the nation. They interpreted them forcefully as manifestations of divine judgement on a

[59] See below pp. 53–5.
[60] N. Sykes, *Edmund Gibson, Bishop of London, 1669–1748* (1926), p. 149.
[61] [J. Trapp], *Thoughts upon the Four Last Things* (1734), Advertisement to the Reader.

guilty people.[62] Each crisis provoked loud calls for 'a general reformation'. The '45 rebellion, the Seven Years War, the Wilkite agitations and still more the American rebellion and the traumatic loss of the thirteen colonies were for the clergy deeply disturbing events, whose providential significance was discussed in innumerable sermons. When James Creighton was called on to announce the royal proclamation of a national fast at a critical point of the American war, he felt waves of fire coursing through his body as he mounted the pulpit and thereafter fell into a long period of anxiety and depression.[63] The 'somnolence' of late eighteenth-century Anglicanism was not apparent to him and his like.

The laity

It should be clear by now that, while the eighteenth-century Church may have lacked a missionary culture, it was not without pastoral zeal. But how far did the Church succeed in engaging the laity? What, indeed, did lay men and women want from the Church? What was the nature of popular belief and how did it relate to the orthodox Christianity taught from the pulpit? Did the Church have social and cultural, as opposed to narrowly ecclesiastical, meanings? These are questions which historians are only beginning to address, in essays such as that here by Jonathan Barry, and it is impossible to offer more than tentative and generalized answers. The traditional clerical bias of ecclesiastical history has nowhere been so pronounced as in studies of the eighteenth century, yet, paradoxically, in few periods is the contribution of lay men and women to Anglican piety so striking. Did any pulpit moralist shape Georgian religion more than Mr Spectator? Did any preacher do more to promote Christian beneficence and philanthropy than the devout Jonas Hanway? Did any clerical propagandist do as much as Wilberforce's *Practical View* or Hannah More's *Thoughts on the Manners of the Great* to recommend 'vital religion' to the upper orders? The religious life of Samuel Johnson has been the subject of a number of studies, and we have glimpses of the deep personal piety of other, more unexpected figures, such as the Duke of Newcastle, who prepared to receive the sacrament with at least as much care as he managed Parliamentary elections.[64] Religion and politics were not necessarily discrete spheres of activity in the lives of

[62] See D. Napthine and W. A. Speck, 'Clergymen and Conflict 1660–1763', *SCH*, 20 (1983), 231–51; H. Ippel, 'Blow the Trumpet, Sanctify the Fast', *Huntington Library Quarterly*, 44 (1980), 43–60; F. Deconinck-Brossard, *Vie politique, sociale et religieuse en Grande-Bretagne 1738–60* (2 vols., Paris, 1984), I, 321–94.

[63] *Arminian Magazine*, 8 (1785), 300–1.

[64] On Johnson see N. Hudson, *Samuel Johnson and Eighteenth-Century Thought* (Oxford, 1988), and the works cited therein. For Newcastle see Sykes, *Church and State*, pp. 277–82, 437–9.

individuals: a concept of public service, informed at least in part by a religious world-view, impelled a significant number of politicians to support the campaign for the reformation of manners in the 1690s.[65] However, we still know remarkably little about the religious opinions of the English elite, who, it should be remembered, owned nearly half of the advowsons of the Church, and still less about those of the mass of English men and women.

One problem in discussing the religion of the laity is that the measurable aspects of worship tell us very little. Reception of communion is now accepted as a badge of church membership and there is a temptation to use it as such in the eighteenth century. Consequently, the low figures given for communicants in visitation returns – about 5 per cent of the population in Oxfordshire between 1738 and 1811, for example – have been seen as evidence of dissatisfaction with, if not rejection of, the established Church.[66] But other evidence suggests that attitudes towards the sacrament were far more complex than such a simplistic interpretation suggests. Some pious laymen undoubtedly practised frequent reception; the religious societies of the 1690s advocated weekly communion, while the members of the society of St Giles Cripplegate, which was in being from 1722 to 1762, adopted the practice of monthly communion. Infrequent reception, however, could also be a mark of piety: Samuel Johnson, commonly regarded as a devout High Churchman, received the sacrament only once a year. The lists of communicants kept by the incumbents of Lower Heyford, Oxfordshire, in the 1730s and 1750s reveal that even among regular church-goers few kept to the rubric of communicating at least three times a year. To some extent Protestant ideas may have contributed to this reluctance; Bishop Peploe condemned weekly communion as 'popish'. Infrequent communion did not necessarily indicate a low view of the sacrament. On the contrary, some felt that a formidable amount of preparation, often entailing many hours of meditation, was necessary, while in Restoration Wiltshire fear of damnation through unworthy reception was an important reason for people staying away from the Lord's Table. Among the lower orders, these fears were accentuated by a belief that only the more educated or respectable members of society could be worthy.[67]

Figures for attendance at services, if they existed, would be a better

[65] D. Hayton, 'Moral Reform and Country Politics in the Late Seventeenth-Century House of Commons', *PP*, 128 (1990), 48–91.

[66] R. Currie, A. Gilbert and L. Horsley, *Churches and Churchgoers* (Oxford, 1977), p. 22.

[67] J. W. Legg, *English Church Life from the Restoration to the Tractarian Movement* (1914), pp. 36, 312, 34; Marshall, 'Administration of Hereford and Oxford', pp. 123–4; W. K. L. Clarke, *Eighteenth-Century Piety* (1944), pp. 11–12; D. Spaeth, 'Common Prayer? Popular Observance of the Anglican Liturgy in Restoration Wiltshire', in *Parish, Church and People*, ed. S. J. Wright (1988), pp. 135–9.

indicator of commitment to the Church than the number of communicants. Even so, they would need to be used with care. Attendance at week-day services was notoriously poor. Sunday services were also avoided by many if there was no sermon: even among the better-educated laity few agreed with the Reverend George Woodward 'that their main business at Church is to attend to the prayers rather than the sermon, which is the lowest part of the service'.[68] Nevertheless, the relatively limited provision for public worship in the Georgian Church might be seen to suggest the alienation of the laity, and it requires explanation. There were undoubtedly lazy clergy who failed to perform their duties to the satisfaction of their congregations. Equally, there was clearly a significant body of apathetic and uninterested parishioners. But even making allowance for both, the most obvious explanation for the number of services offered by the Church and clergy is that they were providing as many as were wanted by the laity. A constant refrain of visitation charges and returns is that of bishops exhorting their clergy to institute more services and the clergy excusing themselves by saying that, even if they were to do so, their parishioners would not attend. If we are to explain the different religious cultures that existed in different parts of the country, we perhaps need to focus more on lay demand for worship than clerical supply.

Many laymen were clearly satisfied merely to attend church on Sundays, and probably not always then. But it is becoming increasingly clear that for others public worship was only one part of their religious lives. The societies of the age of Horneck and Woodward were a manifestation of lay dissatisfaction with the repetitive routine of parish services on Sundays and of the desire for something more informal, more untrammelled and personal. Even in the mid-eighteenth century some Anglican societies continued to exist, and not merely in Evangelical parishes, to provide a forum for the devotional energies of a minority. These societies, in contrast to those of the Methodists, were incorporated within the parochial structure and were subject to some clerical supervision. But the self-consciously devout minority to whom such societies appealed did not necessarily have much regard for parochial or even denominational boundaries in their search for religious fulfilment. In mid-century Bristol William Dyer attended 'services in his parish church of Redcliffe, other Anglican churches and the cathedral, as well as early morning Methodist gatherings and an evening gathering led by an independent preacher'.[69] The idea that religion became 'commercialized' in this period certainly reflects the tendency of a minority, in the

[68] *A Parson in the Vale of the White Horse. George Woodward's Letters from East Hendred 1753–61*, ed. D. Gibson (Gloucester, 1983), p. 82.

[69] J. Barry, 'The Parish in Civic Life: Bristol and its Churches 1640–1750', in *Parish, Church and People*, ed. Wright, p. 161.

cities at least, to 'shop around' in search of a full spiritual life.[70]

Less visible to historians is the piety of the closet, the parlour and the fireside, but biographical evidence suggests that it was more typical than is often assumed. Even family prayers, allegedly revived by nineteenth-century Evangelicals, were not uncommon: the Duke of Newcastle and the Marquis of Rockingham both had divine service performed daily in their households, while the poet, Gilbert West, himself read prayers to his family every morning. Further down the social scale the diary of Thomas Turner, a Sussex shopkeeper, is studded with entries about his reading by himself, to his wife, and even to a poor neighbour, religious books such as Tillotson's *Sermons*, Sherlock's *On Death* and Young's *Night Thoughts*.[71] The astonishing market for devotional literature in the eighteenth century suggests that Turner was far from being an untypical representative of the Georgian middling classes. Bishop Gibson's *Family Devotion*, first published in 1705, had reached its 22nd edition by 1754; even more popular were *The Whole Duty of Man* and Nelson's *Festivals and Fasts*. Much of this literature, significantly, was based on the Book of Common Prayer, which was itself used not merely as a service book, but also as a manual for family and private devotions. At a still humbler level was the Methodist cottage meeting, one of the most common and least studied foci of popular evangelical piety. Here was an important area in which women in their own kitchens or by their own hearthsides could exercise a pastoral leadership which was denied them in public worship. In the northern towns Evangelical clergy tried to foster such home-based piety to counter the secularizing effects of industrialization which made church attendance difficult on Sundays. They – or their curates – gave week-night cottage lectures and even led class meetings, initiatives warmly recommended by J. B. Sumner as bishop of Chester in the early nineteenth century.[72]

Many Georgian laymen and women, therefore, had a rich religious life outside the confines of their parish churches. The full implications of this fact will remain unclear until more work has been done on the subject, such as that which is beginning to illuminate lay piety during the Restoration.[73]

[70] For the application of the concept of 'commercialization' to religion see J. Gregory, 'Anglicanism and the Arts', in *Culture, Politics and Society in Britain 1660–1800*, ed. J. Black and J. Gregory (Manchester, 1991), pp. 82–109, and ch. 8 below.

[71] Legg, *English Church Life*, p. 102; *The Travels through England of Dr Richard Pococke*, ed. J. Cartwright (2 vols., Camden Society, 1888–9), I, 66; *The Diary of Thomas Turner 1754–65*, ed. D. Vaisey (Oxford, 1984), *passim*.

[72] D. Valenze, *Prophetic Sons and Daughters. Female Preaching and Popular Religion in Industrial England* (Princeton, 1975), *passim*; Smith, 'Religion in Industrial Society', chs. 2–3.

[73] D. Spaeth, 'Parsons and Parishioners: Lay–Clerical Conflict and Popular Piety in Wiltshire Villages, 1660–1740', PhD dissertation, Brown University, 1985; C. J. Sommerville, *Popular Religion in Restoration England* (Gainesville, 1977); E. Duffy, 'The Godly and the Multitude in Stuart England', *The Seventeenth Century*, 1 (1986), 31–55.

Tentatively, however, two points can be made. First, Georgian Anglicanism, in its piety though not in its theology, was in large part a creation of the laity. The emphasis on public, especially sacramental, worship in the nineteenth and twentieth centuries has encouraged a perception of the eighteenth-century Church which emphasizes its public worship. If that worship appears to have been lacking, perhaps it was because it formed only one part, in many cases possibly only a small part, of the religious life of men and women who had little time for clerical pretensions and who emphasized the lay character of the Reformation Church. At the very least, it can be said that the gap left in the nation's spiritual life by the infrequency of church services did not go wholly unfilled. Second, Georgian Anglicanism embraced considerable variations in the religious ideas and practices of the laity. The patterns of public worship alone would suggest that the normal practice of an Anglican in North Wales was very different from that of one in Kent. In turn, the religion of both was different from that of the anti-clerical Anglesey squire William Bulkeley. Some anti-clericalism was clearly deist and anti-Christian in origin, but much of it was not. Bulkeley's condemnation of 'priestcraft' was clearly anti-clerical in character. He resented the 'pretensions' of the clergy to power, to wealth and to special knowledge of religion; he denounced their 'Pride' and their 'neglect of Duty'. Yet, alongside his contempt for the clergy went respect and love for the Church.[74] The tension between the two remained unresolved in much anti-clerical thought, though it was often eased by the assertion of the Protestant doctrine of the priesthood of all believers, the denial of the need for any mediator between God and man. Such ideas gave rise to distinctive forms of piety, emphatically lay, but nonetheless Anglican.

Some form of household piety may not have been uncommon, especially among the middling classes, though the devout were only ever a small minority. Of some importance, therefore, are the religious beliefs of the not insignificant section of the population who did no more than attend their parish churches more or less regularly, or perhaps not at all. There has been a slow growth of interest in the theme of popular religion, especially since the publication of Keith Thomas's *Religion and the Decline of Magic* (1971). Particular attention has been given to the continued existence of 'folk religion', a residue of pagan magic and superstition which in some areas exercised a powerful hold over the minds of the common people well into the nineteenth century. These beliefs are often seen as sharply distinct from 'orthodoxy', an assumption which ignores the large degree of syncretism between the two: the belief of some that confirmation was desirable as often as possible was certainly not orthodox, but neither was it magical. In

[74] G. N. Evans, *Religion and Politics in Mid-Eighteenth-Century Anglesey* (Cardiff, 1953), pp. 99–101.

practice, as James Obelkevich has recently noted, people 'held folk beliefs and Christian beliefs side by side without any feeling of inconsistency'.[75] There was, moreover, a powerful strain of popular Anglicanism within English society. Any fashionable stereotype of the Church as an agency of social control neglected or despised by its plebeian constituents needs to be treated warily and set alongside the powerful loyalties which it attracted; loyalties attested by the great 'Church and King' riots from Sacheverell to Priestley, and still more by the innumerable little pro-Church mobbings of Methodist itinerant preachers.[76] The existence of that loyalty, however, is easier to define than its meaning. Popular Anglicanism was not primarily theological. In eighteenth-century Lancashire, as Jan Albers demonstrates below, it is more helpful to define religion culturally, as a form of identification linking rich and poor 'in a common world-view and a communal sense of purpose'. For many their church was inextricably linked with a nexus of social and political interests with which they identified. Some might go to enjoy the familiar cadences of the liturgy, others to participate in group activities such as church choirs, bell ringing or rush bearing, which were often still strongly associated with it, despite the insistence of E. P. Thompson and others that the Church had forfeited its influence over popular culture.[77] Inevitably the motives of most were mixed, and 'the Church' was a metaphor for many attachments: personal, familial, social, economic and political.[78] But, above all, the church was a focus for the identity of the parish, the place where 'the whole Village meet together with their best Faces, and in their cleanliest Habits'. At the most basic level, that of the rites of passage, the whole community, even including Dissenters, participated in its services. Not for nothing is the Italian word for local patriotism *campanilismo*, for the church tower, the *campanile*, is the proudest and most visible symbol of the historical continuity of the parish community. The church could attract the kind of tribal loyalty given to kin or to parent; powerful feelings were drawn to it by the presence of ancestors in its graveyard. It was 'Mother Church'. The language of the eccentric

[75] J. Obelkevich, 'Religion', in *The Cambridge Social History of Britain 1750–1950*, ed. F. M. L. Thompson (3 vols., Cambridge, 1990), III, 319.

[76] G. Holmes, 'The Sacheverell Riots', *PP*, 72 (1976), 55–85; C. Haydon, 'Anti-Catholicism in Eighteenth-Century England, *c*.1714–*c*.1780', DPhil dissertation, University of Oxford, 1985, *passim* (esp. chs. 5 and 7); G. Ditchfield, 'The Priestley Riots in Historical Perspective', *Transactions of the Unitarian Historical Society*, 20 (1991), 3–16; D. Wykes, '"The Spirit of Persecutors Exemplified": The Priestley Riots and the Victims of the Church and King Mobs', ibid., pp. 17–39; J. Walsh, 'Methodism and the Mob in the Eighteenth Century', *SCH*, 8 (1972), 213–27.

[77] E. P. Thompson, *Customs in Common* (1991), pp. 49–55; R. W. Malcolmson, *Life and Labour in England 1700–80* (1981), ch. 4.

[78] J. Trifitt, 'Believing and Belonging. Church Behaviour in Plymouth and Dartmouth 1710–30', in *Parish, Church and People*, ed. Wright, pp. 179–202.

plebeian lay preacher William Huntington is startlingly Freudian when he describes returning to his parish church after long absence: it was, he said, like 'getting again into the bowels of my old solid mother'.[79] The parish church engaged not only loyalty to Anglicanism but also the other powerful *isms* with which the Church of England was inextricably bound up: localism and atavism.

Norman Sykes argued that 'the eighteenth century witnessed a steady and progressive laicisation of religion'. As he pointed out, however, laicization is not secularization.[80] In many respects the close relationship of gentry and clergy made the alliance of church and state more of a *social* reality at the end of the eighteenth century than at any time since the middle ages. The life-style of the clergy, supported by rising incomes, came to resemble more closely that of the gentry and solid bourgeoisie. The clergy threw themselves into local administration and improvement as JPs, land tax commissioners, turnpike trustees and surveyors of the highways. The growing influence of the clergy on the commissions of the peace is striking, even if it can be explained in part by the reluctance of country gentlemen to act as JPs. In the early eighteenth century there were few clerical justices, but their numbers increased from around 1740, until, by 1831, one clergyman in every six was an active magistrate. Above all, late Georgian clergy were no longer inclined to view themselves as a separate estate, as their clericalist, Atterburian predecessors had, but as members of a propertied hierarchy, a trend reflected most visibly in the abandonment by many of distinctive clerical dress.[81] It could even be argued that the laity had succeeded in creating the Church they wanted – eighteenth-century clergymen, unlike both Puritans and Laudians in the seventeenth century and Tractarians in the nineteenth, made little effort to force their distinctive conception of the true nature of Anglicanism on their congregations. If, in many ways, by the late eighteenth century the Church had become more enmeshed in the structures of the local community than at any time since the Reformation, this may well have brought pastoral benefits. The enhanced social status of the clergy may have given them greater authority, while their more active involvement in the routines and responsibilities of landed life may have brought them into a more intimate association with their rural flocks. There is, after all, considerable evidence for the local popularity of those hunting parsons who so shocked Victorian sensibilities. But if there was pastoral profit, there was also pastoral loss. First, as Professors Ward and Evans have shown, the gentrification of the clergy could alienate them dangerously from their disgruntled plebeian flocks.

[79] *The Spectator*, ed. D. F. Bond (5 vols., Oxford, 1965), I, 460; T. Wright, *The Life of William Huntington* (1909), pp. 21–2. [80] Sykes, *Church and State*, p. 379.

[81] Virgin, *Age of Negligence*, p. 94; Langford, *Public Life*, pp. 410–20, 431–6.

This had implications for the establishment as clerical authority was denounced for prostituting itself in support of the vested interests of a propertied governing class.[82] Second, if the Church had become enmeshed in the structures of local communities, this could be a weakness rather than a strength. The clergy had become, perhaps, too much like the laity; alongside the laity they often practised the 'nominal Christianity' castigated by Wilberforce in his *Practical View*. From this perspective the late Georgian clergy were unable to provide spiritual and moral leadership for the community. The critiques of the eighteenth-century Church that were developed in the early nineteenth century are informed, in part, by these pastoral failings, but too often these failings have been allowed to obscure its strengths and successes.

Schools, tendencies and parties

In the 'long' eighteenth century covered by the essays in this volume, the Church passed through a variety of moods. With apparent paradox, it has been blamed for the opposite extremes of febrile factionalism and dull torpor. This is partly because the course of Anglican history in the period has been seen as falling more or less into two contrasting parts. The half century following the Revolution has been seen as one of vehement controversy between High and Low Churchmen – a contest closely related to the clash of Tory and Whig parties – which diminished gradually as these political conflicts abated. Within the Church, as in the party political arena, the 'rage of party' has been seen as slowly giving way to a state of comparative peace, an ecclesiastical analogue to that 'growth of political stability' which has preoccupied modern historians of the period. The collapse of Jacobitism, the patriotic consensus evoked by the Seven Years War, the non-partisan aspirations of George III – each had its part in diminishing religious as well as political tensions. This model of church life in the 'long' eighteenth century as divisible into two zones, one of anxiety and the other of tranquillity, with a transitory phase sandwiched in between, is a schema which has considerable plausibility, but still needs a great deal more scrutiny. Party political conflicts undeniably set parson against parson, but they were not the only source of division within the Church (although they are those most studied by recent historians). Differing views on issues of doctrine and spirituality were always capable of causing friction in the clerical body, even, as the Feathers Tavern furore made plain, during an allegedly tranquil period.

[82] E. Evans, 'Some Reasons for the Growth of English Rural Anti-Clericalism *c.*1750–*c.*1830', *PP*, 66 (1975), 84–109; W. R. Ward, 'The Tithe Question in England in the Early Nineteenth Century', *JEH*, 16 (1965), 67–81.

Different devotional schools have always existed in the Church of England. This is inevitable in any national church, particularly so in one with a mixed inheritance of Catholic and Reformed elements. In 1878, C. J. Abbey wrote confidently: 'From the beginning of the Reformation to the present day, the three principal varieties of Church opinion known in modern phraseology as "High", "Low", and "Broad" Church have never ceased to co-exist within its borders . . . In the eighteenth century there were, from beginning to end, men of each of these three sections.'[83] There is much to support Abbey's assertion.

These different styles of churchmanship have recently begun to excite an interest which is reflected in this volume. As several essays show, terms such as 'High Church', 'Low Church', 'Latitudinarian', 'Orthodox', 'Methodist' and 'Evangelical' all had their currency in the eighteenth century. Those who identified themselves with particular subgroupings in the eighteenth-century Church often ascribed themselves a pedigree and located themselves within a tradition. Latitudinarians often traced their Anglican ancestry back to Locke and Chillingworth. Evangelicals appealed continually to the English Reformers and the respectable, episcopalian Calvinism of early seventeenth-century bishops like Davenant, Hall and Ussher. High Churchmen saw themselves standing foursquare on 'the old way' of Laud and Hammond, transmitting to posterity an apostolic order and a static deposit of doctrine handed down from the Catholic antiquity of the ante-Nicene Fathers.

Yet it is often easier to point to the existence of such labels than exactly to define their meaning. This is partly because they were ascribed pejoratively by opponents more often than they were used as terms of self-definition. Nonetheless, there certainly were devotional 'schools' in the Church, emphasizing different elements in its inheritance. Certainly, too, there was periodic friction between them, but for the most part, such group conflicts were over specific and sometimes transitory issues. W. A. Speck and others have shown how vehement could be the collision of 'High Church' and 'Low Church' at the hustings in the early decades of the century.[84] Yet Jeremy Gregory's essay provides a valuable counterpoint, in suggesting the non-partisan nature of much churchmanship and the dominance of a 'mainstream' Anglicanism, whose minor cross-currents did little to inhibit a high degree of clerical fraternity, co-operation and consensus. He deplores the 'conflict' model of church history which has overemphasized the debates and arguments which have taken place within the Church. It is certainly unwise to treat the history of the Church of England merely in terms of a perpetual struggle between opposing forces. That there was

[83] Abbey and Overton, *English Church*, II, 411.

[84] W. A. Speck, *Tory and Whig. The Struggle in the Constituencies 1701–15* (1970).

partisanship in the eighteenth-century Church is clear, but this is not to say that there were 'church parties' in the high Victorian sense, well-organized, possessed of a keen sense of group identity and more or less permanently mobilized for combat.

How many of the 10–15,000 clergy who staffed the Church at a given time belonged to any recognizable school of churchmanship in the eighteenth century is impossible to determine. The views of most parish clergy lie shrouded in obscurity. Any attempt to quantify clerical groupings along the line of W. J. Conybeare's famous survey of mid-Victorian church parties is fraught with difficulties.[85] A devotional or theological style could be powerful at one level of churchmanship yet not at another. The views of the episcopate, for example, might well be unrepresentative of the outlook of the lower clergy, as the strife between the upper and lower houses of Convocation showed in Anne's reign.

It is clear, however, that the balance of strength between different schools of Anglican churchmanship – High, liberal and Reformed – shifted considerably between 1688 and 1833. The causes of these shifts were complex and need a great deal more investigation. Government policy played its part in altering the balance of forces within the Church. The departure, whether voluntary or enforced, of some 2,000 Puritan clergy between 1660 and 1662 shattered the hegemony of the 'Calvinistic' Reformed tradition which had been dominant for decades after the Reformation. The departure after 1689 of 300–400 Nonjurors had profound effects on the future of the Laudian tradition. Changes of dynasty brought consequential changes in the hierarchy of the Church, as new regimes attempted to remodel the episcopate through their control of crown patronage. Under George I and George II episcopal appointments were generally confined to those who could be relied on to support the Whig interest and led therefore to a significant strengthening of the Low Church tradition in the upper echelons of the Church. The Crown or the bishops appointed deans and chapters, which produced, by 1740, an overwhelmingly Whiggish archidiaconate. Episcopal patronage had its effect in changing the character of a diocese. In Canterbury, where 105 livings were in the archiepiscopal gift, after 1715 there was a visible shift from Tory to Whig sentiment among the parish clergy, evident in their votes for Parliament and Convocation.[86]

Changes in cultural mood were, of course, vital. The new science

85 W. J. Conybeare, 'Church Parties', *Edinburgh Review*, 98 (1853), 273–342.

86 M. Watts, *The Dissenters from the Reformation to the French Revolution* (Oxford, 1978), p. 219; E. G. Rupp, *Religion in England 1688–1791* (Oxford, 1986), p. 5; P. Langford, 'Convocation and the Tory Clergy, 1717–61', in *The Jacobite Challenge*, ed. E. Cruickshanks and J. Black (Edinburgh, 1988), p. 114; J. Gregory, 'Archbishop, Cathedral and Parish: The Diocese of Canterbury 1660–1800', DPhil dissertation, University of Oxford, forthcoming.

profoundly influenced theological discourse from the late seventeenth century, as Isabel Rivers and others have recently shown.[87] In the early nineteenth century, the incoming tide of Romanticism infused 'High and Dry' churchmanship with the new passion and extremism which were to be characteristic of the Tractarians. Shifts in the power structures and ethos of Oxford and Cambridge colleges – 'the nurseries of the clergy'[88] – affected the doctrinal perceptions of the ordinands who passed through them. At a time when the Church possessed none of the diocesan seminaries which modern Anglicans take for granted, the universities had a vital role in the formation of clerical opinion: they were the left and right ventricles at the heart of Anglicanism, pumping out the stream of young clergy along the arteries of the parochial system. Changes of intellectual climate here could swiftly affect the temper of churchmanship. Though Oxford managed to keep the High Church flame alight after 1715, Cambridge became for some decades the stronghold of the new natural philosophy and of Latitudinarianism. From its colleges issued a stream of ordinands reared on a curriculum based largely on Locke, Newton and Samuel Clarke.[89] The crucial importance of the universities in moulding clerical opinion was well recognized by early Evangelicals, struggling to establish themselves in a hostile world. In 1799 John Newton wrote that 'since ordination is now scarcely obtainable but by those who bring a College testimonial, let us earnestly pray the Lord to pour down his Holy Spirit upon both our universities'. Already his prayer seemed to be answered, as Evangelical influence in Oxford and Cambridge gained a new authority among opinion-forming elites.[90]

For many years the mid- and late Georgian Church was held to have been dominated by a tepid yet all-pervasive 'Latitudinarianism'. This perspective has begun to alter as historians examine the resilience and strength of other traditions. This is especially the case with High Churchmanship, whose great residual vitality has been emphasized in recent studies. J. A. W. Gunn, F. C. Mather, Peter Nockles and Richard Sharp have disposed of the idea that High Churchmanship was virtually smothered in the Hanoverian Church until its embers were fanned into flame by the Oxford Movement. A coherent and unbroken chain of teaching has been discerned linking the Caroline divines and the Nonjurors to the 'Hutchinsonian' school of Bishop Horne and Jones of Nayland, and thence to divines like Daubeny, Sikes and the Hackney Phalanx in the pre-Tractarian Church.[91] If the

[87] I. Rivers, *Reason, Grace, and Sentiment, vol. I: Whichcote to Wesley* (Cambridge, 1991), pp. 53–9.

[88] J. Gascoigne, *Cambridge in the Age of the Enlightenment* (Cambridge, 1989), p. 82.

[89] Ibid., *passim.*

[90] J. Newton, *Memoirs of the Rev. W. Grimshaw* (1799), p. 101.

[91] J. Gunn, *Beyond Liberty and Property, The Process of Self-Recognition in Eighteenth-Century Political Thought* (Kingston and Montreal, 1983); F. Mather, *High Church*

fortunes of High Churchmanship ebbed and flowed, it seems always to have commanded the allegiance of sizeable sections of the clergy. In Anne's reign the churchmanship of Restoration Anglicanism was still immensely powerful among the lower clergy; parish priests turned out *en masse* in their black coats to vote for proctors in the lower house of Convocation who would support Atterbury's campaign to save a 'Church in danger' from Whiggery and Low Churchmanship. Like the Tory party with which they were often associated, the more partisan High Churchmen were starved of preferment after 1715 and for some decades were kept out of crown livings and cathedral chapters. Nonetheless, in the Walpole era they still had their strongholds – Oxford colleges such as Magdalen, which kept alive the study of the Fathers, and the Collegiate Church in Manchester, a focus for Jacobites and Nonjurors. They owned a lively mouthpiece in the *Weekly Miscellany*, edited by William Webster, which between 1732 and 1741 poured out defiant jeremiads against the spirit of the age. Their piety was kept quietly alive in rectories and manor houses by family tradition and perpetuated by means of local networks of Tory patronage. The bellicose High Church champions of Anne's reign continued to be commemorated by plebeian admirers: prints of Sacheverell are prominently displayed on the wall in Hogarth's depiction of low life and others of Atterbury were still sold in the 1750s. In church services, Caroline ceremonial survived long into early Georgian England. Bishops carried mitres, incense was burned in cathedrals, congregations continued to bow at the name of Jesus. By the mid-century, however, Mather finds 'a marked retreat from the customary'; a 'trend ... towards greater informality in worship'; signs of a slow deterioration that reached its nadir about 1800.[92]

Paradoxically, the theological tradition of High Anglicanism seems to have followed a contrary trajectory, strengthening rather than diminishing in the later decades. From the 1750s, the coterie of 'Hutchinsonians' around George Horne and Jones of Nayland gave the traditional doctrines and piety a new focus and breathed into them a devotional warmth which helped to offset the stiffer piety characteristic of many old-style Churchmen. In the reign of George III High Churchmanship benefited increasingly from the conservative reaction in church and state. In the early years of the Whig hegemony, when the established order felt threatened by Jacobitism, Tory High Churchmen had been seen as potential subversives; after 1760 their principles became more fashionable. Theories of sacral royalism and

Prophet. Bishop Samuel Horsley (1733–1806) and the Caroline Tradition in the Later Georgian Church (Oxford, 1992); P. B. Nockles, 'Continuity and Change in Anglican High Churchmanship in Britain, 1792–1850', DPhil dissertation, University of Oxford, 1982; R. Sharp, 'New Perspectives on the High Church Tradition', in *Tradition Renewed*, ed. G. Rowell (1986), pp. 4–23.

[92] Mather, 'Georgian Churchmanship', p. 261.

high views of episcopacy and tradition looked more attractive in an age of revolutions. When the Unitarian Joseph Priestley attacked the doctrine of the Trinity on the grounds that it was not a tenet of the primitive Church, he provoked an orthodox response from High Church champions like Samuel Horsley, whose arguments gave a new prominence to the authority of patristic tradition. Horsley's defence of Trinitarian orthodoxy helped gain him a bishopric and even won him the praise of the elderly Gibbon.[93] By the close of the century he was one of a cluster of late Georgian bishops who have been classified as 'High Church'. High Church divines were once more strongly represented in the cathedral closes and in the pulpits of the major London churches. In 1818 Charles Daubeny noted approvingly how the 'sound part' of the clergy had 'for some time been recovering lost ground'. On the eve of the Tractarian revival their principles were sufficiently widely held to sustain a market for no less than five periodicals.[94]

It is worth noting, however, that though historians are confident that 'high' Anglicanism existed as a potent force throughout the eighteenth century, they are not always so confident in defining what it was. What makes the taxonomy of church groups particularly difficult is the way in which political definitions became periodically entangled with religious ones. This was particularly the case in the half century after the Revolution, and especially with the concept of 'High Churchmanship'. This might well connote attachment to particular devotional practices or theological categories – to exalted views of the sacraments, reverential views of the episcopal office or the value of ante-Nicene tradition – but for many Englishmen in the early eighteenth century High Churchmanship suggested the Tory party at prayer. Jan Albers's essay in this volume vividly illustrates how the terms 'High Church' and 'Low Church' were used for political stereotyping; their significance was often symbolic, providing convenient code words by which Whig and Tory partisans could define their political identity. The political use of partisan terminology did not necessarily coincide with the religious usage. Terms like High and Low Church may often have been related to different modes of Anglican devotion and theology, but this was not invariably the case. One might be a 'High Churchman' in a political sense and not in a doctrinal sense. William Jane of Christ Church, Oxford, for example, would have been accounted a political High Churchman. By his oratory he helped smash plans to comprehend the Nonconformists in 1689; as a close Tory ally of Atterbury in the Convocation controversy he fought in the front rank of the campaign

93 Mather, *High Church Prophet*, ch. 4; E. Gibbon, *Memoirs of My Life*, ed. B. Radice (Harmondsworth, 1984), p. 181.

94 C. Daubeny, *The Nature of Schism* (1818), pp. 154–5; Nockles, 'Continuity and Change', p. xxxiii.

to elevate the rights and privileges of the clergy; yet he was confidently classified by Edmund Calamy as 'a Calvinist with respect to doctrine'.[95] Not all political supporters of the High Church cause were devout; one doubts whether the mobs who pulled down meeting-houses in the riots of 1710 or 1714–15 shouting 'High Church forever' spent much time attending the sacrament or in closet meditation on the works of Bishop Ken. On the other side of the political fence, one might well be an early Hanoverian court Whig and nonetheless display some of the characteristics of religious High Churchmanship. 'Walpole's Pope', Bishop Edmund Gibson, set out in his *Codex Juris Ecclesiastici Anglicani* (1713) such firm views of sacerdotal authority that he was compared to Archbishop Laud.[96] Archbishop Potter, on most counts, must be construed a High Churchman. The presence in high places of such 'Tories in the Church and Whigs in the State' irritated Whig anti-clericals. Later in the century, High Churchmanship still showed mutations which are now attracting the attention of historians. There were different yet overlapping emphases within its broad parameters. F. C. Mather has acknowledged the existence of a 'High and Dry' school of men like Thomas Randolph, Margaret professor of divinity at Oxford, a type 'not uncommon in the late eighteenth century Church, which was donnish in manner, ostentatiously loyal to the Crown, zealous for the rights of bishops and clergy, and punctilious about conformity to statutes and articles of belief – "high", in fine, in the political sense – but hostile alike to emotionalism in religion and to the sacerdotalism of the Hutchinsonians and the Nonjurors'. By 1800 this school produced what Mather terms 'practical High Churchmen'; earnest, deeply concerned for the defence of the Church against heterodox Latitudinarians and 'enthusiastic' evangelicals. This group made up about half the bench of bishops by 1800.[97] Alongside this school, and sharing many of its concerns, existed a doctrinally 'Catholic' strain of High Churchmanship, represented on the bench by Horne and Horsley, more openly committed to the principle of apostolicity and engaged in a fervently sacramental piety. Peter Nockles's essay below examines some of the taxonomical difficulties involved in distinguishing between these strands and shows the need for a nuanced approach to party labelling in the pre-Tractarian Church.

It is 'Latitudinarianism' which is most often seen as the characteristic mode of Anglican piety in the eighteenth century. Curiously, it is here that most work needs to be done. Despite some valuable recent research and the creation of a periodical, *Enlightenment and Dissent*, devoted in part to

[95] Bennett, *Tory Crisis*, pp. 47, 58–9; E. Calamy, *An Historical Account of My Own Life* (2 vols., 1829), I, 275.

[96] S. Taylor, 'Sir Robert Walpole, the Church of England and the Quakers Tithe Bill of 1736', *HJ*, 28 (1985), 52–3.

[97] Mather, *High Church Prophet*, pp. 17, 211–12.

liberal Anglicanism, the tradition which was allegedly most powerful in the eighteenth century is the least studied. When Norman Sykes wrote confidently of 'the dominance of the Latitudinarian tradition in the Hanoverian Church', he was stating what for most church historians of his time would have seemed a truism. But here again we encounter problems of definition. What was Latitudinarianism? The word itself seems to have been very rarely used by contemporaries. As described by Sykes, it was an elastic term. At times he used it to imply commitment to the tenets of theological liberalism – the school of Tillotson and his followers – but at other times to connote little more than a low-key piety, whose tone was 'homespun and practical', 'rational and ethical rather than emotional, dogmatic, or mystical', adjectives which could fit the preaching and pastoral outlook of a vast number of priests over the centuries.[98]

Was Latitudinarianism, then, a theological position, even a movement, with definable doctrines and principles? Or was it a state of mind? Some historians have stressed the latter. Gerald Cragg described it as 'a temper rather than a creed'. Writing in 1971 Donald Greene suggested that as a term Latitudinarianism had 'no doctrinal significance'. What it *did* signify was 'the desire of many Anglicans . . . – very often bishops and archbishops – to broaden the terms on which adherence to the Church of England was possible, so that it could again "comprehend" the many Protestants, differing little if at all in essential doctrine, who had been forced out by the restrictive legislation of 1662'. Seen in this light, the defining characteristic of Latitudinarianism is not a set of beliefs, but moderation; the practice of Christian charitableness and tolerance. The modern synonym for what the Latitudinarians meant by 'comprehension' is something like ecumenism.[99]

Other recent studies of Latitudinarianism have tended to treat it in very different terms, as a school of liberal religious thought with a set of well-defined tenets. Its intellectuals often ascribed themselves a pedigree that ran back through Samuel Clarke to John Locke and beyond the Civil War to Chillingworth and the Great Tew circle, and sometimes further still to Erasmus.[100] There could be a self-consciously principled, even, at times, a programmatic side to Latitudinarianism. Belief in the sufficiency of the Bible alone as the standard and rule of faith; in the right of private judgement; in the simplicity and accessibility of biblical teaching; in the essentially moral and practical nature of Christianity as a faith founded on

[98] Sykes, *Church and State*, pp. 268, 283.

[99] G. Cragg, *From Puritanism to the Age of Reason* (Cambridge, 1950), p. 81; D. Greene, 'The Via Media in an Age of Revolution: Anglicanism in the Eighteenth Century', in *The Varied Pattern*, ed. P. Hughes and D. Williams (Toronto, 1971), pp. 312–13.

[100] B. Young, '"Orthodoxy Assail'd": An Historical Examination of some Metaphysical and Theological Debates in England from Locke to Burke', DPhil dissertation, University of Oxford, 1990, ch. 1.

the truths of natural religion, though elevated above them by revelation; in the need to be charitable to fellow Protestants but ever vigilant against the threat of sacerdotalism ('the raising of the power and authority of sacred functions beyond what is founded on clear warrant in scripture'): these were principles which Bishop Burnet listed as the characteristics of a 'Low Church man' in 1713, and they were still those of an Edmund Law or a Francis Blackburne two generations later.[101] Though Latitudinarianism was never organized as a party, it was a sufficiently coherent intellectual force to possess its own networks of patronage and its centres of propaganda, particularly Cambridge University. John Gascoigne's careful study of *Cambridge in the Age of the Enlightenment* shows the development in the university of a powerful academic consensus, based on a marriage between Newtonian science and the liberal theology popularized by disciples of Hoadly and Samuel Clarke. Woven into the syllabus and expounded in lectures, Latitudinarian principles shaped the education of generations of Cambridge ordinands under the first two Georges.

But there was divergence as well as consensus in Latitudinarian religion. A multitude of clergy remained content to uphold a simple, eirenic, anti-dogmatic stance, accepting the Anglican formulae but interpreting them with latitude. They kept the spirit of 'free inquiry' within limits of orthodoxy. Some of them had doubts about the importance or truth of speculative doctrines such as the Trinity, but did not push their views, opting for a quiet life. Yet there was also an activist, progressive impulse in liberal Anglicanism which drew some of its leaders along a path which led not to complacency but to controversy and impelled a few into secession from the Church. If the Latitudinarians believed in tolerance and reconciliation, they also believed in the need for 'free inquiry' and the pursuit of religious truth, wherever the quest might lead them. A dedication to religious progress was characteristic of the activist Latitudinarian intellectual. Low Churchmen, wrote Burnet, 'think no humane constitution is so perfect but that it may be made better'. Edmund Law, future bishop of Carlisle, adumbrated a theory of progression in religion which claimed that religious knowledge had 'held pace in general with all other knowledge'.[102] Many liberals urged that the Church should be made more inclusive, either by efforts to negotiate the comprehension of the Dissenters, or at very least by assuaging some of their animus against the establishment. The Church's doctrinal formulae could be purified. Some of the dogmas which had expressed the religious views of earlier ages had now become obsolete and

[101] G. Burnet, *A Discourse of the Pastoral Care* (3rd edn, 1713), New Preface.

[102] Ibid., p. 9; E. Law, *Considerations on the Theory of Religion* (Cambridge, 1745; 3rd edn, 1755), p. 212; D. Spadafora, *The Idea of Progress in Eighteenth-Century Britain* (New Haven, 1990), ch. 3.

hindered the advance of religious knowledge. Too many of the simple truths of the Bible had been obscured by centuries of scholastic systematizing, like the painting of some Old Master hidden away beneath the layers of dirt and varnish, and they needed to be uncovered so that their pristine purity could be seen in a full light. It had been the God-given task of the Reformers to remove much of this incrustation, but the work of the Reformation was still incomplete; a 'second Reformation' was necessary to scrape off the remaining traces of sacerdotalism and superstition.

Some Latitudinarians approached this task gingerly, fearing to arouse controversy which might prove counter-productive and damage the very cause of enlightened moderation it was intended to promote. There must have been many liberals like John Jortin the church historian, whose urge to reform was firmly held in check by his devotion to the principles of charity and forbearance. Jortin professed his trust in a progress which would come gently and inexorably through the advance of 'polite learning, as humanity helps to open and enlarge the mind . . . and give it a generous and liberal way of thinking'. Reformers, he urged, should be content to address themselves to 'small defects'; they should not demand controversial changes which would stir up the spirit of fanaticism, which had only recently begun to subside. Progressive Anglicans should be content to move slowly: 'let us be thankful for what we have', was his counsel.[103] Other liberals, however, were not content to trust in the inevitability of gradualism, but adopted more militant postures. Latitudinarian views did not necessarily imply eirenicism. A commitment to the principle of religious moderation did not necessarily mean a commitment to amiable passivity. There were Latitudinarians who felt that moderation had to be fought for, perhaps passionately. In the politically charged decades of the early eighteenth century, when Low Churchmen felt themselves under attack, there were few gladiators to match the pugnacious Bishops Hoadly and Peploe who took the offensive against what they considered to be the unwarranted claims of sacerdotalism. Later in the century there were always liberals who felt that if some of the phraseology of the Liturgy was obnoxious, it must be improved: if the terms of subscription to antiquated Articles were restrictive, then they should be officially relaxed. Both these objectives, given the legally established position of the Church of England, could only be accomplished by Parliamentary statute. This entailed political action, the lobbying of Parliament – and the inevitable storm of controversy. In his *Free and Candid Disquisitions* (1749) John Jones urged the authorities in church and state to purge the Liturgy of its anomalies, excise the ferocious dogmatism of the Athanasian Creed and remove some relics of popish ritual. But where Jones

[103] J. Jortin, *Remarks on Ecclesiastical History* (2 vols., 1846), II, 419.

was content to recommend, Francis Blackburne, archdeacon of Cleveland, moved on further, entering the field of political activism. His challenging treatise *The Confessional* (1766) condemned as prevarication the comfortable mental reservations used by many clergymen when subscribing. Putting his belief into practice, in 1770 he launched the famous Feathers Tavern petition to Parliament for a relaxation of the terms of subscription.

As Martin Fitzpatrick's essay in this volume shows, the *Confessional*, and the petition it inspired, represented a turning point in the movement of liberal Anglicanism. The rejection of the petition by a huge majority of MPs impelled a few of the disappointed petitioners, like Blackburne's son-in-law Theophilus Lindsey, into a Unitarian secession. It forced some advanced liberals – like John Jebb and Christopher Wyvill – to look critically not only at the present state of the Church but also at the political constitution of which their Church was a part, and so contributed to campaigns for Parliamentary reform. The petition divided the Latitudinarian camp. Many leading figures like Bishop Edmund Law and William Paley, though sympathizing with its objectives, did not sign it. It was one thing to hold discreetly liberal views; it was another to form a cabal or political pressure group to push them through Parliament: this looked like the formation of a party and in the eyes of many clergymen overstepped the bounds of acceptability. Thomas Balguy, for instance, though a liberal, and the dutiful son of John Balguy, a prominent Hoadlyite theologian, vehemently attacked the Feathers Tavern campaign in an archidiaconal charge as a movement which would end not in the reform but in the eventual abolition of the Church. He allowed that the Articles might need judicious tinkering, but he deplored any attempt to remove all 'human formularies' in the name of free inquiry.[104] A gap opened up between those whose religious liberalism consisted in a relaxed commitment to tolerance and comprehensiveness and those for whom it was a militant creed. Only 200 clergymen signed the petition and only a tiny handful – nine – took the issue as far as secession. In Cambridge the 1770s began the disintegration of the liberal consensus which had dominated for decades. The failure of the petition, together with the political polarization caused by the American crisis, marked a partial retreat from advanced liberalism in religion as well as in politics.[105]

While liberal Anglicans disagreed on the expediency of political activism, so too were they divided on the issue of theological heterodoxy. High Church polemicists had always maintained that Latitudinarianism was a

[104] T. Balguy, *Discourses* (Winchester, 1785), p. 253.

[105] R. Barlow, *Citizenship and Conscience* (Philadelphia, 1962), p. 150; G. Ditchfield, 'The Subscription Issue in British Parliamentary Politics, 1772–9', *Parliamentary History*, 7 (1988), 75 n. 41; Gascoigne, *Cambridge*, ch. 7.

cloak for heresy. This charge had plausibility, especially when it came to the doctrine of the Trinity, whose apparent lack of a clear-cut scriptural warrant perturbed some liberals and persuaded others to place it among the *adiaphora* of non-essential truths. While regius professor of divinity at Cambridge, Richard Watson avoided terms like 'Trinity', 'sacrament' and 'original sin' lest he use 'unscriptural words to propagate unscriptural dogmas'.[106] At the same time, a great many liberals do not appear to have approximated to the stereotype popularized by Leslie Stephen, in whose jaundiced opinion 'the intellectual party of the Church was Socinian in everything but name'.[107] Even Blackburne himself, vilified by High Churchmen as heterodox, dissociated himself from Unitarian seceders like his son-in-law Lindsey and wrote a lively essay entitled 'An Answer to the Question Why Are You Not a Socinian?' Blackburne was opposed to the reductionism of much of the 'rational religion' of his age. He rounded on Low Churchmen like Clarke and John Balguy, who rested their system on some 'invisible light of nature'. He disliked those – among whom he ranked Bishop Butler himself – who overemphasized the role of reason in such a way as to leave revelation 'no higher office than holding the candle to it'. He believed such intellectualistic 'rational Christianity' to be 'the foster father of modern infidelity' and a staging post to Deism.[108] Blackburne is possibly representative of many liberals who combined some surprisingly orthodox views with a devotion to the principle of *sola scriptura*. This allowed him to fight for the protection of colleagues whose pursuit of truth led them to speculative 'heterodoxy' on questions which did not appear to be determined by Scripture.

By the 1780s the balance of strength in the Church appeared to be tipping rapidly against programmatic and doctrinal Latitudinarianism. In 1783 John Disney, resigning his rectory and his orders, sadly admitted that though he still believed that the Anglican Liturgy would be reformed, he did not expect it in his generation. At the apex of the Church, George III took a firm stand against those whose Trinitarian views were rumoured to be shaky. When Pitt proposed the theologian William Paley for a bishopric, the King was said to have refused, muttering 'Not orthodox, not orthodox.'[109] Latitudinarians already on the bench, like Watson of Llandaff, moved no higher. The tide was turning against what was increasingly

[106] Gascoigne, *Cambridge*, p. 240.

[107] L. Stephen, *History of English Thought in the Eighteenth Century* (3rd edn, 2 vols., 1902), I, 426. On the 'intellectual party' in the late eighteenth century see A. M. C. Waterman, 'A Cambridge "Via Media" in Late Georgian Anglicanism', *JEH*, 42 (1991), 419–36.

[108] F. Blackburne, *Works, Theological and Miscellaneous* (7 vols., Cambridge, 1805), I, cxx, 315, lxxxiv.

[109] J. Disney, *Reasons for Resigning the Rectory of Panton* (2nd edn, 1783), p. 27; Gascoigne, *Cambridge*, p. 242.

regarded as an overemphasis on natural religion at the expense of revealed. Paley's works, which had long been prescribed texts in the universities, began to be suspect in the early nineteenth century.[110] The French Revolution had brought in its train a powerful reaction against the permissive spirit of 'indiscriminate liberality' whose dangerous fruits now appeared to be evident. 'Liberality of sentiment', Horsley complained, had been used as a cloak for 'profane indifference'. In conservative eyes, the democratic politics of the Unitarian seceders and their allies suggested a sinister link between doctrinal heterodoxy and political radicalism. The atheism of the French Revolution seemed to provide a sombre object lesson on what happened to a society when the solvent forces of rationalism were allowed to go unchecked. In the 1790s many clerical liberals gave up swimming against the tide of patriotic loyalism. Some deserted the Foxite opposition which they had formerly supported and extolled the necessity for order and strong government: 'Pigeon' Paley, regarded by some as too much of a leveller, published two pamphlets in 1792 which led one disgusted liberal critic to write him off as 'a disciple of Filmer'. Campaigners for the relaxation of subscription kept a low profile; this seemed hardly the time to press the claims of 'free inquiry'.[111] The old Latitudinarian reformist tradition was not dead – it found a celebrated political exponent in Sydney Smith – nor was the liberal theological tradition extinct, for it found fresh, fruitful and orthodox forms in the Oxford Noetics. But both had lost much of their power. The Noetics took trouble to emphasize that though they fought for 'moderation', it was a moderation without the 'indifference' which extreme liberalism encouraged.[112]

It is easier to trace the fortunes of liberal Anglican intellectuals than to chart the strength of the 'pragmatic', pastoral Latitudinarianism which Norman Sykes held to be dominant among the parish clergy of the Hanoverian Church. His evidence for this claim looks thin; it is largely drawn from a small sample of clerical diaries, among which that of Parson Woodforde is most prominent. Sykes evidently agreed with those who saw Woodforde's famous diary as 'representative of the country clergy of Georgian England'.[113] Throughout the history of the English Church there has always been a large group of clergymen who appear to have been

[110] G. Cole, 'Doctrine, Dissent, and the Decline of Paley's Reputation 1805–25', *Enlightenment and Dissent*, 6 (1987), 19–30.

[111] S. Horsley, *Charges* (Dundee, 1813), p. 38; *Letters to William Paley* (1796), p. 54. For a valuable discussion of the liberal retreat in the 1790s see N. Murray, 'The Influence of the French Revolution on the Church of England and its Rivals, 1789–1802', DPhil dissertation, University of Oxford, 1975, ch. 3.

[112] M. Morgan, 'Rational Religion and the Idea of the University: A Study of the Noetics 1800–36', PhD dissertation, University of Adelaide, 1991, *passim*.

[113] Sykes, *Church and State*, p. 270.

concerned above all with the day-to-day routines of parish life and to have had no distinctive theological position. Much research remains to be done, however, before we can judge whether Sykes was right or wrong in identifying the prevailing mood of such men in the eighteenth century as the low-key Latitudinarianism of a Woodforde.

We are still a long way from measuring the extent to which Latitudinarian ideas and sentiments were diffused. They certainly left a deep mark, even on many who did not regard themselves as liberals. A great deal of the influential moral theology which showed the Hanoverian Church at its most productive came from liberal pens. The Latitudinarians shaped the religious language and the apologetic assumptions not just of liberals but of clerics of all persuasions. Isabel Rivers has drawn attention to the ways in which the plain, rational language and the rhetorical method of the early 'Latitude-men', heavily influenced by the diction of the new science and by the reaction to Commonwealth 'enthusiasm', ousted the more emotional and affective preaching style of Puritanism to become the accepted standard for clerical discourse.[114] The Latitudinarians may not have captured the Church of England, but for more than a century they helped to mould its language. Some indication of their victory can be seen in the chorus of sharp disapproval, coupled with sheer astonishment, with which clerics of all persuasions greeted the Methodist adoption of the affective style in the early years of the Evangelical Revival.

Not only the style but also the content of Hanoverian homiletic owed much to the Latitudinarians. Their emphasis on natural religion was shared by clergy of other schools. They largely set the agenda for a great deal of Anglican apologetic. It would be going much too far to accept the sweeping judgement of Mark Pattison that 'the title of Locke's treatise, *The Reasonableness of Christianity*, may be said to have been the solitary thesis of Christian theology in England for great part of a century'.[115] Yet the assumption that the case for the Christian revelation stood or fell by its consonance with reason was widely approved, as much by Bishop Butler, so revered by the Tractarians, as by Archbishop Tillotson, whom they disliked.

It would be a grave error to see Latitudinarian Anglicanism as merely a stage in the onward march of secularization. There were no doubt negative and reductionist strands in liberal Anglican thought – diminished reverence for the sacraments, for church tradition and for festivals. In the opinion of some worried church leaders like Secker, the stress on the practical encouraged a disinclination to engage with the central dogmas of the Christian faith; not only the Trinity, but also the Atonement and sanctification by the

[114] Rivers, *Reason, Grace, and Sentiment*, ch. 2.
[115] Pattison, 'Religious Thought', p. 46.

Holy Spirit. Secker feared that 'many, if not most of us, have dwelt too little on these doctrines in our sermons'. The sense of the mysterious and the numinous in religion was dangerously attenuated.[116]

Yet whatever their critics believed, Latitudinarian writers saw themselves not as undermining the foundations of revealed religion, but as strengthening them against the onslaught of sceptics and infidels. Although Churchmen of other schools sometimes accused liberals of preaching 'mere morality', they nonetheless avidly used their Christian apologetic. The physico-theology of the early Boyle lecturers, describing the proofs of God's power and benevolence which natural science had uncovered in the mechanisms of nature, was pirated by evangelicals like the Calvinist James Hervey and gratefully used by High Churchmen like Thomas Frewen, described below.[117] There were certainly High Churchmen who attacked Locke as 'a Socinian or an atheist', but others, like those of the Hackney Phalanx, gratefully employed Lockean arguments concerning the 'reasonableness of Christianity' to fend off Deists and Unitarians. As Pietro Corsi has recently shown, they made similar use of the Oriel Noetics.[118] Few works of apologetic can have had as much influence as Paley's *Evidences* which soon became a prescribed text on university reading lists and went through innumerable editions. Among the liberals of the Church of England there was a positive desire to Christianize the Enlightenment, rather than merely to anathematize it, and leave it – as in France – to become subversive and overtly irreligious.[119]

What, then, of the Reformed tradition in the Church? No shift in the balance of forces within the Church was as spectacular as that which occurred with the ejection of Puritan ministers at the Restoration. Though some Calvinists conformed and a few reached the episcopate, the old Reformed piety went into precipitous decline. By Anne's reign it had few leading exponents: one of them – John Edwards of Cambridge – bemoaned the fact that the old divinity was now out of favour, 'an unwelcome doctrine ... upon the point of expiry'.[120] By 1730 the old Calvinist clergyman was not merely an endangered, but almost a vanished, species. Yet so large and sudden a vacuum in Anglican spirituality could not continue to be unfilled. With the outbreak of the Evangelical Revival, life slowly flowed back into

[116] *Works of Secker*, V, 442.

[117] See J. Hervey, *Theron and Aspasio* (3 vols., 1755), and *Meditations and Contemplations* (26th edn, 1797).

[118] Clark, *English Society*, p. 47; P. Corsi, *Science and Religion* (Cambridge, 1988), pp. 73, 22, 89.

[119] R. Porter, 'The Enlightenment in England', in *The Enlightenment in National Context*, ed. R. Porter and M. Teich (Cambridge, 1981), pp. 1–18; S. Gilley, 'Christianity and Enlightenment', *History of European Ideas*, 1 (1981), 103–21.

[120] J. Edwards, *The Preacher* (1709 edn), 3rd Part, p. viii.

what was recognizably the old Reformed tradition, though it was often expressed in fresh ways. The Church of England was unable to contain all the energy of the new movement. Much of it found an outlet in 'Methodism', in its various forms, but from the earliest days there developed a distinctively Anglican wing of the Revival, largely separate from Methodism and often highly critical of it. The mainstream Evangelical clergy became increasingly uneasy at the Methodists' breach of church order; at their cavalier invasion of the 'dark' parishes of 'unconverted' clergymen; at their formation of societies which held aloof from the parson and took their orders from travelling lay preachers. The sanctioning of plebeian laymen as Methodist itinerants and leaders offended not only the priestly dignity but also the class feelings of many Evangelicals: Samuel Walker of Truro spoke for many when he told Wesley 'It has been a great fault all along, to have made the low people of your counsel.'[121] Most of the Evangelical clergy were Calvinists, albeit moderate Calvinists, and disliked Wesley's evangelical Arminianism.

From the 1750s local coteries of 'Gospel clergymen' emerged who were committed to a 'regular' parish ministry, like the Cornish circle around Walker of Truro or the Yorkshire group around Henry Venn of Huddersfield.[122] The numbers of such 'Gospel clergy' were at first tiny, but grew rapidly after the 1780s. The first-generation London Evangelical William Romaine, who annually set aside a day on which to pray for each of them by name, began his list with only twenty names; by the time of his death in 1795 he prayed for 500. Estimates of Evangelical clerical numbers for the early nineteenth century vary considerably, but by 1830 they were clearly a formidable phalanx. One Dissenting estimate puts their strength in 1839 as possibly 3,000 clergymen.[123] By the early nineteenth century they had their bastions in the universities. Colleges like St Edmund Hall at Oxford and Magdalene and Queens' at Cambridge fell for a time under Evangelical influence, becoming veritable 'schools of the prophets'. At Cambridge, the celebrated 'conversation parties' of Charles Simeon of King's College moulded generations of ordinands, giving him an influence (in Macaulay's judgement) which far exceeded that of any primate and extended out to the remote corners of the country.[124] They had their representatives in the episcopate: Ryder was appointed to Gloucester in 1815, C. R. Sumner to

[121] Quoted Walsh, 'Religious Societies', pp. 300–1.

[122] G. C. B. Davies, *The Early Cornish Evangelicals* (1951); J. Walsh, 'The Yorkshire Evangelicals in the Eighteenth Century', PhD dissertation, University of Cambridge, 1956.

[123] W. Cadogan, *A Funeral Sermon Occasioned by the Death of the Rev. W. Romaine* (1795), p. 25; *Eclectic Review*, n.s., 5 (1839), 139.

[124] G. O. Trevelyan, *Life and Letters of Lord Macaulay* (2 vols., 1876), I, 68n.

Llandaff in 1826 and J. B. Sumner, later archbishop of Canterbury, to Chester in 1828.

The extension of the movement in the Church was not merely the work of the clergy but was due largely to the mobilization of the laity. In the great voluntary Evangelical societies lay men and women were given active roles largely denied them in the parochial life of the Church. Elizabeth Elbourne's essay in this volume shows how the Evangelical movement tapped the energies of the professional and commercial classes, bankers and civil servants, to form the CMS. In Wilberforce and Hannah More it gained accomplished writers who in their tracts put the evangelical message into forms which made it palatable to middle-class lay readers. Wilberforce's *Practical View* and More's *Practical Piety* put a case for 'vital religion' which was remarkably free from theological jargon, appealing to the psychological needs, social interests and above all the moral sense of their readers. Genteel treatises like these slipped into drawing rooms closed to volumes of calf-bound sermons. In Parliament, Wilberforce's group of 'Saints' gave the cause a potent centre of propaganda and publicity, setting moral standards which irritated many but also impressed others, outside as well as inside the political world. On reading James Stephen's essay on the Clapham Sect in 1838, the worldly Whig Charles Greville wrote in his diary that 'a certain uneasy feeling, a conscience-stricken sensation, comes into my mind . . . I see men who filled with glory their respective stations either in active or contemplative life; and then I ask myself how I have filled mine . . . a station . . . which might have been both useful and respectable if it had been filled as it ought.'[125]

Controversies and debates

The major schools of churchmanship – High, liberal, Evangelical – existed as identifiable tendencies in the Georgian Church. For the most part their relationship was one of peaceable coexistence. Periodically, however, issues arose which sharpened their dividing lines and even threatened to create embryonic church parties. As yet we know relatively little about these controversies, save for the clash of High and Low Churchmen in the half century following the Revolution, which dangerously polarized sections of the clerical body. This divide ran simultaneously along so many ideological fault-lines that it seems in retrospect remarkable that the Church held together so well. There was the dynastic issue, kept alive by the Nonjurors, whose presence was a standing rebuke to the conscience of sensitive High Churchmen who had conformed and a continuing provocation to Low

[125] Quoted I. Bradley, *The Call to Seriousness* (1976), p. 171.

Church supporters of Hanover. There were divisions over pastoral strategy: should the Church attempt to retain what it could of its old coercive power, tightening up the discipline of the church courts and curtailing the toleration of Dissenters to the bare minimum? Or should it accept the Toleration Act as irrevocable and seek to win back dissidents by persuasion, through voluntary societies and missionizing? Behind the ideology of Tory High-flyers lay the vision of the Church as the symbol and guarantor of a unitary state; Low Churchmen accepted more readily, though often reluctantly, that religious pluralism had come to stay.

The Bangorian controversy brought to a head some of the important issues separating Anglicans. Ignited by his sermon, *The Nature of the Kingdom of Christ* (1717), it revolved around the crippled figure of Bishop Hoadly, a highly placed and provocative Latitudinarian. Though the controversy produced much wearisome logomachy, it raised important questions. Was the Church of Christ a visible or an invisible body? Should a terrestrial Church be regarded as essentially a voluntary society (as Locke and some advanced Low Churchmen claimed) whose members had a God-given right of private judgement, to join it or leave it, and individually to assess the truth of its doctrines? Or was the Church (as High Churchmen insisted) a corporate, visible, universal society, which demanded dogmatic obedience by virtue of its apostolic commission? Were Christians to be judged for the 'sincerity' of their belief or for their allegiance to the dogmas of the Church? Was the sacrament of the Lord's Supper – as Hoadly maintained – a simple memorial feast, or was it a sacred mystery, a sacrifice, in which the real presence of Christ was communicated to the believer? The Hoadleian theology seemed to leave little room for the role of the priesthood as mediators between God and man.[126]

By mid-century the doctrinal warfare between advanced Latitudinarians and High Churchmen had been dampened down, but the embers still smouldered. Two long-running issues continued periodically to disturb the clerical mind and act as a polemical focus for group identity. The first was the doctrine of the Trinity; the second was the issue of subscription to the Thirty-Nine Articles. Since the Articles clearly affirmed the Trinity and the Liturgy endorsed the vehemently Trinitarian Athanasian Creed, the two issues often became entangled. The Trinity had not been a source of much clerical anxiety before 1688 (George Bull's *Defensio Fidei Nicaenae* (1685) had been directed against *foreign* Socinians) but the situation changed sharply thereafter. Although the Toleration Act expressly excluded non-

[126] The fullest accounts are still J. Hunt, *Religious Thought in England* (3 vols., 1870–3), III, 32–49, and Stephen, *English Thought*, II, 152–67. See also H. Rack, '"Christ's Kingdom Not of this World": The Case of Benjamin Hoadly versus William Law Reconsidered', *SCH*, 12 (1975), 275–91.

Trinitarians from its protection, the relaxation of censorship which followed the Revolution made it easier to dabble in heterodoxy, and some Anglican intellectuals became open or covert Arians. Cambridge became a centre for Trinitarian heterodoxy. From it issued a succession of advanced liberals: the eccentric William Whiston who, as Macaulay remarked, 'believed everything but the Trinity'; Samuel Clarke, author of *The Scripture Doctrine of the Trinity* (1712); and some alleged crypto-Arians, of whom one or two, like Hoadly and Rundle, became controversial bishops. Few were prepared to go as far as Robert Clayton, bishop of Clogher, whose *Essay on Spirit* (1751) led to the threat of prosecution, from which he was saved by death. Clayton's opinions were thought not only extreme, but eccentric: in his view the Logos was the Archangel Michael and the angel Gabriel was the Holy Spirit.[127]

The *Essay on Spirit* was far more important as an irritant than as propaganda; it did more to unite the orthodox than to win converts to heterodoxy and it inspired several important rejoinders, among them Jones of Nayland's *Catholic Doctrine of the Trinity*, whose appearance was a minor milestone in the resurgence of High Church self-consciousness. The same effect was produced by the Feathers Tavern petition, which appeared – not without some plausibility – as a campaign for greater doctrinal permissiveness in the Church on behalf of uneasy Arians or Socinians. By pushing too far, advanced liberals helped to provoke a widespread conservative reaction which united Anglicans of different devotional groups against them. In 1772 the Calvinist Augustus Toplady, who was planning a polemical life of Archbishop Laud, dropped the idea, lest it might encourage mud-slinging not only at Arminianism, but at Christian orthodoxy itself: 'we bid fair at present not for having an high Church', he wrote, 'but for having no Church at all'.[128] This was even more the case when the controversy entered another phase in 1782 with Joseph Priestley's Unitarian *History of the Corruptions of Christianity*. Priestley's case (that the Trinity was not a doctrine of the Church in its earliest days but a later accretion) had some scholarly force, but it fell on deaf ears and merely united the clerical body still further in defence of orthodoxy. This time the heretic was not a renegade Anglican, but an outsider, a Dissenter, and a political radical, against whom all orthodox Anglicans could rally. The overall effects of a century of Trinitarian controversy are hard to assess, but it is at least arguable that they were as productive of unity as of dissension. The doctrine of the Trinity had its attendant metaphysical difficulties, but these do not seem to have been sufficient to trouble most Churchmen, who

[127] Abbey and Overton, *English Church*, I, 480–529, quotation at p. 490.
[128] A. Toplady, *Works* (6 vols., 1794), VI, 168.

appear to have accepted it simply, and to have seen those who abandoned or qualified it as deviants from the historic Christian faith.

The issue of subscription was a more serious cause of anxiety and division, for it posed problems which potentially affected all the major groupings of the Church. Those most troubled by the obligation of subscription were liberal Churchmen who believed that confessional formulae riveted on to the Church man-made metaphysical systems beyond the warrant of the Scriptures, inhibited the exercise of private judgement and tied the Church to obsolete theological formulations.

The critics of Latitudinarianism often spoke as though it was only the liberals who wriggled at the requirement that clergymen should subscribe to the Articles in their 'literal and grammatical sense'. This was not the case. Many Churchmen, including Daniel Waterland, the critic of Arian subscription, felt some embarrassment about the unfashionably Calvinistic tone of some of the Articles, particularly the 17th on Predestination. In 1772, the year of the Feathers Tavern petition, Beilby Porteus, future bishop of London, petitioned the Archbishop of Canterbury for a review of the Liturgy and Articles, and in particular for a change to make the 17th 'more clear and perspicuous, and less liable to be wrested by our adversaries to a Calvinistic sense'.[129] A good deal of thought and not a little agony was devoted to the casuistry of subscription. The anti-Trinitarian William Hopkins, who subscribed five times in his career, felt at the end of his life that he might have been guilty of quasi-blasphemy, which, he wrote, was 'something very shocking to my soul'. The philosopher David Hartley was dissuaded from taking holy orders by the requirement. Many subscribers, however, reassured themselves with the argument of Bishop Burnet that, though the Articles demanded 'assent', they were framed in such a way as to be taken in different and even contradictory senses. Others adopted Samuel Clarke's solution, that anyone might subscribe to them if he believed them to be broadly reconcilable with Scripture.[130] Perhaps only the Evangelicals accepted them joyfully in their literal sense, claiming that they alone held unequivocally to the title deeds of the English Reformation.

Unfortunately, however, if the Evangelicals delighted in their attachment to the Articles, some were uneasy about the Liturgy. The Prayer Book contained statements which they found hard to square with Reformed orthodoxy, particularly the rubrics for baptism (which seemed to affirm baptismal regeneration) and burial (which appeared to imply that every deceased person was a regenerate soul). In 1757 Walker of Truro contem-

[129] D. Waterland, *The Case of Arian Subscription Considered* (Cambridge, 1721), pp. 39–42; R. Hodgson, *The Life of Beilby Porteus* (1811), p. 39.

[130] Langford, *Public Life*, p. 109; *DNB*, IX, 67; G. Burnet, *An Exposition of the Thirty-Nine Articles* (1699), p. 8; J. Ferguson, *Dr Samuel Clarke* (Kineton, 1976), pp. 179–86.

plated leaving the Church after he had pronounced the optimistic words of the burial rubric – 'a sure and certain hope' of resurrection – over a local debauchee. Several early nineteenth-century Evangelical seceders, in Puritan style, cited the popish imperfections of the Liturgy as a major cause of their disaffection.[131]

At the close of the eighteenth century, the epicentre of the debate over the Articles had shifted away from its location in the Trinitarian and Feathers Tavern controversies. It now centred no longer on Latitudinarians, but rather on the rival claims of Evangelicals and High Churchmen to be the standard-bearers of Anglican orthodoxy. A signal-gun was the publication of *The True Churchmen Ascertained* (1801) by the combative John Overton of York, who argued that only Evangelicals still adhered to the principles of the English Reformation. The controversy – an indication that the Evangelicals were now being taken seriously – smouldered and fizzed for years, like a Chinese cracker. It provided the staple for many a Bampton lecture and episcopal charge. Though the debate was known as 'the Calvinist controversy' predestination was only one of several issues at stake, and not the most important, for, if it was a doctrine to which most Evangelicals subscribed, it was not one generally regarded as an essential dogma. John Newton spoke for many when he remarked that 'Calvinism should be in our discussions like a lump of sugar in a cup of tea; all should taste of it, but it should not be met with in separate form.'[132] More central was the debate on the nature of justification and of regeneration, which prefigured the Gorham controversy. However, the argument remained comparatively subdued and intermittent. It never approached the temperature level of mid-Victorian church party conflicts. The *Christian Observer* stressed that this was not 'a *bellum usque ad internecionem* [a war to the death] ... It is about a certain tract of territory; a sort of borderers' war, respecting boundaries not easy to be settled.'[133] Though the debate about the Reformed and the Catholic elements in the Anglican inheritance was under way, it was, as yet, muted.

By 1800 theology and ecclesiology were not the only factors making for partisan feelings. The different Anglican schools of churchmanship were now evolving ganglions which prefigured the party formations of the Victorian Church. The Evangelicals led the way here. More than other groupings, they were perceived as having some of the attributes of a church 'party'.[134] From an early stage they possessed a sense of distinctiveness. Initially this was forced upon them by rancorous opposition to their alleged

[131] Davies, *Early Cornish Evangelicals*, pp. 193–6; G. Carter, 'Evangelical Seceders from the Church of England, *c.*1800–50', DPhil dissertation, University of Oxford, 1990, *passim.*

[132] J. Scott, *The Life and Times of the Rev. T. Scott* (6th edn, 1824), p. 446.

[133] *Christian Observer*, 7 (1808), 736. [134] Ibid., 2 (1803), 33.

'enthusiasm', which banded them together in their adversity. More fundamentally, it stemmed from the experience of conversion, the 'great change' which marked the Evangelical off from his unregenerate colleagues and pushed him towards those who shared a similar experience. The Calvinistic doctrine of predestined particular election, of being personally singled out by God for salvation, heightened the sense of apartness felt by many Evangelicals. The appearance of partisanship also resulted from a degree of organizational articulation which was highly unusual in the Hanoverian Church. From the beginning of the Revival, Evangelicals had been well aware of the pastoral and evangelistic utility of voluntary societies. Though the primary aim of the early Methodist and the later Evangelical societies was to revitalize the Church and to reform the nation, they also created something like an embryonic party organization, whose nation-wide networks gave them the attributes of a confederacy. At first the 'Gospel clergy' had been scattered sparsely across the landscape, but they had gradually banded themselves together to form clerical clubs, like those at Elland in Yorkshire and Rauceby in Lincolnshire; regional conclaves which took on the role of unofficial synods, in which something like a party line was hammered out on issues of faith and order. These provincial associations gave the Evangelical clergy the rudiments of a national framework, for they corresponded with each other – an exchange of letters between the Rauceby and Bristol societies and the Eclectic Society in London, for example, contributed to the formation of the Church Missionary Society.[135] The great Evangelical voluntary societies, while often interdenominational, like the Bible Society and the Religious Tract Society, had a largely Anglican leadership. Their interlocking directorates and large networks of 'auxiliaries' up and down the kingdom gave the Evangelicals the appearance of a formidably coherent pressure group.[136] Such affiliations, outside episcopal control, appeared alarming in a Church which was now becoming uneasy about its own decentralization. The 'Gospel clergy' had ceased to be a congeries of despised provincial clerics and were moving from the periphery towards the centre of Anglican culture, a transition paralleled by the growing influence of that prominent, London-based group of politicians, administrators and businessmen known as the Clapham Sect.

The clergy of other schools were bound together more by informal ties of sentiment than by such organizational bonds. Yet the value of association was becoming obvious to all, and by the early nineteenth century High Churchmen, responding to the pastoral challenge of the times and to Evangelical competition, were coalescing into more coherent groupings.

[135] See C. Hole, *The Early History of the Church Missionary Society* (1896), pp. 23–34.
[136] F. K. Brown, *Fathers of the Victorians* (Cambridge, 1961).

The so-called 'Hackney Phalanx', led by the layman Joshua Watson and H. H. Norris, exerted an influence not unlike that of the Clapham Sect. They too extended their influence through voluntary associations which were not interdenominational, as were some of the Evangelical societies, but sternly Anglican and aimed at the promotion of 'Church principles', like the National Society for the Education of the Poor (1811) and the Church Building Society (1817).

Church periodicals provided another important point of union. The founding of *The Orthodox Churchman's Magazine* (1801), still more that of *The British Critic* (1793) and *The Christian Remembrancer* (1818), focused High Church opinion. The Evangelicals published their equivalents, such as the moderate *Christian Observer* (1802), the organ of the Claphamites and their clerical friends, and *The Record* (1828) which expounded a sterner, less accommodating variety of 'vital religion'. Periodicals played an important part in articulating nascent party feeling. Through their reviews, articles and hagiography they helped to disseminate a particular Anglican viewpoint, moulding group opinion as well as reflecting it: they provided a centre for cohesion and collective loyalty, giving a sense of kinship to readers scattered across the country.

The identity of Anglicanism[137]

On the eve of the Oxford Movement the centripetal forces within the Church were still vastly more powerful than the centrifugal. At the parochial level, Anglicanism drew on a massive, unreflecting attachment to the established Church as the Church of the nation, rooted in English history. Its intelligentsia was seldom riven into rival factions. Under George II and George III the Church of England may or may not have been a Latitudinarian Church, but it was certainly a broad Church. Throughout much of the period covered by this volume the forces making for consensus greatly outweighed those making for conflict. Historians too often neglect the silent majority. They frequently distort the course of Anglican history by focusing on the writings of controversialists and extremists, ginger-groups like the Feathers Tavern petitioners or coteries like the Hackney Phalanx and the Clapham Sect, and overlook the huge body of religious literature which bears the imprint of no particular subgrouping in the Church.

The day-to-day routines of parish life went on regardless of partisan attachments. If Anglicans differed in their politics and styles of

[137] Though the adjective 'Anglican' can be traced to the early seventeenth century, it is not a word generally employed in the period covered by this volume. Nonetheless, as this section will show, Anglican and Anglicanism can be usefully applied to describe the distinctive characteristics which contemporaries saw as defining the Church of England.

churchmanship, they were united in their pastoral endeavours and in their fundamental loyalty to the Prayer Book and ultimate willingness to accept the Articles. Though dividing on some doctrinal or political issues, Churchmen could often unite on others, especially those touching non-partisan campaigns for moral reform or philanthropy. Craig Rose's essay underlines this point, showing how – even in the faction-torn reign of Anne – Whig politicians and High Tory clerics could meet together to launch the SPCK. Much the same held true at the end of the eighteenth century, when a new movement for the reformation of manners mobilized support from a very broad spectrum of opinion.[138] Jeff Chamberlain's study shows how one member of the High Church dynasty of the Frewen family, despite his nostalgic Toryism and residual Jacobitism, could welcome a firm Whig, Matthias Mawson, as bishop of Chichester because of his reputation as a good man and a conscientious pastor. No doubt examples could be piled up to validate the existence of massive Anglican consensus and solidarity in the eighteenth-century Church. Even those who appear to stand for highly distinctive styles of churchmanship often show cross-bench attachments which make it difficult to label them as partisans. Archbishop Tillotson, for example, often regarded as the epitome of Latitudinarianism, died in the arms of Robert Nelson, the saintly Nonjuror. The reading lists of Georgian Anglicans show a catholicity which might have surprised some of their Victorian successors. The books read by Anna Larpent in the late eighteenth century combined Latitudinarian moral theology with High Church devotional manuals. Bishop Cleaver of Chester may be classified as a High Churchman, but in 1791 his suggested reading list for his clergy included not only the Fathers and Nonjurors on *jure divino* episcopacy, but also the German biblical critic Michaelis on the New Testament and a pungently Calvinist work, John Edwards's *The Preacher*.[139]

Though dramatic alterations of political regime affected the complexion of the Church they could not lead to a sudden and drastic remodelling such as that which affected the civil administration. There could be no purge of parish livings or cathedral chapters similar to that imposed on the commissions of the peace. The patronage of the Crown was limited to less than 10 per cent of church livings, while the other 90 per cent remained in the hands of private patrons and corporations both clerical and lay, like the Oxford and Cambridge colleges or the City livery companies. The dispersal of patronage among so many hands enabled temporarily unfashionable styles

[138] J. Innes, 'Politics and Morals. The Reformation of Manners Movement in Later Eighteenth-Century England', in *Transformation of Political Culture*, ed. Hellmuth, pp. 57–118.

[139] MS Huntington Library, San Marino (we owe this reference to Professor John Brewer); W. Cleaver, *A List of Books Intended for the Use of the Younger Clergy* (Oxford, 1791).

of churchmanship to survive and flourish. In the eighteenth century the number of advowsons in the gift of clergymen seems to have increased in some areas, encouraging the creation of clerical dynasties – like the Frewens – which enabled a family devotional tradition to be maintained across the decades, regardless of alterations at Westminster or Canterbury. Similarly, both Evangelical and High Church laymen used the patronage and influence at their disposal, not for the purpose of nepotism, but to advance like-minded clerics.[140]

The cohesion of the eighteenth-century Church was strengthened by a cult of religious moderation. Here in the opinion of Norman Sykes (a moderate in his own opinions) was one of the main self-defining characteristics of the Hanoverian Church. This had not always been the case. After the Revolution moderation possessed offensive Whiggish implications of lukewarmness and laxism; 'No Moderation' was a High Church slogan in the election of 1702.[141] Thereafter, for many decades, it was more usually encouraged as a cardinal Christian virtue. After 1715, as the Vicar of Bray put it, 'moderate men looked big'. Philippians 4.5 became a much-used text, which was seen as epitomizing the spirit of Hanoverian churchmanship: 'Let your moderation be known unto all men.' The promotion of eirenicism and tolerance chimed in nicely with the values of the English Enlightenment. It also fitted the requirements of Whig oligarchs who pursued their goal of political stability by avoiding contentious ideological issues. The cult of moderation was in part a defensive response to the political use by Tories of the cry of 'Church in Danger'; the Sacheverell business was burned into political memory. Whig politicians did not need to be reminded by Hume that 'moderation is of advantage to every establishment'. 'Extremes of all kinds are to be avoided.'[142]

The very intensity of clerical controversies in the post-Revolutionary decades provoked a reaction towards moderation. By the 1740s there were signs that they were beginning to subside. Philip Doddridge noted gratefully in 1744, 'I think our Clergy grow more moderate.' By mid-century Horace Walpole could comment on the absence of 'religious combustibles' on the contemporary scene. In the 1760s the change of mood had gone still further. In Lancashire, which had been notorious for its clerical divisions,

140 D. Hirschberg, 'The Government and Church Patronage in England, 1660–1760', *JBS*, 20 (1980–1), 112–13; Albers, 'Seeds of Contention', I, 39–40; C. Dewey, *The Passing of Barchester* (1991); Walsh, 'Yorkshire Evangelicals', pp. 233–4.

141 G. Bennett, 'The Era of Party Zeal 1702–14', in *The History of the University of Oxford, vol. V: The Eighteenth Century*, ed. L. Sutherland and L. Mitchell (Oxford, 1986), p. 62.

142 Quoted R. Greaves, *On the Religious Climate of Hanoverian England* (Inaugural Lecture, Bedford College, London, 1963), p. 3. For the famous song 'The Vicar of Bray', first printed in 1734, see *The New Oxford Book of English Verse*, ed. H. Gardner (Oxford, 1972), pp. 425–7.

Jan Albers has noted that the clergy now saw themselves increasingly as a 'united front, acting as a government party rather than as the guardians of partisan animosities'.[143] Can we see here the results of a generational break; the arrival into holy orders of a cohort of younger clergy, reared under the Whig hegemony and predisposed to accept the principles of religious moderation?

A major reason for the decline of clerical in-fighting lay in the slow abatement of the political party conflicts with which the tensions in the Church had possessed a symbiotic relationship. As the Nonjurors dwindled in number and Jacobitism lost its relevance, the dynastic issue ceased to trouble Anglican consciences. George III's war on party had its effect on the Church, as Tory clergymen rallied to heartfelt support of the dynasty and eagerly anticipated opportunities for preferment. As Paul Langford has noted, the political cleavages which had divided social life in the early eighteenth century, splitting fox hunts, book clubs and assemblies, gave way to a more relaxed bipartisanship which affected clerical as well as lay life.[144]

In the age of the Whig hegemony there were not so many opportunities for clerical party feeling to manifest itself. After the passage of the Septennial Act there were fewer electoral occasions for the ventilation of contentious church issues. The suspension of Convocation after 1717 deprived angry High-flyers of a forum in which to mobilize clerical opinion as they had in the palmy days of Atterbury. This silencing of the Church's synodical voice worried some clerical leaders, but Archbishop Secker himself considered it on balance in the best interests of the Church. Though church issues were exploited by the Tory opposition, they were deliberately played down by Whig political leaders who had no intention of reawakening the 'Church in Danger' furore which had shattered their hopes in 1710. Episodes like the Convocation controversy, 'the Sacheverell madness' and the Bangorian conflict remained evergreen in Whig memory. The possibility that these passions were not extinct but only dormant gave Whiggish Churchmen cause for unease and inclined them to caution. Commenting on the well-orchestrated public outcry at the Jewish Naturalization Bill in 1753, Archbishop Herring wrote gloomily 'what a thin covering of embers had kept down the fire of high-church!'[145]

The 'moderation' of the Hanoverian Church was to some extent the

[143] G. Nuttall, *Calendar of the Correspondence of Philip Doddridge DD (1702–51)* (1979), p. 194; H. Walpole, *Memoirs of King George II*, ed. J. Brooke (3 vols., New Haven, 1985), III, 8; Albers, 'Seeds of Contention', II, 326.

[144] Langford, *Public Life*, ch. 2, esp. pp. 118–31.

[145] N. Sykes, *From Sheldon to Secker* (Cambridge, 1959), pp. 222–3; L. Colley, *In Defiance of Oligarchy. The Tory Party 1714–60* (Cambridge, 1982), pp. 104–17; J. Disney, *Memoirs of the Life of Arthur Ashley Sykes* (1789), p. 99.

result of a self-conscious strategy. Governments generally avoided making provocative episcopal appointments. In the early decades of the Whig hegemony there were one or two controversial elevations, such as that of Hoadly, whose views were seen as extreme by many fellow Low Churchmen, but even then Samuel Clarke was passed over and in 1730 Hoadly himself was denied translation to Durham. A storm of protest prevented the suspected Arian Thomas Rundle from getting an English see, though he was later fobbed off with an Irish one. After 1742, when Newcastle controlled the patronage, there was no recurrence of such provocation; clerics notorious as controversialists were not preferred. Throughout the period those who reached the very top were generally safe men, moderates, like Wake, Gibson, Secker, Porteus and Moore. Moderate conservatism, rather than any active commitment to Latitudinarianism, characterized the governors of church and state.[146] Great caution was shown over issues of church reform. Under George I, Whig leaders were forced in 1717 to back away from the repeal of the Test Acts, demanded by their Dissenting friends, lest they alienate their fearful supporters and antagonize the episcopate. In the early 1730s Walpole gave little support to those Whigs who were pushing a package of provocatively anti-clerical measures, including the repeal of the Test Act. In the 1740s and 1750s plans for an Anglican episcopate in America foundered not only because ministers were anxious about the political repercussions in the colonies, but because they might arouse contention at home. The hopes of Latitudinarian activists that 'a farther reformation' might be achieved by revising the Thirty-Nine Articles and the Liturgy were severely hampered by a general suspicion that such improvement might revive dormant politico-religious animosities. Archbishop Herring, who was strongly believed to favour such reform in the abstract, was careful to give it no official countenance. Archbishop Potter spoke for many church leaders when he remarked that 'the unsettling any religious Establishment often proves a greater Evil, than any of those Inconveniences, or Defects, which it is intended to remedy'. Governments still pursued this prudent maxim after 1760, and even in the more troubled 1770s, as G. M. Ditchfield's essay reveals, the religious policy of Lord North's government was characterized by a cautious liberalism.[147]

The ideal of moderation was encouraged by constant invocation of the idea of Anglicanism as a *via media*. This had a long pedigree, but it attained

[146] Sykes, *Gibson*, pp. 134–7, 265–76; Taylor, 'Church and State', ch. 5; Mather, 'Georgian Churchmanship', p. 282.

[147] G. Townend, 'Religious Radicalism and Conservatism in the Whig Party under George I', *Parliamentary History*, 7 (1988), 24–44; Taylor, 'Walpole and the Church', pp. 51–77; idem, 'Whigs, Bishops and America: The Politics of Church Reform in Mid-Eighteenth-Century England', *HJ*, 36, 2 (1993); Disney, *Sykes*, pp. 98–9; J. Potter, *Works* (3 vols., Oxford, 1753), I, 416.

its full flowering in the Hanoverian Church.[148] The note was firmly struck in 1711 in one of the *Spectator*'s most influential essays. Addison applauded the way in which the national Church occupied a median position between the opposite ideals of religious unity and religious freedom. In a dream, his Mr Spectator finds himself in the Great Hall of the Bank of England surrounded by emblems of England's strength: there, 'at the Upper-end of the Hall was the *Magna Charta*, with the Act of Uniformity on the right Hand, and the Act of Toleration on the left'. Spectator is shaken by the appearance of various spectres of discord, then relieved by the sight of benign apparitions, a procession of well-matched couples who epitomize the factors which bring stability to the body politic. Well to the fore comes 'Moderation leading in Religion'. Addison was a Whig and in 1711 this was still a propagandist position, but what for him was a 'Vision' was increasingly to become a reality after 1715.[149]

The belief that the Church of England pursued an Aristotelian mean between ecclesiastical extremes was attractive to Hanoverian Churchmen. The traumas of the seventeenth century, when the Church had been assailed on two fronts, had sharpened up the idea of Anglicanism as a middle way and given it strong historical plausibility: in those dark days, lamented John Wilder in 1739, 'this truly Apostolical Church [was] wounded, mangled, and by Papists and Puritans, alike Crucified, like our Saviour, between Two Thieves'.[150] In the eighteenth century it gained added strength from its consonance with classical and Enlightenment ideals of balance, proportion and harmony. It blended with the powerful cultural ideal of 'politeness'. The metaphor of Anglicanism as a golden mean was conveniently applicable in a wide variety of contexts. Ecclesiologists stressed the central path of the Church of England between the claims of Rome and Geneva; between the infallibilist authoritarianism of Rome and the excessive individualism of radical Protestants, with their extreme view of the right of private judgement. One of the uses of the idea of the *via media* was that it allowed Anglicanism to be defined negatively rather than positively. Apologists often contented themselves with explaining what the Church of England was not, rather than what it was. This avoided many of the difficulties involved in defending a Church which was professedly both Catholic and Reformed, clearly separated off from the Roman Church, yet distinct from other Protestant churches by her strong continuities with the medieval past, above all by her retention of the historic episcopate. Calendrical occasions existed which encouraged the negative delimitation of the

[148] See, e.g., D. Campbell, *The Church Her Own Apologist* (1818), adapted from T. Puller, *The Moderation of the Church of England* (1679).

[149] *Spectator*, ed. Bond, I, 14–17.

[150] J. Wilder, *The Trial of the Spirits* (Oxford, 1739), pp. 21–2.

boundaries of Anglicanism. On 30 January the clergy were enjoined to use the rubric commemorating the execution of King Charles I, which gave an opportunity to distance the Church from Protestant sectaries and enthusiasts; on 5 November they celebrated her preservation from popery and superstition.

In the age of Deism and Methodism, the median role of the Church was traced along another continuum, as marking the proper line between what Bishop Gibson, in a celebrated pastoral letter, saw as the contrary distortions of 'Enthusiasm' and 'Lukewarmness'. Evangelicals themselves put the conception of the 'middle way' to good use. The Evangelical moderates claimed that their theology kept a median path between the Scylla of high Calvinist fatalism and the Charybdis of Arminianism. Charles Simeon assured his readers, 'I have laboured to maintain that spirit of moderation which so eminently distinguishes the Established Church.'[151] The idea of the 'middle way' was set in what was virtually a cyclical theory of English church history. It became an Anglican commonplace that a religious exaggeration in one direction produced a dangerous pendular swing the other way. Puritan rigorism was largely to blame for Restoration laxism; the excesses of free-thought in the 1720s and 1730s were held to be responsible for provoking the 'enthusiastic' extravagance of the early Methodists. The message was clear: like the Marquis of Halifax's famous 'Trimmer', the good English Churchman should whenever possible avoid extremes and take up the middle ground.

The triumph of 'moderation' was assisted by a growing sense of security. It was easier for eighteenth-century Churchmen to maintain a stance of relaxed tolerantism once the Church of England no longer felt itself under much pressure from its rivals. The fears of many High Churchmen that the Toleration Act would lead to a great expansion of Nonconformity gradually proved to be groundless. By the 1730s Nonconformist leaders like Watts and Doddridge were publicly bemoaning 'the decay of the Dissenting interest'.[152] It was clear that Nonconformity had been largely marginalized: though often perceived as a nuisance it was not seen as a threat to Anglican hegemony. Meanwhile, the fear of Rome, which had appeared so menacing in the age of Popish Plots, slowly receded and might have receded more rapidly if Jacobitism and the prospect of a Catholic Pretender had not kept it artificially alive. In the seventeenth century the intellectual challenge of Roman Catholicism had stung a succession of heavyweight apologists like Stillingfleet into defending the integrity of Anglicanism; in the eighteenth century Anglican apologetic was usually pitched at a lower level. The

[151] E. Gibson, *The Bishop of London's Pastoral Letter ... By Way of Caution against Lukewarmness ... and Enthusiasm* (1739); C. Simeon, *Horae Homileticae* (21 vols., 1832–3), I, Dedication. [152] Watts, *Dissenters*, pp. 382–93.

main threat of Rome to the Church was no longer seen to lie in her appeal to the elite but in the furtive proselytizing of her disguised priests among the poor, for whom her quasi-magical superstition still held some attraction. Most anti-Roman publications were not learned treatises but popular tracts.[153]

Even when Churchmen were at their most quarrelsome, they were quietly confident in the superiority of their own Church over all others. The Anglican Church was seen to be constitutionally sound and closer than any other to the model of apostolic purity. She was 'the best visible church on earth'. Though she might have her imperfections, she was vastly superior to her rivals to left or right. Most Churchmen would have agreed with the Restoration apologist Joseph Glanvill when he declared 'we are freed from the idolatries, superstition and other corruptions of the Roman Church on the one hand; and clear from the vanities and enthusiasms that have overspread some Protestant churches on the other. Our church hath rejected the painted bravery of the one and provided against the sordid slovenliness of the other.'[154] After the departure of the Nonjurors, the absence of any large-scale secessions suggests that eighteenth-century clergy were ideologically contented with their lot. There were a few seceders. One or two 'Methodistical' parsons moved into formal Dissent, like the Countess of Huntingdon's former chaplain, Thomas Wills; perhaps half a dozen Evangelical clergy departed in the so-called 'Western Schism' of 1815. On the other side, a handful of liberals made their exit into Unitarianism in the 1770s. But these losses were almost certainly counter-balanced by movement the other way, with the migration to Anglicanism of conforming Dissenting ministers (some fifty between 1714 and 1731), foreign Protestants and Roman Catholics.[155] The Church had its complement of incipient mutineers, but extremely few deserters.

Unlike many of their predecessors and successors, eighteenth-century English clerics were sufficiently relaxed in their churchmanship to feel little need to defend the integrity of their Church or to define its identity. After Wake, the Hanoverian Church produced little that was constructive or fresh in the way of ecclesiology. The scholarly spade work had already been conveniently done by forebears who had written in an atmosphere of polemical urgency which no longer existed. The Church was confident of her doctrinal and ecclesiological superiority over her rivals. She believed that her authority was traceable back beyond the Rome-inspired mission of

[153] Haydon, 'Anti-Catholicism', ch. 3.

[154] T. Biddulph, *Practical Essays on the Services of the Church of England* (3 vols., 1810), I, 17; J. Cope, *Joseph Glanvill* (St Louis, 1956), p. 13.

[155] Carter, 'Evangelical Seceders', ch. 4; Watts, *Dissenters*, p. 384; E. Duffy, 'Over the Wall: Converts from Popery in Eighteenth-Century England', *Downside Review*, 94 (1976), 1–25.

Augustine of Canterbury to the autonomous patriarchates of Celtic Christianity, perhaps even to Joseph of Arimathea and St Paul.[156] Archbishop Wake assured his Gallican correspondents in 1718, 'the Church of England is free, is orthodox; she has a plenary authority within herself. She has no need to recur to other churches to direct her what to believe or what to do'. Wake was confident enough in the superiority of Anglicanism to desire the export of its 'orderly episcopacy' to the Protestant Churches on the Continent.[157]

A high degree of consensus bound the clergy to the polity, Articles and Liturgy of their Church. This did not mean that all saw eye to eye. No single ecclesiology united all Churchmen. As the Bangorian controversy showed, there were different views of what constituted a Church. A few High Churchmen saw episcopacy as essential; most others probably saw it as pertaining to the *bene esse* but not the very *esse* of a Church. Evangelicals warmly defended episcopacy as ancient and apostolic, liberals like Paley justified it on grounds of utility, and even an advanced Hoadlyite like A. A. Sykes allowed that the Scriptures supported the idea of 'a regulated, and even an episcopal ministry'.[158] But all accepted it. The dogmatic tolerance of the Church rested on a generous view of the division between fundamentals and non-essentials. Though divines differed sharply at times over the precise interpretation of the Thirty-Nine Articles, this did not matter in practice as much as might have been expected. Writing in 1718 to the Swiss cantons who were deeply split over the issue of doctrinal uniformity, Wake assured them that in the English Church bishops and clergy of different persuasions could subscribe to the Articles because 'we have left every one to interpret them in his own sense; and they are indeed so generally framed, that they may, without an equivocation, have more senses than one fairly put upon them'.[159]

As we have seen, such eirenicism did not prevent religious conflicts from disturbing the peace of the Church. Yet not all of these were disruptive of its stability, for if controversies could sometimes divide the Hanoverian clergy, they could also unite them. Joseph Trapp remarked ruefully in 1721, 'were we only attacked from Without, not betrayed from Within; the united Powers of Earth and Hell could not hurt our Cause ... *Nothing can ruin the Church, but the Church*'.[160] But when the struggle was with an external

[156] Spurr, *Restoration Church*, ch. 3; J. Champion, *The Pillars of Priestcraft Shaken. The Church of England and its Enemies 1660–1730* (Cambridge, 1992), pp. 55–63. Similar arguments were still being used a century later. See G. Williams, 'Some Protestant Views of Early British Church History', *History*, 38 (1953), 219–33.

[157] Quoted N. Sykes, *William Wake, Archbishop of Canterbury* (2 vols., Cambridge, 1957), I, 266, and G. Every, *The High Church Party 1688–1718* (1956), p. 168.

[158] Disney, *Sykes*, p. 9. See also N. Sykes, *Old Priest, New Presbyter* (Cambridge, 1956), ch. 6.

[159] Sykes, *Wake*, II, 32–3. For different interpretations of the Articles see pp. 48–9 above.

[160] J. Trapp, *The Dignity and Benefit of the Priesthood* (1721), p. 36.

enemy, clergymen often fought together as a pack. The deist challenge of the 1720s and 1730s threw Churchmen into gloom and panic, but it also drew High Churchmen and Low together against the common foe and mitigated the disruptive effects of the Bangorian controversy. Much the same held true for the French Revolutionary years, when alarmed Churchmen of all persuasions manned the ramparts of the establishment, shoulder to shoulder, against the perceived assaults of Methodist sectaries, Jacobin infidels and radical Unitarians.

Though the Hanoverian clergy were at times divided by particular theological issues, they were bonded together by a firm commitment to the defence of the national Church, by law established. Increasingly, too, they were united by their involvement in the defence and maintenance of the propertied order. This was visible both at the ideological and at the governmental level. A new mood was evident in Anglican homiletics during the American Revolution, when, as James Bradley's recent study has shown, the clergy rallied to the support of the government's policy of coercion, in opposition to the Dissenters who often petitioned for conciliation. In the troubled 1780s and the panicky 1790s there was a marked shift away from political and constitutional questions which had preoccupied the clergy earlier in the century, such as the origins of government, the nature of political obligation and the right of rebellion, in favour of a new concentration on social theory. Robert Hole has demonstrated that the homiletic stress was now on themes of social control: on hierarchy, restraint and obedience. On these themes there was little to separate the politico-theology of High Churchmen like Horsley from Evangelicals like Hannah More, or, indeed, from that of many liberals.[161] Meanwhile, the clergy became increasingly involved not merely in the theoretical defence of the propertied order, but, as has been seen, in its actual administration, above all as JPs.[162] This helped to mitigate the effects of any clash between rival devotional schools. As clergymen of all sorts sat side by side on the bench upholding the social order, doctrinal divisions lost much of their power to fragment the clerical body.

Conclusion

In the century and a half of Anglican history covered by this volume the Church underwent a variety of changes of mood and ethos. Even in the

[161] J. Bradley, 'The Anglican Pulpit, the Social Order, and the Resurgence of Toryism during the American Revolution', *Albion*, 21 (1989), 361–88; idem, *Religion, Revolution and English Radicalism* (Cambridge, 1990); R. Hole, *Pulpits, Politics and Public Order in England 1760–1832* (Cambridge, 1989); Clark, *English Society*, ch. 4.

[162] See above pp. 7, 28.

years of greatest stability under George II and George III it had its complement of crises, controversies and fresh pastoral challenges. Its churchmanship was not static. The balance of strength between its traditional devotional schools altered significantly, while within those schools there were important shifts of outlook and idiom. New Evangelical was not the same as old Puritan. Nor was the Romantic Tractarian the same being as the old, static High Churchman. The liberal Oxford Noetics of the 1820s distanced themselves from the Cambridge Latitudinarians of the previous century.

At the same time, there is a strong degree of structural unity about the history of the Church in the 'long' eighteenth century. This is most obviously the case with its legal and constitutional position. After the Revolution of 1688 the Church operated within a juridical framework which lasted, with minor adjustments, until the eve of the Reform crisis. The Toleration Act sanctioned religious pluralism, within limits, and allowed orthodox Protestant Dissent to compete with the established Church for the souls of the English people. The Test Acts ensured that the established Church nonetheless maintained a powerful social and political ascendancy and that Anglicans alone possessed rights of first-class citizenship. This somewhat ungainly compromise congealed into a durable system. At first, many Churchmen had reacted with shock to the replacement of the principle of uniformity by that of toleration, but the post-Revolutionary system became accepted as a hallowed part of 'our matchless constitution in Church and State'. The balance of Toleration and Test Acts was elevated by Warburton above the realm of historical event into that of a theoretical ideal, with near-universal validity. 'That most just of all Public Laws, the Law of TOLERATION . . . is certainly of DIVINE ORIGINAL', he wrote: it was 'a sovereign Law of Nature.'[163] Ironically, the Revolution settlement of church and state which had alarmed so many Tories under William and Anne was defended as sacrosanct by their great-grandsons by the time of the French Revolution: it was now hallowed by the patina of prescription as well as by a century of proven utility.

In some ways what has been termed the 'constitutional revolution' of 1828–32 brought a decisive break with the old legal order. The repeal of the Test and Corporation Acts in 1828, Roman Catholic Emancipation in 1829, the reform of the electoral system in a direction that gave greater strength to popular opinion – these successive hammer blows made a huge psychological impact on Anglican Churchmen.[164] The old 'Protestant Constitution' had gone; the confident hegemony of the established Church

[163] W. Warburton, *The Doctrine of Grace* (1763), pp. 189–90.

[164] G. Best, 'The Constitutional Revolution, 1828–32, and its Consequences for the Established Church', *Theology*, 62 (1959), 226–34.

was shaken. A Parliament open to rivals of the Church of England, to Catholics and Dissenters, could no longer be deemed 'a lay synod of the Church of England'.[165] It was clear to many that another seismic shift had taken place in church–state relations, comparable to that of the Revolution of 1688. The constitution had lurched further towards officially sanctioned pluralism – and hence towards a state system effectively governed by principles of indifferentism and secularism. From now on, in the opinion of John Keble in his famous Assize Sermon of 1833, the Church of England was only '*one sect among many*'.[166]

By the 1830s the consensual Anglicanism of the late Hanoverian era had begun to fragment. Recognizable 'church parties' were beginning to surface. The Oxford Movement introduced a new note of ultraism into High Churchmanship: 'CHOOSE YOUR SIDE' was the brusque injunction of Newman in the first of the *Tracts for the Times*. The Evangelicals in turn responded to the aggressive Catholic revival with shrill cries of 'No Popery'.[167] Nor was conflict confined to skirmishes between the Reformed and Catholic tendencies in the Church. Within those groupings themselves new fissures appeared. In the late 1820s the interior harmony of the Evangelical party began to fracture. The Apocrypha controversy which rent the Bible Society revealed the extent of the gap between the moderates of the Wilberforce–Simeon school, represented by the *Christian Observer*, and the sterner, more dogmatic Calvinists represented by the *Record*. The threat of revolution at home and abroad excited currents of pre-millennial excitement which further divided the Evangelical camp. At the same time the Oxford Movement created similar cleavages within Anglican High Churchmanship. The 'safe men' of the old Orthodox school were sharply criticized for their lethargy and complacency by the new Tractarian leaders. In scarcely veiled language, the preface to Hurrell Froude's *Remains* (1838) hinted at some of the issues which separated the new High Churchmen from the old: the Tractarians' less than reverential attitude to 'human establishments' of religion and their actively irreverent treatment of the sixteenth-century Reformers.[168] By the 1830s the existence of 'party feeling' was attracting the attention of clerical writers, particularly liberal Churchmen; in 1822 Richard Whately published a warning tract on *The Use and Abuse of*

[165] Quoted O. Brose, *Church and Parliament. The Reshaping of the Church of England 1828–60* (Stanford and London, 1959), pp. 30–1. The second Test Act of 1678 applied only to Catholics, so Protestant Dissenters had been able to sit in Parliament in the eighteenth century. Froude and others like him, however, feared that Catholic Emancipation and the extension of the franchise would make Parliament more susceptible to pressure from non-Anglicans.

[166] J. Keble, *National Apostasy Considered* (Oxford, 1833), Advertisement, p. iii.

[167] *Tracts for the Times*, 1 (1833), 4; P. Toon, *Evangelical Theology 1833–56* (1979), chs. 1–3.

[168] D. Bebbington, *Evangelicalism in Modern Britain* (1989), ch. 3; *Remains of Hurrell Froude* (2 vols., 1838), I, xiv–xv; Nockles, 'Change and Continuity', *passim*.

Party-Feeling in Matters of Religion. The intensification of partisan conflict led to debates over the ecclesiology, history and doctrine of the Church of England which made the identity of Anglicanism more problematic for some Churchmen. It was no longer so easy unquestioningly to accept the natural superiority of the Church of England over its rivals: now a more confident Roman Catholicism and a more militant Protestant Nonconformity posed challenges seldom encountered by the Church since the seventeenth century. The 1830s, 1840s and 1850s witnessed secessions from the Church on a scale unparalleled in the eighteenth century, mostly to Rome, though not a few made their exit into Protestant Dissent.

Nonetheless, as is the case with most enduring institutions, there was much in the established Church that remained unchanged. In many ways it is impossible to make a caesura between the Georgian and the Victorian Church of England. The formal worship of the 1662 Prayer Book carried on unaltered, though there were periodic suggestions for its emendation. Clerical subscription to the Articles remained obligatory until 1865, when it was relaxed in ways which would have delighted many old Latitudinarians.[169] Though the church reforms of the 1830s shocked many conservative Churchmen, they can be seen as part of a continuing process which can be traced back to the 1780s. Through voluntary societies, occasional acts of Parliament and a quiet strengthening of diocesan administrative structures, the Church was visibly adapting itself to social change well before 1830. There is a good case to be made for a 'gradualist' chronology of church reform, as well as for a 'cataclysmic' one which stresses the impact of Whig reforms.[170] Moreover, despite those reforms, it is not difficult to find areas of Victorian church life in which the allegedly eighteenth-century abuses of the Church quietly flourished much as before. The patronage system long resisted attempts at reform: in the 1870s hundreds of advowsons were on the open market and the *Ecclesiastical Gazette* carried advertisements from agents offering livings with light duties in sporting country.[171] The tenor of the cathedral close in mid-Victorian Barchester suggests that there had been no dramatic change in an area of clerical life where the Hanoverian Church is often portrayed at its least spiritual. Despite the tonic effects of church reform, it is not difficult to find examples of rowdy, sluggish or slovenly clergymen who fitted Victorian stereotypes of the Hanoverian age. Clerical pugilists still survived and clerical sportsmen flourished in parts of rural England. In the 1850s the poverty and low moral tone of the clergy in the hill country of Wales and the Lakes led W. J. Conybeare to the

169 Chadwick, *Victorian Church*, II, 133.
170 Virgin, *Age of Negligence*, pp. 264–7; Best, *Temporal Pillars*, ch. 4.
171 W. Evershed, 'Party and Patronage in the Church of England, 1800–1945', DPhil dissertation, University of Oxford, 1986, p. 43.

conclusion that Macaulay's well-known account of the rustic clergy in the reign of Charles II 'would apply almost verbatim to the mountain clergy in the present century'. The state of parish churches provided much to shock the medieval revivalists of the Cambridge Camden Society in the early Victorian period. Their magazine, *The Ecclesiologist*, was filled with critical reports: naves which housed fire engines, a furniture-store in a chancel, one altar used as a hat-stand, another covered in filthy baize rags.[172]

By now abuses of this kind were being regarded as unwelcome hangovers from a past order of things, and more particularly as relics of a negligent Hanoverian Church. By the early 1830s structures and attitudes which had been complacently accepted in the late eighteenth century had come to be widely regarded as in urgent need of reform. Within a generation a dramatic change in perception had taken place, which affected the Church as it did other national institutions. The Evangelical and Tractarian movements, like secular radical movements, had a vested interest in displaying the eighteenth century as a dark backcloth against which to depict the achievements of reform. This downgrading of the Hanoverian Church was all the more plausible now that a picture of the overall structure of church life was at last available as a result of various statistical inquiries, above all those of the great Parliamentary commissions, of which the Ecclesiastical Revenues Commission of 1835 had pride of place. Henceforth new, quantifiable criteria for the 'success' or 'failure' of the Church were available, which enabled the religious life of the previous era to be shown up as demonstrably defective. With the formation of the Ecclesiastical Commission in 1835, a centralized and permanent agency for improvement was now in being.

As a result, the *idea* of 'the eighteenth-century Church' as a definable entity, stagnant and corrupt, had been firmly created. It was a conception which rapidly gained ground. Even Sydney Smith seems to have accepted that he himself represented an era of churchmanship that was both deficient and *passé*: 'whenever you meet a clergyman of my age,' he told the young Gladstone in 1835, 'you may be quite sure he is a bad clergyman'. Whether he was correct in this self-condemnation, or, indeed, whether he was justified in attempting to make such a comparison of his own generation with that of Gladstone's, is a question to which much of this volume is addressed.[173]

[172] W. J. Conybeare, *Essays Ecclesiastic and Social* (1855), p. 4; *The Ecclesiologist*, 2–5 (1842–6), *passim*. [173] W. E. Gladstone, *Gleanings* (7 vols., 1879), VII, 220.

Part I

The pastoral work of the Church

2 The eighteenth-century Reformation: the pastoral task of Anglican clergy after 1689

Jeremy Gregory

Recent historical scholarship has emphasized the pastoral initiatives developed by both Protestant and Catholic churches throughout Europe in the century after the Reformation.[1] The fledgling Anglican Church has been shown to have participated in this preoccupation, in its concern for a more pastorally orientated clergy and in its attempt to inculcate Anglican doctrines and religious practices in the hearts and minds of parishioners.[2] But in the period after 1660, what might be called the second century of the Church of England, the pastoral focus of the Anglican clergy has been seen in a far less favourable light. Whilst the pastoral endeavours displayed in the decades immediately after 1660 have begun to gain recognition, it is still commonly supposed that the initial post-Restoration energy and enthusiasm gave way to complacency and inertia after 1689 or 1714, only to be reasserted during the Evangelical and Tractarian Revivals.[3] This essay explores some of the ways in which Anglican clergy in the century and a half between the Toleration Act of 1689 and the Tractarian movement saw their pastoral task and highlights some of the ways in which they hoped to implement it.

Some of the latest work on the functioning of the Church in this period, echoing older views, has tended to downplay the pastoral problems and concerns faced by Anglican clergy in the parishes. One recent study of the role of the Church between 1700 and 1840 has dubbed this an 'age of

1 See, for example, E. Cameron, *The European Reformation* (Oxford, 1990).

2 P. Collinson, *The Religion of Protestants* (Oxford, 1982); R. O'Day, *The English Clergy. The Emergence and Consolidation of a Profession 1588–1642* (Leicester, 1979); *Continuity and Change. Personnel and Administration of the Church of England 1500–1642*, ed. R. O'Day and F. Heal (Leicester, 1976).

3 For the Restoration period see R. A. Beddard, 'The Restoration Church', in *The Restored Monarchy*, ed. J. R. Jones (1979), pp. 155–75; D. Spaeth, 'Common Prayer? Popular Observance of the Anglican Liturgy in Restoration Wiltshire', in *Parish, Church and People*, ed. S. J. Wright (1988), pp. 125–51; J. Spurr, 'Anglican Apologetic and the Restoration Church', DPhil dissertation, University of Oxford, 1985. For the decline of this endeavour at the end of the seventeenth century, see A. Whiteman, 'The Re-establishment of the Church of England, 1660–3', *Transactions of the Royal Historical Society*, 5th ser., 5 (1955), 131.

negligence' in pastoral terms.[4] On the other hand, in J. C. D. Clark's interpretation of events the Anglican hegemony he perceives in the intellectual sphere was matched by an almost effortless Anglican dominance in the parishes of England. But in some ways Clark's work seriously underestimates the problems faced by clergy in their pastoral task. It might also be suggested that Clark's analysis has done little more than to reinterpret the traditional notion of eighteenth-century stasis. Instead of seeing the period as one which saw the triumph of rationalism and stability over religious fanaticism, we are now asked to see a new kind of stability based on this being an age of largely unperturbed and unproblematic faith. Anglicanism, so he assumes, was unquestioned and its essential tenets seem almost magically to have percolated right down the social scale. In brief, the new eighteenth century is becoming as much of a myth as the old, a 'cosy' world where everyone shared in the same beliefs and assumptions.[5]

This was certainly not the view from the parishes where clergy were more often daunted by the problems of their task than comforted by the ease of their situation. Clark ought to have followed through the implications of his own methodology. He is surely right to argue that the world after 1688 needs to be seen as a continuation of the world before. Yet there is a curious disjunction in his analysis. For the thrust of sixteenth- and early seventeenth-century scholarship has been to demonstrate the problems and difficulties faced by the churches all over Europe, gradually whittling away the confident assertions of the older histories and stressing instead the slowness of implementing the Reformation, seeing it as a long-drawn-out struggle with limited impact, failing above all to capture the people.[6] And those problems continued, inspiring renewed waves of Reformation vigour reaching far into the seventeenth century.[7] In France the Tridentine reforms of the clergy, which aimed at making them into a more pastorally

[4] P. Virgin, *The Church in an Age of Negligence 1700–1840* (Cambridge, 1989). See also R. W. Malcolmson, *Life and Labour in England 1700–1780* (1981), pp. 83–93.

[5] Clark, *English Society*, esp. pp. 87, 277, although this assumption permeates the whole work. For Laslett's contention that in this period 'all our ancestors were literal Christian believers, all of the time', see *The World We Have Lost* (1965), p. 74. The most recent edition significantly modifies this statement: *The World We Have Lost – Further Explored* (Cambridge, 1983), p. 71.

[6] J. Bossy, *Christianity in the West 1400–1700* (Oxford, 1985); J. Delumeau, *Le Catholicisme entre Luther et Voltaire* (Paris, 1971, English translation, 1978). On the limited impact of the Reformation in sixteenth-century England, see *The English Reformation Revised*, ed. C. Haigh (Cambridge, 1989).

[7] For example, H. J. Cohn, 'The Territorial Princes in Germany's Second Reformation, 1559–1622', in *International Calvinism 1541–1715*, ed. M. Prestwich (Oxford, 1985), pp. 135–63; K. von Greyerz, *The Late City Reformation in Germany* (Wiesbaden, 1980), pp. 196–203; B. Nischan, 'The Second Reformation in Brandenburg', *Sixteenth-Century Journal*, 14 (1983), 173–87; and *Die reformierte Konfessionalisierung in Deutschland*, ed. H. Schilling (Gutersloh, 1987).

efficient force, were only getting under way, through the creation of seminaries, in the late seventeenth century, and arguably only in the eighteenth century were the effects of this being seen in the parishes.[8] These various kinds of reformers, whether Protestant or Catholic, displayed a common aim in attempting to turn the unconscious assumptions and unreflecting habits of belief of people throughout Europe into a formulated faith.

Similarly we should not underestimate the extent to which many Anglican clergy after the mid-seventeenth century saw themselves as continuing, and in some cases fulfilling, the Reformation ideals of spreading Christianity and Anglicanism to the 'dark corners of the land'. Such efforts had not ended in 1559, 1603 or 1640. The pastoral activities of Anglican clergy after 1660, and especially after 1689, can profitably be viewed as part of that continuing drama, 'the English Reformation'. Perhaps it might be thought that by the early eighteenth century this would only be true of regions far removed from the centres of power and influence. But even Kent, supposedly in the forefront of the sixteenth-century Reformation, was still considered a *pays de mission* in the eighteenth century. For all the efforts of Collinson's 'godly pastors' the south-east of England contained large pockets of religious ignorance.[9] In 1716, for example, Ralph Blomer, a prebendary of Canterbury Cathedral, told his fellow clergy that 'we have, in truth (I am sorry to observe it) a sufficient share of this duty of Preaching Christ to the Gentiles, without looking beyond the Bounds of our own Country. We have among ourselves a certain Leaven of Paganism, that is working upon the very vitals of Christianity.'[10] And if this indicates a certain similarity of aims with the pastoral concerns of the period conventionally labelled 'Reformation', it can also be argued that the pastoral task, the problem of spreading and maintaining religious orthodoxy and thus the need to reform 'rival' versions of belief, was far greater in the eighteenth century than it had been in the sixteenth century. Now clergy had to fight on a whole range of fronts, ranging from Catholics to all kinds of Protestant Nonconformists. The Toleration Act of 1689 made the pastoral task and responsibilities of Anglican clergy appear even more central to the

[8] R. Briggs, '*Idées* and *Mentalités*; the Case of the Catholic Reform Movement in France', *Journal of the History of European Ideas*, 7 (1986), 9–19; P. T. Hoffman, *Church and Community in the Diocese of Lyon 1500–1789* (New Haven, 1984), p. 5. See also *Church and Society in Catholic Europe of the Eighteenth Century*, ed. W. J. Callahan and D. Higgs (Cambridge, 1979).

[9] On Kent in the Reformation see the magisterial study by P. Clark, *English Provincial Society from the Reformation to the Revolution* (Hassocks, 1977). Also, P. Collinson, 'Cranbrook and the Fletchers: Popular and Unpopular religion in the Kentish Weald', in *Reformation Principle and Practice*, ed. P. N. Brooks (1980), pp. 173–202.

[10] R. Blomer, *A Sermon Preach'd in the Cathedral . . . Church of Canterbury . . . on Friday June 15th, 1716* (1716), p. 10.

well-being of the established Church; lacking the exclusive support of the state, pastoral pressure was seen as the most effective method of making any headway against the presence of Dissenters. G. V. Bennett saw the Toleration Act as making the Church of England 'partially disestablished' and thereby having to compete with other religious groups.[11] The Anglican Church had to accept that the 'commercialization of religion' in the eighteenth century necessitated entering the market-place. Clergy could no longer rely on the combined efforts of the spiritual and secular courts to impose Anglicanism in the parishes, and it was only through pastoral directives, through the efforts of individual clergy, through their powers of persuasion rather than legal coercion, that the Church was likely to make any impression against its rivals.

Certainly we ought to recognize that the work for the clergy in the parishes after 1689 indicates the only limited success of the Reformation in earlier periods. And it is worth pointing out that although English historians have, on the whole, been reluctant to pursue questions on the sixteenth- and seventeenth-century historical agenda into the eighteenth, continental scholars, who are perhaps more convinced by notions of the *longue durée*, have found it worthwhile. We will have an improved understanding of what the Reformation implied, and its broad social consequences, if we track its influence and its ideology well into the eighteenth century.

In the clerical propaganda of the period the understanding demanded of parishioners was a distinctive feature of the Anglican Church, marking it off from the superstition of popery and the mindless enthusiasm of Nonconformists. Locke's concept of mind as a *tabula rasa* placed the decisive role on the religious teacher, and this only added to the impetus, desire and need for clergy to involve themselves in this aspect of their pastoral office. Parishioners had to be educated in their religious understanding so as to save them from being seduced by rival creeds. Archbishop Secker urged his clergy in the mid-eighteenth century to remember that Christianity was a religion not merely of clergy and intellectuals, but of all men.[12] It was this, so the propaganda ran, which separated the Church of England from the oppression of Roman Catholicism, which denied the laity any true understanding of the faith. As John Cooke told the lower house of Convocation in 1704: 'the barbarous policy of the Church of Rome may be discovered: to shut off the Scriptures from the people, to keep them, as if mad and distracted, in darkness, knowing they must necessarily rave against their

[11] G. V. Bennett, 'Conflict in the Church', in *Britain after the Glorious Revolution*, ed. G. Holmes (1989), pp. 155–75.

[12] T. Secker, *Eight Charges Delivered to the Clergy of the Dioceses of Oxford and Canterbury* (1769), p. 22.

keepers, the priests, whenever they come into the light'.[13] In England it was believed that 'enlightenment' would march arm in arm with Anglicanism; a proper understanding of religion would bring people out of ignorance into civilization. A report reached Archbishop Wake in 1724 of Allington Firth in Kent where the people were 'living as brutally as if they were in the remotest part of the world'. The writer referred to the 'blessing of bringing people to the light that have so long been in their own darkness'.[14] There was thus a curious harmony between clerical perceptions of some of their parishioners and their understanding of the task of missionaries overseas. At home and abroad Anglican clergy were concerned to find the best ways of converting people to Anglicanism.[15]

Instead, the pastoral task of Anglican clergy, in opposition to perceptions of Catholic atrocities, involved using a range of educational strategies and devices which, although initiated in earlier periods, were developed and extended during the eighteenth century. The principal method by which they tried to establish the most simple and rudimentary understanding of their faith and its obligations was through catechizing. This was essentially a series of questions and answers designed to disseminate basic tenets of the faith, and had been central to the pastoral endeavours of the Reformation period.[16] Archbishops after 1689 continued to urge their clergy to continue this practice. Wake, for example, observed in 1724 that 'it is with a very sensible concern that I hear so many complaints of the gross ignorance of the common people in the things of God, and of the too general neglect of catechising, which seems to have been the chief occasion of it'.[17] It has been suggested that eighteenth-century clergy gradually let the habit die out, so that by the end of the period it was dropped altogether.[18] This is clearly not true of the Canterbury diocese where visitation returns show that in 1806 most parishes still had some kind of catechizing.[19] In some parishes there is indeed improvement throughout the century.[20] It is true that from the end

[13] J. Cooke, *Thirty Nine Sermons on Several Occasions* (2 vols., 1739), II, 497; C. J. Sommerville, 'The Distinction between Indoctrination and Education in England, 1549–1719', *Journal of the History of Ideas*, 44 (1983), 387–406.

[14] Christ Church, Oxford, Arch.W Epist. 10, fo. 6: anon. to Wake.

[15] On Anglican missionary activity, see P. J. Marshall and G. Williams, *The Great Map of Mankind. British Perceptions of the World in the Age of Enlightenment* (1982), pp. 98–127, and D. A. Pailin, *Attitudes to Other Religions. Comparative Religion in Seventeenth- and Eighteenth-Century Britain* (Manchester, 1984).

[16] I. M. Green, '"For Children in Yeeres and Children in Understanding": The Emergence of the English Catechism under Elizabeth and the Early Stuarts', *JEH*, 37 (1986), 397–425.

[17] N. Sykes, *William Wake, Archbishop of Canterbury* (2 vols., Cambridge, 1957), I, 182.

[18] J. H. Overton and F. Relton, *The English Church from the Accession of George I to the End of the Eighteenth Century (1714–1800)* (1906), p. 294.

[19] LPL, V/G 3/2 a–d.

[20] This mirrors evidence from elsewhere: D. McClatchey, *Oxfordshire Clergy 1777–1869* (Oxford, 1960), p. 144; A. Warne, *Church and Society in Eighteenth-Century Devon* (Newton Abbot, 1969), p. 49.

of the seventeenth century records indicate that most parish clergy in the Canterbury diocese limited the practice of catechism to specific periods in the year, most commonly Lent, but how far this represents a decline on the early seventeenth century is difficult to judge. Visitation returns suggest that clergy were willing to catechize, but that they found opposition from certain parishioners, who were unwilling to send their children and servants. The incumbent of Upper Hardres informed Wake in 1716 that he catechized 'every Sunday from Easter to Harvest, a season when I find children in the country can most conveniently come to church'.[21] Wake and Secker both wrote commentaries on the Catechism which were used by the parish clergy to some effect. Thomas Turner, the well-read shopkeeper of East Hoathly observed in 1758: 'in the even. finished reading Wake's Catechism, which I think a very good book and proper for all families'.[22]

Turner represents the view of an articulate, south-eastern layman. But it is clear that some clergy found that such catechisms were far too difficult and complex for most parishioners to understand. The incumbent of Doddington told Wake in 1728, 'I have tried your Grace's explanation, but few attain to more than the late Dr Isham's Short Exposition',[23] pointing to a hierarchy of understanding in the parish. Other expositions used by the Canterbury clergy were those by Bishop Beveridge, Bishop Mann, Bishop Williams and Dr Marshall. Clergy often noted that they wanted shorter and simpler ones for use in the parish. By far the most popular in Kent was *The Church Catechism Explained, By Way of Question and Answer and Confirmed by Scripture Proofs*, written by John Lewis. Lewis was an active parish priest, receiving support from both Tenison and Wake. He was vicar of St John's, Margate, (1706–46) as well as being incumbent of the neighbouring parish of Minster in Thanet (1708–46). His exposition was warmly welcomed by Thomas Bray who had it printed under the auspices of the SPCK in 1700. Lewis's catechism was popular not only in Kent but also in the rest of England. By 1714 it had run through seven English editions and by 1812 it had reached forty-two editions. In 1738 it was the most popular catechism in the diocese of Oxford and in Bristol in the 1760s. In 1713 it was translated into Welsh.[24] Lewis compiled it specifically for the

[21] Christ Church, Oxford, MS Wake Visitation A, 1716, sub 'Upper Hardres'.

[22] W. Wake, *The Principles of the Christian Religion Explained* (1699); T. Secker, *Lectures on the Catechism of the Church of England* (2 vols., 1769). Secker's *Lectures* had reached fifteen editions by 1824, and had spawned various abridged editions: see R. Lee, *An Analysis of Archbishop Secker's Lectures on the Church Catechism* (1831); *The Diary of Thomas Turner 1754–65*, ed. D. Vaisey (Oxford, 1984), p. 149.

[23] Christ Church, Oxford, MS Wake D, 1728, sub 'Doddington'.

[24] G. H. Jenkins, *Literature, Religion and Society in Wales 1660–1730* (Cardiff, 1978), p. 81; *Articles of Enquiry Addressed to Clergy of the Diocese of Oxford at the Primary Visitation of Dr Thomas Secker, 1738*, ed. H. A. Lloyd Jukes (Oxfordshire Record Society, 38, 1957), p. 14 n. 5; E. Ralph (ed.), 'Bishop Secker's Diocese Book', in *A Bristol Miscellany*, ed. P. McGrath (Bristol Record Society, 37, 1985), pp. 21–69.

poor and uneducated and had consulted neighbouring clergy whilst writing it, an indication of the attempt by some clergy to get to grips with the problems of disseminating religious knowledge by pooling their pastoral experience. Lewis pointed out how essential it was that parishioners should understand the tenets of the faith. Repeating the catechism was not an exercise in memory, but in reasoned understanding: 'where the Grounds and Principles of our holy religion have never been well laid, preaching rarely proves effectual; nor can it otherwise be expected, than that our flocks should be rendered an easy prey to every seducer'.[25] Lewis argued that without such basic knowledge other parts of the clerical function were a waste of time: 'the preaching of the sermons without catechizing is like building without laying the foundations; without this way of instruction, the mind is rendered like a ship without ballast and can keep no steady course, but rolls and is tossed to and fro with every wind of doctrine and is in continual danger of oversetting'.[26] He set out the questions to be answered with texts from Scripture, so that pupils could learn the Bible too. He stressed, speaking from experience, that sermons had little value without proper preparation of the congregation beforehand.

Lewis, with the other commentators, emphasized the duty of parents and masters to send their dependants to be catechized; this was the concomitant to the religious freedom which the laity had gained at the Reformation, and he made it clear that the laity had religious duties as well as religious rights. If they were remiss in fulfilling such duties they would have to answer 'to the great judge of the quick and the dead'.[27] Of course the precise role that the laity should be allowed to play in religious life was a matter of controversy throughout the period, the threat of schism and Nonconformity ensuring that Anglican clergy kept it within strict bounds. Nevertheless, the laity had their role in educating their children in basic religious beliefs, and some clergy reported that children were catechized at home. Canon Charles Smyth termed 'Evangelicalism' as the 'religion of the home',[28] but it is clear that there was nothing original in encouraging family religious life, so long as it remained preparatory and complementary to that supplied by the Church and did not become a substitute for regular attendance at the parish church. Indeed it was something which mainstream Anglican clergy relied on, taking pains to ensure that each family in the parish was supplied with a catechism for family use. John Johnson, the High Church vicar of Cranbrook, observed in 1716 that 'many people are ... exceeding backwards in sending their youth to be catechised, yet I find they commonly teach them catechism in their houses'.[29]

[25] J. Lewis, *The Church Catechism Explained* (1700), Preface, p. iii. [26] Ibid., p. vii.
[27] Ibid. [28] C. Smyth, *Simeon and Church Order* (Cambridge, 1940), p. 13.
[29] Christ Church, Oxford, MS Wake, sub 'Cranbrook'.

The Anglican interest in family religion as a pastoral strategy requires some attention. It has been fashionable to link worship within the family to groups usually associated with opposition or at least criticism of mainstream Anglicanism, such as Puritans and Evangelicals. Lawrence Stone has suggested that family devotional piety indicated a privatization of religion, encouraging the break up of communal ideals represented by the parish church, whereby the household took over the responsibility of the parish. For him developments in the family marked a growth of an attitude of indifference towards the authority of the clergy and worked against patriarchy and clerical importance.[30] But 'the spiritualization of the household' was central to the Anglican pastoral endeavour too. Theophilus Dorrington, for example, in his *Family Devotions* (1693) stressed the importance of family worship, especially if parishioners could only get to church once on a Sunday, and for the old and the sick who might be tempted not to go to church at all. Dorrington also believed that family exercises could be antidotes to Dissent. Anglican clergy like Dorrington, who had been brought up as a Presbyterian, were alive to the temptations and attractions which some forms of Dissent offered the individual.[31] Margaret Spufford has indicated that the strength of Nonconformity lay in the fact that whereas every villager was automatically a member of the all-inclusive Church, membership of Nonconformist groups might imply some kind of conscious choice.[32] In some ways the encouragement of Anglican family devotion was a counterfoil to this, allowing individual initiative and piety to be developed as part of church policy. But Dorrington was aware of the need to have set prayers, laid out by the clergy. He did not want to encourage prayers which 'depended upon sudden and unprecedented thoughts and Experience'.[33]

How far the duties of family devotion and prayers were actually performed is impossible to assess. Perhaps this was less likely in the lower orders where communal forms were more important than family solidarity. Nevertheless evidence from chap-books indicates that family piety might have reached lower-class families.[34]

Clergy realized that it was not only children who required instruction in

[30] C. Hill, *Society and Puritanism in Pre-Revolutionary England* (1966 edn); E. S. Morgan, *The Puritan Family* (New Haven, 1944); J. Morgan, *Godly Learning* (Cambridge, 1986); L. Stone, *The Family, Sex and Marriage in England 1500–1800* (1977); M. Todd, *Christian Humanism and the Puritan Social Order* (Cambridge, 1987).

[31] T. Dorrington, *Family Devotions for Sunday Evenings* (4 vols., 1693–5).

[32] M. Spufford, *Contrasting Communities. English Villagers in the Sixteenth and Seventeenth Centuries* (Cambridge, 1974), p. 344.

[33] Dorrington, *Devotions*.

[34] M. Spufford, *Small Books and Pleasant Histories* (1981); D. Valenze, 'Prophecy and Popular Literature in the Eighteenth Century', *JEH*, 29 (1978), 75–92; J. Ashton, *Chap-books of the Eighteenth Century* (1882).

the basic doctrines of the Church. The incumbent of Throwleigh informed Secker in 1758 that besides catechizing children on Sunday afternoons he also catechized 'in the form of a sermon to bring people, for they are backward'.[35] Others claimed that they did not need to catechize publicly since, as one incumbent in the diocese noted, 'my constant preaching may be called catechizing, for I never meddle with politics, nor controversy'.[36] The Vicar of Wingham told Wake in 1716 that 'sometimes for the entertainment of the elder part of the congregation I have read to them Bp. Beveridge's large explication'.[37] Henry Brailsford, a minor canon at the Cathedral and incumbent in the diocese, published in 1689 'for the parishioners of St. Mildred's, Canterbury' an abridgement of Bishop Pearson's exposition of the Creed.[38] This is representative of the means by which parochial clergy attempted to diffuse the great works of Christian scholarship to their parishioners, but it also raises the question of how far doctrine could be represented accurately for mass consumption. Indeed, trends in sermon writing and delivery in the period can be linked to these pastoral problems. The often noted move to a plain style in the post-Restoration period, which came to be the hallmark of eighteenth-century sermons, can be explained in part by the perceived need to get the message across in a clear manner. And the constant need to repeat essential religious truths is one explanation of the clergy's habit of preaching sermons more than once.[39] The problem of disseminating basic truths made some clergy appreciate the books written by those who are usually seen as Evangelical clergy, hostile to mainstream Anglicanism. In the 1760s George Berkeley admired Thomas Haweis's sermons and found that Henry Venn's *Complete Duty of Man* was an 'excellent book' which was a great help to him in his parish at Bray: 'I bless God, many persons here seem disposed to receive his word with gladness, but it is shocking . . . how few of the many I have talked to have believed Jesus to be God.'[40]

The role of eighteenth-century charity schools as an attempt to inculcate religious knowledge and in teaching parishioners to read as part of a clerical campaign to ensure a better understanding of the Anglican position has not yet been fully appreciated. It has been recently questioned whether there was a charity school 'movement' at all; evidence from Leicestershire has suggested that it was little more than the continuation of a process which

35 LPL, MS 1134/d, sub 'Throwleigh'.
36 Christ Church, Oxford, MS Wake B, sub 'St. Dunstan's, Canterbury'.
37 Christ Church, Oxford, MS Wake A, sub 'Wingham'.
38 H. Brailsford, *The Poor Man's Help* (1689), dedication.
39 C. Smyth, *The Art of Preaching* (1940), pp. 90–166.
40 H. Venn, *The Complete Duty of Man: Or, a System of Doctrinal and Practical Christianity* (1763); BL, Add. MS 39311, fo. 252: G. Berkeley to Mrs Berkeley, 24 Nov. 1769.

had roots in the early seventeenth century.[41] Certainly the aims behind the establishment of such schools echoed Reformation concerns to strengthen allegiance to the Church and to religious principles, yet the lack of adequate educational provision in Kent for the poor shows how incomplete this aspect of the Reformation had been. It is not easy to establish precise figures for educational provision at the Restoration but it would appear that only a few parishes in the Canterbury diocese, probably no more than twenty-five, had some regular provision for parochial education,[42] and there were large areas of the diocese completely without such provision. By the end of the eighteenth century there had been a dramatic transformation with nearly half of all parishes in the diocese providing some kind of education for their children. Moreover these new schools were situated in the areas of high population growth such as the parishes which bordered the north Kent coast, and there were now schools in the Romney Marsh area, which in 1660 had been neglected. The new schools were almost solely designed for the education of the poor and went rather further than the creations of the earlier religious reformers in that much of this provision was open to girls as well as boys. The older schools, headed by the King's School, Canterbury, taught a largely classical syllabus and attracted the sons of neighbouring gentry, prosperous tradesmen and clergy. Several of the grammar schools in the diocese also taught the classics and they suffered some measure of decline because this kind of education was not universally popular. In contrast, the new charity schools aimed to serve the needs of a less well-educated cultural and social milieu. Much of the progress had occurred in the more rural parishes. The role of the clergy in all this needs to be stressed; not only were they often instrumental in finding the finance for these schools, either by generous benefaction as was the case with Richard Foster who established a school at Crundale,[43] or more likely by raising subscriptions, but they were often also the teachers or guardians of the schools. The origins of the new charity schools lay in the need to defend Anglican doctrines against Catholicism; they were White Kennett's 'little garrisons against Popery'. They were enjoined upon clergy in the diocese by the SPCK who saw its task as co-ordinating the movement and supplying clergy with advice and books. But it would be wrong to give the SPCK the credit for actually instigating the erection of a school in any particular

[41] The standard work is still M. G. Jones, *The Charity School Movement* (Cambridge, 1938); J. Simon, 'Was there a Charity School Movement?', in *Education in Leicestershire 1540–1940*, ed. B. Simon (Leicester, 1968), pp. 55–100; R. W. Unwin, *Charity Schools and the Defence of Anglicanism* (Borthwick Papers, 65, 1984).

[42] R. Hume, 'Educational Provision for the Kentish Poor, 1660–1811: Fluctuations and Trends', *Southern History*, 4 (1982), 122–44.

[43] Canterbury Cathedral Archives, MS U3/116/25/1; Christ Church, Oxford, MS Wake B, sub 'Saltwood'.

parish; this was usually done by the local incumbent who had the task of encouraging the laity to give funds to supply tuition and books for the children, and, in many cases, clothing as well. The influence of clergy in some parishes was crucial: it was during Josiah Woodward's incumbency that four charity schools were established by subscription at Maidstone, each teaching thirty children.[44]

It has been argued that the specifically religious role of the charity schools, the education of parishioners in religious principles, died out by the 1730s.[45] Certainly a hindrance to the campaign was the Mortmain Act of 1736 which forbade death-bed benefactions. Nevertheless the use of the schools continued to be advocated by clergy. William Marsh observed that they were the most successful means of breaking down the ingrained religious ignorance of his rural parishioners. He recommended to Secker in 1758 that

> as many pious and wealthy people are disposed to bequeath charitable legacies at their death they could not do a better thing than to leave £10 or £1 p.a. in small country parishes, for some to teach poor people's children to read, and say cat, for want of which, ignorance is entailed on this sort of folk, for many generations.[46]

The cause of parochial education received new impetus during the last two decades of the eighteenth century with the creation of the Sunday school movement. Recent scholarship has tended to equate this movement with the Evangelical Revival,[47] but it is clear that its support came from right across the clerical spectrum. In Kent the creation of such schools received a great deal of support from George Horne, the dean of Canterbury, and leader of the High Church Hutchinsonians. In a sermon preached in 1785, which was dedicated to George Hearne, the pioneer of religious education in the area and rector of St Alphege, Canterbury, Horne outlined the benefits of Sunday school education: 'It is one mark of that wisdom by which the world is governed', he said, 'that the assistance afforded is proportionable to necessities of the times'. Horne quoted Jonas Hanway, the well-known philanthropist, on the innocence of children, who were ready to be moulded by religious opinions. He observed that this work 'implores, above all the patronage and assistance of the clergy under whose direction and superintendence, it should, if possible be carried out'. Horne attacked some of the evangelicals of the period by insisting that 'if ever a Reformation be brought about in this kingdom, it will be by the labours and diligence of the parochial clergy, each in his own parish'. He suggested that

44 SPCK, CR 1/3, Abstract Letterbook, 1711–12, fo. 111.

45 R. Thompson, *Classics or Charity? The Dilemma of the Eighteenth-Century Grammar School* (Manchester, 1971), p. 67.

46 LPL, MS 1134/a, sub 'Bicknor'.

47 T. Laqueur, *Religion and Respectability. Sunday Schools and Working Class Culture 1780–1850* (New Haven, 1976).

the success of the Sunday schools would make the next age less corrupt and more religious.[48]

The diocese was not in an area of the country noted for its Evangelical clergy, yet many parishes had instituted a Sunday school by the time of Archbishop Manners Sutton's primary visitation of 1806. In speaking in terms of an 'Evangelical Revival' as the main leaven in the dough of the eighteenth-century Church, historians have misjudged the significance of mainstream Anglican churchmanship and its ability to initiate pastoral developments. Rather than talking of an Evangelical reaction, we might note how far the Evangelical concern to reach out to the poor and uneducated was a continuation of much that had gone on before. Indeed, the Sunday schools need not be separated from the charity schools; both institutions had common aims and received similar support. In many cases the Sunday schools developed in parishes alongside the existing charity schools, or replaced them, being more suited to the emerging industrial and 'modern' working hours.

Charles Moore told Archbishop Moore in 1786 that 'by the voluntary contributions of my parishioners, I was enabled, about a year ago to open schools of instruction on a Sunday for all the children of the poor'. Moore believed that 'the labour and industry of the lower classes is no hinderance to piety and religion. Indeed the more diligent and industrious they are in trades and occupations on working days, the more consistent they are in their public devotion on Sundays.' George Hearne described part of the day's work:

> I examine the most forward of the children and explain the Catechism and the use of the Prayer Book. I exercise them in repeating after me the Lord's Prayer, and the Creeds, and all the responses. We have gone through, likewise, Fox, on Public Worship, and his Introduction etc., and Crossman's Introduction etc., the Church Catechism Broke into short questions, and Mann's Catechism. The books in common use are The Child's First Book, Fisher or Dixon's Spelling Book, the Catechisms before mentioned, particularly Mann's; the Divine Songs of the pious and excellent Dr. Isaac Watts, and every child is furnished with a Common Prayer Book and Testament to carry to Church.[49]

The list is interesting not only because it reveals something of the sheer

[48] G. Horne, *Sunday Schools Recommended, a Sermon . . . with an Appendix on the Method of Forming and Conducting Them* (Oxford, 1786), pp. 15, 20; idem, *A Charge Intended to have been Delivered to the Clergy of Norwich at the Primary Visitation of George, Lord Bishop of the Diocese* (Norwich, 1791), p. 21.

[49] LPL, V/G 3/a, sub 'Boughton Blean'; G. Hearne, 'appendix' in Horne, *Sunday Schools*, p. 35. The works mentioned by Hearne are F. Fox, *The Duty of Public Worship Proved* (1713); idem, *An Introduction to Spelling and Reading* (7th edn, 1754); H. Crossman, *An Introduction to the Knowledge of the Christian Religion* (Colchester, 1742); *The Church Catechism Broke into Short Questions* (1730); I. Mann, *A Familiar Exposition of the Church-Catechism* (5th edn, 1771).

range of educational materials available to the late eighteenth-century cleric in his attempt to spread the Anglican message, but also because it is indicative of the pastoral method of such clergy, disseminating religious principles through endless repetition, and giving primacy to the written word.

Seeing the clergy's endeavours in the parishes as part of a continuing process of implementing the Reformation helps account for some of their failures. In searching for a new basis for a Christian polity, in willing participation rather than through political might, clergy were heavily dependent on a religion of the word, attempting to propagate Christian beliefs through reading skills. And, through the efforts of the SPCK, the word increasingly came to mean more than just the Bible, as clergy distributed tracts, books and pamphlets to the populace. Popular devotional works and catechisms sold at prices within the economic range of all but the most deprived. But this method presupposed that parishioners were literate, and, as the incumbent of Orlestone complained to Wake in 1724, 'the people of this parish are so meanly educated that very few grown persons, masters, parents or servants, are able to read or write'.[50] This helps to explain the intensity with which the illiterate were exhorted to learn to read. In their efforts to inculcate understanding, clergy were perhaps responsible for widening a division within the parish, between the religious elite and those who were considered 'spiritually ignorant'. The greater the emphasis clergy placed on 'understanding' as a criterion for religious commitment, the more likely it was that divisions would occur in the parish. 'Success' or 'failure' depended on how high a level of commitment individual clergy demanded from their parishioners: different concepts of spirituality would vary from incumbent to incumbent. Under pressure from active archbishops, clergy in the diocese of Canterbury, themselves largely all graduates, were reluctant to accept the lowest common denominator. The consciousness of a growing separation between elite and popular culture compelled clergy to launch a campaign to improve their social and intellectual inferiors, and it was a hard task to achieve the positive aim of turning the ordinary practitioner of religion into a Christian in a sense conceived by his or her betters. In this situation the function of the parish clergy was to close the gap between orthodox Christianity and the dubious beliefs of the people.

There was, of course, nothing new in the existence of differing standards of religious attainment amongst parishioners. There had never been a single level of knowledge and sophistication. Clergy were well aware that there were parishioners whose beliefs could not have been called Christian. Keith

[50] Christ Church, Oxford, MS Wake C, sub 'Orlestone'.

Thomas has alerted us to a great unchurched lump of men and women to whom the basic concepts of Christianity were strange and alien and Peter Clark has described the popular beliefs which confronted clergy in sixteenth-century Kent: 'subdued within it were currents of magic and animism, an unconcern for any idea of a Christian deity, and a whole range of submerged communal emotions and relationships'. James Obelkevich has noted similar belief systems in nineteenth-century Lincolnshire.[51] There is no reason to suppose that the clergy of the eighteenth century were not faced by the same kind of non-Christian sentiments and beliefs, and it was these they tried to replace with Anglicanism. We do the Church no justice unless we see that it saw itself as an institution fighting grimly against what it termed irreligion, superstition and unbelief. In its attempt to reform and educate, and indeed to 'Christianize' popular culture, the Church was acting in a long tradition, yet it was often the demands placed by the clergy on understanding the fundamentals of Christianity which increased the polarity.

In an analysis of pre-industrial society, Peter Laslett has argued that all parishioners would have held Christian beliefs and that religious stratification was unknown in such a society, being the product of nineteenth-century industrialization and urbanization,[52] whereby religion became a 'middle class matter'. Such a view greatly underestimates the problems encountered by Anglican clergy in their efforts to educate their parishioners in their version of Christianity. Religious classes within the parish were as much the product of clerical activity in the seventeenth and eighteenth centuries as of nineteenth-century social developments. The world which was lost through industrial and urban change should not be seen as an homogenous religious culture. In the mid-seventeenth century Ralph Josselin, for example, gave up trying to preach for all in his Essex parish, splitting his parishioners into three categories.[53] It was essentially an elite within the parish, the size and social composition of which varied according to individual circumstances, who attained the kind of religious commitment desired by the Church hierarchy, and complaints of the growth of irreligion in the period stemmed from the gulf between standards set by the Church and the religious elite, and the reality attained by many of the parishioners. William Marsh complained to Archbishop Moore in 1786 of 'the want seemingly of that inward and sincere regard for religion in the greatest part of the people, which the nature of it requires'.[54] There was thus a tension

[51] K. V. Thomas, *Religion and the Decline of Magic* (1971); Clark, *Provincial Society*, p. 153; J. Obelkevich, *Religion and Rural Society. South Lindsey 1825–75* (Oxford, 1979), pp. 283–91.
[52] Laslett, *World We Have Lost – Further Explored*, pp. 71–2.
[53] *The Diary of Ralph Josselin 1616–83*, ed. A. Macfarlane (British Academy, Records of Social and Economic History, n.s., 3, 1976), pp. 236, 252, 376, 424.
[54] LPL, V/G 2/a, sub 'Bicknor'.

between the clergy's role as ordained ministers of a comprehensive Church and as leaders of a religious community.

In their attempts to regularize the religious beliefs and behaviour of their parishioners, Anglican clergy shared similar ideals to the 'godly' of the early seventeenth century: both were concerned with trying to transform the attitudes and practices of the majority of the parish.[55] Post-Restoration Anglicanism inherited more from so-called Puritanism than the traditional interpretation of a two-culture polarity allows. The Anglican hierarchy did not want Anglicanism to be a cosy and lax alternative to the rigorous standards of the Puritans, and in their own way they were just as concerned with the sluggish. Puritanism may have been politically defeated in 1660, but the Puritan mentality made headway in eighteenth-century England, not by attacking orthodox Anglican religion, but by being assimilated within it. It is this, as much as the traditional concentration on the abuses committed by clergy, which explains the disaffection which was sometimes shown towards the Church. In trying to impose their standards on the parish the clergy might offend what were seen as traditional customs and modes of behaviour, in the same way as seventeenth-century Puritans aroused hostility. Archbishop Wake received a complaint in 1725 about a Mr Squire whose strict ideals led to some battles with parishioners: 'His predecessor, Mr Green, was as bad a preacher as well could be. His tongue was too big for his mouth, so that what he said was perfectly unintelligible. Besides he'd often fall asleep in his desk, and nod in his pulpit. But for all this he was beloved, for he had the sociable quality of drinking and playing with the Graziers and Butchers.'[56] Denominational histories have perhaps exaggerated the differences between religious groups, but, from the standpoint of the parish, such distinctions look increasingly blurred. Eighteenth-century Anglicanism, as much as Puritanism, Methodism, Evangelicalism or Tractarianism, represented an attempt to mould religious sensibilities. Indeed we might do well to explore the relationship between Anglican pastoral ideals and achievements and the pastoral missions of earlier Puritan and later Evangelical and Tractarian groups. Closer examination reveals much in common between the Church of England and its so-called rivals. It is possible to argue that Puritan, Evangelical and Tractarian ideals were only reiterating Anglican pastoral commonplaces.

It is, however, too easy in analysing the pastoral task of the Anglican clergy to accept their comments and criticisms of parishioners at face value.

[55] For example, K. Wrightson and D. Levine, *Poverty and Piety in an English Village. Terling 1525–1700* (New York, 1979).

[56] Christ Church, Oxford, Arch.W.Epist. 10, fo. 191: Lewis to Wake, 31 May 1725. For a contrast between Puritanism and Anglicanism, see C. Hill, 'Occasional Conformity', in *Reformation, Conformity and Dissent*, ed. R. B. Knox (Epworth, 1977), pp. 199–220. If Hill's view of the Restoration is correct, that the populace preferred the Church of England because they thought it was lax, then they were to be disappointed.

In measuring affection for the Church we should beware of assuming that those who did not match up to the increasingly high standards set by the clergy were in fact the illiterate and irreligious multitude of clerical imaginings. Some visitation returns give the impression that true Protestant religion was out of the reach of the uneducated and those considered to be the 'uncivilized'. Other clergy were aware of a sense of increasing secularization. In 1784 Archdeacon Backhouse moaned to a congregation at Deal that 'a just and awful sense of the Divine influence, has diminished, is diminishing and ought to be increased'.[57] But laments such as this concerning the immorality and ungodliness of parishioners may have resulted not so much from a decline in the standards of the populace, but from a more exalted concept of what was tolerable and from a sense of nostalgia for an assumed religious past. The impression of unrelieved gloom and failure is also a product of the kinds of sources available to the historian. Inevitably clergy in their correspondence and reports concentrated on their problems and difficulties, and thus we are likely to miss what has been called the 'unspectacular orthodoxy' of many parishioners.[58]

In any case it is wrong to suggest that popular religious beliefs were completely divorced from official Anglicanism. In many ways the conventional way of explaining religious differences in terms of elite and popular cultures imposes too rigid a distinction on the reality faced by clergy in the parishes. The activity described above indicates rather that the clergy through catechizing and the spread of education helped to construct a ladder joining the clerical and lay elite with the rest of the population. This indicates a gradation, rather than a polarity of religious knowledge. And the gap between the 'religious' and the 'irreligious' did not necessarily mirror the gap between rich and poor; clergy pointed to the existence of other groups of parishioners who were the trouble-makers. One such group was the youth of the parish. The role of the youth groups as a disruptive factor in the parish has been well studied in France and elsewhere on the Continent for the sixteenth and seventeenth centuries, and it is clear that eighteenth-century Anglican clergy were not immune from such problems.[59] Clergy often complained that it was the older children who were the most successful in avoiding catechism and religious instruction. In a similar category came servants. It was traditional that they should be given religious education and they were supposed to be sent to catechism.

[57] W. Backhouse, *God The Author of Peace and Lover of Concord. A Sermon Preached ... Thursday, 29 July 1784* (Canterbury, 1784), p. 11.

[58] M. Ingram, 'Religion, Communities and Moral Discipline in Late Sixteenth and Early Seventeenth-Century England: Case Studies', in *Religion and Society in Early Modern Europe 1500–1800*, ed. K. von Greyerz (1984), p. 181; Spaeth, 'Common Prayer?', p. 125.

[59] S. Brigden, 'Youth and the Reformation', *PP*, 45 (1982), 37–67; Collinson, *Religion of Protestants*, pp. 224–30.

The incumbent of Shadoxhurst informed Wake in 1726 that he found the servants a particular worry, 'they are stubborn and resolute, pretend to be too big and ashamed to be catechised in public, and declare in plain words that they will not obey or be compelled to it'.[60] The incumbent of Littlebourne reported in 1786 that 'some servants are absent, owing to the general dissipation of the times in which higher wages and no restraint enable them to indulge'.[61] In trying to fulfil their duties, clergy were, then, hampered by forces and factors largely outside their control. A gradual loosening of patriarchal ties within the family, affecting parental control over children, as well as control over servants, has been seen as a distinctive feature of this period. How far this social development was a phenomenon new in the eighteenth century can be doubted, yet clergy certainly seemed to think that they lived in difficult times.

An enduring feature of the pastoral concern of the eighteenth-century clergy was that it was not the monopoly of any one brand of churchmanship. During the early years of the eighteenth century, for instance, when religious parties were at their height, it is clear that the leaders of both the Whig and Tory clerical groupings shared a common interest in pastoral matters. Whatever the divisions between the laity, polarities between members of the clergy were not so clear-cut. In the Canterbury diocese, both Tenison and Wake, who had clear Whig credentials, supported and gave preferment to staunch Tory High Churchmen like John Johnson, the vicar of Cranbrook, and the Whig John Lewis, the vicar of Margate. Johnson recognized that the pastoral problems he faced in Cranbrook transcended politics. He told Wake, 'I am sensible my enemies will impute all the hardships I am under to my disaffection (as they call it) to the present government, but it is true that my difficulties in serving the cure were well nigh as great in the reign of Her late Majesty.'[62]

The tragedy of party conflict and fervour in the Canterbury diocese, as elsewhere, was that it detracted from a uniform policy of pastoral reform. It is fashionable to suggest that clerical differences in the early eighteenth century were all-embracing and to neglect the fact that their similarities were to prove just as important. The wish for renewed pastoral vigour was not the sole prerogative of the Tory faction. Both Lewis and Johnson submitted for Wake's consideration detailed proposals for reform. They both stressed the need for better pastoral oversight and for a united clerical policy on matters concerning relations with Dissenters and with

[60] Christ Church, Oxford, MS Wake A, sub 'Shadoxhurst'.
[61] LPL, V/G 2/c, sub 'Littlebourne'.
[62] Studies which concentrate on clerical differences along party lines include: G. Every, *The High Church Party 1688–1718* (1956), and W. A. Speck, *Tory and Whig. The Struggle in the Constituencies 1701–15* (1970); Christ Church, Oxford, MS Wake C, sub 'Cranbrook'.

parishioners. Through visitation procedures, pastoral directives and correspondence with individual clergy in their diocese, the archbishops attempted to procure a united pastoral front. No doubt this had always been part of archiepiscopal policy; it had clearly been dear to Laud's heart. Nevertheless, the party divisions of the early eighteenth century made the need to find a common outlook and a common purpose even more pressing. Ralph Blomer wrote to Wake in 1716: 'May your Grace have the satisfaction of seeing us more and more united, and the honour of being the principal agent in so great and Christian a work!'[63] It was in large measure the pastoral concerns of the eighteenth-century archbishops which united their clergy and served to soften clerical party rivalry. The pastoral concerns of the Whig Church, headed by archbishops such as Wake, Potter, Secker, Cornwallis and Moore, served to reconcile many clergy to the Hanoverian regime. The desire to improve the standard and frequency of parochial worship, the attempt to reduce the numbers of non-attenders at services, the importance placed on receiving the sacrament, the desire to extend parochial education, the concern shown to the fabric of the churches were central aspects of Hanoverian churchmanship.[64]

It would be greatly to underestimate the task of the church hierarchy to suggest that parish clergy fulfilled their obligations of the pastoral office. Whilst some parish clergy were clearly more aware of the pastoral difficulties and obligations than were church dignitaries, others had to be prodded into action. Secker informed his clergy that if they did not perform their pastoral function well, they could not expect promotion.[65] Part of the problem was, as many clergy reiterated, that incumbents were often more popular amongst their parishioners if they did not appear to be too demanding, and parish clergy could resent what they felt to be undue interference by archbishops.

The Anglican pastoral system needed constant vigilance from archbishops and archdeacons. The information collected at visitations enabled conscientious archbishops to see where improvement was needed. Such pressure from the hierarchy to increase the pastoral commitments of their clergy continued the process of 'clerical professionalization' which has recently been analysed in the early seventeenth century and it also has clear similarities to the aims of the Catholic hierarchy in the eighteenth century in Europe.[66] It may also very well be that the suggestion that in eighteenth-century France the long-term result of such pastoral involvement must have been positive was true of the pastoral work of eighteenth-century

[63] Christ Church, Oxford, Arch.W.Epist. 6, fo. 176: R. Blomer to Wake, 20 Apr. 1716.

[64] Cf. L. Colley, *In Defiance of Oligarchy. The Tory Party 1714–60* (Cambridge, 1982), p. 113.

[65] For example, LPL, MS Secker 3, fos. 201, 253.

[66] O'Day, *English Clergy*.

Anglican clergy as well.[67] What is difficult to know is how parishioners responded to this educational endeavour. Certainly one may doubt to what extent it changed people's lives, or if they actually abandoned more traditional beliefs. Yet the essential truths of the Christian doctrine may have been better known by more parishioners at the end of the period than at the start. In 1830, for example, the majority of cottages in the parish of Hernehill contained a Bible or Prayer Book or Anglican hymn book, whereas in the mid-seventeenth century it had been known for its illiterate and uneducated parishioners.[68] Anthropologists have postulated a distinction between 'belief' and 'faith', where faith is a term used for an optional belief, needing education and instruction to sustain it.[69] In the archbishops' efforts to exhort their clergy to fulfil their pastoral role and in the clergy's efforts to educate their parishioners in a better understanding of Anglicanism, the Church of England was attempting to make the eighteenth century not into an age of reason, or of unreflecting belief, but into an age of faith.

[67] Briggs, '*Idées* and *Mentalités*', p. 14. Also C. Langlois, *Le Diocèse de Vannes au XIXe siècle 1800–30* (Paris, 1974). Such interpretations are revising the more traditional view that eighteenth-century Europe witnessed a 'de-christianization'. For a classic statement on this theme, see M. Vovelle, *Piété baroque et déchristianisation en Provence au XVIIIe siècle* (Paris, 1973), and idem, *Religion et Révolution* (Paris, 1976).

[68] B. Reay, 'The Last Rising of the Agricultural Labourers: The Battle in Bossenden Wood, 1838', *History Workshop*, 26 (1988), 95.

[69] C. Larner, *Witchcraft and Religion* (Oxford, 1984), p. 121.

3 The clergy in the diocese of London in the eighteenth century

Viviane Barrie-Curien

This essay attempts to reassess some long-held assumptions about the Church of England in the eighteenth century. A clerical living is often supposed to have been a career for the upper classes – indeed increasingly so – and furthermore the clergy are seen to have been complacent and neglectful of their pastoral task. However, eighteenth-century ecclesiastical history still remains under-researched, and a new perspective at a local level, that of the diocese of London, provides a different picture of the Church, both in the recruitment of its clergy and in its work in the parishes.

The status and the role of the clergy have lately been investigated by historians of the Reformation and of the early seventeenth century.[1] They have stressed the crisis that followed the Reformation, when the Church started to appear as a career fit only for the sons of the comparatively humble, the *menu peuple*, thereby creating a shortage of personnel.[2] The end of Elizabeth's reign brought about an improvement in the social status of the clergy, when some younger sons of the gentry and many sons of clergymen started to enter the Church.[3] But the Civil War inflicted a further blow on their still uncertain respectability, and the Restoration Church

[1] A review of the current bibliography can be found in Viviane Barrie-Curien, 'The English Clergy, 1560–1620: Recruitment and Social Status', *History of European Ideas*, 9 (1988), 451–63. Rosemary O'Day's work has been particularly helpful in recent years in its identification of the clergy as a distinct social and professional group.

[2] Christopher Hill, *Economic Problems of the Church* (Oxford, 1956), pp. 14ff; Rosemary O'Day, *The English Clergy. The Emergence and Consolidation of a Profession 1558–1642* (Leicester, 1979), pp. 28ff; idem, 'The Reformation of the Ministry, 1558–1642', in *Continuity and Change. Personnel and Administration of the Church of England 1500–1642*, ed. Rosemary O'Day and Felicity Heal (Leicester, 1976), pp. 56–7; Margaret Bowker, *The Henrician Reformation. The Diocese of Lincoln under the Episcopacy of John Longland 1521–47* (Cambridge, 1981), pp. 121, 131, 137.

[3] C. H. Mayo, 'The Social Status of the Clergy in the Seventeenth and the Eighteenth Centuries', *EHR*, 37 (1922), 258–66; Patrick Collinson, *The Religion of Protestants* (Oxford, 1982), pp. 100–2; Peter Tyler, 'The Status of the Elizabethan Parish Clergy', *SCH*, 4 (1967), 84–5; Michael Zell, 'Economic Problems of the Parochial Clergy in the Sixteenth Century', in *Princes and Paupers in the English Church 1500–1800*, ed. Rosemary O'Day and Felicity Heal (Leicester, 1981), p. 29; Ian Green, 'Career Prospects and Clerical Conformity in the Early Stuart Church', *PP*, 90 (1981), 73–5, 78; O'Day, *English Clergy*, pp. 161–2.

could not become an attractive career.[4] The early eighteenth century was a time of increasing difficulties, both for the Church as an institution, and for the clergy as a social and professional group; they felt themselves severely criticized by laymen, while their financial straits knew no improvement.[5] After 1760, however, their professional, financial and social position underwent a change for the better. According to many historians, clergy then came from the gentry and even from the aristocracy, who thought the Church a desirable career for their younger sons and managed to keep the best preferments for them and the sons of 'small' men were discarded.[6] Clerics acquired an even greater respectability during the nineteenth century, when the Church became an acceptable profession for the upper middle and upper classes.

This essay will begin by testing such generalizations by examining the social origins of a random sample of 500 clergymen beneficed in the diocese of London between 1714 and 1800 – that is about a quarter of the 2,000 men who held ecclesiastical preferment in the diocese, which covered Essex, Middlesex, the City of London and a third of Hertfordshire.[7]

The figures for their social recruitment, as shown by Table 1, do not entirely support the idea of an elitist profession. Three main groups can be identified, chiefly through the Institution Books of the diocese and the matriculation registers of Oxford and Cambridge,[8] where the clergy were educated: the sons of the gentry, those of clergymen and those of 'plebeians'. The nobility is represented by a small minority of 1.2 per cent, even though one finds among its sons two descendants of Charles II. The gentry account for nearly 38 per cent of the sample, which makes them a dominant group, but the sons of the clergy are almost as numerous – over 35 per cent. Over 19 per cent, nearly a fifth, are sons of 'plebeians', presumably shopkeepers, traders, freeholders, husbandmen, yeomen and small farmers. Moreover, as the breakdown into subgroups shows, 'gentry' here means chiefly the sons of mere gentlemen, who account for more than a quarter of the whole sample; the sons of esquires represent a little less than

[4] Mayo, 'Social Status', pp. 258, 265; Norman Ravitch, *Sword and Mitre. Government and Episcopate in France and England in the Age of Aristocracy* (The Hague, 1966), p. 118; idem, 'The Social Origins of French and English Bishops in the Eighteenth Century', *HJ*, 8 (1965), 309–25.

[5] Sykes, *Church and State*, pp. 188, 212.

[6] Ibid., pp. 156–7; G. M. Trevelyan, *English Social History* (1944 edn), pp. 359–60; G. E. Mingay, *The Gentry* (1976), p. 138.

[7] On the diocese of London and its clerical personnel, two printed sources remain invaluable: R. Newcourt, *Repertorium Ecclesiasticum Parochiale Londinense* (1710); G. Hennessy, *Novum Repertorium Ecclesiasticum Parochiale Londinense* (1898).

[8] PRO, Exchequer MSS, Institution Books, series B and C, RR, 9/69–79; *Alum. Cantab.*; *Alum. Oxon.*

10 per cent, and those of knights and baronets – the titled gentry – 2.6 per cent. Among the sons of clergymen, only 6.2 per cent have a father belonging to the higher clergy, that is, a canon or above. The Church in the diocese of London does not therefore appear to have been an aristocratic body. On the contrary, one is struck by the high percentages of sons of parish clergy, of plebeians and of mere gentlemen. The diocese thus went on attracting and integrating a large proportion of working-class or lower middle-class people (as the nineteenth century would call them), probably through the channels of private patronage, as well as through school and university scholarships.

The social recruitment of the clergy naturally underwent some changes through the eighteenth century. It has been generally assumed that an increasing proportion of them were drawn from the upper gentry and the nobility as early as the 1760s. Tables 2 and 3 break down this recruitment into periods of twenty years each, by taking the number of clergymen who were instituted to any kind of benefice or office in the diocese of London during each period. These tables do indeed show that between the beginning and the end of the century the gentry increased from 31 per cent to almost 57, the sons of 'plebeians' went down from 28.5 per cent to just over 12, and those of the parish clergy decreased from almost 26 per cent to 19.5, while those of the higher clergy rose from under 3 per cent to over 5. The nobility, though still very scarce in absolute numbers, was also more numerous in the second part of the century, and the sons of peers and baronets taken together, while totally absent from the diocese before 1700, constitute 4 per cent of the sample in its last twenty years. However, this evolution did not happen before 1781, and it was brought about chiefly by the high proportions of the sons of esquires and baronets, while those of knights tended to disappear. Indeed, given the very small absolute number of sons of baronets, one may even say that the change occurred through the esquires alone, who, although wealthier than mere gentlemen, nonetheless did not belong to the country gentry. The Church therefore was still nothing like an aristocratic body. It still contained a fair proportion of sons of 'plebeians' (who were by no means excluded from this diocese, although it was both important and rich), and they were still managing to enter on an ecclesiastical career at the end of the century. It is likely that in other, poorer dioceses in the north or west of England, the increase of the gentry class was not yet perceptible in the eighteenth century, and did not emerge until the early Victorian age.

These 500 clergymen, particularly those born in the gentry, can be further characterized through an examination of their geographical origins. 57 per cent of the whole sample came from London, the county of Middlesex, and from provincial towns, the population of which reached 2,000 or more in

1801, according to the census taken in that year.[9] This already very high proportion reaches 67 per cent when it comes to the sons of the gentry, 30 per cent of whom were born in provincial towns and the rest in London and Middlesex. One may safely conclude that the Church did *not* attract a majority of landed gentry, not even enlisting their younger sons. Rather it recruited the sons of professional people – doctors, lawyers, merchants and traders, who lived in towns – sometimes called 'pseudo-gentry', whose wealth and respectability earned them the status of gentlemen or even esquires, but who could not on any account be classified as country squires. Thus, after adding the 127 sons of 'urban gentry' to the sons of merchants, lawyers and doctors already identified as such, the figures of Table 1 should be altered as follows.

Father's status or occupation	*Number of clergymen*	*Percentage*
Nobility	6	1.2
Landed gentry	62	12.4
Professions	153	30.6
Clergy	177	35.4
Schoolmasters	5	1.0
'Plebeians'	97	19.4

We have used the term 'professions', though the nineteenth century was soon to call them the 'middle classes'. It is apparent that they accounted for nearly a third of the recruitment, and that, as the landed gentry amounted then to no more than 12.4 per cent of the sample, the simple association between the landed order and the Church of England cannot be sustained, at least as far as the recruitment of the London diocese is concerned. Almost 63 per cent of the sons of 'plebeians' also came from towns, which suggests how education, then mainly urban, had helped them on in the course of their career. The sons of clerics, on the other hand, were mostly the children of country clergymen, very often beneficed in the county of Essex, a fact which emphasizes the degree of self-recruitment and the extent to which sons succeeded to their fathers' livings. Indeed, a high proportion of the clergy came from within the diocese, and 'self-recruitment' can thus be used in a geographical as well as in a social sense. The Church in the Hanoverian age thus drew its personnel mainly from an urban middle class and also from its own ranks, hence its capacity for generating ecclesiastical dynasties. Moreover, the towns involved in the recruitment of the profession were situated chiefly in the south and east of the country. This underlines the part played in church history by the older towns of pre-industrial England. If

[9] Parliamentary Papers, Abstracts of the Answers and Returns Made Pursuant to an Act, Passed in the 41st Year of His Majesty George III, 'An Act for Taking an Account of the Population of Great Britain and the Increase and Diminution thereof', 1802, part I.

one takes into account the market-towns, which must have numbered between 1,000 and 2,000 inhabitants in 1801, the dependence of the Church for its clergy on the small centres, which had been in existence, often prosperously, since about the twelfth century and the economics of which were still based on traditional activities, would be even more striking. On the other hand, industrial new towns, London apart, do not seem to have had any notable influence on clerical recruitment.[10]

How did the clergy of the diocese of London fulfil their pastoral duties in their 600 parishes? Some insight into this question can be gained by studying the replies to eight questionnaires sent to incumbents before pastoral visitations between 1723 and 1790. Although some of the answers have been lost and some whole questionnaires are obviously missing, the material we have is often very illuminating about the religious life of the parishioners and the clergy alike.[11] Unfortunately, the returns do not include London until 1790, so we know chiefly about country parishes. But several separate inquiries bear on the capital alone.

The Church of England clergy of the eighteenth century often stand accused of neglecting the cure of souls, and of allowing too much pluralism and non-residence to offer any serious pastoral care. The duties of an incumbent were, at least theoretically, numerous and demanded a constant presence in his parish.[12] Some bishops, especially at the end of the century, kept exhorting their clergy to greater zeal and professional conscientiousness, reproaching them in particular with their frequent non-residence.[13] Non-residence was very often the consequence of pluralism, and both were so often branded as responsible for the decline of the popularity of the

[10] The same phenomenon is visible among the French Catholic clergy of the eighteenth and nineteenth centuries. While presenting an image of themselves as rooted in country parishes and dedicated to pastoral work in rural areas, French priests came mostly from towns and tended to belong either to families of *notables* or to clerical families, many benefices being handed down from uncle to nephew.

[11] Guildhall Library, MS 25750: Visitation Returns for Middlesex, Essex, Hertfordshire and Buckinghamshire, 1723 (2 vols.); MS 25751: Visitation Returns for Middlesex, Essex, Hertfordshire and Buckinghamshire, 1727 (1 vol.); MS 25753: Visitation Returns for Middlesex, Essex, Hertfordshire and Buckinghamshire, 1738 (3 vols.); MS 25754: Visitation Returns for Middlesex, Essex, Hertfordshire and Buckinghamshire, 1742 (4 vols.); MS 25755: Visitation Returns for Middlesex, Essex, Hertfordshire and Buckinghamshire, 1747 (3 vols.); LPL, Fulham Papers, boxes 55 and 56: 'Visitation Returns, 1766'; Fulham Papers, box 54: 'Visitation Returns, 1770'; Fulham Papers, boxes 82, 83 and 84: 'Visitation Returns, 1778'; Fulham Papers, boxes 81, 85, 86 and 87: 'Visitation Returns, 1790'.

The diocese of London is fortunate in being well provided with visitation returns for the first half of the eighteenth century, whereas most dioceses have not kept any before the 1760s. See for instance the case of the diocese of Norwich, as studied by W. M. Jacob, '"A Practice of a very Hurtful Tendency"', *SCH*, 16 (1979), 321.

[12] 'Glimpses of the Church of England', *Church Quarterly Review*, 72 (1911), 317.

[13] Sykes, *Church and State*, pp. 370–1; R. A. Soloway, *Prelates and People. Ecclesiastical Social Thought in England 1783–1852* (1969), pp. 233–4, 355.

Church that any study of the pastoral work of the clergy must start with a description of their deployment.

Pluralism was by no means a novelty in the eighteenth century; it was commonplace before and just after the Reformation.[14] Legislation on this issue dated back to a statute of 1529 and to the Canons of 1604.[15] Both allowed a very wide interpretation, and there was no attempt to reform the law until the nineteenth century, when several acts were passed to enforce clerical residence, in 1813 and 1817, and again in 1838 and 1850.[16] Pluralism afforded an automatic dispensation from residence on one of the two livings. It was not, however, the only reason for non-residence, although it was far and away the most frequent. An incumbent whose parsonage-house was out of repair was allowed to live elsewhere, as were the chaplains of the nobility. Fellows of university colleges could stay in Oxford or Cambridge and keep a curate in their stead. Last, but not least, clergymen could be non-resident for medical reasons.[17] These various provisions, which also dated back to the 1529 statute, were not modified or abolished until 1803.[18]

Pluralism in the London diocese seems on the increase in the eighteenth century according to the evidence of visitation returns, as shown in Table 4. The figures drawn from the incumbents' replies show that more and more of them managed to combine several preferments in the course of the century. Parishes held together with one or two others amount to less than 40 per cent of their total in 1723 and 1727, reach 50 per cent in 1738, and stay just above this figure in the following years. Moreover, many incumbents also held curacies, sometimes just to help a neighbouring parson, but often for a whole lifetime, although this sort of pluralism was on the decrease after

[14] Arthur Warne, *Church and Society in Eighteenth-Century Devon* (Newton Abbot, 1969), pp. 42–3.

[15] Sykes, *Church and State*, pp. 147–8, 184; Diana McClatchey, *Oxfordshire Clergy 1777–1869* (Oxford, 1960), pp. 38–40. Nobody could hold two livings if one of them was worth more than £8 a year. However, the archbishop of Canterbury could grant dispensations for specific reasons: royal chaplains, spiritual persons members of the King's Privy Council, chaplains attached to spiritual or temporal peers, doctors and bachelors in canon law, qualified for one according to the 1529 Statute. The 1604 Canon included a further clause relating to dispensation; that the cleric should be at least an MA, own a preaching licence and commit himself to reside in one of the two livings for at least part of the year, that the two benefices should be not more than thirty miles distant from one another, and that a curate should be in charge of the parish in which the incumbent chose not to live.

[16] McClatchey, *Oxfordshire Clergy*, pp. 45, 75.

[17] Sykes, *Church and State*, pp. 216, 219–20; McClatchey, *Oxfordshire Clergy*, pp. 32–3; Warne, *Church and Society*, p. 40. Assertions that the climate of the part of the country in which their livings were situated did not agree with them, or that they could not live in London for want of fresh air, can be frequently found, usually supported by doctors' evidence and certificates.

[18] McClatchey, *Oxfordshire Clergy*, p. 32.

1747.[19] However, pluralism was often deemed not as damaging to the cure of souls as is usually reckoned. Most of the time it involved neighbouring parishes, only a mile apart, or less, in many cases, or at least livings were in the same diocese, so that parishioners were able to see their incumbents every week or at least for part of the year, since many clergymen in fact shared their time between their two benefices. The chief motivation for pluralism was economic necessity. Poor parishes were held together all the more easily as they were usually thinly populated, and incumbents of wealthy livings did not normally feel the need to hunt for a second institution. This explains why many would-be reformers of the Church kept advocating the redistribution of its resources to assist the poorer benefices, for this alone could put an end to the evils of pluralism, the first of which was non-residence.

Non-residence affected the deployment of the clergy in each diocese in different ways. The diocese of London can be deemed a peculiar case because of the existence of the metropolis. The first extant information we have for the City of London itself comes from a metropolitan visitation by Archbishop Tillotson in 1693.[20] There follows in 1711 an archideaconal visitation,[21] a series of churchwardens' certificates concerning the use of the Book of Common Prayer in the London churches in 1715[22] and, after the visitation returns of 1790, we end up with an inquiry by Bishop John Randolph in 1812.[23] The information is set out in Table 5, which shows that most London parishes enjoyed the presence of several clergymen, with only a very small minority being served by just one. In addition to the incumbent and his curate, they often had lecturers and readers, which implies a considerable increase of pastoral care, particularly of preaching, enabling London parishioners to hear several sermons or lectures every day. Moreover, lecturers became increasingly common as the century wore on. The number of parishes where the incumbent was absent was always high, ranging from 10 to over 30 per cent, although it was on the decrease at the end of the century. But this was compensated for by the large number of

[19] This meant that clergymen entering the race for preferment at the end of the century were more likely to become pluralists, but that there was a higher pressure on livings for the unbeneficed clergy, who had to be content with combining several curacies, a notoriously frequent phenomenon from the 1770s onwards.

[20] Guildhall Library, MS 9538: Original Visitation Presentments for the City of London, metropolitan parochial visitation, 1693 (1 vol.).

[21] Guildhall Library, MS 9248: London Archdeaconry, Visitations, copy presentments for the City of London, July 1711.

[22] Guildhall Library, MS 9581: 'Churchwardens' Certificates Returned upon Bishop John Robinson's Order Touching Observance of the Requirements of the Act of Uniformity of Public Prayers and Administration of Sacraments, 1714–1715 (chiefly those of City Parishes)'.

[23] LPL, Fulham Papers 552: 'Bishop Randolph's Inquiry in and about London, 1812, about Curates, Lecturers and Chapels'.

clerics in the metropolis. Visitation returns offer us a very different picture of the country parishes between 1723 and 1790, revealed in Table 6. One of the bishops' queries bore on the residence of the incumbent and his curate. The great majority of churches were served by only one clergyman; the increase in Table 5 in the number of livings served by both a parson and a curate in 1790 is only due to the presence of the London data for that year. On the other hand, more and more parishes were taken care of by their curate alone, in the absence of the incumbent: these amount to 15 per cent in 1723, to a fifth in 1738, to a quarter between 1742 and 1778, and reach 29 per cent in 1790.

Unsurprisingly, the incumbents tended more and more to live away from their livings. Tables 7 and 8 show that in 1723, 1727 and 1738, two-thirds or three-quarters of the parishes had resident incumbents, but less than 60 per cent enjoyed this position in 1742, and less than 50 per cent from 1778 onwards. Moreover, clergymen chose to live increasingly far away from their church, for instance in a diocese non-contiguous to that of London, where, no doubt, they held other livings. It would appear, then, that the end of the century represented the lowest ebb in the clergy's professional conscientiousness, despite their improved status. But one must bear in mind that for most of the century at least the phenomenon already noticed in relation to pluralism applies to non-residence as well; many of the non-residents lived nearby in another parish and went on serving their cure. This appeared to many, including bishops, a safeguard against the worst evils of absenteeism. Though the incumbent, and sometimes also the curate, was technically non-resident, he was in fact close enough to discharge at least a minimum of pastoral duties. This was particularly easy in London, and also in towns like Colchester, Chelmsford or St Albans, where living in the next parish often meant being a few streets away. But it could also be managed in Essex, as in many parts of the south-east of England, where the parishes were very numerous, small and so close together – often no more than a mile or so apart, and sometimes even less – that the parson could walk from his house to his church in a few minutes. This pattern of settlement, along with the large number of curates even in the country, meant that a majority of rural parishes had either their incumbent or their curate resident either in the parish or in the next village.[24]

Nevertheless, the proportion of churches without a clergyman nearby remained a concern for bishops and laity alike. The reasons for non-residence were usually given by the guilty clerics in the visitation returns, but they also appear in an episcopal inquiry conducted in 1736 on pluralism

[24] It was much more difficult to deal in the same way with absenteeism in the large parishes of the north of England.

and non-residence,[25] in some early nineteenth-century applications for licences of non-residence and in their notifications[26] and in a Parliamentary inquiry giving figures for the years 1804–7.[27] Table 9 shows that the chief motivation was always pluralism, which accounted for at least half of the cases of non-residence. It was followed either by the lack of a convenient or comfortable parsonage-house, or by medical reasons, the latter becoming more and more prominent as an excuse once parsonages were repaired and enlarged, whereas the climate of the south-east part of the diocese was past any improvement. Teaching posts elsewhere, either in a university or a school, or as private tutor in a gentry family, came as the last explanation of non-residence. All these reasons are borne out by the visitation returns, which become particularly graphic when non-resident clergymen described the various fevers, agues and breathing difficulties, which afflicted the inhabitants of villages situated on the North Sea coast or in the lower Thames valley, all plagued by marshes and by very difficult soils and weather, with poor roads or none during winter. Incumbents were equally eloquent when finding fault with their parsonages, especially those built of plaster and thatch, so small and out of repair that they had sometimes been let previously to day-labourers or to poor farmers.[28] Even so, pluralism remained at the root of the somewhat haphazard deployment of the clergy, which therefore continued as long as no remedy was found for clerical poverty. But both these evils were mitigated to a certain extent, at least in the diocese of London, owing to the proximity of livings and the great number of curates.

What did the clergy offer their parishioners, and what did the latter expect? Neither the people's nor the bishops' demands seem to have been very exacting in the eighteenth century. The practice of week-day services

[25] Guildhall Library, MS 25752: 'Episcopal Visitations, clerical returns for Middlesex, Essex, Hertfordshire and Buckinghamshire, 1736' (2 vols.).

[26] Guildhall Library, MS 11181: 'Licences for Non-Residence, 1804–1809'; MS 11182: 'Papers, Chiefly Notifications, Monitions and Correspondence, Relating to Non-Residence, 1804–1813'; MS 11182A: 'Entry-Book of Licences for Non-Residence, 1814–1815'; LPL, Fulham Papers 102: Diocesan Papers/Benefices, 'Pluralism, 1762–1880'; Fulham Papers, box 551: Diocesan Papers/Individual Bishops, 'Beilby Porteus, 1787–1809; Letters Arranged in roughly Alphabetical Order, mainly Applying for Licences for Non-Residence, 1803–1809; Unsuccessful Applications for Licences for Non-Residence, 1804–1805'; Fulham Papers, box 552: Diocesan Papers/Individual Bishops, 'John Randolph, 1809–1813; Applications for Licences for Non-Residence, 1812'; Fulham Papers, box 100: Diocesan Papers/Benefices, 'Certificates and Notifications of Non-Residence, 1803–1804, 1857, 1872'; Fulham Papers, box 148: Diocesan Papers/Benefices, 'Certificates and Notifications of Non-Residence, 1810–1812'; Fulham Papers, box 138: Diocesan Papers/Benefices, 'Applications for Licences for Non-Residence, 1809–1811, 1818, 1820, 1824'.

[27] LPL, Fulham Papers, box 452: Diocesan Papers/Benefices, 'Non Residence, 1804–1826'; 'Abstracts ... of Returns Relative to the Clergy ... 1804–1807, 1808'; 'Applications for Non-Residence Licences'.

[28] These complaints about parsonage-houses indicate the new social status of the clergy, who obviously wished to live in houses such as gentlemen might have had.

had been given up except in towns,[29] and Sunday services were the only ones concerning which the bishops issued injunctions. Constrained by pluralism and non-residence, they required no more than two services per Sunday with only one sermon, preferably in the morning.[30] Communion, sometimes described by obviously High Churchmen as the Holy or the Blessed Eucharist, but more commonly termed the Sacrament of the Lord's Supper, was celebrated but seldom for a variety of reasons. Canon 21 prescribed it three times a year, at Christmas, Easter and Whitsun, but several bishops advised a fourth celebration at Michaelmas, to bridge the long gap between Whitsun and Christmas.[31] Most country churches, therefore, had Holy Communion three or four times a year, while only in cities and some market-towns was it offered every month, and in London every Sunday.[32] Attendance showed pronounced regional variations. In the south-east and south-west of England, the laity did not communicate very often or in great numbers, except on Easter Sunday. Was this because of deep Protestant convictions or even Puritan scruples? In the north of England, where Catholicism and traditional practices had survived longer, reinvigorated by the Nonjurors at the end of the seventeenth century, many people came to the sacrament.[33] Communion therefore remains less

[29] J. H. Overton, *Life in the English Church 1660–1714* (1885), p. 175, quoting James Paterson, *Pietas Londinensis* (1714); Sykes, *Church and State*, p. 242; McClatchey, *Oxfordshire Clergy*, pp. 246–7; Gordon Rupp, *Religion in England 1688–1791* (Oxford, 1986), pp. 513, 516.

[30] Sykes, *Church and State*, p. 250; Rupp, *Religion in England*, p. 513; F. C. Mather, 'Georgian Churchmanship Reconsidered: Some Variations in Anglican Public Worship 1714–1830', *JEH*, 36 (1985), 265–7; Viviane Barrie, 'Recherches sur la vie religieuse en Angleterre au XVIIIe siècle', *Revue Historique*, 266 (1981), 375–8; Viviane Barrie-Curien, 'La Pratique Religieuse en Angleterre dans la seconde partie du XVIIIe siècle', *Revue Historique*, 275 (1986), 345.

[31] C. J. Abbey and J. H. Overton, *The English Church in the Eighteenth Century* (2 vols., 1878), II, 15; L. Elliott-Binns, *The First Evangelicals* (1928), pp. 106, 251; Sykes, *Church and State*, p. 250; Warne, *Church and Society*, p. 45; Rupp, *Religion in England*, p. 517.

[32] J. Wickham Legg, *English Church Life from the Restoration to the Tractarian Movement* (1914), pp. 21–3, 31–3; Elliott-Binns, *First Evangelicals*, p. 106; Sykes, *Church and State*, pp. 252, 255; McClatchey, *Oxfordshire Clergy*, pp. 86–7; J. H. Pruett, *The Parish Clergy under the Later Stuarts. The Leicestershire Experience* (Urbana, Chicago and London, 1978), pp. 121–2.

[33] Sykes, *Church and State*, pp. 251–3; Rupp, *Religion in England*, pp. 516–17; Warne, *Church and Society*, pp. 45–6; Mather, 'Georgian Churchmanship', pp. 272–4. According to *Archbishop Herring's Visitation Returns 1743*, ed. S. L. Ollard and P. C. Walker (5 vols., Yorkshire Archaeological Society, 1927–31), I, v-xxiv, the figures of communicants as given by visitation returns cannot be trusted, as they merely meant the number of people old enough to take the sacrament, who had been confirmed aged at least thirteen, and not of those who actually attended communion. However, see Sykes's comment, *Church and State*, p. 252, on this point. As far as the diocese of London is concerned, figures given seem to be those of actual communicants, as they are so small compared to the number of houses and families in the parishes also given in the returns, that they could not possibly account for all people aged over thirteen, even in such thinly populated villages as those of Essex and Hertfordshire in the eighteenth century.

revealing of religious beliefs than the frequency of services and the attendance at sermons.

The diocese of London offers a good instance of religious practice where the emphasis was laid on preaching and not on communion. But visitation returns yield data displayed in Table 10, which could be termed pessimistic. Very few parishes bothered with a week-day service, except in London, in Middlesex and in country towns. What must have seemed much more grievous in the eyes of ecclesiastical authorities was that even the two Sunday services were not kept everywhere, and that such neglect was on the increase. In 1723, 44 per cent of parishes had fewer than two Sunday services; the figure was just over half in 1747, and reached two-thirds from 1766 onwards. The proportion of churches which followed the norm set by bishops represented a majority in 1723, but a minority as soon as 1727, and, after stabilizing somewhat in the 1740s, dropped again in 1766. By 1790 it was no more than a quarter of the total.

The figures in Table 11 show that this decline in the number of services was due mainly to the difficulties of pastoral work in the villages, and especially in the marshes near the sea or the Thames estuary, called 'the hundreds of Essex', though other country parishes inland, some way from the coast, experienced the same decrease in church services. As for provincial towns, they took noticeably divergent courses, some of their churches increasing their number of services through the century, while in others the same decline took place as in the villages. London, however, maintained a tradition of great pastoral activity, with two-thirds of its parishes having many week-day services in 1790, and none fewer than two per Sunday. The county of Middlesex, in which services followed much the same pattern as in the provincial towns in the first part of the century, ended up being very similar to the City, particularly in Westminster, thereby achieving a religious and pastoral integration parallel to its geographical merging into London. This is apparent not only in the frequency of services, but also in the great number of lectures in metropolitan parishes, both on Sundays and on weekdays. Two series of data at each end of the period reveal this latter phenomenon. In 1715, according to the churchwardens' returns to Bishop John Robinson's inquiry, no London parish went without at least one lecture on Sunday, and only 14.2 per cent of the Middlesex churches had none. In 1812, an inquiry about curates and lecturers showed that 88 per cent of the London and Middlesex livings had at least one lecture; in total there were ninety-eight lectureships for seventy-five churches, and less than 30 per cent of them were endowed, the others being supported by the parishioners' voluntary gifts. This suggests a powerful popular demand for sermons.[34] Thus, to brand the end of the eighteenth century and the

[34] Guildhall Library, MS 9581; LPL, Fulham Papers 552; see nn. 22 and 23.

beginning of the nineteenth as a nadir in religious life and in pastoral care does not do justice to the Church or to the laity. In some provincial towns and in large cities the Church increased its pastoral work to match the rise in population, and thus compensated for the decline in the frequency of services in villages where the number of inhabitants, never very high, was either decreasing or stagnant.

Nevertheless, even the not too demanding requirement of the bishops for two Sunday services was not observed in the majority of villages. The reasons and explanations for this phenomenon throw some light on the structures of parochial and religious life in rural England. Table 12 shows the frequency of these reasons given by the guilty incumbents or curates in the course of pastoral visitations. The most frequent reason is the existence and extent of pluralism. Also commonly cited were an 'immemorial custom' to have only one service a week; the low revenues of the parish, which were in fact an explanation of pluralism; and the smallness of the population, which did not make a second service necessary. The general impression is that parishioners did not wish for more services than they already had, and felt they did not need them. Some clergymen actually claimed to have tried two services per Sunday, and to have abandoned the second for want of a congregation.[35]

This is not to say that the behaviour of the clergy did not play a part in the pattern of Sunday services. Pluralism in particular had a very negative influence on the number of services, whether the incumbent held another living, or whether he served another church as curate. Since the issue of parochial revenues was bound up with that of pluralism, it often followed that the poorer the living was, the fewer services were held in its church. Moreover, the closer an incumbent's two parishes were, the more likely both of them were to have only one service each, as the parson would try to serve both himself, instead of keeping a curate in one, who might have taken duty twice. Clerical non-residence, be it due to pluralism, bad health or the lack of a satisfactory parsonage-house, also determined the frequency of divine worship. Again, when the incumbent lived in a contiguous village, he was available to take duty once on Sunday, but certainly not twice; when far away, he was seldom to be seen, but employed perforce a curate who might be resident and able to give his parishioners two services. That is not to say that for other parts of a clergyman's duty – visiting the sick, helping the poor, teaching the children catechism – it was not preferable to have the incumbent nearby.

[35] One can find many instances of these attempts in the visitation returns of various Essex parishes. In 1723, the incumbent of Bromfield angrily maintained that the Toleration Act of 1689 was responsible for this neglect of the afternoon services, since it allowed church attendance to become voluntary.

A variety of other unavoidable circumstances also affected the patterns of Anglican worship. The first was the presence of Nonconformists in many parishes, probably more than are revealed by the visitation returns. In others, the clergy reported that the population consisted mainly of farmers and labourers, both too poor and too busy to come twice to church, particularly when they had cattle to look after even on Sundays. This social argument is all the more convincing as there were few resident landed gentry in many parts of Essex and Hertfordshire who would have seen to it that their tenants attended both services.[36] Another explanation for poor attendance related to the structure and configuration of the villages, many of which consisted of a long and narrow main road, with scattered houses, farms and cottages, almost all a long distance away from the church. Thus, people would not come to services more than once a Sunday, especially in winter when the roads became almost impassable. This pattern of settlement reflected the fact that the villages had either slowly lost some of their inhabitants down the centuries, or had never been nucleated; in either case, they had no real geographical centre focused on the church. A last, and very important, factor was that only one of the two Sunday services had a sermon, the second one consisting only of prayers, since most clergymen would not write two different sermons for the day. To many lay people a service without preaching was no service at all. They preferred to resort to a nearby parish church for the second service rather than attend their own to hear only the prayers, and therefore clergymen used to work out arrangements to deliver their sermons at different times, so that the inhabitants of two or three villages could go to one another's churches to enjoy as much preaching as possible. Visitation returns give many instances of this keen interest in preaching which resulted, paradoxically, in non-attendance at the second Sunday service in one's own parish.[37] Eventually the second service was given up, and many parishes began to operate in a sort of network, throwing together the hearers, incumbents and curates available within a small area, where villages were close enough and clerics sufficiently numerous to allow such arrangements. This practice made pluralism more acceptable; it was a way to keep an incumbent busy for that part of the day when his flock went elsewhere and those who also had to do duty in another

[36] The statistics show that in parishes where 'families of note', as visitation returns call them, were constantly resident, services and sacraments were offered more often than in those without any local landed gentry or aristocrats.

[37] In 1727 the Rector of Cold Norton admitted that 'parishioners prefer to resort to one of the neighbouring churches, and there are many very close, to hear a sermon when I am only reading prayers, to which I have vainly tried to bring them'. In 1766 the Rector of Mashbury explained bluntly that people 'prefer to attend the whole duty in neighbouring churches than half duty in their own'. In 1778 the Vicar of Marks Tey stated that 'it is difficult to get a congregation when there is no sermon'.

parish often found fellow clergy to take over to the laity's satisfaction. In short, the omission of the second Sunday service in most country churches was not a symptom of indifference, but, on the contrary, of concern for what seemed to laymen the essential part of divine worship. It suggests the persistence in this part of England of the Puritans' emphasis on preaching, of their rejection of mere ceremonies devoid of a sermon, and it is perhaps reminiscent of their organization of parishes in larger units run by local clergy and lay folk.[38] It also reveals that townsmen were not the only ones to enjoy sermons: country people took to them too.

Townspeople, on the other hand, were almost the only ones in the eighteenth century to set great store by communion. This sacrament is actually less revealing of people's religious outlook than the Sunday services, since the requirement of three or four celebrations a year was so easy to fulfil that very few parishes failed to meet it, and it is difficult to work out its motivation and significance. As Table 13 reveals, a minority of churches kept a weekly sacrament, in Middlesex and chiefly in London, which explains the increase in 1790. Monthly communion was also an urban phenomenon, common enough in provincial cities and in Middlesex. But country parishioners had the sacrament offered to them at the three festivals only, and increasingly at Michaelmas as well.

However, the frequency of communion met with some changes in the course of the century. Monthly communion kept increasing in Middlesex, particularly in churches where it had previously taken place six or eight times a year, and by 1766 some of them were celebrating it every Sunday. Yet even in 1790, the services were never as numerous as in the City of London, except in Westminster. Provincial towns saw an augmentation of monthly sacraments between 1723 and 1747, when they were celebrated in two-thirds of the churches. But this practice declined in the second part of the century, when communion four, six or eight times a year became usual. On the other hand, very few town parishes had it only three times – some of them never provided sacraments, though this was only the case when the churches had been demolished, thereby compelling the inhabitants to resort elsewhere for services and communion. In the country, more and more parishes adopted a quarterly celebration, instead of having it only at each of the three great festivals. Altogether, fewer than 5 per cent of parishes in the whole diocese failed to fulfil the minimum required of them. This is one of the main characteristics of eighteenth-century piety, at least in the country. Whereas services and sermons appear to have been very important, communion did not seem essential to the majority of the laity and even to most

[38] Essex, like East Anglia, was central to the development of the Puritan and even Presbyterian movement in the last decades of the sixteenth century. See Patrick Collinson's study of the Dedham classis, in *The Elizabethan Puritan Movement* (1967).

clergymen. It may be part of the Protestant and Puritan inheritance in the south-east of England, although infrequent communion seems to have been the rule in Roman Catholic countries as well, except in cities.

The reasons for the rarity of communion were seldom to be found in the visitation returns, inasmuch as it did not seem out of order to most of the clergy. Since three times a year was the rule, and since so few churches had it less often, there was little occasion to give explanations for what was customary. In a few cases, however, the laity's attitude was blamed. The first explanation offered was, of course, the presence of Dissent in some parishes, although, curiously enough, it does not occur very often in visitation returns.[39] Another frequent argument was that lay people wishing to take the sacrament were scarce: villages (it was said) had few inhabitants above confirmation age, parishioners did not like sacraments or understand their value, communion had fallen into disuse in the course of the seventeenth century, especially during the Civil War. Perhaps the medieval idea, that communion truly belonged to priests rather than the laity, still lingered. Some clergymen tried their best to encourage their flock to come in greater numbers, but did not meet with much success. The second half of the century did not bring any noticeable change; farmers, labourers and cottagers displayed particular reluctance to communicate, and clergymen maintained that their lack of education was responsible for their ignorance of the sense of sacraments.[40] Nevertheless, one should note some improvements in a few parishes, due no doubt to the energetic exhortation of their incumbents; there are instances of slow and gradual mental changes, which may owe something to evangelical tendencies in the Church of England as early as the 1730s.[41]

[39] In Chickney in 1742, 'there are nine houses almost all inhabited by Dissenters separated from the Church of England, and when the celebration of Holy Communion was made public, there was not a competent number of parishioners to communicate with the incumbent. This is the reason why the sacrament of the Lord's Supper has not been administered here of late.' In 1747 at Stanstead, St Margaret, communion was never celebrated 'as there are too few inhabitants in this small parish, and even the chief ones are Quakers and the others Dissenters'. Presbyterians were mentioned in 1778 at East Mersey and at Little Totham. The Rector of Bishop's Wickham hinted at occasional conformity in 1738: 'Although I have often preached on the need for frequent communion, it is seldom that I have a competent number of communicants, as none of the churchwardens receive communion, except to be qualified for office.'

[40] The Rector of Little Chishall, recently instituted in 1723, 'cannot learn whether communion has ever been administered in the last forty years; when I gave the sacrament, only three or four people took part of it, whom I had difficulty in persuading to receive it'. The Rector of Little Braxted explained in 1727 how he had tried several times but 'could not gather the number of communicants required by the rubric'.

[41] In 1747 in Little Dunmow, the curate explained that 'the sacrament had fallen into disuse several years ago, but, the Lord be praised, it is now administered four times a year'. The same phenomenon occurred in Lexden, where communion, which had not been celebrated for many years, was brought back at the three festivals in 1727, and six times a year from 1738 onwards.

Given the low level of lay demand, the frequency of communion was very dependent on the number of inhabitants within the parish. The population had to reach 500 or more to sustain more than four celebrations a year. Nucleated villages tended to have fewer than scattered hamlets, in which it was more difficult to gather the whole population together – people therefore came a few at a time to a communion offered more frequently. Another very important factor was the presence of what visitation returns termed 'families of note' in the parish. When the local gentry were resident, communion tended to be more frequent, either because the gentry wanted to receive it more often, or because they attracted more villagers to church and persuaded them to communicate.[42]

The behaviour of the clergy and of the laity allows some insight into the main characteristics of ecclesiastical structures, of the clergy's deployment and of their organization. All were deeply rooted in an ancient parochial geography, which dated back at least to the Reformation and often to the thirteenth century. One can be cautiously optimistic about religious practice and clerical professionalism in the eighteenth century. Large cities like London and its immediate surroundings in Middlesex were well provided for. As for country livings, they obviously suffered from long-lamented evils; not only from pluralism and non-residence, but also from poverty and depopulation. But in many parishes, solutions were found – not all simple or easy, but warranted by old custom, and made possible by local conditions such as the high density of churches, the proximity of villages and the small number of inhabitants, as well as by the low level of the demands of laity and church authorities alike. But these structures could not have functioned in other parts of the country, such as the north, or Wales, or the new populous towns of the eighteenth century, where the crisis of the Church in the nineteenth century was to break out.

[42] This analysis of the two main aspects of religious practice lacks an important element: figures of church attendance. Neither visitation returns nor other inquiries reveal anything about the number of people who came to services. However, the former give figures of communicants, which represent between approximately 4 and 10 per cent of the population of each parish.

Appendix

Table 1 *The social recruitment of the clergy of the diocese of London in the eighteenth century**

Father's status or occupation	*Number of clergymen*	*Percentage*
Nobility	6	1.2
Gentry	189	37.8
Merchant	9	1.8
Doctor (in medicine)	5	1.0
Lawyer	12	2.4
Clergy	177	35.4
Schoolmaster	5	1.0
Plebeians	97	19.4
Father's status or occupation	*Number of clergymen*	*Percentage*
Nobility	6	1.2
Baronet	8	1.6
Knight	5	1.0
Esquire or armiger	48	9.6
Gentleman	128	25.6
Merchant	9	1.8
Doctor (in medicine)	5	1.0
Lawyer	12	2.4
Higher clergy	31	6.2
Parish clergy	146	29.2
Schoolmaster	5	1.0
Shopkeeper or craftsman	27	5.4
Farmer or husbandman	8	1.6
Unspecified 'plebeian'	62	12.4

* The figures are worked out from a random sample of 500 clergymen beneficed in the diocese of London between 1714 and 1800.

Table 2 *The social recruitment of the clergy in the diocese of London in the eighteenth century, by twenty years' periods (in absolute numbers)**

Father's status	*Before 1700*	*1701–20*	*1721–40*	*1741–60*	*1761–80*	*After 1781*
Nobility				2	2	2
Gentry	11	23	41	23	36	55
Merchant	2		2	1	3	1
Doctor (in medicine)		1	1	1	2	
Lawyer	2		2	4	3	1
Clergy	10	26	40	36	39	26
Schoolmaster		2	1	1	1	
Plebeian	10	9	26	22	18	12
Total	35	61	113	90	104	97

*The social recruitment of the clergy in the diocese of London in the eighteenth century, by twenty years' periods (in percentages)**

Father's status	*Before 1700*	*1701–20*	*1721–40*	*1741–60*	*1761–80*	*After 1781*
Nobility				2.2	1.9	2.0
Gentry	31.0	37.7	36.2	25.5	34.6	56.7
Merchant	5.7		1.7	1.1	2.8	1.0
Doctor (in medicine)		1.6	0.8	1.1	1.9	
Lawyer	5.7		1.7	4.0	2.8	1.0
Clergy	28.5	42.6	35.3	40.0	37.5	26.8
Schoolmaster		3.2	0.8	1.1	0.9	
Plebeian	28.5	14.7	23.0	24.4	17.3	12.3

* These figures are worked out from a random sample of 500 clergymen beneficed in the diocese of London between 1714 and 1800.

Table 3 *The social recruitment of the clergy in the diocese of London in the eighteenth century, by twenty years' periods (in absolute numbers)**

Father's status	*Before 1700*	*1701–20*	*1721–40*	*1741–60*	*1761–80*	*After 1781*
Nobility				2	2	2
Baronet		1	1		2	5
Knight	1	1	2		1	
Esquire	1	3	6	4	8	26
Gentleman	9	18	32	19	25	24
Merchant	2		2	1	3	1
Doctor (in medicine)		1	1	1	2	
Lawyer	2		2	4	4	1
Higher clergy	1	2	6	9	5	5
Parish clergy	9	24	34	27	34	19
Schoolmaster		2	1	1	1	
Trader or craftsman	3	5	5	8	4	2
Farmer or husbandman			3	3	2	
Plebeian	7	4	18	11	12	10
Total	35	61	113	90	105	95

*The social recruitment of the clergy in the diocese of London in the eighteenth century, by twenty years' periods (in percentages)**

Father's status	*Before 1700*	*1701–20*	*1721–40*	*1741–60*	*1761–80*	*After 1781*
Nobility				2.2	1.9	2.0
Baronet		1.6	0.8		1.9	5.1
Knight	2.8	1.6	1.7		0.9	
Esquire	2.8	4.9	5.3	4.4	7.6	26.8
Gentleman	25.7	29.5	28.3	21.1	24.0	24.7
Merchant	5.7		1.7	1.1	2.8	1.0
Doctor (in medicine)		1.6	0.8	1.1	1.9	
Lawyer	5.7		1.7	4.4	3.8	1.0
Higher clergy	2.8	3.2	5.3	10.0	4.8	5.1
Parish clergy	25.7	39.3	30.0	30.0	32.6	19.5
Schoolmaster		3.2	0.8	1.1	0.9	
Trader or craftsman	8.5	8.1	4.4	8.8	3.8	2.0
Farmer or husbandman			2.6	3.3	1.9	
Plebeian	20.0	6.5	15.9	12.2	11.5	10.3

* These figures are worked out from a random sample of 500 clergymen beneficed in the diocese of London between 1714 and 1800.

Table 4 *Pluralism in the diocese of London in the eighteenth century (information derived from pastoral visitations)*

Percentages of parishes at each visitation held by their incumbent alone or in plurality	*1723*	*1727*	*1738*	*1742*	*1747*	*1766–70*	*1778*	*1790*
Held alone	59.0	60.4	50.2	48.9	47.8	53.2	45.7	47.3
With another one	39.8	37.5	48.7	48.9	51.6	45.0	49.4	49.8
With two others	1.0	2.0	0.9	2.2	0.2	1.7	4.9	2.7

Percentages of parishes at each visitation served by their incumbent alone or with curacies	*1723*	*1727*	*1738*	*1742*	*1747*	*1766–70*	*1778*	*1790*
With no curacy	84.9	73.2	83.0	79.7	78.5	86.1	89.4	91.5
With one curacy	14.5	23.6	16.4	19.1	19.9	11.2	9.7	7.6
With two curacies	0.5	3.1	0.4	1.0	1.5	0.7	0.9	0.8

Table 5 *The clergy's deployment in London parishes from the end of the seventeenth to the beginning of the nineteenth century (in percentages)**

Parishes served by	*1693*	*1711*	*1715*	*1790*	*1812*
Incumbent	6.6	2.9	4.7	19.0	10.6
Curate	1.6	2.9		24.0	
Lecturer			11.9		
Incumbent and curate	1.6	2.9		51.0	20.0
Incumbent and lecturer	23.3	32.3	64.2		20.0
Curate and lecturer	20.0	30.8	7.1	5.0	
Incumbent and reader	3.3				
Incumbent, curate and lecturer	30.0	20.5	11.9		32.0
Incumbent, lecturer and reader	11.6	4.4			
Curate, lecturer and reader	1.4				
Incumbent and over two assistants	1.6	1.4			17.3

* Percentages are worked out on the basis of the number of parishes represented in each inquiry or visitation.

Table 6 *The clergy's deployment in the parishes of the diocese of London in the eighteenth century, derived from visitation returns (in percentages)**

Parishes Served by	*1723*	*1727*	*1738*	*1742*	*1747*	*1766–70*	*1778*	*1790*
Incumbent	68.9	70.7	66.0	58.1	59.2	52.6	47.9	32.8
Curate	15.5	13.1	21.0	27.6	24.5	26.9	25.4	29.5
Incumbent and curate	15.0	15.7	12.7	13.4	16.2	20.2	26.7	37.0
Incumbent and lecturer	0.5	0.4		0.4				0.2
Curate and lecturer			0.2					0.6
Lecturer				0.2		0.2		

* Percentages are worked out on the basis of the number of parishes represented in each pastoral visitation.

Table 7 *Clerical residence in the diocese of London in the eighteenth century, derived from visitation returns (with detailed places of residence) (in percentages)*

Incumbent's place of residence at each pastoral visitation	*1723*	*1727*	*1738*	*1742*	*1747*	*1766–70*	*1778*	*1790*
In his parsonage-house	53.0	58.3	52.2	52.6	52.5	45.4	44.4	36.8
In his parish, but not in the parsonage	11.6	13.8	9.7	6.8	6.5	4.6	5.2	5.1
In the contiguous parish or in the same town	12.1	11.1	11.8	14.5	15.0	12.8	12.0	17.1
In the same deanery	3.9	4.1	4.7	3.8	3.8	4.6	6.9	4.0
In the contiguous deanery	6.0	6.0	9.0	7.3	7.2	9.4	8.3	6.9
In the same county	2.6	0.4	3.0	2.5	2.2	5.1	2.9	2.1
In the same diocese	5.2	3.2	3.7	5.0	5.0	7.4	6.3	8.4
In the contiguous diocese	5.0	1.3	4.2	5.3	4.7	5.4	6.0	8.2
Far away	0.2	1.3	1.2	1.7	2.7	5.4	8.0	11.4

Table 8 *Clerical residence in the diocese of London in the eighteenth century, derived from visitation returns (with simplified places of residence) (in percentages)*

Incumbent's place of residence at each pastoral visitation	*1723*	*1727*	*1738*	*1742*	*1747*	*1766–70*	*1778*	*1790*
In his parish	64.6	72.2	62.0	59.6	59.0	50.0	49.6	41.9
In the contiguous parish or in the same town	12.1	11.1	11.8	14.4	15.0	12.8	12.0	17.1
In the same diocese	17.9	13.8	20.6	18.7	18.3	26.4	24.4	21.4
In a contiguous diocese	5.0	1.3	4.2	5.3	4.7	5.4	6.0	8.2
Far away	0.2	1.3	1.2	1.7	2.7	5.4	8.0	11.4

Table 9 *The reasons for non-residence among the clergy of the diocese of London in the eighteenth century and at the beginning of the nineteenth century (in percentages)**

	1736	*1804–5*	*1805–6*	*1806–7*	*1803–12*	*1804–12*
Pluralism	63.2	29.5	31.5	41.8	48.4	85.3
Ill-health	19.3	14.1	13.7	12.5	12.4	
Parsonage out of repair or non-existent	10.3	30.2	18.6	13.2	26.6	4.8
Teaching posts or cathedral functions	5.8	7.6	9.2	5.6	11.8	4.8

* The above figures are drawn from an episcopal inquiry about pluralism and non-residence in the diocese of London in 1736, from a Parliamentary inquiry on non-resident clergy for the years 1804–5, 1805–6 and 1806–7, from 233 applications and notifications of non-residence ranging from 1803 to 1812, and from another series of 41 notifications of non-residence for the years 1804–13.

Table 10 *The frequency of divine service in the parishes of the diocese of London in the eighteenth century, derived from visitation returns*

	1723	*1727*	*1738*	*1742*	*1747*	*1766–70*	*1778*	*1790*
Percentages of parishes at each visitation with week-day services	11.4	12.8	8.5	8.8	8.0	6.7	8.3	12.8
Frequency of Sunday services and sermons in parishes at each visitation (percentages)								
More than prescribed	7.8	9.4	6.2	2.7	3.4	13.8	15.2	24.3
As prescribed	47.8	41.5	43.4	45.5	45.3	23.6	20.3	20.7
Less than prescribed	44.3	49.1	50.3	51.9	51.3	62.6	64.3	55.0

Table 11 *The frequency of divine service in the different regions of the diocese of London in the eighteenth century, derived from visitation returns**

	Mean frequency†	*Middlesex*	*Provincial towns*	*Thames valley*	*Coast*	*Inland*	*London*
			1723				
>Norm	7.8	24.3	21.7	9.3	1.9	5.5	
Norm	47.8	65.8	65.8	32.5	28.8	55.9	
<Norm	44.3	9.7	13.0	58.1	69.2	38.5	
			1727				
>Norm	9.4	17.5	25.0	10.2	3.3	9.2	
Norm	41.5	77.5	50.0	43.5	20.2	46.2	
<Norm	49.1	5.0	25.0	46.1	76.4	44.4	
			1738				
>Norm	6.2	20.4	16.6	2.1		6.1	
Norm	43.4	71.4	58.3	39.1	25.8	46.4	
<Norm	50.3	8.1	25.0	58.6	74.1	47.4	
			1742				
>Norm	2.7	11.6	3.4		0.8	2.4	
Norm	45.5	79.0	68.9	37.7	26.4	48.7	
<Norm	51.9	9.3	27.5	62.2	72.8	48.7	
			1747				
>Norm	3.4	19.5	7.6	2.0		1.5	
Norm	45.3	71.7	73.0	40.0	28.5	46.9	
<Norm	51.3	8.6	19.2	58.0	71.4	51.5	
			1766–70				
>Norm	13.8	26.0	59.0	11.0	7.0	10.0	
Norm	23.6	67.0	14.0	19.0	17.0	24.0	
<Norm	62.6	7.0	28.0	70.0	76.0	65.0	
			1778				
>Norm	15.2	53.0	33.0	16.0	8.0	9.0	
Norm	20.3	39.0	22.0	16.0	12.0	22.0	
<Norm	64.3	8.0	44.0	67.0	80.0	69.0	
			1790				
>Norm	24.3	64.0	43.0	9.0	8.0	10.0	66.0
Norm	20.7	31.0	21.0	19.0	10.0	21.0	34.0
<Norm	55.0	5.0	36.0	72.0	83.0	69.0	

* Percentages are worked out on the basis of the number of parishes in each region, and give the proportion of those which follow each type of religious practice.

† The mean frequency of divine service is represented by the proportion of parishes in the whole diocese, notwithstanding their location, which follow each type of religious practice.

Table 12 *The reasons for the neglect of divine service on Sundays in the diocese of London in the eighteenth century, as given by the clergy in visitation returns (in percentages)**

	1723	*1727*	*1738*	*1742*	*1747*	*1766–70*	*1778*	*1790*
Pluralism†	49.0	51.0	48.3	39.6	43.7	50.3	48.3	43.5
Custom	3.8	5.4	7.6	12.5	10.8	21.7	24.0	29.0
Other churches nearby	13.3	8.6	9.3	11.5	7.0	13.7	8.0	13.2
Low parochial revenues	14.6	6.5	8.2	15.0	15.6	12.9	8.7	4.3
Parishioners' unwillingness	6.3	8.6	4.3	4.0	4.8	4.9	6.9	7.4
Too few people in the parish	6.3	6.5	12.0	10.5	12.4	4.5	4.0	2.4
Incumbent's great age or illness	3.1	3.2	2.1	4.0	2.1			
Particular cases	1.2			0.5		3.0		
Several reasons at a time	1.9	9.7	7.6	2.0	3.2			

* Percentages are worked out on the basis of the number of reasons given by the incumbents of the churches where the number of Sunday services is below the prescribed norm at each pastoral visitation.

† Pluralism here may mean either that the incumbent had another benefice, or that he was curate to another church, and that in any case he had to read divine service and to preach twice each Sunday at each place.

Table 13 *The frequency of communion in the parishes of the diocese of London in the eighteenth century derived from visitation returns (in percentages)*

Frequency of celebration of communion in parishes at each pastoral visitation (percentages)	*1723*	*1727*	*1738*	*1742*	*1747*	*1766–70*	*1778*	*1790*
Weekly	0.0	0.8	0.0	0.4	0.0	0.3	0.3	0.8
Monthly	10.9	18.4	12.2	13.7	13.0	10.1	12.7	23.7
From 8 to 6 times a year	9.3	9.8	9.0	8.9	8.9	5.5	7.0	4.5
4 times a year	30.0	34.3	41.1	41.0	45.8	63.1	61.4	56.1
3 times a year	44.3	33.9	34.1	32.6	30.5	18.3	15.2	10.1
Very seldom or never	3.1	2.5	3.4	3.3	1.6	2.8	3.4	4.7

4 The reception of Richard Podmore: Anglicanism in Saddleworth 1700–1830

Mark Smith

One of England's more remote areas, Saddleworth, always has been and still remains a borderland shared between a number of distinct jurisdictions. In secular terms, eighteenth-century Saddleworth formed one of the most westerly parts of the West Riding of Yorkshire, occupying the moorland valleys of the upper Tame and its tributaries on what was otherwise the Lancastrian side of the Pennine ridge. In ecclesiastical terms, Saddleworth was a parochial chapelry within the parish of Rochdale, and represented the easternmost extension of the Lancastrian part of the archdeaconry of Chester in the Chester diocese.

Its inhabitants had, from the fifteenth century at the latest, got their livelihood from a combination of pastoral agriculture and domestic textile manufacture, characteristic of the northern moorland economy. During the eighteenth century, they participated in the great leap forward of the Yorkshire woollen industry, benefiting, in particular, from a plentiful supply of water power to turn fulling and scribbling mills and the new spinning machinery. Between 1740 and 1792, the local production of woollen cloth increased by over 400 per cent in quantity and almost 800 per cent in value, and this was not the only economic development. Proximity to the dynamic textile economy of its neighbour Oldham led, during the nineteenth century, to a penetration of the western parts of Saddleworth by the cotton industry, and by 1838 some thirty-nine local cotton mills were together employing a workforce of over 2,000.[1]

This economic growth was accompanied by a rapid advance in the size of the population. In 1726, the population of Saddleworth was estimated at no more than 1,500 people, but by 1782 it had increased markedly to almost 7,000. At the first census, in 1801, the population return stood at 10,665 and thirty years later it had reached almost 16,000 – a tenfold increase over the century.[2] However, the social geography of the area remained recognizably

[1] J. Aikin, *A Description of the Country from Thirty to Forty Miles Round Manchester* (1795), pp. 556–8.

[2] B. Barnes, 'The Upper Tame Valley', BA dissertation, University of Manchester, 1971, p. 17.

similar to that obtaining at the start of the period. Isolated farmsteads and little folds of houses had grown into hamlets and hamlets into villages. There was also a discernible thickening of the population along the valley bottoms and the border with Oldham, but the inherited pattern of small communities remained intact. Along with the geography of community in Saddleworth went a strong sense of communal identity both in the individual villages and in the four ancient districts, or 'meres', within which they were federated. In practice, this sense of community must have been expressed most frequently in the simple neighbourliness that made village life viable. However, it became most visible in the great communal festivals like the rush bearings, when carts from outlying hamlets, expressions of communal pride guarded by the local youth, converged, not always without violence, on the parochial chapel.[3]

As economic change produced temporary dislocations in the life of the Saddleworth villages, communal identities began to be expressed in terms of radical politics. To a certain extent, this response cut across local solidarities as the divergent interests of employers and their workmen became increasingly evident. As early as 1795, for example, one local radical, Daniel Neild, was using a version of the labour theory of value derived from Adam Smith in an attempt to forge an alliance between local shopkeepers, landowners and operative clothiers against the industrial employers. However, the small size and relative instability of many local enterprises limited the progress of economic differentiation along class lines and, as the support of 'many respectable people' for local labour combinations showed, communal solidarity retained throughout the period a capacity to transcend emerging class antagonisms. Nevertheless, in the early nineteenth century radical feeling was expressed with increasing ferocity, and the men of Saddleworth marched to Peterloo, along with their neighbours from the village of Lees, behind a black banner bearing the declaration 'Equal Representation or Death'.[4]

Although the local radicals seem in practice to have been far more violent in their rhetoric than in their deeds, the rhetoric both exemplified and reinforced Saddleworth's long-standing reputation as a particularly violent society. Even in an area not noted for polite manners, Saddleworth had a

[3] M. Brierley, *A History of Saddleworth* (1883); Parliamentary Papers, 1852–3, 86, Parts 1 and 2.

[4] *Manchester Mercury*, 29 Apr. 1829; D. Newton, 'Aspects of Historical Geography in the Saddleworth Area', BA dissertation, University of Durham, 1971, pp. 55–60; F. R. Raines, *Diary* (extracts published in the *Oldham Chronicle*, 23 Jan. 1926 – 27 Feb. 1926), 28 Sept. 1828; S. Bamford, *Passages in the Life of a Radical*, ed. W. H. Chaloner (1967), Part 1, p. 203; A. J. Brooks, 'More Light on Radical Saddleworth's Secret History', *Bulletin of the Saddleworth Historical Society*, (1982), 68–72; D. Neild, *Addresses to the Different Classes of Men in the Parish of Saddleworth* (1795).

dark reputation. Contemporary observers were shocked by the savagery of local blood-sports, and intercommunal violence, especially between young men from rival meres, was common.[5] Given the reputed nature of the flock he would have to pastor, the prospect of succession to the perpetual curacy of Saddleworth (value £60 per annum) may not have seemed particularly enticing when the Vicar of Rochdale offered the living to his assistant curate, Richard Podmore, in 1771.[6]

His predecessor, John Heginbottom, who had held the curacy since 1726, had adopted a belligerent approach to pastoralia. According to one Saddleworth historian, 'When Mr Pigot [the patron] gave him the living he observed – "Mr Heginbottom, the Saddleworth people are a very turbulent and unmannerly set, what will you do with them?" He replied – "Preach the Gospel, and if that will not do" – clenching his fists and throwing himself into a Boxing attitude – "this will!"'[7] Heginbottom is recorded as having tried out his alternative technique on at least one local farmer, but his prospective successor proved to be made of rather less stern stuff. Podmore graduated from Christ's College, Cambridge, in 1760 and was nominated by his old tutor, Dr Wray, as assistant curate of Rochdale in 1767. Four years later Wray took advantage of the death of Heginbottom to advance his protégé a further step.[8] Podmore, who was known as a rather nervous and timid man, may not have been a particularly wise selection and his nervousness must have been increased when he heard that his election was by no means popular with the local inhabitants whose own choice would have been Heginbottom's assistant curate, Samuel Stones.

Various Saddleworth men seem to have tried to put pressure on the Vicar of Rochdale to change his mind and may even have threatened violence, but, perhaps mindful of an earlier dispute with Heginbottom about jurisdiction in the chapelry, Dr Wray remained obdurate and feeling began to run high in the Saddleworth villages. Podmore must have made the journey up the valley to take up his new cure with some trepidation and when he finally reached the chapel it was to find that his worst fears had been realized. The whole community seemed to have been mobilized to oppose his institution and, according to a local diarist,

> with great difficulty Mr Podmore obtained an entrance into the church in consequence of an immense mob which assembled, determined to prevent his taking possession of the living. However, he managed to read himself in without receiving any bodily injury, but so great were his apprehensions that his opponents would resort to violent measures, that he escaped through the north door of the church in disguise.

[5] R. Poole, 'Oldham Wakes', in *Leisure in Great Britain 1780–1939*, ed. J. K. Walton and J. Walvin (1983), p. 78; *Manchester Mercury*, 29 Apr. 1826.

[6] *Alum. Cantab.*, Part II; Chetham's College Library, Manchester, Raines MSS, I.

[7] Raines MSS, XXXVIIa. [8] *Alum. Cantab.*; Raines MSS, XXXVIIa.

The nervous shock was too much for Podmore. There is a strong local tradition that for some time afterwards he was confined in an asylum, and certainly he later retired to the more congenial surroundings of a living or two in Kent. He retained the perpetual curacy of Saddleworth for twenty-one years without visiting the parish again and without ever preaching in the parochial chapel.[9]

This anecdote is fairly typical of the way in which much of the local history of the Hanoverian Church has hitherto been written. We are back in a familiar world of pastoral scandal moderated by amiable eccentricity. The patron pays scant attention to local needs, the pastor is not only non-resident but mad, and the people appear at the church mainly in order to riot. However, as with much of the anecdotal history of the eighteenth-century Church, the anecdote conceals more than it illustrates. When one looks behind the story to examine the pastoral effectiveness of the Church of England in Saddleworth and the more usual nature of popular communal involvement with the Church, the rough reception of Richard Podmore emerges as a rather unusual episode in a century of sustained expansion.

Most obviously, this expansion took the form of an increase in church room to accommodate the rapidly growing population of the Saddleworth villages. Initially, this increase was provided by a more intensive use of existing structures. At the start of the century, the ancient parochial chapel of Saddleworth seems to have provided sittings for about 260 people, or around 20 per cent of the population of the district. It was soon recognized that this level of accommodation was inadequate, and in 1711 a gallery was erected at the west end of the church. Over the next few years, seating was extended along the ground floor of the building until the chancel was crowded with seats almost as far as the communion rail, and a second gallery was built along one of the chancel walls. Finally, in 1728, further galleries were constructed along the north and south aisles and a loft built for the choir and organ. The result by 1730 was a doubling of seating capacity in the church and an increase in the proportion of the population accommodated to around 30 per cent – all achieved without troubling the church building statistics.[10]

However, as settlements in the outlying districts of the chapelry continued to grow, the need for more accommodation closer at hand became apparent. The first new churches built to supply this need were erected, not in Saddleworth itself, but in the neighbouring parish of Ashton. St John's, Hey, was built in 1743 according to its consecration deed, 'for the ease and convenience of the inhabitants of the hamlet of Lees and other neighbouring inhabitants ... of the chapelries of Saddleworth and Oldham, who by

[9] Raines MSS, I, XXXVIIa; *Alum. Cantab.*

[10] A. J. Howcroft, *The Chapelry and Church of Saddleworth and Quick* (1915).

reason of the distance of their several chapels and parish churches, cannot especially in winter time, without great inconvenience, repair to the same to hear Divine Service'. St George's, Mossley, which performed much the same function on the southern borders of Saddleworth, was opened fourteen years later in 1757.[11]

Accommodation provided in churches beyond the borders of the chapelry was necessarily limited in its value and a quickening in the pace of population growth after the middle of the century pointed clearly to the need for more accommodation in Saddleworth itself. The result was the consecration in 1765 of St Thomas's in the district of Friarmere, built with 500 seats to serve in particular the rapidly growing township of Delph. It was followed in 1786 by the largest church in the locality, Holy Trinity, Dobcross, built to seat 840 people mainly drawn from the district of Shawmere. Two years later, the last of the ancient divisions of Saddleworth gained its own chapel with the opening, in Quickmere, of St Anne's, Lydgate, with some 660 seats.

The aggregate result of this impressive church building effort was an increase from 260 seats in 1700 to around 2,760 in 1790: a multiplication of the available church room by over 1,000 per cent over the century. The growth in available accommodation even outstripped the local demographic revolution during this period, and consequently there was a slight rise in the proportion of the population that could be accommodated to around 36.5 per cent in 1788. Moreover, the calculation of available church room according to seating capacity seems, according to contemporary accounts, to produce a significant underestimate. Raines, the curate of Saddleworth at the end of the century, for example, seems regularly to have attracted congregations far in excess of the notional 517 seats available in his chapel, and the most popular services could attract up to 2,000 people, many standing in the aisles, baptistry and even filling up the vestry for want of room in the main body of the church. If anything deterred Saddleworth people from church attendance during this period, it certainly does not seem to have been shortage of accommodation.[12]

However, the consecration of St Anne's marked the end of the local church building effort and no increases in church accommodation are recorded for the remainder of the period. As a consequence, the proportion of seats to the population as a whole had fallen to about 17.4 per cent by 1830, less than half its peak eighteenth-century level.

There is no evidence to suggest that Saddleworth was particularly unusual within the diocese of Chester in the vitality of its church building

[11] S. Andrew, *A History of Hey* (1905), p. 9; Manchester Central Library, Rushton Visitation Returns, I, 142.

[12] Rushton Visitation Returns, LXII; Raines, *Diary*, 27 July 1828.

effort. The neighbouring district of Oldham, for example, increased its number of church buildings from two to seven between 1730 and 1770 and its density of seating from under 40 per cent to over 50 per cent, despite a demographic increase much larger than that experienced in Saddleworth. However, here too, significant increases in accommodation dried up towards the end of the century and, by the mid-1820s, the density of seating had fallen dramatically to around 15 per cent. Looking further afield, a brief survey of church building in the forty parishes of the south Lancastrian deaneries of the diocese of Chester reveals that a total of at least sixty-one new churches were built between 1690 and 1799, with another forty-seven existing churches being rebuilt and many more being extended with large increases in accommodation.

Even more significant is the chronology of church building. Some seven churches were built or rebuilt between 1690 and 1704, twelve in each of the next two periods of fifteen years, and another fourteen between 1740 and 1754. Thereafter, as the rate of population growth began gradually to accelerate, so did the process of church building. A further nineteen churches were built or rebuilt between 1755 and 1769, eighteen between 1770 and 1784 and twenty-six in the last fifteen years of the century, of which twenty-one were entirely new structures. However, at this point the local church building enterprise seems to have petered out, and during the next fifteen years the total of churches built or rebuilt reached only nine. Nevertheless, demographic growth continued apace, and the consequence in many parishes was a serious decline in the proportion of the population that could be seated in church. In the large parish of Bolton le Moors, for example, the proportion fell from over 20 per cent in 1801 to 15.2 per cent in 1811 and 12 per cent in 1821.

The reasons for this failure to maintain momentum are not altogether clear and, as we shall see from the state of the Church in Saddleworth, it certainly seems inappropriate to attribute it to any general lack of zeal. The best available explanation seems to be the effect of general economic uncertainty caused by the Napoleonic wars on a church building enterprise that rested in the final analysis on the resources of a local economy experiencing quite novel growth combined with an unprecedented degree of turbulence and instability. Certainly the years following the defeat of France saw a remarkable resurgence of church building which was only partly due to the additional stimulus of Parliamentary grant and forty-two more churches were built or rebuilt between 1815 and 1829.[13] By this time

[13] E. Baines, *History, Directory, and Gazeteer of the County Palatine of Lancaster* (1824); A. J. Dobb, *Like a Mighty Tortoise. A History of the Diocese of Manchester* (1978); *Notitia Cestriensis or Historical Notices of the Diocese of Chester by the Right Reverend Francis*

the Church was having to run simply in order to keep still, and the shortage of accommodation became a general cry of church reformers in the 1830s and of ecclesiastical historians ever since. However, in Saddleworth at least, and perhaps much more widely in the industrial north, this shortage was a product not so much of a long century of neglect as of an unprecedented period of sustained demographic growth combined with an enforced pause in church building around the turn of the century, just when it most required acceleration.[14]

Even where its existence is admitted, eighteenth-century church extension is frequently criticized on the grounds that the failure to sub-divide large parishes weakened the pastoral structure of the Church of England and that the new chapels of ease were built for a population already becoming alienated from the Church and in any case excluded by the prevalence of appropriated seats. In Saddleworth, however, these criticisms seem to be wide of the mark. The curates of the new chapels do not seem to have expended great quantities of energy on demarcation disputes and the arrangement worked smoothly, even when, as in the case of St John's, Hey, the chapel was in a different parish to much of the population that it served. The parishes like Manchester, which contained a single great centre of population with a multiplicity of churches of its own as well as a number of out-townships, may have experienced particular problems, and by the late 1840s, when it was beginning increasingly to attract the attention of clerical reformers, the chapelry system had perhaps begun to outlive its usefulness. Nevertheless, throughout the eighteenth century, there were, in many cases, great advantages in retaining the old parish boundaries. They maintained ancient community relationships that enabled resources to be mobilized for church building from over a much wider area than would have been possible with parochial subdivision, as many nineteenth-century church builders, in newly created 'Peel Districts', discovered to their cost. At the same time the construction of chapels of ease often allowed the Church to participate in shaping the new communal identities which were already beginning to grow in the places where they had been planted. As a transitional arrangement for communities gradually approaching maturity, it was ideal. The pattern of a mother church with a number of subordinate chapels also served a valuable function in a church generally lacking in structures of intermediate ecclesiastical authority. The incumbents of mother churches seem to have acted effectively as rural deans in

Gastrell DD, ed. F. R. Raines (Chetham Society, 19, 1849, 21, 22, 1850); V. D. Davies, *Some Account of the Ancient Chapel of Toxteth Park Liverpool from the Year 1618 to 1883* (1884); Rushton Visitation Returns, I–LXXVI.

[14] See C. W. Chalklin, 'The Financing of Church Building in the Provincial Towns of Eighteenth-Century England', in *The Transformation of English Provincial Towns*, ed. P. Clark (1984), p. 295.

some large parishes, and the vicar of Rochdale certainly carried out a visitation of the Saddleworth churches in this capacity in 1813.[15]

The problems caused by appropriated seats also seem to have been exaggerated. In the chapels of ease, seats were allocated in proportion to the amount subscribed towards their erection and the rent appropriated towards the support of the minister. However, Saddleworth presented no opportunity for the sort of clerical speculation in seat rents to which one or two churches in Manchester and Liverpool seem to have owed their origin, and great care was taken to ensure that seats surplus to the requirements of their owners were re-let at the original rent, thus avoiding both profiteering and the potential problem of a large number of unoccupied seats. Early nineteenth-century records suggest that local pew owners were often willing to allow their property to be used freely for the benefit of the poor. In 1821, the curate of Holy Trinity, Dobcross, for example, reported that he had no accommodation set aside for the poor, but that all were nevertheless admitted. Moreover, in Saddleworth seat ownership was not confined solely to the well-to-do. Although the bulk of the cost of the new chapels was necessarily borne by local men of substance, there was also a multiplicity of small subscriptions from the community at large and at St John's, Hey, and St Thomas's, Friarmere, for example, those who could not afford to subscribe money did so in kind or with their own labour and received seats in return. This sort of communal enthusiasm for the acquisition of a chapel makes clear the vitality of church feeling even in the industrial villages of Saddleworth and provides a context in which the concept of the appropriated seat takes on a rather different character.[16]

The participation of the local population in church life more generally was in great measure dependent on the degree of pastoral impetus provided by their clergy. Heginbottom, whose belligerent approach to evangelism we have already noticed, seems to have both been popular and, by contemporary standards at least, conscientious. He remained constantly resident on his cure from his appointment in 1721 to his death in 1771, despite its relatively low value and the disrepair of the parsonage-house in which he had to bring up a large family. Divine service was regularly performed and Heginbottom was a memorable preacher as well as a conscientious and welcome visitor of the sick and the poor with the result, according to one of his successors, that 'He was much beloved of his flock and during his time

[15] Raines MSS, XV, 210; M. A. Smith, 'Religion in Industrial Society: The Case of Oldham and Saddleworth, 1780–1865', DPhil dissertation, University of Oxford, 1987, pp. 134–6; W. R. Ward, *Religion and Society in England 1790–1850* (1972), pp. 221–7; B. F. L. Clarke, *The Building of the Eighteenth-Century Church* (1963), p. 193.

[16] Raines MSS, XXXIV: T. Wray to Mr Speed, 24 Mar. 1768; Chester RO, EDV/7, Diocesan Visitation Returns, 1821, no. 341; Andrew, *History of Hey*, p. 9; Anon., *Friarmere Parish 1768–1968* (1968), p. 2.

there was not a Dissenter in Saddleworth.' Heginbottom's popularity probably did not stem solely from his conscientious performance of church duty, however, and his predilection for drinking, often in company with his close friend Tim Bobbin, the local dialect writer, occasionally provoked episcopal censure. His practice of fiddling at parish dances on Sunday evenings and providing a barrel of beer for those parishioners who helped him gather in the harvest on his glebe were clearly not to the taste of the nineteenth-century historian of his incumbency, but they must nevertheless have provided a level of contact with his flock without which his more regular ministry would have been the poorer.

After Heginbottom's death, the chapelry endured almost sixty years of non-resident incumbencies. The story of Richard Podmore has already been told, but his eventual successor, Charles Zouch, proved to be an almost equally poor choice. He arrived with something of a reputation for eccentricity and the Bishop of Chester was only induced to license him after some fairly intensive lobbying by his father, the vicar of Sandal, and his uncle, who was a canon of Durham. He found neither the income nor the house associated with the curacy to his liking and within two months had managed to provoke a number of his parishioners into complaining to the patron about alterations he had made to the service. By 1794, after almost two years' residence and having given what were generally considered to be unmistakable proofs of his insanity, he was removed to a private lunatic asylum at Billington near Whalley, where he seems to have remained quite happily until his death in 1831.[17] Saddleworth may be counted as unfortunate in having two mad parsons in succession, but it was not the only local cure to have suffered from non-resident incumbencies. Bowness Cleasby, the incumbent of St Anne's, Lydgate, was twice non-resident for long periods during his incumbency, while under episcopal censure for assorted unsavoury incidents in his private life, and St Thomas's, Friarmere, was always at risk of non-residence because of the lack, until the early 1820s, of a suitable parsonage-house. Finally, St John's, Hey, was held in plurality with the chapel of St Peter's, Oldham, by its Evangelical perpetual curate, William Winter, for twenty-seven years from 1810 until 1837.[18]

Saddleworth, therefore, suffered its fair share of the formal abuses described by Peter Virgin. It is less than clear, however, that the parishioners of Saddleworth suffered greatly thereby. Non-resident incumbents did not necessarily produce unserved cures and the resident stipendiary curates who filled the place of the Saddleworth non-residents seem, in general, to have done their work quite adequately. In most cases, the value

[17] Raines MSS, I, XXXVIIa.
[18] Raines MSS, II, XV; Raines, *Diary*, 15 July 1828; Andrew, *History of Hey*, p. 7.

of the livings was already low and even after gradual enhancement by the operation of Queen Anne's Bounty, only varied from £85 to £108 per annum in 1813. Stipends for curates would in general have been correspondingly lower, the one exception to this rule being St John's, Hey, where William Winter, the Evangelical pluralist, seems to have maintained a curate in charge on an income equal to or slightly higher than that enjoyed by the previous incumbent.[19]

However, low stipends do not seem to have forced local curates into pluralism on their own account or into seeking alternative employment that conflicted with their parochial duties. The most common means of supplementing incomes was the familiar one of taking in a few private pupils or teaching in the village school, an occupation which in itself must have brought valuable contacts with the local community. If one considers Philip Rycroft's evidence from Craven in West Yorkshire, that rising incomes towards the end of this period created a new and damaging social distance between the clergy and the bulk of the people they served, then one might even be tempted to argue that low stipends were, at least from this point of view, a beneficial side effect of non-residence and contributed greatly to the easy relationship that many of the local stipendiary curates seem to have had with their parishioners![20]

Clear evidence of the conscientious performance of church duty by resident incumbents and curates is provided by the survival of six sets of episcopal visitation returns for Chester between 1778 and 1825. These reveal a standard Sunday pattern already established in each Saddleworth chapel in 1778 of two services, one in the morning and one in the afternoon with a sermon at each, except on sacrament Sundays when one of the sermons was omitted. This represented good practice even by later, nineteenth-century standards and seems, judging by John Addy's analysis of the 1778 returns, to have been quite common throughout the Chester diocese. If pressure on church room was increasing, then late eighteenth-century clergymen were at least making the best possible use of the resources available to accommodate the growing demand. The number of sermons preached in local churches comfortably exceeded the canonical minimum and it is clear that the popularity of Anglican services in the later eighteenth century came to depend increasingly on the effectiveness of the preaching. Poor preachers might find their congregations drifting away to one of the

[19] Chester Diocesan Visitation Returns, 1811, no. 150, 1821, no. 388; Parliamentary Papers HOL 1818, Vol. 93, 42–9; Raines, *Diary*, *passim*; Andrew, *History of Hey*, p. 25; C. C. W. Airne, *St Anne's Lydgate. The Story of a Pennine Parish 1788–1988* (1988), pp. 17–18; P. Virgin, *The Church in an Age of Negligence 1700–1840* (Cambridge, 1989), *passim.*

[20] Andrew, *History of Hey*, p. 31; Airne, *Lydgate*, p. 18; P. Rycroft, 'Church, Chapel and Community in Craven, 1764–1851', DPhil dissertation, University of Oxford, 1988, p. 146.

other chapels or even to the meeting-houses of the Dissenters who were beginning to make their presence felt in the area for the first time. Conversely, a good preacher could expect very large congregations, and Evangelicals, who began increasingly to make the running from the 1770s, were, as one might expect, particularly to be found in the forefront of the development of a popular preaching style in the locality. Raines, the moderately Evangelical stipendiary curate of Saddleworth, seems regularly to have preached to congregations in excess of a thousand, including a number of people who had formerly attended the Calvinistic Independent chapel at Delph.[21]

The popular preference for word over sacrament meant that there was no great demand for a departure from the standard practice of holding no more than four communion services a year. If anything, there was a trend towards less frequent celebrations over the period from 1778 to 1825, with some churches which had been holding as many as eight services at the beginning recording only four or five at the end. Even though some clergymen worked hard to increase the number of communicants, participation in the rite remained, even at Easter, the preserve of a minority within local congregations and the only element in the church service seriously to rival preaching in its popularity was the music, which, in Saddleworth, was both popular and of a high standard. The area had a long and flourishing musical tradition and choirs, together with groups of instrumentalists, seem to have formed in local churches as soon as they opened. At St John's, Hey, for example, so many men were anxious to join, that a system of vice-members was created and fines and expulsions for non-attendance were imposed. The Hey chorus singing was adjudged 'superior to any previously known' at a great northern music festival held in Liverpool in 1766 and members of the choir were frequently called upon to assist other musical groups throughout the country. Sacred music concerts seem to have become enormously popular occasions as local music societies began to pioneer the northern tradition of oratorio performance, and services at which collections were being made to support the singers could fill local churches to capacity and beyond.[22]

The standard of pastoral work undertaken by Heginbottom's successors

[21] Chester Diocesan Visitation Returns, 1788–1825; Raines, *Diary*, 20 July 1828, 27 July 1828, 31 Aug. 1828; J. Addy, 'Bishop Porteus' Visitation of the Diocese of Chester 1778', *Northern History*, 13 (1977), 175–94. See also F. C. Mather, 'Georgian Churchmanship Reconsidered: Some Variations in Anglican Public Worship 1714–1830', *JEH*, 36 (1985), 255–83.

[22] Chester Diocesan Visitation Returns, 1788–1825; Raines MSS, I; Raines, *Diary*, 27 July 1828; Andrew, *History of Hey*, pp. 14–25; C. E. Higson, 'Lees Chapel Otherwise Hey Chapel in Lees', *Transactions of the Lancashire and Cheshire Antiquarian Society*, 34 (1916), 179–200.

also seems to have been quite high. The clergy catechized their congregations assiduously, generally for six months of the year and especially when the time for confirmation approached. They were also indefatigable visitors of their parishioners. John Buckley of St Thomas's, Friarmere, for example, explained in 1825 that he always visited the sick and made visits at other times also. The general standard of this activity may have improved during the period, again under Evangelical influence, and the diary of Francis Raines, the curate of Saddleworth from 1828 to 1829, describes a regular round of visits which must have cost him considerable effort. Other local clergy increasingly found themselves called upon to support a number of Evangelical initiatives, the most notable of these being the widespread introduction of Sunday schools which provided an outlet for missionary enthusiasm and displaced energy during the enforced pause in church building of the early nineteenth century. So successful was this enterprise that some churches found themselves operating large networks of schools, and St John's, Hey, for example, stood by the turn of the century at the head of seven schools scattered among the nearby villages. An alternative means had thus been found for the provision of a religious focus within the multiple nuclei of Saddleworth's dispersed population and, moreover, a means which mobilized the laity in support of the pastoral effort. By this development, the clergy also found themselves being dragged, not without some unease, into co-operation with local evangelical Dissent. The Saddleworth Sunday School Union, which was one of the most important manifestations of this new ecumenism, finally broke down in 1817 with a dispute over the church catechism, but good relationships continued, as did some pan-evangelical organizations like the local branch of the British and Foreign Bible Society, and a foundation had been laid for further co-operation later in the century.[23]

There is evidence that some of the more old-fashioned populist clergy in the Heginbottom mould had begun to feel under pressure when compared with the more exacting standards of the newer Evangelicals. Raines records an encounter with one such – a clergyman from Rochdale who 'made some ill tempered remarks on Low Churchmen, or the "tight laced gentlemen" and "Saints" as he termed them, I clearly saw it was all directed at me'. Certainly men like Raines had a clear idea of the sort of behaviour now to be expected of a serious clergyman and his family, and he noted in July 1828, following a visit to one of his clerical neighbours in Saddleworth, 'Called with Mr Alkin (the curate of Lydgate) at the Rev. Mr Mills's. The magistrate was from home; his lady very polite, though very fashionable

[23] Chester Diocesan Visitation Returns, 1788–1825; Raines, *Diary*, *passim*; Andrew, *History of Hey*, pp. 25–6; M. Brierley, *A Chapter From a MS History of Saddleworth* (1891).

and aping the modern fine lady. Routs, cards and dancing, for a churchman's wife with a church income of not more than £150 per annum is inconsistent and reprehensible.' Raines's Evangelicalism was moderate in its theology and non-partisan in its approach; he consciously rejected the term Low Churchman with its Erastian connotations and was on occasion (though perhaps only as a debating point) willing to describe himself as a 'High Churchman'. The conflict between men like Raines and their rather more old-fashioned neighbours was not so much a matter of party as of style.[24] This clash of styles took its most dramatic form in the career of Samuel Stones, the assistant curate engaged by Heginbottom to lighten the load during his old age and in 1771 the popular choice to succeed to the perpetual curacy. Stones seems to have been a reasonably conscientious curate and was no doubt a congenial companion for the old man. However, according to the *Wesleyan Methodist Magazine*,

> To religion, in its regenerating power, its spiritual and hallowing influences, this individual was an entire stranger; paying far more attention to his dogs and gun than some of his hearers deemed fitting for his holy calling. One evening, a plain but good man ventured in true Saddleworth style to remonstrate with his Pastor on this matter, – insisting that, 'it would beseem' that gentleman 'better' if he would 'mind the study more, and the gun less'... This event proved the turning point in the curate's career. The homely remark was as a 'nail fastened in a sure place'. The gun and dogs were given up; he betook himself to thoughtfulness and prayer, and soon became a christian indeed. The Gospel of Christ thus made to him 'the power of God unto salvation', he began to proclaim in its simplicity, and with marked success. An extensive religious awakening followed, meetings for prayer and supplication were convened in the houses of his parishioners; and many, by the force of truth, were 'turned from darkness unto light and from the power of Satan unto God'.[25]

It was not simply into a riot but also into a religious revival that Richard Podmore walked with such trepidation in 1771, and when the mob assembled to resist his arrival it was, for once, siding with the Methodists in order to throw out the parson. It is Stones rather than Podmore who should stand as a paradigm of the Anglican Church in Saddleworth, awakened during the late eighteenth century not so much from corruption or negligence as from a relatively relaxed populist style, into a new Evangelicalism no less popular in its appeal, but sharper in its confrontation with secular culture and more ready to grapple strenuously with the novel challenges of industrial society.

How far one can generalize from the experience of the Church in Saddleworth remains an open question. It seems unlikely that non-resi-

[24] Raines, *Diary*, 29 July 1828, 29 Aug. 1829.
[25] *Wesleyan Methodist Magazine* (1853), 786.

dence was everywhere of so little practical consequence as in Saddleworth, but the local evidence does show that formal abuse was not necessarily incompatible with pastoral excellence. Similarly, the vitality of the local church building effort in Saddleworth and throughout south Lancashire demonstrates that there was nothing intrinsic in the structures of the Hanoverian Church which precluded an active and largely successful response to the challenges with which it was faced. In fact, as a number of recent studies have suggested, it seems that it was in precisely those places where the challenge was at its most acute, where conditions were most difficult and the clergy least well provided for, that the Church was to be found at its most active. Of course, in the last analysis, everything depended on local initiative and determination, both clerical and lay, and it is perhaps as well that the men of places like Saddleworth had acquired the habit, because in this respect, at least, very little was to change in the next century.[26]

[26] Smith, 'Religion in Industrial Society', ch. 2; Rycroft, 'Craven', pp. 116–35; M. Cragoe, 'The Tory and Anglican Gap in Welsh Historiographical Perceptions: The Case of Carmarthenshire 1832–86', DPhil dissertation, University of Oxford, 1990, p. 285; Virgin, *Age of Negligence*, pp. 153–7; Mather, 'Georgian Churchmanship', *passim*.

Part II

Crisis and reform

5 The Church, the societies and the moral revolution of 1688

John Spurr

'It is not surprising', writes D. W. R. Bahlman, 'to find a movement for the reformation of manners starting in the Church immediately after the revolution [of 1688].'[1] Other historians have agreed that 'by the 1690s many Anglicans had come to the conclusion that the reaction against strict attitudes to morals and religion which had accompanied the restoration of Charles II had gone too far, and there took place what was in effect a revival of "puritanism", in a devotional and moral, rather than in an ecclesiastical sense within the established church'.[2] It has become a commonplace that running alongside the dynastic, constitutional and ecclesiastical revolutions of 1688 was a revolution in expectations about public manners or a 'moral revolution' as Bahlman dubbed it. And it has become as firmly accepted that this moral revolution crystallized the pastoral dilemma facing the Church of England. Should the Church accept that she was just another voluntary body competing in the religious free market created by the Toleration Act of 1689? And should she recognize that the secular authority was now the primary agent of moral reformation? Or could she, with political help, resurrect the pastoral and moral control over the nation to which she had aspired since 1662? The quandary of the Church was exposed by her half-hearted involvement in the Societies for the Reformation of Manners (henceforth referred to as SRM), which were only endorsed by the primate in 1699, almost a decade after they were first formed, and by the reactionary and authoritarian demands of the fractious lower house of Convocation. Bahlman's portrait of a Church paralysed by indecision, torn between participation in the moral revolution or maintaining her denominational and disciplinary identity, has been deeply influential, not only on studies of the moral revolution, but also on general interpretations of the Church's history after 1688.[3] Although some observers might wonder

1 D. W. R. Bahlman, *The Moral Revolution of 1688* (New Haven, 1957), p. 22.

2 M. R. Watts, *The Dissenters from the Reformation to the French Revolution* (Oxford, 1978), p. 423; also see T. Isaacs, 'The Anglican Hierarchy and the Reformation of Manners, 1688–1738', *JEH*, 33 (1982), 391–411; A. G. Craig, 'The Movement for the Reformation of Manners 1688–1715', PhD dissertation, University of Edinburgh, 1980, pp. 256–71.

3 See Bahlman, *Moral Revolution*, pp. 27–8; G. V. Bennett, 'Conflict in the Church', in *Britain after the Glorious Revolution*, ed. G. Holmes (1969), p. 165.

whether the Church faced quite the clear-cut choice suggested by this formulation, the purpose of this essay is simply to examine one source of Anglican unease: the role of 'voluntarism' in the life of the national Church. The clergy were divided over the utility and the desirability of the Anglican laity forming voluntary associations for pious purposes. Clerical attitudes were formed against the background of more than a century of extra-parochial, mainly puritan, religious association, and against the fears of 'conventicles' and other dissident gatherings during the reigns of Charles II and James II. But, as I shall show, there were Anglican religious societies in Restoration England, and there was a tradition of Anglican voluntarism linking the voluntary religion of the pre-1640 Church and the religious associations of the 1690s.[4]

I

From the outset, the Church of England was expected to play a major part in the moral revolution. For all her faults, she was the obvious, perhaps the only, agency capable of achieving the reformation of the nation's morals. The royal commission for the Convocation of December 1689 recognized the central role of the Church when it drew attention to the 'divers defects and abuses in the ecclesiastical courts and jurisdictions; and particularly there is not sufficient provision made for the removing of scandalous ministers, and for the reformation of manners either in ministers or people'.[5] In February 1690 William III wrote to Bishop Compton of London about the notorious 'overflowing of vice' and the need for 'a general reformation of the lives and manners of all our subjects'.[6] Here William was simply doing what all new or insecure monarchs did and making a play for English *dévot* support. Charles II had issued a series of proclamations against vice in 1660–3, and James II issued another on 29 June 1688.[7] Among the other influences upon the King was that of Queen Mary, who took the warnings of divine providence and the advice of Bishops Burnet and Lloyd to her timorous heart.[8] King and Queen were

[4] On the tradition see P. Collinson, 'The English Conventicle', *SCH*, 23 (1986), 223–59; idem, *The Religion of Protestants* (Oxford, 1982), ch. 6; E. Duffy, 'Primitive Christianity Revived: Religious Renewal in Augustan England', *SCH*, 14 (1977), 287–300; J. D. Walsh, 'Religious Societies: Methodist and Evangelical 1738–1800', *SCH*, 23 (1986), 279–302; H. D. Rack, 'Religious Societies and the Origins of Methodism', *JEH*, 38 (1987), 582–95; W. O. B. Allen and E. McClure, *Two Hundred Years. The History of the SPCK 1698–1898* (1898); F. W. B. Bullock, *Voluntary Religious Societies 1520–1799* (St Leonards on Sea, 1963).

[5] E. Cardwell, *A History of Conferences* (3rd edn, Oxford, 1849), p. 442.

[6] *His Majesty's Letter to the Lord Bishop of London* (1690), dated 13 Feb. 1689/90; cf. Bahlman, *Moral Revolution*, pp. 15–16.

[7] G. V. Portus, *Caritas Anglicana* (1912), pp. 32–3.

[8] For Mary's dependence on the clergy see *Memoirs of Mary, Queen of England (1689–93)*, ed. R. Doebner (1886), esp. pp. 14, 21, 37, 51.

treated to a series of Anglican sermons hammering home the message, 'righteousness exalteth a nation, but sin is a reproach to any people'.[9]

Meanwhile the bishops spread the message beyond the court. In September 1690 Bishop Stillingfleet of Worcester commended to his clergy the 'design' of the King's letter of February 1690, and instructed them to work for the reformation of drunkards and other sinners.[10] It was Stillingfleet, acting as the intermediary of 'certain Pious Gentlemen', who in July 1691 obtained the vital letter from Queen Mary to the Middlesex Justices which led to the first wave of prosecutions for vice.[11] In November seven bishops defended Bulkeley and Hartley, the reforming JPs, against charges of exceeding their powers.[12] Across the country preachers and clerical pamphleteers took up the cause of reform; the bishops were urged to act and rumours circulated of a proclamation for the suppression of debauchery. In the New Year of 1692 the bishops petitioned the King for the execution of the laws against profanity and on 21 January a proclamation to that effect duly appeared.[13] In March Bishop Compton wrote to his diocesan clergy reminding them of the King's letter of February 1690 and pointing out that 'the Secular Powers are not less concerned ... to discourage Idleness and Debauchery upon a Temporal Account; than we are to do it upon a Religious one' – a message which was repeated in April by Bishop Patrick making his primary visitation at Ely, and by Bishop Kidder of Bath and Wells at his visitation in July.[14]

Anglican interest in moral reform had several sources. Since the turmoil of mid-century, the Church had become obsessed with the chastisements and mercies of divine providence and with the national reformation for which they so clearly called. This Anglican providentialism saturated the rhetoric to which William and Mary were subjected and dominated reforming manifestos such as Bishop Fowler's *Vindication* of the SRM.[15] Greeting

[9] Proverbs 14. 34; see Simon Patrick, *Works*, ed. A. Taylor (9 vols., Cambridge, 1858), VIII, 421; William Lloyd, *A Sermon Preached before the King and Queen at Whitehall, 12 March 1689/90* (1690).

[10] Edward Stillingfleet, *The Bishop of Worcester's Charge to the Clergy of his Diocese in his Primary Visitation ... 1690* (1691), p. 16.

[11] Edward Fowler, *A Vindication Of An Undertaking of Certain Gentlemen, in Order to the Suppressing of Debauchery, and Profaneness* (1692), pp. 6–7.

[12] See Bahlman, *Moral Revolution*, pp. 19–21; Craig, 'Movement for Reformation of Manners', pp. 49–52, 57–9. Fowler's *Vindication* was a product of this controversy.

[13] William Talbot, *A Sermon Preached ... upon the Monthly Fast-day, September 16 1691* (1691), esp. pp. 26–7; John Tillotson, *Sermons* (12 vols., 1757), III, 117–18, also see 49; F. W., *A Letter to a Bishop From a Minister Of His Diocese* (1691), p. 17; *HMC*, Portland MSS, III, 483, 486.

[14] Henry Compton, *The Bishop of London's Eighth Letter to his Clergy* (1692), pp. 8–9; Patrick, *Works*, VIII, 548–9; Richard Kidder, *The Charge of Richard, Lord Bishop of Bath and Wells* (1693), p. 14.

[15] See J. Spurr, '"Virtue, Religion and Government": The Anglican Uses of Providence', in *The Politics of Religion in Restoration England*, ed. T. Harris, P. Seaward and M. Goldie (Oxford, 1990), esp. pp. 39–40.

the proclamation of January 1692, the preacher Thomas Watts asserted that nothing could avert divine vengeance against England except 'either an Universal Reformation, and unanimous Piety: or a due execution of primitive Discipline' for which 'our holy Establish'd Church' had so long hoped 'in vain'.[16] But as the Church well knew the revival of effective 'Primitive discipline' over both laity and clergy depended on the help of the secular authorities to remedy her financial problems, to restore the terror of her courts and their penalties and to rationalize her pastoral provision. The Church perhaps also needed a moral revolution to vindicate the political revolution of 1688. It was no good arguing that God had intervened to spare the nation from popery and arbitrary government, if the nation was so clearly determined to squander the deliverance and ignore its duties to God.[17] In addition the moral revolution promised a welcome diversion from the Church's own troubles. Here was a cause which might unite the clergy and bind the laity to the Church of England during difficult times; for suddenly she was no longer the national Church but merely the established Church; and she faced, both nationally and parochially, the effects of the Toleration Act. The Act was abused, as Bishop Compton complained, by those

> who have forsaken the Church, not to go to a Meeting; but either to the Ale-house, or to loyter in the fields, or to stay at home, and that sometimes to follow worldly business. To suppress these grievous disorders, as much as may be; we thought the first step to be made was to call upon the Civil Magistrate. For the Laws are many and strict against Tipling, Swearing, and the like. So that if the Justices would but seriously and conscientiously set themselves to the execution of them; it could not miss of having a very good effect. Especially if they would distinguish the prophane withdrawers from those that are protected by the Act of Toleration.[18]

The Anglican clergy looked forward to working with William and Mary – many were the invidious comparisons drawn between these 'two good angels' and their immediate predecessors; 'we have already liv'd to see what Influence a *Prince's Life* can have on his *Subjects*', observed one preacher, who went on to hope that 'we may begin to be seasoned with *better principles* from an Imitation of our *present King*' whose personal example and '*Resolutions* likewise to *Countenance Piety and Vertue, and discourage Wickedness and Vice*' demonstrated that virtue was both feasible and potentially fashionable.[19] Furthermore the Anglican clergy could now expect the co-operation of Parliament, the Justices and aldermen, the subordinate lay authorities.

[16] Thomas Watts, *New Prayers and Meditations* (1692), sig. A2.

[17] See Patrick, *Works*, VIII, 461; G. M. Straka, *Anglican Reaction to the Revolution of 1688* (Madison, Wis., 1962).

[18] Compton, *Bishop of London's Eighth Letter*, p. 8.

[19] Tillotson, *Sermons*, III, 185–6; Charles Lidgould, *A Sermon Preach'd... July the 24th, 1698* (1699), p. 19.

Given such strong motives for Anglican involvement, why did the Church allow her role to dwindle? It seems that most of the clergy had not anticipated that the laity would steal a march on the Church and organize themselves in pursuit of moral revolution, nor that they would combine across denominations to do so. There was a genuine fear that the association of Anglicans and Dissenters in the SRM would harm the Church. Thomas Caryl, the vicar of St Mary's, Nottingham, believed that his local society was honest and well meaning, but nevertheless he feared 'it will not easily do so much good in this town, as those of the like nature may do in London; especially when I consider in what danger those churchmen (whom I believe to be the minority) among 'em will be in, of being first work'd into an indifferency and afterwards quite drawn off from the Establishment'. Archbishop Sharp of York refused to license any of his diocesan clergy to preach to the societies for fear that they might be persuaded to preach to the society in a Nonconformist meeting. An even more legalistic line was taken by Archdeacon Nicolson of Carlisle, who argued in 1700 that 'these societies were conventicles, and unlawful assemblies in the voice of the statute law, till their meeting houses were licensed: and that (even then) though they might be within the privileges of the Act of Toleration, they were without the pale of the Established Church'.[20]

The creation of conventicles, of voluntary lay associations, went to the heart of one of the late seventeenth-century Church of England's abiding problems. Although such voluntary associations of the pious are a feature of all churches, they seem at odds with the Church of England's view of herself as a *national* church and with her characteristics of public worship and common prayer. Professor Collinson has explored the English tradition of voluntary religion surrounding the officially sanctioned worship of the Church and has identified its contribution to mainstream, non-separating, Puritanism before 1640. But what survived of that Puritanism after the Civil War and Interregnum found little welcome in the national Church after 1662: the Church would no longer harbour dissidents on her fringes and so most withdrew into Nonconformity. Yet it would be a mistake to suppose from this that piety and zeal were the preserve of Puritans and Nonconformists: not only were some Restoration Anglicans pious, they were also eager to associate with like-minded laymen in giving expression to their devotion.

II

The best-known instance of a voluntary religious association in the Restoration Church is the society which began in 1678 or 1679 when several

[20] See A. T. Hart, *The Life and Times of John Sharp* (1949), pp. 181–3.

young London men applied to Anthony Horneck, preacher at the Savoy chapel, for spiritual direction. Horneck advised weekly meetings and drew up rules to guide them. In one account Horneck was 'an eminent Friend, or rather Father' to the societies 'from their first Rise'; but his biographer, the cautious Bishop Kidder, could not decide whether Horneck 'did move these young men at first to enter into such societies, or whether they first applied to him'. Whoever first suggested the formation of societies, the devout impulse behind them was a result of Horneck's 'awakening' sermons and 'Mr Smithies'' Sunday morning lectures, 'chiefly designed for the instruction of youth', at St Michael Cornhill.[21] These two London preachers deserve our attention.

'This Dr Horneck (being a German borne) is a most pathetic preacher, a person of a sai[n]tlike life; & hath written an excellent Treatise of *Consideration*.'[22] Anthony Horneck was a Rhinelander educated in the University of Heidelberg before his arrival aged twenty in England in 1661. This precocious young man was incorporated MA at Oxford as a member of the Queen's College, was ordained into the Church of England and became in turn vicar of All Saints, Oxford, tutor to Lord Torrington (the son of Albemarle), rector of Doulton in Devon and finally, in 1671, preacher at the Savoy chapel where he also ministered to the parishioners of St Mary-le-Strand until his death in 1697. During the 1680s, alongside Churchmen like Tenison and Patrick, Horneck was assiduous in combating popish proselytizing. In 1685 a visitor to London reported that 'he constantly preaches every afternoon at Black Friars' and his popularity was so great that he sometimes found it 'no easie matter to get through the Crowd to the Pulpit'. Horneck's fame as a preacher was matched by his reputation as a devotional writer and ascetic. And not only did he nurture the religious societies, he also endorsed the moral revolution; his sermon at Gilbert Burnet's consecration as bishop of Salisbury on Easter Day 1689 included a rousing call for episcopal help in the work of reformation.[23]

'Mr Smithies', the lecturer, was William Smythies, curate to Edward Fowler at St Giles Cripplegate. The son of an Essex vicar, he entered Emmanuel College, Cambridge, in July 1651; but he obviously had his differences with the Puritan authorities since he quickly disappeared into

[21] See Josiah Woodward, *An Account of the Rise and Progress of the Religious Societies in the City of London* (2nd edn, 1698), pp. 17, 34–5; Richard Kidder, *The Life of the Reverend Anthony Horneck* (1698), p. 13; J. Wickham Legg, *English Church Life from the Restoration to the Tractarian Movement* (1914), pp. 291–3, 308–9.

[22] *The Diary of John Evelyn*, ed. E. S. De Beer (5 vols., Oxford, 1952), IV, 306–7.

[23] These details are gleaned from Horneck's published works; his biography by Kidder; Woodward, *Account of Religious Societies*; *State Papers and Correspondence Illustrative of the Social and Political State of Europe*, ed. J. M. Kemble (1857), pp. 193–6: Thomas Burnet to Electress Sophia of Hanover, 29 July 1697; LPL, MS 1029, item 7; Bodl., MS Wood F 39, fo. 43.

private life – later claiming that 'when I had hid myself in a private place in the *Essex-Hundreds*, I was routed thence by one of *Oliver*'s Agents, because my Name was then *Malignant*'.[24] Smythies appears to have returned to the university to take his BA in early 1660 and then became rector of Tacolneston, Norfolk, until 1671. In 1673 he arrived at St Giles as curate where he remained until his death in 1704. During the Tory reaction of the early 1680s, Smythies was embroiled in controversy when first he, and then Fowler his vicar, were attacked by some of their parishioners and by the Tory press – as his name had been 'Malignant' thirty years before, now it was 'Trimmer'. He defended himself and his ministry strenuously: 'I have always set myself against the two great evils of the age, *Divisions* and *Debauchery*'; in the pulpit, 'the Subjects of Charity, the Sacraments, and Instruction of Youth, are those which I have chiefly insisted upon'.[25]

This controversy incidentally provides a clue about another of the earliest religious societies. In 1684 Smythies was accused by Roger L'Estrange of praying, reading and catechizing in a 'Private Meeting' in Ave-Mary Lane. Smythies was indignant:

> Tis true, that there are some young Persons that are my Morning-Auditors, who meet once a month at a *Club*, and always give somewhat to the Poor, which I have had the disposal of. They have made an Order amongst themselves, that no disloyal Person shall come amongst them, nor any but those that are *Communicants*. But that I, or any *Clergyman* ever came amongst them to Pray, Read, etc. or ever was but one half hour with them at their *Club*, is utterly false.[26]

The club in Ave-Mary Lane was not unique. In 1681 the 'devout young men' of St Martin-in-the-Fields drew up articles of association, restricting membership to those who 'frequent our parish church' and who have received the sacrament or declared 'they will do it as they have opportunity', and 'if any person shall neglect coming to the holy sacrament three times together without a very good reason, he shall be excluded'. The society met at five o'clock every third Sunday of the month, 'in decent order with our hats off', their 'monitor' read 'some prayer as shall be useful for our purpose', the stewards read a chapter out of the Bible, and then any of the society repeated the heads of a sermon 'or anything else that is useful for us'. The other purpose of their meeting was to take a collection for the poor to be distributed by 'the Doctor' – presumably Dr Thomas Tenison, then rector of St Martin's.[27]

Given the undeniable danger posed to such associations by Tory zealots

[24] William Smythies, *A Reply to the Observator* (1684), p. 2.

[25] Ibid.; William Smythies, *The Spirit of Meekness* (1684), sig. A5v; Smythies, *A Reply to a Letter* (1685), p. 5. Mark Goldie and I are preparing an account of the stirs at St Giles.

[26] William Smythies, *A Letter to the Observator* (1684), p. 7; also see [Roger L'Estrange], *The Observator*, no. 134; Anon., *The Observator Reproved* (1684).

[27] BL, Add. MS 38693, fo. 137.

like L'Estrange, it would not be surprising if other secret societies had existed of which no trace now remains. Certainly several sources suggest these societies continued to grow during the later 1680s. 'In King James's reign, the fear of popery was so strong, as well as just, that many, in and about London, began to meet often together, both for devotion and for their further instruction', wrote Burnet. 'Things of that kind had been formerly practised only among puritans and the dissenters: but these were of the church, and came to their ministers, to be assisted with forms of prayer and other directions: they were chiefly conducted by Dr Beveridge and Dr Horneck.'[28] William Beveridge was rector of St Peter Cornhill, and a future High Church bishop. According to Josiah Woodward, some societies went underground, becoming 'clubs' and meeting in alehouses; others, however, grew bolder in the face of danger, and at St Clement Dane public prayers were set up at 8 p.m. daily and a monthly evening lecture provided to confirm communicants in the holy purposes and vows they had made at the holy table.[29]

The societies and their activities became more visible after the Revolution. Visiting London in the winter of 1689–90, Robert Kirkman, a Scottish Episcopalian minister, described the religious societies of 'young men, apprentices of divers trades, exemplary in piety and virtue' who met at St Clement Dane and St Lawrence Jewry: 'There be two societies where about sixty in each contribute for daily prayers, and meet one hour twice a week for conference about cases of conscience, questions of divinity to be resolved, advice for advancing a trade, getting a maintenance, helping the sick of their society visiting and exhorting them, and the like.'[30] The religious societies became a feature of London life in the 1690s. 'They procure Sermons by way of preparation for the *Lord's Supper*, or to engage a sutable [*sic*] Holiness of Life after it, every *Lord's Day* about five in the Evening, in many of the largest Churches in the City: Their *Charity* is extended to deserving Objects in all the Parts of the *City* and *Suburbs*.'[31] We know of 14 such societies, with a total of 298 members, in London in 1694; by 1698 the number of societies had increased to 32 and the next year to 39.[32] 'For a greater encouragement to devotion', said Burnet, the societies

> got such collections to be made, as maintained many clergymen to read prayers in so many places, and at so many different hours, that devout persons might have that

[28] Gilbert Burnet, *History of My Own Time* (6 vols., 2nd edn, Oxford, 1833), V, 18; also see T. Birch, *The Life of Dr John Tillotson* (2nd edn, 1753), p. 214; Woodward, *Account of Religious Societies*, pp. 39–40.

[29] Woodward, *Account of Religious Societies*, pp. 40–1.

[30] Quoted in Craig, 'Movement for Reformation of Manners', p. 79.

[31] Woodward, *Account of Religious Societies*, p. 131.

[32] See Bodl., MS Rawl. D 1315 (1694); Woodward, *Account of Religious Societies*, pp. 63–4; [Josiah Woodward], *An Account of the Societies for the Reformation of Manners* (1699), p. 15.

comfort at every hour of the day: there were constant sacraments every lord's day in many churches: there were both greater numbers and greater appearances of devotion at prayers and sacraments, than had been observed in the memory of man.[33]

In 1692 Edward Stephens, a weariless promoter of frequent communion and reformation of manners, brought together 'a little company of constant weekly communicants' for daily communions; 'out of respect to the Church' they met 'in private under a tacit connivance, rather than make use of the late Act of Tolleration', until Edward Fowler allowed them to make public use of St Giles Cripplegate.[34]

The relationship between these devotional societies and the SRM has been the subject of some debate.[35] Yet there seems to be no reason to doubt the claim of Josiah Woodward, who chronicled both movements, that the two acted in concert. The help and information given by the religious societies to the SRM did not contradict their principles of Anglican piety nor did it compromise their separate existence. Even the real competition between secular and ecclesiastical jurisdictions was dismissed by many Anglicans: Anthony Horneck 'was for Reformation of *Manners*, and a strict regard to the Discipline and holy Constitutions of the Church'.[36] It was, however, the eventual fate of the religious societies to be swallowed up by more aggressive movements. In 1700 the SPCK was 'pleased to take them into their Protection' and urged its clerical members 'to reduce the Religious Societies to Parochial ones; ... consequently every Minister will have the charge of his own Flock'. Later still, Methodism was to 'cannibalize' some of the surviving religious societies.[37]

III

What inspired the Anglican voluntary tradition of the later seventeenth century? Perhaps no special inspiration was necessary. As Woodward remarked, the formation of pious fellowships 'has been the practice of serious *Young Men* in all Ages, and among all the various Denominations

33 Burnet, *History of Own Time*, V, 18.

34 LPL, MS 930, item 35: Edward Stephens to Archbishop Tenison, 21 Feb. 1694/5. On Stephens's role in the reform movement see Portus, *Caritas*, pp. 36–8.

35 Largely due to imprecision about whether the connexions are shared members or ideological affinities. Bahlman and Isaacs deny any connexion; but Duffy and Rack discern a common purpose; also see T. C. Curtis and W. A. Speck, 'The Societies for the Reformation of Manners', *Literature and History*, 3 (1976), 47; Craig, 'Movement for Reformation of Manners', ch. 3.

36 Kidder, *Life of Horneck*, pp. 42, 45; also see Burnet's views quoted by Isaacs, 'Anglican Hierarchy', pp. 396–7.

37 See Allen and McClure, *Two Hundred Years*, pp. 59–60; Walsh, 'Religious Societies'; Rack, 'Religious Societies'; *Diary of an Oxford Methodist – Benjamin Ingham, 1733–4*, ed. R. P. Heitzenrater (Durham, N.C., 1985).

of *Christians*'.[38] Fraternities, sodalities, guilds or fellowships are a perennial structure of lay religious life, and seem particularly pertinent to urban adolescent males, to the youths and apprentices to whom we now attribute such a large role in events like the English Reformation. Several commentators have observed the parallels, without implying any direct connexion, between the English religious societies and St Vincent de Paul's charitable work in Paris in the 1630s, or the sodalities of Gaston de Renty. Others have discerned a connexion, via Horneck, with German Pietism. There were, however, models much closer to home. As Gilbert Burnet said, 'things of that kind had been formerly practised only among puritans and the dissenters'. In the 1660s Thomas Vincent, the ejected minister of St Mary Magdalen, Milk Street, was 'monitor' to a 'convention' of young men.[39] In Newcastle in the early 1680s, about thirty young men 'met together once a week for mutual assistance and improvement in religion; for which they spent some time in prayer and conference'. Sad to say, one of the fellowship informed on them to 'bloody' Judge Jeffreys who hauled them into court at the Newcastle assizes of July 1684. Convinced that these were 'thirty young fanaticks' Jeffreys would brook no denial, and the pious youths languished in gaol until February of the next year.[40]

The Newcastle group took their rules from a book by Isaac Ambrose (1604–64), the meditative Presbyterian of Lancashire. Ambrose's group agreed that 'every Wednesday (especially during winter) we will meet for a conference about soul-affairs' and to discuss 'choyce heads of practical divinity', cases of conscience and controverted points of doctrine.[41] Their rules give a flavour of their meetings; any difference in opinion was to be fully debated, and then submitted 'to the judgment of the Society, as it shall be made good out of the Word'. A complex procedure was provided for admonishing and disciplining any member who fell into sin or scandal. 'For better regulating of this Society, we will have a Moderator' who 'shall propound the question and matter of our Discourse the week before it be discussed; and at every meeting begin with Prayer, and end with Thanksgiving'. As far as admission to 'our Society' was concerned,

> we will not be too strict nor too large; not too strict in excluding any, in whom we have any good hopes of sincerity, and real desire to increase their knowledge, and mutual love, though they may be *but weak* in gifts: nor too large in admitting such, who may be either *heretical in opinion*, or enordinate [*sic*] in *life*: And by this Rule,

[38] Woodward, *Account of Religious Societies*, p. 30.

[39] Thomas Vincent, *Words of Advice to Young Men* (1668).

[40] See *Memoirs of the Life of Mr Ambrose Barnes* (Surtees Society, 50, 1866), pp. 424–5, 196–7. The support of Barnes, a Nonconformist alderman, for these youths suggests that Jeffreys's suspicions were justified.

[41] Isaac Ambrose, *Compleat Works* (1674), pp. 243–4: 'of preparatives to Christian-society'; *Memoirs of Barnes*, p. 424.

those that are to be admitted shall be voted by the major part of us. [margin: Rom. 14.1, 2, Thess. 36.14, Tit. 3.10]

A Puritan pattern did not necessarily mean a dissident practice. Some of the societies may well have done no more than discuss a sermon which they had heard in church – as Adam Martindale, the Nonconformist minister did with 'an house full of parishioners of the devoutest sort'. 'Repetition', that is, repeating the heads of a sermon, formed a link, an 'umbilical cord' in Collinson's words, between a pious meeting and the church; it was, after all, precisely what the devout young men of St Martin-in-the-Fields proposed to do.[42] The Churchmen were building on a tradition and on existing institutions; William Smythies preached at St Michael Cornhill under the terms of John Rainey's bequest of 1631, which set up an archetypal Puritan 'lecture' of the early seventeenth century in requiring the preacher to 'chiefly Aim at the suppressing of Sin, and building up the Kingdom of Grace in the hearts of the Auditors'.[43] Anglicans too were concerned with growing in holiness and grace, with that most Puritan of goals, 'edification' – even if they understood it in a rather different way from the Dissenters.[44] Yet we must acknowledge that, even while they emulated them, the Anglican religious societies were simultaneously in competition with the Puritan models of religious association.

The Church of England had always paid lip-service to the notion of religious sociability. At the height of her troubles in the 1650s, those still loyal to their distressed Mother the Church were urged to form 'holy fraternities' of 'Mourners in Sion'; in the insecure 1660s, Richard Allestree proclaimed private reformations insufficient, 'there must be combinations and publick *Confederacies in Vertue*, to ballance and counterpoise those of *Vice*'.[45] A work of 1680, *The Country Parson's Advice to his Parishioners*, argued that English Christianity, and the tottering Church, would benefit greatly if the 'good men of this Church' in the several parts of the kingdom would form 'Fraternities, or friendly Societies'.[46] Such appeals, however, were far less significant in promoting religious societies than was the piety and theology of Restoration Anglicanism.

Restoration Anglicans were exhorted to take up holy living in conjunction with a lively faith, to add the power of godliness to its form, to follow the primitive Christians in fulfilling 'the whole duty of man'. This insistence

42 Collinson, 'English Conventicle', pp. 243, 259.

43 Smythies, *The Worthy Non-Communicant* (1683), sig. A4v; also see A. H. Johnson, *A History of the Drapers Company* (5 vols., 1914–22), III, 472; IV, 319.

44 See J. Spurr, 'Schism and the Restoration Church', *JEH*, 41 (1990), 421–3.

45 [Richard Allestree], *The Causes of the Decay of Christian Piety* (1667), p. 434.

46 *The Country Parson's Advice to his Parishioners* (1680), p. 81. For the later influence of this book, see *Diary of Oxford Methodist*, ed. Heitzenrater, pp. 168–9; J. S. Simon, *John Wesley and the Religious Societies* (1921), p. 9.

on 'a practical & operative faith' was aimed squarely at Puritan or Nonconformist teachings which seemed to lean towards antinomianism.[47] At the risk of caricature, one can say that the Anglicans preferred a constant striving to an instantaneous and – as they saw it – presumptuous assurance of personal salvation. Anglican pastors worked for the repentance of sinners; they admonished them to 'enter into their closets' and get on their knees. Anglican piety was a regime of introspective, almost morbid, self-examination, penitence and thanksgiving, of private and household devotion, and it was the necessary foundation of 'holy living'. Moral reformation might follow in the wake of personal piety: 'we cannot think that profaneness, drunkenness, whoredom, thefts, robberies, and other enormities would so abound as they do, if persons were religiously bred up and the people every where accustomed to pious performances in the houses where they live'.[48] But this was incidental to the primary purpose of private devotion, which was to prepare the individual for the public worship of the Church and above all for the Lord's Supper, that 'little epitome of the whole gospel'.[49]

The Anglican model of holy living was promoted through a huge and diverse literature which embraced works of moral exhortation and guidance such as *The Whole Duty of Man* and far more specific manuals like *A Week's Preparation towards a Worthy Receiving of the Lord Supper*. While the devotional writers stoked the fires of piety, the Church struggled to provide a public outlet for the consequent devotion. The provision of daily prayers was increased in the capital. In 1664 Pepys had been surprised to discover that daily prayers were read at St Dunstan's, Fleet Street, but by 1683 there were five parish churches in the City with a single daily service, seven with morning and evening prayer, and eight chapels with daily services. Daily services at 6 a.m. and 7 p.m. had been established at St Paul's, Covent Garden, in 1680. These were in addition to the services at 10 a.m. and 3 p.m. which were funded by an association of pious persons. By 1687 there were nearly thirty parish churches in London offering daily prayers.[50] The provision of communions was also increasing. There is some evidence that monthly celebrations were not unheard of in London during the 1660s and 1670s. In 1673 the vestry of St Bartholomew Exchange debated whether to revive the office of 'lecturer to preach a preparation sermon for the better taking of the sacrament of the Lord's Supper

[47] *Diary of Evelyn*, ed. De Beer, V, 3–4; also see J. Spurr, *The Restoration Church of England 1646–89* (New Haven, 1991), ch. 6.

[48] Anon., *Domestick Devotions for the Use of Families and of Particular Persons* (1683), p. 73.

[49] Patrick, *Works*, I, 174–5.

[50] See [Thomas Seymour], *Advice to Readers of the Common Prayer* (1683), p. 168; Patrick, *Works*, IX, 476; Anon., *Rules for our More Devout Behaviour in the Time of Divine Service* (2nd edn, 1687), pp. 78–82.

monthly'.[51] In the early 1680s there was a clerical drive for more frequent celebration of the sacrament, which finally bore fruit in Archbishop Sancroft's 1684 circular ordering weekly communions in all the cathedrals. The clergy welcomed this order; a delighted Archdeacon Granville of Durham rushed into print to stir up the parish clergy to imitate 'an example so pious and worthy of their high station, by celebrating the holy communion more frequently, than of late hath been accustomed in parish churches'.[52] In the London parishes, the celebration of weekly eucharists, like the reading of daily prayers, was gaining ground during the 1680s.

The sacrament was a focus for all Anglican spiritual regimes, especially those of the fraternities of the contrite. Membership of the religious society at St Martin-in-the-Fields was dependent on reception of the sacrament; Woodward referred – unfortunately without naming the town – to a provincial religious society which had grown out of a Saturday meeting to prepare for the sacrament.[53] Woodward's specimen rules for a society – which seem to have been adopted verbatim at St Giles Cripplegate – required a monthly reception. Other rules attributed to Horneck stipulate only that 'they should meet together once a Week, and apply themselves to good Discourse, and *things wherein they might edify one another*'; but their clerical director was to 'direct what practical divinity shall be read at these meetings', and if that director was Horneck it seems likely that he would suggest works like his own devotional manuals, *The Happy Ascetick* (1681), *The Exercise of Prayer* (1685) or *The Crucified Jesus* (1686). Like hundreds of other such works, including one by William Smythies, Horneck's writings were calculated to channel fervent private devotion towards the Church's public worship and sacraments: his work of 1683, *The Fire of the Altar*, was subtitled 'certain directions how to raise the soul into holy flames before, at and after receiving the blessed sacrament of the Lord's supper'. At the Savoy, Horneck administered the sacrament on the first Sunday of every month and preached a preparation sermon on the preceding Friday. Although two celebrations were held on each Sunday – at 8 a.m. and after the morning sermon – and other clergymen helped distribute the bread and wine, these communions were protracted affairs; 'the number of the Communicants held a great proportion to that of his Auditors, and their Devotion was very exemplary'.[54] In 1685, we find Edward Fowler, vicar of St Giles Cripplegate, reporting to Sancroft that 'God hath blessed mine and my assistant's endeavours here, with not only as numerous and regular a

[51] *The Vestry Minutes of St Bartholomew Exchange*, ed. E. Freshfield (1890), pp. 121–2.
[52] Denis Granville, *Compleat Conformist* (1684), dedication, and appended *Letter*, pp. 1, 10–11. This paragraph draws on my *Restoration Church*, ch. 7.
[53] Woodward, *Account of Religious Societies*, p. 19.
[54] Kidder, *Life of Horneck*, pp. 9–10. Smythies's book was *The Worthy Non-Communicant*.

congregation as is perhaps to be found in England, but also very comfortable weekly communions.'[55] His assistant was of course William Smythies. Comfortable the weekly communions may have been, but we should remember that this piety was part of the theology of holy living and it too fed off the sinner's sense of unworthiness. Woodward explained the origin of the societies by describing how these young men 'were about the same time touch'd with a very affecting sense of their Sins'.[56]

It was the preaching of Horneck and Smythies that first 'awakened' the young men of the societies to their sins. A contemporary described Horneck's preaching as 'most florid, fervent, and pathetique, bot [*sic*] all upon the Mystique way, which did take much with the common sort of serious people, who are many tymes wrought upon by zealous raptures of communion with God, the grace of God, Indwelling in Christ, the joy of the Holy Ghost, and other misterious notiones, which they fancie, rather than feel or understand'.[57] Josiah Woodward was 'made privy to the Spiritual Sorrows of one' of the young men of the religious society,

> who with floods of Tears lamented, that he had not till then had any affecting Apprehensions of the *Glorious Majesty* and *Perfections* of *God*, nor of his Infinite Love to Men in his Son *Jesus Christ*: And that he had not before felt any just Conviction of the *Immense Evil* of every Offence against God, tho it be but (said he) in the wilful Neglect or Misperformance of any Duty to him. But now he saw and groan'd under all this, in very sharp and pungent Convictions. And withal perceiving the universal Corruption of *Humane Nature*, and the deplorable Crookedness and *Deceit of Man's Heart*; and with what a world of Temptations we are encompass'd, being withal besieg'd by many invisible Legions of *Infernal Spirits*: When he consider'd all this, his Soul was even poured out within him, and he was in danger of being overwhelmed with *excessive Sorrow*.[58]

This sense of personal sin was a central component of Restoration Anglicanism. The Churchmen consciously adopted the strategy of convincing their congregations 'that they live in the practice of great Sins, which they shall certainly suffer for, if they do not Repent'.[59] Far from demoting religion to the mere pursuit of virtue, the theology of 'holy living' demanded a rigorous pursuit of Christian perfection while constantly reiterating the impossibility of overcoming sin. It was complained that Horneck 'hath made the way to heaven so hard and laborious; that many good ladies that followed up most to his precepts, were thrown into a thousand melancholique sufferings and fears, for not having doone all that they thought they were obleidged to doe, lyk the primitive Christians'.[60] Restoration Anglicanism was a

[55] Bodl., MS Tanner 31, fo. 225. [56] Woodward, *Account of Religious Societies*, p. 31.
[57] *State Papers*, ed. Kemble, p. 193.
[58] Woodward, *Account of Religious Societies*, pp. 32–3.
[59] Stillingfleet, *Bishop of Worcester's Charge*, p. 17. [60] *State Papers*, ed. Kemble, p. 194.

demanding, if not daunting, regime, which has been described, not inappropriately, as 'a system of religious terrorism'.[61]

In the last resort Anthony Horneck's preaching and devotion was as off-putting to some as it was attractive to others. His mystical language seemed to smack of 'enthusiasm', and while this clearly awoke fears of fanaticism in some critics, for others it conjured up the spectre of popery. In fact Horneck's own theological affinities are a mystery; but he apparently found no difficulty in conforming to the Church of England. His congregation came from across the Cities of London and Westminster and across the social spectrum – it was remarked that Horneck's 'parish' extended from Whitehall to Whitechapel. 'Godly sisters, daughters and mothers in Israel' – including Bishop Stillingfleet's pious wife – and young men seem to have predominated. While this self-selected group of *dévots* flocked to the Savoy from their own parishes, the community whose souls were officially in Horneck's care, the parishioners of St Mary-le-Strand, remained in the words of their pastor obdurately 'enamoured' of their sins, sunk in debauchery and negligent of the Lord's Supper.[62] One is bound to wonder, too, why it was that in 1689 the parishioners of St Paul's, Covent Garden, were 'averse in a high degree to Dr Horneck' when he was proposed as their minister.[63]

Horneck's ministry epitomized the advantages and disadvantages of the Anglican pattern of ideal piety. It clearly worked for some, moving them to real devotion and a fulfilling internal life. But it needed a clerical and liturgical apparatus – daily public prayer and frequent communions – that simply was not available outside London. Horneck's appeal was to a section of the pious of London. It was probably easier to gather a congregation from across the parishes in the capital where the parochial system was already weaker than it might have been in other towns. Horneck appealed to those who felt their piety marked them out from their neighbours. 'The first Design of those who join'd in this *Religious Fellowship*', says Woodward, 'lookt no further than the *mutual Assistance* and *Consolation* one of another in their *Christian warfare*; that by their interchanged Counsels and Exhortations, they might the better maintain their Integrity in the midst of a *crooked and perverse Generation*.'[64] To borrow a phrase, brotherhood entails otherhood. Voluntary association allowed the embattled godly to withstand the world. Anglicans accepted that many

[61] Watts, *Dissenters*, pp. 426–7 (the phrase was originally Lecky's); this point is expanded in Spurr, *Restoration Church*, ch. 6.
[62] Horneck, *The Fire of the Altar* (1683), epistle dedicatory.
[63] Birch, *Tillotson*, p. 208: Lady Russell to Tillotson, Sept. 1689.
[64] Woodward, *Account of Religious Societies*, pp. 50–1.

conformists were half-hearted or worse in their religion; and some Anglicans took the next step and recognized that the Church had no monopoly on piety. They lamented the loss to Nonconformity of so many divines who could have been 'Instruments of reforming the parochial Churches by Example, Admonition, and Assisting the Exercise of Discipline'.[65] A few Restoration Churchmen were even prepared to believe that a concern for piety and the reform of manners could bridge the denominational gap. The incumbent of Barthomley, Cheshire, took strength from the fact that 'We have (Blessed be God) more than Fifty Righteous in every City, both *Conformist* and *Nonconformist*, who cry Night and Day for the Averting of Gods Wrath; the Reforming our Manners, the Healing our Divisions, and the Continuance of the Publick Profession of his truth amongst us.'[66]

Are such views straws in a wind blowing from the eighteenth century? Are they precursors of that post–1689 religious world where the zealous of different denominations might have much more in common with each other than with the lukewarm or the lax of their own denomination? Whatever the answer, it is clear that the Anglican piety of the Restoration was far from tepid. The Church's own theology and piety encouraged a devotional tendency which, when developed by men like Horneck and Smythies, served to undermine her parish congregations and her much-vaunted status as the Church of the whole nation. It is difficult to avoid the conclusion that much of the dilemma posed by the moral revolution was of the Church's own making.

[65] [Seymour], *Advice to Readers of Common Prayer*, p. 114.
[66] Zachary Cawdrey, *A Preparation for Martyrdom* (1681), pp. 7, 8.

6 John Locke, Jonas Proast and religious toleration 1688–1692

Mark Goldie

I

After the publication in autumn 1689 of *A Letter Concerning Toleration*, John Locke allowed himself, for the first time in his career, to become embroiled in a public polemical exchange with one of his critics. His tract was attacked by two High Church clergymen who upheld the coercive uniformity exacted by the Restoration Church. Locke ignored the more senior of them, Thomas Long, archdeacon of Exeter,[1] but responded with the utmost seriousness to an elegant and forceful pamphlet by an Oxford divine called Jonas Proast. Locke's *Second* (1690), *Third* (1692) and unfinished *Fourth* (1704) *Letters on Toleration* were all critiques of Proast, and they fill nearly six hundred pages in his *Works*.[2]

Locke had written the *First Letter*, or rather its Latin original, the *Epistola de tolerantia*, in Holland in 1685, under the shadow of Louis XIV's Revocation of the Edict of Nantes.[3] It is an olympian essay which has acquired a pre-eminence in the canon of his work. The subsequent *Letters* have a more precise contextual location in English church politics, and

For commenting on a draft of this essay I am most grateful to Anthony Claydon, Ole Grell, John Marshall and Stephen Taylor. Locke's four *Letters Concerning Toleration* are cited as *First Letter*, *Second Letter*, etc., with page references to *The Works of John Locke* (10th edn, 10 vols., 1801), vol. VI. Locke's letters are cited as *Corr.* from *The Correspondence of John Locke*, ed. E. S. De Beer (9 vols., Oxford, 1976–).

[1] Thomas Long, *The Letter for Toleration Decipher'd* (1689).

[2] The sequence of the Locke–Proast exchange is: Locke, *A Letter Concerning Toleration* (1689, publ. October); Proast, *The Argument of the Letter Concerning Toleration Briefly Consider'd and Answer'd* (Oxford, 1690; dated 27 March; licensed 9 April); Locke, *A Second Letter Concerning Toleration* (1690; dated 27 May; licensed 24 June); Proast, *A Third Letter Concerning Toleration* (Oxford, 1691; dated 21 February; licensed 20 April); Locke, *A Third Letter for Toleration* (1692; dated 20 June; publ. November); Proast, *A Second Letter to the Author of the Three Letters for Toleration* (Oxford, 1704; dated 14 June; licensed 19 June); Locke, *Fourth Letter*, printed in *Posthumous Works* (1706), pp. 235–77. Locke's *Letters* will appear in the Clarendon Edition of the Works of John Locke, under the editorship of John Marshall.

[3] For the historical circumstances of the *Epistola* see the modern editions by Mario Montuori (The Hague, 1963), Raymond Klibansky and J. W. Gough (Oxford, 1968) (hereafter Klibansky and Gough) and James H. Tully (Indianapolis, 1983).

more can be said about their circumstances than has hitherto been recognized. Jonas Proast was not an isolated target. In assaulting him, Locke placed himself firmly amid the developing quarrel between High and Low Church factions within the established Church. He publicly associated himself with the Latitudinarian wing, and more particularly with the circle of John Tillotson, archbishop of Canterbury from 1691 to 1694.[4]

The point is worth stressing, for it has recently been argued that Locke's natural home was amongst Dissenters and sectaries, amid Puritan rebels rather than Anglican bishops. Locke, James Tully has written, is 'erroneously grouped' with the Latitudinarians.[5] Yet for all Locke's theoretical radicalism – whether political in the right of revolution, theological in his Socinianism or ecclesiological in his intense anti-clericalism – he always remained a member of the Church of England, took its sacrament and attended its services. In 1672–3 he was secretary for ecclesiastical patronage under Lord Chancellor Shaftesbury; in 1673 he entered the Council of Trade in place of Benjamin Worsley who, as a Dissenter, refused to take the Tests; and in 1696 he again qualified himself to sit on the Board of Trade. After the Revolution he sometimes used his influence to secure preferment for his clerical associates, and he numbered at least three bishops amongst his friends.[6] Of the English clergymen who appear in his correspondence, forty-six were Anglicans and four were Dissenters. It is true he also had Dissenting friends, such as the Quaker Benjamin Furly and the Presbyterian John Shute, and true that in 1704 the Presbyterian Edmund Calamy proudly claimed Locke's authority for his *Defence of Protestant Nonconformity*.[7] But Locke's catholic sympathies and acceptance of tolerated sects should not be mistaken for a key to his own religious identity. He stood squarely with people like his close colleague Edward Clarke, who was always a Churchman, but whose Whiggery damned him amongst the clergy. Mary Clarke's comment to her husband could equally well apply to Locke:

[4] There are dangers in the labels 'Latitudinarian', 'High' and 'Low' Church. This essay implicitly defends their use for this period; the first two terms were available by the 1680s. For some cautions see John Spurr, '"Latitudinarianism" and the Restoration Church', *HJ*, 31 (1988), 61–82.

[5] J. H. Tully, 'Locke', in *The Cambridge History of Political Thought 1450–1700*, ed. J. H. Burns and Mark Goldie (Cambridge, 1991), p. 645; also his 'Governing Conduct', in *Conscience and Casuistry in Early Modern Europe*, ed. E. Leites (Cambridge, 1988), p. 20. The presupposition can lead to mistakes: Tully states that Locke's ally Samuel Bold was 'a Dissenter', whereas he was an Anglican vicar of a Dorset parish. See also Richard Ashcraft, *Revolutionary Politics and Locke's 'Two Treatises of Government'* (Princeton, 1986).

[6] See, more fully, John Marshall, 'John Locke and Latitudinarianism', in *Philosophy, Science and Religion in Restoration England 1640–1700*, ed. Richard Kroll, Richard Ashcraft and Perez Zagorin (Cambridge, 1992).

[7] Edmund Calamy, *An Historical Account of My Own Life* (2 vols., 1829), II, 30–1; and *A Defence of Moderate Nonconformity* (1703), Part II, Introduction.

the parsons that I hear preach seem to intimate as if it [the Church] was as much in danger of falling into the hands of the dissenting party as ever it was into the popish, and many are possessed that you are a meeter, though I tell all that I hear say so, that I have often heard you say you never was at a meeting in your life . . . and your being a moderate man gave them such thoughts.[8]

In Locke's contest with Proast, the crucial polarity was not between Anglicanism and Dissent, but between the High Church ideals of the deposed Archbishop William Sancroft, and a new type of churchmanship which sought to seize the pastoral initiative in the aftermath of the Act of Toleration. If Tillotson was to make headway, then the squadron of Oxford theologians who provided the doctrinal backbone to Sancroft's church, and to whom Proast was adjutant, had to be defeated. In this task Locke was Tillotson's servant.

This essay falls into two parts. Before turning to examine Locke's attitude to the Toleration Act, we need to begin with Proast, the chaplain of All Souls College, Oxford.[9] Proast's career is of significance in showing his setting within Oxford, the bastion of High Churchmanship, and in explaining how his involvement in a university fracas in 1688 subsequently became entangled with his attack on Locke. A long donnish battle, fought in Oxford and Lambeth Palace, provided a bitter personal backdrop to the theoretical controversy with Locke. Proast, the defender of religious persecution, was to spend the 1690s feeling persecuted by the Church's new governors.[10]

II

Proast's antecedents – he was born about 1642[11] – were far removed from his own religious preferences, for he was the son of a Leiden-educated pastor of the Dutch Calvinist congregation at Colchester. Pastors of the ilk of Jonas Proost senior had aroused the suspicion of Archbishop Laud for their contacts with Puritan divines. Proost had attended a nonconforming

[8] Somerset RO, MS DD/SF 4515. A 'meeter' is one who attended Dissenting meeting-houses.

[9] There is no entry for Proast in the *DNB*, although this has now been remedied in the *Missing Persons* Supplement (Oxford, 1993). Locke scholars have not hitherto provided more than a line or two identifying him.

[10] For the philosophical and theological issues between Locke and Proast see Mark Goldie, 'The Theory of Religious Intolerance in Restoration England', in *From Persecution to Toleration*, ed. O. P. Grell, J. Israel and N. Tyacke (Oxford, 1991), pp. 331–68; Jeremy Waldron, 'Locke: Toleration and the Rationality of Persecution', in *Justifying Toleration*, ed. S. Mendus (Cambridge, 1988), pp. 61–86. More briefly: H. R. Fox Bourne, *The Life of John Locke* (2 vols., 1876), II, 182–7, 238–40, 523–4; Maurice Cranston, *John Locke* (1957), pp. 331–2, 366–8.

[11] He was nearly seventy at his death in 1710: *Remarks and Collections of Thomas Hearne*, ed. C. E. Doble, *et al.* (11 vols., Oxford Historical Society, 1885–1921), II, 374.

academy and had moved to the London Dutch congregation in the middle of the Civil War.[12]

Oxford weaned Proast junior from his Puritan roots, and he remained a university man, becoming chaplain successively at the Queen's College and All Souls.[13] In 1688 occurred the signal event of his career, to which we shall return: his expulsion from All Souls. He was restored in 1692, but, after unconscionable behaviour, departed again in 1698. He now became archdeacon of Berkshire, although continuing to live in Oxford until his death in 1710.[14] He engaged in scholarly pursuits with three High Church friends, the Jacobite antiquary Thomas Hearne, to whom he fed such gossip as that the astronomer Edmund Halley 'believed a God, and that was all'; the medievalist Thomas Tanner, who succeeded him at All Souls; and the principal of St Edmund Hall, John Mill, who spent many years working on a variorum Greek New Testament, which, ironically, radicals would use to deconstruct biblical authority and which Locke eagerly awaited.[15] Proast's Tory friends thought him admirable, Hearne judging that 'he was a truly honest, wise man, and a good scholar'.[16]

Aside from a vindication of himself in the All Souls case, Proast's only verifiable published works are his three tracts against Locke. But he also left two short unpublished polemics, dating from 1688. They show that he was an antagonist not only of Locke but also of King James II. His *Brief Defence of the Society of St Mary Magdalen College* took up the cudgels against James's notorious ejection of the Magdalen fellows who resisted the appointment of a popish president. He specifically challenged James's henchman, Bishop Thomas Cartwright, and his propagandist Nathaniel Johnston, who upheld the king's prerogative in governing the universities. It is an ingenious tract which argued that, notwithstanding the king's

[12] O. P. Grell, 'A Friendship Turned Sour: Puritans and Dutch Calvinists in East Anglia, 1603–1660', in *Religious Dissent in East Anglia*, ed. E. Leedham-Green (Cambridge, 1991), pp. 45–67; *Register of Baptisms in the Dutch Church at Colchester from 1645 to 1728*, ed. W. J. C. Moens (Huguenot Society of London, 12, 1905), p. 89; *Collections of Hearne*, ed. Doble *et al.*, I, 241. Pastor Proost [*sic*] senior was born in 1572 and was about seventy when his son was born; he intended to send his son to Leiden or Utrecht and have him follow in his footsteps.

[13] Matriculated, Queen's, 1659; BA, 1663; MA, Gloucester Hall, 1666; incorporated MA, Cambridge, 1670. *Alum. Oxon.*, III, 1215; *Alum. Cantab.*, III, 401; Anthony Wood, *Fasti Oxoniensis*, ed. P. Bliss (2 parts, 1815–20), II, 290.

[14] *Collections of Hearne*, ed. Doble *et al.*, II, 71, 374, 377; Montagu Burrows, *Worthies of All Souls* (1874), p. 301.

[15] Mill's *New Testament* (1707), in preparation from 1678, gave 30,000 textual variants and was a milestone in scriptural studies. Proast probably helped Mill, as did Hearne. In *A Discourse of Freethinking* (1713), Anthony Collins used Mill to undermine Scripture. For Locke's interest see *Corr.*, II, 407; IV, 733; V, 3. See Adam Fox, *John Mill and Richard Bentley* (Oxford, 1954). For Proast's friendship with Tanner see Bodl., MS Ballard 4, fo. 101; Tanner 23, fo. 132; 24, fo. 85.

[16] *Collections of Hearne*, ed. Doble *et al.*, II, 374; III, 472–3.

intrinsic absolute authority, he was bound by the concessions and limitations made by his predecessors and embodied in college statutes. This principle of *concessio* was often used by royalists to explain why the king was absolute in essence but limited in practice. In defence of the idea of a royal covenant of self-limitation he cited Pufendorf's *De Jure Naturae*, a text little used in England before the Revolution.[17] Proast's other manuscript is a single sheet called *The Case of Reading the Declaration for Liberty of Conscience*. It reveals that, like nine-tenths of Churchmen, Proast resisted James's demand that the Declaration of Indulgence – the prerogative edict of toleration – be read from the pulpits. It is plain that his objection had less to do with the constitutional impropriety of the King's suspension of the penal laws, than with a revulsion against religious toleration as such.[18]

Proast thus emerged into public view as a fashionable All Souls High Tory of the 80s. He was a characteristic product of the Restoration purge of the universities, that brilliantly successful project for retuning the minds of the clergy. In metaphysics, they remained committed to Scholasticism and suspicious of Cartesian and Lockean epistemology. Proast remarked that he preferred Aristotle to Locke, 'that old Conductor of Human Understanding'.[19] In politics they inclined to absolutism, though protective of the Church. In ecclesiology, they remained imbued with a militant desire to destroy the Dissenters. Their time of triumph was the period 1681–5, when they set about achieving a purified Anglican and Tory polity, and when an unprecedentedly savage onslaught upon the Dissenters was undertaken. Their spiritual father was Archbishop Sancroft, who instigated the publication in 1680 of Sir Robert Filmer's *Patriarcha*. Two of Locke's friends would point out a parallel between Filmer and Proast, as ideologists respectively of the civil and ecclesiastical spheres. In 1690 Benjamin Furly, having read Proast ('a ninny') and Locke's *Second Letter*, remarked that Proast 'is as ingeniously corrected, as Sir R. F. in the Treatises of Government'. Likewise, in 1703, John Shute wrote that Locke's books had devastated both elements of the old Tory ideology: 'a pen which has baffled the boldest champion of slavery, and exposed the sophistry of a ... refined

[17] Bodl., MS Tanner 338, fos. 302–12 (cf. Tanner 29, fo. 105). The tract is dedicated to John Hough, ejected president of Magdalen, and dated 26 October 1688. By then there was no point in publishing it, since, the day before, the King had restored the fellows. The tract's target was Nathaniel Johnston's *The King's Visitatorial Power Asserted* (July 1688).

[18] Bodl., MS Tanner 28, fo. 32; printed in John Gutch, *Collectanea Curiosa* (2 vols., 1781), I, 328. Hearne also mentions '*A Brief Assertion for Lay Deprivation*, as tis thought by Mr Proast' (*Collections of Hearne*, ed. Doble *et al.*, IV, 31), but I have not found it. LPL, MS 934, item 34, is possibly another Proast MS: *The Due Way of Ending the Controversy between the Two Houses of Convocation* (1706).

[19] Proast, *Second Letter*, p. 11.

scheme of persecution; ... two ... adversaries, over whom you have had a glorious triumph'.[20]

The Anglican Zion of Charles II's last years was shattered as much by James II's revolution as by William III's. To modern scholars accustomed to seeing Locke in simple opposition to a generation of time-serving absolutists, it is important to stress how total was the political and moral desertion of James by most Tories and Churchmen. They hated popery as much as Puritanism and Whiggery; and James, a Catholic who decreed toleration, managed to embody all these evils. Tories challenged James's schemes at every opportunity. The resistance of Magdalen College is famous, but in a lesser known skirmish Jonas Proast was valiant for Anglican truth. In his expulsion from the chaplaincy of All Souls he became a minor martyr in the Anglican counter-revolution against James.[21]

III

In 1687 All Souls acquired a new warden by royal mandate. During a vacancy of some months several candidates were proposed, chiefly John Dryden, the convert poet; also Robert Plot, a Catholic antiquary; Thomas Watson, soon bishop of St David's; and Matthew Tindal, a future Deist and follower of Locke but now a brief convert to Catholicism. The King chose instead Leopold Finch, the twenty-four-year-old son of the Earl of Winchelsea, who caught the public eye by raising a company of undergraduates to fight the Duke of Monmouth. Finch was a Protestant High Tory and continued so in the 1690s, yet his temperament and 'pragmaticalness' placed him at odds with mainstream Church Toryism. As a Victorian commentator put it, he exhibited 'an injudicious mixture of exuberant loyalty and dissipated habits ... tempered by dabbling in the classics'.[22] Sancroft, who was visitor (the external adjudicator) of All Souls, had blocked his appointment to a fellowship in 1681, had deplored his appointment to one in 1682 and was disgusted at his elevation to the wardenship, considering him morally unfit to be an ordained minister and tutor of young students. But pious opposition to Finch's appointment was arrested by the thought that the alternative was the papist Dryden. Accordingly, Sir Thomas Clarges and Lord Weymouth, leading lay Churchmen, restrained Sancroft's ire. Instead of an overt campaign against Finch, the fellows adopted a stratagem which preserved their conscientious distaste alongside political prudence. The king's mandate would normally be taken as an

[20] Locke, *Corr.*, IV, 145; VIII, 133–4.

[21] See Mark Goldie, 'The Political Thought of the Anglican Revolution', in *The Revolutions of 1688*, ed. R. A. Beddard (Oxford, 1991), pp. 102–36.

[22] C. G. Robertson, *All Souls College* (1899), p. 157.

instruction to elect the person nominated: in this case they simply admitted Finch as warden but did not elect him. Finch has gone down in the chronicles of All Souls as the unelected warden.[23]

Finch belonged to that small class of Tory collaborators who supported James far further than did the bulk of the Anglican elite. Proast was among the members of All Souls who deplored their new warden as an unprincipled praetorian in an impending popish holocaust. It was reported that, on All Souls day 1687, Finch was carousing in an Oxford inn with 'soldiers and trumpeters ... [while] the English Church [was] languishing'.[24]

In the following year a university election took place to fill the post of Camdenian professor of ancient history. It occurred on 2 April 1688, just before the Church's national refusal to read the King's Declaration of Indulgence. The successful candidate was Henry Dodwell, the shining star of a new generation of High Church theologians. An ardent and massively scholarly defender of Anglican doctrine, he was passionate equally for the purging of Dissenters as of papists. A fellow of Trinity College, Dublin, he made annual trips to Oxford, where 'frequenting coffee-houses where the clergy resort, they found so much satisfaction, content, and learning in his discourse, as also affableness and love to the clergy, that they thereupon chose him'.[25] There were two other candidates for the Camdenian chair. One was Charles Aldworth, the recently ejected vice-president of Magdalen College, who was to succeed Dodwell in 1691 after his deposition as a Nonjuror. The third rival was Leopold Finch. Consequently the election was a trial of strength between the church party and the King's party within the university. Although the church vote was split between Dodwell and Aldworth – the former being seen by some as an Irish carpetbagger – Dodwell won by a margin of six votes in a poll of nearly three hundred. Bishop William Lloyd rejoiced: 'if ever I saw the hand of God in an election it was in this'.[26]

Dodwell's chief canvassers were John Mill and Jonas Proast. Finch thought the election was marred by 'all imaginable foul play' and protested that Proast had been reimbursed by nearly £20 'for horse-hire and other charges'. College heads prided themselves on dragooning the support of their own fellows. So Finch thought it 'a high offence' that Proast did not

[23] LPL, MS 688, fos. 7, 126–7; Bodl., MS Top. Oxon., c.126, fos. 3–5; Robertson, *All Souls*, ch. 8; Burrows, *All Souls*, pp. 291–301 and chs. 16–17 generally; G. V. Bennett, 'Loyalist Oxford and the Revolution', in *The History of the University of Oxford, vol. V: The Eighteenth Century*, ed. L. S. Sutherland and L. G. Mitchell (Oxford, 1986), p. 43.

[24] Robertson, *All Souls*, p. 158, quoting Anthony Wood.

[25] *The Life and Times of Anthony Wood*, ed. Andrew Clark (5 vols., Oxford, 1891–1900), III, 263.

[26] LPL, MS 688, fo. 129; Bodl., MS Eng. Letters c.28, fo. 18; c.29, fo. 102; *Collections of Hearne*, ed. Doble *et al.*, I, 97; *Life and Times of Wood*, ed. Clark, III, 263; Burrows, *All Souls*, pp. 307–10. Dodwell got 104 votes, Finch 98, Aldworth 86.

vote for him. Worse still, Proast persuaded at least two other fellows to vote for Dodwell – enough votes to determine the outcome. Finch was so enraged that next day he peremptorily expelled Proast 'for contempt'.[27]

Naturally Proast turned to the Visitor for justice. Sancroft referred the matter to Bishops Lloyd and Baptist Levinz. Lloyd was a friend of Dodwell's and had taken him on diocesan tours to help hector Dissenters. He attested that 'Mr Proast is a man of not only an unblamable, but an exemplary good life; he is also a learned man and very industrious; every way so far from being a blemish that he is an ornament of his college.' The bishops' findings were scarcely in doubt, and in May counsel for both sides argued the case before Sancroft. But national events precluded further action, and when Sancroft and Lloyd were in the Tower in June for their stand against the Declaration of Indulgence, Finch took the opportunity to have Proast's college rooms broken into and his possessions ejected. After the bishops' acquittal, Sancroft appointed the Dean of Arches, Sir Thomas Exton, to make an inquiry into the College. At this point Sancroft got a heavy-handed letter from Sir Thomas Clarges, warning that if Exton found against Finch it would inexorably lead to a new confrontation between the King and the Archbishop 'about prerogative and power'. Sancroft was unmoved. Proast's affair looked set to succeed the Magdalen College and Seven Bishops cases, with the stakes becoming dangerously high. Clarges and other laymen were struggling to avert further confrontation, and seem to have feared that the next battle might provoke James to depose Sancroft. However, the contest did not materialize: Exton fell ill and died, and the Revolution deposed James.[28]

Like many Tories, Proast was at first aghast at the Revolution. He was reputed to have 'damned all that gave the Prince of Orange the least countenance'. When the new oath of allegiance appeared, he 'ran about town saying he was damned if he took it'. But, having persuaded some fellow clergy to become Nonjurors, he himself took the oath, putting in a conditional declaration that he swore only that 'for the necessity of government, and by the laws of the land, there is an allegiance or obedience due to King William and Queen Mary'. His qualms were soon forgotten: he thought it better to salvage a Williamite Toryism than to go into the Nonjuror wilderness.[29]

[27] LPL, MS 688, fo. 68; Jonas Proast, *The Case of Jonas Proast* (n.p., n.d. [1690]), pp. 1–2; Leopold Finch, *The Case of Mr Jonas Proast* (n.p., n.d. [*c.* 1690]), pp. 7–9; Bodl., MS Top. Oxon., c.126, fo. 6; *Collections of Hearne*, ed. Doble *et al.*, I, 97; *Life and Times of Wood*, ed. Clark, III, 263; Bennett, 'Loyalist Oxford', pp. 39–40. Finch claimed Proast had already stepped out of line at the 1685 election for a new university MP, when Proast could not bring himself to vote for 'Clark, Fellow of All Soul's'.

[28] A. Tindal Hart, *William Lloyd 1627–1717* (1952), p. 79; Bodl., MS Tanner 340, fos. 412–14; LPL, MS 688, fo. 92; Proast, *Case of Proast*, pp. 3–4; Burrows, *All Souls*, pp. 307–10.

[29] LPL, MS 688, fo. 131. Similarly, Proast's friend Mill got notoriety as 'Johnny Wind-Mill': 'Wilt thou take the oaths, little Johnny Mill? / No, no, that I won't; yes, but I will.'

Since Proast was so obviously a victim, if at one remove, of James's high-handed dealings with Oxford, he should have expected, like the fellows of Magdalen, rapid restitution at the Revolution. As Proast insisted, Finch had used 'arbitrary power' after the manner of the fallen King, and Proast now looked to William of Orange as 'a deliverer of the oppressed'.[30] But matters were complicated by post-Revolution church politics and new impediments quickly stood in Proast's way. From the outset, Tory and Whig, High Church and Low, fought to claim the soul of the Revolution. The rehabilitation of reputations became a key part of political theatre. Whigs paraded their martyrs, such as Titus Oates, and Tories lauded theirs, such as John Hough, the deposed president of Magdalen. But Proast was caught in the crossfire, for Sancroft's successors at Lambeth had no love for his sort of churchmanship, and when Proast launched his defence of religious intolerance against Locke it became imperative to give no countenance to the view that the Revolution was a victory for the type of Anglicanism that had dominated the 1680s.

Sancroft quickly sank into torpor in the face of James's overthrow; he was suspended in 1689 and driven from Lambeth in 1691. In the interim, some of his authority devolved upon the dean of Canterbury. It was to Dean John Sharp that Proast wrote in October 1689 and December 1690, arguing that Sharp was empowered to restore him. But the dean and chapter declined to act, lest they injured the archbishop's visitorial power. Locke, in the *Third Letter*, was to go out of his way to praise Sharp as 'a very judicious and reverend prelate'.[31]

In 1691 the vacant sees were filled, and Proast now had to deal with Tillotson. The new Archbishop's Latitudinarian views appalled High Churchmen: people of Proast's leanings were apt to regard him as a dire enemy of the Church seated upon its primatial throne. Tillotson was denounced as a Socinian heretic. Moreover, he had sacrilegiously usurped the episcopate from a man removed for political reasons, a matter that preyed upon the consciences not only of Nonjurors but also many conforming Anglicans. Tillotson suffered public attacks and poison pen letters throughout his short reign, harassed, so Gilbert Burnet claimed, to an early death. His fiercest enemy was Proast's hero Henry Dodwell, the now-deposed Camdenian professor. When Tillotson was about to assume his see, Dodwell wrote to him vilifying him as 'the aggressor in the new designed schism, in erecting another altar against the hitherto acknowledged altar of your deprived fathers and brethren'; his consecration was 'null and invalid and schismatical'.[32] There was a desperate bitterness in the

[30] Proast, *Case of Proast*, pp. 2–3.

[31] Ibid., p. 3; Finch, *Case of Proast*, pp. 16–17; Locke, *Third Letter*, p. 146; A. Tindal Hart, *The Life and Times of John Sharp* (1949), p. 133.

[32] See Thomas Birch, *The Life of Dr John Tillotson* (2nd edn, 1753), p. 246; cf. pp. 194–5, 216–17, 312–13.

Dodwell camp: they had heroically withstood King James, but were cast aside when James was vanquished.

Tillotson was a leading advocate of toleration in 1689. He had long been an associate of Locke's, a friendship that deepened after the Revolution. When Tillotson died, Locke remarked that now 'I have scarcely anyone whom I can freely consult about theological uncertainties.'[33] By the time that Tillotson was pressed to settle the Proast case, he and Locke had become intimate allies in the Low Church cause, and Proast had published two attacks on Locke and toleration. It is therefore scarcely surprising that, as Hearne complained, the Archbishop was 'very dilatory in doing [Proast] justice', and only 'after a great deal of trouble and pains at last was [he] restored'.[34] It is plain that Tillotson deliberately protracted the case and, when forced to find in favour of Proast, gave him the least satisfaction possible. Judgement was given in September 1692, when (as we shall see) Locke and Tillotson were in regular contact and Locke had just completed his *Third Letter*, a swingeing attack on Proast and the pre-Revolution Church. Tillotson refused to order payment of Proast's arrears, rubbing salt in the wounds of the Oxford martyr and his High Church friends, and provoking Proast to appeal to the Privy Council and the civil courts.[35] The code of honour of public polemic demanded of Proast a great burden of words if he was to match Locke's massive *Third Letter*. Simultaneously, personal honour demanded a wearing campaign of further litigation over his chaplaincy. In fact Proast was successfully silenced and did not venture into print against Locke for another dozen years. The Archbishop and the philosopher had crushed the mouthpiece of Oxford intolerance.

For Proast there were two consolations: a week before Tillotson's judgement, Proast was, by the patronage of a High Church friend, appointed to an ecclesiastical office in the diocese of Salisbury.[36] Better still, at about the same time, he was offered (though did not accept) the rectory of Shottesbrooke in Berkshire, the home of a Nonjuror 'college' presided over by Dodwell.[37] Both appointments were under the nose of that redoubtable Whig and ally of Tillotson, Gilbert Burnet, bishop of Salisbury.

[33] Locke, *Corr.*, V, 238. [34] *Collections of Hearne*, ed. Doble *et al.*, I, 97.

[35] Finch, *Case of Proast*, p. 17, indicates that Proast appealed to the courts and Privy Council; I have found no evidence that he did so. In 1696 he also threatened to petition Parliament: LPL, MS 688, fo. 93.

[36] Proast was appointed the 'official' of Berkshire, an ecclesiastical legal office. His patron was William Richards, whom he succeeded as archdeacon of Berkshire. *Life and Times of Wood*, ed. Clark, III, 403–4; *Collections of Hearne*, ed. Doble *et al.*, II, 71.

[37] BL, Lansdowne MS 446, fo. 123: dispensation to hold Shottesbrooke living, 2 Feb. 1693. The offer passed to John Mill's vice-principal, White Kennett. Shottesbrooke was frequented by George Hickes and Edmund Gibson; the patron was Francis Cherry. Thomas Hearne had been a poor boy of the parish sent to the care of Kennett, Mill and Proast in Oxford. See G. V. Bennett, *White Kennett 1660–1728* (1957), pp. 17–22.

In March 1694 Tillotson finally ordered restoration of Proast's 'chamber and commons'. But the order was ignored and Proast saw nothing of the £188 he claimed he was owed. Within days of Tillotson's death in December, Proast applied to the new Archbishop, Thomas Tenison. But Tenison could not stomach Proast either, calling him 'full of an evil spirit'. If less theologically provocative than Tillotson, Tenison kept the hierarchy on a Low Church trim for a generation, to the enduring frustration of High Church activists. Whatever the original justice of Proast's cause, it was convenient for Lambeth Palace to keep him waiting and fretting.[38] By October 1696 Proast was libelling Tenison. 'Must it be said, my Lord, that justice forsook Lambeth, when Archbishop Sancroft removed from thence? ... that good old gentleman behaved himself in my cause, like one that believed the scriptures.' Tillotson, Proast continued, had done nothing for nearly three years, and now Tenison acted 'most barbarously, against all humanity as well as justice'. These latter-day archbishops treated him 'like a dog'.[39]

Not until 1698 was the case finally laid to rest, by which time an entire volume of depositions, libels and representations had silted up in Tenison's files.[40] Throughout the proceedings Proast had demanded that Warden Finch be expelled because he had never been elected. Like all too many of James's Tory collaborators – and unlike many of James's Tory enemies – Finch had quickly made his peace with the new monarchs, taken the oath of allegiance and charmed his way into court favour. Proast wanted James's collaborator ousted. Finch in turn refused to reinstate a chaplain who called him a 'pretended Warden'. In the end the moral victory went to Proast. In a donnishly byzantine compromise, Finch formally resigned his wardenship to the Visitor, and then the fellows formally elected him as their warden; Proast was paid £100. Finch died in office in 1702, sunk beneath drink and debt.[41]

[38] LPL, MS 931, item 48; *Life and Times of Wood*, ed. Clark, III, 447; Anthony Wood, *Athenae Oxonienses*, ed. P. Bliss (4 vols., 1813–20), I, cxviii; Edward Carpenter, *Thomas Tenison* (1948), pp. 273–5. Hearne thought Tenison one of the 'virulent enemies of the Church of England and universities, such as are for bringing in a Comprehension and establishing everything that makes for the Whigs and Presbyterians': *Collections of Hearne*, ed. Doble *et al.*, II, 115.

[39] LPL, MS 688, fos. 92–3.

[40] LPL, MS 688; also Vicar-General's papers, VVI/4/5.

[41] LPL, MS 688, fos. 19, 23, 25, 35–6, 42–4, 67, 130–1; Proast, *Case of Proast*, p. 2; Finch, *Case of Proast*, pp. 1–3; *Life and Times of Wood*, ed. Clark, II, 272n; *Collections of Hearne*, ed. Doble *et al.*, I, 97; Robertson, *All Souls*, p. 159; Burrows, *All Souls*, pp. 309–10; Carpenter, *Tenison*, pp. 273–5; BL, Harleian MS 3361, fos. 2–6; Bodl., MS Ballard 21, fo. 56; MS Tanner 23, fos. 107, 120–1; cf. fos. 117, 122, 124, 132. In the 1698 hearing Proast was represented by Stephen Waller, son of the poet Edmund, and Finch by John Shadwell, son of the poet Thomas.

IV

Neither Locke nor the archbishops were under any illusion that Proast's tracts constituted an isolated philosophical engagement. They manifestly emerged from the Oxonian High Church citadel and voiced the doctrines of a party: a blow against Proast was an affront to his sponsors. Proast had been put up to writing against Locke by Arthur Charlett, master of University College from 1691, a consummate manipulator who dominated Oxford Toryism, and who had 'complained aloud of the injury' done to Proast at All Souls. Hearne claimed that originally Proast's first tract against Locke carried a dedication to Charlett.[42] Proast's tracts bore the imprimatur of Oxford's vice-chancellor Jonathan Edwards, who attacked Locke in his *Preservative against Socinianism* (1693), and who later took part, with John Mill, in the banning of Locke's *Essay Concerning Human Understanding* in the university.[43] Proast's publisher was Henry Clements, the bookseller who later published for the most notorious of Queen Anne High Churchmen, Francis Atterbury and Henry Sacheverell. Proast, Charlett, Mill, Hearne, Edwards and Dodwell formed a close-knit group – powerful heads of colleges and their high-minded scholar protégés, some inhabiting the twilight world of Nonjuror self-exile. Allies too were people like Robert South, who wrote to Charlett in 1695 bewailing the destruction of religion by 'Whigs and latitudinarians'.[44]

Although Locke's *Epistola* and *First Letter* were published anonymously, it is almost inconceivable that Proast did not speedily know against whom he was writing. To Locke's intense anger the secret was quickly out. In March 1690 James Tyrrell reported from Oxford that people there were saying that Locke was the author of the *Two Treatises*, the *Letter Concerning Toleration* and *A Discourse of Humane Reason* (the last in fact by William Popple, the translator of Locke's *Letter*). By April, Philip van Limborch in Amsterdam had heard that Locke's authorship of the *First Letter* was 'a matter of common knowledge' in England.[45]

Locke's *Second* and *Third Letters* were laced with an overt anger. Proast was, with good reason, made to stand proxy for the whole High Church party, the 'party you write for'. The penal laws were instruments 'employed

[42] LPL, MS 688, fo. 27; *Collections of Hearne*, ed. Doble *et al.*, II, 5.

[43] On the ban in 1703 see Cranston, *Locke*, pp. 466–9.

[44] Quoted in Bennett, 'Loyalist Oxford', p. 42n. For the scholarship of this circle see David Douglas, *English Scholars 1660–1730* (1939); *University of Oxford*, ed. Sutherland and Mitchell, ch. 29. See also Mark Goldie, 'John Locke and Anglican Royalism', *Political Studies*, 31 (1983), 61–85.

[45] Locke, *Corr.*, IV, 36, 56; cf. 61–2, 65–6, 116–17; Klibansky and Gough, pp. xxii-xxiv; Cranston, *Locke*, pp. 332–3. Locke's authorship was leaked by Robert Pawling, if he is the 'merchant' referred to; see *Corr.*, IV, 56, 66, 116.

in favour of your party: for so it must be called and not the Church of God'. It is 'care of a party . . . rather than care of the salvation of men's souls' that animates Proast's work. His is a work 'clearing the way to secular power'. Locke, sarcastically allowing himself 'for once [to] suppose you [are] in holy orders', devoted a snidely needling passage to the 'men of art' of Proast's sort, referring to 'the safe retreat' and 'the strong guard you have in the powers you write for'. He affected to quail at taking up the gauntlet against Proast's party, for perhaps he should 'make a truce with one who had such auxiliaries'.[46]

Locke had acute personal reasons for taking a jaundiced interest in the Oxford caucus. In the frightening period before his flight to Holland in 1683 he had been subject to clerical surveillance and was expelled from Christ Church. He had close contact with the Whig burgesses who controlled the city until broken by the Tory dons in the purge of 1682. One of these, the Presbyterian Robert Pawling, was Locke's landlord in London after the Revolution, and Locke asked him to deliver one of the presentation copies of the *Third Letter*.[47] Another of Locke's friends was the physician David Thomas: one of Thomas's sons, William, was kept out of All Souls in November 1689 'for no preferment is to be got but by High Churchmen'. In the following April, when it came to getting a place at New College for another son, Locke's godson John, Locke thought it 'advisable to procure the king's letter', which seems to have done the trick.[48]

Locke's chief Oxford contact was James Tyrrell, who, in turn, was close to the lawyer-theologian Matthew Tindal. One of Charlett's correspondents reported that, on 30 January 1695, Tyrrell and Tindal heard a sermon at St Mary Magdalen against Hobbes and Locke: they were 'very attentive, and too probably one or both of these may have given Mr Locke some account thereof'.[49] Tindal was a fellow of All Souls, who, despite his growing notoriety as an enemy of religion, retained his fellowship from 1678 until his death in 1733. In 1705 he produced a devastating piece of Erastian anti-clericalism, misleadingly entitled *The Rights of the Christian Church*, in which the conjoint influence of Hobbes and Locke was detected. In 1730 he published a textbook of Deism, *Christianity as Old as Creation*. Warden Finch, as well as fighting Proast, was simultaneously at war with Tindal and the Whig fellows.[50] And, symmetrically, Proast hated Tindal as much as he hated Finch. Proast claimed that Tindal had, around 1696,

[46] Locke, *Second Letter*, p. 99; *Third Letter*, pp. 172, 356–7, 367, 542–4.

[47] The conflict between the Oxford dons and the Whigs is best followed in *Letters of Humphrey Prideaux . . . to John Ellis*, ed. E. M. Thompson (Camden Society, n.s., 15, 1875), pp. 104, 129, 131, 134, 139, 142.

[48] Locke, *Corr.*, III, 726; IV, 50; cf. I, 283–4; III, 702, 715, 726, 753; IV, 13, 45, 50, 52, 82.

[49] Quoted in Bennett, 'Loyalist Oxford', pp. 47–8.

[50] Bennett, in *University of Oxford*, ed. Sutherland and Mitchell, pp. 40, 47–8, 78, 82, 391.

while strolling in the quad before dinner, declared 'that there neither is, nor can be, any revealed religion'. This report was published by George Hickes in the preface to William Carroll's *Spinoza Reviv'd* (1709), which assaulted Tindal and Locke for irreligion.[51] All Souls thus contained a triad of the rival political and philosophical forces loose in the post-Revolution world, and was all but destroyed by it.

V

We can now rise from the mire of personal animus to consider Locke's response to the Toleration Act. The Act, passed in May 1689, was a partial and begrudging rather than a categorical achievement. It merely suspended the penal clauses in the laws for religious uniformity. As High Churchmen pointed out, it did not repeal those laws nor remove the guilt of schism. Locke referred to it as 'the late relaxation of the penal laws against Protestant Dissenters', and the 'penalties ... lately taken off'.[52]

The Act was the broken-backed remainder of a larger package of reform which came to grief at the hands of High Churchmen. There were two further elements in that package. The first was the abolition of the requirement in the Test and Corporation Acts under which the taking of the Anglican sacrament once a year was a condition for holding public office. King William himself incautiously proposed its abolition in March, and provoked the anger of Tories – Sancroft's advisor Sir Thomas Clarges amongst them. The Whigs' weapon in attempting to secure repeal was to link it to an alleviation of the harsh terms to be imposed on those bishops and clergy who refused the new oath of allegiance. A ruthless *quid pro quo* was implied: if conscientious Dissenters were freed from the Test, then Nonjurors would not suffer expulsion from their sees, parishes and professorships. But, in an atmosphere of increasing intransigence, nothing was conceded: Dissenters remained excluded and Nonjurors were ousted. The sacramental Test remained until 1828.[53]

The second intended element in the package was the achievement of comprehension. A liberalizing of the conditions of church membership as laid down in the Uniformity Act of 1662 would have allowed many Puritans

[51] William Carroll, *Spinoza Reviv'd* (1709), sigs. b1v-b2r; V. H. H. Green, 'Religion in the Colleges, 1715–1800', in *University of Oxford*, ed. Sutherland and Mitchell, p. 435. In 1704 Proast presented a copy of his *Second Letter* to Tindal, who snidely 'thanked him for writing so seasonably, since it showed so plainly what is aimed at by the clergy': Locke, *Corr.*, VIII, 370. In 1730 a country clergyman sent Bishop Gibson some of Proast's slanders on Tindal as ammunition in the latest deist furore (LPL, MS 1741, fos. 62–3).

[52] Locke, *Third Letter*, pp. 288, 417; cf. pp. 396, 415–16.

[53] Henry Horwitz, *Parliament, Policy and Politics in the Reign of William III* (Manchester, 1977), pp. 21–3, 26, 29; Edward Cardwell, *A History of Conferences* (3rd edn, Oxford, 1849), p. 406; Bennett, 'Loyalist Oxford', pp. 25–6.

to return to a united fold. An anarchic plurality of separated sects was scarcely anybody's ideal: far rather a national catholic communion free of the taint of schism. Before 1689 Latitudinarians had striven for comprehension, but High Churchmen had countenanced neither comprehension nor toleration, until, in the face of James II, they reluctantly struck a deal for the sake of Protestant solidarity. It is doubtful whether Sancroft and his associates were inwardly persuaded: in September 1688 Bishop Francis Turner told Sancroft of his fear that some noted divines intended overtures for comprehension and thus 'to offer all our ceremonies in sacrifice to the Dissenters'.[54] Nonetheless, the politic agreement was carried forward in William's early months, and some senior Churchmen, like Bishop Lloyd, seem to have been fully converted. The intention was that toleration would be an addendum to comprehension, an indulgence to the insignificant few, mainly Baptists and Quakers, who would feel unable to reunite even with a broad-bottomed establishment.[55]

Parliament quickly passed a Toleration Act for the interim, and the Lords got as far as passing a Comprehension Bill. But then the Commons petitioned William, asking that comprehension be referred to the Church's synod, Convocation. Reluctantly, and fatally, Tillotson and Burnet advised the King to accede. High Churchmen then proceeded to betray their promise of 1688: the duress of popery was gone, the counter-duress of a Calvinist king had arrived, and the demands of clamouring Dissenters rankled once more. In April 1689 the Marquis of Halifax told Burnet that 'the Church people hated the Dutch, and had rather turn Papists than receive the Presbyterians among them'. Convocation would, Burnet lamented, 'be the utter ruin of the Comprehension scheme'.[56]

Tillotson spent the summer drawing up a scheme of concessions for the Dissenters and a revised Prayer Book, and in September a preparatory commission was convened. It included Burnet, Tenison and two of Locke's friends who soon became bishops, Edward Fowler and Richard Kidder. Its High Church members quickly withdrew in protest. J. G. Graevius wrote to Locke of his hopes concerning 'the consultations of a number of divines... in London, they being men of known moderation'.[57] But in the October elections to Convocation Tillotson's party was disastrously defeated. Burnet noted that 'great canvassings were everywhere, in the elections of Convocation men, a thing not known in former times'. In Oxford Henry

[54] Quoted in Cardwell, *Conferences*, p. 404.

[55] See George Every, *The High Church Party 1688–1718* (1956), chs. 2–3; Roger Thomas, 'Comprehension and Indulgence', in *From Uniformity to Unity 1662–1962*, ed. Geoffrey F. Nuttall and Owen Chadwick (1962), pp. 191–253; H. Horwitz, 'Protestant Reconciliation in the Exclusion Crisis', *JEH*, 15 (1964), 201–17.

[56] Birch, *Tillotson*, pp. 163–5; Cardwell, *Conferences*, pp. 408–11.

[57] Locke, *Corr.*, III, 795.

Dodwell was a busy canvasser, and doubtless Proast too. The Oxford contingent elected to Convocation included Jonathan Edwards, who licensed Proast's books; seven other heads of houses, including Proast's friend John Mill; and the divinity professor William Jane. When Dean John Sharp proposed Tillotson as prolocutor (chairman), he was overwhelmingly defeated by Jane.[58]

Hard on the heels of Convocation came the general election of February and March 1690: that too saw a conspicuous swing toward the Tories. The old Tory leader Danby, now Marquis of Carmarthen, spoke of his high hopes for 'the Church party'. During the next two years Whigs had cause to feel that the Revolution had merely restored the Restoration Tories, with the Commons dominated by such figures as 'Sir Thomas Clarges of the High Church'.[59]

These are the circumstances in which Locke's *First* and *Second Letters* were published. In the summer of 1689 the Unitarian merchant, William Popple, translated Locke's *Epistola de tolerantia* into English. In the autumn High Churchmen published Convocation manifestos, and Popple's translation appeared. Convocation sat from November to February; a second edition of Locke's *Letter* appeared in March; and Proast's first response to it appeared in April. Archdeacon Thomas Long, in a tract hectoring Convocation on the evils of toleration, drew attention to his own recent attack on Locke.[60]

If Locke's *Letters* were primarily a defence of the toleration achieved in 1689, it is scarcely surprising that they also shared the distress of Low Churchman and Dissenters at what was *not* achieved. In June 1689 Locke told Limborch that the Toleration Act was 'not perhaps so wide in scope as might be wished ... Still, it is something to have progressed so far.' In 1690 he complained of 'the laws about religion, still in force'. When Popple added a preface to his translation of the *Letter*, he complained that 'we have need of more generous remedies than what have yet been made use of', and he demanded 'absolute liberty'. Locke scholars have often objected that the latter remark was incompatible with Locke's strictures against 'licence' in the *Essay Concerning Human Understanding*. But it is plain that Popple had no metaphysical abstraction in mind, but the now emasculated full toleration package. Locke himself, in the *Second Letter*, called for 'a perfect toleration'.[61]

[58] Every, *High Church Party*, p. 57; Birch, *Tillotson*, pp. 165ff, 183ff; Bennett, 'Loyalist Oxford', pp. 26–9; Cardwell, *Conferences*, pp. 412–14.

[59] Lord Sidney, quoted in Horwitz, *Parliament*, p. 61; see ch. 3 generally.

[60] Thomas Long, *Vox Cleri* (1690), p. 46.

[61] Locke, *Corr.*, III, 633; for Popple's Preface see Klibansky and Gough, pp. 164–5; Locke, *Essay*, 4.3.18; Locke, *Second Letter*, pp. 45, 63; cf. 'universal toleration': *Third Letter*, pp. 372, 465. See Caroline Robbins, 'Absolute Liberty: The Life and Thought of William

Both the failure of the repeal of the Test and of comprehension are reflected in Locke's pages. He wanted to abolish the Test, though would probably have retained a doctrinal test for Catholics. He deplored the use of the sacrament as an instrument for excluding the scrupulous from civic life, and for making hypocrites out of the less scrupulous who cynically conformed. The Test was a weapon for bullying people at every level. In the 1680s, as well as expelling Dissenters from local office, Tory magistrates forced the poor to come to church as a condition of receiving relief, and issued inn-keepers' licences only to Anglican conformists. Locke wrote of 'men ... driven to take the sacrament to keep their places, or to obtain licences to sell ale, for so low have these holy things been prostituted'. It is a point he harped upon, asserting that 'those who threatened poor ignorant and irreligious ale-sellers, whose livelihood it was, to take away their licences, if they did not conform and receive the sacrament, may be thought perhaps to have something to answer for'.[62]

Locke was closely associated with those Whigs who sought to repeal the Test. One of the lords who protested at the retention of the Test was Viscount Mordaunt, who came over in William's invasion. Mordaunt was the first highly placed person Locke visited when he returned from Holland in February 1689, and it was through Mordaunt that he was soon offered an ambassadorship.[63] Locke also approved of the plan for a bargain over the fate of the Nonjurors. In April 1690, when Parliament debated a bill to require office-holders to accept William and Mary as 'rightful and lawful' rulers, Locke drew up a paper defending the imposition of tough conditions of political loyalty on Tories who doubted the new monarchs' legitimacy. If Dissenters were to be marginalized by the religious Test, so too must fastidious *jure divino* Churchmen by the oath of civil allegiance.[64]

Locke's response to the failure of comprehension is more complex. In his correspondence he made two overt references to the scheme, in letters to Limborch in March and September 1689. The first remark gives little away,

Popple, 1638–1708', *William and Mary Quarterly*, 24 (1967), 190–223. Thomas Long took 'absolute liberty' to be a Jesuitical plot 'to crumble us into innumerable and irreconcilable sects': *The Letter for Toleration*, sig. A2, pp. 1, 5. When John Shute defended 'absolute toleration' he meant the abolition of the Test: *The Rights of Protestant Dissenters* (2 parts, 1704–5), part II.

62 Locke, *Second Letter*, p. 73; *Third Letter*, p. 342. There are two further clues to Locke's attitude to the Test. In Holland he read with approval John Phillips's tract against Samuel Parker's case for allowing Catholics into office: *Corr.*, IV, 172; Phillips, *Sam. Ld. Bp. of Oxon, his Celebrated Reasons for Abrogating the Test ... Answered* (1688). Shute's *Rights of Protestant Dissenters*, which may be presumed to have had Locke's endorsement, defended abolition of the Test for Protestants but not for Catholics.

63 Birch, *Tillotson*, pp. 160–2; Locke, *Corr.*, III, 573–6; Cranston, *Locke*, p. 312.

64 James Farr and Clayton Roberts, 'John Locke on the Glorious Revolution: A Rediscovered Document', *HJ*, 28 (1985), 385–98.

but does reveal his distaste for the expected resistance of the High Church party.

> The question of toleration has now been taken up in parliament under a twofold title, namely Comprehension and Indulgence. The former signifies extension of the boundaries of the Church, with a view to including greater numbers by the removal of part of the ceremonies. The latter signifies toleration of those who are either unwilling or unable to unite themselves to the Church of England on the terms offered to them. How lax or how strict these provisions are likely to be I hardly yet know; this at least is my impression, that the episcopal clergy are not very favourably inclined to these and other proposals that are now being mooted here; whether this is conducive to their own advantage or to that of the state is for their consideration.

Locke's second remark apparently shows little enthusiasm for comprehension, partly because there would inevitably remain discountenanced sects beyond its pale.

> In the matter of Comprehension there is already something on the anvil ... What this measure is likely to effect, should it come into force, is not yet clear to me, nor can I feel any hope that ecclesiastical peace will be established in that way. Men will always differ on religious questions and rival parties will continue to quarrel and wage war on each other unless the establishment of equal liberty for all provides a bond of mutual charity by which all may be brought together into one body.[65]

On the face of it, Locke did not much care for comprehension. His primary purpose was to defend the lifting of penal laws from the sects, and, in the manner of such outspoken enemies of the established Church as William Penn, he attacked the domineering propensities of 'established sects under the specious names of national Churches'. Discountenanced sects often exhibit brotherly love and a free spirit, where national churches 'usually breathe out nothing but force and persecution'. Often Locke seems stoically accepting of denominational diversity, for such is the 'incurable weakness and difference of men's understandings'. A people must rest content if they can achieve charity and an agreement on fundamentals, 'though divided into different societies or churches, under different forms'. 'Differences in ways of worship will not hinder men from salvation, who sincerely follow the best light they have', for though there is but one true religion, it is not only to be found in the Church of England. Locke's commitment to voluntaryism was categorical: the sects had a right to exist.[66]

Yet there is a countervailing theme, a more positive attitude to comprehension. Locke did not defend sectarian diversity as a virtue in itself. He expressed embarrassment at the proliferation of 'sects which so mangle Christianity' and spoke a traditional language in talking of the 'guilt of

[65] Locke, *Corr.*, III, 583–4, 689. [66] Locke, *Third Letter*, pp. 237, 239, 328, 372.

schism'.[67] Like other Latitudinarians, he found dogmatic separatism as distasteful as High Church formalism. There might be a pointless brutality in forcing people to kneel to receive the sacrament, but there was equally a pointless scrupulosity in objecting to the practice. Locke was not much interested in the Dissenters' obsessions with sacramental posture, clerical dress and episcopal re-ordination. He had more in common with Church of England theologians who, on the one hand, shared his speculative liberalism on the subject of the Trinity, like Isaac Newton and Tillotson's friend Thomas Firmin, and, on the other, those who were concerned to supersede formalist wrangling and pursue instead a religion of moral reformation, like Tillotson himself. Tillotson and Locke both believed that ceremonial scruples were damaging distractions from the real business of promoting Christian living.

In the *Second Letter* Locke announced that membership of the Church of England is what 'I confess of myself'. The *Second* and *Third Letters* were intramural partisan pieces. He voiced the characteristic sentiments of those who sought comprehension, with their familiar stress on the evils of imposing 'things indifferent'. 'Who sees not, but the bond of unity might be preserved, in the different persuasions of men concerning things not necessary to salvation, if they were not made necessary to Church communion?' Kneeling at the Lord's Supper has been a 'matter of great scruple', but such things are inessentials; God laid down nothing concerning them and so they are 'alterable'. The imposition of 'the cross in baptism, kneeling at the sacrament, and such like things', being ceremonies 'not instituted by Christ' and 'impossible to be known necessary to salvation', such are 'what I argue against'. Locke constantly protested at 'needless impositions' and 'arbitrary limits of communion'. He reversed the charge of schism made against the Dissenters, by placing the guilt upon those who sanctify 'the shibboleth of a party, and erect it into an article of the national church': it is they who are 'authors and promoters of sects and divisions'.[68]

Locke sometimes used the term 'toleration' in its older, generic sense, to refer to the comprehending of Christians within the Church as well as the freeing of those outside it. He did so in his letter to Limborch quoted above, and Limborch in reply likewise referred to 'Christian toleration, which is well represented under the two heads of Comprehension and Indulgence'. In the *Third Letter* Locke remarked that 'under toleration' dubious dogmas would not be erected into formal terms of church communion. He also

67 Ibid., p. 239.

68 Locke, *Second Letter*, p. 99; *Third Letter*, pp. 145, 156, 238–9, 248, 328–9. Cf. Klibansky and Gough, pp. 5, 16, 103, 107–9, 157–9. Referring to English prelatists and Scots Presbyterians Locke hoped for 'some relaxation in the attitudes of extremists on either side' (*Corr.*, III, 598).

wrote that what 'the defenders of toleration complain of' is the laws 'that put a distinction between outward conformists and nonconformists'. The meaning of 'toleration' was not therefore exhausted by the notion of sectarian pluralism.[69]

The publishing history of Locke's *First Letter* provides one significant indication that Locke understood the toleration of sects not as a self-sufficient policy but as complementary to comprehension. When the Latin version was shipped to England, it was made available for sale in tandem with another book. In about late July 1689 100 copies of the *Epistola* were sent to Samuel Smith's bookshop in London, bound up with a treatise by Samuel Strimesius, called *Dissertatio Theologica de Pace Ecclesiastica*. Strimesius, professor of theology at Frankfurt-on-the-Oder, penned this 'dissertation on Peace in the Church' in about 1684, amid the atmosphere of ecumenical hope engendered by Leibniz's conversations with Bossuet. It sought to find common doctrinal ground, to remove unnecessary impediments to reunion. Limborch reprinted Strimesius's book to accompany Locke's. Encapsulating the two books, Limborch remarked that the *Dissertatio* 'may justly be called Comprehension, the other treatise Indulgence or Toleration; the argument of each seems in all respects similar to deliberations on matters of religion under each of these heads'. Locke did not demur from this coupling: he thanked Limborch for sending copies of 'the treatise on toleration and peace in the Church'. In September Limborch reported that Strimesius had been denounced 'as an Arminian, indeed a Socinian', and his book suppressed by his enemies. He hoped that England would be saved from such 'bitter zeal'.[70]

Just as comprehension was the missing half of the legislative package of 1689, so Strimesius's *Dissertatio* was, so to speak, intellectually the missing half of Locke's *Epistola*. Locke was not disposed to celebrate toleration, in the sense of unlimited division and plurality, as a self-sufficient good. He stood in the tradition of Reformation eirenicism: toleration was a preliminary tactic in the search for 'the Peace of the Church'. He told Limborch that with the passing of the Toleration Act 'the foundations have been laid of that liberty and peace in which the Church of Christ is one day to be established'.[71]

We can now see Locke's apparently negative view of comprehension, expressed to Limborch in September 1689 and quoted above, in a different light. That letter was written when it was already apparent that the High

[69] Locke, *Corr.*, III, 588; Locke, *Third Letter*, pp. 239, 318.

[70] Samuel Strimesius, *Dissertatio Theologica de Pace Ecclesiastica* (Frankfurt, 1688; reprinted, 1689); Locke, *Corr.*, III, 608, 615–16, 633, 682–3, 696, 699. The 1705 Amsterdam edition of the *Epistola* included the title of Strimesius's book on the general title page: Klibansky and Gough, p. xxxvii.

[71] Locke, *Corr.*, III, 633.

Church party would concede as little as possible. Even the Presbyterians who earnestly sought a comprehension thought the terms offered in 1689 'very narrow and stingy'. It must also be remembered that there were some for whom comprehension was an excuse for *not* tolerating those beyond its pale. Locke was nervous of any threat to the fragile stability of the new Toleration Act. Nothing that was likely to emerge that winter could arouse his enthusiasm. But he remained committed to a wider ideal of comprehension, one that could only be secured by 'equal liberty for all [which] provides a bond of mutual charity'. It is surely in the same spirit that Popple, in his preface to the *First Letter*, amid the din of High Church fusillades, remarked: 'It is neither Declarations of Indulgence, nor Acts of Comprehension, such as have yet been practised or projected amongst us, that can do the work. The first will but palliate, the second increase our evil.'[72] The Toleration Act was certainly desirable, but it was not the plenary fulfilment of a vision of Christian England.

VI

We have seen how the *Second* and *Third Letters* attacked the High Church party and responded to the defeat of comprehension. We next need to indicate a further and somewhat more constructive theme that is especially apparent in the *Third Letter*. This is the theme of pastoral care and moral reformation, and in pursuing it Locke revealed himself to have been drawn, by 1692, yet closer to Tillotson and Burnet, such that he publicly identified himself with their plans for the renewal of the post-Revolution Church. In doing so he joined a circle at the heart of which stood Queen Mary II, whose importance in the religious history of this time has not yet been fully appreciated. She was a woman of decided views, a Latitudinarian queen.

After the filling of the bishoprics voided by the Nonjurors, ecclesiastical government fell into Latitudinarian hands. As well as Tillotson, Locke numbered Kidder and Fowler as friends amongst the new bishops. The Queen was much involved in 'the filling of bishoprics', for the Calvinist William left church matters to his Anglican wife. She in turn relied on Burnet and Tillotson. The Archbishop and the Queen were to die within a few weeks of each other at the close of 1694, a double blow but for which, lamented Burnet, 'we might have seen a glorious face put on our Church'. Locke's intimate friend Edward Clarke was auditor to the Queen and wrote him a bitter lament at her death. The Queen well knew that the filling of the sees escalated the 'great division in the Church' and set Nonjurors and High Churchmen about her ears. She also knew Tillotson's theological notoriety:

72 Horwitz, *Parliament*, p. 24; Locke, *Corr.*, III, 689; Popple, Preface, in Klibansky and Gough, pp. 164–5.

one day she caught Dean George Hooper off guard with a teasing question, 'Why is Archbishop Tillotson a Socinian?' She was at loggerheads with her sister Anne, who was abetted by Henry Compton, the Tory bishop of London, who resented being beaten to the primacy by Tillotson. 'All the High Churchmen', wrote Mary, were 'making a party' with Compton and her sister. They 'laugh at afternoon sermons', which she had instituted at Whitehall and of which 'most sober people' approved.[73]

When Mary arrived in 1689 she was disturbed to find 'so much formalism and little devotion', and set about producing a stream of prayers and meditations. In concert with Tillotson and Burnet she concerned herself with reform: curbing the profanation of the Sabbath, limiting pluralism and non-residence, and funding poor clergy. Tillotson avoided Convocation, suspended in 1690 as an unmanageable talking shop for High Church zealots, and likewise evaded the Church-dominated House of Commons. He turned instead to royal proclamations, such as that issued early in 1692 against 'vicious, debauched and profane persons'. Much of this activity was characteristic of that concern for superseding formalist with ethical Christianity, a shift which separates seventeenth- from eighteenth-century sensibilities and which the Latitudinarians did much to sponsor. It was part of what has been called 'the moral revolution of 1688'.[74]

Throughout 1692 Locke was deeply preoccupied with religious toleration. His *Third Letter* was not only his most prolonged printed reflexion on the topic, but also constituted his most public identification with Tillotson's campaign for moral reformation. It is not clear exactly when he wrote it. He worked on it in February and April, when he discussed it with Newton, Limborch and Jean Le Clerc. There are signs that he wrote most of it speedily during May and June. The printed tract carries the date 20 June, but he continued revising it after that, taking advice from Newton during July. Locke opened the book with the claim that his friends insisted he write this reply, and his text contains several reported conversations, such as the remark that 'a friend of mine finding me talk thus, replied briskly'.[75] These need not necessarily be literary affectations, for Locke was discussing such matters in the Dry Club, a group of liberal Churchmen who met under the aegis of William Popple. In November Popple reported the names of new

[73] *Memoirs of Mary, Queen of England (1689–93)*, ed. R. Doebner (1886), pp. 24, 37, 39; cf. pp. 26, 38, 43, 57; Burnet, *The New Preface . . . to the . . . Pastoral Care* (1713), p. 18; Hester W. Chapman, *Mary II, Queen of England* (Bath, 1972), p. 227; Somerset RO, MS DD/SF 284. Tyrrell hoped to see Locke at Mary's funeral, but the hard winter kept Locke at Oates (*Corr.*, V, 260, 285; cf. 249–50). Most of Mary's letters and memoirs are reproduced in Marjorie Bowen, *The Third Mary Stuart* (1929). See also Birch, *Tillotson*, pp. 312–14.

[74] *Memoirs of Mary*, ed. Doebner, p. 12; Birch, *Tillotson*, *passim*; Dudley Bahlman, *The Moral Revolution of 1688* (New Haven, 1957).

[75] Locke, *Corr.*, IV, 387–8, 451, 485; Locke, *Third Letter*, p. 357; cf. pp. 141–2, 179, 222.

members in the same letter as his list of proof-reading errata for the *Third Letter*.[76]

Locke may well have discussed ideas for the *Third Letter* with Tillotson also, for they saw a good deal of each other that summer. In April Tillotson secured the prestigious rectory of St Andrew Undershaft for one of Locke's oldest clerical friends, Gabriel Towerson.[77] More importantly, just as the *Epistola* had been associated with Strimesius's *Dissertatio*, so the *Third Letter* is connected with two other books, by Burnet and by Limborch, and it was the circumstances of both books that brought Locke regularly to Lambeth Palace.

As well as his general hopes for moral reformation, Tillotson wished to address more precisely the circumstances of a Church which had now to cope with legalized rivalry from the Dissenters. Anglican defenders of toleration had long contended that the only legitimate way to win them was by pastoral and catechetic energy and not by magistratical compulsion. The way of Christ is gentleness, and the rod has no ability to convince the intellect. The Restoration Church had, by contrast, been wedded to a model of coercive discipline: Tillotson needed a catechism for the post-Revolution pastorate. He turned to Burnet and commissioned a book from him, 'to prepare the scene for many noble designs for the perfecting of our ecclesiastical constitution'. The result was *A Discourse of the Pastoral Care*, a handbook for the conduct of parish ministers, directing them, not to dogma and ritual, but wholeheartedly to 'the completing of our Reformation, especially as to the lives and manners of men'. It had the Queen's authority, and later Burnet would say 'I writ this book by her order, as well as by our primate's.' She read and approved the manuscript and agreed to accept the dedication, which addressed her as Defender of the Faith and declared that as the Church had had its Constantine and Theodosius, so also it had its Pulcheria. The book was published in 1692 and was reprinted many times throughout the next century.[78]

Locke wrote his *Third Letter* with Burnet's *Pastoral Care* at his side. On six separate occasions he cited and quoted from it. Locke called Burnet 'that eminent prelate' and 'a very knowing bishop of our Church'. Burnet served as a counterpoise to Proast, offering a new model of churchmanship, 'adapted to our present circumstances'. Locke followed Burnet in arguing that in the Restoration world the use of force amounted to an admission of

[76] On the Dry Club see Locke, *Corr.*, IV, 571, 581, 621; Cranston, *Locke*, pp. 361–2, 406.

[77] Locke, *Corr.*, I, 155; Birch, *Tillotson*, pp. 371–2.

[78] Birch, *Tillotson*, pp. 264–8; Burnet, *A Discourse of the Pastoral Care* (1692), sigs. A3r, A4r; Burnet, *The New Preface*, p. 19; T. E. S. Clarke and H. C. Foxcroft, *A Life of Gilbert Burnet* (Cambridge, 1907), pp. 309–14. Editions appeared in 1713, 1726, 1736, 1762, 1777, 1805, 1807, 1818, 1821 and 1824. Pulcheria (399–453): devout empress, acclaimed by the bishops at the Council of Chalcedon.

pastoral failure. In Proast's Church, ministers 'not over-busying themselves in the care of souls, find it for their ease, that the magistrate's coactive power should supply their want of pastoral care'. Locke cited Burnet's most explicit passage about the Dissenters and the penal laws, 'the law has been so much trusted to, that that method only was thought sure; it was much valued, and others at the same time much neglected'. But now we must learn to use only 'reason and persuasion' and not 'grudge or envy them their liberty'. Mercifully, Locke says, 'some bishops' are against having 'men driven by the whip'; they prefer to recommend catechetical instruction, the arguing of a cause on equal terms. With palpable passion Locke denounced Proast's 'itching of your fingers to be handling the rod' and threw at him what Burnet 'tells you' about the duty of the gentle shepherd. Proast's brand of clergy prefer 'invectives from the pulpit, instead of friendly and Christian debates with people in their houses'. Content with haranguing Dissenters, they are blind to 'the ignorance and irreligion of conformists themselves'. Burnet spoke of the ordination of ministers as involving a contract: 'according to the nature of all mutual compacts' ministers who are guilty of 'total failure' of pastoral duty 'forfeit all the authority and privileges' of their status. Proast and his crew had broken the sacred contract of their calling, and Burnet's book had, Locke judged, offered a shocking catalogue of clerical inadequacy. It had struck a chord in the nation, for what the Bishop complains of is 'so visible, that it is in every one's mouth'.[79]

Burnet still believed it desirable to convert Dissenters to the Church: only the method had changed. We are not 'to think that the Toleration, under which the law has settled the Dissenters, does either absolve them from the obligations that they lay under before, by the law of God and the Gospel, to maintain the unity of the Church, and not to rent it by unjust or causeless schisms, or us from using our endeavours to bring them to it, by the methods of persuasion and kindness'. By such means they will come to see 'upon how slight grounds, they have now so long kept up such a wrangling, and made such a rent in the Church'. Equally, Burnet saw no abatement of the task of moral discipline, and twice Locke quoted his adage that 'party is the true name of making converts, except they become at the same time good men as well as votaries to a side or cause'. An unrighteous Anglican is no true convert to Christ's Church. Lamenting 'our want of the Godly discipline that was in the primitive church', Burnet urged that the minister must admonish the sinful, refuse the sacrament to the scandalous and set about 'the correction of manners'. Reflecting a widespread Anglican fear of

[79] Locke, *Third Letter*, pp. 151, 171, 173, 433–4, 481, 527–9, 543; quoting Burnet, *Pastoral Care*, pp. 115, 118, 120–2, 187–9, 201–2, 205. Locke cited from the octavo edition of Burnet's book. Burnet's book was licensed on 5 May, which helps date Locke's composition of the *Third Letter*. Cf. *Second Letter*, p. 86.

the 1690s, he ruefully judged that 'the truth is ... it is very hard to restrain ecclesiastical tyranny on the one hand, without running to a lawless licentiousness on the other'.[80]

Locke himself was emphatic about the duty to punish vice. 'The magistrates ... may and ought to interpose their power, and by severities, against drunkenness, lasciviousness, and all sorts of debauchery.' As 'for the toleration of corrupt manners, and the debaucheries of life ... I do not plead for it; but say it is properly the magistrate's business by punishments to restrain and suppress them.' The asymmetry in Locke between religious tolerance and moral intolerance remains a puzzle.[81]

In appealing to 'so great an authority' as Burnet, Locke lent his weight to the newly and precariously predominant Latitudinarian junto now governing the Church from the Queen's closet. Not for the first time was Locke engaged in the paradoxical business of conniving at the use of the royal prerogative to reform the ecclesiastical estate: he had done so in policy papers for Shaftesbury and Charles II in 1670–2.[82] By endorsing Burnet he underwrote what was to become a pattern of the eighteenth-century Church: Whig prelates in hot contention with Tory divines, and secured more by the blessing of an Erastian court than by popularity amongst the clerical rank-and-file. This pattern became abundantly clear a generation later when in 1713, under Robert Harley's Tory government, Burnet reissued his *Pastoral Care* with a boisterous new preface, restating his 'Low Church notions', vilifying those who had driven Tillotson to an early grave, and those who set up priestly authority against the state.[83] He praised Queen Mary's religiosity in such a way as to imply criticism of Queen Anne's High Church preferences. He duly met with a volley of High Church assaults, new demands 'to make heresies and schisms penal', and claims that his and Tillotson's latitude licensed 'our new sect of freethinkers': Locke, Collins, Toland, Tindal, Clarke, Whiston and Hoadly.[84]

[80] Burnet, *Pastoral Care*, pp. 190, 201–3; Locke, *Third Letter*, pp. 528, 543; cf. pp. 323, 343, 379.

[81] Locke, *Third Letter*, pp. 416, 469. Locke applauded the Societies for the Reformation of Manners: *Corr.*, VII, 225. See also: John Dunn, 'The Claims to Freedom of Conscience', in *From Persecution to Toleration*, ed. Grell, Israel and Tyacke, pp. 171–93.

[82] John Marshall, 'John Locke in Context', PhD dissertation, Johns Hopkins University, 1990, ch. 3.

[83] Burnet, *The New Preface*, pp. 12, 14, 18, and *passim*.

[84] *The Oxford-Scholar's Answer to the Bishop of Sarum's New Preface* (1713), p. 11; *Mr Asgill's Congratulatory Letter to the L--d B--p of S--m* (1713), pp. 7–8; *Antidotum Sarisburiense* (1713), p. 37. The implication of the foregoing pages is that Latitudinarianism, comprehension and reformation of manners form a nexus, as against High Church preoccupations. This seems to me where the evidence of Locke's *Letters* leads. Craig Rose argues similarly in 'Providence, Protestant Union and Godly Reformation in the 1690s' (forthcoming). But Anthony Claydon emphasizes bipartisan support for Mary's programme (PhD dissertation, University of London, forthcoming). Recent literature on the reformation of manners movement is cited elsewhere in this book.

It is true that Locke's opinion of Burnet was mixed, not least because of the latter's reputation for abrasiveness and opportunism. They seem to have avoided each other during their Dutch exile, and Locke was not complimentary when reporting Burnet's elevation to a bishopric in 1689. But Burnet was an energetic lobbyist for toleration and comprehension, and he kept up an amicable correspondence with Locke's friends Limborch and Le Clerc. Locke's exchanges with Limborch frequently mention Burnet in connexion with the political fortunes of toleration. If in personal life there was little love lost between them, in public they shared an outlook.[85] The *Third Letter* is an explicit endorsement of Burnet's pastoral philosophy and in turn of the Queen's and the Archbishop's projects. It is also an exhaustive mauling of Proast, published a few weeks after Tillotson outraged Proast by a backhanded restitution.

The relationship between Locke and Tillotson in 1692 proves to be closer still. The *Third Letter* was also connected with a major work by Limborch, Locke's chief correspondent on theological matters. For some years, since discovering the records of the thirteenth-century Inquisition of Toulouse, Limborch had been preparing his *Historia Inquisitionis*. As well as documenting popish cruelties, he sought to show that religious persecution by any church was the spawn of popery. Quoting Luther, he remarked that the spirit of popedom lurked in everybody.[86] Similarly, a central theme in Locke's *Letters* was the moral, and almost the physical, equivalence between the English repression of Dissent and the contemporary archetype of popish persecution, Louis XIV's attack on the Huguenots. Repeatedly Locke equated Anglican intolerance with 'dragooning', in reference to the notorious activities of French troops. What seemed worrying about Proast's case was its eloquent pretence that English penal methods were categorically different from those of papists. Proast claimed that Anglican laws were intended as a gentle chastisement to assist persuasion and catechesis. They did not extend to destruction of life or limb, they were edificatory, a schoolmasterly discipline to encourage Dissenters to think again. It was this 'new way of persecution' that Locke's friends insisted he respond to, in order to show that it was but the old way sanitized, 'though it come short of the discipline of fire and faggot'.[87] Locke constantly attacked Proast's attempt to distance Anglican persecution from the brutality of

[85] Locke, *Corr.*, III, 589, 597–8; Clarke and Foxcroft, *Burnet*, pp. 228, 267–8, 359. See also Fox Bourne, *Locke*, II, 150, 155, 249; Cranston, *Locke*, pp. 285, 316–17, 321, 363, 415 (Cranston is mistaken in asserting, p. 321, that Burnet was rumoured to be the author of Locke's *First Letter*).

[86] Philip van Limborch, *Historia Inquisitionis* (Amsterdam, 1692). An English edition, by the Presbyterian Samuel Chandler, appeared in 1731 under the title *The History of the Inquisition*; Chandler used his introduction to bewail the failure to repeal the Test since 1689.

[87] Locke, *Third Letter*, pp. 142, 194, 262, 283, 285, 409, 413, 530; *Second Letter*, pp. 69, 87.

Rome. Locke knew well enough that both Anglicans and French papists drew their arguments from St Augustine's teaching, and that one of the most influential versions of the Augustinian case amongst Anglican divines had been produced by Thomas Long, who was the other critic who published an attack on Locke's *First Letter*.[88]

Limborch's *Historia Inquisitionis* was ready by May 1692, but took a long time to print. On 2 June Locke wrote to him in terms which show that he linked the publication of the *Historia* with his own impending *Third Letter*. Limborch's book 'I am impatient to see; nor do I know any other that is likely to be more profitable to the Christian world; for those who do not love and promote Christian liberty as is right nevertheless shrink from fire and sword, and want the monstrous cruelty of the Holy Office to be kept far from themselves'. Locke plainly had Proast in mind here. Locke wanted to show that Anglican persecution was but a branch and remnant of popery: his *Third Letter* was intended to be thought of as an addendum to Limborch's great indictment of Romish persecution. 'Theological zeal, as I see it, is always and everywhere the same and proceeds in the same way.'[89]

On 17 June Limborch told Locke that he wished to dedicate his work to Tillotson, as being a person 'far beyond all theologians with whom I am acquainted', whose 'writings and ... actions bear witness to the fact that he favours the teaching which I have undertaken to maintain'. On 30 June Locke met Tillotson, who agreed that Limborch's book was 'most opportune at this time', and readily assented to the dedication, provided he could check the text before publication. In the next several weeks Locke discussed the draft dedication with Tillotson, Limborch and Le Clerc, at the same time as revising his *Third Letter*. He went to see Tillotson several times, and the final text of the dedication reached Limborch in September.[90]

Early in November copies of the *Historia* were shipped over, appropriately protected from the aggression of popish France by a 'convoying warship'. Limborch sent Locke five presentation copies: for Locke himself, for Tillotson, Burnet, Kidder and Locke's long-standing patron, the Earl of Pembroke. On hearing of the book's arrival, Locke travelled to London especially to make personal presentations to Tillotson, Burnet and Pembroke, though Kidder he could not track down when he visited the House of Lords. Locke flatteringly implied to Limborch that affairs of state ground to a halt whilst the attention of great men was absorbed by the *Historia*. That was on about 19 November: almost simultaneously Locke's *Third*

[88] Thomas Long, *The History of the Donatists* (1677). Locke referred to Proast's 'friend St Austin' (*Third Letter*, pp. 292, 529), and Long quoted Augustine on the Donatists against Locke (*Letter for Toleration*, pp. 14–15). For the use of Augustine see Goldie, 'Theory of Religious Intolerance'.

[89] Locke, *Corr.*, IV, 400, 458; cf. 277–8, 328.

[90] Ibid., IV, 463, 469, 481, 486–7, 496–7, 525.

Letter was published. At the close of the year Limborch was anxious to have letters of approval from Tillotson and Burnet as cynosures to 'protect me, if need be, against those whom everything of ours displeases', and on 8 January Locke called on Tillotson again, who gave him a letter for Limborch, and copies of his newly published *Sermons Concerning the Divinity and Incarnation.*[91]

Limborch's dedication, the text of which Locke had nursed, lavished praise on Tillotson as the mentor and father of a newly charitable church. 'Providence seemed to have chosen him, in order that, under his influence and conduct, the whole body of the reformed churches, laying aside their intestine disputes, might unite and support the liberty of the Gospel and the Christian religion against the machinations and shocking cruelty of the Church of Rome.' 'All protestants' ought to find 'a common spiritual father' in this man of 'universal charity and benevolence', and 'learn to detest all cruelty against, and punishments of those, who dissented or were in error, if they were otherwise persons of piety'.[92] Later, Locke himself, in his *Vindication of the Reasonableness of Christianity*, would call Tillotson 'that ornament of our Church, and every way eminent prelate'; and later still recommended Tillotson's sermons as 'masterpieces' of practical divinity.[93]

As Anglican persecution was the English appendix to the tyranny of the Roman Inquisition, so Locke's *Third Letter* was the English corollary to Limborch's *Historia Inquisitionis*. It was Locke's most thorough assault on the Restoration hegemony of the High Churchmen, who had preferred a regime of violence on behalf of inessential dogmas rather than a pastoral commitment to Christian unity and holy living. He damned Proast's Church and heralded Tillotson's.

VII

A dozen years separate Locke's *Third Letter* from Proast's final return to the fray in 1704. The circumstances of that belated eruption are a further chapter in the same church politics and provide a coda to this essay. The struggle over Occasional Conformity provides the context for Locke's last engagement with national politics before his death. In each of the three years from 1702 to 1704 the Tory party attempted to pass legislation outlawing what they took to be the hypocritical practice by which Dissenters qualified themselves for office by taking the Anglican sacrament

[91] Ibid., IV, 525–6, 556, 564, 579, 580, 588, 589–90, 605, 637.

[92] Limborch, *History*, epistle dedicatory.

[93] Birch, *Tillotson*, pp. 273–4, 344; Locke, *Corr.*, VIII, 57. Cf. Fox Bourne, *Locke*, I, 264, 309; II, 236–8.

annually. The attempted Bill was thwarted by the government, the House of Lords and the moderate bishops. The accompanying furore brought forth Henry Sacheverell's *Character of a Low Churchman* (1702), Daniel Defoe's *Shortest Way with the Dissenters* (1702) and Matthew Tindal's *Rights of the Christian Church* (1705).

Proast was provoked to take up his pen by a charge that, through his long silence, he had abandoned his claim that the magistrate may coercively exact religious conformity. Although once more picking up the gauntlet, neither he nor Locke had anything new to say.[94] Proast did, though, add an addendum to his final attack on Locke, a side blow against a new Whig tract called *The Rights of Protestant Dissenters*, by John Shute, 'who seems to be a disciple of yours'. Shute was indeed a close friend of Locke in his last years, and Francis Atterbury heard a rumour that *The Rights* was by Locke himself. Shute soon became the highest placed Dissenter in public office, and was a campaigner for the abolition of the Test.[95]

The Occasional Conformity affair also elicited *The True Character of a Churchman* from an intemperate Whig called Richard West. It vindicated toleration, comprehension and Burnet's reputation. West was Burnet's chaplain, and later marked himself out by an outrageous sermon before the House of Commons defending the execution of Charles I.[96] When Jonas Proast died in 1710 West succeeded him as archdeacon of Berkshire. Hearne, bemoaning the passing of Proast, called West a man 'famous for his preaching up anti-monarchical, rebellious doctrines', and, outraged at his new preferment, remarked that Burnet evidently thought it good to reward him 'by advancing him to spiritual preferment instead of a gallows'.[97] Thus Proast, the Tory divine whom Locke had taken so much trouble to refute, gave way to a scabrously Whig Low Churchman. It was by such small turns of the wheel of preferment that the Church of Sancroft gave way to that of Tillotson.

94 It was the occasion of the only known correspondence between the two men: *Corr.*, VIII, 364–5.

95 Shute (later Viscount Barrington), *Rights of Protestant Dissenters*; Proast, *Second Letter*, p. 21; Locke, *Corr.*, VIII, 311–12. Shute was commissioner of customs from 1708 until sacked by the Tories in 1713; he negotiated in vain in 1717 for repeal of the Test.

96 Richard West, *The True Character of a Churchman* (1702); *A Sermon Preached before the ... House of Commons* (1710). See *Alum. Oxon.*, IV, 1601; Bennett, 'Loyalist Oxford', pp. 36, 64n.

97 *Collections of Hearne*, ed. Doble *et al.*, II, 385; cf. Bodl., MS Ballard 4, fo. 101: Tanner to Charlett, 15 May 1710.

7 The origins and ideals of the SPCK 1699–1716

Craig Rose

On 8 March 1699 Dr Thomas Bray and three of his acquaintances met in the Lincoln's Inn rooms of one of their number, the barrister John Hooke, and formed themselves into the Society for Promoting Christian Knowledge.[1] Thus was established the foremost voluntary society within the Church of England. While there has been much writing on the early years of the SPCK, there has been little detailed analysis of the ideals which coloured its work.[2] This essay seeks to remedy this deficiency through an analysis which draws not only upon the SPCK's copious records, but also upon the theological and devotional works of leading SPCK members, Thomas Bray and Robert Nelson. An examination of their much-neglected works makes it possible to reconstruct the ideal of evangelical philanthropy, which was central to the early work of the SPCK. But this essay will also attempt to set the Society in a broader political and religious context. We shall begin with a review of the political complexion of the SPCK's membership.

I

Within two years of its foundation, the membership of the SPCK had grown to some ninety Subscribing or Resident members.[3] Subscribing members were admitted to the Society only upon the recommendation of an existing member, and were based for at least part of the year in London. As their title suggests, they paid an annual subscription and enjoyed voting

I am grateful to Mark Goldie for his comments on an earlier version of this essay. I would also like to thank Dr Gordon Huelin, the SPCK archivist, for his assistance during the research for this essay and for permitting me to quote from the SPCK Archives.

[1] SPCK, Society Minutes, 8 Mar. 1699.

[2] W. O. B. Allen and Edmund McClure, *Two Hundred Years. The History of the SPCK 1698–1898* (1898), and W. K. Lowther Clarke, *A History of the SPCK* (1959), are the standard histories of the Society. L.W. Cowie, *Henry Newman* (1956), provides a useful general survey of the SPCK's early years.

[3] See the list of the Society's Subscribing members in 1699–1701, published in *A Chapter in English Church History*, ed. Edmund McClure (1888), pp. 1–4.

rights at Society meetings. The SPCK also had many Corresponding members dotted throughout the country. Like the Subscribing members, they gained admission to the Society only by recommendation, but they did not pay an annual subscription and enjoyed only observer status at SPCK meetings.[4] The following brief review of the political composition of the SPCK's early membership pays attention only to the Subscribing members; they formed the London-based core of the Society and directed its policies.

The Resident members of the SPCK were politically a motley crew and represented a very wide spectrum of opinion within the Church of England. Of the Society's five founder members, two were to become MPs. Sir Humphrey Mackworth was a renowned Welsh High Tory, one of the principal agitators for the Occasional Conformity Bills of 1702–4 and a Tacker in 1704.[5] The west countryman Colonel Maynard Colchester was Whig MP for Gloucestershire in 1701–8.[6] The third founder member, Lord Guilford, was the son of Charles II's Lord Chancellor and had inherited the Tory politics of his father.[7] 'I cannot list myself under either of the two common denominations, Whig or Tory', wrote the fourth founder member, John Hooke, in 1710. Instead, he described himself as loyal to the Queen and the Church of England.[8] As we shall later see, Thomas Bray, the Society's chief founder, is equally difficult to place in any party category.

Although not among its founders, the SPCK's most active members in its fledgling years were probably Robert Nelson, Sir John Philipps, Henry Hoare, John Chamberlayne and Henry Shute. Nelson was a noted Non-juror and Jacobite;[9] Philipps was Whig MP for Pembroke Boroughs;[10] Hoare was a scion of a prominent Tory banking family in London;[11] Chamberlayne, the Society's first secretary, was a writer and courtier with predominantly Whiggish connexions;[12] while Shute, the Society's treasurer, was described in 1721 as being thought 'too much what in the late Reign was call'd a Low Ch[urc]h man'.[13]

4 Glenice Siddall, 'The Movement to Reform and Improve Social Manners and Morality . . . 1678–1738', MA dissertation, University of Birmingham, 1976, pp. 25–6.

5 Mary Ransome, 'The Parliamentary Career of Sir Humphry Mackworth, 1701–13', *University of Birmingham Historical Journal*, 1 (1947–8), 232–54.

6 History of Parliament Trust (hereafter HPT), draft biography of Colchester. I am grateful to Dr Eveline Cruickshanks for permitting me to consult this and other draft biographies.

7 G. V. Bennett, *The Tory Crisis in Church and State 1688–1730* (Oxford, 1975), p. 231; Linda Colley, *In Defiance of Oligarchy. The Tory Party 1714–60* (Cambridge, 1982), p. 55; *DNB*.

8 BL, Add. MS 70242: John Hooke to Robert Harley, 12 Aug. 1710.

9 For Nelson's life, see C. F. Secretan, *Memoirs of the Life and Times of the Pious Robert Nelson* (1860).

10 HPT, draft biography. His two sons became leading Tories.

11 For the Hoare family, see H. P. R. Hoare, *Hoare's Bank* (1955). Henry Hoare was the son of the prominent London Tory, Sir Richard Hoare.

12 *DNB*. For Chamberlayne's Whiggish connexions, see BL, Egerton MS 929, fo. 90; BL, Stowe MS 226, fo. 276.

13 SPCK, Newman Private Letters, Mar. 1720 to Oct. 1724, fo. 27.

The Society's clerical members included many moderate comprehensionist clerics, notably Nicholas Stratford, bishop of Chester; Simon Patrick, bishop of Ely; William Lloyd, bishop of Worcester; Richard Kidder, bishop of Bath and Wells; and Edward Fowler, bishop of Gloucester.[14] Younger men like Charles Trimnell, Edmund Gibson and White Kennett came to be closely associated with Whiggery.[15] On the other hand, Thomas Manningham, bishop of Chichester from 1709, was a noted Tory.[16] John King, rector of Chelsea, was a close friend of the leading Tory Churchman William Dawes, and a staunch defender of the Church from the attacks of both Dissenters and anti-clericals.[17] Philip Stubbs, later archdeacon of St Albans, wrote passionately against occasional conformity.[18] Against Richard Mayo, son of a Presbyterian minister and chaplain of the Whiggish St Thomas's Hospital, can be set Sir George Wheeler, born in 1650 to Royalist exiles in Holland, tutored by George Hickes at Oxford, and considered a 'Worthy Gent' by the Nonjuror Thomas Hearne.[19] After 1701 the Society could also number among its members such distinguished Tory clerics as John Robinson, Francis Gastrell, William Stratford and William Higden.[20]

The political and religious complexities of the SPCK's membership are epitomized by the Society's chief founder, Dr Thomas Bray. In 1685 he had been presented to the rectory of Over Whitacre in Warwickshire by Lord Digby, a future sympathizer of the Nonjuring and Jacobite cause.[21] Bray's neighbouring clerics, John Kettlewell and Digby Bull, also Digby men, were both deprived as Nonjurors in 1690.[22] Upon the removal of Bull from the parish of Sheldon, Bray was placed in the living by Lord Digby.[23] Despite these Nonjuring connexions, Bray himself was a fervent supporter of the Hanoverian Succession.[24] Indeed, by 1716 he believed the Nonjuror schism to be 'no other than Rebellion against the Government under the Cloak of Religion' and advocated the transportation of Nonjuring

14 For all of whom, see *DNB*.

15 G. V. Bennett, *White Kennett 1660–1728* (1957); Norman Sykes, *Edmund Gibson 1669–1748* (1926). For Trimnell, see *DNB*.

16 *DNB*; Norman Sykes, 'Queen Anne and the Episcopate', *EHR*, 50 (1935), 433–64, at p. 448 n. 3.

17 *Remarks and Collections of Thomas Hearne*, ed. C. E. Doble *et al.* (11 vols., Oxford Historical Society, 1885–1921), XI, 82; John King, *Animadversions on a Pamphlet, Intituled a Letter of Advice* (1701); John King, *The Case of John Atherton, Bishop of Waterford* (1710).

18 Philip Stubbs, *For God or For Baal* (1702).

19 *DNB*. For Wheeler, see also *Collections of Hearne*, ed. Doble *et al.*, VIII, 161.

20 Bodl., MS Rawl. D839, fo. 195.

21 H. P. Thompson, *Thomas Bray* (1954), p. 3. For Lord Digby, see John Findon, 'The Nonjurors and the Church of England 1689–1716', DPhil dissertation, University of Oxford, 1978, p. 103.

22 Thompson, *Bray*, p. 9.

23 Ibid., p. 4.

24 *The Memoirs of William Whiston* (1753), p. 134.

clergy.[25] Yet he held the highest notions of the dignity and power of the episcopal clergy and in this respect had much in common with Henry Dodwell, the Nonjuror theologian.[26] As Commissary of Maryland from 1695 to 1700, Bray's endeavours to gain a maintenance for the colony's Anglican clergy won Dodwell's warm approval.[27] Bray was implacably hostile to Quakers, Socinians and Deists, since they challenged the fundamental tenets of Christianity. His attitude towards moderate Dissenters was more complex. In theory he maintained that all schismatics from the Church of England had ceased to be members of the Christian Church; in practice he was tolerant of Presbyterians and Independents.[28]

What implications are to be drawn from the bipartisan nature of the SPCK? To some extent, it doubtless signifies that the Society meant different things to different men. But there is also a wider explanation. In recent years, historians have stressed the essential unity of the Restoration Church, a unity only shattered by the conflicting responses of Churchmen to the Revolution of 1688 and its aftermath. John Findon has detected no differences in principle prior to 1690 between those clergy who took the oaths and their Nonjuring brethren; the latter suffered only because they ate 'of the tree of undue scrupulosity'.[29] According to other historians, divisions between High and Low Churchmen only emerged after 1689 when clergymen quarrelled over the best means to 'salvage the wreck' of the Church establishment. Whereas High Churchmen campaigned for a return to the *status quo ante* 1688, Low Churchmen urged adaptation to new circumstances.[30] Even after 1688, it has been suggested, there remained a fundamental consensus within the Church of England: most Churchmen, both High and Low, advocated the Church's continued predominance in English society, would accept no further concessions to Dissenters and were orthodox in doctrine.[31] The Whig Churchman Edmund Gibson, himself an SPCK member, held notions of ecclesiastical power that were as 'High' as those of any Tory.[32] He supported the Whigs only because he saw this as the best means to protect the Church in the post-Revolution world. When

[25] Christ Church, Oxford, Arch.W.Epist. 15, fo. 175. This is part of a memorial from Bray to Archbishop Wake, 20 Sept. 1716.
[26] Bray's views on the power and rights of the clergy are discussed below, pp. 178–9, 182–3. For Dodwell's theology, see Findon, 'Nonjurors', pp. 160–3.
[27] Bodl., MS Cherry 23, fo. 153. For Bray's visitation of Maryland in 1700, see Thompson, *Bray*, pp. 44–56.
[28] See below, pp. 185–8.
[29] Findon, 'Nonjurors', pp. 47, 51, 185.
[30] John Spurr, 'Anglican Apologetic and the Restoration Church', DPhil dissertation, University of Oxford, 1985, p. 123; Geoffrey Holmes, *The Trial of Dr Sacheverell* (1973), pp. 29–33; Bennett, *Tory Crisis*, pp. 20–2.
[31] Gordon Rupp, *Religion in England 1688–1791* (Oxford, 1986), pp. 72–6.
[32] Clark, *English Society*, pp. 137–9; Sykes, *Gibson*, pp. 181–2.

he believed that the Whigs were attacking the Church, he severed his links with Walpole's ministry.[33]

An interpretation of the post-1688 Church which stresses an underlying consensus between High and Low Churchmen does not explain the motives of all SPCK members. For example, the Whig MP Grey Neville was a far from loyal son of the Church. His Low Churchmanship had descended into Nonconformity by 1709, and he withdrew from the Society.[34] But such an interpretation does illuminate some paradoxical links within the SPCK. Samuel Brewster, a Lincoln's Inn barrister, was one of the SPCK's most active members. He also corresponded with leading Nonjurors, left money in his will to George Hickes, defended Jacobites captured during the '15 and was reputedly author of one of the more notorious Jacobite pamphlets.[35] At first glance, Brewster appears to have little in common with another active SPCK member White Kennett, the very epitome of a Whig Low Churchman. However, it is often forgotten that Kennett's Whiggery was a distinctly post-Revolution phenomenon: in his youth he had written against the exclusionist Whigs. Ironically, he was drawn to Whiggery only after he had been presented to the rectory of Shottesbrooke, Berkshire, by the Nonjuring Cherry family in 1694. At Shottesbrooke Kennett had a stormy relationship with Henry Dodwell, the leading light in the famous Nonjuror colony. Yet Kennett's contacts with the Shottesbrooke Nonjurors were not entirely without profit, for in 1700 he was presented to the living of St Botolph Aldgate by one of Dodwell's coterie, Samuel Brewster, barrister of Lincoln's Inn.[36]

In order to maintain the SPCK's bipartisan membership, the Society attempted to remain aloof from the political strife of the Augustan age. In this endeavour, it was largely, though not completely, successful. After 1710 party animosities were so acute that not even the SPCK was unaffected. Though the Society had 'industriously avoided the unchristian Distinctions that have been so fashionable of late years', wrote the SPCK secretary Henry Newman in 1715, 'yet they Could not escape being call'd the Presbyterian Club whilst they met in the Parish of St Andrew's Holborn

[33] Stephen Taylor, 'Sir Robert Walpole, the Church of England and the Quakers Tithe Bill of 1736', *HJ*, 28 (1985), 51–77.

[34] Neville joined Thomas Bradbury's Fetter Lane Independent congregation; see Greater London RO, N/C/31/3/1–2, 10, 13 Mar. 1709. For his withdrawal from the Society, see Bodl., MS Rawl. D839, fo. 195.

[35] For a letter from Henry Dodwell to Brewster, 29 Aug. 1700, see Bodl., MS Cherry 23, fos. 153–5. Brewster does not appear to have been a Nonjuror himself; see BL, Add. MS 45511, fo. 82: Nelson to Brewster. For his will, see PRO, Prob. 11/569, fo. 121. Brewster's defence of the Jacobite prisoners is revealed in Samuel Brewster, *Jus Feciale Anglicanum* (1725), pp. i-xii. For Brewster's reputed authorship of the Jacobite pamphlet *Ex Ore Tuo Te Judico. Vox Populi, Vox Dei* (1719), see Paul K. Monod, *Jacobitism and the English People 1688–1788* (Cambridge, 1989), p. 40.

[36] Bennett, *White Kennett*, pp. 5–6, 17, 24.

[Henry Sacheverell's parish] as they did till of late'.[37] At the other end of the political spectrum, extremist Whigs might suspect the Society of harbouring High-flying predilections. To help allay such suspicions, in August 1716 the Society prudently decided to impose the oaths on all existing and future members.[38] But these problems simply emphasize the Society's non-partisan nature. In July 1716 a proposal that the Society include a collect for the Royal Family in its regular prayers was not given a universal welcome. One member aired his disquiet in the following revealing terms:

That the use of such Prayers tho he could join in them himself carry'd in them something like a Test insinuating as if there were some Members that could not pray for the King, which he thought was a treatm^t that did not become a Society that had hitherto acted in consert for promoting the Interests of Religion separate from any Political Considerations.[39]

The non-partisan stance of the SPCK in an intensely partisan era is of real interest and importance. In fact, a study of the SPCK's ideals and policies sheds light on those matters which could still bring together some High Churchmen and some Low Churchmen after 1689. First, it will be necessary to throw into sharper profile the ideas and schemes of the SPCK's chief founder, Thomas Bray.

II

The problems that beset the Church of England during the reigns of William III and Anne have been well documented in recent years, notably by Gareth Bennett and Geoffrey Holmes. The Toleration Act of 1689 had apparently shattered the Church's coercive machinery. Many churchwardens refused to present parishioners for non-attendance at church, and many Churchmen feared that the ecclesiastical courts' sway over the behaviour of the laity had been greatly weakened. The Anglican clergy felt threatened by an apparent resurgence in Dissent. This was a particular problem in the London suburbs, where the shortage of church accommodation hindered an effective response to the Nonconformist challenge. Socinians and Deists questioned the veracity of the Trinity and Divine Revelation, and after the lapse of the Licensing Act in 1695 a flood of heterodox propaganda poured from the presses. There was also much downright anti-clericalism, the priestly rites being denounced as mere superstitious 'priestcraft'. The poverty of many parochial livings, exacerbated by the impact of war taxation, provided a further cause for clerical discontent.[40]

[37] SPCK, Newman Society Letters, 1715–16, fo. 29. [38] SPCK, Minutes, 30 Aug. 1716.
[39] SPCK, Newman Society Letters, 1715–16, fos. 86–7.
[40] Bennett, *Tory Crisis*, pp. 3–20; Holmes, *Trial*, pp. 26–41.

Thomas Bray, chief founder of the SPCK, spent the early 1690s as a parish priest in Warwickshire. His numerous writings and projects were all clearly shaped by the unprecedented force of the assault on the Church of England. Before 1689, wrote Bray, attacks on the Church had come from Dissenters, and had been 'slight Skirmishes made only upon its outworks; namely, against its Rites and Ceremonies'. But now 'alas the Enemy has... enter'd through our Breaches into the very heart of our City (as St Austin calls the Church of God)'. The very essence of Christianity was challenged: 'All the Grand and Fundamental Articles, both of Natural and Revealed Religion, are now either most furiously storm'd by Atheists, Deists, and Socinians on the one hand, or secretly and dangerously undermined by Enthusiasts and Antinomians [Quakers] on the other.'[41] Bray believed that these ideas had gained ground particularly since 'the Liberty of the Press', for now 'all degrees of persons do freely Read the most poisonous Authors'.[42]

The most dangerous aspect of the attack on the Church was the denigration of its priests and their functions. Writing in 1702, Bray claimed that 'all Veneration to the Priestly Character is worn off, few considering us as Authorised by God, to transact Matters of the greatest moment between God and Man; namely to ratifie by Sacraments the Covenant of Grace on his behalf, to proclaim his Laws, and to bless the People in his Name'.[43] Five years earlier, he had condemned those who 'traduce the whole Order [of the priesthood] as useless, and as a burden to the World'.[44]

Bray's response was to stress the dignity and importance of the priesthood. 'The Lawful Governors and Teachers in the Church of Christ', he wrote,

> are the principal Parts in the Mystical Body, as the Heart, the Liver, and the Brain, are in the Natural. For as in the Natural, from those principal Parts are sent forth that Portion of Blood and Spirits, which give Life and Strength to every single Member; so from Christ's Ministers, is Communicated to all the Members of the Mystical Body, that Nourishment, which maintains the spiritual Life in them ... And indeed, the Graces of the Holy Spirit are convey'd by those Ordinances, which they only have power to Administer.[45]

The laity should know its place, for the 'highest Profaneness' occurred when laymen 'do Sacrilegiously usurp the sacred Office of the Ministry'.[46] Instead of holding the clergy in contempt, young people should seek the priest's leadership and direction: 'You shall seek the law at his Mouth, that is, you must apply your selves duely to those whom God has Ordained to

[41] Thomas Bray, *A Course of Lectures upon the Church Catechism* (Oxford, 1696), epistle dedicatory (unpaginated). [42] Thomas Bray, *Bibliotheca Catechetica* (1702), p. vii.
[43] Ibid., pp. vi-vii. [44] Thomas Bray, *Bibliotheca Parochialis* (1697), pp. 2–3.
[45] Bray, *Lectures*, pp. 64–5. [46] Ibid., pp. 185–6.

open and Interpret the Scriptures, for the discovery of his Will, and of what he has Prescribed, as necessary to Salvation.'[47]

In order to effect an enhancement of the influence of, and a renewed respect for, the Church of England and its clergy, Bray outlined a number of schemes. Lending libraries for the use of the parochial clergy should be established in rural deaneries. The local clergy would meet there regularly to discuss affairs and co-ordinate actions; thus the ancient discipline of rural deaneries would be revived.[48] More importantly, the libraries would provide poor clergymen with all books essential 'to enable 'em fully to instruct the People in the meer Necessaries of Salvation'.[49] If the clergy were not so equipped, it would be impossible for them to refute the insidious doctrines now abroad. Consequently, they 'must needs fall into the Lowest Contempt' with their parishioners. Money for the libraries was raised by public subscription, and later Bray extended the project to provide fully equipped libraries for all parochial livings worth less than £20 per annum.[50]

Above all, Bray advocated the establishment of a central directing body to promote the influence of the Church of England. He first planned a chartered *de fide propaganda*, to carry out missionary work abroad and reinvigorate the Church at home. This would remove the reproach that 'whilst the Papists, the Dissenters, and the very Quakers have such Societies for carrying on their Superstitious Blasphemies, Heresies and Fooleries we have nothing of this nature yet set up, in order to promote the pure and primitive Christianity which we profess'.[51] This project proved too ambitious. It was not until 1701 that the chartered Society for the Propagation of the Gospel was established to carry out Anglican missionary activity overseas.[52] But the domestic part of the scheme had been implemented two years earlier with the foundation of the unchartered Society for Promoting Christian Knowledge.

III

In its fledgling years, the ideals, aims and policies of the SPCK clearly bear the hallmarks of Thomas Bray. Like the good doctor, the Society had one central concern: the implementation of a programme of evangelical philanthropy, which would reassert the spiritual and political primacy of the

[47] Thomas Bray, *A Pastoral Discourse to Young Persons* (1704), preface (unpaginated). This tract can be found in a collection of works by Bray entitled *The Whole Course of Catechetical Institution* (1704).

[48] *Publick Spirit Illustrated in the Life and Designs of the Reverend Thomas Bray* (1746), pp. 20–3.

[49] Thomas Bray, *An Essay towards Promoting all Necessary and Useful Knowledge* (1697), p. 12.

[50] Bray, *Bibliotheca Catechetica*, pp. vi-vii.

[51] Quoted in Thompson, *Bray*, pp. 36–7.

[52] Ibid., pp. 72–3.

Church of England in the nation. In its endeavours, the Society saw itself as a subordinate auxiliary of the clergy. According to Henry Newman, the SPCK's task was to render 'the labours of the Clergy more easy and Successful'.[53] While some historians have seen the establishment of the SPCK as a sign of the diminishing importance of the Anglican clergy,[54] the Society itself laid emphasis on the clergyman's predominant role in both civil and spiritual affairs. In May 1700 John Chamberlayne congratulated Archdeacon Booth of Durham, a Society Correspondent, upon his appointment as a JP. Such an appointment, wrote the SPCK's first secretary, 'will soon take away the popular prejudice that our Clergy should not be entrusted with any Civil Power, but keep only to their Church and Profession'.[55] Indeed, the SPCK's *schema* placed the laity in an avowedly subordinate position to the clergy. Not until February 1700, for example, did the Society agree to admit laymen as Corresponding members.[56] The Society was happy to recommend coercive measures in order to boost declining church attendance. In October 1700 John Chamberlayne outlined the following scheme to a Correspondent:

> Let the Justices of the Peace require the Church Wardens to give them an account of all such Persons in their respective Parishes who frequent no Place for Divine Worship, and at ye same Time let others of Zeal and Integrity be imployed to make ye same Enquiry. If the Church Wards (as usually they do) return Omnia Bene, then may the Justices Instance ABC, and demand their opinion of such persons. By this means the Church Wardens have in some Places been brought to inform agst all such offenders lest their negligence be punished.[57]

However, advocacy of coercive measures was quite rare. The Society had been founded in response to the new challenges faced by the Church after 1689. Its methods were similarly attuned to the post-Revolution predicament of the Church and were essentially voluntary in character. Above all, the Society promoted the spread of Christian knowledge, 'the only Knowledge which can conduct us safe through the Mazes and Labyrinths of this World, to our Rest and Happiness in the other'.[58] To this end, the Society distributed 'small usefull Tracts' to their Correspondents, which the latter were to use 'for the Instruction of the Poorer sort in the Knowledge of God and of our Holy Religion, and for their Assistance in a Christian Practice'.[59] The distribution of religious literature was, in fact, the SPCK's chief expense.[60] But its primary weapon in the campaign to spread Christian knowledge was catechetical education.

[53] Cambridge University Library (hereafter CUL), Add. MS 5, no. 153.

[54] Cowie, *Newman*, p. 37; M. G. Jones, *The Charity School Movement* (Cambridge, 1938), pp. 5–6.

[55] *Chapter in Church History*, pp. 65–6.

[56] SPCK, Minutes, 22 Feb. 1700.

[57] *Chapter in Church History*, p. 85.

[58] Bray, *Essay*, preface (unpaginated).

[59] CUL, Add. MS 5, no. 153.

[60] SPCK, Newman Society Letters, 1710–11, fo. 35.

Thomas Bray believed that 'a constant Course of Catechising our Youth in the Fundamental Principles of Christianity, is the only means that can effectually obviate and Cure those Great and prevailing Evils' that confronted the Church.[61] The 'Seeds of Virtue, and the Principles of Religion', Bray wrote, 'can never be too soon sown in their Hearts, that, if possible, Religion may have the first Possession of their Souls, which is the great Advantage before that evil Examples and bad Customes have corrupted them'.[62] John Chamberlayne expressed a similar viewpoint. If children were early instructed in the principles of Christianity, they 'could not possibly (with the ordinary assistance of God's good Spirit) degenerate into such vile and unXtian practices as they now generally do'. While the SPCK's concern was extended to all echelons of society, the Christian education of poor children was given top priority. Inevitably, the 'Barbarous Ignorance' of Christianity was most observable 'among the common People, especially ... those of the poorer sort'.[63] Christian knowledge was especially requisite for the poor since the less they had 'of outward Comforts, the more reason they have to provide themselves of Spiritual Consolations, that they may not be Miserable in both Worlds'.[64] At the same time, they were the least able to provide themselves with such an education. Hence the SPCK's emphasis on the provision of catechetical charity schools 'for the Benefit of such Poor Children ... whose Parents or Friends are not able to give them Learning'.[65]

An education based on the Anglican Catechism provided all knowledge necessary to attain salvation. It also reinforced allegiance to the Church of England. In the answer to the second question of the Catechism, the catechumen affirmed that he was a 'Member of Christ'. But to be sure of being a 'Member of Christ', wrote Bray, the catechumen must be 'secure of being within the Pale of a right Constituted Gospel-church'. The episcopal Church of England was such a church, and therefore it was inadmissible 'to separate your selves from this, wherein you are undoubtedly under a true Gospel Ministry'.[66] The doctrinal orthodoxy enshrined in the Catechism also served as a guard against heresies and errors.[67] Furthermore, a catechetical education would make children 'Advocates against the Obloquies, and Detractions of those, who are always upon the wicked Topick of Reviling the Clergy for their Office sake'.[68]

A sound knowledge of the Catechism was also a necessary requirement for 'the Renewing and Ratifying in Confirmation, that Covenant and Vow

[61] Bray, *Lectures*, epistle dedicatory (unpaginated). [62] Ibid., p. 9.

[63] *Chapter in Church History*, p. 83. [64] Bray, *Lectures*, p. 180.

[65] *An Account of the Methods whereby the Charity-Schools have been Erected and Maintained* (1705), p. 5. [66] Bray, *Lectures*, pp. 41–2. [67] Ibid., pp. 18–19.

[68] Thomas Bray, *An Introductory Discourse to Catechetical Instruction* (1704), preface (unpaginated).

which was made in Baptism'.[69] As Robert Nelson explained, the Church required 'that none be presented to the Bishop for Confirmation, till they can give an Account and Reason of their Faith'.[70] Indeed, the Catechism was defined as 'an Instruction to be learned of every Person, before he be brought to be Confirmed by the Bishop'.[71]

According to Thomas Bray, the rite of confirmation was 'both greatly Necessary, and of singular Benefit in the Church of Christ'. Like the Catechism itself, confirmation helped both to save souls and strengthen the Church of England. The first part of the rite consisted of the ratification of the baptismal vow by 'an open Profession from the Mouth of One formerly Baptized, and now come to Years of Discretion, made before the Bishop and Congregation of Christ's Church'.[72] Baptism was the first and essential step towards salvation. Without that sacrament, 'there is no admittance to the Privileges of the Gospel'.[73] Reaffirming the vow in confirmation enabled the candidate to receive the 'ordinary Gifts of God's holy Spirit'.[74] Moreover, the solemn declaration before the bishop and congregation was a 'very singular Means to fix you in your Religious Purposes' and a 'perpetual Warning not to desert the Banner of the Captain of our Salvation'.[75] Conversely, neglecting confirmation was tantamount to having 'Renounc'd the Covenant of Grace, and to have Repented it was ever made in your behalf'.[76]

Confirmation was no less important in its emphasis on the role of the bishop. The second part of the rite consisted of the bishop's 'solemn Prayers to God, to enable the Party [being confirmed], by the Grace of his Holy Spirit, to do the same, and in his Episcopal and Fatherly Benediction, or Blessing of him, together with his Laying on of Hands, after the Example of the Holy Apostles, to certify him of God's Favour and graciousness towards him'.[77] Thomas Bray firmly believed in the *jus divinum* of episcopacy. In 1703 he proposed the establishment of bishoprics in Jamaica, Barbados, Virginia and Maryland, partly to show that Anglicans genuinely believed 'the Truth and Force of our own Arguments brought to prove the Jus Divinum of Episcopacy'.[78] Not surprisingly, he stressed the efficacy of the episcopal prayer and benediction during the rite of confirmation: 'much benefit', he wrote, 'may, without doubt, be expected from the Devout Prayers and Paternal Benediction, or Blessing of a Father of the Church, for God will ever have a particular Regard to his own Institutions, and will bless those Means of conveying his Grace, which he himself has Appointed'. Similar benefits could be expected from the bishop's laying on

[69] Bray, *Lectures*, p. 13. [70] Robert Nelson, *The Practice of True Devotion* (1715), p. 220.
[71] Bray, *Lectures*, p. 1. [72] Ibid., p. 9. [73] Ibid., p. 291.
[74] Nelson, *True Devotion*, pp. 222–3. [75] Ibid., p. 218. [76] Bray, *Lectures*, p. 10.
[77] Ibid., p. 9. [78] Quoted in Thompson, *Bray*, p. 71. See also Bray, *Lectures*, p. 41.

of hands, an action 'after the Example of the Holy Apostles'. When performed by their episcopal successors, the laying on of hands 'may be expected to have still such Graces accompanying it, as in this present State of the Church, will be needful for you'.[79]

The role of the bishop in confirmation had far-reaching implications. Above all, according to Robert Nelson, confirmation preserved the 'Unity of the Church'. The realization that only a bishop could perform this rite would make young people 'sensible of their Obligation to live in Episcopal Communion, and convince them that their Obedience is due to such Pastors and Ecclesiastical Governors as are endued with all those Powers that were left by the Apostles to their Successors'.[80]

Confirmation was also a necessary qualification for participation in Holy Communion, the 'most inestimable Priviledge in the World'. The last five questions of the Catechism dealt with the doctrine of the Lord's Supper, and a thorough catechetical education would show children that 'the oft'ner they come, they do more and more secure themselves those inestimable Benefits, made over to us by the Covenant of Grace'. Therefore a catechetical education, leading to confirmation, would ultimately 'have our People Daily crowding to the Lord's Table, which they do now so profanely turn their Backs upon'.[81]

Catechetical education, especially for the children of the poor, was one of the two key elements in the SPCK's plan to reinvigorate Anglicanism. The second was the advocacy of practical devotion and piety, or, as Thomas Bray put it, 'a powerful, Practical, and Working Faith'.[82] Belief alone was not enough. Just as the 'most regular Life that can be, except it be Acted upon Christian Principles, is but meer Morality', so 'the most Orthodox Belief that is, if it be Barren in good Works, is but a dead Faith'.[83] Only the truly devout could look forward with confidence to salvation. Such a person would be constantly inquiring, 'Lord, what wouldst Thou have me do?'[84] Holy and devout living consisted of the performance of those 'Duties which we owe to God and our Neighbour'.[85] Duty to God was fulfilled by worshipping Him sincerely in church and home and by constantly seeking Him. The duty owed to 'our Neighbour' consisted of doing good to fellow men. In a general sense, this simply meant loving one's neighbour. More particularly, it meant the performance of works of charity, 'doing good to the Bodies and Souls of Men', as Robert Nelson succinctly defined it.[86] The promotion of good works was the principal element in the SPCK's plan to gain salvation for those with superfluous wealth.

[79] Bray, *Lectures*, pp. 11–12. [80] Nelson, *True Devotion*, pp. 219–20.
[81] Bray, *Lectures*, p. 16. [82] Ibid., p. 262.
[83] Ibid., p. 3. [84] Nelson, *True Devotion*, p. 10.
[85] Bray, *Lectures*, p. 262. [86] Nelson, *True Devotion*, p. 119.

Nelson's *Address to Persons of Quality and Estate* was published posthumously in 1715. The theme of the book was 'the great Business of their [the wealthy's] Salvation, wherein their eternal happiness lies at Stake'.[87] To this end, he outlined a number of charitable projects worthy of support. These philanthropic projects, wrote Nelson, 'may properly be looked upon as so many Spiritual Banks, where their Money is secured by the Word of infallible Truth, and where the Profit is as durable as their Souls, and as large as their Wishes'.[88] Elsewhere in the book, Nelson spoke of the rich 'Working out Your Repentance, by showing Mercy to the Poor; of Covering Your Sins by Charity; of Making an Atonement for them by Alms'.[89] Thomas Bray paraphrased Scripture to air a similar viewpoint: 'He that gives Alms to the Poor, He that Cloaths the Naked, or Feeds the Hungry, will find it upon his Account at the Day of Judgment.'[90] Conversely, those who failed to perform charitable works 'shall certainly perish among the Reprobate'.[91] On the SPCK's poor box similar sentiments were expressed in verse:

> The Proof of Faith is Charity
> Without this all's Hypocrisy
> Nor can you hope God's Love to know
> If you shall None to others Show[92]

Although charity to meet the bodily needs of the poor was important, it was rendered insignificant if 'at the same Time [you] neglect to help him in the more important Concerns of his Soul'.[93] Just as the 'Soul of Man is Infinitely more valuable than the Body', so a charity aimed at saving others 'must needs be of a far more exalted Nature, than that which Terminates only upon the welfare of this Mortal Life'.[94] Indeed, those whose charity helped to save others could look forward to the 'Highest Stations in the Kingdom of Glory, of becoming Courtiers and Favourites to the King of kings'.[95] Charity schools once again provided the perfect outlet for such philanthropy. As Nelson asked, 'if we have any Regard to our own eternal Happiness, shall we neglect this means [charity schools] of turning many unto Righteousness?'[96]

The SPCK set an example of holy living, for many of its members were enthusiastic performers of good works. Sir Humphrey Mackworth believed that 'it was not sufficient to Eschew Evill but wee must also doe good & that it was not convenient to hide my Talent i'a Napkin'.[97] Between 1702 and

[87] Robert Nelson, *Address to Persons of Quality and Estate* (1715), p. 100.
[88] Ibid., p. 104. [89] Ibid., p. 74. [90] Bray, *Bibliotheca Parochialis*, p. 5.
[91] Nelson, *Address*, p. 239. [92] Bodl., MS Rawl. D839, fo. 73.
[93] Nelson, *True Devotion*, p. 93. [94] Bray, *Bibliotheca Catechetica*, p. 2.
[95] Ibid., p. 12. [96] Nelson, *Address*, p. 165.
[97] Quoted in D. Rhys Philips, *The History of the Vale of Neath* (Swansea, 1925), p. 233 n. 6. I am grateful to Dr David Hayton for this reference.

1704 Mackworth introduced bills into the Commons to employ the poor.[98] In 1704 he set up two charity schools in the Vale of Neath, chiefly for the children of his colliery workers.[99] He also claimed to have become involved in his corrupt mining ventures 'purely out of a design to doe more good in ye world, to my children and to ye poore and to the whole towne & countrey abt Neath who were growne Very poore, & would employ & trade'.[100] Another Welshman, Sir John Philipps, founded twenty-two charity schools in Pembrokeshire.[101] Maynard Colchester established the first Gloucestershire charity schools in the 1690s.[102] Sir William Hustler and Sir George Wheeler founded charity schools respectively in Wakefield and Spitalfields.[103] Henry Newman wrote of Richard Mayo that 'all the surplusage of his income not spent in his family was laid out in Charity'.[104] According to Thomas Hearne, Henry Hoare was 'well known to excel in the Spirit, and in the Works of Charity'.[105] He was the treasurer of two London charity schools and the moving spirit in the establishment in 1716 of the Westminster Charitable Society.[106] Samuel Brewster appears to have organized a major project to secure the religious reformation of his country seat, Stoke Nayland in Suffolk.[107] Such charitable works were natural for those who believed, like Brewster, that 'ye evangelical vertues are so linked as not to be separated & therefore may properly be compared to a Tree whereof Faith is ye root, Hope ye body, Charity ye branches & good works ye fruit'.[108]

IV

In earlier parts of this essay, we have seen that the SPCK's brand of Anglicanism stressed the dignity of the clergy and the importance of the priestly functions. It was also rigidly orthodox in doctrine. Thomas Bray roundly denounced Socinianism and Deism as emanating from the 'most Depraved and Corrupt Minds', and poured scorn on those who set up 'their own Imaginations and Fleshly Reasonings against those Spiritual Notions, and those Mysterious Articles of Faith, which are delivered to us in the Scripture'.[109] Indeed, Bray regarded Socinianism and Deism as the most

[98] Ransome, 'Mackworth', pp. 244–6. [99] Philips, *Vale of Neath*, p. 169.
[100] Quoted in ibid., p. 233 n. 2. [101] HPT, draft biography of Philipps.
[102] HPT, draft biography of Colchester.
[103] HPT, draft biography of Sir William Hustler; SPCK, Minutes, 25 Jan. 1700.
[104] SPCK, Newman Society Letters, 1716–17, fo. 42.
[105] *Collections of Hearne*, ed. Doble *et al.*, VI, 287.
[106] For Hoare's charity school treasurerships, see Bodl., MS Rawl. C743, fos. 106–7. For further information on his role in the charity school movement and the Westminster Charitable Society, see C. M. Rose, 'Politics, Religion and Charity in Augustan London *c.*1680–*c.*1720', PhD dissertation, University of Cambridge, 1989, pp. 137, 170.
[107] BL, Harleian MS 3777, fos. 249, 251–2. [108] BL, Add. MS 45511, fo. 103.
[109] Bray, *Lectures*, pp. 235–6.

serious of the many threats faced by the Church, for they challenged the very fundamentals of Christian belief. Bray's attitudes were reflected in the SPCK. William Whiston was a friend of Bray, and an early Corresponding member of the Society. However, his growing attachment to the anti-Trinitarian doctrine of Arianism created problems. Realizing that the Society 'thought themselves only capable of supporting things as they then stood in the Church of England, by Law established', Whiston resigned from the SPCK in 1710 lest his continued membership arouse dispute.[110] Eight years later, the Society was deeply embarrassed when it printed Archbishop Wake's edition of the Psalms. Samuel Clarke, the Arian divine, had tampered with the manuscript, and the book consequently insinuated 'an Opinion dissonant to the Doctrine of the Established Church concerning the Ever Blessed Trinity'. The SPCK suppressed all copies of the book in its possession and requested Correspondents to return those copies which had been sent to them.[111]

How did the SPCK view non-Anglican Christian denominations? It has been claimed that anti-Catholicism was one of the SPCK's key policies.[112] This was not the case. The Society was certainly hostile to Roman Catholicism. In October 1699 the SPCK's members were asked to 'endeavour to inform themselves of the practices of the Priests to pervert his Majesty's subjects to Popery'.[113] During the last years of Queen Anne's reign, the SPCK maintained a secret committee to monitor Catholic missionary activity.[114] The Society also distributed anti-Catholic literature to Correspondents upon request.[115] But anti-popery can in no sense be described as an issue of central importance to the Society. It came to the fore only at moments of acute danger to the Protestant Succession. In fact, hostility to Quakerism loomed much larger in the SPCK's deliberations.

Towards the Quakers, the Society bore the deepest of animosities. The very first item in the SPCK minutes concerned the progress that had been made 'towards the instruction and conversion of Quakers', and the further steps necessary 'to redeem that misguided people to the knowledge and belief of Christ'.[116] In October 1700 John Chamberlayne described the conversion of the Quakers as one of the SPCK's central objectives.[117] The tone of the Society's policy was once again set by Thomas Bray. Like Socinians and Deists, the Quakers had rejected fundamental Christian beliefs. The Quaker, wrote Bray, treated the Scriptures as 'a dead Letter',

[110] *Memoirs of Whiston*, p. 151. For his friendship with Bray, see ibid., pp. 134–5.
[111] CUL, Add. MS 9, no. 267.
[112] Siddall, 'Movement to Reform', pp. 68–70. See also C. M. Haydon, 'The Anti-Catholic Activity of the SPCK, *c.*1698–1740', *Recusant History*, 18 (1986–7), 418–21.
[113] SPCK, Minutes, 26 Oct. 1699.
[114] Siddall, 'Movement to Reform', pp. 79–84.
[115] SPCK, Minutes, 12 Sept. 1700, 10 June 1708.
[116] SPCK, Minutes, 8 Mar. 1699.
[117] *Chapter in Church History*, p. 84.

and 'Blasphemously entitles every foolish and deceitful Imagination of his own corrupt Heart, to the Motion of the Holy Spirit'.[118] Consequently, Bray looked upon the Quakers 'as a Heathen Nation'.[119] To effect their conversion, the Society employed George Keith, himself a former Friend, as a roving missionary. Books were sent to Correspondents for use 'in detecting the vile errors of the Quakers'.[120] The Society also kept a close watch on the Quaker schools at Wandsworth and Clerkenwell.[121]

The SPCK was more charitable towards other non-Anglican Protestants. It had strong links with continental Protestant groups. Wilhelm Mecken and Anton Böhme, Lutheran chaplains to Prince George of Denmark, were Subscribing members of the SPCK.[122] It was upon Böhme's initiative that from 1709 the SPCK partly financed a Danish mission to southern India.[123] In the early 1730s the Society promoted the settlement of the Salzburger refugees in Georgia.[124] In the ranks of the Society's Correspondents could be found the Swiss theologians Jakob Scherer and J. F. Ostervald, and the German, Hermann Francke.[125] The Society had much in common with Ostervald and Francke. Ostervald rejected dogmatic Calvinism and instead stressed the importance of practical piety. His catechism was translated into English and printed by the SPCK.[126] Francke was the founder of a famous catechetical school at Halle, and in May 1699 an account of it was given to the Society.[127] Such links were also seen as a means to spread the influence of the Church of England. The Society was suitably gratified by Ostervald's efforts to introduce the Anglican liturgy at Neuchatel.[128] Under the SPCK's guidance, the Salzburger refugees agreed to a form of public worship modelled on that of the Church of England.[129]

The Society enjoyed cordial relations with the Presbyterian Church of Scotland. In 1708 the SPCK conferred honorary membership upon several prominent figures in the Kirk.[130] The Society would not infringe upon the

[118] Bray, *Lectures*, p. 84. [119] Quoted in *Chapter in Church History*, p. 22.

[120] SPCK, Minutes, 2 Apr. 1702. [121] SPCK, Minutes, 10 Dec. 1702.

[122] For Böhme, see *DNB*, and J. J. Rambach, *Memoirs of... Anthony William Boehm* (1735). From the time of his wife's accession to the throne, Prince George's chaplains conducted services according to the Book of Common Prayer.

[123] For the Danish mission, see Cowie, *Newman*, pp. 104–31.

[124] Ibid., p. 231.

[125] Eamon Duffy, '"Correspondence Fraternelle": the SPCK, the SPG, and the Churches of Switzerland in the War of the Spanish Succession', *SCH*, Subsidia 2 (1979), 251–80, esp. pp. 254–5, 257–8. [126] Ibid., pp. 252–3, 262; Cowie, *Newman*, p. 25.

[127] SPCK, Minutes, 11 May 1699; Jones, *Charity School Movement*, p. 36. A detailed examination of the SPCK's relations with Francke is provided in Daniel L. Brunner, 'The Role of Halle Pietists in England (*c*.1700–*c*.1740)', DPhil dissertation, University of Oxford, 1988.

[128] SPCK, Minutes, 23 Dec. 1703; Duffy, '"Correspondence Fraternelle"', pp. 267–8, 273.

[129] Cowie, *Newman*, p. 232. [130] Clarke, *SPCK*, p. 89.

territory of the Scottish SPCK, established in 1709. For example, in 1713 the Society declined to help an episcopalian charity school in the Highlands, since that might be 'Construed as an Invasion of the province of ye Society Erected at Edinburgh for promoting Xtian Knowledge'. In this case, the SPCK's respect for a lawful national church also came into play. As Henry Newman wrote, 'the Society would be tender of doing any thing that might occasion a Jealousy in those p[ar]ts as if they were designed to undermine ye Established Religion of N[orth] Brit[ain]'.[131]

The SPCK's attitude towards moderate English Dissenters was complex. In theory, Thomas Bray argued that schismatics from a lawful church had removed themselves from the pale of the Christian church and were on a par with excommunicates.[132] In practice, he was less extreme. Presbyterians and Independents at least accepted orthodox Christian belief in divine revelation, the Trinity and infant baptism. In America in 1700 Bray had not ventured into Congregational New England, for it was his policy 'not to intermeddle, where Christianity under any form has gained Possession'.[133] He bitterly opposed the High Church assault upon Dissent in Anne's last years.[134] John Hooke, another SPCK founder member, held similar views. Although he did not support 'an Absolute unlimitted Toleration', he opposed 'Persecuting Good Loyal Protestants who agree with ye Church in fundamentalls'. He supported the comprehension of moderate Dissenters within the Church.[135]

Some members of the SPCK believed disputes between Christians to be uncharitable and counterproductive. Although it was important to contend for the faith, Robert Nelson regarded excessive controversy as a hindrance to practical piety. Among the many 'ill effects of Parties', he believed, was

> the great decay of the Spirit and Life of Devotion; for while Men are so deeply concerned for their several Schemes, and pursue them with the Vigour of their Minds, and the bent of their affections: the solid and substantial Part of Religion is apt to evaporate, and Charity, the very bond of peace, and of all Virtues, without which, whoever liveth, is counted dead before God, is but too frequently made a Sacrifice of these Differences that divide us.[136]

[131] SPCK, Newman Society Letters, 1713–14, fos. 72–3.
[132] Bray, *Lectures*, p. 53.
[133] Quoted in Thompson, *Bray*, p. 58.
[134] Christ Church, Arch.W.Epist. 15, fo. 381. This is part of an unsigned and undated memorandum to Archbishop Wake on the early history of the charity schools. It can confidently be attributed to Thomas Bray, since it is in an identical style and hand to an earlier memorandum in the same volume (fos. 164–78), definitely written by Bray. The author's stress on the role of the SPCK in the London charity school movement also points to Bray.
[135] BL, Add. MS 70242: John Hooke to Robert Harley, 12 Aug. 1710.
[136] Nelson, *True Devotion*, pp. iv–v.

In 1711 William Melmoth similarly deprecated 'the unnatural Heats and Animosities which are sprung up among us, and which must unavoidably enervate the force of true Religion'.[137]

Not all SPCK men were of such eirenic dispositions. Humphrey Mackworth was one of the principal agitators for the Occasional Conformity Bills. Like John Comyns, a fellow SPCK member, Mackworth was a Tacker in 1704.[138] Samuel Brewster's scheme to reinvigorate the religious life of Nayland seems in part to have been a response to local Nonconformists. Though the scheme was facing financial difficulties, Brewster wrote in 1709, he 'was resolved to go thro yt ye Dissenters might not have ye pleasure of laughing at an abortive project'.[139]

In general, though, the SPCK held a charitable opinion of moderate Dissenters. Of course, the Society wanted them to conform to the Church of England, but there was to be no active proselytizing. In 1705 and 1708 the Society cold-shouldered requests from Correspondents that it issue propaganda against moderate Dissenters.[140] Twenty years later, Henry Newman clearly enunciated the SPCK's policy on this issue:

> The Society have purposely declin'd (as foreign to promote Christian Knowledge) to concern themselves with the Controversie between the Established Church & the Dissenters except in the Instances you mentioned of defending Infant Baptism: the common result of disputes among Protestants being rather a lessening of Charity than conviction of truth.

The SPCK secretary continued with some reflexions on the issue. Newman stressed that these were his 'private Opinion', and not said in the Society's name. Nevertheless, they probably give a useful insight into SPCK thinking. The case for the Church of England had been so well argued 'that it can hardly be read by any Reasonable Dissenter, but he will be asham'd to own himself an Enemy of the Establish'd Church if he does not entirely conform'. But militant proselytizing was misguided and ineffective: 'It is generally observ'd where a minis^{r} of the Establish'd Church has set himself with great Zeal to preach up conformity, there the Dissenters are most numerous.' Indeed, Newman believed that 'The Dissenters of all sorts generally encrease by all resemblances of persecution but dwindle when left to cool reflection, and to see themselves out liv'd in respect of good Morals by those of the Establish'd Church.' If stress were laid on the 'Truths we all agree in', mutual charity would eventually eliminate the lesser

137 William Melmoth, *The Great Importance of a Religious Life Consider'd* (1711), preface (unpaginated).

138 Ransome, 'Mackworth', p. 237.

139 BL, Harleian MS 3777, fos. 251–2. See also BL, Add. MS 45511, fo. 81.

140 SPCK, Minutes, 22 Nov. 1705, 12 Aug. 1708.

controversies. In the meantime, the Church of England should concentrate on encouraging its own members to lead holy lives, rather than preaching down Dissent. For 'if Christianity it self loses ground among the Professors of it in the Establish'd Church', asked Newman, 'whereof have we to boast?'[141]

[141] SPCK, Newman Society Letters, Feb. to Nov. 1727, fos. 25–6.

8 Cultural patronage and the Anglican crisis: Bristol *c.* 1689–1775

Jonathan Barry

There has recently been a great revival of interest both in the post-Restoration Church and in the cultural life of English towns during a period dubbed by Peter Borsay 'the English urban renaissance'. Yet, by and large, the two themes have not been considered in direct relationship. Those who have considered the Church have been preoccupied with its political and ideological significance, above all with the notion of a 'confessional state'. With the exception of Jeremy Gregory, few have concerned themselves with the cultural life of the Church. Cultural historians have either asserted or assumed that the 'urban renaissance' was largely secular, indeed a symptom of the secularization of the elite. Church patronage is ignored since cultural changes are seen as arising from the combined interests of lay patrons, eager to establish or consolidate their status through cultural prestige, and of commercially minded providers of culture, tapping growing surplus incomes. Although it has been recognized that voluntary groups, notably the numerous clubs and societies of the period, played a key part in cultural life, their secular foundations and motivations have been assumed.[1]

Insofar as religion has been discussed, it has been as a negative factor. Religious animosities supposedly delayed the growth of the stability necessary for such a cultural renaissance, whilst one of the renaissance's purposes and effects was to furnish a cultural world safely distinct from the contentious field of denominational religion. The classicism implicit in a 'renaissance' may itself be taken to indicate a retreat from Christian divisions into the modern paganism of Augustan culture.

This essay has a double aim. First it questions this standard view by indicating the continued centrality of the Church, and the various forms of its patronage, in cultural life, through a case-study of Bristol. It concentrates on the arts, though the same case can be made for the press, education and the sciences, for example. Secondly, it considers what light cultural patronage throws on the Church's position within a religiously divided

[1] P. Borsay, *The English Urban Renaissance* (Oxford, 1989); J. Gregory, 'Anglicanism and the Arts', in *Culture, Politics and Society in Britain 1660–1800*, ed. J. Black and J. Gregory (Manchester, 1991), pp. 82–109; P. Clark, *Sociability and Urbanity* (Leicester, 1986).

society. What effect did Anglican cultural patronage have on its standing? How far did the Church's involvement in such cultural patronage compromise, as well as reinforce, its claims to represent the sole legitimate ideological expression of the community?

By reconstructing the dilemmas and debates which these issues generated within Bristol, some answers emerge to the broader question of how the Church responded to what G. V. Bennett dubbed 'the Anglican crisis' in the opening chapter of his book, *The Tory Crisis in Church and State*. Of Bennett's alternative adjectives, Anglican seems preferable to Tory because, as we shall see, Whigs like Arthur Bedford shared with Tories a sense of the dilemmas involved, but I am indebted to Bennett's formulation of the challenges faced by the Church after 1688. As he put it: 'a great and critical choice lay before Anglicans. Were they ready to accept the place in English society of a basically voluntary body working within the legal conditions of the establishment or were they going to agitate for a return to the past when Church and State had conjoined in a single authoritarian regime?'[2] If the Church were to pursue the voluntary road, then its cultural patronage was arguably going to be a decisive factor, but how strong an advantage would it gain?

In offering Bristol as a case-study, I hope that I am not offering too hopelessly unrepresentative an example.[3] Bristol was of course a cathedral city, and also one generously provided with parish churches, seventeen in all, unlike many rapidly growing urban centres. The Church was thus well placed to play a major part in the city's cultural life. On the other hand Bristol was no Barchester; it was hardly dominated by its cathedral close, nor even by the splendours of St Mary, Redcliffe. Not only was the city growing rapidly, from some 15,000 inhabitants in 1660 to over 20,000 by 1700 and up to 50–60,000 by 1775, but the commercial wealth of its residents was supplemented by the thriving trade of the Bristol Hotwells, a leading summer spa. Bristol was one of the strongest centres of Nonconformity, harbouring the largest Quaker meetings outside London, strong Presbyterian, Congregational and Baptist groups and, from 1739, a significant Methodist presence, Calvinist as well as Wesleyan.

The Anglican Church not only faced formidable rivals, but suffered from internal weaknesses. The bishopric was not only notoriously poor but involved a uniquely split-site diocese, joining Bristol and its hinterland with Dorset. As a consequence many diocesan clergy were non-resident, though energetic bishops or deans could (and did) try to enforce attendance at such

[2] G. V. Bennett, *The Tory Crisis in Church and State 1688–1730* (Oxford, 1975), p. 22.

[3] A fuller account of Bristol's religious condition, in which the points below are substantiated, is given in J. Barry, 'The Parish in Civic Life: Bristol and its Churches 1640–1750', in *Parish, Church and People*, ed. S. J. Wright (1988), pp. 152–78.

critical periods as the 1680s and the early eighteenth century. A substantial group combined cathedral posts with service in Bristol's parishes. Pluralism thus reduced the numbers of active clergy, but their assiduity in parish duties was generally ensured by dependence on their congregations for voluntary subscriptions and fees to supplement very low fixed stipends. The Church in Bristol was influenced by a number of competing forces – not just cathedral and parish but also the patronage of congregations and vestries, of the powerful city corporation, which controlled many of the livings and lectureships and had its own civic chapel, and also of guilds, societies and other groups which might support the clergy.

Growing out of this complex religious position was the contentious and central place of religion in Bristol politics for at least a century after the Restoration.[4] The city corporation, generally Tory or divided in its allegiance until around 1700, became increasingly Whig thereafter, until the great realignment of positions after about 1760. This Whiggery was associated with a strong Presbyterian presence on the corporation and it left the parishes as potential centres of Tory opposition, along with other voluntary groups and the Corporation of the Poor (a city-wide elected body for managing the central workhouse and outdoor poor relief after 1697). Despite this, however, it would be simplistic to see a straight Nonconformist–Anglican divide in Bristol. There was a considerable Whig Anglican party, personified from the 1730s by Josiah Tucker, long-time dean of Gloucester.[5] The claim to represent the Church was just that, a claim, and was never monopolized, ideologically or practically, by any group.

For our purposes the most significant point is that Church support and legitimacy were still highly valued in post-Restoration Bristol. We must set cultural patronage in a wider context, in which the Church was still the premier location for public activity, its personnel still the key intelligentsia, and its organization still by far the strongest basis of association.[6] Indeed, other forms of association deferred to this primacy by involving the Church in their public activity. Thus guilds, charitable societies, freemasons' lodges, the Bristol Infirmary and the like all followed the model set by the corporation in making an Anglican church service and sermon an integral part of their annual feasts.[7] The publication of these sermons was relatively frequent, offering a valuable extra piece of patronage for the clergyman and

4 J. Barry, 'The Politics of Religion in Restoration Bristol', in *The Politics of Religion in Restoration England*, ed. T. Harris, P. Seaward and M. Goldie (Oxford, 1990), pp. 163–90, documents the early phases of this.

5 G. Shelton, *Dean Tucker and Eighteenth-Century Economic and Political Thought* (1981).

6 This, like many of the other generalizations hereafter, cannot be documented here; readers are referred to J. Barry, 'The Cultural Life of Bristol 1640–1775', DPhil dissertation, University of Oxford, 1985, esp. pp. 183–245.

7 Ibid., pp. 171, 180–1, 309.

enabling him to establish the authorized meaning of that group's activity, sometimes controversially.

The cultural life on which attention has recently focused has largely been the public and commercial world of the performing arts – musical performances, the theatre, spectacles involving the visual arts, and published literature. In itself, this focus may draw our attention away from major areas of cultural life where religion and the Church were important. Music historians have often associated a decline in domestic music-making with a shift to lay attendance at professional concerts. Bristol probate evidence shows the expected decline in the ownership of such items as virginals after the Civil War, and fewer references occur elsewhere to makers of such instruments, a decline not apparently reversed until the mid-eighteenth century. But it is hard to explain this through concert-going, for which there is little evidence before the 1720s. It may be that the churches were an earlier source of public music – organ-builders are the one group of musical instrument-makers to appear consistently in the records from the 1680s. Music teaching was dominated by the church organists until the very end of our period, when music masters who combined the trade with running a musical shop or instrument-making appear. Even then church organists still dominated the field, together with parish clerks and those attached to the cathedral choir. Although the organ-builders made harpsichords as well, and the music masters mostly taught on such instruments, it seems significant that the organ remained the centre, as it were, of the musical world.[8]

The domestic ownership of cultural items may not follow the same trajectory as public performance, as we can see in the case of literature and the visual arts. Religious subjects continued to dominate Bristol publishing, and if probate records contain a declining number of specific references to Bibles, and especially to service books, after 1640, this may just reflect the growing tendency to publish such works in smaller editions unlikely to be named. Certainly Bristol's clergy played their part, not just in the outpouring of sermons, but in producing other types of religious literature, including hymns, poems, stories and the like. In this field a trickle became a flood with the Evangelical Revival, both Anglican and Nonconformist. The popularity of hymn collections reminds us of the important role of household worship, not least in Anglican families.[9]

Religious publishing also had important ties with the visual arts, as many of the more substantial publications were illustrated with prints. Illustrated

[8] Ibid., pp. 186–7, 215–16, 363; J. G. Hooper, 'A Survey of Music in Bristol', typescript in Bristol Central Library, Bristol Collection, reference 23031 (2nd edn, 1963).

[9] J. Barry, 'The Press and the Politics of Culture in Bristol, 1660–1775', in *Culture, Politics and Society*, ed. Black and Gregory, pp. 49–81.

Bibles were the most lavishly advertised of the serial publications available from the 1730s. Religious themes were probably also prominent in the massive explosion of prints to adorn household walls indicated in early eighteenth-century inventories. Religious subjects were quite often mentioned in notices of prints and pictures for sale. Of course, Anglicans had no monopoly here; most of the prints were Catholic or Calvinist in origin and Nonconformist ministers like Watts and Whitefield are mentioned specifically. Ames, a Bristol engraver, produced prints of many of Bristol's leading Nonconformist ministers of the later eighteenth century. On the other hand we also know of prints of three heroes of the Tory party in Bristol: the philanthropist Edward Colston; the MP Thomas Coster, victor at the 1734 election; and Sir John Phillips, defeated in the election of 1754.

For many Bristolians cultural and religious activity came together during those rites of passage which the Church still dominated. Births were celebrated by peals of bells, while weddings were occasions for music and dancing, as well as the provision of wedding rings. There was also a considerable pietistic literature, notably poetry, produced on the theme of love and marriage. The most important link came through funerals, on which Bristolians spent lavishly. Costs included lengthy tolling of the funeral bell, while the procession might be accompanied by music. Quite apart from lengths of cloth for the pall and for the gloves, scarves and hatbands of the mourners, sumptuous funerals included the handing out of special mourning rings and the decoration of the coffin and church with heraldic escutcheons. This gave business to a series of arms or herald painters. Though the last such man to be recognized nationally by the heralds died in 1709, the practice continued, whilst a kindred trade, that of the monumental mason, grew steadily in importance. The leading practitioners in eighteenth-century Bristol were the Patty family, who stocked a variety of ready-made monuments as well as carving exquisite pieces to order. Such items were of course expensive, and the lavish pomp of funerals was never accepted as desirable by everybody. Nonconformists, particularly Quakers, not only challenged the Anglican monopoly over this rite of passage but also, perhaps because of its Anglican association, often rejected the associated cultural practices. All religious groups, however, found death a central literary theme, indeed it was probably *the* major theme of Bristolian literary efforts, ranging from epitaphs and elegies on monuments to long elegies printed in the newspapers or as separate publications.

Did these occasions for cultural activity, so bound up with religion, and the Church, give way to more secular and this-worldly concerns? Can we infer this, for example, from the growth in portrait painting – celebrating the living – or the growth in societies, some of them overtly cultural in aim, such as catch clubs or musical groups, others incorporating music and literature in their celebrations? Perhaps, although we should note the leading role often played by the clergy in many of these developments. The Reverend Nathaniel Ingelo, whom the Broadmead Independent church dismissed because of his involvement in music-making during the late 1640s, went on to direct the King's Chapel. A century later the Bristol Catch Club included a number of clergymen, while Thomas Chatterton's father, a schoolmaster and cathedral chorister, composed songs for the club at the Pineapple of which he was a member. The earliest society in Bristol whose purposes we might define as purely cultural was the St Stephen's Ringers, established earlier as a guild for parish bell ringers, though evolving in the eighteenth century into a genteel club. The development of change-ringing led to the formation of clubs of young men in other parishes who met regularly to attempt marathon sessions of grandsire triples both 'for pleasure' and in anticipation of remuneration or hospitality from gratified parishioners. In the 1700s Arthur Bedford was hopeful that the formation of properly regulated parish music societies among young people would be an important first step in the reformation of manners and the establishment of religious societies.[10]

In short, religious interests, and the Church's activities in particular, still played a central role in forms of cultural life which have attracted little historical attention, compared to the growth of a commercial and public world of the polite arts, on which the rest of this essay will focus. Here too, the place of the Church in the growth of the city's artistic life has been unduly neglected. For reasons of space no discussion of the relationship between the Church and the theatre will be possible.

The central place of church organists and singers in the city's musical life has already been mentioned. For them church positions offered both a basic income and a public audience; when they developed a concert life, they did so in close association with the Church. One of the earliest concerts recorded, in 1726, was a benefit for the cathedral organist, Nathaniel Priest, and the following year a benefit concert for him on St Cecilia's Day was preceded by morning anthems at the cathedral. A rival concert was held the same evening by the gentlemen of a 'musical society' for another organist, Mr Smalley. In 1728 Smalley was defeated in the contest to become organist at St Mary, Redcliffe, whereupon he disappeared from the city's musical life.[11] The organists continued to organize many of the city's concerts, including the establishment of winter subscription concerts; in the 1770s

[10] *Records of a Church of Christ*, ed. R. Hayden (Bristol Record Society, 27, 1974), p. 102; E. H. W. Meyerstein, *Life of Thomas Chatterton* (1930), p. 9; H. E. Roslyn, *History of the Ancient Society of St Stephen's Ringers, Bristol* (Bristol, 1928); *Felix Farley's Bristol Journal*, 9 Feb. 1760, 10 Apr. 1762; A. Bedford, *Great Abuse of Musick* (1711), pp. 230–1, 257.

[11] *Farley's Bristol Newspaper*, 9 July 1726, 28 Oct., 1, 15 Nov. 1727, 10 Feb. 1728.

two alternative concert series reflected loyalties to rival organists. Similarly, they played a role in the growth of assembly rooms and balls. The Old Assembly Room was given a small organ in 1746 and in 1757 the New Assembly Room was equipped with a grand organ belonging to Edmund Broderip (one of a clan of West Country church organists), which was probably played by him at concerts. The Bristol Catch Club included several organists and Broderip's nephew Robert, another Bristol organist, published a collection of catches for the Club at the end of the century.[12]

Churches could also be used as concert halls, and several times after 1750 Bristol musicians were involved in performances in Keynsham parish church – conveniently placed for both Bath and Bristol.[13] No public concerts are recorded in Bristol's parish churches, but the cathedral was certainly employed. Apart from morning anthems on days when major concerts were held in the evenings, full oratorios were occasionally performed. The only performance of Handel's *Messiah* given in a sacred building in his lifetime was that at the cathedral in 1758, and another followed at Easter in 1774, as a benefit finale for one of the subscription series, with funds going to the Bristol Infirmary.[14] Many of the concerts put on by Bristolians (as opposed to visiting musicians staying at the Hotwells) had a charitable purpose, often occurring on St Cecilia's Day. The most elaborate were the music festivals that coincided with the feast for the Bristol Society for the Sons of the Clergy, a body dedicated to helping impoverished widows and families of the Anglican clergy by bringing together clerical families and their lay friends. At their height in the late 1750s these feasts were raising more money than the more durable, and hence better known, Three Choirs Festival in the neighbouring dioceses.[15]

Religious music was also regularly performed in secular settings. Anthems and oratorios by Purcell, Handel and Boyce were featured not just in concerts but in the theatres. Handel's *Messiah* was performed at the opening of the New Assembly Room in 1756, and *Judas Maccabeus* the next year when the new organ was unveiled. Admittedly an avowedly 'concerto spirituale' staged in 1772, which included Allegri's *Miserere*, failed to attract a large audience, but it so enraptured some who attended that they each offered a guinea for a repeat performance.[16]

[12] *Oracle and Country Advertiser*, 8 Nov. 1746; *Bristol Weekly Intelligencer*, 5 Feb. 1757; R. Broderip, *A Collection of Duets* (Bristol, 1795); Bristol Central Library, Bristol Collection, reference 21952 (a collection of catches).

[13] *Bristol Weekly Intelligencer*, 17 Aug. 1751; *Bristol Journal*, 20, 27 Aug. 1774.

[14] W. Dean, *Handel's Dramatic Oratorios and Masques* (1959), p. 45; *Felix Farley's Bristol Journal*, 12 Aug. 1758; *Bristol Journal*, 12, 19, 26 Mar. 1774.

[15] J. E. Jackson, *Sermon at the Cathedral* (Bristol, 1846), appendix; *Felix Farley's Bristol Journal*, 13 Aug. 1757, 12, 19 Aug. 1758, 7 July 1759, 9 Aug. 1760.

[16] *Farley's Bristol Newspaper*, 18 Nov. 1727; *Bristol Weekly Intelligencer*, 27 Dec. 1755, 3 May 1757; *Felix Farley's Bristol Journal*, 13 June 1761, 13 June 1772; *Bristol Journal*, 23 May 1772, 4 Sept. 1773.

It seems clear that, by associating their performances with the Church, whether by using religious music, religious settings or performing for a good cause, musicians were to some extent legitimating their actions. One commentator on the Handel performance at the opening of the New Assembly Room expressed his fear that this was merely a token gesture, at best to be repeated annually while otherwise the rooms were devoted to dissipation and luxury. Secular music-making evidently required a figure like Handel as a symbol of cultural respectability, reassuring the public of the Christian as well as moral function of music, a task surely also performed by the close ties with local Anglican church life. For many of those involved, such as the vicar of St Mary, Redcliffe, Thomas Broughton, author of one of Handel's scriptural libretti, and for many of the organists, the association of religion and music was no doubt a genuine one.[17]

Similar links may be traced, more briefly, in the visual arts and literature. The churches of Bristol required a great deal of upkeep which gave important work to the city's painters and skilled craftsmen. Although the churches lacked the paintings and sculptures of Catholic countries, they were rich in church furniture, often highly ornate. James Stewart's sketches of the interiors of several mid-eighteenth-century parish churches reveal a riot of carved wood, in pews, pulpits, altar-pieces and the like, as well as much ornamental metalwork, including ornate gates and rails, candelabra and lecterns. Churches had painted and carved representations of the royal arms as well as benefaction tables, texts of scriptures and monuments, requiring regular gilding, carving, repairing and repainting. The organs in churches were given elaborate cases, often associated with screens and galleries. The architect Strahan was paid nine guineas in 1728 to design the Redcliffe organ-case, and published a print of the design. Altar-pieces were also commissioned, notably that for which Hogarth was paid £525, again at St Mary, Redcliffe. This commission provided hundreds of pounds of further work to local painters and carvers working on the surrounds and creating a fitting marble altar. No other project was on quite this scale, but the cumulative effect of many smaller works was a major support for local skill. Altars also required plate and chalices, mostly produced locally.[18]

The Church offered further work to architects. Though Nonconformist groups were more likely than Anglicans to require new buildings, such as Wesley's New Room and the Friends' Meeting House in Quakers' Friars, both the work of the Quaker George Tully, Anglican churches required

[17] *Felix Farley's Bristol Journal*, 10, 17 Jan. 1756, 19 Aug. 1758; Dean, *Handel's Dramatic Oratorios*, pp. 414–33.

[18] Bodl., MS Gough Somerset 8; M. J. H. Liversidge, *William Hogarth's Bristol Altar-Piece* (Bristol, 1980).

repair, extension and even, in the eighteenth century, rebuilding and new foundation. The 1710s saw small-scale work on All Saints and other churches, then in the 1750s and 1760s St Werbergh's and St Nicholas's were rebuilt and the new parish church of St George's, Kingswood, constructed, followed in the mid–1770s by the rebuilding of St Michael's by Patty. Such large projects attracted public attention both to the architects and to the styles adopted, prompting discussion of the contrasts between different styles in church building and their religious effects.[19]

Church patronage for literature was less direct, not involving the financial support of professional artists so much as inspiration and an audience for amateur writers, including many clergy. An important connexion between the two was provided by Bristol Grammar School, staffed by Anglican clergymen. The headmasters between 1712 and 1743, William Goldwin and Alexander Stopforth Catcott, both poets, encouraged composition in both Latin and English. Goldwin's *Poetical Description of Bristol* (1712) was intended to inspire emulation in his pupils, and in 1737 similar motives led Catcott to publish the verses written by the pupils for the annual visitation by the corporation. One of his pupils was the eccentric clergyman Emanuel Collins, who expressed his appreciation for his mentor in his *Miscellanies* of 1762. In 1739 Catcott planned to put on a play performed by the school boys, but at the last moment the corporation banned it, compensating Catcott for any wasted expense. Attitudes later changed and in 1773 and 1774 the boys put on two plays, enthusiastically reviewed in the papers, the latter even including females![20]

Partly because of their classical education, the clergy were not only themselves the most active literary figures, but often acted as patrons for other enthusiasts. Charles Wesley was at the centre of one circle of women writers, while contemporaneously Hannah More was helped by Josiah Tucker and Sir James Stonhouse, both Anglican clergymen, through whose contacts More became involved with David Garrick and London literary circles. Thomas Chatterton equally looked to the clergy, along with the other learned professions, for patronage; his failure to gain recognition led to an outpouring of vitriolic satire which nonetheless reveals his sense that

[19] A. Gomme, M. Jenner and B. Little, *Bristol: An Architectural History* (1979); C. W. Chalklin, 'The Financing of Church Building in the Provincial Towns of Eighteenth-Century England', in *The Transformation of English Provincial Towns*, ed. P. Clark (1984), pp. 286–7, 290, 296–301; *Michael Rysbrack*, ed. K. Eustace (Bristol, 1982); Bodl., MS Gough Somerset 2, fos. 153–8.

[20] W. Goldwin, *Poetical Description of Bristol* (1712); A. W. Oxford, *William Goldwin* (Bristol, 1911); A. S. Catcott, *Exercises Performed at a Visitation of the Grammar School* (Bristol, 1737); E. Collins, *Miscellanies in Prose and Verse* (Bristol, 1762), pp. 137–42; Bristol Archives Office (AO), Corporation Vouchers, 1739; *Bristol Journal*, 17 Apr. 1773, 9 Apr. 1774.

these people were the city's literary intelligentsia, even if myopic and corrupt.[21]

Chatterton's failure to win recognition partly stemmed from his unwillingness to publish the moral and religious literature that the clergy largely wrote themselves and encouraged in others. He should have emulated the teacher who inspired him to write, a young man called Phillips, whose death prompted an obituary noting that he had a genius 'devoted to the service of religion and virtue'. Many others followed suit, composing hymns and other religious poetry, fictional and factual lives, prayers, elegies, verse paraphrases of the Bible and even religious philosophies in verse. A late seventeenth-century Anglican example was Dean Samuel Crossman, who wrote both hymns and exemplary stories and lives. Thereafter, though Anglican examples are not absent, the initiative rather shifted to other groups, unless one classifies the massive output of the Wesley brothers and other Methodists, much printed in Bristol, under the Anglican heading. Quakers, for example, developed the autobiography or brief life as a literary genre, while the local Quaker Anthony Purver prepared a new translation of the Bible, a task also essayed by the Unitarian minister Edward Harwood. Two Nonconformist ministers, John Needham and Thomas Janes, published collections of moral and sacred poems, including their own work. One of the aims of these was to give children a suitable anthology of uplifting verse; Needham's may have been intended for use in the school of his Baptist co-pastor William Foot. But it was commonplace for the pious, both lay and clerical, to seek to harness literature to religious ends.[22]

Though common, this task had its problems and tensions. These concerned the correct use of the arts, both for general religious purposes and for specific denominational ends. Anglicans shared the doubts of other Protestants about how the arts might corrupt, while they also found themselves in competition with Dissenters in the exploitation, or non-exploitation, of particular artistic genres to strengthen their own church. All this coexisted with the pious hope that the arts might foster non-denominational Christianity within a divided city.

The oldest, but apparently the least worrying, of the dilemmas concerned the classical, and hence pagan, basis of so much culture. Some Bristolians

[21] A. R. Young, *Mrs Chapman's Portrait* (Bath, 1926), pp. 78–90; W. Roberts, *Memoirs of Life and Correspondence of Hannah More* (2nd edn, 4 vols., 1834); Meyerstein, *Life of Chatterton*; T. Chatterton, *The Complete Works*, ed. D. S. Taylor (2 vols., Oxford, 1971), I, 365–76, 412–19, 421–2, 452–68, 526–42, 546–59, 670–2.

[22] *Felix Farley's Bristol Journal*, 4 Nov. 1769; S. Crossman, *Young Man's Calling* (1675); A. Purver, *A New and Literal Translation* (2 vols., 1764); E. Harwood, *Liberal Translation of the New Testament* (1768); J. Needham, *Select Lessons in Prose and Verse* (3 edns, Bristol, 1755, 1765, 1778); T. Janes, *Beauties of the Poets* (1777).

criticized this dependence. Goldwin, though teaching the classics, stressed the primacy of biblical over pagan learning, quoted Old Testament poetry as his precedent and urged his pupils to study Christian verse.[23] Arthur Bedford in his various treatises on the use of music also insisted on the biblical heritage and basis of correct musical practice.

In doing so, Bedford was seeking to defend the complex church music he loved from accusations that it was a popish relic. It was the Roman Catholic associations of culture, notably in the visual arts and music, that caused the most concern. Despite their willingness to spend on decoration, Bristol's churches remained largely bare of direct religious representations. In 1731 the churchwardens of Clifton were successfully prosecuted in the church courts for putting up superstitious pictures, while a few years later Bishop Butler was criticized, especially by Presbyterians, for using stained glass and a marble cross in his private chapel. Musicians also faced suspicion of popery, reinforced no doubt by actual examples, such as Elway Bevin, cathedral organist to 1637, or the organ builder Renatus Harris at the end of the century. Visiting musicians from the Continent sometimes publicized the fact that they came from Protestant countries. Above all, as Bedford knew, the music of organs and complex plainsong was distrusted by many as popish compared to the simple metrical psalms and hymn-singing of parish churches.[24]

The basis of such concerns lay in the primacy of 'the Word' in Protestantism. Written texts were permitted where paintings were forbidden, while complex church music was criticized for distracting attention from the words. Those who defended artistic usages had to explain how the arts could heighten, not obscure, the effect of the words. Next to the Hogarth altar-piece at Redcliffe was a Bible open at the passage relating to the scene depicted.[25] The appeal of the arts to the senses was seen by many as contrasted with the appeal of the Word to the reason. The problem could also lie, however, with words, which might themselves distract from the Word. Rhetoric was equally distrusted, an attitude reflected in the regular disclaimers of literary merit by Bristol writers. Many drew a distinction between the religious 'kernel' of their message and its rhetorical shell and justified the latter only as a concession to a regrettable human sensuality. Verse, in particular, was justified as a means to reach those unwilling to read plain prose and to help memory. As the Bible seemed threatened by a flood of other publishing, authors such as Harwood or More sought to restate

[23] Goldwin, *Poetical Description*, preface; idem, *Light of an Exemplary Life* (Bristol, 1734).

[24] LPL, MSS, Court of Arches no. 4654, G102/90, D1054; BL, Add. MS 5811, fo. 95; W. Barrett, *History and Antiquities of the City of Bristol* (Bristol, 1789), p. 285; J. G. Hooper, *Life and Works of Elway Bevin* (Bristol, 1971); *New Grove Dictionary of Music and Musicians*, ed. S. Sadie (1980), under Bevin and the Harris family; Barry, 'Cultural Life', p. 198; A. Bedford, *Temple Musick* (1706), pp. 209–29.

[25] Barrett, *History*, p. 575.

biblical truths in polished literary forms. But to do so risked accusations that one was venturing on sacred subjects with unworthy aim or inadequate talent, and often it set off denominational or theological controversy.

As a general rule, Anglicans showed less anxiety about using the arts than Dissenters, although there is no clear contrast, rather a spectrum of opinions, varying slightly in each specific artistic dimension. The least distinction, as already indicated, can be seen in the field of literature. From the late seventeenth century both Anglicans and Dissenters, and both Whig and Tory Anglicans, were prepared to use poetry and prose to support their cause. In 1684 a Tory diatribe, *A Satyrical Vision*, claimed that Whigs were enemies of the muses, but this was no more reliable than Goldwin's claim, in his panegyrical *Poetical Description*, that he, like his Addisonian model, was rising above party dispute, rather than endorsing a mildly Whig *status quo*. In subsequent generations a succession of Tories opposed to the Whig supremacy both local and national returned to satirical mode to attack the establishment, culminating in Chatterton's work.[26] But such writing was generally overshadowed by less controversial literary pieces, stressing where possible the common Christian message and the role of literature as a means of transcending denominational boundaries.

This was much less possible in music and the visual arts, where the popish question was more pressing, and where artistic patronage and usage was much more closely tied to specific issues of church practice. In the seventeenth century the clearest example had concerned church music, and above all organs. The Civil War and Interregnum had seen the dismantling of a rich organ-playing inheritance in Bristol's churches, and until the 1680s only the cathedral had restored its organ. Then, as part of the Tory reaction, organs were placed in two parish churches, while the cathedral commissioned a new organ costing £850 from Harris in 1682. Nonetheless, most Anglican parishes, weakened and divided by events since 1640, lacked the resources or will to use the arts to differentiate their church life significantly from that of the mainstream Nonconformists, leaving the cathedral very much the principal representative of a different tradition.[27]

In the two decades after 1700, however, there was a resurgence in Anglican art. The parish churches were repaired and beautified with new ornaments; marble altars and pictures at the altars were installed, along with organs in the majority of parishes, often in conjunction with new galleries and other church furnishings. The chief mover in this process was Edward Colston, a Tory philanthropist who gave large sums to particular

[26] 'Phileroy', *A Satyrical Vision* (1684); G. Lamoine, *La Vie littéraire de Bath et de Bristol 1750–1800* (2 vols., Lille, 1978); D. S. Taylor, *Art of Thomas Chatterton* (Princeton, 1978).

[27] *Calendar of State Papers Domestic 1683–4*, p. 205; *HMC*, 5th Rep., App., p. 323; H. W. Hunt, *Bristol Cathedral Organ* (Bristol, 1907).

church projects and promised help to any parish church making such changes. As he intended, other Anglicans followed suit with legacies and subscriptions. Such measures formed part of a co-ordinated programme of Anglican resurgence, other elements of which were charity schools and Lenten lectures. Their common aim, to attract Bristolians back to the churches, was the avowed purpose of the many bells recast at this period with inscriptions of loyalty to the Church. At the same time the cathedral authorities were improving the church interior and upgrading their choir. Arthur Bedford, vicar of Temple, not only arranged for organ-playing in his own church and other improvements, but also sought to bring the artistic traditions of cathedral and parish closer together by reviving counterpoint singing in parish services. Bedford expounded at length in his books and his letters to the SPCK his belief that church music could provide the central thrust in Anglican revival, not only by improving church attendance but also by interesting the young in church music.[28]

This pattern, once established, was then maintained, with Anglican churches investing considerable sums in paintings, sculpture, architecture, music and bells. The most ambitious parish was St Mary, Redcliffe, where the vestry, already possessing the finest Gothic church in the region, made every effort to improve their services with new bells, a magnificent organ complete with the latest mechanisms and stops, and two new altar-pieces – that of 1708 being replaced by Hogarth's in 1756. There were even detailed discussions about a new spire. Although Anglican art generally adopted neo-classical forms, at Redcliffe and in some other parishes there was a new respect for the Gothic tradition, reflecting a new willingness to appeal to the medieval, even the Roman Catholic, legacy.[29]

How successful was this growing effort by the Church to capitalize on its cultural strengths and differentiate itself from other churches by cultural means? Arguably, it brought considerable success, though the evidence is only circumstantial. It seems significant that a stagnation in Nonconformist fortunes followed the early eighteenth-century Anglican campaign. In 1772 the newspaper report about the opening of the new organ at St Peter's commented on the presence of many Nonconformists, even Quakers, in the packed church.[30] It is tempting to look to such occasions, bringing the

[28] Here as elsewhere the evidence is largely drawn from churchwardens' accounts and other parish and cathedral records, supplemented by the records of gifts in Barrett, *History*, and *Bristol Charities*, ed. T. J. Manchee (2 vols., Bristol, 1831). See also Hooper, 'Survey'; J. Speller, 'Bristol Organs in 1710', *Organ*, 57 (1978–9), 85–90; T. Garrard, *Edward Colston* (Bristol, 1863); H. T. Ellacombe, *Church Bells of Gloucestershire* (Exeter, 1881); BL, Add. MS 5811, fo. 91; Bedford, *Temple Musick*, *Great Abuse* and *Excellency of Divine Music* (London, 1733); Bristol AO, P/Tem./Ka/4, fo. 65 and *passim*.

[29] Barrett, *History*, p. 573; *Felix Farley's Bristol Journal*, 4 June 1768; *Bristol Memorialist* (Bristol, 1816), pp. 79–80; Chatterton, *Works*, I, 640, 666–9.

[30] *Bristol Journal*, 4 Apr. 1772; *Bristol Gazette*, 9 Apr. 1772.

better-off of all denominations into regular contact with Anglican services, to explain the drift back to Anglicanism in these sectors of the population.

The Church may have been less strongly placed in the struggle to attract a broader public through congregational singing. Despite the building of organs the parish churches apparently retained the old method, whereby the parish clerk gave out the line before it was sung, together with the old tunes. Arthur Bedford, lamenting the fact that the devil had all the best tunes, had toyed with the notion of resetting carols and hymns to popular melodies, but it was left to the Methodists, in particular, to appeal to the public through vigorous hymn- and psalm-singing, often to lively tunes borrowed from secular ballads and operas. Once the Wesleyans had begun the trend, however, others felt bound to follow. The Baptists developed a strong hymnal tradition, while in 1758 the Lewin's Mead Presbyterian congregation decided to 'introduce a better means of singing psalms in public worship'. Faced with such competition, an increasing number of parish churches bought the new versions of the psalms for congregational use. Christmas Day 1770 was celebrated in several parishes with hymns sung from specially printed sheets, while a new emphasis was placed on singing by charity school pupils. Edmund Broderip's brother, the organist at Wells, published an edition of *Psalms, Hymns and Spiritual Songs* in both 1745 and 1769 and in 1772 the music-seller Naish advertised the volume *Divine Music*, composed by the late Bristol cathedral organist Combes and others, containing twenty psalm tunes in three parts adapted to be sung to the new version of the Psalms at the cathedral and 'in most places of public worship in Bristol'.[31]

Music offers the clearest illustration of the way in which cultural patronage by the churches was related to denominational rivalry, though similar trends are discernible in literature and the visual arts. Musical examples also provide the best evidence for the final theme of this essay, namely whether, in the patronage of artistic work by the Church, it was the interests of religion or those of the arts that fared best. We are fortunate to have the thoughts on this very issue of a contemporary Bristolian, Arthur Bedford. His starting-point was precisely the dilemma which G. V. Bennett identified for the Church after 1688, namely how it could re-establish its authority in an age of toleration and with a relatively free market in ideas and culture. In

[31] S. Seyer, *Serious Address to Members of the Church of England* (Bristol, 1772), p. 11; Bedford, *Great Abuse*, pp. 179–86, 229–31; Chatterton, *Works*, I, 447; E. Sharpe, 'Bristol Baptist College and the Church's Hymnody', *Baptist Quarterly*, n.s., 28 (1979–80), 7–16; Bristol AO, 6687 (1), 3 Jan., 26 Dec. 1758, 26 Dec. 1770, and 6687 (2), 1759, 1772–5; Bodl., G.A. Glos B4b (1); *Hymns for Christmas Day 1770* (Bristol, 1770); *Bristol Oracle and Country Advertiser*, 2 Feb. 1745; *Bristol Journal*, 4 Feb. 1769, 7 Mar. 1772; Hooper, 'Survey', pp. 271–80.

his writings about music (as well as the theatre) he explored ways in which the Church could regain the cultural initiative.[32]

Bedford identified two main problems. First was the boom in music publishing, which was flooding the market with products appealing to the lower tastes even of the educated, in part by the lure of fashion, and thus threatening to eclipse the inheritance of English religious music. The danger was directly parallel to the threat posed to religion by the outpouring of Arian and deist works since the end of licensing in 1695. Bedford wavered in his response between advocating renewed censorship and market restrictions or reliance on a massive programme of education for the young, in music as in religion, to cultivate better tastes. Meanwhile he appealed to all good Christians to exercise better judgement, so using consumer power to encourage publishers to produce better pieces.[33]

Second, Bedford blamed organists and choirs for not providing music of the correct quality or kind, so confirming the prejudice of many Churchmen against music. Organists were no longer giving their religious role priority, by composing and playing the serious divine music which would support and uplift the Church's ministry. Instead they were introducing into church playful voluntaries and musical trills which showed off their virtuosity but disrupted church services and destroyed the harmony of word and music. Their allegiances were not wholeheartedly to the Church, since they were also active as music and dancing masters and as players in theatres and taverns, where they learnt techniques and musical styles which they transferred to the church, whilst using their churches as concert-halls to impress prospective pupils. The only solution was to prevent organists from engaging in these other employments and to discipline choristers, who were notoriously irreverent and spent much of their time performing in theatres and alehouses. Once church music was revived its power would win converts and educate people to higher musical tastes.[34]

How accurate was his analysis? There was certainly a great deal of competition in music publishing with the traditional church music Bedford loved. Popular ballads and garlands had now been supplemented by the monthly collections and other volumes of fashionable songs and melodies. An impressionistic survey of the works advertised in Bristol, and of concert works performed, does not support the idea that serious church music was forced out of the market, if only because of Handel's enormous popularity,

[32] Since this essay was written, an important study of Bedford's musical ideology has appeared, namely W. Weber, *The Rise of the Musical Classics in Eighteenth-Century England* (Oxford, 1991), pp. 47–56 and *passim*.

[33] Bedford, *Great Abuse*, pp. 179–83; Bristol AO, P/Tem./Ka/4, fos. 65, 74, 106, 184.

[34] Bedford, *Great Abuse*, pp. 206–16, 235–57.

but certainly the English musical tradition before Purcell was largely ignored. The strength of church music probably owed something to the continued influence of church organists and settings in the organization of concerts. Despite this side of the coin, which Bedford had ignored, other Bristolians agreed that organists were being corrupted by their links with secular music. Both William Goldwin and John Wesley expressed dislike of the way in which organ voluntaries were interfering with the words of the service, while Thomas Chatterton contrasted the Italianate frills and flourishes of Edmund Broderip with the direct playing of another Bristol organist, Edward Allen, whose music he claimed appealed to the soul rather than to the senses. Bedford's allegations about organists' and choristers' indiscipline are supported by the continuing difficulties of the cathedral authorities. In 1682 the organist was expelled after a series of offences including keeping an alehouse and corrupting the choristers and there were repeated orders concerning absenteeism, lateness, drunkenness and insufficient practice.[35]

In explaining the musicians' divided loyalties, Bedford had stressed the attractions of teaching and secular playing. But as the SPCK secretary pointed out to him, it is hard to see how else such musicians could earn a living, given the inadequacy of church stipends, in Bristol as elsewhere. Ever since its foundation in 1542 the cathedral had been inadequately funded. Laud's survey of 1634 had criticized the pluralism of the lay singers, many of whom held posts in parish churches or other occupations that precluded proper attendance. One lay singer was reputed to earn £200 p.a., of which only £8 came from his official salary. After the Restoration pay was increased to £12 p.a., plus an annual dinner and it remained at this level until 1740 when some of the lay singers were given £16 p.a., a salary extended to all six in 1761. The four choristers were paid £4 p.a. and the two probationary choristers £2 p.a. from the seventeenth century until 1767, when a new scheme was introduced offering them £7 p.a., but withholding the extra money until they left the choir, when it would be paid as a lump sum if they were adjudged to have behaved well. The insufficiency of these salaries is suggested by the need to supplement them considerably when a talented singer threatened to leave. In 1718 Arbuthnot told Swift that Bristol had an extremely fine singer whom he hoped to poach, and it can be no coincidence that at that very time the salary of one of the lay singers, Carter, was increased to £45 p.a., made up partly by leaving other posts vacant, partly by using Carter to copy music and partly from general funds.

[35] Bristol Central Library, Bristol Collection, reference 6485 ('A Clergyman's Wish', by Goldwin); J. Wesley, *Journal*, ed. N. Curnock (8 vols., 1909–16), V, 290; Chatterton, *Works*, I, 516–17, 640–1; Bristol AO, DC/A/8/1, 17 Dec. 1682.

His stipend was later reduced to £30, a level occasionally granted to others.[36]

A similar position holds for the organists. Before 1640 cathedral organists had received £10 p.a., plus £3 6s 8d as master of the choristers, while parish organists only received £3 or £4 p.a. After 1660 the cathedral stipend rose to £17 and then £20 by 1669, while the few parish salaries recorded before 1700 suggest an income of £5–10 p.a. By leaving other positions vacant and giving up a rental income, the cathedral authorities raised their organist's pay to £40 p.a. by the 1720s, a level at which it remained until 1775. As a consequence most cathedral organists also held parish posts, in many cases two of them. In 1745 James Morley held three positions, bringing in £72 p.a. in all, though presumably he had to pay deputies. Parish salaries generally rose in the early eighteenth century to about £20 and then stabilized, although a few organists received less until the 1740s. Churches occasionally grumbled about the ensuing pluralism, but were not prepared to raise salaries.[37]

This is hardly surprising given the heavy expense of both purchasing and maintaining organs. They generally cost between £200 and £400, and annual upkeep included £2 for an organ-blower and perhaps £5 for an organ-builder. In a few cases the organist offered to bear this cost himself in return for a larger salary. St Augustine's parish, which did not have an organ until one was given by the prospective Tory radical MP, Henry Cruger, in 1772, managed to raise the £20 organist's salary, but also looked to its parishioners to encourage the organist by a private subscription.[38] It was but a short step from this to the benefit concerts which had rewarded the cathedral organists since at least 1726.

It is clear that, in music at least, the Church had to accept a partnership with other forms of support, because the resources were lacking to offer complete support to talented musicians. The consequent pluralism and dependence on lay financial support, and hence approval, were not unique to the Church's cultural position, of course, but reflected its general urban condition. Through such compromises the Church was able to sustain a level of services which its legal endowments and official status could not themselves support – the growth of alternative means of support for

[36] Bristol AO, P/Tem./Ka/4, fo. 184, DC/A/8/1, 16 May 1730, DC/A/8/2, 1 Dec. 1767, DC/A/9/2/1, 1719; *HMC*, 4th Rep., App., pp. 141–4; *Correspondence of Jonathan Swift*, ed. H. Williams (5 vols., Oxford, 1963), 11 Dec. 1718.

[37] J. G. Hooper, 'Organists and Masters of Choristers of Bristol Cathedral', *Friends of Bristol Cathedral Annual Reports* (1967–8), 17–27, (1968–9), 16–23; Bristol AO, P/AS/ChW 1735–55 and /V/1a 1734, P/XCh/ChW/1e 1746–56, P/Tem./La/2 1771.

[38] Bristol AO, P/AS/V/ib 1761–2, P/St Aug/ChW/1b 1772–5; Barrett, *History*, p. 401; *Felix Farley's Bristol Journal*, 23 Mar. 1771.

musicians might be said to have offered commercial sponsorship to maintain the Church. In some cases this clearly generated conflicts of interest, robbing the Church of full control over its employees and over the cultural forms which it sought to exploit.

Yet equally, as this essay began by showing, cultural provision was still heavily dependent on the Church, as well as vice versa. Both in practical terms and in the legitimation of new cultural activity, the Church's support was important, not least because of a long-lasting distrust of a totally commercial culture controlled by market forces alone. This interdependence lies at the heart of understanding eighteenth-century England as neither a confessional state where the established Church could afford to ignore voluntary support, nor a secular consumer society without any use for an established Church, but rather as a commercial society with genuine religious pluralism, that is with a genuine pluralism based on genuine religious allegiances. The Church of England weathered its crisis to emerge secure but altered in such conditions; its cultural patronage not only illustrates how this occurred but perhaps goes some way to explain why it did so.

9 Latitudinarianism at the parting of the ways: a suggestion

Martin Fitzpatrick

The discussion that follows arises from an attempt to understand the problems faced by church reformers in the mid-eighteenth century. It relates the most controversial reformist work of the time, Archdeacon Blackburne's *Confessional*, to the Latitudinarian tradition and at the same time places it in the context of Enlightenment thinking. It begins by suggesting that although Latitudinarians and liberal Dissenters were facing similar problems, those facing the former were more acute. In order to demonstrate this, I have the temerity to attempt a brief characterization of the Latitudinarian tradition, before trying to demonstrate that the tensions in the tradition which had broadly been creative in the seventeenth century were ceasing to be so by the mid-eighteenth century. Blackburne's work attacked key elements in the Latitudinarian synthesis, and, in consequence, Latitudinarian reformers were forced to regroup leaving them in a weak position to resist the tide of conservative orthodox reaction which swept the country in the 1790s.

I

It is not difficult to see many links and parallels between Latitudinarians and Old Dissenters in the eighteenth century. They shared in many ways a common theological, philosophical and political outlook. They emphasized the relationship between religion and morality, between piety and civic virtue. They were tolerant of differences, stressed the common core of Christianity and placed the creeds and dogma at the margins of their concerns. They were not prepared to allow philosophical differences to outweigh their commitment to moderation and, in their different contexts, to the *via media.* Many still hoped for a comprehensive establishment. They were the English counterparts of the moderate Enlightenment which Henry May has discerned in America.[1] But, like their American counterparts, in one respect they were quite immoderate, and that was in their opposition to

[1] H. E. May, *The Enlightenment in America* (New York, 1976).

Roman Catholicism. Their vision of a better world was profoundly Protestant. Many aspects of their outlook and relationships were unchanged in the late eighteenth century. Dissenters and Latitudinarians continued to coexist for the most part in mutual admiration. Richard Watson included Dissenting and unorthodox tracts in his collection of *Theological Tracts*, and earned the admiration of Dissenters as different as Edward Harwood and Joseph Priestley.[2] William Paley's *The Principles of Moral and Political Philosophy* (1785) was described by John Disney as 'a most excellent work' and was subsequently cited by Samuel Heywood in his *The Dissenters Right to a Compleat Toleration Asserted*, one of the most important treatises on toleration in the late eighteenth century.[3] Such mutual admiration led to the formation of the Society for the Promotion of Scriptural Knowledge in 1784. Yet in the late eighteenth century Latitudinarianism and Old Dissent were undergoing changes. Both were subject to radical forces which would strengthen Old Dissent and weaken Latitudinarianism. Much of this process has been well described by John Gascoigne, but he has emphasized the general coherence of the late eighteenth-century world of Anglican Latitudinarians and of Rational Dissent.[4] My emphasis is slightly different. I see the development of a more radical Enlightenment, and the loss of Latitudinarians to Dissent as marking the end of the Anglican–Latitudinarian compromise. I believe that at the heart of the break up of that compromise were intellectual forces which it could no longer hold in check, and that, although Latitudinarians found ways of adapting to the new situation, the loss of their bolder reforming spirits to Dissent, coupled with the nature of their revised beliefs, made it difficult for Latitudinarians to resist the tendency in the 1790s to regard reformers as dangerous enemies to the church and state.[5]

II

Even as Latitudinarianism was in the process of formation, its adherents were accused of unorthodoxy. Chillingworth was accused of Socinianism.[6]

[2] R. Watson, *Anecdotes of the Life of Richard Watson, Bishop of Landaff* (2nd edn, 2 vols., 1818), I, 222–6; T. J. Brain, 'Some Aspects of the Life and Works of Richard Watson, Bishop of Llandaff, 1737–1816', PhD dissertation, University of Wales, 1982, pp. 126–7.

[3] John Disney Manuscript Diary, 29 Sept. 1784; [S. Heywood], *The Dissenters Right to a Compleat Toleration Asserted* (1787), pp. 100–1, 106–11. See also the conclusion of *Bishop Hoadly's Refutation of Bishop Sherlock's Argument Against a Repeal of the Test and Corporation Acts* (Birmingham, 1787). I am grateful to Dr D. O. Thomas for allowing me to consult Disney's diary.

[4] 'Anglican Latitudinarianism and Political Radicalism in the Late Eighteenth Century', *History*, 71 (1986), 22–38.

[5] See N. U. Murray, 'The Influence of the French Revolution on the Church of England and its Rivals, 1789–1802', DPhil dissertation, University of Oxford, 1975, pp. 80–124.

[6] H. Baker, *The Wars of Truth. Studies in the Decay of Christian Humanism in the Earlier Seventeenth Century* (Gloucester, Mass., 1952, repr. 1969), p. 273.

Later figures were undoubtedly heterodox: Samuel Clarke was an Arian as was William Whiston. Recently, in a robust defence of Latitudinarianism Roger Emerson has stressed the extent to which its doctrinal content was profoundly traditional: 'it was an Anglicanism that could not include the Socinians or Arians although it could tolerate them'.[7] Indeed, it is true that Whiston was expelled from Cambridge and his biographer, James E. Force, makes an active distinction between Newtonianism and Latitudinarianism.[8] Nonetheless, something important in the Latitudinarian character is missed if it is portrayed as doctrinally orthodox but reticent on matters of doctrine for pragmatic or emollient reasons. There were, I believe, a number of elements at play in the Latitudinarian religious view. First, there was an emphasis on simplicity and rationality; second, there was the belief that reason and revelation spoke the same language and produced the same enlightenment, for the 'understanding of man is the candle of the Lord';[9] third, that the essential truths were contained in the Bible; fourth, the optimism that these essential truths were accessible to all men; fifth, that apart from these truths, all other truths were matters of opinion; finally, that men may know God in various ways, and that God would not be offended by a belief sincerely held. Such views were formed from a combination of Protestantism and Christian humanism. They ran counter to the religious absolutism of the Roman Catholics and the Puritans, but they also embodied within them far more tolerant attitudes and a far weaker doctrinal emphasis than most Anglicans were prepared to accept before the Glorious Revolution and a substantial number afterwards. It was a synthesis which depended as much on faith as logical coherence. It could be easily threatened by too great an emphasis on any one component at the expense of the others: too great an emphasis upon rationality could lead away from Christian orthodoxy to natural religion; too great an

[7] R. Emerson, 'Latitudinarianism and the English Deists', in *Deism, Masonry and the Enlightenment*, ed. J. A. Leo Lemay (Delaware, 1987), pp. 41–2. That Emerson overplays Tillotson's devotion to the creeds of the Church is suggested by Tillotson's comment in a letter of 1694, regarding the Athanasian Creed, 'I wish we were well rid of it'. Cf. Robert Wallace, *Antitrinitarian Biography* (3 vols., 1850), I, 273–5, cit. D. G. Wigmore Beddoes, *Yesterday's Radicals. A Study of the Affinity between Unitarianism and Broad Church Anglicanism in the Nineteenth Century* (Cambridge and London, 1971), p. 127 n. 26, see also p. 18. On Tillotson's attitude towards the heterodox see, G. Reedy, SJ, *The Bible and Reason. Anglicans and Scripture in Late Seventeenth-Century England* (Philadelphia, 1985), pp. 126–30, 134–5.

[8] J. E. Force, *William Whiston: Honest Newtonian* (Cambridge, 1985), p. 119.

[9] Prov. 20. 27. This was the text for Nathanael Culverwell's, *An Elegant and Learned Discourse of the Light of Nature with Several Other Treatises* (Oxford, 1669) in which he defended the use of reason from its detractors and abusers; on the relationship between reason and revelation amongst the Latitudinarians, besides Reedy, *The Bible and Reason*, see P. Harrison, *'Religion' and the Religions in the English Enlightenment* (Cambridge, 1990); D. A. Pailin, *Attitudes to Other Religions. Comparative Religion in Seventeenth- and Eighteenth-Century Britain* (Manchester, 1984), pp. 23–44, and H. G. Reventlow, *The Authority of the Bible and the Rise of the Modern World* (1984), pp. 223–85.

emphasis upon individual conscience could lead to a religious individualism which was incompatible with any formal ecclesiastical organization.[10] Yet, in a sense, Latitudinarianism was an attempt to cope with these very problems. The shift of religious authority from tradition to the Bible was much approved by its early figures. Chillingworth declared in *The Religion of the Protestants* (1637) that 'the Bible, I say the Bible only, is the religion of Protestants'. He argued thus in part to hold in check the differences which were dividing the Anglicans. His very next sentence is:

> Whatsoever else they believe besides it, and the plain, irrefragable, indubitable consequences of it, well may they hold it as a matter of opinion: but as matter of faith and religion, neither can they with coherence to their own grounds believe it themselves, nor require the belief of it of others, without most high and most schismatical presumption.[11]

Later, Samuel Clarke, who cited this text, suggested that Protestants would have been spared serious divisions had they held to these simple beliefs.[12] Indeed, Latitudinarian 'liberality' arose primarily from a desire to create a united, comprehensive Protestant Church, and their commitment to toleration of Dissent was secondary to promoting tolerance within the Anglican Church.[13] For some, if schism could be overcome there would be a glorious prospect for universal Christian enlightenment,[14] but for all Latitudinarians it was important that men maintained a measured attitude to the truths of reason and revelation. If the claims were pitched too high it could lead to dogmatism and to a flight from reason. Thus though they vested authority in the Bible, they accepted that it could be interpreted in different ways, that it was obscure on many issues and silent on others. There were, they conceded, many things which one could not know with certainty. These were the 'things indifferent' which horrified Puritan and High Anglican alike. Rather like Descartes and his philosophical followers, they combined scepticism with certainty.[15] Whatever the religious or philosophical coherence involved in such a stance, it did cause difficulties in relation to the doctrines of the Church as embodied in the Thirty-Nine

[10] Baker, *Wars of Truth*, p. 192.

[11] W. Chillingworth, *The Works of William Chillingworth* (10th edn, 1742), para. 56, p. 354; Baker, *Wars of Truth*, p. 222.

[12] S. Clarke, *The Works of Samuel Clarke DD, vol. IV: The Scripture Doctrine of the Trinity* (1738), p. iv.

[13] J. van den Berg, *The Idea of Tolerance and the Act of Toleration* (Dr Williams's Trust, 1989), p. 8.

[14] Culverwell, *Light of Nature*, treatise 'The Schisme', pp. 23–4.

[15] See, e.g., Chillingworth, *Religion of Protestants*, in *Works of Chillingworth*, ch. 2, sects. 150–2, pp. 123–4; Culverwell, *Light of Nature*, pp. 1–3; R. Orr, *Reason and Authority. The Thought of William Chillingworth* (Oxford, 1967), pp. 71–114, explains the nature of Chillingworth's adherence to the Bible; see also, Baker, *Wars of Truth*, pp. 223–7; J. Gascoigne, *Cambridge in the Age of the Enlightenment* (Cambridge, 1989), pp. 44–6.

Articles. These Articles were regarded as impediments to the essential faith and harmful to the wider cause of Christianity. For Chillingworth,

This vain conceit, that we can speak of the things of God better than in the words of God: this deifying our own interpretations, and tyrannous inforcing them upon others; this restraining of the word of God from that latitude and generality, and the understandings of men from that liberty, wherein Christ and the Apostles left them, is and hath been the only fountain of all the schisms of the church, and is, and hath been that which makes them immortal [i.e. schisms].[16]

If one had to have a creed, then the simplest was the best, which was, according to Chillingworth, the Apostles' Creed.[17] He and other Latitudinarians had conscientious difficulties in subscribing to the Thirty-Nine Articles. In the eighteenth century, many Latitudinarians found that Samuel Clarke's formula for subscribing provided a way out of their difficulties. He argued in his introduction to his *The Scripture Doctrine of the Trinity* (1712) that Protestants, unlike the Roman Catholics, regarded their doctrines as 'human and fallible' and required subscription to their church articles only insofar as their meaning was consonant with Scripture and, crucially, that it was up to individuals to decide whether or not this was so: 'every person may reasonably agree to such forms, whenever he can in any sense at all reconcile them with Scripture'.[18] But not all with Latitudinarian sympathies were convinced by this loose formulation. William Whiston regarded Clarke's view as prevaricating, and John Jackson, who usually defended Clarke in all things, on this issue dissented from his mentor. He decided to refuse all preferment which involved subscribing again to the Thirty-Nine Articles. Other Latitudinarian clergymen followed suit, while others contemplating taking orders decided against a career in the Church. It is easy to minimize the real conscientious difficulties that Anglicans faced on this issue. Even Hoadly, who, having offered Jackson preferment, insisted upon his re-subscribing the Articles, was not perhaps betraying his own principles. As John Gascoigne has pointed out, the principles of the Latitudinarians were intended to be healing principles;[19] it was hard for them to see them applied in such a way as might introduce new rifts into a Church which had with difficulty survived the Glorious Revolution. Whiston might argue that he preferred integrity to orthodoxy,[20] but the majority of eighteenth-century Latitudinarians did not want to face that stark choice: in keeping with the tradition, they wanted reconciliation not confrontation. Yet this was possible only so long

16 Chillingworth, *Religion of Protestants*, ch. 4, sect. 16, p. 203, cit. imperfectly [F. Blackburne], *The Confessional* (3rd edn, enlarged, 1770), p. 52 n.

17 Baker, *Wars of Truth*, p. 223; Orr, *Reason and Authority*, pp. 88, 138.

18 Clarke, *Scripture Doctrine of the Trinity*, pp. ii, ix-xii; J. P. Ferguson, *Dr Samuel Clarke* (Kineton, 1976), p. 179.

19 Gascoigne, *Cambridge*, p. 132.

20 Ferguson, *Samuel Clarke*, p. 190.

as the delicate balance of the elements within Latitudinarianism was maintained. Although the subscription controversy died down, it cast a shadow over the lives of many Anglicans who maintained an uneasy loyalty to their preferred church. Moreover the issue did not die down completely; it continued to smoulder in the background with occasional bursts of activity, such as that caused by the Reverend John Jones's *Free and Candid Disquisitions Relating to the Church of England* (1749), which argued for reform on a broad range of church issues and for a modified form of subscription.[21] But the work which really stirred the flames into dangerous life was Francis Blackburne's *The Confessional: Or a Full and Free Inquiry into the Right, Utility, Edification, and Success, of Establishing Systematical Confessions of Faith and Doctrine in Protestant Churches*, published in 1766.[22] Before discussing it, however, I want to examine a work known to Blackburne which was not about the subscription issue, but which was representative of the mid-eighteenth-century Enlightenment in England and of advanced Latitudinarian thinking. I want to do so, because it is indicative of how intellectual change would make the Latitudinarian compromise difficult to sustain.

David Hartley was the son of a clergyman. He was educated at Cambridge and it was intended that he would follow in his father's footsteps. However, while at university he developed scruples about subscribing to the Thirty-Nine Articles and chose instead to make a career for himself in medicine. In 1749, he published his great work, *Observations on Man, His Frame, His Duty and His Expectations*. This systematic and developed exposition of the Lockean doctrine of the association of ideas was potentially disruptive of Latitudinarian thinking.[23] In particular, Hartley allowed no room for the distinction between speculative and certain truths. In effect, he adapted the Christian humanist belief that 'ideally all man's faculties may be fused in the pursuit of that goodness which constitutes the highest truth'[24] to the new spirit of the scientific revolution. He developed the idea not merely of the progress of knowledge but also of spiritual progress. This allowed no room for scepticism, and made the furtherance of truth of paramount importance. In that cause, Hartley argued for free inquiry and vigorous open debate: 'It is a great insult offered to the truths of

[21] [J. Jones], *Free and Candid Disquisitions Relating to the Church of England and the Means of Advancing Religion Therein* (2nd edn, 1750), ch. 6, pp. 102–3. See R. B. Barlow, *Citizenship and Conscience* (Philadelphia, 1962), pp. 116–17.

[22] [J. Disney], *A Short View of the Controversies Occasioned by the Confessional*... (1773), lists 101 works.

[23] On the problems of interpreting Hartley, see I. C. Douglas, 'David Hartley and the Perfectibility of Man', MPhil dissertation, University of Leeds, 1989.

[24] Baker, *Wars of Truth*, p. 93.

religion, to suppose that they want the same kind of assistance as impostures, human projects, or worldly designs. Let every man be allowed to think, speak, and write, freely; and then the errors will combat one another, and leave truth unhurt.'[25] This plea came at the end of an argument against 'creeds, articles or systems of faith'[26] and its corollary that one should not be subject to civil penalties for beliefs or lack of them. As a good Latitudinarian, he believed that the essential truths of Christianity were clear enough, and that it was sufficient for each man to take the Scriptures for his guide. Preachers should avoid controversy and preach practical subjects. More arcane matters were most fittingly the subject of printed controversy.[27] Like Edmund Law, Hartley believed in the progress of religious knowledge.[28] Formulations of faith merely served to impede that progress; they neither guarded nor preserved the faith. Ultimately, Hartley expected all religious institutions to be swept away at the inauguration of the millennium. Yet the radicalism of his position remained embryonic. His attitude towards change was passive. He placed himself in the hands of God. He mapped out an ideal state but did not recommend any positive steps to bring it about. In that respect, his millenarianism resembled, to a degree, that of the Newtonian divines whom Margaret Jacob has studied.[29] No sooner had Hartley argued against human formulations of faith and for free inquiry, than he cautioned his readers against criticizing those who subscribed to such creeds. He suggested that 'in certain cases', 'it may be necessary to submit to some forms'. As Christians one should not condemn each other but should devote oneself to serving God, for, '[that] is the only thing of importance; *circumcision and uncircumcision are equally nothing. Let every man abide in the same calling wherein he was called.* Only, where a plain act of insincerity is required, this approaches to the case of eating in the idol's temple, and gives great offence to others.'[30]

Such views did not in any immediate way threaten the Latitudinarian position. Indeed, one can see Hartley struggling to maintain something of a *via media*, trying to reconcile the need for change with the demands of obedience.[31]

But his work contained a potent long-term threat, which was realized in the work of Francis Blackburne, who had, as a young man entering the

[25] D. Hartley, *Observations on Man, His Frame, His Duty and His Expectations: In Two Parts* (5th edn, 1810), II, 368. [26] Ibid., II, 363.

[27] Cf. Kant's view that the public use of reason should lead to the progressive reformation of religious establishments. *Kant's Political Writings*, ed. H. Reiss (Cambridge, 1970), pp. 56–9.

[28] R. S. Crane, 'Anglican Apologetics and the Idea of Progress, 1699–1745', in his *The Idea of the Humanities* (2 vols., Chicago and London, 1967), esp. I, 259–77.

[29] See M. Jacob, *The Newtonians and the English Revolution* (Hassocks, 1976).

[30] Hartley, *Observations*, II, 369. [31] Ibid., pp. 383–5.

Church, swallowed Samuel Clarke's argument for subscription; this had brought on a lifetime of spiritual dyspepsia. To ease his troublesome conscience he spent many years collecting information on the issue of subscription. This he fed into his *Confessional.* It gives the work a scholarly character, a diffuse form and a comparatively blunt controversial edge. It was a work of erudite iconoclasm; page after page is given over to confutation of the various arguments and schemes for formulation of belief adopted by Protestants since the Reformation. Here we find no crisp proposals for reform. Blackburne's precise proposals tend to be buried deep within the work. Yet the core of his stand is stated clearly enough at the beginning:

JESUS CHRIST hath, by his gospel, called all men unto liberty, the glorious liberty of the sons of God, and restored them to the privilege of working out their own salvation by their own understandings and endeavours. For this work of salvation sufficient means are afforded in the holy scriptures, without having sufficient recourse to the doctrines and commandments of men. In these scriptures all things needful for spiritual living and man's soul's health are mentioned and shewed. Consequently, faith and conscience, having no dependence upon man's laws, are not compelled by man's authority.[32]

Blackburne in this way took his stand on the Reformation principles of obedience to conscience and the sufficiency of the Scriptures.[33] Hartley had kept in check the elements in his work which might destabilize Latitudinarianism by retaining a Christian humanist eirenicism. Blackburne, in combining Hartley's attitude towards truth with his Reformation principles, was led to attempt to reshape Latitudinarianism. It is not so much that he did not share an attachment to many aspects of the Latitudinarian synthesis, rather that, given his enlightened emphasis on truth above all things, he was bound to seek the creation of a new set of priorities. Thus he accepted the view that the Scriptures were open to a variety of interpretations,[34] but, since he followed Hartley in believing that all truth was important, he could not fall back on the distinction between essential truths and things indifferent, and, since he followed the Christian humanist belief that the true and the good were intimately related, he also confuted the Lockean distinction between practical conduct and speculative opinion. He thought that there were few truths or errors of a religious kind which could be described as 'merely speculative'.[35] In consequence, *The Confessional* upset the finely balanced Latitudinarian scales which on the one side allowed Latitudinarians to dissent privately from some of the doctrines of the Church and on

[32] [Blackburne], *Confessional*, pp. 1–2.

[33] See 'Luther's Answer before the Emperor and the Diet of Worms, 18 April 1521', in E. G. Rupp and B. Drewery, *Martin Luther* (1970), p. 60.

[34] [Blackburne], *Confessional*, pp. 4–5.

[35] Ibid., pp. 392–3.

the other to feel justified that their conduct was in the interests of their Church. If one goes through *The Confessional* one can extract the following radical propositions which show just how far Blackburne was upsetting the balance:

1 No church has the right to 'require assent to a certain sense of scripture, exclusive of other sense, without an unwarrantable interference' with the cardinal tenet of the Reformation, the right of private judgement.[36]
2 No case can be made for confessions of faith based merely on their utility or expediency.[37]
3 It was historically inaccurate to suggest that the compilers of the Thirty-Nine Articles had intended them to be subscribed in a Latitudinarian manner. They believed them to be true 'in one precise uniform sense'.[38]
4 All creeds, confessions and ecclesiastical forms which were not 'agreeable to the word of God' should be phased out.[39]
5 Church establishments should be entirely independent of the state.[40]
6 The proper application of scriptural principles would lead to reforms in the role and emoluments of the clergy.[41]
7 The Anglican Church should become sufficiently comprehensive to include heterodox as well as orthodox Protestants.[42]
8 The magistrate's right to discriminate on a religious basis was limited to the right to restrain 'overt acts of opposition to the righteous regulations of civil society'.[43]

One can see that it would not be difficult to draw up the whole programme of religious radicals in the late eighteenth century from Blackburne's work: the total separation of church and state; complete liberty of conscience; and universal toleration. The least important part of that programme, that for a reformed, more liberal and comprehensive Church, was, however, his prime concern. Indeed, his own aims were far more limited than the principles which he enunciated. Moreover, such was the weight of Latitudinarian passivity that he felt he had to justify doing anything at all. Others before him had made radical declarations of principle, but had gone on to show that they were inapplicable to the world as it is.[44] Even the powerful intellect of Hartley had lent itself to the cause of accepting the *status quo*, if only on an interim basis. Blackburne's first task, therefore, was to demonstrate the need for deeds to follow arguments. He cited Hartley against himself, pointing out that he warned those who failed in their duty that they

[36] Ibid., pp. 50–1. [37] Ibid., pp. 61–81. [38] Ibid., p. 90. [39] Ibid., pp. 419–20.
[40] Ibid., advertisement and pp. xvi-xvii, 256–7.
[41] Ibid., p. 403. See also preface, 1st edn, pp. xiii–xiv, 254. [42] Ibid., pp. 38–9, 401.
[43] Ibid., p. 122. Cf. R. Price, *Britain's Happiness and the Proper Improvement of it* (1759), pp. 7–9.
[44] Blackburne uses Hoadly to illustrate this point. *Confessional*, pp. 374–5, and preface, 1st edn., pp. liv-lv.

would bring down upon their heads 'the prophetical censures in the highest degree'.[45] The whole passage runs as follows:

> when it so happens, that persons in high stations in the church have their eyes enlightened, and see the corruptions and deficiencies of it, they must incur the prophetical censures in the highest degree, if they still concur, nay, if they do not endeavour to reform and purge out these defilements. And though they cannot, according to this proposition, expect entire success; yet they may be blessed with such a degree as will abundantly compensate their utmost endeavours, and rank them with the prophets and apostles.[46]

Here we see Blackburne drawing out the argument for reform from Hartley and ignoring his hesitations. His own researches into the history of the Church Articles had convinced him, too, that the spirit of compromise and the politics of expediency had generally done more harm than good. There was therefore an empirical as well as a rational basis for his belief in the importance of acting upon one's own convictions. Nonetheless, his actual proposals for reform were much less bold than one might expect either from his stark proclamation of the case for Christian liberty in his opening chapter or from the detailed arguments within his work. The reasons for this are threefold. In his idiosyncratic way he was devoted to the Anglican Church; Dissent held few attractions for him. He was offered the lucrative pulpit of the London Old Jewry on the death of Samuel Chandler in 1766. Since he had sworn a self-denying ordinance against accepting any preferment in the Church which involved re-subscribing to the Thirty-Nine Articles, this was an obvious way of bettering his material position. His stipend was £150 per annum, the Old Jewry was worth £400 per annum.[47] The second and third reasons are related. Blackburne was a genuine Latitudinarian in that his great desire was to see a more comprehensive Church of England. However, he had a special incentive for wishing to see this development. Latitudinarians were traditionally hostile to Roman Catholicism and objected to its claims to exclusive possession of religious truth. Blackburne's hatred of papists was, however, somewhat excessive. He was closely associated with that arch-anti-papist of the mid-eighteenth century, Thomas Hollis of Lincoln's Inn. Hollis came to believe that the Anglican Church had gone soft on popery, and that increasingly it was in

[45] Ibid., pp. 374–5; Hartley, *Observations*, II, 383–4.

[46] Hartley, *Observations*, II, 383–4.

[47] F. Blackburne, *Works, Theological and Miscellaneous* (7 vols., Cambridge, 1805), I, lxxii-lxxv; T. Belsham, *Memoirs of the Late Theophilus Lindsey, MA* (1812), pp. 17–18 n.*, p. 496. Blackburne had contemplated leaving the Church in the 1750s but had concluded that the Church, despite its faults, was superior to Dissent. He sought to convince Theophilus Lindsey of the need to remain within the Church; when he did eventually leave in 1773 he was mortified. See Dr Williams's Library (DWL), MS 12.52, esp. fos. 32, 36, 100. I am grateful to the Trustees of Dr Williams's Library for permission to cite manuscripts in their possession.

the hands of crypto-Catholics.[48] He was able to make connexions which can only be described as those of a slightly disordered imagination. He linked the Anglican attempt to create a colonial episcopate with a resurgence of Catholicism in England and on the Continent. Yet his ideas were not sufficiently crazy for others to shun them. The European campaign against the Society of Jesus was reaching its height and Hollis collected and distributed many of the tracts against the society. What he feared was that the Enlightenment, rather than undermining Catholicism, would take a Catholic form. The signs were that the new knowledge instead of leading to the reform of Catholicism was being accommodated within it. Blackburne cited the *Encyclopédie* as an example of such a process. Its contributors were heterodox in their thoughts but not in their behaviour for they still 'complied with the forms of the church'.[49] More importantly, Blackburne was convinced that Roman Catholicism was on the increase in England. He had had *The Confessional* on the stocks for a long time, but had judged that the climate was not right for a favourable reception. That view did not change, but he came to believe that it was a matter of urgency that the Church should be reformed in order to strengthen its Protestant character, and, encouraged by Thomas Hollis, he decided to publish in 1766.[50]

The Confessional was a modest success. It quickly went into a second edition which was followed by a third in 1770, and it engendered a controversy in which the Archbishop of Canterbury took part anonymously.[51] However, as noted, as a manifesto for reform it was curiously limited. Just as Blackburne's attitude to toleration proved to be less enlightened than the principles which he enunciated, so too his proposals for church reform were more confined than the principles upon which they were based. Despite what I have said about the logic of his principles driving him to take action which would threaten the Latitudinarian *via media*, it has to be conceded that the impulse for publication did not arise solely from intellectual principles and that the measures which he undertook subsequently were not in themselves contrary to Latitudinarian ideas. After all the pages of close confutation, Blackburne's proposals for reform were contained on little more than a single page. He suggested that the clergy should be required to subscribe only to certain requirements already made at the office of ordination, the doctrinal part of which embodied an

48 On Hollis, see C. Robbins, *The Eighteenth-Century Commonwealthman* (Cambridge, Mass., 1959); C. Robbins, 'The Strenuous Whig, Thomas Hollis of Lincoln's Inn', *William and Mary Quarterly*, 3rd ser., 7 (1950), 406–53; P. Marshall, 'Thomas Hollis 1727–74; the Bibliophile as Libertarian', *Bulletin of the John Rylands Library* (1983–4), 246–63; W. H. Bond, *Thomas Hollis of Lincoln's Inn. A Whig and his Books* (Cambridge, 1990).

49 [Blackburne], *Confessional*, preface, 1st edn, p. lxxiii n.

50 [F. Blackburne], *Memoirs of Thomas Hollis* (2 vols., 1780), I, 302.

51 *The Autobiography of Thomas Secker, Archbishop of Canterbury*, ed. J. S. Macauley and R. W. Greaves (Lawrence, Kans., 1988), fos. 72–4 and p. 176.

agreement that the Scriptures were sufficient for salvation. No commitment was to be made to any theological system or particular set of doctrines; the subscriber should profess his belief in the divine authority of the Scriptures and undertake conscientiously to pursue scriptural knowledge and his pastoral role.[52]

Blackburne can be forgiven for hesitating to publish his work, for in it he had committed himself unequivocally to following up his words with action.[53] He declared that those who saw the need for reform should be prepared to 'try their strength', for 'Men's endeavours in this, as well as in the other cases, are not to be suspended by the improbability of success, or even by trials apparently fruitless. We are not judges what success our pious endeavours may have in due time. *The Kingdom of GOD cometh not with observation*.'[54]

The task which Blackburne set himself was an impossible one, and he was well aware of that. In July 1769, he wrote to the Dissenting minister William Turner of Wakefield, 'I have not the remotest prospect of anything which deserves the name of Reformation in our very unedifying establishment. But while we believe it to be the cause of Christianity – we must press towards the mark as we can, and work our way with such talents and Instruments as we are supplied by providence.'[55] And press on he did. In collaboration with like-minded Churchmen, notably his son-in-law, Theophilus Lindsey, vicar of Catterick, and John Jebb, fellow of Peterhouse, he formed the association, known as the Feathers Tavern Association, in July 1770, with a view to petitioning Parliament for clerical relief from subscription and for lay relief in the universities. What then followed is, at least in outline, a fairly familiar story. After travelling the length and breadth of the land collecting signatures, only some 200 clergymen and a further 50 laymen signed the petition. This was presented to the Commons in February 1772 and duly defeated by a large margin, only 71 MPs voting for it. On re-presentation in 1774, it was not put to the vote.[56] Some leading figures among the Latitudinarians, such as Edmund Law, did not even sign it. Was this then a storm in the Latitudinarian tea cup?

In one sense it was. Latitudinarianism certainly did not die. At this time Richard Watson was just beginning to emerge as the leading advocate for church reform and William Paley as a compelling theoretician of Latitudinarianism. Both were sympathetic to the petition. Watson, who was always a somewhat self-conscious individualist,[57] had, however, advocated an

[52] [Blackburne], *Confessional*, pp. 421–4. [53] Ibid., pp. 414–17.
[54] Ibid., p. 417. [55] *Monthly Magazine*, Dec. 1796, p. 888.
[56] See G. M. Ditchfield, 'The Subscription Issue in British Parliamentary Politics, 1772–9', *Parliamentary History*, 7 (1988), 45–80.
[57] Watson, *Anecdotes*, I, 208.

approach to the bishops rather than Parliament. Paley had refused to sign the petition, quipping that he could not afford to keep a conscience, but he did support the movement in print. And when it failed, they remained, as did most supporters of the petition, within the Church of England. That was certainly in keeping with the whole ethos of Latitudinarianism. Watson's work is also testimony to the way in which the traditional Latitudinarian synthesis could be restated. He combined a belief in the value of free inquiry as a means of testing truth[58] with an acceptance of the limitations of human reasoning. Free inquiry did not so much lead one to the truth, rather it led one to be both undogmatic and, on many issues, agnostic. He wrote in his *Anecdotes*,

The most undecided men on doubtful points, are often those who have bestowed most time in the investigation of them, whether the points respecting divinity, jurisprudence, or policy. He who examines only one side of a question, and gives his judgment, gives it improperly, though he may be on the right side. But he who examines both sides, and after examination gives his assent to neither, may surely be pardoned this suspension of judgment, for it is safer to continue in doubt than to decide amiss.[59]

It is no coincidence that he wrote these reflexions immediately after citing the Reverend Edward Harwood's testimony that, after expending much energy in examining the Athanasian, Arian and Socinian schemes, he could subscribe to none of them, but would 'die fully confirmed in the great doctrines of the New Testament, a resurrection, and a future state of eternal blessedness to all sincere penitents and good Christians'.[60] This, no doubt, was Watson's position too. Such things were things indifferent to him. *Plus ça change, plus c'est la même chose*? Perhaps, but if one examines Paley's thought, one can see an important change of emphasis occurring in Latitudinarianism. Paley was very much in favour of Blackburne's ambition to create a more comprehensive Church with a simplified set of doctrines; he also thought that freedom of inquiry might produce greater agreement, and hoped that a moderate, liberal Church would reduce the need to dissent to a minimum.[61] But he aimed to found the Church not upon Scripture but upon utility. On that ground alone the governors of the Church should adjust to the needs of a more enlightened age.[62] Whereas expediency was a dirty word for Blackburne, Paley looked on it with approval. He even thereby justified the radical outlook and actions of Blackburne and the reformers, for without men of spirit who were

[58] Ibid., I, 217. [59] Ibid., I, 227.
[60] Ibid.; *Gentleman's Magazine*, Nov. 1793, pp. 994–5.
[61] W. Paley, 'A Defence of the Considerations on the Propriety of Requiring a Subscription to Articles of Faith' (1774), in *Sermons and Tracts by the Late Rev. William Paley DD* (1808), pp. 41–4. [62] Ibid., p. 44.

incautious and imprudent, no change would ever occur until 'the renovation of all things'.[63] Whereas Blackburne wanted to reform the Church so that it would conform to scriptural practice, Paley believed that the New Testament did not prescribe a particular ecclesiastical constitution, so that it was in order to adjust it on the basis of expediency and considerations of public utility. By founding his position on utility he made it possible for Latitudinarian aspirations to be perpetuated in an age which had moved away from the theology and metaphysics of the tradition. In doing so, he was not entirely original, for Hoadly in his *Reasonableness of Conformity* had argued that since the Church was not of this world then the question of the human establishment of religion could only be decided on the basis of utility and not of Christian idealism.[64] The most influential Latitudinarian theologian of the mid-century, Edmund Law, master of Peterhouse from 1756/7 and bishop of Carlisle from 1769, was Paley's first patron and something of a mentor.[65] Law developed what John Gascoigne has called a form of religiously based utilitarianism.[66] In his *Considerations on the State of the World with Regard to the Theory of Religion* (1745) he attacked the idea of 'one fixt, immutable and universal Law of Nature'.[67] As Hartley did a few years later, he portrayed man as continually advancing in knowledge of God's works. Yet he later wrote, in support of Blackburne's stand on subscription, of 'The Christian religion as originally constituted, as very plain and practical; level to all capacities, and calculated for the common good of mankind, in every station and condition, both here and hereafter.'[68]

This is a restatement of the Reformation theme of the corruption of Christianity and of the Latitudinarian belief in the availability of the central truths of Christianity to all mankind. They were the views which his friend Blackburne could recognize as his own. Moreover, it might be thought that there were utilitarian dimensions to Blackburne's thought, for the subtitle of the *Confessional* uses the word utility.[69] That was deliberate, for Blackburne's purpose was to show that articles of religion cannot be justified on

[63] Ibid., p. 58. Paley thought that if the governors of the Church proved inflexible they might find themselves 'in the situation of a master of a family, whose servants knew more of his secrets than it is proper for them to know'.

[64] Hoadly, *Reasonableness of Conformity*, cit. [Blackburne], *Confessional*, p. 375.

[65] M. L. Clarke, *Paley. Evidences for the Man* (1974), pp. 13–14; D. L. LeMahieu, *The Mind of William Paley* (Lincoln, Nebr., and London, 1976), pp. 15–18.

[66] Gascoigne, *Cambridge*, p. 129.

[67] E. Law, *Considerations on the State of the World with Regard to the Theory of Religion* (Cambridge, 1745), p. 7; Crane, 'Anglican Apologetics', pp. 259–74; R. Brinkley, 'A Liberal Churchman: Edmund Law', *Enlightenment and Dissent*, 6 (1987), 3–18.

[68] E. Law, *Considerations on the Propriety of Requiring Subscription to Articles of Faith* (Cambridge, 1774), p. 2.

[69] Cf. Gascoigne, *Cambridge*, p. 133, with [Blackburne], *Confessional*, pp. 246–50, 254, 264–5.

the basis of utility. On this point, his historical arguments harmonized with Law's views that the canons, creeds and dogmas of one generation were inappropriate for the next and impeded the progress of religion. Blackburne used the principle of utility against itself: the useful thing to do is not to take utility into account. It is not useful for the magistrate to interfere in religious matters, for, in doing so, he makes religious truth less accessible to the many, and hence makes religion less efficacious in producing virtuous citizens: 'The use of religion to society, I apprehend to be, that men, having in their hearts the fear of God, and of his judgements, may be restrained from evil, and encouraged to be virtuous, in such instances as are beyond the reach of human laws.'[70]

Such a view of the salutary effect of religion led Warburton to defend the alliance between church and state.[71] Indeed, there emerged from utilitarian-style arguments a coherent stance over the relations between church and state which foreshadowed Burkeian-style arguments for conservation. Paley, who systematized this strain of religious utilitarianism, used it to justify social hierarchy, and to persuade the poor, that is 'the labouring part of mankind', that 'some of the necessities which poverty ... imposes, are not hardships but pleasures'.[72] This he combined with the bland argument that 'religion smooths all inequalities, because it unfolds a prospect which makes all earthly distinctions nothing'.[73]

Blackburne had died by the time Paley preached such views, but such cautious ethical utilitarianism in which religion provided but a distant prospect of happiness would not have been to his taste. *The Confessional* and the Feathers Tavern petition affirmed religious rights irrespective of the utility of granting them. Religion took precedence over secular concerns: 'if the rule of pure religion be taken from the christian scriptures, the temporal peace and safety of any Christian in civil society is but a secondary consideration to the obligation he is under to hold fast his integrity, in *truth* and *sincerity*'.[74] Here one can see how far Blackburne had strayed from the Latitudinarian *via media*. By failing to distinguish between different forms of truth and by insisting upon liberty of conscience, he had led himself and others up a cul de sac, and created an intolerable dilemma for the petitioners once their petition had failed. Although he had not followed Hartley in arguing against all forms of subscription, his argument in favour was weak and defensive. The logic of his position was against subscription in any form. And even if it were not, he had so thoroughly demolished the case

[70] [Blackburne], *Confessional*, p. 253.
[71] W. Warburton, *The Alliance between Church and State* (2nd edn, 1741), pp. 7–19.
[72] Paley, 'Reasons for Contentment, Addressed to the Labouring Part of the British Public' (1792), in *Sermons and Tracts*, p. 164.
[73] Ibid., p. 175.
[74] [Blackburne], *Confessional*, pp. 255–6.

for subscribing to the Articles that the honest course would appear to have been to have left the Church. At the end of Chapter V of *The Confessional*, he summed up in a way which clearly demonstrated that the Latitudinarian balance between rationality and individual conscience would not bear close scrutiny:

There is one particular weakness and want of forecast, common to all these pleaders for latitude. If you take their several schemes, as they are founded upon the church's declarations, nothing can be more righteous or reasonable than to comply with the terms prescribed by the church; and then, *perfectly consistent is the reasonableness of conformity, with the rights of private judgement*. But go back to their principles of Christian Liberty, on which they oppose the advocates for Church-authority; and you will find there is nothing more inconsistent with those principles, than the Authority which the Church of *England* actually claims and exercises.[75]

He went on to point out, in conclusion, that once it had been shown that the powers and privileges which the Church exercised did not rest upon right, then 'consistency required' that those who had, falsely, maintained that position 'should have withdrawn from a church which usurped an authority that did not belong to her, and to have borne their testimony against her in DEEDS as well as WORDS'.[76]

Evidence suggests that Blackburne had forebodings that the failure of his reform campaign would lead some to leave the Church. His own words pointed in that direction. Yet he was unable to apply the same rigorous logic to his own situation. He frequently consoled himself that reform would come in 'God's good time'.[77] Meanwhile, he persuaded himself that he was not acting contrary to conscience. He wrote to Theophilus Lindsey on 25 February 1757,

I would not subscribe again, even tho' I were reduced to beg a piece of bread by my children. But as the thing is done, and done in *ignorance* and *unbelief*... I wrong or deceive nobody by holding my benefice by that Title, provided I bear testimony to every one and on all fitting occasions, that I do not hold myself any longer bound by those terms.[78]

It was in this spirit that some of his friends introduced their own liturgical reforms, relying on the enlightened spirit of the age, and hoping that this might be the means of introducing reforms on a wider scale once it was seen that their effects were not harmful. This was what Lindsey's friend, William Chambers did, but as Grayson Ditchfield has remarked, we do not know if such experimentalism would have been accepted for any length of time

[75] Ibid., p. 268. [76] Ibid., pp. 268–9.
[77] DWL, MS 12.52, fo. 36: Blackburne to T. Lindsey, 25 Feb. 1757; DWL, MS 12.45, fo. 5: Blackburne to J. Wiche, 5 Dec. 1765; Belsham, *Memoirs of Lindsey*, App. III, pp. 493–5 (Blackburne to T. Lindsey, 15 Nov. 1757).
[78] DWL, MS 12.52, fo. 36.

since Chambers died in 1777. It certainly did not work for another clergyman, Edward Evanson.[79] Moreover, this was not an option open to young men who had not entered orders. If ordinands were persuaded by Blackburne's arguments, they could hardly subscribe to the Articles in ignorance. They could not conscientiously become ordained. This was not an entirely new dilemma, but Blackburne posed it in acute form. Nor could the option recommend itself to Blackburne's more radical supporters. His demonstration that it was improper to subscribe to the Articles in a Latitudinarian spirit forced on them a crisis of conscience. Thus *The Confessional* unwound many of the strands in Latitudinarianism and impelled Latitudinarians towards the creation of a new synthesis which would cope not only with the radical claims emerging from some of its onetime adherents, but also with some of the insistent questions raised by the development of science and of biblical scholarship. Paley's theological utilitarianism was unquestionably more in keeping with the coming age of Bentham than traditional Latitudinarianism, and would exert an immense influence on subsequent generations.[80] Certainly the Latitudinarian flag remained flying, and the emergence of the Broad Church movement in the mid-nineteenth century was very much in the Latitudinarian tradition. Indeed, one might say that the tradition triumphed in 1865, when the requirement to subscribe to every one of the Thirty-Nine Articles as being agreeable to the Word of God was relaxed and replaced by a more general adherence to the doctrines of the Church as being agreeable to the Word of God. For Blackburne, this would have been a prevaricating solution, but at least it has the merit of accommodating the tradition of the Church with individual conscientious scruples.

III

To sum up, most of Blackburne's ideas were not new. There were many precedents within the Latitudinarian tradition for his unease about subscription and about the relationship between church and state. Where Blackburne differed was in his insistence on the primacy and unitary nature of truth. This lay at the roots of his radicalism and left him in a thoroughly exposed position within the Church. He spent many pages towards the conclusion of *The Confessional* demonstrating that Hartley was under a misapprehension in thinking that, in any age in the history of the Church,

[79] Belsham, *Memoirs of Lindsey*, pp. 65–86 n.*; G. M. Ditchfield, 'The Revd. William Chambers, DD (*c*. 1724–1777)', *Enlightenment and Dissent*, 4 (1985), 3–12.

[80] R. Hole, *Pulpits, Politics and Public Order in England 1760–1832* (Cambridge, 1989), pp. 73–82; cf. G. A. Cole, 'Doctrine, Dissent, and the Decline of Paley's Reputation 1805–25', *Enlightenment and Dissent*, 6 (1987), 19–30.

there were those who worshipped God 'in spirit and in truth', yet had innocently concurred in supporting 'what is contrary to the pure religion' as a result of their own 'invincible prejudices'.[81] To Blackburne, this looked like an *apologia* for those who knew the truth but who failed to act upon it. Yet, anxious as he was to show that the logic of Hartley's views was against prevaricating, and despite the force of his own opinions on the subject, was that not what he was forced to do himself in the end? That is a reminder of the powerful loyalties which many Latitudinarians displayed towards their Church in the face of taunts of disloyalty and heterodoxy, and at the cost of intellectual consistency. Blackburne himself would have been very welcome amongst the Dissenters. He was very much at ease with them. He sent one of his sons to the Warrington Academy; and much of his radicalism came from his contact with Thomas Hollis's connexion of Old Commonwealthmen, many of whom were Dissenters. In broader terms, he was a man who reflected the fissiparous tendencies in the later Enlightenment, he was caught between the moderate and radical Enlightenments. The force of his affections lay with the former; the force of his arguments lay with the latter. His most dynamic followers, those who made the Feathers Tavern petition possible, left the Church, notably Theophilus Lindsey, John Jebb and John Disney. Latitudinarianism was always going to have a difficult time in the late eighteenth century with the growth of High Churchism and Evangelicalism within the Church and political radicalism and a self-conscious conservatism in the state. Its constituency within the Church was hard to maintain, more especially as most Whig Churchmen were politically conservative.[82] Its combination of moderate scepticism and rationality was too easily separated out into conservatism and radicalism. Only in the robust individualism of a Richard Watson do we see the attempt to apply old-fashioned Latitudinarianism to the problems of the late eighteenth century. Nonetheless, it was a pity that the splinter movement occurred just at the beginning of acute tension over reform in church and state. Many of the arguments in the subscription controversy foreshadowed later arguments in the debate over the French Revolution, and the challenge which Theophilus Lindsey presented to Anglicanism undoubtedly led to exaggerated fears as to the extent to which political radicalism threatened the constitution in church and state. Had reformism developed without this dimension, then it might have been possible to keep the threat of political and religious radicalism in perspective. The *trahison des clercs* of Lindsey and his followers, which led to the setting up of a Unitarian Church in Essex Street, London, using a revised liturgy derived from the efforts of Samuel

[81] [Blackburne], *Confessional*, p. 406.

[82] P. Langford, 'The English Clergy and the American Revolution', in *The Transformation of Political Culture*, ed. E. Hellmuth (Oxford, 1990), pp. 275–307.

Clarke, created alarms and fears out of all proportion to the enterprise. The Church entered the 1790s with its 'liberal' wing critically weakened by the loss of coherence of traditional Latitudinarianism. A movement which had emerged as a moderate response to the factionalism and fanaticism of the early modern period, could no longer cope with the new rifts emerging in government and society as they entered the age of revolutions. In an acute if unkind phrase, Philip Anthony Brown described the political moderates in the 1790s as men who were 'anxious to wash but not to get wet'.[83] That was very much to be the fate of the Latitudinarians in the late eighteenth century. If Blackburne may be held partly responsible for this, it was at least his virtue that he took the risk of getting wet, even if he found it difficult living with the consequences. One is left to ponder what his attitude would have been had he lived into the 1790s. We would not be the first to do so: a correspondent in the *Monthly Magazine* in 1797 ruminated 'What would he have thought, had he lived to see the present times – to see his former coadjutors and compatriots in the cause of ecclesiastical and civil reformation, almost all turn apostates, and not only so, but, in many instances, persecutors of their once associates and friends!'[84]

[83] P. A. Brown, *The French Revolution in English History* (3rd impr., 1965), p. 55.
[84] *Monthly Magazine*, 1797, pp. 355–6.

10 Ecclesiastical policy under Lord North

G. M. Ditchfield

I

In adopting as its subtitle 'Was there a "resurgence of Toryism" in the 1770s?', this essay threatens to take up a very familiar theme. As long ago as 1942, G. H. Guttridge claimed to identify a 'New Toryism' in ministerial policy after 1760 in his *English Whiggism and the American Revolution* and on its re-issue in the early 1960s, Professor Christie effectively demolished the idea.[1] But there are perhaps two reasons why another study of at least one aspect of the subject, namely the ecclesiastical one, might be justified now. First, neither in his original essay nor in his more recent analysis of the personnel of the House of Commons in the 1770s, in which he illuminated a considerable degree of continuity between the Pelhamite ascendancy and that of North,[2] did Professor Christie seriously consider ecclesiastical matters. Secondly, in the last few years, other works have postulated a Tory revival of at least some sort in the time of North. One thinks of J. A. W. Gunn's *Beyond Liberty and Property* and Paul Langford's demonstration that many representatives of old Tory families backed North's coercive policy and, by imbuing it with the 'mindless authoritarianism' of the country gentry, helped to create the conditions 'without which an unprecedented war against colonists could not have been fought'.[3] In 1989 Dr Bradley took this line of argument much further, writing of a 'Resurgence of Toryism' during the American Revolution.[4] Despite the careful avoidance of a correlation between Toryism and support for divine right

I wish to thank Professor Bryan Keith-Lucas, Dr Paul Langford, Professor F. C. Mather and Dr David Wykes for valuable comments on a draft of this essay.

1 Ian R. Christie, 'Was there a "New Toryism" in the Earlier Part of George III's Reign?', *JBS*, 5 (1965–6), 60–76, and reprinted in idem, *Myth and Reality in Late Eighteenth-Century British Politics* (1970), pp. 196–213.

2 Ian R. Christie, 'Party in Politics in the Age of Lord North's Administration', *Parliamentary History*, 6 (1987), 47–68.

3 J. A. W. Gunn, *Beyond Liberty and Property. The Process of Self-Recognition in Eighteenth-Century Political Thought* (Kingston and Montreal, 1983); Paul Langford, 'Old Whigs, Old Tories and the American Revolution', *Journal of Imperial and Commonwealth History*, 8 (1980), 123–7.

4 James E. Bradley, 'The Anglican Pulpit, the Social Order and the Resurgence of Toryism during the American Revolution', *Albion*, 21 (1989), 361–88.

monarchy, we are left in no doubt that by 'Toryism' is meant a High Church mentality in control of the instruments of government, not the oppositional Tory party, with its quasi-libertarian ethos, of the Walpole–Pelham period. Dr Bradley writes of 'a resurgence of Tory ideas', signifying 'a threatening, authoritarian note', an 'authoritarian emphasis', 'hostility to Dissent' and a 'perceived threat of arbitrariness', all of which were 'genuinely menacing to Dissenters and Commonwealthmen'.[5]

Such allegations would have been easily recognizable to late eighteenth- and to nineteenth-century Dissenting historians, such as Bogue and Bennett, or Skeats and Miall. In their eyes, the drift to war in America was accompanied by a harsher approach to domestic civil liberties, informed by Anglicanism, fuelled in tract and sermon by the clergy and involving (to quote the first of them) 'an aversion to all who were without the pale of the establishment, whom they designated by the title of schismatics and fanatics'.[6] That such charges should be revived, and in a much more sophisticated manner, suggests that they merit careful examination. Much of the evidence which is adduced in support of them is derived from studies of the outpouring of propaganda from the clerical elite, notably sermon literature.[7] This essay, however, takes a somewhat different approach by seeking to test them against the crucial touchstone of the way in which policy in these matters under North's administration was applied in practice. For since this alleged 'arbitrariness' is said to have been religious in inspiration, then if it had any substance in fact it would surely be found, among all branches of policy, in the ecclesiastical, and of all ministries, in that which is inextricably associated with the American conflict. In the twelve years of its existence, North's administration provided sufficient evidence in three areas to make possible a realistic assessment of its ecclesiastical policy. These areas, attitudes toward doctrinal unorthodoxy within the Church of England; the treatment of non-Anglicans; and the response to ecclesiastical problems in the imperial context, where the ministry faced a major crisis over the American Episcopalians, will be considered in turn.

II

A proposition which has recently become familiar is that from about 1770 Anglican orthodoxy came to be defended in pulpit and Parliament not

[5] Bradley, 'Resurgence of Toryism', pp. 373, 364, 362 n. 6, 385.

[6] David Bogue and James Bennett, *History of Dissenters from the Revolution in 1688 to the Year 1808* (4 vols., 1808–12), IV, 147, 153; H. S. Skeats, continued by C. S. Miall, *History of the Free Churches of England 1688–1891* (1891), p. 381.

[7] See particularly Bradley, 'Resurgence of Toryism', and Robert Hole, *Pulpits, Politics and Public Order in England 1760–1832* (Cambridge, 1989). Dr Hole, in suggesting (p. 51) that, at least from 1782, many Anglican sermons 'became noticeably more conservative and authoritarian', places this process at a slightly later date than does Dr Bradley.

simply because its propagation was socially expedient but because its doctrine was true, and that, accordingly, a stricter adherence to the Articles of religion was insisted upon. In particular, Dr Clark diagnoses a much stronger emphasis upon Trinitarian orthodoxy in response to attacks upon it from Latitudinarian and anti-Trinitarian directions, attacks which concentrated particularly upon clerical subscription to the Thirty-Nine Articles.[8] Indeed, Blackstone in the first edition of his *Commentaries* (1765–9) described anti-Trinitarianism as 'one species of heresy, very prevalent in modern times'; the reference was still there in the tenth edition in 1787.[9] A key element in the selection of bishops was their Trinitarian orthodoxy; the elevation of Porteus is often ascribed to his endorsement of ministerial American policy in a Fast Day sermon, but George III was equally impressed by his doctrinal reliability. The King gave the same reason for offering the see of Gloucester to Thomas Balguy in 1781.[10] The Latitudinarians Hinchliffe and Shipley and the Socinian Law, all nominated by Grafton in 1769, by contrast, were offered no further preferment. Lower down the clerical scale one senses something similar. The *Kentish Gazette* commented in January 1772 'A correspondent observes, that the Thirty-nine Articles, for these six months past, have been more *read* and more *noticed*, than for half a century before', while the following year, the Reverend William Jones, best known as 'Jones of Nayland' but at that time Jones of Pluckley, reportedly stated with satisfaction that 'the clergy would now preach upon the Articles'.[11] Hence neither the rejection by the Commons of the Feathers Tavern petition for relaxation of subscription for Anglican clergy in 1772 and 1774 nor the defeat of the Parliamentary move for the abolition of lay subscription in the universities should cause astonishment.

Yet the rhetoric of many Churchmen, of which the anti-Socinian works of Horne and Newton are prime examples, was not accompanied by any thorough-going policy of enforcement. The *de facto* acceptance of heterodoxy can be demonstrated in several ways. The first concerns the universities. In Cambridge, with its Latitudinarian tradition, Arian and even Socinian theology was openly propounded. Cambridge provided an

[8] Clark, *English Society*, pp. 229, 251.

[9] W. Blackstone, *Commentaries on the Laws of England* (1st edn, 4 vols., Oxford, 1765–9), IV, 49.

[10] Hole, *Pulpits, Politics and Public Order*, p. 48; *The Correspondence of King George III 1760–83*, ed. Sir John Fortescue (6 vols., 1927–8), III, nos. 1943 and 1981, V, no. 3383.

[11] *Kentish Gazette*, 25–8 Jan. 1772; diary of the Rev. Joseph Price, vicar of Brabourne, Beaney Library, Canterbury. The MS of the diary is in shorthand, but there is a typewritten transcript by F. W. Higenbotham. The foliation of each is the same; this reference is to fo. 174. Most of the diary is published in *A Kentish Parson. Selections from the Private Papers of the Revd. Joseph Price, Vicar of Brabourne, 1767–86*, ed. G. M. Ditchfield and Bryan Keith-Lucas (Kent County Council, 1991).

important intellectual stimulus to Unitarianism not only through those of its clerical alumni who seceded from the Church, like Theophilus Lindsey, John Disney and William Frend, but through many who remained within its bosom. Edmund Law at Peterhouse presided over a Unitarian coterie; he and Peter Peckard (originally an Oxford man but from 1781 master of Magdalene) both joined the Unitarian Society for Promoting Knowledge of the Scriptures in 1783;[12] a similar group emerged at Jesus. The Reverend Joseph Price, vicar of Brabourne, while pursuing the (sadly incompatible) aims of marrying a rich widow and securing a fellowship at Peterhouse, found ample evidence of heterodoxy on his visits to Cambridge. Apart from John Jebb, whose lectures, Price was told, had promoted 'Socinianism and Fatalism', he recorded that the Reverend William Oldham, fellow of Peterhouse, 'Says he laughs at the 39 Articles in his room'.[13] Richard Watson, who 'talked openly ... as a Socinian' and criticized North's American policy, and William Paley, whose Trinitarian orthodoxy was subsequently called into question,[14] were the best-known, but far from the only, representatives of the Latitudinarian tradition. In 1775 there was much resistance in the university to the presentation of a loyal address to the King. Despite the Parliamentary failure of reform of the subscription laws, significant changes in Cambridge were made; in 1772 a declaration of *bona fide* membership of the Church of England replaced subscription to the Articles for BAs (there remained no subscription at matriculation) and was extended to several other degrees in 1779.[15]

It is true that moves to modify lay subscription on matriculation at Oxford failed in the university Convocation in 1772–3.[16] Yet North, as its Chancellor, tried to persuade Oxford to relax its rules on subscription; the university actually feared that North's ministry would intervene in its internal affairs to make it soften, not harden, this important outwork of orthodoxy. Inasmuch as North wished to interfere at all with the universities, it was to push Oxford very gently in what would later be called a 'liberalizing' direction, in response to the argument that it was absurd to expect very young men to express agreement with doctrinal articles which they might not understand.[17] North did not seek to take further powers

[12] JRL, Lindsey Correspondence: Theophilus Lindsey to W. Tayleur, 4 Dec. 1783.

[13] *A Kentish Parson*, ed. Ditchfield and Keith-Lucas, pp. 71–2, 66.

[14] John Seed, 'The Role of Unitarianism in the Formation of a Liberal Culture, 1775–1851. A Social History', PhD dissertation, University of Hull, 1981, p. 30; G. A. Cole, 'Doctrine, Dissent, and the Decline of Paley's Reputation, 1805–25', *Enlightenment and Dissent*, 6 (1987), 19–30.

[15] John Gascoigne, *Cambridge in the Age of the Enlightenment* (Cambridge, 1989), pp. 201–2, 206–9.

[16] L. G. Mitchell, 'Politics and Revolution 1772–1800', in *The History of the University of Oxford, vol. V: The Eighteenth Century*, ed. L. S. Sutherland and L. G. Mitchell (Oxford, 1986), pp. 166–77.

[17] Ibid., pp. 171–3; P. D. G. Thomas, *Lord North* (1976), p. 148.

over Cambridge, despite that university's reputation for Whiggery, Latitudinarianism and heterodoxy – a marked contrast with the plans of Sunderland and Stanhope to regulate Oxford in 1719 or of the Pelham ministry to take greater control after the '45.[18] No doubt these heretical elements at Cambridge seemed less dangerous to the existing regime than early eighteenth-century Oxford Toryism had been. The contrast is nonetheless illuminating. Which policy, it may be asked, showed more of an 'authoritarian emphasis'?

A second illustration of the acceptance of diversity may be found in the campaign of Porteus, Wollaston and others to ease what they saw as the Calvinistic rigour of some of the Articles. It is impossible to be sure how much support their discreet (and unsuccessful) approach to Cornwallis commanded; according to one source a report in the *Gentleman's Magazine* of their meeting with the Archbishop, which stated that 'he took it for granted there were many of the Clergy of the same opinion', was a misrepresentation of what he actually said.[19] But the application attracted the interest of such respectable and career-conscious men as Thomas Percy and James Yorke.[20] 'Many very worthy Sons of the Church of England, think some thing of this Sort, would be the very best answer to the disaffected Petitioners', wrote Percy.[21] Subsequently, when Lindsey cited these overtures to bestow a retrospective justification upon his own proposals for liturgical reform, Porteus tried to distance himself from the clergymen of the Feathers Tavern. However, the two groups did have in common a dissatisfaction with things as they stood, a wish to modify Article 17 ('Of Predestination and Election') and 'to diminish schism and separation by bringing over to the National Church all the moderate and well-disposed of other persuasions'.[22] Their initiative did not damage their careers; Percy became dean of Carlisle and bishop of Dromore, Yorke became bishop in rapid succession of St David's, Gloucester and Ely, while George III regarded Porteus's 'very proper conduct ... on the attempt to alter the Liturgy' as an added reason for his nomination to the see of Chester.[23]

Thirdly, the open existence of heterodoxy at parish level, although a minority affair, is amply documented. Blackburne's circle is well known. Joseph Price of Brabourne noted Arian sentiments and admiration for

[18] J. Black, 'Regulating Oxford: Ministerial Intentions in 1719', *Oxoniensia*, 50 (1985), 283–5; Paul Langford, 'Tories and Jacobites, 1714–51', in *University of Oxford*, ed. Sutherland and Mitchell, ch. 4.

[19] *Gentleman's Magazine*, 42 (1772), 546; manuscript diary of Joseph Price, fo. 168.

[20] Sykes, *Church and State*, pp. 383–4; *The Correspondence of Thomas Percy and Richard Farmer*, ed. C. Brooks (Louisiana State University Press, 1946), pp. 159–60.

[21] *Correspondence of Thomas Percy and Richard Farmer*, ed. Brooks, p. 160.

[22] R. Hodgson, *The Life of Beilby Porteus* (1811), pp. 38–40, quoted in Sykes, *Church and State*, p. 384.

[23] *Corr. George III*, ed. Fortescue, III, no. 1943.

Samuel Clarke's non-Trinitarian version of the Book of Common Prayer among several of his fellow clergy in east Kent; the Reverend John Conant, rector of Hastingleigh, 'wants to have the Apostles' Creed to be the only test of receiving orders or taking a benefice', while the Reverend Thomas Thompson, vicar of Elham, was 'favourable in fancy to Arians' and 'half a dissenter owing to having been in America'.[24] William Chambers, rector of Thorpe Achurch, Northamptonshire, a close friend of Lindsey, experimented freely with Unitarian variations on the Prayer Book and remained unmolested until his death in 1777.[25] But the most extreme case was that of Edward Evanson, vicar of Tewkesbury, whose openly Unitarian preaching led to his prosecution, at the instigation of the local town clerk, in the church courts in 1777–8. The prosecution failed on a technicality in the Court of Arches and on appeal to the Court of Delegates. Its significance, however, is to be found not only in Evanson's victory over his critics but in the support which he attracted. The solicitor-general, Alexander Wedderburn, defended him *gratis*, appeared against the attorney-general, Thurlow, in the Court of Delegates and made Evanson his domestic chaplain. Wedderburn (and Germain) had spoken and voted for the Feathers Tavern petition in 1772.[26] When Evanson finally resigned from the Church he did so on his own initiative for reasons of conscience. He enjoyed much local support and remained on the best of terms with his diocesan, Warburton.[27] Evanson's case heightened an already strong reluctance to use the church courts as a defence against heterodoxy. The very few clergymen who left the Church of England on Unitarian grounds were not obliged to do so. They resigned as a result of separate, only loosely connected, individual decisions, over a decade, not *en bloc*, in response to a suddenly imposed crisis. Hence the vast majority of the 250 or so signatories to the Feathers Tavern petition remained. Even the seceder Jebb could acknowledge that 'many persons who hold similar opinions to mine, can continue in the Church with great advantage to the cause of Christianity; acting at the same time in perfect conformity to conscience'.[28]

Hence when we are confidently and rightly informed that this was an age of powerful Trinitarian reassertion, and when this phenomenon is presented as one aspect of an Anglican-inspired 'authoritarian' mentality, several important qualifications should be registered. First, neither North's

[24] *A Kentish Parson*, ed. Ditchfield and Keith-Lucas, pp. 40, 119, 120.

[25] G. M. Ditchfield, 'The Revd. William Chambers, DD (*c.*1724–1777)', *Enlightenment and Dissent*, 4 (1985), 3–12.

[26] Neast Havard, *A Narrative of the Origin and Progress of the Prosecution against the Rev. Edward Evanson* (1778); *Sermons by Edward Evanson* (2 vols., Ipswich, 1807), I, lxi-lxv; *Parl. Hist.*, XVII, 264–7, 294–5, 296–7.

[27] *Sermons by Edward Evanson*, I, lxv.

[28] *The Works, Theological, Medical, Political and Miscellaneous of John Jebb ... with Memoirs of the Life of the Author, by John Disney* (3 vols., 1787), I, 106.

ministry nor the episcopal hierarchy made strenuous efforts to restrict this parochial diversity. In denying the need for the Feathers Tavern petition, North himself recognized, and indeed seemed to congratulate the regime upon, the latitude inside and outside the Church, citing the open, though strictly illegal, questioning of the doctrine of the Trinity.[29] There had certainly been no increase in the enforcement of the law since mid-century. For, secondly, we need to remember that before 1760 several Anglican clergy who engaged in Trinitarian speculation of various, and sometimes quite mild, sorts faced serious obstruction in their careers. William Whiston was removed from his Cambridge chair, John Cater was refused ordination at Oxford in the 1720s, John Jackson was denied an incumbency and was several times on the verge of prosecution and Bishop Clayton of Clogher went to his death in 1758 with proceedings pending against him.[30] These cases should be set against claims that the principal Anglican priority of 1775–83 was 'obedience and submission to those in authority'.[31] 'Obedience and submission' had been required just as strongly before 1760 and the rejection of the Feathers Tavern petition was entirely consistent with previous ecclesiastical policy. Thirdly, one should note that re-emphasis upon the Trinity was not a purely Anglican phenomenon. The age of North saw many orthodox Dissenters oppose relaxation of the subscription laws for their own pastors lest, to quote one of their broadsheets, it 'encourage the propagation of the principles of those persons who deny the *Doctrine of the ever blessed Trinity*' and it saw a handful of Dissenting ministers deprived of their offices for offending on this point. The Baptist New Connexion seceded from the General Baptist body for the same reason – Evanson's main opponent in Tewkesbury indeed affirmed that one family had been driven by Evanson's preaching to 'the Anabaptist meeting, where they had been informed that the Divinity of Christ was strongly insisted upon'.[32]

Such cases hardly suggest that ecclesiastical practice in North's time amounted to repression or arbitrariness. Latitudinarians and Arians in the Church were not likely to be preferred (though there were significant exceptions), but the same was true, for much of the century, of High

[29] *Parl. Hist.*, XVII, 273.

[30] For Whiston, Jackson and Clayton see *DNB*; for Cater see V. H. H. Green, 'Religion in the Colleges, 1715–1800', in *University of Oxford*, ed. Sutherland and Mitchell, p. 436. For the importance which Newcastle placed upon Trinitarian orthodoxy in his selection of bishops see Stephen Taylor, 'Church and State in England in the Mid-Eighteenth Century: The Newcastle Years 1742–62', PhD dissertation, University of Cambridge, 1987, pp. 103–5.

[31] Bradley, 'Resurgence of Toryism', p. 364.

[32] Staffordshire RO, Dartmouth MSS, D 1778 V 617b: broadsheet issued by the 'Society of Protestant Dissenting Ministers, and Others, meeting at the New York Coffee House, Sweetings's Alley, Cornhill, London', 16 Feb. 1773; Seed, 'Role of Unitarianism', pp. 54–5; Havard, *Narrative*, p. 15.

Churchmen and Hutchinsonians. As Dr Clark observes, Socinianism was 'open and unpunished', and in his acceptance of a 'parochial picture of diversity and anomaly'[33] lies a warning that the powerful rhetoric of orthodoxy which emanated from some elements of the clerical (and lay) elite should not be mistaken for the reality of ecclesiastical practice.

III

Does policy towards non-Anglicans suggest a different conclusion? Most important in this respect is Protestant Dissent, for, as Dr Bradley observes, 'Hostility towards Dissent was traditionally a sign of High-Anglican and Tory ideals.'[34] Indeed there might be *prima facie* grounds for the historian to expect a greater measure of such hostility in the 1770s. For by that time Dissenters, no longer inhibited by the fear of Jacobitism, and with at least some of their number increasingly influenced by heterodox theology, were rather more critical of the existing regime than had been the case under the Whig ascendancy of 1714–60.[35] A severe governmental response to these changes in Dissent would not, in such circumstances, be difficult to explain and some contemporaries believed that it was happening. George Hardinge neatly summed up his phobia of a reactionary union of court and bench when he told Horace Walpole that the bishops 'oppress the dissenter at the ... beck of the white wands and the King's Friends'.[36]

Yet in the 1770s there was a greater easing of the law towards Dissenters than at any time since 1714–22. The sequence of annual Indemnity Acts, important for their symbolic, if not their practical, value, was not interrupted. It is true that the Relief Bills of 1772–3, to exempt Dissenting ministers and schoolmasters from subscription to the doctrinal articles of the Church of England, were defeated in the House of Lords. But in 1779 a not dissimilar bill passed into law with virtually no demur in the upper chamber.[37] Nor, unlike the exemption from the sacramental provisions of the Test Act granted to Irish Presbyterians in 1780, can it be interpreted as a grudging concession wrung from a reluctant government by the pressures of war. Once a very general affirmation of Protestant Christianity had been included in the Bill, the idea received much ministerial and episcopal

[33] Clark, *English Society*, p. 320; J. C. D. Clark, 'On Hitting the Buffers: The Historiography of England's Ancien Regime', *PP*, 117 (1987), 200.

[34] Bradley, 'Resurgence of Toryism', p. 375.

[35] Clark, *English Society*, pp. 217, 317.

[36] *The Yale Edition of Horace Walpole's Correspondence*, ed. W. S. Lewis (48 vols., New Haven, 1937–83), XXXV, 387.

[37] G. M. Ditchfield, 'The Subscription Issue in British Parliamentary Politics, 1772–9', *Parliamentary History*, 7 (1988), 53–64. Hole, *Pulpits, Politics and Public Order*, p. 54, is incorrect in stating that this Bill met the same fate as its unsuccessful predecessors of 1772–3.

support. 'Much more may be said in favour of the Dissenters' plea', Bishop Newton had written in 1773, drawing the obvious parallel with the Feathers Tavern petition,[38] while Bishops Ross, Hurd and Porteus expressed public and private sympathy. Porteus thought the Act (19 Geo. III c. 44) 'both wise and just, & no less consonant to the principles of sound Policy than to the genuine Spirit of the Gospel'.[39] Many Dissenting ministers privately endorsed this verdict, especially when North virtually promised that those who omitted to sign the declaration would not be prosecuted.[40] The prospect of such a measure encouraged some bishops to portray the constitution in libertarian terms. Though retaining a few reservations about the 1779 Act, Hurd wrote 'Nobody, however, will or ought to be punished for religious opinions.' Newton boasted 'We connive at several abuses of the law rather than give the least handle to unreasonable jealousies and suspicions.' Porteus gave as the most compelling reason for the insistence on the declaration of belief in the Scriptures as the need for a guarantee that Dissenters' preaching should 'contain nothing injurious to Civil Society or to the established form of Government'.[41]

Though Thurlow had brusquely dismissed the Dissenters' petition in 1772,[42] Lord Mansfield was far more sympathetic. The Baptist minister Samuel Stennett, a prominent spokesman for the pressure group which pursued the claim, recalled: 'Lord Mansfield said to the dissenters who solicited his assistance, "If you won't subscribe you shall not be Archbishop but you shall not go to prison", i.e. he was a friend to their [application].'[43]

Mansfield duly voted for the Bill in the Lords in 1772 and 1773. In the public eye he was firmly identified with the ministry and was the object of much opposition paranoia, the successor to Bute as the Caledonian *éminence grise* behind the tyrannical machinations of the court. Yet in 1767 his opinion that 'It is now no crime for a man who is within the description of that act [i.e. the Toleration Act] to say he is a Dissenter' had been decisive in leading to the historic House of Lords ruling, in *City of London* v. *Allen Evans*, and even his much-derided judgement in Somersett's case (1772) has been reinterpreted in a more sympathetic, and genuinely anti-slavery, light in a recent article by James Oldham.[44] The decade did not witness a marked deterioration in relations at local level. Dr Jacob's study of Norfolk, for

[38] Thomas Newton, *Works* (6 vols., 1787), III, 485.

[39] LPL, MS 2098, fo. 94 (diary of Bishop Porteus).

[40] Ditchfield, 'Subscription Issue', pp. 64–5.

[41] F. Kilvert, *Memoirs of the Life and Writings of the Right Reverend Richard Hurd, DD* (1860), p. 135; Newton, *Works*, III, 466; LPL, MS 2098, fo. 88.

[42] J. S. Watson, *The Reign of George III* (Oxford, 1960), p. 156.

[43] *A Kentish Parson*, ed. Ditchfield and Keith-Lucas, p. 11.

[44] *Parl. Hist.*, XVI, 313–27; James Oldham, 'New Light on Mansfield and Slavery', *JBS*, 27 (1988), 45–68.

instance, reveals 'clear signs of a growing religious pluralism' and he points to 'remarkable tolerance' between the Anglican Tories and Dissenting Whigs in Norwich.[45] In Lancashire and Cheshire it was the move for repeal of the Test and Corporation Acts in 1787, not the events of a decade earlier, which produced serious conflict between Church and Dissent.[46] The same is true in other counties: there are numerous examples of local co-operation over Sunday schools, civic improvements and anti-slavery.[47] Instances of individual hostility, of course, cannot be denied, nor can the unpopularity incurred by some 'rational' Dissenters through their pro-Americanism. But the era of North is notable for the absence of any Church and King, anti-Dissenting backlash, with popular support, sponsored by local elites and encouraged by the government. That phenomenon belongs to the 1790s.

The section of Protestant non-Anglicanism which historically had experienced the most painful encounters with the law was the Society of Friends. In 1772 a bill to mitigate their liability to tithes indeed failed in the House of Commons. However, much evidence from many quarters suggests that over a long period Quakers and contemporary society had reached a mutually acceptable *modus vivendi*. This process was not halted, let alone reversed, under North. Only one Quaker was imprisoned for non-payment of tithe in the 1770s; he was the only Friend to suffer this fate between 1759 and 1789. Dr Evans's figures for Staffordshire reveal that the total number of 'Sufferings' in the 1770s was 58, the lowest figure for any decade in the century; this compares with 115 in the 1730s and 80 in the 1760s. The total amount taken in distraint of property for non-payment of tithe in that county in the 1770s was £38 1s 6d; only the 1750s had a lower figure.[48] These statistics indicate a decline in the need or willingness to prosecute, not merely a fall in Quaker numbers. The specifically Quaker grievance over tithe was diminishing – despite the beginning of that well-known upward curve in the number of clerical magistrates. The Epistles from the Yearly Meeting of Friends in London deplore the loss of life in North America but contain no hint of growing domestic persecution. The Epistle of 1778 reflected upon 'the many mercies we, with our fellow-subjects, have long and largely enjoyed'.[49] There is some truth in the claim of a group of

45 W. M. Jacob, 'Clergy and Society in Norfolk, 1707–1806', PhD dissertation, University of Exeter, 1982, pp. 414–18.

46 G. M. Ditchfield, 'The Campaign in Lancashire and Cheshire for the Repeal of the Test and Corporation Acts, 1787–90', *Transactions of the Historic Society of Lancashire and Cheshire*, 126 (1977), 109–38.

47 See, for instance, John Money, *Experience and Identity. Birmingham and the West Midlands 1760–1800* (Manchester, 1977), pp. 126–7, 190–1.

48 Eric J. Evans, 'A History of the Tithe System in England, 1690–1850, with Special Reference to Staffordshire', PhD dissertation, University of Warwick, 1970, pp. 427–32.

49 *Epistles from the Yearly Meeting of Friends, Held in London, to the Quarterly and Monthly Meetings in Great Britain, Ireland and Elsewhere, from 1681 to 1857* (2 vols., 1858), II, 34.

Anglican incumbents that 'The clergy have of late treated the Quakers with great lenity.' That claim was made in a memorandum to Cornwallis in protest against the Quaker Tithe Bill in 1772. It invoked traditional liberties, complaining that by extending the summary method of tithe recovery to all tithes (unless the entitlement to the tithe were in question) and by removing the right of appeal from Quarter Sessions, the Bill would deprive many clergymen, whose incomes might be at stake, of 'that great Bulwark of British Liberty, *Trial by Juries*'.[50] The irony is that the denial of trial by jury in civil cases was one of the grounds on which the Parliamentary opposition was soon to denounce the Quebec Act as popish and arbitrary. There was also an extension of legal recognition of Quakers' idiosyncrasies when Mansfield ruled in King's Bench in the case of *Atcheson* v. *Everett* in 1776 that a Quaker's testimony on his affirmation was admissible in an action for debt. His words are worth quoting: 'I think it of the utmost importance, that all the consequences of the act of toleration should be pursued with the greatest liberality, in ease of the scrupulous consciences of dissenters ... But so as those scruples of conscience should not be prejudicial to the rest of the King's subjects.'[51]

What of the Catholic minority in Britain under North? To Dr Haydon we owe the identification of a more sympathetic attitude on the part of the governing orders towards Catholicism in 'enlightened' and post-Jacobite conditions, together with a warning that the extent of this process should not be exaggerated.[52] Older suspicions indeed persisted among the elite, including the clerical elite. A favourite example concerns the Reverend William Allen, rector of Little Chart in Kent, and the Jesuit James Darrell, who acted as chaplain to his own family at Calehill: 'Mr and Mrs Darrell being from home, James the priest sent for Allen to dine with him. A. would not go, lest James would give him something that did not agree with his constitution, i.e. would poison him.'[53]

But if the defeat of Jacobitism tended to make some Dissenters less friendly towards government, it opened the way for greater governmental understanding of Catholicism. The need to govern a Catholic population in newly conquered colonies had the same effect. The Quebec Act of 1774 was passed with little dissension. The English Catholic Relief Act of 1778, the first of its type, was associated with a similar Relief Act for Ireland and the proposal (though not the passage) of one for Scotland. When every qualification is made about low Parliamentary attendances and the lateness

[50] LPL, Cornwallis Papers, III, fo. 72.

[51] H. Cowper, *Reports of Cases Adjudged in the Court of King's Bench ... 1774 to 1778* (1783), p. 388.

[52] Colin Haydon, 'Anti-Catholicism in Eighteenth-Century England, *c*.1714-*c*.1780', DPhil dissertation, University of Oxford, 1985, ch. 6.

[53] Manuscript diary of Joseph Price, fo. 97.

of the session, one has to recall that North's ministry refused to repeal the Act of 1778 after the Gordon Riots and brushed aside the 'Bill to secure the Protestant Religion in Great Britain from any encroachment of Popery' in July 1780, which even some of its own supporters would have liked to see enacted. The ministry did not share the widespread fears of growing Catholic numbers. Its inquiry into Catholic numbers was designed to calm such fears, and the Address of Convocation to George III in 1780 assured him that 'Popery is less prevalent than it has been in this part of your dominions.'[54] The ministry used the Act for preventing abuses of the Lord's Day in 1781 (21 Geo. III c. 49) to undermine the vehemently anti-Catholic debating societies in London by forbidding them to meet on Sundays, their most active day.[55]

This policy was entirely consistent with a declining willingness to use the penal code against Catholics and with their improved treatment at law. In the case of *Foone* v. *Blount* (1776), Mansfield ruled in King's Bench that although the Act of 1700 (11 and 12 Will. III c. 4) had laid down that a Catholic could not purchase landed property or enjoy the full benefits of its inheritance, a Catholic beneficiary of a will was entitled to receive a monetary legacy even if the sum necessary to pay such a legacy could only be raised by the sale of the deceased person's landed estate. His words on that occasion belong to the same category as his judgement in *Atcheson* v. *Everett*:

> The statutes against Papists were thought, when they passed, necessary to the safety of the state: upon no other ground can they be defended ... The legislature only can vary or alter the law: but from the nature of these laws, they are not to be carried by inference beyond what the political reasons which gave rise to them, require.[56]

In 1780 Mansfield's directions to the jury in an action brought against a defendant, alleged to be a Catholic priest, for saying mass, ensured the acquittal of the accused.[57] Mansfield's reputation for judicial leniency towards Catholics led to allegations that he, and members of the administration, were crypto-papists.[58] Their attitudes have been contrasted with the militant anti-Catholicism of many of North's radical critics. To the latter, an apparently pro-Catholic policy was yet more evidence of the 'arbitrary' and intolerant intentions of the ministry and the political system which sustained it. It is easy to stigmatize such attitudes as, by later standards, 'illiberal'. Yet one must take seriously the judgement of a recent historian

[54] *Gentleman's Magazine*, 50 (1780), 617.
[55] Haydon, 'Anti-Catholicism', pp. 255, 292.
[56] Cowper, *Cases in King's Bench*, p. 466. Four years earlier, a private Act of Parliament (12 Geo. III c. 122) had eased the problems of inheritance facing a Catholic lady in the Fenwick Case: Haydon, 'Anti-Catholicism', ch. 6.
[57] J. Campbell, *Lives of the Chief Justices of England* (3 vols., 1849–57), II, 514–16.
[58] Haydon, 'Anti-Catholicism', pp. 271–2.

that 'For consistency on religious toleration, Mansfield is the man, not Wilkes.'[59] When Mansfield's close alignment with the ministry, and the coexistence of a more sympathetic Catholic policy with a softening of legal restrictions on Dissenters are *both* borne in mind, the comment is not without significance for policy towards non-Anglicans as a whole in North's time.

IV

The issues discussed in this essay cannot be isolated from the particular sense of danger experienced by the Church of England in the age of the American Revolution. Dr Bradley indeed recognizes the existence of perceived and real threats, the former, in his view, being heresy (to which he gives little attention) and luxury (which was far from an exclusively Anglican preoccupation). The real threats he sees as social discontent and the growth and radicalization of the press, although one does wonder whether they were entirely novel phenomena in the 1770s.[60] These real and perceived threats, the argument goes, crystallized in the challenge to order and authority presented by the rebellion in America.

But that rebellion threw up a more specific threat, real and perceived, to the Church of England. It arose from the crisis in which the American Episcopalian clergy were engulfed. In the decades leading up to the outbreak of hostilities, there had been substantial growth in Anglican numbers in the American colonies, as indicated by increases in church building, ordained clergy and centres of clerical education, with new colleges in New York and Philadelphia.[61] Despite pressure from some English bishops and practical arguments in its favour, North's ministry followed the example of previous Whig administrations by refusing to set up an Anglican episcopate in North America. In 1771 the Secretary of State for the Colonies, Lord Hillsborough, admitted that the likelihood of political opposition on both sides of the Atlantic effectively ruled out this possibility.[62]

Despite, or, according to some, because of, this refusal, many Episcopal clergy and their congregations suffered physical violence as the challenge to British rule developed. Particularly in the northern colonies, those clergy who declined to omit prayers for the King were forced to close their churches and abandon their parishes. The letterbook of Henry Caner,

[59] Philip Lawson, 'Anatomy of a Civil War: New Perspectives on England in the Age of the American Revolution, 1767–82', *Parliamentary History*, 8 (1989), 146.

[60] Bradley, 'Resurgence of Toryism', pp. 380–7.

[61] Frederick V. Mills, 'Anglican Expansion in Colonial America, 1761–75', *Historical Magazine of the Protestant Episcopal Church*, 39 (1970), 315–24.

[62] J. M. Sosin, 'The Proposal in the Pre-Revolutionary Decade for Establishing Anglican Bishops in the Colonies', *JEH*, 13 (1962), 83–4.

minister of the King's Chapel, Boston, describes the mounting 'insult' and 'distress' experienced by the loyalist clergy. By January 1776 Caner's congregation consisted only of soldiers; two months later, with the rapid British evacuation of the city, he was obliged to embark at short notice, leaving his church and possessions to be looted by the rebels.[63] Samuel Seabury, later the first bishop of the Protestant Episcopal Church of America, was imprisoned. There were rather plaintive gatherings of dispossessed clergy in New York (where eight of them died), in Nova Scotia and, soon, in England.[64] Very quickly, horror stories about their ill-treatment found their way into the proceedings of the SPG and from there to the newspaper and periodical press. The perception of such men as martyrs, invoking images of the 1640s and comparisons with John Walker's *Sufferings of the Clergy*, was not slow to follow.[65]

Of course, not all the Episcopalian clergy in North America were loyalist – David L. Holmes's figures are 150 'Loyalists' and 123 'Patriots' – and there was considerable variation between colonies. The clergy most likely to be loyalist, however, were those sponsored by the SPG, which in 1776 alone was assisting in the financial provision of seventy-seven missionaries in the thirteen states.[66] These clergy tended not only to be the most loyal, but also the most likely to have been born in England, to have the best connexions in English clerical circles and to be best able to present their case effectively to an English audience. Though not all of them suffered, many, along with their lay followings, did.[67]

The SPG not only subsidized missionaries but in its anniversary sermons every February provided opportunities for the Episcopalian case to be heard and read. From the late 1760s this occasion grew in importance, to join the other sermon days as a demonstration of official attitudes.[68] The

[63] Bristol University Library: MS letterbook of the Rev. Henry Caner (hereafter Caner letterbook). The book consists of copies of his outward letters from 1728 to 1778; the pages are numbered only to 18 Apr. 1767. The references here are to Caner's letters to Bishop Terrick of 7 Oct. 1774 and 27 Apr. 1776. See also Mary Beth Norton, *The British Americans. The Loyalist Exiles in England 1774–89* (Boston and Toronto, 1972), pp. 51–2.

[64] C. F. Pascoe, *Two Hundred Years of the SPG* (1901), pp. 73–7; H. P. Thompson, *Into All Lands. A History of the Society for the Propagation of the Gospel in Foreign Parts 1701–1950* (1951), pp. 92–7.

[65] Pascoe, *Two Hundred Years*, p. 76; *Gentleman's Magazine*, 46 (1776), 171; *General Evening Post*, 24–7 Feb. 1776; *Kentish Gazette*, 10–13 Apr. 1776; *Chester Chronicle*, 11, 25 July, 16 Aug. 1776.

[66] David L. Holmes, 'The Episcopal Church and the American Revolution', *Historical Magazine of the Protestant Episcopal Church*, 47 (1978), 283; Pascoe, *Two Hundred Years*, p. 79.

[67] Pascoe, *Two Hundred Years*, pp. 74–8; Jonathan Boucher, *A View of the Causes and Consequences of the American Revolution; in Thirteen Discourses, Preached in North America between the Years 1763 and 1775: With an Historical Preface* (1797), p. xlix.

[68] See Henry P. Ippel, 'British Sermons and the American Revolution', *Journal of Religious History*, 12 (1982–3), 191–205.

most prominent names among the Anglican hierarchy appeared on this occasion regularly to denounce the rebel attacks on the Episcopalians: Ewer (1767), Lowth (1771), Moss (1772), Barrington (1775), Hinchliffe (1776), Markham (1777), Brownlow North (1778), Yorke (1779), John Thomas of Rochester (1780), Hurd (1781). The same plaint was taken up in other sermons.[69] This verbal and literary support was soon translated into material terms. The Address of Convocation to George III in 1780 thanked the King for his 'royal munificence' to the Society.[70] Well before that, a fund-raising scheme to assist the suffering and, in many cases, exiled clergy had begun. Opened, with press advertisements, in February 1776, it stood at £6,416 16s 1d when it closed the following July. Although this amounted to only one third of the £19,532 8s 11d raised at the same time, but with an obviously more general public appeal, for wounded soldiers and their families,[71] both funds involved an expression of support for the ministry. To subscribe for the Episcopalian clergy was implicitly to endorse North's American policy. This was quickly apparent to advocates and opponents of the fund alike. To one of the former, 'The Episcopalians in America ... have, in all this unhappy Contest, approved themselves the true and firm friends of the Constitution ... to countenance and support such Men, were Justice and Charity out of the Question, is, in some sort, to countenance and support the cause for which they have suffered.'[72] A critic of the subscription dismissed it as 'an engine of Court policy', 'a movement of the cabinet', 'a stroke of ministerial policy to arouse our religious resentments'.[73] Certainly the subscription received emphatic ministerial endorsement. A bevy of senior governmental figures appeared in the published lists of contributors: Lord North, £25; his father the Earl of Guilford, a lifelong courtier, £20; Lords Dartmouth, £30, and Hillsborough, £26 5s 0d, former secretaries for the colonies; Lord Bathurst, lord chancellor, £25; Lord Gower, lord president of the council, £25; Richard Rigby, paymaster, £25; Charles Jenkinson, £10; Lord Hertford, lord chamberlain, £20.[74] The list also includes Mansfield, whose donation of £10 shows that it was possible to combine succour for the Episcopalian clergy (and backing for North's

[69] See, for instance, John Butler, *A Sermon Preached before the House of Lords ... Feb. 27 1778* (1778); James Cornwallis, dean of Canterbury and nephew to the Archbishop, *A Sermon Preached at the Anniversary Meeting of the Sons of the Clergy ... May 15, 1777* (Canterbury, 1777).

[70] *Gentleman's Magazine*, 50 (1780), 617.

[71] James E. Bradley, *Popular Politics and the American Revolution in England* (Macon, Ga., 1986), p. 153.

[72] Letter of 'A Layman' in *Public Advertiser*, 14 Mar. 1776.

[73] Letter of 'Americanus' in *London Evening Post*, 2–5 Mar. 1776.

[74] The lists of subscribers were printed in most London and some provincial newspapers. For present purposes the lists in *Public Advertiser*, 27 Feb., 6, 12, 19, 26 Mar., 3, 9, 16, 29 Apr., 14, 29 May, 5 June, 2–4 and 23 July 1776, have been used.

American policy) with practical steps towards the extension of domestic religious toleration. The ministerial commitment is also evident in the disbursements from the fund; not only did some 100 dispossessed clergy receive £50 each,[75] but North intervened in other cases. He granted a pension of £100 p.a. to the Reverend Samuel Peters, who had been driven from his mission in Hebron, Connecticut, in 1774, and, when explaining the arrears of the Civil List to the Commons on 16 April 1777, stated that £27,000 had been paid as charity to American loyalists, though we do not know how much of this was spent on the Episcopalian clergy.[76]

The clerical initiative behind the fund was unmistakable. The main contributors and organizers were individual Anglican clergy. Every bishop contributed, led by the two archbishops with £30 each. The lists also include well over 600 lower clergy, who gave sums varying from half a guinea to five guineas. In general, the subscription was best supported in the south-east of England and the east and west midlands, with the dioceses of Canterbury and Norwich prominent,[77] least supported in the north of England. There was a predictably strong Oxonian presence, the Welsh clergy were well represented and some £900 was subscribed by the Church of Ireland. It was a cause which demanded financial sacrifice, however small, rather than simply a signature to a petition. By the spring of 1776 the fund had received sufficient coverage in the newspapers to stimulate a public debate; there were complaints that the sufferings of the Episcopalians had been exaggerated and that the poorer English clergy would have been worthier beneficiaries of such generosity.[78]

There was a long tradition of fund-raising for Protestant minorities and refugees in Catholic Europe.[79] The published Civil List accounts for 1776 include £500 for 'certain Foreign Protestants'.[80] But this subscription involved a rather different British perception of threatened religious minorities abroad; Catholic regimes, it seemed, were not the only persecutors and it might not be fanciful to detect here the potentialities for the much more widespread fund-raising for the far more numerous French *émigré* Catholic

[75] See Caner letterbook, Caner to Mather Byles, 1 July 1776 and to Moses Badger, 1 July 1776.

[76] Wayne N. Metz, 'A Connecticut Yankee in King George III's Court: A Loyalist Anglican Clergyman in England, 1774–1804', *Historical Magazine of the Protestant Episcopal Church*, 52 (1983), 31; *Parl. Hist.*, XIX, 106.

[77] *Kentish Gazette*, 10–13, 13–17, 17–20 Apr. 1776; *Norfolk Chronicle: Or Norwich Gazette*, 2, 30 Mar. 1776.

[78] See especially *Kentish Gazette*, 30 Mar.–3 Apr. 1776; *Public Advertiser*, 5 Mar., 23 Apr., 20 July 1776; *Chester Chronicle*, 13 July, 9 Aug. 1776.

[79] See, for example, J. Black, 'The Catholic Threat and the British Press in the 1720s and 1730s', *Journal of Religious History*, 12 (1982–3), 375; D. W. Bebbington, *Evangelicalism in Modern Britain* (1989), p. 39.

[80] *Journals of the House of Commons*, XXXVI, 395.

clergy in the 1790s, so amply documented by Dr Bellenger.[81] The strong Anglican feelings over the Episcopalians were genuine, not simply manufactured for the purposes of anti-Dissenting propaganda. The direct or indirect inspiration of many of the 'authoritarian' sermons of the 1770s discussed by Dr Bradley was not only the American Revolution in general but the treatment of the Episcopalians in particular. Four examples of authors cited by Dr Bradley stand out particularly in this respect. The first is Miles Cooper's *National Humiliation and Repentance Recommended . . . in a Sermon* (Oxford, 1777); it needs to be stressed that Cooper had been president of King's College, New York, and had barely escaped after being threatened by a mob.[82] The second is East Apthorpe's *Sermon on the General Fast* (1776); Apthorpe had been a missionary for the SPG in Cambridge, Massachusetts, between 1759 and 1764 and, in Bridenbaugh's words, 'provided the Yankees with one of the most potent symbols in their successful campaign against episcopacy'.[83] The third is Andrew Burnaby's *Sermon Preached before the Honourable House of Commons* (1781); Burnaby was best known for his *Travels through the Middle Settlements in North America. In the Years 1759 and 1760*, published, with an immediate second edition, in 1775. Slipped in among the descriptive passages is the warning that 'religious zeal . . . like a smothered fire, is secretly burning in the hearts of the sectaries' (p. 158). By this time Apthorpe and Burnaby both held Anglican livings, at Croydon and Greenwich respectively, and it is not surprising that each gave five guineas to the subscription. The fourth example is Archbishop Markham's *Sermon Preached before . . . the SPG . . . February 21, 1777* (1777); Markham lamented not only the misfortunes of loyalists in general but specifically dwelt upon 'the ministers of our church pursued with a licentiousness of cruelty, of which no Christian country can afford an example'.[84]

From the perspective of American Episcopalian clergy in exile, and of their Anglican supporters in the British Isles, public affairs looked very different from the way in which they appeared to Dissenting radicals and Commonwealthmen. To them, the British government was not too harsh, but too weak; before the revolution it had lacked the will to impose episcopacy; thereafter it was guilty of neglect towards those who had endured most in its interests. As the exiles scrambled for the poorest English curacies, encountered resentment from competitors for church patronage in an already overcrowded clerical profession and were told successively by the Bishop of London and the Secretary of State for the Colonies that the other bore responsibility for them, their bitterness perhaps becomes under-

[81] Dominic Bellenger, 'The *Emigré* Clergy and the English Church, 1789–1815', *JEH*, 34 (1983), 392–410.

[82] Thompson, *Into All Lands*, p. 95.

[83] Carl Bridenbaugh, *Mitre and Sceptre. Transatlantic Faiths, Ideas, Personalities and Politics* (New York, 1962), p. 111.

[84] Markham, *Sermon before the SPG*, p. xiv.

standable. 'The worst rebel in America would be more noticed & more assisted here than the best friend of Government', wrote Caner.[85] To them, the threat of arbitrariness and authoritarianism lay not in North's policies nor in Anglican attitudes more generally, but in the rebel treatment of loyal clergy (and sometimes laity). An 'Address to the British Government', printed in the *London Evening Post* for 13–16 April 1776, bemoaned 'the arbitrary power of the Hancocks, the Adams's and the other sovereigns of the Congress', while 'the poor, loyal episcopal party, the Issachar of the new, as they have been of the old world, were to be dragooned into submission under Presbyterian taxers'. Jonathan Boucher commented 'that an established Church, which gives such ample and liberal toleration to sectaries of every name, should herself not be tolerated, is a phenomenon in political history peculiar to the American world'.[86] Some Episcopalian loyalist clergy, moreover, including Boucher himself, had initially sympathized with colonial grievances; the Reverend Jacob Duché, for instance, had been chaplain to the first and second Continental Congresses.[87]

Much is known about the hostile reactions of many American colonists and their English Dissenting sympathizers to attempts to establish a colonial episcopacy;[88] perhaps not quite enough is known about the Anglican response to the failure of these attempts and to the violent overthrow of Episcopalianism in some colonies during the 1770s. It is not surprising that the Episcopalian clergy and their sympathizers identified the failure to establish episcopacy as a cause of the rebellion.[89] Nor is it surprising that they perceived a threat from English Dissenters, who, to the well-publicized if not always representative heterodoxy and pro-Americanism of some of their numbers, seemed to add an intolerance towards those outside their own ranks. The Episcopalian jeremiad is relevant to the present discussion in two respects: it helps to explain what Dr Bradley disapprovingly terms 'the shrillness of Anglican sermons during the American Revolution';[90] and it renders all the more noteworthy the practical acceptance of theological diversity and the relaxations of the law which have been outlined in this essay.

V

None of this is to suggest that North's ministry pursued some kind of 'liberalizing' policy in a modern sense, still less that it did so consciously,

85 Caner letterbook: Caner to S. Gardiner, 30 Sept. 1776.
86 Boucher, *View of the Causes*, p. 107.
87 Clark, *English Society*, p. 273 n. 215; Norton, *The British Americans*, pp. 23–4.
88 A. L. Cross, *The Anglican Episcopate and the American Colonies* (Cambridge, Mass., 1902), the works of Bridenbaugh and Sosin cited above and the articles in *Church History*, 45, 3 (Sept. 1976).
89 Clark, *English Society*, p. 326.
90 Bradley, 'Resurgence of Toryism', p. 386.

nor is it to suggest a return to a depiction of a dominant Latitudinarian mentality in Church and ministry. There is no doubt that an emphasis upon order and authority is to be found in much of the Anglican preaching and writing in this period, though it is important to appreciate that it drew its inspiration from Whig as well as Tory sources, and was not peculiar to the post-1760 period. Nor is the thrust of this essay necessarily at odds with Dr Clark's concept of eighteenth-century England as a 'Confessional State', with the system of religious tests at the very centre of politics. And one recognizes that sympathetic gestures towards Catholics and Episcopalians, which later generations might regard as 'tolerant', were open to an 'authoritarian' interpretation in the later eighteenth century.

But this essay seeks to register a note of caution in the use of such expressions as 'authoritarian', 'arbitrary' or 'repressed' in discussions of ecclesiastical policy under North.[91] If 'arbitrariness' is taken to mean despotism, caprice and lack of restraint, and if Toryism is taken to mean threats to Dissenters and to traditional liberties, then these formulations are highly misleading for the 1770s. In practical terms, Professor Christie's verdict, that 'liberty was not waning but broadening in the years after 1760',[92] is as appropriate in the ecclesiastical as in the secular sphere, if indeed the two may be separated. It was, perhaps, not broadening as rapidly as some, probably unrepresentative, expectations demanded. But Dissenters and Commonwealthmen, unlike their successors in the 1790s, or many American Episcopalians in the 1770s, suffered no physical menace. Just as Dr Bradley's study of the petitions and addresses of 1775 shows Anglican lay opinion not only genuinely divided, but free to express its divisions, over American conciliation,[93] so there was an accepted measure of diversity in ecclesiastical practice. The use of force in America and the 'authoritarian tone' of many Anglican sermons was not accompanied by an attack on domestic liberties – quite the reverse. In terms of personnel, North's ministry has more of a 'court Whig' than a Tory appearance and in terms of policy it showed a broader tolerance than many of its predecessors. Not all of this is immediately apparent from an exclusive concentration upon sermon literature; but the evidence of policy permits no other conclusion. Here we return to the familiar theme of the opening paragraph. The lesson, perhaps, is that rhetoric and practice were very different. That, of course, is a statement of the obvious: but at few points is it more obvious than in respect of ecclesiastical policy under North.

[91] For examples of these terms as applied to North's ministry, see Langford, 'Old Whigs, Old Tories', p. 126 and Bradley, *Popular Politics*, pp. 213–15. One wonders what term would be appropriate for the Whig ministry's treatment of its Tory opponents after 1714.

[92] Christie, 'New Toryism?', in idem, *Myth and Reality*, p. 203.

[93] Bradley, *Popular Politics*, ch. 3.

11 The foundation of the Church Missionary Society: the Anglican missionary impulse

Elizabeth Elbourne

I

In October 1795 the editors of the fledgling interdenominational journal, the *Evangelical Magazine*, founded by the LMS director John Eyre with the partial aim of promoting missions, informed its readers of the spectacular success of a week of meetings held in September to form the London Missionary Society. The first private British missionary society designed exclusively to convert the heathen had been founded three years previously by the Particular Baptists. The LMS, however, was the first interdenominational society and the first to make such a large-scale bid for public support. The *Evangelical Magazine* was undoubtedly a biased reporter, but its account is nonetheless striking. 'It is with infinite satisfaction and joy unspeakable, that we now inform our anxious readers that their wishes are not only gratified, but our own expectations far, very far exceeded.'[1] Crowded morning and evening services had been held throughout the week, at one of which thousands had been turned away. On the final evening, some of the ministers present 'could not, for a time, proceed for tears of joy'.[2]

By 25 September the Anglican Evangelical banker Henry Thornton was able to write informally to a future leading organizer of the Church Missionary Society, John Venn, on the rapid fund-raising success of the new society:

> I have heard today . . . that £10,000 is said by Mr Haweis to be already collected for the Missionary Society . . . what a striking thing it is that a Bishop of London [Beilby Porteus] is hardly able (as I suspect) to scrape a few hundred Pounds together for the Missionary Plans in his hands among all the people of the Church Establishment & that £10,000 shd be raised in such a few days by the Irregulars who are also so much poorer a Class of People than the others.[3]

This emotional and financially successful inauguration, the culmination of a year's publicity in the *Evangelical Magazine* and in pulpits throughout

[1] *Evangelical Magazine*, Oct. 1795, p. 421.
[2] Ibid., p. 424.
[3] Church Missionary Society Papers, University of Birmingham, Acc.81, Venn MSS, C.68: Henry Thornton to John Venn, 25 Sept. 1795.

the country, contrasted markedly with the first public meeting of the 'Society for Missions to Africa and the East instituted by Members of the Established Church', soon to be known by the less cumbersome title of the 'Church Missionary Society' (CMS).[4] This was an anniversary sermon, preached in 1801, two years after the actual private inauguration of the Society. A relatively meagre four to five hundred came to hear the Reverend Thomas Scott preach on the damnation of the heathen; not yet having any missionaries in its employ, the Society did not attempt to take a collection. 'Perhaps this may be ascribed in a measure to a very heavy rain and its not being sufficiently made public', wrote Mrs Scott to her son, 'but your father thinks that many frown on the Society'.[5] Only subscribers were invited to the General Meeting which followed the service, in contrast to the LMS policy of holding public meetings. Despite a steady growth in subscriptions, it would be at least twelve years before the CMS would win widespread popular support, or indeed send its first English missionary overseas. Why the disparity?

Most immediately, the awkward position of Evangelicals determined to remain within the establishment in the late 1790s and early 1800s made the foundation of the CMS a tentative enterprise, fraught with problems. Members sought to take the techniques and ideology of domestic evangelical revival and apply them to politically safe ends within the restrictions of church order; this was intrinsically difficult and attracted establishment suspicion. A more fundamental reason for the early disparity between the success of the LMS and the CMS was the feebleness, in the early years of the latter, of an Anglican missionary culture, which would provide both the personnel and the financial support necessary to sustain missions abroad. Both the ecclesiastical and imperial authorities opposed an evangelical missionary movement; thus, the eventual success of the CMS and its allies in 1813 in persuading Parliament to limit the East India Company's (EIC) capacity to refuse missionaries admission to India and to set on foot an Indian ecclesiastical establishment both constituted a significant readjustment of Britain's imperial vision and signalled an astonishing growth in Anglican popular missionary culture.

This essay will focus on the events around the actual formation of the CMS before briefly discussing more speculatively some implications of the successes of the early 1810s. It will argue that the leading clerical progenitors of the CMS are not readily definable in a neat package labelled

[4] The title 'Church Missionary Society' was used informally for many years for the more cumbersome 'Society for Missions to Africa and the East', before becoming official in 1812. Charles Hole traced the development of the term in *The Early History of the Church Missionary Society* (1896), pp. 42, 189, 215, 231. I shall use the abbreviation 'CMS' throughout, although I am aware that this is strictly speaking anachronistic.

[5] 28 May 1801, cited in Henry Venn, *Founders of the Church Missionary Society* (1848), p. 20.

'Anglican Evangelical'; they had close and ambivalent relationships with Methodism, even though they upheld a high view of church order. They did not have a well-defined national 'Evangelical party' behind them in 1799. Rather, the CMS helped to *create* a network of self-defining 'Evangelicals', just as it helped to form local support groups which could be called upon for political ends by the 'Saints' in Parliament and which would enable Evangelical politicians to claim the out-of-doors support of the 'religious world'. These networks were also important because they enabled missionary societies to shape the popular conception of the 'heathen' inhabitants of areas under British influence. The early days of the CMS thus saw the slow growth among Anglican Evangelicals of a popular 'missionary culture' with ramifications both for national politics and for the popular understanding of the non-Christian world.

In the development of Evangelical networks, the CMS was of course only part of a complicated, multi-faceted process;[6] other societies, such as the powerful interdenominational British and Foreign Bible Society (founded in 1804) and even a rejuvenated High Church Society for the Propagation of the Gospel, were institutionally central to the creation of Anglican missionary culture, while much broader forces created a receptive climate. Nonetheless, a careful study of the CMS's foundation provides a means of addressing broader, if not readily answerable, questions.

II

The CMS was the brainchild of a small, tightly interlinked group of Evangelical clergy in London, patronized by the 'Clapham Sect'. The Society was established in the London meetings of the Eclectic Society, an association typical of the clerical discussion societies which were beginning to build Evangelical networks on a modest scale.[7] By 1799, members included many who are now considered to have been key early Evangelical leaders: John Venn, the rector of Clapham, Thomas Scott, author of the *Commentary on the Whole Bible*, Henry Foster, Richard Cecil, John Newton and Josiah Pratt, subsequently the long-standing secretary of the CMS. Others included the Reverend George Pattrick, William Jarvis Abdy, Basil Woodd, William Goode and John Davies, as well as the layman John Bacon, the noted sculptor. Charles Grant and the Reverend Charles Simeon, perhaps the leading Cambridge Evangelical of the early nineteenth century, were among the country members. With the notable exception of Simeon, all these men joined the early directorate of the CMS.

[6] For an overview of Evangelical 'national reform' see Ford K. Brown, *Fathers of the Victorians* (Cambridge, 1961), esp. pp. 234–84 on missions.

[7] *Eclectic Notes*, ed. John H. Pratt (1856), p. 1.

The initial relationship between the Clapham Sect and the group of clergy centred on the Eclectic Society was one of patronage: many Claphamites purchased livings for 'serious' clergy and lent respectability to their London churches. Indeed, several of the 'Eclectics', including Newton, Abdy and Venn, had been brought to London by men who subsequently became lay patrons of the CMS.[8] Additional ties of spiritual friendship and the more material bonds of matrimony linked the two sets further and drew the London Evangelical clergy more closely together.

John Venn's CMS connexions, for example, ranged from the familial to the professional. He had a friendship with the Jowett family dating from his school days, university connexions with Simeon, and ties to the Thorntons inherited from his father. After graduating from Sidney Sussex, Venn was appointed to the living of Little Dunham by Edward Parry, later to become a leading EIC director and an honorary official of the CMS – and a man whose own family connexions, including a future Chancellor of the Exchequer and a former Governor of Bengal, would lend weight to the CMS. The Thorntons, with their extensive banking and imperial interests, were a further source of patronage. In 1804 Venn was presented to the sinecure rectory of Great Tey, Essex, by his 'hond patron' Samuel Thornton, vice-president and banker of the CMS.[9]

The clerical initiators of the CMS were thus not so much the proverbial founders of the Victorian Evangelical party, come together through conviction alone: rather they were originally acquaintances, representative of, but not necessarily in contact with, a broader current in the Church, able to assume a prominent role through location and patronage links. Furthermore, from the very beginning these London Evangelicals, for the most part from comfortable but not unusually affluent commercial or clerical backgrounds,[10] were linked in the most intimate way to men of significant governmental and imperial experience. The CMS may have begun inauspiciously, but it was well placed to become a mouthpiece for the 'Saints'' Christian imperial agenda.

London Evangelical clergy and the lay Claphamites had already collaborated in a range of associations designed to promote Christianization and the improvement of public morals, from the 1788 Society to Effect the

[8] Hole, *Early History*, pp. 621, 635; John Venn, *Annals of a Clerical Family* (1904), p. 127; CMS, Acc.81, C.68: 'Extract from the will of the late John Thornton Esqr of Clapham in the county of Surrey Dated 2 Apr 1790'.

[9] CMS, Acc.81, F3: John Venn (Senior), Annals; Hole, *Early History*, p. 626.

[10] For example, Elliott was upholsterer to the King, while Jowett had a lucrative skinner's business. Venn's father came from a fairly well-off clerical line; Cuthbert, in contrast, succeeded his clerical father as rector of a very small parish in Essex. Newton was the child of a captain in the merchant service involved in slave-trading. On the other hand, Pattrick was a farmer's son and Scott the son of a grazier: their experiences of self-education mirror the classic profile of the early Dissenting missionary.

Enforcement of his Majesty's Proclamation Against Vice and Immorality onwards. The CMS was thus only one among the numerous private societies which were central to the Anglican Evangelical reformation of manners movement.[11] Nonetheless, it represented a particularly apt dovetailing of interests: the Anglican Evangelical need for a respectable missionary society and the imperial need for a means to Christianize colonies without opening the back door to enthusiasm.

Many late eighteenth-century Anglican Evangelical clergy naturally tended to be joined to evangelicals outside the Church of England by bonds of theological sympathy, of personal friendship and (in some cases) of active co-operation. This was particularly so because of the uncertainty about the ecclesiastical status of Methodism. The term was still an elastic one: as late as 1798 Richard Cecil drew a nice distinction between the sense of 'Methodist' as meaning 'any man who is more earnest and active about the salvation which is in Jesus Christ than his neighbours' and as implying a member of 'that numerous body of people, whose zeal for the propagation of Christianity is not connected with any particular regard to the order and discipline observed by the Church of England, nor even that of the regular Protestant Dissenters'.[12] At the same time, the term 'evangelical' had pan-denominational and pan-European significance, denoting for many participation in a self-consciously international movement of Protestant renewal.

The essential insight which animated missionary activity was shared by all evangelicals: man was degenerate in his spiritual essence until rescued by the atoning grace of Christ. Wickedness was man's natural state. Thus the conviction that the heathen were damned was a necessary extension of a conviction about the damnation of all people, including purely 'nominal' Christians who did not possess a *true* and saving knowledge of Christ. The very beliefs which propelled the domestic revivalism so politically troubling to High Churchmen also pointed towards the evangelism of the heathen, in a way which Anglican Evangelicals tended to support but were circumstantially constrained from upholding too publicly.

Individual Anglican Evangelicals had thus watched the formation of the Particular Baptist Missionary Society in 1792, that of the LMS in 1795 and the establishment of several support societies in Scotland with great interest leavened in many cases by personal contact with the participants. The first

[11] Joanna Innes, 'Politics and Morals. The Reformation of Manners Movement in Later Eighteenth-Century England', in *The Transformation of Political Culture*, ed. Eckhart Hellmuth (Oxford, 1990), pp. 57–118; Donna T. Andrew, *Philanthropy and Police. London Charity in the Eighteenth Century* (Princeton, 1989); Brown, *Fathers*, esp. pp. 83–91, 317–60.

[12] Richard Cecil, *Memoirs of the late Hon. and Rev. W. B. Cadogan, MA, John Bacon Esq. RA and the Rev. John Newton* (1812; revised by J. Pratt; memoir of Cadogan first published separately, 1798), pp. 26–30.

secretary of the CMS, Thomas Scott, for example, maintained a lively correspondence with John Ryland, president of the Bristol Baptist College from 1793 to 1825 and secretary of the Baptist Missionary Society (BMS) between 1815 and 1825. He reported in 1809 that he was devoting much of his time to missionary activity, 'excited to emulation by the example of your missionaries in India'. In 1814 he was to write 'I do most heartily rejoice in what your missionaries are doing in India . . . May all India be peopled with true Christians – even though they be all baptists.'[13] Politics, however, dictated the initial maintenance of a proper distance from non-Anglican efforts. As Scott wrote to another friend shortly after the foundation of the LMS:

> My situation . . . as a minister of the establishment prevents me, by considerations of expediency, from fully uniting with a society which is looked upon with jealousy by our staunch churchmen, especially our rulers. At the same time I feel it incumbent on me to be cautious about how I commit myself in a business which is under the management of persons varying in their views and in their measure of respectability. Hence I am constrained to be considerably a stranger to the persons selected for missionaries, and to the interior of the management; though I am privately a steady advocate for the institution, and contribute my mite to the cause. In my situation, I cannot make any public collections, or take any other ostensible measures: but my few steady friends liberally support them.[14]

In short, CMS leading lights were already in the 1790s eagerly following the progress of Dissenting missionary activity but were either too nervous to participate in the interdenominational LMS, or too distrustful of the overambitious scale of its early activities. They doubtless remembered that Porteus, the most pro-evangelical of the bishops, had refused Wilberforce's request to ordain for the South Seas two missionary candidates, graduates of the Countess of Huntingdon's college in Wales, who had been sponsored by Thomas Haweis; some may have known that in 1798 Porteus professed himself unable to subscribe to the LMS. An Evangelical missionary society, however sternly Anglican, was clearly a politically risky proposition, particularly as it posed an implicit challenge and rebuke to the SPG and SPCK.

In addition to the inevitable association with sectarians,[15] missionary activity necessarily required itineracy. This was an explosive issue in 1798–1800 when Pretyman-Tomline and other High Churchmen were pressing for an act outlawing itineracy in Great Britain. The LMS and BMS made things more difficult by hailing the ways in which domestic and foreign

[13] *Letters and Papers of the Late Reverend Thomas Scott*, ed. John Scott (1824), pp. 251, 254: Scott to Ryland, 24 June 1809, 3 Dec. 1814.

[14] Ibid., pp. 184–5: Scott to 'A friend in Scotland', 2 July 1796.

[15] E.g., 'On the Probable Design of Providence in Subjecting India to Great Britain', *Christian Observer*, Feb. 1809, p. 221.

evangelism fed off each other and by claiming some of the credit for the spectacular growth in Calvinist itineracy in rural England from the 1780s onwards which had helped to provoke the establishment clamp-down in the first place.[16] In 1799, for example, Samuel Greatheed of Newport Pagnell reported to LMS directors that 'a number of pious mechanics and a few Ministers devoting themselves to the service of Christ among the Heathen, a general Enquiry was excited among Ministers and private Christians whether it was not their duty to do likewise'. Although most concluded in the negative, the formation of missionary associations inspired the revival of village preaching and the foundation of interdenominational associations for the domestic propagation of the Gospel. Despite the beneficial impact of these activities, Greatheed concluded, 'much pains are taken by high-church politicians to make it believed that these exertions are made with seditious purposes'.[17]

Although Michael Angelo Taylor, MP for Durham, was persuaded to drop his bill restricting itineracy, partly under threat from his own Dissenting constituents and Methodist election agent, itineracy remained under profound suspicion.[18] In this context the increasingly visible London Evangelicals came under direct attack. The *Anti-Jacobin Review* lobbed a series of damaging articles in their direction in 1799 and 1800, alleging that they were probably seditious and at the least arousing unrest among the common people.[19] By 1802 the Blagdon controversy had erupted over the schools of Hannah More, and a previous supporter of More's, William Cobbett, had launched his *Annual Register* with an all-out attack on Evangelical clergy – 'cool, of consummate cunning, of great industry and perseverance, and supported by men of no little wealth', akin to the '"*Gospel-Preaching Ministry*", so loudly clamoured for by the apprentices and chimney-sweeps of London, in their petitions to the regicide parliament'.[20]

The atmosphere was one of anti-Methodist moral panic. Several of the founding members of the CMS had experienced harassment. John Venn, for example, had been refused admission to Trinity College, Cambridge, 'thru the fear of Methodism', while the master and fellows of his second choice, Sidney Sussex, 'were very averse and injurious for a season, on account of his being the son of a Methodist clergyman'. George Pattrick

[16] Deryck Lovegrove, *Established Church, Sectarian People. Itinerancy and the Transformation of English Dissent 1780–1830* (Cambridge, 1988), pp. 14–40.

[17] LMS Archives, School of Oriental and African Studies, London, 1/6/A: Greatheed to Eyre, 13 Feb. 1799.

[18] W.R. Ward, *Religion and Society in England 1790–1850* (1972), pp. 47–53.

[19] For example, *Anti-Jacobin Review*, 2 (1799), 361–71.

[20] *Christian Observer*, Mar. 1802, pp. 179–84; William Cobbett, *Cobbett's Annual Register*, 20–7 Feb. 1802, p. 173; Brown, *Fathers*, pp. 187–233.

was dismissed from the chaplaincy of Morden College, Blackheath, following complaints from the inmates. William Jarvis Abdy, according to a rather cryptic comment by Josiah Pratt's son, suffered at first at St John's, Horsley-down, 'in opposition to his efforts for the spiritual benefit of his flock amounting almost to persecution'. Apparently, however, Abdy 'gradually made his way by patient continuance in well-doing'. As a child, William Goode had seen his beloved family minister forced to leave a Buckinghamshire parish because 'he had acquired the character of what then went by the name of a Methodist', and Goode's family had fled for a while to an Independent chapel.[21]

Even their Claphamite supporters were sometimes suspicious of the ecclesiastical loyalty of Evangelical ministers. Henry Thornton wrote to Wilberforce in 1801 that he found it 'curious' that Pratt should collaborate so much with Dissenters:

it tends to prove what I have often thought that the evangelical mins in the Church who are warm on points of doctrine & talk much of '*seeing clearly*' & indeed most of those who are serious find themselves so naturally connected with Dissenters that consid'g human Nature it is scarcely possible for them to be very staunch friends of the Church under the present Circumstances of the Establishment.[22]

Despite, or perhaps because of, such ubiquitous suspicion, the CMS Evangelicals determinedly professed themselves loyal to church and state, and their theology was far from antinomian or dangerously enthusiastic. 'To preach Christ crucified and him alone' did not have to be subversive. By 1799, as the heat went out of the controversy between Arminianism and Calvinism, Anglican Evangelicals moved to a fusion between the two, despite the roots of most in Calvinism. Henry Jowett wrote in 1795, 'My wish is to preach as the most evangelical or if you will the most Calvinistic Arminians, because they seem to me to come nearest the model of Scripture', while John Newton hoped that he was 'upon the whole a SCRIPTURAL preacher'.[23] Bernard Semmel is probably right that this doctrinal moderation allowed Evangelicalism to be turned to more conservative social ends after the 1790s.[24] For example, in practice (i.e. in accounts of their own conversion experiences), CMS Evangelicals such as Basil Woodd and William Goode allowed for saving grace without a specific moment of new birth.[25] This affirmation of spiritual enlightenment through gradual educa-

21 CMS, Acc.81, F5: Henry Venn, 'Memoirs of the Revd. John Venn – Period first from Birth to College'; Venn, *Annals of a Clerical Family*, p. 102: Berridge to John Thornton, 24 Nov. 1781; J. Scott, *The Life of the Rev. Thomas Scott* (1822), p. 30; Hole, *Early History*, p. 635; *Eclectic Notes*, ed. Pratt, p. 22; William Goode, *A Memoir of the Late Rev. William Goode, MA* (1828), p. 4.

22 Bodl., MS Wilberforce c.51, fo. 30: Thornton to Wilberforce, 21 Nov. 1804.

23 CMS, Acc.81, C.19: Jowett to Venn, 6 May 1795; Cecil, *Memoirs*, p. 403.

24 Bernard Semmel, *The Methodist Revolution* (1973), p. 109.

25 Goode, *Memoir*, p. 4.

tion left the door open to arguments for the value of hierarchy, helping to explain CMS reluctance to ordain the uneducated.

In a similar conciliatory and middle-of-the-road vein, the 'Eclectics' tended to adopt a cautious, but not condemnatory, posture towards some of the inspirational elements of Dissent and Methodism. In an Eclectic Society discussion of dreams, for example, Richard Cecil commented that:

> If important events follow a dream, then we may regard it as one of the links in the chain of Providence. I think that dreams are not philosophically or fairly to be referred to accident ... Yet we must not lean too much towards the superstitious side. Mr. Wesley's people do this. Dreams can afford no implicit ground of comfort and guidance.

John Venn added that dreams, like everything else, could be used by both God and Satan. '*But foresake not the written word for them.*'[26] It is not recorded, however, whether he added the story which his children knew, that he had had a dream of his mother on the morning of her death before the messenger arrived with the news.[27]

CMS Evangelicals were also relatively cautious in their use of millenarian rhetoric. Across the denominational divide, a belief fuelling missions was that missionary activity would hasten the millennium and that the evangelization of the heathen was part of God's providential plan for human history. Although classic distinctions between 'pre-' and 'post-millenarianism' were not employed with doctrinal rigidity, the moderate Evangelicals of the CMS and the Clapham Sect were essentially optimistic about the amelioration of society, whereas the LMS harboured several more 'extreme' evangelicals.[28] Although both the LMS and CMS employed the language of national retribution in the 1800s,[29] for the CMS missionary activity was gradually to usher in the reign of Christ on earth, rather than being a sign of imminent destruction. LMS rhetoric opened the door to a greater *possibility* (however little fulfilled) of political extremism: early LMS missionaries in South Africa, for example, taught that God was about to overthrow the white government as punishment for the oppression of indigenous inhabitants. CMS anniversary sermons more readily employed millenarian language as the political situation improved, since God's blessing on England was a sign of development toward the millennium. Millenarianism, in other words, tended to be used by CMS propagandists to support existing authority relationships, rather than to predict their imminent overthrow.

If, in the context of the 1790s, caution in the face of 'enthusiastic'

[26] *Eclectic Notes*, ed. Pratt, pp. 81, 82–3, 85.
[27] CMS, Acc.81, F5: 'Memoirs of the Revd. John Venn'.
[28] The following draws on Boyd Hilton, *The Age of Atonement* (Oxford, 1988), pp. 14–19.
[29] E.g., *Christian Observer*, Mar. 1802, p. 202.

elements seems to indicate opposition to popular radicalism, the impression is in this case correct. Just before setting up the CMS, the Eclectic Society considered 'what can be done at the present moment to counteract the Designs of Infidels against Christianity?' Pratt proposed a society to oppose the effects of infidelity. It would need to be well funded and secret: 'strike, but conceal the hand'. Ideally, it would control the press, since 'literature is at present the great engine acting upon society'. This project was approved by the Society, and efforts were made to get it under way, fortunately in a less alarming guise: members wrote several pamphlets and tracts on the model of Hannah More's *Village Politics*, as well as launching a series of rotating weekly sermons which was to last three years on 'the Signs and Duties of the Times'.[30]

The 'Eclectics' thus welcomed, indeed depended on, the respectability which the Claphamites were able to bring to the project of a missionary society. Claphamite motivation was probably as much political as theological, to make a distinction which they would have found arbitrary. Several of this group had extensive imperial experience both on the spot in Africa and India, and through their joint involvement in founding and running from London the short-lived evangelical colony of Sierra Leone. They also had what one might term imaginative experience through their participation under the leadership of William Wilberforce in the struggle to abolish the slave trade and to project on to the political stage a galvanizing image of an economically and spiritually redeemed Africa. Several came to the Society with concrete projects for the conversion of peoples among or near whom they had lived, firmly convinced of the beneficial impact of a well-ordered Christianity in introducing civilization and commercial talent. For example, both John Shore (later Lord Teignmouth), former governor-general of India, and the EIC magnate Charles Grant had written on the urgent necessity of converting India to Christianity and had been involved in failed efforts to force the EIC to open India to missionaries. All the same, Grant, in the very year in which he published his *Observations on the State of Society among the Asiatic Subjects of Great Britain*, refused to grant a licence to William Carey and his companion to travel to British India as missionaries for the BMS, despite Scott's intercession: 'his strong disapprobation of Mr. T., on what ground I knew not, induced his negative'.[31] After his 1796–9 tenure as governor of Sierra Leone, Zachary Macaulay had returned with the children of local African chiefs, planning to educate them in England, Christianize them and send them back to West Africa as emissaries of Christ. The plan was surely inspired in part, however, by the

[30] *Eclectic Notes*, ed. Pratt, pp. 13–16.

[31] Eustace Carey, *Memoir of William Carey* (1836), p. 42: Thomas Scott to [Mr Ivimey?], 31 Jan. 1815.

Governor's distrust of evangelical enthusiasm among the ex-slave 'Nova Scotian' settlers,[32] which was not entirely in accord with the Claphamite vision of Sierra Leone as 'an emporium of commerce, a school of industry, and a source of knowledge, civilization and religious improvement' for Africa.[33]

III

The meeting of 18 March 1799, at which the CMS was actually begun, was at least the fourth Eclectic Society meeting on the topic, although the first one for which records survive.[34] The atmosphere was cautious. John Venn proposed resolutions which members agreed breathed 'a quiet, humble, dependent spirit'. First, success in mission would come from the Spirit of God. A foundation must be laid in prayer, and God's providence must be followed, not anticipated. Second, success would depend on the persons sent on the missions, whom God would bring forth. Third, 'it is better that a Mission should proceed from small beginnings and advance according to circumstances'.[35]

This cautious approach was in deliberate contrast with that of the LMS, which had already purchased a ship for some £5,000 and dispatched two large-scale missions to the South Seas. In addition to more central political reasons, this divergence doubtless reflected temperamental differences and some genuine mistrust of the intense providentialism of the LMS. As Scott had written privately in 1796, 'it appears to me that many [in the LMS] are too sanguine, do not sufficiently count their cost, have not wisdom equal to their zeal, and lean more to favourable providential appearances, and second causes, than to the omnipotent activity of the Holy Spirit'.[36]

Venn next pressed the need for a 'community of sentiments' among co-workers to enable co-operation. Pratt put this more succinctly: 'it must be kept in evangelical hands'.[37] As for specific action, the Eclectic Society

[32] Macaulay forbade the black settler David George to go to Jamaica as a Baptist missionary, although he himself claimed in a letter to John Newton that this was not due to party spirit on his part – that he himself 'should not know what name to call myself among Men', and that he did not interfere with local religion, despite 'the gross ignorance of all our Black preachers with scarce an exception & their vain notions of a light within superseding Biblical light'. LPL, MS 2935: Macaulay to Newton, 3 June 1797.

[33] 'Report of the Company's Directors, Delivered to the General Court of Proprietors, on the 24th of March Last', cited in 'Report of the Committee, Delivered to the Annual Meeting, Held June 12, 1810', *Proceedings of the Society for Missions to Africa and the East*, II, 326.

[34] Eclectic Society interest in missions shadowed the opening of actual colonial possibilities; members discussed the best method of propagating the Gospel in Botany Bay in 1783, in the East Indies in 1789 and in Africa in 1791. Josiah and John Henry Pratt, *Memoir of the Rev. Josiah Pratt* (1849), pp. 463–4.

[35] *Eclectic Notes*, ed. Pratt, p. 96.

[36] *Letters and Papers of Thomas Scott*, ed. Scott, p. 185: Scott to 'A Friend in Scotland', 2 July 1796.

[37] *Eclectic Notes*, ed. Pratt, p. 98.

should not yet seek to raise funds. Rather, members should admonish their people to promote the knowledge of the Gospel among the heathen; pray; consider the best method of starting a mission; and each speak to 'at least three of his Christian friends'. The exhortations of Charles Simeon underscore the reader's sense of the Anglican Church slowly following the non-Anglican lead: 'We cannot join the [London] Missionary Society; yet I bless God that they have stood forth. We must now stand forth – we require something more than Resolutions ... We have been dreaming these four years, while all England, all Europe, has been awake.'[38] 'We have set on foot a new society for missions to Africa and the East by members of the established church', wrote Scott to a friend. 'Probably we shall engage a set of men (to support it), and draw most of our resources from quarters, which are out of the reach of other societies.'[39]

An equally discreet foundation meeting of 12 April appointed seven Claphamites to act as vice-presidents.[40] Despite this noteworthy early support the Claphamites were not unequivocal, and few came steadily to meetings. Wilberforce, who was later to argue that the establishment of missions to India was second in importance to the abolition of slavery, prevaricated about accepting the presidency – perhaps unsurprisingly given his delicate position of opposition to Pitt's old tutor, Pretyman-Tomline, over itineracy. The fledgling Society placed the office of president in abeyance, elected Wilberforce a vice-president and rotated an honorary presidency among the vice-presidents.

As a first step towards the creation of Evangelical networks which would be a key function of the CMS, the Society quickly established a list of thirteen country members, all of whom again seem to have been personal contacts. The committee also tackled the crucial problem of gaining episcopal approval. An *Account of a Society for Missions to Africa and the East Instituted by Members of the Established Church* was drafted to be sent to the Archbishop of Canterbury and to the only Bishops, Porteus and Shute Barrington, who might have been expected to offer support. A quietly defensive covering letter hoped for favourable regard on 'this attempt to extend the benefits of Christianity, an attempt peculiarly necessary at a period at which the most zealous and systematic efforts have been made to eradicate the Christian religion'.[41] The *Account* emphasized the social benefits of the spread of Christianity before it urged the spiritual: 'The husband and wife, the father and son, the master and servant, at once learn from it their respective duties, and are disposed and enabled to fulfil

[38] Ibid., pp. 96–8.
[39] *Letters and Papers of Thomas Scott*, ed. Scott, p. 224: Scott to 'A Friend in Scotland', 25 May 1799.
[40] CMS, G/C1, vol. I: Committee Minutes, 12 Apr. 1799.
[41] CMS, G/CA3, vol. I: Venn to Moore, July 1799.

them ... A mild and equitable spirit is infused by it into legislation and civil government. Rulers become the fathers of their people, and subjects cheerfully yield obedience.' The *Account* also explained the rather clumsy system of missionary ordination on which the Society had settled in order to ease the apparent threat to church order of ordaining the under-educated lower-class men expected to volunteer to be missionaries: they were to be ordained as catechists to the mission field, would not have the right to administer sacraments and could not function as priests were they to return.[42]

These papers were to be presented by a carefully selected delegation, headed by Wilberforce, who also approached the Archbishop informally. Moore's eventual reply via Wilberforce, delayed until July 1800, was a masterpiece of prevarication:

> his Grace regretted that he could not with propriety at once express his full concurrence and approbation of an endeavour in behalf of an object he had deeply at heart. He acquiesced in the hope I expressed that the Society might go forward, being assured he would look on the proceedings with candour, and that it would give him pleasure to find them such as he could approve.[43]

The rather desperate Society, reduced by now to dissolving meetings for lack of a quorum, seized on this limited message as a full signal to go ahead; they printed 2,000 copies of the *Account* and asked country members to begin to distribute it. The construction of Evangelical networks began again: country members sent in names of men who might be willing to receive copies or to do publicity work themselves,[44] although estimates of Evangelical strength varied greatly. The consensus, however, was that the largest Evangelical constituency was the poor. It was judged extremely difficult to raise funds in times of such hardship – and of hostility to the Evangelicals in some areas. Most strikingly, despite the CMS's efforts to use this new network of contacts to discover potential missionaries, minister after minister wrote to say that he could think of no suitable person.

An initial explanation for the lack of missionary candidates is that the ministers themselves had preconceptions of what a suitable candidate would look like, whereas LMS candidates were self-selecting. This is insufficient, however, to explain the twelve-year dearth which followed, during which the CMS was driven to employing German Lutherans from the Berlin Academy for lack of British offers. A further suggestion is that evangelically minded young men seeking to become preachers were tending to drift to the Methodists, or indeed being chased to them by local church

42 LPL, Fulham Papers, Porteus Papers, XXXVII.
43 CMS, G/AC3, vol. I: Wilberforce to Venn, 24 July 1800.
44 Crouch and Fry of St Edmund's Hall, for example, punctiliously listed 105 potential sympathizers, subdivided by county. CMS, G/CA3, vol. I: Crouch to Scott, 1 Feb. 1801.

authorities. An instructive example is that of a young farmer's son, suggested by the Reverend J. Mayor for missionary work, who had been 'exceedingly successful in awakening numbers'.

> He has been driven on (by a family who see themselves at length got into Mr. Wesley's connection) to proceed from private admonition in his circle, to preach publicly in houses at distant parts of parishes, and to favour Mr. W's sentiments, to which he has been tempted the more by men preaching in our parts, who tend rather to the Antinomian way. He has been also persuaded to shelter himself from a prosecution threatened by a clergyman by taking the Oaths and being licensed as a dissenting minister.[45]

Mayor's hopes that the young man might be tempted back to church allegiance were not realized, however. Having spent much energy stifling evangelism from below, it was not easy for church figures, no matter how Evangelical, to re-animate it. It was also damaging that the CMS could not offer ordination and full responsibility to such a person. Furthermore, there did not yet exist a cult of missions among the self-consciously Anglican laity – one that would sentimentalize missions, make heroes of missionaries and provide information about the places to which they would go in order to make the idea less terrifying. The 1802 CMS report wondered whether the reputation of Sierra Leone deterred applicants: 'perhaps without sufficient foundations', Africa was reputed to be unhealthy and wholly 'rude and barbarous in its manners'. Indeed, the Company of Directors of Sierra Leone had been looking for a chaplain for the past five years.[46]

The few early offers which did occur tended to be thwarted by family opposition or by last-minute cold feet. The language in which they were couched was less uniformly rhetorical and stereotypical than the letters of even ten years later, suggesting that there was not yet a popular rhetoric of mission. In 1800, for example, George Smith wrote to implore the Macaulay brothers to intervene with his fiancée's mother, resistant as she was to the desire 'which I have had of late more fully, to go as a Missionary to the East Indies if my way could be made clear'.

> I have no wish but just to live and do all the good I can – I wrote to the Young Woman's Mother that if she would not consent for her Daughter to go or give us 20 pounds a year to what I have in an English Circuit, to make her Daughter comfortable, we must do violence to our own feelings and I must go alone. I only wish to do my duty to God and the Young Woman as I have real affection for her. I have had no answer but a charge from her Mother of deserting her Daughter after having gain'd her affections. I have grieved so much that with a cold I had taken and distress of mind I have been under the Doc^rs Hand and confined to my Room for a fortnight.

[45] CMS, G/AC3, vol. I: Mayor to Scott, 22 Jan. 1800.
[46] 'Report of the Directors', 1802, in *Proceedings of the SMAE*, I, 137–8.

He added, 'I have always been of the Church of England and I should not like to go out without Episcopal Ordination – unless I went out as a Methodist Preacher.'[47] Three days later, however, Smith had just received 'a letter from the Young Woman – that if I see it my duty to stay at home and Labour, she will trust on the providence of God and comply with my wishes – and as I know there is real affection on both sides I think my duty and happiness to Marry her and do all the good I can in England'.[48]

Compare this with the standardized rhetorical flourishes of a typical letter in 1812:

> if you are in wants of young men to go abroad on the all important Errand of Proclaiming the unsearchable Riches of Christ to the Poor Perishing Heathen, & if after suitable inquiry and Examination I am approved of, I will thro divine grace with diffidence, Sincerity and Pleasure give up myself to God & to you for the Great, Arduous and Awfully Responsible yet delightful & Honourable work of a Missionary.[49]

IV

The difficult years between these two letters were nonetheless characterized by the growth of self-confidence through the nurture of supportive congregations, in a process given a significant fillip by the local mobilization involved in the fight to abolish the slave trade and by the growing success, despite opposition, of the British and Foreign Bible Society. Throughout the period, the CMS employed German Lutherans to man missions in Sierra Leone and New Zealand, following the model of the SPCK in southern India.[50] Nonetheless, the Society remained very nervous of exposure and felt too threatened to adopt LMS methods of domestic proselytizing, such as fund-raising tours and an open use of the press – beyond a discreet alliance with the *Christian Observer*, edited first by Pratt and then by Macaulay. In a revealing letter of 1806, Pratt pleaded with Berlin seminarians *en route* to Africa through Liverpool not to preach in English, which would reveal them as Dissenting ministers. They should preach '*only in German* and to *your countrymen*, in *some large private room* . . . I love all my Dissenting and Methodist brethren who sincerely love our Saviour; but, as a Society, we are surrounded by those who wait for our halting, and we are bound therefore to adhere strictly to our profession as Churchmen.'[51]

[47] CMS, G/AC3, vol. I: Smith to Macaulay, 26 Nov. 1800.
[48] CMS, G/AC3, vol. I: Smith to Macaulay, 29 Nov. 1800.
[49] CMS, G/AC3: P. Shurr to Pratt, 8 July 1812.
[50] Hans Cnattingius, *Bishops and Societies. A Study of Anglican Colonial and Missionary Expansion 1698–1850* (1952), pp. 41–8.
[51] Pratt to missionaries at Liverpool, 30 Jan. 1806, cited in J. and J. H. Pratt, *Memoir*, pp. 34–5.

Early CMS anniversary sermons were thus relatively defensive. Scott in 1801 and Simeon in 1802 attacked the prevalent notion that the heathen did not in fact need saving – that faith in Christ, in other words, was not essential to salvation which could be achieved through good works. The chief early target was the Enlightenment vision of the noble savage.

Several modern travellers (who, by the help of their coadjutors the infidels, have often seemed to labour at proving that Christianity is useless or needless) have launched out in commendation of the virtuous Hindoos, Chinese, or inhabitants of the South-Sea Islands: yet, it is undeniable, that the more these have been known the fuller has been the proof, that they are exceedingly prone to vices of every kind; as well as given up to idolatry, or sunk in total ignorance concerning God and religion.[52]

It was the debate over India, however, which was both to provide a focus for popular activism and to enable the CMS, in engaging the orientalists head-on, to pass from vague generalities to damaging specifics.[53] Although there is not room here to enter into the intricacies of the extended debate over the admission of missionaries to India under the terms of renewal of the EIC charter in 1813, it is important to stress the centrality of the Evangelical success to the development of Anglican missionary culture. India was the great exemplar of the value of non-Christian civilization: to devalue her morality in the popular imagination was a key step in encouraging popular support for mission and portraying God's hand in the growth of the British empire. The debate also saw the elaboration of a more complicated rhetoric of necessary linkage between Christianity and civilization, as proponents of foreign missions sought to counter fear of social disruption by arguments from social utility.

After the disaster of the so-called 'Vellore Massacre' in 1806, missions came under widespread attack for dangerously provoking indigenous sensibilities. In response, CMS annual reports and anniversary sermons and the review pages of the *Christian Observer* targeted Indian customs in what became a ritualized litany of attacks on pagan cruelty, from suttee and Juggernaut to female infanticide and the self-mutilation of Hindu seers.[54] In 1812 the CMS was instrumental in organizing some 800 to 900 petitions from around the country pleading the need of India, most modelled on a pre-circulated CMS petition arguing that 'the natives of India, both Mohammedan and Hindoo' were 'in a state of mental and moral degradation'.[55]

52 Thomas Scott, 1801 Anniversary Sermon, in *Proceedings SMAE*, I, 44.

53 David Kopf, *British Orientalism and the Bengal Renaissance* (Berkeley and Los Angeles, 1969), pp. 129–44.

54 For an overview from the perspective of the *Christian Observer*: 'Review of Buchanan on Christianity in India', Apr. 1813, pp. 239–53.

55 'Christianity in India', *Christian Observer*, Apr. 1813, p. 263.

Wilberforce fought hard to make this a Church of England battle, successfully pleading with his Methodist and Dissenting connexions to stay out of the fray until the cause had been clearly stamped with the establishment imprimatur.[56] The Evangelical triumph in forcing through the establishment of a colonial episcopate in India and the admission, albeit regulated, of missionaries opened the floodgates to domestic missionary activity; government approval, coupled with the defeat of Sidmouth's Bill of 1811, made missionary activity newly respectable.

A second cause of greater self-confidence was the approaching end of the war, removing the sting from charges of disloyalty to the state. Military success at last made it possible for the CMS to state with some plausibility that God favoured missions: the chief pieces of evidence were the providential success of British commerce and the development of empire, with all the routes these activities opened to the transmission of the Gospel. The 1812 CMS annual report closed on a citation from the official *Report of the Formation of the Cambridge Auxiliary Bible Society*:

> Great Britain now stands alone among the nations, with the wreck of Europe scattered at her feet: and, though the dangers of war have been imminent beyond all example of former times, yet it has pleased Providence to give her strength to resist all the efforts of her enemies, and to establish an empire co-extended with the bounds of the ocean ... [W]e humbly hope that our country has been exalted among the nations for nobler purposes; that the empire of Britain shall be an empire of mercy ... Judging from the events passing around us, the *signs of the times*, is it presumptuous to indulge the humble and pious hope, that to Great Britain may be entrusted the high commission of making known the name of Jehovah to the whole earth?[57]

From 1812 on, CMS officials were able to adopt techniques of fund-raising and publicity pioneered by the Dissenting societies. They formed associations around the country, went on itinerant tours to promote missions and began to publish CMS magazines, founding the *Missionary Register* in 1813 and the *Quarterly Papers* in 1816. In another move which would have been impossible during the early period, the *Quarterly Papers* were aimed at exciting missionary support among children and the working classes. They were distributed to those who could fund-raise a penny a week among friends, 'conveying in plain language, intelligence of the Proceedings of the Society, with Engraved representations and Printed Accounts of the ignorance and miseries of the unhappy objects of their kind solicitude'.[58] As the general fear of missions as a vehicle for seditious

[56] Bodl., MS Wilberforce D.54, p. 135: Diary, 14 Feb. 1812.

[57] *Report of the Formation of the Cambridge Auxiliary Bible Society*, cited in *Report of the Committee ... May 19, 1812 ...* (1812), pp. 437–8.

[58] 'Advertisement', in *The First Ten Years' Quarterly Papers of the Church Missionary Society* (1826).

working-class enthusiasm diminished, the CMS was now enabled to adopt a 'top-down' approach of soliciting working-class support on behalf of the better-off organizers of the Society. At the same time there was a rise in the class level of candidates in all the established missionary societies.[59]

These innovations brought down pamphlet warfare and open accusations of sectarianism upon the head of the CMS.[60] By now, however, the Society felt strong enough to weather the storm. Donations tell their own story. In 1796 the LMS had an annual income of £11,089, a significant percentage of which came from individual donations in church collections. The CMS garnered only £911 (in addition to its foundation grant) in the first two years of its existence, holding steady at just over £500 per annum in 1802–3 and 1803–4. The bulk of contributions came from wealthy individual donors. By 1812, however, the CMS was earning more in annual donations than the LMS, and its funding pattern now imitated that of the LMS in coming largely from small donors. In these statistics alone one might see the extent of the imaginative change which was occurring in villages and towns throughout Britain, the optimism as the war approached its end and the extent to which the Anglican establishment had succeeded in harnessing and turning Dissenting and Methodist techniques and concerns to the ends of an Anglican 'empire of mercy'.

This institutional account does not entirely explain what happened in communities across the country to cause the pandenominational surge in mission support which enabled Bernard Semmel to term 1813–15 the *anni mirabiles* of missions.[61] Precisely because the CMS was so politically hobbled, it could not alone have generated changing perceptions of the non-Christian world. One would like to know, for example, more about what the hundreds of local projectors of CMS associations and dispatchers of petitions expounding Hindu immorality were reading, in what ways their *imaginative* visions of India changed over time and how, if at all, this affected their politics. There is reason to believe that research into the neglected area of local 'cultures of mission' would yield a rich harvest.

[59] E.g., Bodl., MS Wilberforce c.3 fos. 158–96: Burder to Wilberforce, 10 Feb. 1818.

[60] Most notably, Josiah Thomas, *An Address to a Meeting Holden at the Town-Hall in the City of Bath* (1817).

[61] Semmel, *Methodist Revolution*, p. 152.

12 A Hanoverian legacy? Diocesan reform in the Church of England *c.* 1800–1833

R. Arthur Burns

I

Historians of the nineteenth century most frequently encounter the Hanoverian Church as at best a decadent and more often a corrupt institution, ripe for energetic Victorian reform. However, not only was the relationship between well-established 'abuses' and pastoral efficiency more complex than is usually assumed, but there are also instances where it can be argued that the late Hanoverian Church bequeathed a positive legacy to the Victorians. As an illustration this essay considers a neglected aspect of early nineteenth-century church reform, that which occurred in diocesan structures. It argues that through 'diocesan reform' the Hanoverian Church offered its own response to the challenges it faced, and that the period 1800–33 saw the commencement of an enduring 'diocesan revival' which derived its coherence and legitimation from the then prevalent Orthodox High Church theology.[1]

Before proceeding to describe this reform and its implications for our view of the nineteenth-century Church, the term 'diocesan reform' requires clarification. Peter Virgin recently called for a study of the administrative reforms of the '"new breed" of bishop, who emerged after the Napoleonic Wars'.[2] Certainly, case-studies of bishops of the years *c.*1825–50 suffer from the absence of a wider context in which to assess their individual significance. Any challenge they might offer to the long-standing orthodoxy that Samuel Wilberforce was 'The Remodeller of the Episcopate' is undercut by the consequent tendency to identify a series of 'proto-Wilberforces'.[3]

[1] Recently anatomized by Peter Nockles, 'Continuity and Change in Anglican High Churchmanship in Britain, 1792–1850', DPhil dissertation, University of Oxford, 1982. For a brief summary, see idem, 'New Perspectives on the High Church Tradition: Historical Background, 1730–1830', in *Tradition Renewed*, ed. D. G. Rowell (1986), pp. 24–50.

[2] Peter Virgin, *The Church in an Age of Negligence 1700–1840* (Cambridge, 1989), p. 159.

[3] The subtitle of the chapter on Wilberforce in John William Burgon, *Lives of Twelve Good Men* (2 vols., 1888); cf. Standish Meacham, *Lord Bishop. The Life of Samuel Wilberforce 1805–73* (Cambridge, Mass., 1970), p. 146, where he is credited with 'remodel[ling] . . . the episcopate'. For a more detailed discussion of the deficiencies of existing studies of the episcopate, see R. Arthur Burns, 'The Diocesan Revival in the Church of England, *c.*1825–1865', DPhil dissertation, University of Oxford, 1990, ch. 1.2.

However, a study adopting Virgin's broader remit would still accept an unnecessarily limiting perspective from which to observe developments in diocesan administration; it must be stressed that 'diocesan reform' is not synonymous with 'reform of (or by) the episcopate'. To discuss diocesan reform in an episcopally focused account encourages simplistic explanations in terms of heroic, pragmatic episcopal initiatives which do not accommodate the complex series of influences – both in terms of reforming constituencies and ideological legitimation – which lies behind the developments involved. It also obscures the links between reforms which *were* episcopal initiatives and others with similar motivations and objectives, such as those inspired and implemented by the archidiaconate. I therefore prefer to define 'diocesan reform' as developments originating within the dioceses themselves (rather than in Parliamentary or centralized action on a national scale) and which contributed to the reform, expansion or reinforcement of the structures of the diocesan community. These structures included mental structures – 'diocesan consciousness' – the awareness of the diocesan community as having its own dimensions, membership and identity quite distinct from those of the secular communities with which it was imbricated.

This essay casts more than an occasional glance beyond 1833. Most precisely marking the 'official' birth of Tractarianism, the terminal date for this volume also sits conveniently between the constitutional developments of the late 1820s and the legislative implementation of the recommendations of the Ecclesiastical Commissioners, both of tremendous significance for the history of the Church of England. No one would deny the strength of the continuities which encourage a view of the Hanoverian Church as some kind of 'Annaliste' *structure*. It would nevertheless be unfortunate if the study of the Church during the first thirty years of the nineteenth century were only to be pursued within the framework of the 'long' eighteenth century. If only because of the prominence and convenience of the discontinuities around 1830, we ought to be especially alert to continuities traversing the disjuncture. We should also be sensitive to the origins of this periodization itself, which lie in the polemical investment of subsequent Anglo-Catholic historiography in a negative picture of the Hanoverian Church.[4] As important in this respect has been the legacy of the Ecclesiastical Commission, fossilizing in its reports a statistical image of and an implicit qualitative verdict on the Church of England in 1830 which appear deceptively definitive to the 'fact'-hungry historian, and against which Victorian Churchmen measured their own efforts. They had little else in common, but both the Tractarian and Commission accounts of the con-

[4] See Nockles, 'Continuity and Change', p. xix.

dition of the late Hanoverian Church presented it as a *problem* to which their contrasting projects offered solutions.

Subsequent historians have shared this perspective. Even the most conceptually sophisticated account, Kenneth A. Thompson's *Bureaucracy and Church Reform*, is organized around the polarities of Commission and Tractarian approaches, while both Geoffrey Best and Olive Brose emphasize the unique appropriateness of the Ecclesiastical Commission in tackling the deficiencies of the Hanoverian Church.[5] We will return to this assessment of the reform options of the 1830s later, but it is worth noting here that even genuinely revisionist works have operated within these broad parameters.

II

Any discussion of early nineteenth-century diocesan reform should begin with the revival of the rural dean, the single most significant diocesan innovation in this period.[6] This began from a very small base. The eighteenth-century rural dean awaits his historian, but the outlines of his history seem clear. Both rural deans and the associated ruridecanal chapters had generally fallen into disuse since the seventeenth century. Revivals were instituted in Salisbury in *c.* 1666 and by Benson in Gloucester in 1734, but by 1800 the Salisbury deans were once more in disuse, while in Gloucester the office appears only to have survived in a few places and in a decayed state. In Chester, other diocesan officials and prominent parochial clergy occasionally exercised some aspects of decanal authority.[7] The only English diocese in which the rural dean existed in a fully active form was Exeter.[8] The picture in Wales is more complex. At Bangor Bishop Bethell believed that rural deans had existed in some form since 'time immemorial'.[9] Since the mid-nineteenth century the first modern revival of the rural dean has often been attributed to Samuel Horsley at St David's and St Asaph.[10] However, returns made by rural deans survive from the

[5] Kenneth A. Thompson, *Bureaucracy and Church Reform* (Oxford, 1970); G. F. A. Best, *Temporal Pillars. Queen Anne's Bounty, the Ecclesiastical Commissioners and the Church of England* (Cambridge, 1964); Olive J. Brose, *Church and Parliament. The Reshaping of the Church of England 1828–60* (Stanford and London, 1959).

[6] The account here is a modification of that presented at greater length in Burns, 'Diocesan Revival', ch. 4.1–2. The discussion of diocesan reform which follows is largely drawn from this thesis.

[7] I am grateful to Dr M. A. Smith for pointing out evidence of the latter case from 1813, in Cheetham's College Library, Manchester, Raines MSS, XV.

[8] For deans in Exeter, see Arthur Warne, *Church and Society in Eighteenth-Century Devon* (Newton Abbot, 1969), ch. 4 *passim*.

[9] W. Dansey, *Horae decanicae rurales* (2nd edn, 2 vols., 1844), II, 368.

[10] See, for example, ibid., II, 466–7, 468; H. H. Jebb, *A Great Bishop of One Hundred Years Ago. A Sketch of the Life of Samuel Horsley* (1909), pp. 71–2.

eighteenth century in St Asaph, and Professor F. C. Mather has recently uncovered evidence of the office at St David's from as far back as 1717.[11] It is probable, however, that the near-contemporary tradition concerning Horsley at least reflects an intensification of ruridecanal activity as part of Horsley's attempts to raise clerical standards in the dioceses.[12]

Whatever the precise nature of Horsley's contribution, there followed a series of revivals of the office which gathered pace to 1840. John Fisher, translated from Exeter and so familiar with the institution, revived rural deans in the Salisbury diocese in 1811; John Buckner appointed them in Chichester in 1812; Herbert Marsh revived the office at Llandaff in 1819 and then at Peterborough in 1820. Rural deans at Exeter and Bangor were reinvigorated through changes in the method of appointment; the office was revived at Bath and Wells; John Kaye was involved in their restoration first at Bristol in 1824 and then with the co-operation of Archdeacon Goddard in the archdeaconry of Lincoln in 1829. Sumner restored the rural deans at Winchester in 1829, Bagot those of Oxford in 1831; Blomfield and Howley acted at London and Canterbury in 1833; Carr of Worcester followed suit in 1834. At Gloucester Monk reinvigorated the office where he found it and revived it where he did not.

The chronology and extent of the revival require such emphasis in view of the paucity and unreliable nature of references to it in standard works: in Chadwick's *Victorian Church* it hardly merits a mention; David Edwards and Anthony Russell are not alone in dating the revival from 1835 and after.[13] But by this date rural deans were already operational in seventeen dioceses, including all but five in the southern province.

One explanation for this misdating is a misunderstanding of the significance of William Dansey's *Horae decanicae rurales*, published in 1835. It is assumed that the book inspired revivals by collating historical precedents for decanal activity (as Dansey intended). But the book appeared too late to

[11] For St Asaph, see J. Conway Davies, 'The Records of the Church in Wales', *The National Library of Wales Journal*, 4 (1945–6), 10; D. R. Thomas, *St Asaph* (SPCK Diocesan Histories, 1886), p. 96. F. C. Mather, *High Church Prophet. Bishop Samuel Horsley (1733–1806) and the Caroline Tradition in the Later Georgian Church* (Oxford, 1992), pp. 164–5.

[12] The office had also been revived in a number of Irish dioceses during the eighteenth century, and by 1820 sixteen of the twenty-two dioceses possessed rural deans: see Donald Harman Akenson, *The Church of Ireland 1800–85. Ecclesiastical Reform and Revolution* (New Haven, 1971), p. 132 and references there cited. It is difficult to know how much attention these revivals received in England (although Dansey does not seem to have been too impressed), but the whole question of the relationship between reforms in the *unreformed* Church of Ireland and those of the Church of England is much in need of investigation.

[13] See David L. Edwards, *Christian England, vol. III: From the Eighteenth Century to the First World War* (1984), p. 201; Anthony Russell, *The Clerical Profession* (1980), p. 44. For a recent example, see A. F. Munden, 'The First Palmerston Bishop: Henry Montagu Villiers, Bishop of Carlisle 1856–60 and Bishop of Durham 1860–1', *Northern History*, 26 (1990), 194.

play this role. Instead, the revival was sustained by its self-generated momentum, the experience of active systems of deans being disseminated by personal contacts and episcopal translation, a process that can be traced through the family relationships evident in the documents preserved in Dansey's appendices.[14]

Since the rural deans' authority was dependent on delegation from the bishop and was not defined in statute or canon law, the role of the long-dormant office was open to redefinition. Whereas in Exeter they continued to tour churches, chapels and parsonage-houses annually, forwarding information to the diocesan registry so that a returnable order for repairs could be issued, elsewhere newly revived or reinvigorated rural deans were initially employed for a few specific purposes. Horsley seems to have used his deans chiefly in an attempt to raise the professional standards of the Welsh clergy, checking nomination papers and licences. His successor at St David's, Thomas Burgess, expanded their role, using them as substitutes for the non-resident archdeacons, conveying directives to the clergy and conducting informal inquiries into delinquents; the deans were also requested to provide detailed reports on churches, chapels, churchyards, parsonage-houses, schools, charities, glebe and clerical residence. At Chichester and Salisbury, the few early traces of activity must be balanced against Dansey's failure to find any substantial record of the rural deans' operations; in the latter case, it was once more Burgess who developed the deans' role. However, extensive questionnaires such as Burgess's seem only to have been used to elicit newly comprehensive accounts of the diocese on a one-off basis; subsequent inspection was to take place 'from time to time'. As Herbert Marsh told Dansey in 1834, '*rural deans* still continue to exist, though not in such a state of activity as they were ... Having obtained almost all the information which he wanted, he has not urged them to further exertions.'[15]

By 1835 rural deans were nevertheless an important element in diocesan administration. Increased demand for statistical accounts of diocesan improvement led the commissions issued to rural deans at Winchester and Lincoln in 1829 to specify annual inspection among their duties, and this soon became general practice. Rural deans regularly conducted special investigations for bishops and archdeacons. In addition, they were often required to make provision for vacant benefices and to perform an informal role in clergy discipline: here, as in their supervision of church fabric, the rural deans lacked formal authority, but were encouraged to rectify abuses if clergy or churchwardens could be persuaded to co-operate. From the mid–1830s annual meetings of bishop and rural deans provided the first

[14] Especially in the revised edition of 1844.
[15] Dansey, *Horae decanicae rurales*, II, 463.

tentative form of diocesan consultative machinery since the disappearance of the diocesan synod, and after 1839 the revival of ruridecanal chapters built on this development. Rural deans also took on new tasks during the 1830s and 1840s, both those allocated by legislation, as in the Pluralities Act and Church Discipline Act,[16] and on individual episcopal initiative, as when they helped out diocesan education societies which could not support their own inspectors. By the time they were at full strength, some seven hundred rural deans provided the flexible manpower to supervise, direct and organize improvement and reform in the Victorian dioceses. They were the cutting edge of the diocesan revival.

Unlike rural deaneries, archdeaconries had not generally fallen into disuse, but at the end of the eighteenth century the office was rarely fully efficient. Considerable improvement can be observed by 1833. This was partly a direct consequence of the ruridecanal revival – especially in dioceses where rural deans were placed under the archdeacon's control, the latter was now in a position to obtain much more information about his jurisdiction and ensure that his instructions were carried out. Archidiaconal supervision was otherwise exercised through parochial inspections and archidiaconal visitations. At the end of the eighteenth century, it is clear that visitation articles were ill-calculated to provide the information an active archdeacon required, having often remained unrevised since the seventeenth century. There is ample testimony that parochial visitation was widely neglected. For our purposes it is significant that much of this testimony is provided by incoming archdeacons in the 1820s declaring that they would resume a duty neglected by their predecessors. A steady stream of new appointments commenced or completed parochial visitations, while others revised the visitation articles, as Francis Wrangham did at Cleveland in 1821.[17] Archdeacons of the 1820s and 1830s were going about their business with renewed zeal, frequently venting their frustration when they encountered obstacles to their authority. Taking evidence in 1830, for example, the Ecclesiastical Courts Commission found Charles Goddard voluble about the difficulties of exercising his authority, and his need for summary disciplinary powers.[18] In practice, it was the informal, sometimes almost obsessional, attention to detail of archdeacons such as George

[16] 1 & 2 Vict. c. 106, s. 77; 3 & 4 Vict. c. 86, s. 3.

[17] F. Wrangham, *A Charge Delivered in July 1821 ... to the Clergy of the Archdeaconry of Cleveland* (York, 1821), p. 19. However, such innovations could not rival ruridecanal supervision in terms of effectiveness, and the undoubtedly zealous Henry Manning went as far as to abandon parochial visitation during the early 1840s on the grounds that rural deans made it unnecessary: H. E. Manning, *A Charge Delivered at the Ordinary Visitation of the Archdeaconry of Chichester in July 1843* (1843), p. 12.

[18] *Reports Made by His Majesty's Commissioners Appointed to Inquire into the Practice and Jurisdiction of the Ecclesiastical Courts in England and Wales*, Parliamentary Papers, 1831–2 (199), 24, appendix, pp. 135–8.

Wilkins (who once personally raised the finance to employ a curate for a clergyman whom he could not formally remove from his benefice[19]) in which new zeal found expression – these years witnessing the emergence of a characteristic figure of early Victorian 'Life and Letters', the 'indefatigable' archdeacon. Thomas Hill neatly summed up the condition of the office by 1840: 'it was in the state of transition. Already activity was expected from an Archdeacon, and therefore activity met with sympathy and support. The powers attached to the office were vague, the ideas of men with regard to them still more so; it was simply a position of influence.'[20]

The revision of visitation articles was not the only reform associated with the early nineteenth-century archidiaconal visitation. Responding to the unsettled times, visitation sermons abandoned the safe territory of *Pastoral Watchfulness and Zeal*[21] for more topical and controversial material, including church reform. This development reflected the fact that archidiaconal charges were not a universal feature of early nineteenth-century visitations: the promising young clergy often chosen to deliver the sermons were attempting to supply the deficiency, as Edward Duncombe did at York in 1832 with an ill-received address *On Church Reform*.[22] Elsewhere archdeacons themselves took up the challenge either by restoring the charge where the practice had lapsed, or changing the content of the oration. By 1840 more detailed topical and practical local references were common features of archidiaconal charges, which previously had tended to avoid controversies within the establishment, not least because of a reluctance to tread on episcopal toes. This earlier reticence is further illustrated by the small number of charges published. It was only archdeacons like Blomfield – accused of having pretensions to be the *os* rather than the *oculi episcopi*[23] – who had sought a wider audience for their orations. By the early 1830s, however, archidiaconal charges attracted considerable periodical and public interest, and not merely when they addressed 'episcopal' topics – there was a new interest in the diocesan activity and the expertise of individual archdeacons which could be brought to bear on the challenges of parochial management.

Such developments illustrated the potential of the archdeacon, and where the office was dormant or a sinecure this was increasingly recognized as an obstacle to pastoral efficiency. In Chester, Blomfield came to an *ad hoc*

[19] A. C. Wood, 'A Nottingham Archdeacon's Letter-Book of 1832', *Transactions of the Thoroton Society*, 57 (1953), 46–7.

[20] Thomas Hill, *Letters and Memoir of the Late Walter Augustus Shirley* (2nd edn, 1850), p. 306.

[21] The subject chosen by Edward Berens in 1826.

[22] Edward Duncombe, *On Church Reform. A Visitation Sermon Preached June 14, 1832, in All Saints' Church, Pavement* (1832).

[23] G. E. Biber, *Bishop Blomfield and his Times* (1857), p. 40.

arrangement with the commissary of Richmond which in 1827 enabled J. T. Headlam to conduct his first visitation.[24] On the whole though, it was not until the legislative enactments of the Ecclesiastical Commission that the problem of inefficient archidiaconal jurisdictions could (gradually) be confronted.

Unlike the archidiaconal assembly, the episcopal visitation underwent considerable development before 1840. Although it was the only regular occasion on which diocesan community was acknowledged in the meeting of bishop and clergy, by 1820 the episcopal visitation had stagnated. Linked to a confirmation tour, during the eighteenth century both confirmation and visitation had often been crammed into a single day in each centre. The visitation dinner constituted the convivial (sometimes scandalously convivial) highlight of the occasion.[25] The canonical interval between visitations was frequently exceeded: in Winchester, for example, it had become traditional for each bishop to perform only one visitation during his episcopate. Episcopal charges had become as conventional as the visitations. In the 1850s, commentators seeking to illustrate the decadence of the Hanoverian Church often pointed out both the infrequency with which charges were published and their testimony to the poor performance of the parochial clergy – this latter feature reflecting as much the convention that the 'duties of the ministerial office' were the proper subject for a charge. The conventionality of the remarks was underlined by their generality, usually making no specific reference to the individual diocese.

From the mid-1820s, however, there was a determined effort to reinvigorate episcopal visitation. Confirmations were gradually separated off. Where visitation was irregular, younger bishops introduced a new frequency: thus C. R. Sumner began to visit quadrennially in Winchester from 1829 and Phillpotts introduced triennial visitation at Exeter. Like archdeacons, bishops revised their visitation articles so that these might provide a regularly updated account of the diocese.

Perhaps the most significant development occurred in the charge. As criticism of the Church gained force during the early 1820s, a renewed sense of purpose had already become apparent: more demonstrations of the necessity of establishment; greater concern to rebut anti-clerical attacks in discussions of the ministerial office. But the later 1820s saw a new particularity in reference to the bishop's own diocese, based on the statistical information now available from visitation returns and rural deans. One of

[24] P. J. Welch, 'Bishop Blomfield', PhD dissertation, University of London, 1952, p. 112; J. T. Headlam, *A Charge Delivered to the Clergy of the Archdeaconry of Richmond* (1827), pp. 7–8.

[25] For a scandalous example, see Alfred Blomfield, *A Memoir of Charles James Blomfield* (2 vols., 1863), I, 105.

the earliest of the new type of charge was delivered by C. R. Sumner in 1827 at Llandaff. Philip Jacob was impressed:

I had read many charges . . . but this charge seemed idiosyncratic. It was one of a new order of things . . . In one word it was diocesan. The wants of the diocese and how to meet them – a most pressing topic. So new was this . . . that I was assured by one of the editors of a church magazine, that he and his co-editors solemnly deliberated . . . whether such a line of episcopal topics was to be tolerated or countenanced; and, after deep deliberation, they happily agreed: 'it was to be encouraged'.[26]

Sumner's statistics included not only new churches built and schools opened, but also less expected calculations, such as the number of diocesan clergy surviving from his first visitation. Thus alongside the material progress of the diocese they mapped the condition of diocesan *community*. Sumner's approach was encapsulated in his claim that statistics were 'the register of our moral power'.[27] His innovations were mirrored or paralleled in the charges of Blomfield, J. B. Sumner and others. Nor were the new charges reticent concerning topical issues of the time. Audiences lapped up both types of information, and charges were increasingly offered to a wider public through publication. The eleven published episcopal charges I have been able to trace between 1820 and 1824 were followed by eighteen in the next five years and twenty-two between 1830 and 1834.[28] In the same period the average length of the charge increased by almost 33 per cent, the first hint of the over-inflation which culminated in the three- and four-hour charges of the 1860s. By the mid–1830s as a result of these developments the visitation was once more establishing itself as a crucial and productive element in diocesan management and the corporate life of the diocese.

More generally, changes in episcopal practice during the early nineteenth century contributed to the development of the diocese as a self-conscious community. Although the precise chronology of change varied with the age and inclination of the bishop, by 1840 he had often become a more visible presence throughout the diocese, as new churches were consecrated and confirmations increased in frequency and were separated from visitation; such developments incorporated into the diocesan community areas which had previously been inadequately assimilated. Stricter policing of clerical activity also reinforced the diocesan context of the notoriously independent parochial clergy – notably in the case of concern with pluralism and non-residence, and above all in increased efforts to prevent unlicensed clergy

[26] G. H. Sumner, *Life of C. R. Sumner, DD, Bishop of Winchester* (1876), p. 121.
[27] C. R. Sumner, *A Charge Delivered to the Clergy of the Diocese of Winchester in October 1833* (1833), p. 26.
[28] For these purposes I am not distinguishing between printing and publishing: both resulted in much wider dissemination within and beyond the diocesan community.

from officiating in the diocese, and checking the credentials of those ordained elsewhere.

Among the most familiar developments of the early nineteenth century is probably the appearance of great national societies providing support to the hard-pressed parochial system: the National Society (1811) and the Incorporated Church Building Society (1818), to be joined by the Church Pastoral Aid Society (1836) and Additional Curates Society (1837). During the same period a number of diocesan societies and committees were established, often (but not always) affiliated to the national organizations. While diocesan clerical charities for incapacitated clergy, clerical widows and orphans already existed, there now appeared organizations with a variety of purposes. Thomas Burgess's Church Union Society, founded at St David's in 1804, embraced a wide range of tasks: originally encompassing the distribution of Bibles and tracts, the creation of libraries, education of prospective ordinands, building of schools and care of superannuated curates, it was partly responsible for the establishment of St David's College at Lampeter, opened in 1827. In the same year the translated Burgess was involved in the creation of a similarly named society at Salisbury.[29] By 1830 diocesan education societies and committees, church building committees and societies were active in many dioceses. The major expansion of such organizations came in the late 1830s and 1840s, but these earlier instances represented the first appearance of such institutions adopting a *diocesan* framework.

III

At first sight these developments might appear a rag-bag of reforms of limited consequence. It could be objected that adopting the category of 'diocesan reform' imposes a spurious coherence on unrelated phenomena, investing them with unmerited significance. To refute such an imputation, it is essential to step beyond 1833 and consider the subsequent history of diocesan reform.

Up to 1833 the most prominent diocesan reforms had been those involving the rural dean and the visitation. Indeed, for the reformed visitation, the 1830s represented something of a pinnacle. The controversies provoked by the Ecclesiastical Commission and the intensification of church party inevitably focused attention on the topical material in charges and marginalized their local, diocesan content, particularly as the former grew ever longer and more convoluted as bishops attempted to negotiate between conflicting interests. Some parochial clergy came to resent the

[29] See J. S. Harford, *Life of Thomas Burgess, DD* (1840), pp. 227–30, 434; D. T. W. Price, *Yr Esgob Burgess a Choleg Llanbedr* (Cardiff, 1987), pp. 31–3.

extent to which the controversial and divisive charge increasingly dominated the visitation, and the absence of any chance to discuss it with the bishop, especially since it might be taken as a corporate diocesan statement by the wider public addressed over their heads. In contrast, however, the already useful office of rural dean was developed further during the subsequent half century as additional duties were attached to the office and – most significantly – the ruridecanal chapters were revived.

Most of the other reforms also continued into the years after 1833. Diocesan societies, boards and committees appeared in increasing numbers from the late 1830s. The archidiaconate benefited considerably from the reform of jurisdictions initiated by the Ecclesiastical Commissioners (especially the abolition of peculiars, the creation of additional archdeaconries and the gradual reinvigoration of those that were dormant) and from their reallocation of ecclesiastical resources to reimburse archdeacons for the heavy expenses of office. They also gained from more 'professional' appointments by the episcopate; while on their own account there were significant efforts to reinvigorate the archidiaconal visitation through the addition of consultative sessions and communion.

Other aspects of diocesan reform, however, saw no concrete achievements before 1833. This was most notably the case with the revival of diocesan assemblies, the first of which met at Exeter in 1851, and the reinvigoration of clerical discipline. Developments such as the creation of diocesan theological colleges, attempts to give meaningful content to the relation of the cathedral and diocese, more effective deployment of episcopal patronage and the creation of diocesan calendars and almanacs did not occur until after 1833.

However, there were important links between these later reforms and those outlined above. They are most easily observed in the church reform pamphlets of the early 1830s. Most discussion of these publications has revolved around those few, like Lord Henley's *A Plan of Church Reform*, which anticipated the approach to reform represented by the Ecclesiastical Commission; others have only been used to illustrate the lukewarm response such proposals elicited among the mass of the clergy, and their supposed failure to recognize the need for significant reform.[30] But rejection of the Commission did not necessarily entail a lack of commitment to reform, or the irrelevance of alternative proposals. A less predetermined reading of these pamphlets, and of contemporary episcopal and archidiaconal charges, reveals that the diocesan reforms discussed above had already stimulated widespread consideration of the potential of diocesan institutions in terms of a response to the challenges now acknowledged by the

[30] See, for example, Geoffrey Best's revealing remarks on reform literature: *Temporal Pillars*, p. 280.

clergy. Throughout these documents run considerations of the development of rural deans, visitation, diocesan organizations and archdeacons, and the potential for further reforms based on these institutions, such as the revival of ruridecanal chapters, increased powers and salaries for archdeacons and rural deans, annual episcopal visitations and the reorganization of church charities on a diocesan basis. The same discussions call for the reinvigoration of clergy discipline, the renewal of the cathedral as a truly *diocesan* institution, a concentration of episcopal patronage on diocesan clergy, greater access to diocesan information and the revival of diocesan assemblies. The currency of such ideas is further reflected in a variety of contemporary sources, from the interest displayed in such publications in the religious periodical press, to the statements made by witnesses to the Ecclesiastical Courts Commission.

More importantly, however, the concrete developments of the next three decades confirm the pattern established in this literature. Alongside the work of the Ecclesiastical Commission through the 1830s, 1840s and 1850s, and largely unacknowledged in subsequent historiography, ran a parallel initiative to reform the diocesan structures of the Church of England, the most familiar aspects of which occurred where it overlapped with the improvement of episcopal practice (as in the case of the increased episcopal presence in the diocese) or the work of the Ecclesiastical Commission (as in redrawing of ecclesiastical boundaries). This initiative consciously built on the developments already in place by 1833. To demonstrate this fully would require more space than is available here. But it is worth very briefly sketching these linkages in the case of two areas of reform which were indicated earlier as post-1833 phenomena: clergy discipline and the development of diocesan assemblies.

In the former case, the reinvigorated archdeacons and rural deans played a crucial role in the new procedures adopted for clerical discipline, both formally, in the arrangements made by the 1840 Church Discipline Act for preliminary hearings, and informally, with these officers often negotiating the difficult situations which arose in clerical discipline, not least after the rise of ritualism.[31]

The revival of the diocesan assembly is perhaps the clearest example of all. This has been approached as an appendage to the campaign to revive Convocation. It is often treated as the result of ritualist efforts to break free of the establishment after 1850, or as a means of involving laity in the structures of the Church in response to the prospect of competing against other denominations in a religious free market. The Exeter synod is

[31] For a local study emphasizing the importance of the rural dean to clerical discipline, see Frances Knight, 'Ministering to the Ministers: The Discipline of Recalcitrant Clergy in the Diocese of Lincoln 1830–1845', *SCH*, 26 (1989), 365–6.

dismissed as an idiosyncratic and insignificant precursor.[32] Approached from the context of the diocesan revival, however, an intimate relationship with the developments discussed here is revealed. Much of the pressure for diocesan assemblies stemmed from clerical dissatisfaction with visitations as the only diocesan gatherings. In addition, while the fact that bishops had come to regard and consult rural deans as if they were representatives of the clergy had generated resentment since they were not elected by the clergy, this had also developed a tradition of consultation. Annual diocesan meetings of rural deans and the ruridecanal chapters were in fact vital both in building this tradition and also providing a model and an infrastructure which could serve as the skeleton of a diocesan assembly; their role was central in both the Exeter assembly in 1851 and also the first diocesan conferences of the 1860s. The importance of the diocesan background was not confined to providing a framework – many of those promoting diocesan assemblies saw them as a distinctively diocesan project aimed to reinvigorate that community in the same way that C. R. Sumner had thirty years before presented his efforts to reform the visitation. Even Henry Phillpotts, whose 1851 synod was in fact a crucial link between earlier and later campaigns, saw it as the culmination of a strong and self-consciously diocesan strand in his thought rather than merely a tactical initiative in the Gorham controversy.[33]

The diocesan reforms before 1833 thus led directly to those of the subsequent forty years, and there was no important discontinuity or qualitative change during the 1830s. That there was such continuity, however, should not be that surprising. As Richard Brent has convincingly shown, the changing direction of national ecclesiastical policy was partly a function of the fact that the traditional ecclesiastical counsellors of the Tory governments of the 1820s, the Orthodox Hackney Phalanx, were displaced along with their political associates by liberal Churchmen associated with the Whig administrations of the 1830s.[34] Subsequently, Peel found his most congenial counsellor in Charles Blomfield, who, despite his High Churchmanship, was recognized by contemporaries as rarely bringing his theology directly to bear on administrative reform, and who was committed not only to the reform objectives of the Ecclesiastical Commission, but to the Commission itself as the best means of reform.[35] It has been a tacit

[32] For such approaches, see, for example, M. A. Crowther, *Church Embattled. Religious Controversy in Mid-Victorian England* (Newton Abbot and Hamden, Conn., 1970), pp. 205–16; Owen Chadwick, *The Victorian Church. Part II* (2nd edn, 1972), pp. 359–60; M. J. D. Roberts, 'The Role of the Laity in the Church of England *c.*1850–1885', DPhil dissertation, University of Oxford, 1974, ch. 12.

[33] See Burns, 'Diocesan Revival', pp. 262–76.

[34] Richard Brent, *Liberal Anglican Politics. Whiggery, Religion and Reform* (Oxford, 1987).

[35] For Peel and Blomfield, see Brose, *Church and Parliament*; Best, *Temporal Pillars*, ch. 7; Welch, 'Bishop Blomfield', ch. 10.

assumption of most considerations of post-1833 reform that the approach of the Orthodox party was no longer capable of generating initiatives and was played out (at which point the analysis again draws on the Anglo-Catholic account of the nineteenth century). But particularly now that Peter Nockles has demonstrated the continuing vitality of the Orthodox tradition through the 1830s and 1840s,[36] we can recognize the particular significance of their displacement from the corridors of political power for their contribution to *legislative* reform. Having lost the initiative here, it was almost inevitable that they should often be cast in the role of resisting Parliamentary reforms initiated by others.

However, no such displacement occurred in the diocesan hierarchies. There the legacy of Liverpool's ecclesiastical patronage continued to be felt well past 1850, while the archidiaconate mirrored the episcopate by which it was appointed. In the context of the 1830s and 1840s Orthodox creativity required a new outlet, and in the dioceses Orthodox dignitaries were well placed to implement their vision of ecclesiastical reform. Moreover the central place of ecclesiology in Orthodox theology, with its emphasis on the episcopate and the unity of the Church focused on its visible institutions, as well as respect for the historic tradition of the Church of England on both sides of the Reformation, made this a particularly congenial field. Indeed, those points at which they made most impact on the legislative reform of the Church in the 1830s and 1840s, such as the opposition to centralizing clergy discipline legislation or the successful resistance to the merger of the dioceses of St Asaph and Bangor, were those in which the diocesan principle could serve as the core of a coherent opposition case.

The relationship of diocesan reform and Orthodox theology was complex. The significance of the many Orthodox archdeacons and of several Orthodox bishops in the reforms discussed is already apparent. Many pamphlets discussing both positive proposals for diocesan reform and those offered by the Ecclesiastical Commission did so clearly within the context of an assessment of the ecclesiological appropriateness of the reforms from such a standpoint. Few works speak more eloquently of the Orthodox approach to diocesan reform than Dansey's *Horae decanicae rurales*, which emerged from the group of High Churchmen dominant in the Salisbury diocese, and acknowledged the assistance of H. H. Norris, Bethell, Howley, Marsh and Joshua Watson.[37] The volume is lavishly produced, with a heavy, archaic, gothic typeface – the *British Critic* described it as 'redolent of good old times'[38] – and contains a large collection of documents grouped by diocese testifying to the long history of

[36] Nockles, 'Change and Continuity'.
[37] W. Dansey, *Horae decanicae rurales* (2 vols., 1835), I, xv–xix.
[38] *British Critic*, 19 (1836), 273.

the rural dean throughout the episcopal church, highlighting, for example, the diocesan reforms of Borromeo. The proposals it offered were thus firmly rooted in the past and tradition of the Church. But they were nevertheless highly practical, and sought to make the Church function more effectively.

While many of those involved both before and after 1833 were Orthodox High Churchmen of some description, however, this has to be weighed against the prominence among the reformers of such men as C. R. Sumner, a Claphamite Evangelical. It is apparent that while the ecclesiological emphasis on diocesan episcopacy and the unity of the visible church (as expressed in diocesan community) which provided the overarching legitimation of the diocesan revival does seem to have been derived from a distinctively Orthodox ecclesiology, this legitimation could nevertheless operate effectively beyond its core constituency. In part this reflects the respect for the institutions of the visible church of regular Evangelicals, and in particular Claphamite Evangelicalism, which made the diocesan revival a more attractive and accessible cause for them than it was to be for later Recordites. Thus although its origins lay in Orthodox ecclesiology, the diocesan revival was able to marshal support from a wider constituency in the Church – indeed this was one of its crucial attractions to reformers, who saw it as a means of reuniting a fragmenting Church around theologically neutral institutions which articulated (and in generating 'diocesan consciousness' fostered) *unity*.

IV

The evidence presented here has a number of implications for our view of church reform and the neglect of diocesan developments in current historiography. It might be claimed that diocesan reform was insignificant when compared with the work of the Ecclesiastical Commission or the pastoral initiative inspired by the Tractarians. Yet we have observed an important series of reforms which ultimately equipped the Victorian diocese with an effective infrastructure staffed by a newly professional cadre of episcopal agents, in itself an important contribution to clerical professionalization. Its significance was acknowledged in initiatives to reorganize jurisdictions; in legislation designed to facilitate its progress; and in its considerable impact on the course of other reform initiatives. It also provided a context for the incorporation of the churchgoing laity into ecclesiastical structures. Even within the pragmatic, empirical and utilitarian terms of reference adopted by the Commission, the revival had important quantifiable results in raising clerical incomes, building churches and improving efficiency. It should be remembered that, seen from the diocese, it was often the *diocesan* structures from which the stimuli to centralized action – such as money to elicit grants from central funds ensnarled in the bureaucratic red tape of the Commission – emerged. This diocesan perspective on the effectiveness of centralized reform agencies has been largely invisible to historians working from the centralized records.

By 1865 the concrete achievements of the revival were self-evident. But one should not neglect its less tangible results. The brief and achievements of the Ecclesiastical Commission were a necessary but not a *sufficient* response to the challenges of the mid-nineteenth century. Even in terms of some of the Commission's own objectives, such as the reinforcement of episcopal authority, it is clear that the diocesan reformers' methods were both more appropriate and effective than those of the Commissioners. One only need contrast the scandals associated with the Commissioners' renewal of episcopal residences with the impact of the much less expensive developments described here in creating new theatres for the symbolic assertion of the bishop's role.

On a wider front, before 1833 diocesan reform had provided the first steps in the creation of a communal diocesan identity and purpose which was a key ingredient in the resilience of the Victorian Church in the face of a variety of challenges, and contributed considerably to the recovery of self-confidence and morale apparent by the 1860s. One of these challenges was the rise of church party. While this is not the place to explore the subject, it can be argued that the diocesan revival and its legitimating ideology provided the context for a self-conscious, determined counter-initiative to the rise of party – for if the revival had a rallying-cry it was the call for *unity*, appealing to the past history of the Church as a community of believers within the diocesan context, and playing down the emphasis on theological affiliations which had underlain other contemporary initiatives to increase clerical solidarity. The diocesan revival was one of the few centripetal forces in the mid-century Church of England. In this instance is it too much to suggest that the late Hanoverian Church did not bequeath the Victorians a problem, but rather a positive legacy – indeed not just a positive legacy, but a potential weapon with which to counter a peculiarly *Victorian* problem?

Finally, we should return to a consideration of the general approach to church reform current in the works of Best, Brose, Thompson and others. First, it will already be apparent that I think that studies that ignore the developments in diocesan management are seriously deficient, not least in lacking a proper framework for the understanding of the context for the impact of the Commission and the Oxford Movement.

Secondly, diocesan reform does not sit easily in the periodization which sees the period 1800–33 as a kind of eighteenth-century left-over. It slots more comfortably into that which stresses the significance of the French

Revolution as a stimulus to action on the part of the Church and which recognizes reform commencing in the 1790s and continuing through into the mid-nineteenth century. Inclining to what Virgin has called the 'gradualist' view of church reform, it seems to me that not only do we need to be aware of continuities across the 1830s, but also to beware of adopting the Ecclesiastical Commission's agenda as the only criteria on which to assess the 'efficiency' of the late Hanoverian Church.[39] Recognizing such continuities is one means of avoiding this danger.

A consideration of diocesan reform should also make us pause before accepting Kenneth Thompson's characterization of the reform options of the 1830s. Thompson claims that in the 1830s the Church was confronted with a choice between rational, empirical and pragmatic reform entailing centralization and bureaucratization, and the Tractarian approach, subjugating all other considerations to the transcendental reference of theology, rejecting empirical or 'logico-experimental' criteria. Thompson laments the absence of 'instrumental reforms in the organization of the Church ... [with] a general theory to legitimate them which did not appear to involve merely a rationalization based on the principle of expediency'. He suggests that there was a need for an approach 'which could reconcile expediency in adapting the norms (the concern of the reformers) with legitimation in terms of religious principles (the emphasis of the Oxford Movement)'.[40] Like Brose and others, Thompson caricatures the bishops of the 1830s as empiricist pragmatists in as far as they accepted the Commission reforms, and as reactionaries in as far as they did not.[41] But this dualistic framework cannot accommodate the significance of the approach developed in the diocesan revival during the first thirty years of the century, which in fact *did* combine both sorts of legitimation in an attempt to bring the old order to terms with the new world. The relationship between different approaches to reform was vastly more complex than Thompson's model allows. He approvingly quotes Geoffrey Best's verdict that the 'rapid accumulation and convergence of factors on both the "demand side" and the "supply side" for organizational revolution allowed for no alternative to the Ecclesiastical Commissioners to anyone "who really tried to see the Church and nation as a whole, not abstractly nor in terms of conventional rhetoric, but in the modern way, with the aid of maps, committees, circular inquiries and tabulated statistics"'.[42] We will leave on one side the implicit assumptions here that economic redistribution is a precondition of effective

[39] Virgin, *Age of Negligence*, p. 264. If I had a criticism of Virgin's excellent study, it might be that he succumbs to this temptation.

[40] Thompson, *Bureaucracy and Church Reform*, pp. 42, 47, 49.

[41] Ibid., pp. 28, 48; for other examples, see Brose, *Church and Parliament*, p. 34; Desmond Bowen, *The Idea of the Victorian Church* (Montreal, 1968), p. 52.

[42] Thompson, *Bureaucracy and Church Reform*, p. 14, quoting Best, *Temporal Pillars*, p. 347.

reform, and that the 'modern' is the superior and the 'real' way of looking. Not only does the diocesan revival not fit this formulation, but even considering Best's own 'committees, circular inquiries and tabulated statistics', we have seen in the case of the episcopal visitation that these could play a key role in a quite different approach to reform, and indeed in quite 'unmodern' ways – as when Sumner presented the figures for those surviving since his first visitation, in a conscious attempt to generate community spirit.

Just as Best and others have accused the reform pamphleteers of the 1830s of neglecting the importance of far-reaching institutional reform, it could be said that Best neglects the importance of the *legitimation* such reform requires for its success. It is significant that the Commissioners themselves saw assisting diocesan reform as integral to their task; it was not simply a case of episcopal self-conceit,[43] but that they perceived more readily than later historians the interconnexion of the two approaches. To read reform pamphlets and charges taking note only of those passages discussing or criticizing the Commission, centralization or economic redistribution, while ignoring those concerning clergy discipline, diocesan reform and episcopal authority is to adopt a different agenda for the subject from that accepted by contemporaries.

It is therefore suggested that no really adequate account of church reform in the early nineteenth century can afford to neglect the contribution of the diocesan revival. Best's influential volume must be accepted for what it is (and set out to be) – a brilliantly perceptive monograph on the history of the Queen Anne's Bounty and the Ecclesiastical Commissioners – and not be mistaken for what its discursive approach can make it seem – a comprehensive history of church reform in the period. Nor can historians rely on the Anglo-Catholic accounts of nineteenth-century episcopal practice for information on diocesan history. Instead, before they can arrive at an overall assessment of the nature, chronology, direction and dynamics of church reform in the early nineteenth century, historians need to drag their gaze away from the hypnotic fascinations of Westminster and Oxford, and examine more closely the dioceses of the Church of England.

[43] Best, *Temporal Pillars*, p. 328.

Part III

Identities and perceptions

13 The eighteenth-century Church: a European view

W. R. Ward

My object in this essay is to remind us that, though one might never guess it from modern historical writing, there was still a Protestant world in the eighteenth century to which the Church of England belonged, to which it was acknowledged to belong and to which it regarded itself as belonging. There were of course Anglicans who specially prized features of their Church which they did not find in continental Protestant churches, Restoration High Churchmen who cherished the delusion that the Church of England was the very pattern of the primitive Church, as there are some at present who cherish the delusion that the Church of England is the very pattern of a putative coming Great Church. The mixture of coyness and downright hostility to the word Protestant which is now characteristic of Anglican, and increasingly of British, church opinion generally is hardly to be found. This is not very surprising in view of the fact that the political nation had had to turn first to a Dutch Reformed and then to a German Lutheran monarch and finally to a great deal of diplomacy, secular and ecclesiastical, to keep out the Catholic branches of the Stuart line. It is particularly worth examining the European standing of the Church of England, both in contemporary perception and in historical retrospect, because, if there is one period of Anglican history of which subsequent Anglicans have been ashamed, it is the eighteenth century. It may therefore seem astonishing that in the contemporary perception of the early eighteenth-century Protestant world the Church of England enjoyed a chorus of admiration which, if not quite unanimous, far exceeded anything which has since come her way, and her divines, so suspect at home in the nineteenth century, enjoyed a European hearing such as has been denied them, on the whole justly, for two centuries or more. I would like first to discuss the contemporary perceptions, and then, keeping the European perspective, add some comments in historical retrospect.

In 1748 that marvellous old sceptic David Hume went on a grand tour of Germany and other parts and found himself pleasantly surprised.

> Germany is undoubtedly a very fine Country, full of industrious honest People, & were it united it woud be the greatest Power that ever was in the World. The

common People are here, almost every where, much better treated & more at their Ease, than in France; and are not very much inferior to the English, notwithstanding all the Airs the latter give themselves . . . it gives a Man of Humanity Pleasure to see that so considerable a Part of Mankind as the Germans are in so tolerable a Condition.[1]

The complacency which Hume exemplified as well as reported of the English was well founded. For a century past Germany had been absorbing growing numbers of British publications and the real flood tide of the third quarter of the eighteenth century had still not been reached.[2] The scale of this extraordinary, self-inflicted cultural bombardment has been disguised by the very narrow presuppositions on which the history of theology and high literature are usually pursued; but it clearly went right across the board – technical and scientific literature (doubtless encouraged by the fact that there were many German members of the Royal Society and the Society of Arts);[3] the moral weeklies in the style of Addison and Steele;[4] even English newspapers were held to set a good example, Göckingk, admittedly a newspaper man himself, producing the hyperbolic claim that 'the invention of the newspaper is incontestably one of the greatest blessings of the European nations . . . The general spirit of participation in all public events, which the English call Public Spirit, was by this means spread from nation to nation.'[5] There was philosophy, and, what is especially germane to our theme, religious and theological literature of every conceivable kind, devotional, historical, exegetical, doctrinal, kerygmatic. This was especially important because, although literature of these kinds declined as a proportion of the total book market as new genres were developed, it was always very large. In due course there were also ephemera for the masses of the sort that bibliographers, literary critics and often even public censors have been unwilling to recognize as books; forgotten classics of the English literary underworld with inviting titles such as *The Imprudences of Youth*, *The Son Perverted by his Father*, or *The Furies of Love*.[6]

[1] *The Letters of David Hume*, ed. J. Y. T. Greig (2nd edn, 2 vols., Oxford, 1969), I, 126.

[2] On this subject see Bernhard Fabian, 'English Books and their Eighteenth-Century German Readers', in *The Widening Circle*, ed. F. J. Korshin (University of Pennsylvania Press, n.p., 1976), pp. 117–96.

[3] Hans-Joachim Braun, *Technologische Beziehungen zwischen Deutschland und England von der Mitte des 17. bis zum Ausgang des 18. Jahrhunderts* (Düsseldorf, 1974). It is worth noting that one of the German pastors in London chose the early years of the Industrial Revolution to make the ominous comment: 'The Briton is not himself inventive, but . . . follows the track pointed out to him by the foreigner; he seeks to improve it through his own additions, and pushes everything along with the money he collects through the shipping and commerce of the East & West Indies.' J. G. Burckhardt, *Kirchengeschichte der deutschen Gemeinden in London* (Tübingen, 1798), p. 13.

[4] Wolfgang Martens, *Die Botschaft der Tugend. Die Aufklärung im Spiegel der deutschen moralischen Wochenschriften* (Stuttgart, 1971).

[5] Quoted in H-U. Wehler, *Deutsche Gesellschaftsgeschichte* (Munich, 1987–), I, 308.

[6] Rudolf Schenda, *Volk ohne Buch. Studien zur Sozialgeschichte der popularen Lesestoffe 1770–1910* (Taschenbuch edn, Munich, 1977), pp. 194–200.

It was, indeed, not until the eighteenth century that the English of German theologians was equal to any great amount of translation from the English direct, but they took on board a great deal of English work at second hand, from Latin, French and Dutch,[7] and, as I think has not been recognized, from the enormous number of summaries and book reviews in publications like the *Acta Eruditorum* (Leipzig, from 1682), and in Orthodox[8] journals like the *Unschuldige Nachrichten* (Wittenberg, 1701; transferred to Leipzig the following year) and the *Acta Historico-Ecclesiastica* (Weimar, from 1735). The chief of the indirect routes to the German market was provided by the Netherlands, for, by the end of the seventeenth century, the Dutch occupied the same central position in the world of vernacular translation as they did in the dissemination of news. In the Netherlands it could be confidently maintained 'that the English nation surpasses other nations in the speculative knowledge of theology (oh, that they were so happy in the practice thereof) and have a pleasing gracefulness in it, is taken for an infallible truth by almost all sound judgments who have thoroughly searched their works'.[9] Great quantities of Puritan literature (followed later by *belles lettres*)[10] found their way into Dutch, often *en route* for other languages such as German, Swedish and Hungarian.[11] English theology enjoyed a popularity in the Netherlands in excess of what some English spokesmen considered decent, Bishop Thomas Sprat complaining that 'our famous divines have been innumerable, as the Dutchmen may witness, who, in some of their theological treatises have been as bold with the English sermons as with our fishing; and their robberies have been so manifest that our Church ought to have reprizals against them, as well as our merchants'.[12] The plagiarism has continued to provide employment for

[7] Udo Sträter, *Sonthom, Bayley, Dyke und Hall. Studien zur Reception der englischen Erbauungsliteratur in Deutschland im 17. Jahrhundert* (Tübingen, 1987), pp. 25–35.

[8] The word 'Orthodox' (in upper-case) in this essay is used solely to indicate the parties in the Lutheran and Reformed worlds which adopted that description for themselves. Their common characteristic was a highly articulated systematic theology and a propensity to Aristotelianism. There is no reference in this essay to the Greek or Russian Orthodox churches.

[9] Cornelis W. Schoneveld, *Intertraffic of the Mind. Studies in Seventeenth-Century Anglo-Dutch Translation* (Publications of the Sir Thomas Browne Institute, n.s., 3, Leiden, 1983), p. 70.

[10] J. van der Haar, *From Abbadie to Young. A Bibliography of English most [sic] Puritian [sic] Works I/T Dutch Language* (Veenendaal, 1980); *The Role of Periodicals in the Eighteenth Century*, ed. J. D. van Dorsten (for the Sir Thomas Browne Institute, Leiden, 1984).

[11] Bengt Hellekant, *Engelsk Uppbyggelselitteratur I Svensk Översättming Intill 1700 Talets Mitt* (Stockholm, 1944), pp. 287–8; unpublished paper presented to Anglo-Hungarian Conference of Historians 1977 by L. Makkai, 'Puritanism and Modernism in Seventeenth-Century Hungary', p. 3; J. Wallmann, 'Labadismus und Pietismus. Die Einflüsse des niederlandischen Pietismus auf die Entstehung des Pietismus in Deutschland', in *Pietismus und Reveil*, ed. J. van den Berg and J. P. van Dooren (Leiden, 1974), p. 147.

[12] Thomas Sprat, *Observations on Monsieur Sorbière's Voyage into England* (Oxford, 1665), pp. 270–1.

modern literary detectives, and the translation went on right into the middle of the eighteenth century.[13]

Eighteenth-century churches often participated in the esteem or disesteem of their nations, and to some extent the reputation of the English Church rode on a tide of English popularity, a tide lifted by some very bizarre perceptions. There were plenty of continental Protestants in this period who really thought the English were larger than life. When so sober a man as Sigmund Jacob Baumgarten, who in his youth had thought that the most searching test to which theological propositions could be subjected was that of the logic of Christian Wolff,[14] concluded that historical criteria must now be applied, he created a whole translation factory to put works of British history into German dress[15] because

> England and the lands connected with it are more fruitful in noteworthy people of all conditions and ways of life who attract and occupy the attention of their rational fellow-creatures, or can yield more notable examples of the most glorious virtues or most shameful vices, of the exceptional use and misuse of unusual capabilities and advantageous opportunities and of the most rapid and unexpected changes of good and ill fortune than other nations have to show, whose members have no such share in the supreme power . . . and hence have not reached the levels to which corporately developed scholarship, wit, shrewdness, industriousness, bravery, arts, science, business, riches, extravagance, boldness, folly, enthusiasm and evil have risen in this land.[16]

This belief that the English did nothing by halves creates a curious difficulty in the sources for abnormal religious psychology. The Quakers were English enough, though they proselytized actively in Germany in the seventies and eighties. It was clear to the Orthodox that English passions could be readily fanned to produce the trembling phenomena of primitive Quakerism,[17] and that a slightly stronger breeze would blow similar delusions back to Germany in the shape of Fifth Monarchy men,[18] English

[13] J. van den Berg, 'Eighteenth-Century Dutch Translations of the Work of some British Latitudinarian and Enlightened Theologians', *Nederlands Archief voor Kerkgeschiednis*, 59 (1979), 194–212.

[14] Wolff himself drew from Isaac Barrow, mathematician and divine. Christian Wolff, *Logic or Rational Thoughts on Powers of the Human Understanding* (1770), p. lxxv.

[15] Martin Schloemann, *Sigmund Jacob Baumgarten* (Göttingen, 1974), pp. 156–68 and bibliography of Baumgarten's translations. Cf. S. J. Baumgarten, *Uebersetzung der algemeine Welthistorie die in England durch eine Gesellschaft von Gelehrten ausgefertigt worden* (Halle, 1744), I, 48–9.

[16] S. J. Baumgarten, *Samlung von merkwürdigen Lebensbeschreibungen grosstenteils aus der britannischen Biographie übersetzet* (4 vols., Halle, 1754–7), I, Preface.

[17] Johann Georg Walch, *Historische und theologische Einleitung in die Religions-Streitigkeiten ausser der Evengelisch-Lutherischen Kirche* (5 vols., Jena, 1733–6; repr. Stuttgart and Bad Canstatt, 1972), I, 606–7.

[18] Of whom Germany was alleged to have two kinds: 'primae quidem classi homines immoderatos, crassos, fanaticos & turbulentos, alteri moderatiores atque mitiores inseram'. Johannes Reiskius, *Commentatio de Monarchia Quinta eadem Universali per Mille Annos Derativa* (Wolfenbüttel, 1692).

Behmenists or even the sad illusions of Eva Buttlar.[19] The result was that abnormal phenomena were often known both by those who opposed them and those who experienced them as 'English' phenomena. Unfortunately the German word *englisch* very occasionally in ordinary usage means 'angelic'; and in this connexion the 'very occasionally' becomes 'fairly often'. Take, for example, the case of J. F. Rock the leader of the Inspired.[20] When he first turned from plain separatism to inward mysticism, he underwent much trouble, including loss of appetite, but received spiritual consolation. He said 'I know not whether they were *englische-Annäherungen* or whether it was the presence of the Lord.' Here he clearly means 'angelic approaches'. But a little later when he was seized by the strange physical phenomena of Inspiration he said in a very similar phrase, 'whether they are now *englische Bewegungen* or the genuine workings of God, I leave over to the father of all spirits', and here he probably means movements of a Quakerish kind for which he did not much care at first.[21] Yet often the word quite clearly means 'English' whether the connotations are good or bad. Thus, for example, one of the radical attacks on the Moravians stated: 'they either submit to legal and unevangelical sons of thunder, or the Anti-Christ can be represented among them *in Englischen Lichtes-Schein* [in English illumination]; the spirit of death is indeed nothing other than the spirit of Anti-Christ'.[22] The pejorative implications of this reference can be balanced by the favourable connotations of others.[23]

The fact that the word *englisch* can present a problem in the description of religious experience is an indicator of one of the sources of demand for English religious literature. For, if that market was enhanced by the belief that there was something extravagantly grandiose about the English, and was encouraged by widespread admiration for English political

[19] F. W. Barthold, *Die Erweckten im protestantischen Deutschland während des Ausgangs des 17. und der ersten Hälfte des 18. Jahrhunderts* (*Historisches Taschenbuch* 1852–3, ed. Friedrich von Raumer; repr. Darmstadt, 1968), p. 166; Martin Gruhlichen, *Annales Theologico-Ecclesiastici* (Dresden and Leipzig, 1734), pp. 724, 849; Hermann Rückleben, *Die Niederwerfung der hamburgischen Ratsgewalt* (Hamburg, 1970), p. 90; Nils Thune, *The Behmenists and the Philadelphians* (Uppsala, 1948), pp. 125–6.

[20] The Inspired were a group of Pietists expelled from Württemberg who made contact in the Wetterau with the French Prophets and were transformed by them. Their states of 'inspiration' were marked by psychic and physical abnormalities during which they prophesied. On them see my *Protestant Evangelical Awakening* (Cambridge, 1992), ch. 5.

[21] Max Goebel, 'Geschichte der wahren Inspirations-Gemeinden von 1688 bis 1850', *Zeitschrift für die historische Theologie*, new ser., 19 (1855), 98, 109.

[22] Andreas Gross, *Vernünftiger und unpartheyische Bericht ... über die neuaufkommende Herrnhütische Gemeinde* (3rd edn, Frankfurt, 1740), p. 21.

[23] Thus in an account of Felgenhauer: 'The English or psychic spirits are sent out as good angels to the service of men.' Dr Kayser, 'Hannoversche Enthusiasten des siebzehnten Jahrhunderts', *Zeitschrift der Gesellschaft fur niedersächsiche Kirchengeschichte*, 10 (1905), 59.

institutions[24] – and German Protestants, who were anything but liberal, were alarmed for the safety of the English Church in the rebellion of 1745, Britain being one of the international guarantors of the peace settlements of Ryswick and Utrecht[25] – then the market was in one aspect created as a response to a religious need. In the definition of this religious need we owe a great deal to the bibliographers. They have shown that in the seventeenth century, and right through to the middle of the eighteenth, the demand for devotional literature, what might be called the pabulum of *pietas*, was overwhelming, and that it had never been possible to meet it from the Bible and Protestant sources alone. The most popular of all the authors in this sector of the German book market was Thomas à Kempis, who went through 188 editions in Latin and the vernacular languages in the sixteenth century and 444 in the seventeenth. The most popular Lutheran writer, Johann Arndt, whose *Four* (later six) *Books of True Christianity* from their first appearance in 1605 up to 1740 were published ninety-five times in German, and twenty-eight in Latin, English, Dutch, Danish, Swedish, French, Czech, Russian and Icelandic, was also heavily dependent on pre-Reformation writers. It was further the case that Puritan devotional literature was in a great measure modelled on earlier Catholic literature and it proved among the most durable of English exports to the Continent. Lewis Bayley's *Practice of Piety* which flew the flag everywhere enjoyed up to 1740 fifty-nine editions in English and forty-five in German, French, Welsh, Hungarian, Roumanian, Indian and Italian, and appears to have attained sixty-eight German editions soon afterwards.[26] Bayley, like other Puritan texts, first got into Germany through the Reformed churches of Switzerland, but already in 1631 a Luneburg edition had been produced by one of the two great Lutheran devotional presses, and after that they never let it get out of print. Another English author very fully received in Lutheran Orthodoxy was Joseph Hall, sixty-one editions of whose *Arte of*

[24] 'The English imperial constitution is without doubt one of the best in the world.' Burckhardt, *Kirchengeschichte der deutschen Gemeinden in London*, pp. 9–10.

[25] *Acta Historico-Ecclesiastica*, 10 (1746), 28–63.

[26] These publication statistics are conveniently summarized in Hartmut Lehmann, *Das Zeitalter des Absolutismus* (Stuttgart, 1980), pp. 114–18. See also Johannes Wallmann, 'Johann Arndt und die protestantische Frömmigkeit. Zur Rezeption der mittelalterischen Mystik im Luthertum', in *Chloe. Beihefte zum Daphnis Bd.2*, ed. Dieter Breuer (Amsterdam, 1984), pp. 50–74. On the medieval reference of the Puritan devotional literature see Charles E. Hambrick-Stowe, *The Practice of Piety* (Chapel Hill, 1982), p. 28. On book ownership at a local level, F. Breining, 'Die Hausbibliothek des gemeines Mannes vor 100 und mehre Jahre', *Blätter für württembergischen Kirchengeschichte*, 13 (1909), 48–63; Oskar Sakrausky, 'Evangelisches Glaubensleben im Gailtal zur Zeit der Reformation und Gegenreformation', *Carinthia I*, 171 (1981), 191; Reinhard Wittram, 'Der lesende Landmann. Zur Rezeption aufklärerischer Bemühungen durch die bauerliche Bevölkerung im 18. Jahrhundert', in *Der Bauer Mittel-Osteuropas im sozio-ökonomischen Wandel des 18. und 19. Jahrhunderts*, ed. H. Ischreyt (Cologne and Vienna, 1973), pp. 142–96.

Divine Meditation were translated in this period. A universal success story was the *Gulden Kleinodt der Kinder Gottes* of Emmanual Sonthomb, the anagram for E. Thomson, a member of the Merchant Adventurers of England living in Stade in the early sixteenth century. Thirty of Baxter's works were translated, and Bunyan, nine of whose works were translated, was already a hero in north Germany within a decade of his death. He was among the authors prescribed for reading in the Halle Orphan House on Sundays when there were no public prayers, and he received the radical accolade of a life and bibliographical notice in Gottfried Arnold's *Leben der Gläubigen*.[27] In general the Puritan literature had a far longer run on the Continent than it did at home. English sermons were also in demand, especially Stillingfleet, Tillotson and Watts. The Orthodox Löscher, cautiously commending a gigantic compendium of 1717 in which the views of English theologians of all shades were presented under subject headings alphabetically arranged, warned that 'ships coming in from Ophir or from other distant ports commonly bring in monkeys with them' but admitted that 'the English excel in doctrinal matters, the French in power to move, the Italian in the ability to ornament ... Yet the prize belongs easily to the English because they excel all others in teaching and their eloquence is very instructive.'[28] There were differences of opinion in Lutheran Orthodoxy on the issue of approved preaching methods: understandably, the vogue of the English pulpit necessitated a textbook on the *Engellische Prediger-Methode*.[29] That sober scholar, Hans Leube, in a phrase whose full venom may be appreciated from the fact that it was written just after the Versailles settlement, spoke of 'the victory procession of English devotional literature in the Lutheran Church',[30] and indeed Edgar Mackenzie recently calculated that by 1750 more than 690 British religious works, most of them devotional and the core of them Puritan, totalling some 1,700 editions and impressions, had been put into German.[31] The scale of all this may be judged by the fact that as late as 1740 devotional works constituted 20 per cent of the total book production in Germany as compared with the 5 per cent devoted to *belles lettres*. The dominance of this form of literature indeed misled some German commentators as to its real provenance. Wendeborn, for example, in a work originally written to inform Germans

[27] August Sann, *Bunyan in Deutschland* (Giessen, 1951), pp. 12–15; Gottfried Arnold, *Das Leben der Gläubigen* (Halle, 1701), pp. 830–933.

[28] Johan Christoph Gerstäcker, *Amoenitates Anglicanae. Das ist Engelandische Ergötzlichkeiten* (Magdeburg and Leipzig, 1717), Preface.

[29] Martin Schian, *Orthodoxie und Pietismus im Kampf um die Predigt* (Giessen, 1912), pp. 14, 132–4.

[30] H. Leube, *Die Reformideen in der lutherischen Kirche zur Zeit der Orthodoxie* (Leipzig, 1924), p. 169.

[31] Edgar C. Mackenzie, 'British Devotional Literature and the Rise of German Pietism', PhD dissertation, University of St Andrews, 1984. Cf. Sträter, *Sonthom, Bayley, Dyke und Hall.*

as to things English, recalled that 'The spirit of the Greeks remained a long time in their colonies; and the English manners, as well as the English way of thinking, have preserved themselves longer than a century, with very little alteration in the American colonies', an equating of the Puritan with the national character which would not I think carry the imprimatur of Patrick Collinson.[32]

The general significance of what I have been describing is that despite all the efforts of the confessional theologians to create watertight and mutually exclusive positions, ordinary Protestants had stayed themselves during a terrible century by appeal to a spiritual tradition common to Catholic and Protestant in which the Puritan devotional literature could take its place. It is notable that the men who ushered in new ways of Christianizing their world, Spener and Francke, Baxter and Watts, Doddridge and Wesley, should all appear as middle men of one kind or another. Someone needed to mediate between the world of ecclesiastical precision and the world of spiritual nutriment; and the fact that the reading of Luther's *Preface to the Romans* or his commentary on Galatians proved the royal road to conversion showed that the mediators were going to have to go behind the scholastic orthodoxies of recent generations to do it.[33] It was a serious matter, however, that, in the Church of England as reconstructed after the Restoration, only a minority movement was prepared to take this road. The Church was beginning a long process of introversion which seems now to have left it without retreat except to the Counter-Reformation.

It would be grossly unjust to conclude, however, that that day had already come. The period from the middle of the seventeenth to the middle of the eighteenth century, from Descartes's *Les Passions de l'Âme* (1649) to Adam Smith's *Theory of Moral Sentiments* (1759), was a golden age in the history of moral philosophy, and one in which its concern for the study of the passions and their influence on behaviour ran close to the interests of those, Catholic and Protestant, who were concerned to jack up the general level of religious devotion. From the time when Hobbes had insisted on direct observation without preconceptions, British moralists had been of the first importance.[34] In addition, the English also had an impact on continental Protestant views of the Bible: they were supposed to have a special esteem for Scripture and to be offended when the biblical texts were corrupted.[35] This respect served the turn of the early champions of En-

[32] F. A. Wendeborn, *A View of England towards the Close of the Eighteenth Century* (2 vols., 1791), I, 357; P. Collinson, *The Birthpangs of Protestant England* (1988), pp. 1–27.

[33] On this see Martin Schmidt, 'Luthers Vorrede zum Römerbrief im Pietismus', in his *Wiedergeburt und neuer Mensch* (Witten, 1969), pp. 299–330.

[34] On this see Norman Fiering, *Jonathan Edwards's Moral Thought in its British Context* (Chapel Hill, 1981), p. 5; and, more generally, his *Moral Philosophy at Seventeenth-Century Harvard* (Chapel Hill, 1981).

[35] Carl Heinrich Bogatsky, *Aufrichtige und an aller Kinder Gottes gerichtete Declaration über eine gegen ihn herausgekommene Herrnhütische Schrift* (Halle, 1751), p. 10.

lightenment, Edelmann in his radical phase rejoicing that English scholars had detected some thousands of transcription errors in the New Testament alone, and believing that the English Deists had proved that few of the works of Moses had survived. The Deists had indeed mounted a double-barrelled attack, using Locke's criteria of simplicity and clarity to impugn the doctrine of the Trinity, and radical biblical criticism to undermine the Scripture principle. All these resources were available to men like Edelmann,[36] and the Deists themselves appeared in Germany on a considerable scale in the middle third of the eighteenth century.[37] When Schlegel came to sum up the whole story from the standpoint of the Enlightenment in the later years of the century, he beat the drum about the inspiration to research abroad given by the boldness of English scholars, and given especially in the fields of the philosophy of religion and Old Testament studies.[38] In the field of exegesis, British influence was felt on the conservative right as well as the radical left. The holdings of the library of the Stift at Tübingen are a marvellous record of what the Württemberger church authorities thought was worth buying in every generation since the Reformation. In 1766 the catalogue was classified according to the strict principles of Orthodoxy in which dogmatics, ethics and practical theology were subdivided among Lutherans, Reformed, Remonstrants, Papists, Fanatics and Turks, leaving the Church of England nowhere; but exegesis was entirely exempt from this segregation, and holdings of English exegesis, especially Selden, Lightfoot, John Mill and Edward Leigh, were pre-eminent.[39] International respect for English exegesis was matched also by respect for that rather false dawn of new contractual activity in the English Church which was marked by the founding of the SPCK and SPG,[40] a respect which facilitated a powerful English influence upon the development of rational Orthodoxy in Switzerland.[41]

[36] J. C. Edelmann, *Moses mit Aufgedeckten Angesicht* (1740), repr. in *Samtliche Schriften* (12 vols., Stuttgart, 1970–6), VII, pt 1, 47, 57, 83, 133.

[37] On this see A. O. Dyson, 'Theological Legacies of the Enlightenment: England and Germany', in *England and Germany*, ed. S. W. Sykes (Frankfurt and Bern, 1982), p. 55; C. J. Abbey and J. H. Overton, *The English Church in the Eighteenth Century* (2 vols., 1878), I, 244–62.

[38] J. R. Schlegel, *Kirchengeschichte des achtzehnten Jahrhunderts* (3 vols., Heilbronn, 1784–96), I, 456–92; II, 814.

[39] Martin Brecht, 'Die Entwicklung der alten Bibliothek des Tübinger Stift in ihrem theologie- und geistesgeschichtlichen Zusammenhang', *Blätter für württembergische Kirchengeschichte*, 63 (1963), 31, 59.

[40] Gerhard Reichel, 'Der "Senfkornorden" Zinzendorfs', in *Zinzendorf Werke* (Hildesheim, 1962–), 2nd ser., XII, 339; Samuel Urlsperger, *Der noch lebende Joseph Schaitberger* (Augsburg, 1732), pp. 3, 6. (As a young man, Urlsperger, later a member of the SPCK, had performed a disputation on the relations of faith and reason in Locke and Poiret. S. Urlsperger, *Judicium sine Affectu de Duobus Adversariis Joh. Lockio & Petro Poireto eorumque Pugna de Ratione et Fide pro Materia Disputationis*... (Tübingen, 1708).)

[41] P. Wernle, *Der schweizerische Protestantismus im XVIII Jahrhundert* (5 vols., Tübingen, 1923–42), I, 468–77; W. R. Ward, 'Orthodoxy, Enlightenment and Religious Revival', *SCH*, 17 (1982), 287–90.

This cultural invasion, however clearly demand-led, did not, of course, proceed without resistance. Even an enthusiast for things English like Thomasius selected what he wanted from the flood with discretion.[42] There was a negative as well as a positive side to the English example. The English were clearly as bad as the Dutch in screwing profits from the slave trade.[43] Above all the Lutheran Orthodox, for whom the ark of the covenant was the defence of a system of pure doctrine, could no more compromise with things English than with things Pietist, spiritualist or radical. England was indeed known to be a source of bad books and Socinianism,[44] and when in 1749 government circles interested themselves in obtaining a doctorate for an Anglican at the Hanoverian university at Göttingen, the theology faculty absolutely refused on the grounds that to confer such a dignity on a man who did not subscribe to the Augsburg Confession would damage the reputation of the place.[45] The censorship in Saxony did its best to keep out radical English works,[46] and their apologists were full of warnings against excessive dependence on English models in preaching and scholarship.[47] Even transitional theologians who stood between Orthodoxy and the Enlightenment were prepared to declare war on English radicals who denied or doubted revelation.[48] There had once been proposals for union between the churches of England and Mecklenburg in 1663 which were brushed off by Bishop Cosin,[49] and more famous ones between the

[42] W. Bienert, *Der Anbruch der christlichen deutschen Neuzeit dargestellt an Wissenchaft und Glauben des Christian Thomasius* (Halle, 1934), p. 243.

[43] Theodor Wotschke, 'August Hermann Franckes rheinische Freunde in ihren Briefen', *Monatshefte für Rheinische Kirchengeschichte*, 22 (1928), 315.

[44] H. L. Benthem, *Neueröffneter Engelandischer Kirch- und Schulstaat* (2nd edn, Leipzig, 1732), Preface, p. 9; *Acta Historico-Ecclesiastica*, 9 (1745), 298ff. In 1761 when a private library was auctioned in Hamburg, the Senate purchased copies of the works of Herbert of Cherbury and others in order to confine them 'to the City Library, where . . . with others of similar content, [they] formed a special section under the name of *libri prohibiti*'. J. C. Edelmann, *Selbstbiographie 1749–52*, ed. W. Grossmann (Stuttgart and Bad Canstatt, 1976), p. vi.

[45] J. Meyer, 'Geschichte der Göttinger theologischen Fakultät', *Zeitschrift der Gesellschaft für niedersächsiche Kirchengeschichte*, 44 (1937), 24.

[46] Agatha Kobuch, 'Die Zensur in Kursachsen zur Zeit der Personalunion mit Polen (1697–1762). Beiträge zur Geschichte der Aufklärung', PhD dissertation, Humboldt University, [East] Berlin, 1965, I, 89–90.

[47] *Unschuldige Nachrichten*, 1740, p. 495, App. 'Früchte', 111–12; Martin Greschat, *Zwischen Tradition und neuem Anfang, Valentin Ernst Löscher und der Ausgang der lutherische Orthodoxie* (Witten, 1971), pp. 236–8. It is noteworthy, however, that Löscher himself was prepared to translate and secure the approval of the Leipzig faculty for Humphrey Prideaux's *Alt- und Neue Testament in eine Connexion mit der Juden und benachbarten Völker Historie gebracht* (2nd edn, Dresden, 1726), an 'excellent work [designed] to connect Biblical with profane history in a convincing way'. *Unschuldige Nachrichten*, 1721, pp. 147–9.

[48] Arnold F. Stolzenburg, *Die Theologie des Jo. Franc. Buddeus und des Chr. Matth. Pfaff* (Berlin, 1926; repr. Aalen, 1979), pp. 279–284.

[49] Karl Schmaltz, *Kirchengeschichte Mecklenburgs* (3 vols., Schwerin and Berlin, 1935–52), III, 53.

churches of England and Prussia undertaken by Archbishop Wake, which fell foul of the changed diplomatic situation in the 1720s.[50] But the more isolated Lutheran Orthodoxy became in its strongholds of Electoral Saxony and the imperial cities, the more hysterical became its opposition to any Anglican contamination. The English Church was seen to be riddled with Arianism and Socinianism; 'it was created like the English language which was put together out of many others, such as Lower Saxon, Danish, Latin, French and old British; so also is English theology created from religions of many kinds'.[51]

What these negotiations brought out was that, notwithstanding the depth of the English cultural invasion of Germany, inter-church relations were a curious mixture of religion and politics. Within every church there were confessional high-flyers who thought they could 'go it alone', and believed that, in the interests of truth, they had no option but to do so. In the Lutheran world Orthodoxy was a politics primarily of Saxony and secondarily of Sweden. All the new religious movements in the Lutheran world were anti-Saxon and might expect the patronage of the Hohenzollerns, who had good dynastic reasons for wishing to get round the confessional opposition of Lutheran and Reformed at home. They also had compelling diplomatic reasons, in the first instance, for opposition to both Sweden and Saxony, and, in the longer run, for securing the leadership of as much of the Protestant interest as possible for the contest against the Habsburgs.

It was much the same in England. The High Church party believed that what mattered about the English Church was what distinguished it from the continental churches, and they could never really swallow either the political or religious consequences implied by the coalition politics of the Grand Alliance against France. Their weaknesses were, first, that the only plausible monarch they could lay hands on was Queen Anne, and she was devotedly married into the most intensely Pietist court in Europe, that of Denmark (her consort, Prince George, was a channel of all kinds of Pietist influence in this country); and, second, that the Church of England was much less successful than the Lutheran and Reformed churches in girding its position with a systematic theology. The forces of change in England had much less to push over than on the Continent. The Low Church party believed that the level of confessional conflict in Europe and the Catholic threat to the succession in Britain were such that isolation was not a feasible option, and that a common Protestant front must be achieved both at home and abroad. The weakness in their position was that no Grand Alliance could do without the Habsburgs, and the Habsburgs were champions of the Counter-Reformation who vied in brutality with the Bourbons.

[50] N. Sykes, *William Wake, Archbishop of Canterbury* (2 vols., Cambridge, 1957), II, 1–88 *passim*; Schlegel, *Kirchengeschichte*, II, 274–6.
[51] *Unschuldige Nachrichten*, 1727, pp. 432–9.

Nevertheless, like spoke to like, and those who believed that isolation was neither splendid nor possible held out a hand to each other. The great English religious societies were notable vehicles of propaganda for the Franckean institutions at Halle; they made it their business in one generation to provide a refuge for Palatines and in the next for Salzburgers. The latter were looked after by the Georgia Trustees who commissioned the Wesley brothers to provide them with pastoral care. After a large dose of Moravian influence the Wesleys succeeded in putting the societary tradition in English religion to new use, and John, especially, both in translating hymns and in his theology, became an English vehicle of altogether new kinds of German influence. By a chance that was almost a paradox, a Hanoverian dynasty which in the Electorate surrendered to the Orthodox party by closing preferment to candidates who were not natives, maintained an active Pietist interest at their London court, headed by the King's mistress, the Duchess of Kendal, and the Countess Johanna Sophie of Schaumburg-Lippe, and by continuing the long line of Pietist court chaplains begun by Prince George of Denmark. Two of these chaplains, Böhme and Ziegenhagen, in turn not only played a distinguished part in British religious life but were the major channel by which continental and British help was directed not only to the Halle missions, but also to the mass German immigration into the American colonies. Above all the English press kept the British public fully informed as to the crisis in central European Protestantism and created a frame of mind in which the carnal could worship Frederick the Great as a Protestant hero and celebrate him in a host of public-house signs and figures in Staffordshire china[52] while the spiritual could take up with religious revival as another route to saving the Protestant interest.

The situation in the nineteenth century was in one respect the same and in another entirely different. In both the Lutheran and Anglican churches there was still a party of exclusiveness and a party of openness; the difference in England was that the balance between them had entirely changed in favour of the former. The universities and the clergy of the Church, had, under pressures of the late eighteenth century, been much more fully incorporated into the establishment than their predecessors had ever been, and, in their revulsion against Enlightenment, were more completely isolationist in their defence of English ways and institutions than were their predecessors. What escaped their eye was that the long

[52] M. Schlenke, *England und das frederizianische Preussen 1740–63* (Freiburg and Munich, 1963); M. Schlenke, 'England blickt nach Europa: Das konfessionelle Argument in der englischen Politik um Mitte des 18. Jahrhunderts', in *Aspekte der deutsch-britischen Beziehungen im Laufe der Jahrhunderte*, ed. P. Kluke and P. Alter (Stuttgart, 1978), pp. 24–45.

apprenticeship of Germany to the thought of the West and especially England was (the economic sphere still excepted) now over; contemporaneously with the emergence of Goethe in the field of literature, schools of theology, the philosophy of religion and biblical criticism developed from which England had everything to learn. The response, both High Church and Evangelical, was a renewed dose of that introversion which has become so depressingly familiar in many areas of British life since the end of the last war. The Church of England having in the last generation foiled a Methodist attempt, under ecumenical banners, to reconstitute a national establishment on sixteenth-century lines, discovers that its special peculiarities are not much kept up outside Rome; the last ditch of isolationism is to seek a take-over bid from that quarter. The outside world is re-establishing itself again in English religious life.

I would like to conclude with a brief historical retrospect comparing the eighteenth-century Church of England with its historical counterparts. Marc Raeff, in his optimistically entitled *Well-Ordered Police State*, points out that the prerogative or police states of eastern Europe in the eighteenth century all had a work for their churches to do, a work not only of informing and educating, but also of Christianizing, de-paganizing, de-Protestantizing in Catholic states and de-Catholicizing in Protestant states, above all a work of assimilating and controlling.[53] That work the churches were, of course, glad to undertake, though Orthodox parties often lamented the terms on which it had to be done. The English state lost its prerogative or police powers, insofar as their exercise required a special court, during the period of the Civil War, and the Revolution settlement rendered useless some of the powers of church courts. Nevertheless, the English state, comparatively policeless and not well ordered, had much the same work of assimilation for its churches to carry through in the fringe territories of America, Wales, Ireland and the Highlands of Scotland. The first three were entrusted to the Church of England, and in all it failed. The Church in America suffered from lack of resolute state backing and has, I think, endured excessive abuse by American historians. It made a slow start and did not adapt easily to American conditions, but the fact was that its popular support and organization were far better at the beginning of the War of Independence than they ever had been, and it was beginning to attract new types of support. Its misfortune was to be the church of an imperial power which failed to sustain itself. In Wales an energetic but rather ill-conceived campaign to educate, convert and Anglicize the people backfired badly and evoked by way of resistance a powerful religious revival which was Welsh and Dissenting in character. In Ireland, the

[53] Marc Raeff, *The Well-Ordered Police State* (New Haven and London, 1983), pp. 56–69.

Church, secure in the support of the gentry class, depended too much on deference, and the missions begun on a private-enterprise basis by Wesley helped to ignite religious revivals among both Catholic and Protestant, which turned out on both sides to the disadvantage of the Church of England. But while the Church of England was losing the highlands of Wales and never properly got into those of Ireland, the Church of Scotland, after a ferocious struggle, did win the Highlands of Scotland substantially for the Protestant faith and the English language. Its success was due partly to superior resolution, but largely to the fact that it was able to use its lay agencies to promote religious revival within the alien society.[54] The Church of England was by no means the only church in Europe to find its policies of assimilation resisted by revival; the Church of Scotland was one of the establishments which managed to use the phenomenon. What was distinctive about the Church of England proved in the end to be to its disadvantage.

[54] J. MacInnes, *The Evangelical Movement in the Highlands of Scotland 1698–1800* (Aberdeen, 1951).

14 Portrait of a High Church clerical dynasty in Georgian England: the Frewens and their world

Jeffrey S. Chamberlain

I

Hanoverian England was a hostile environment for High Churchmen. To them it seemed that virtually everything they fought for – divine right hereditary monarchy, religious conformity and scrupulous orthodoxy – was being threatened, if not utterly destroyed. Nevertheless, many refused to capitulate to the pressure applied by the political and ecclesiastical establishments to sell out, and High Churchmanship persisted, despite many countervailing pressures. Since they felt that their most sacred principles were being severely undermined by forces in Church, government and society, High Churchmen clung to their ideals all the more tightly, and determined to hold their ground against the foes who assailed them.

What induced men to remain High Churchmen? If these were men truly out of step with the times, why did they persevere? And how did they interact in a society in which so many stood against what they stood for? Was their opposition rooted in piety or in other social factors?

These are difficult questions to answer for it is no simple task to discern the ethos of parish priests, most of whom left no record of their thoughts. A few cases exist, however, where these issues can be looked at in detail. One of these is the Frewen family, a clerical dynasty which began in the late sixteenth century and lasted well into the nineteenth. This essay relates how the Frewens, as traditionalists, coped with and adjusted to the hostility of Georgian England. It is much more, though, than the story of one seemingly inconsequential clerical family, for the picture that emerges of the Frewens bears upon wider themes since it challenges some long-standing notions of churchmanship in the eighteenth century.

II

The Frewen clerical dynasty began in the Elizabethan period. Though the first parson in the line inclined towards Puritanism,[1] the establishment of

[1] John Frewen, rector of Northiam, was prosecuted for Nonconformity by his own parishioners. Mark Antony Lower, *The Worthies of Sussex* (Lewes, 1865), p. 48.

the family's characteristic piety came from a very different tradition. Accepted Frewen, son of the Puritan John (the 'Puritan' Christian name is itself suggestive), repudiated his father's religious orientation and fell in with William Laud and his circle. Though forced into exile during the Interregnum, he was ultimately rewarded for his loyalism by Charles II: at the Restoration he was appointed archbishop of York. His tenure was brief, but his influence on the Frewens was not – he was a hero to the whole family, and became a model for them of the quintessential Churchman. He was revered by his descendants for his principles, position and piety and they ascribed to him almost mythic saintliness.[2] A manuscript book of his sermons and memoranda was carefully preserved and handed down from one generation to the next, and a miniature given to him by Charles I when he was his chaplain on the Spanish mission was practically venerated as a relic.[3] His spirit seemed to hover over and guide the family in death as in life, since his Laudianism and loyalism persisted among them for generations.

The Frewens maintained this High Church temperament inherited from their 'patriarch' even into the eighteenth century, when Laudianism would seem to have been outmoded. At this time, there were Frewens with livings in both Leicestershire and Sussex. These included the Reverend John Frewen, rector of Sapcote, Leicestershire, in the 1720s and 1730s, and his son Thomas, who succeeded him in that living in 1735. Thomas held the living until he inherited the nearby estate of Cold Overton Hall in 1777, whereupon he presented his brother-in-law, Stanley Burroughs, to the post.

The Sussex representatives of the Frewens included Thankful, rector of Northiam (1669–1749), Stephen, vicar of Fairlight (1677–1722), both of whom were cousins to Thomas of Brickwall, and John, Thankful's son, who was vicar of Fairlight and rector of Guestling (1702–43). Sussex, in fact, served as the centre of the Frewen clan, since Thomas Frewen of Brickwall – not a cleric, but a High Churchman nonetheless – acted as a co-ordinator of Frewen affairs. Brickwall in Northiam was the oldest and most substantial estate in the family, and Thomas was the unofficial head of the various branches of the family. He, in effect, sustained family loyalties through his correspondence and contacts.

III

The Frewens were clearly High Churchmen – both politically and religiously – at the time of the Hanoverian accession. In the highly charged first

[2] When it was suggested that Accepted Frewen had not completely divested himself of his father's Puritanism, Thomas Frewen of Brickwall recoiled in horror and wrote a hagiographic defence of the prelate. *A Just and Plain Vindication of the Late Dr Frewen, Lord Archbishop of York* (1743), p. 6.

[3] Thomas Frewen, *Vindication*; A. L. Frewen, *A History of Brickwall in Sussex and of the Parishes of Northiam and Brede* (1909), pp. 25–6.

decade and a half of the eighteenth century, they consistently lined up on the Tory/High Church side of the conflict. Their voting pattern in Sussex from 1705 to 1741 was consistently Tory, with only one exception.[4]

Several issues seem to have been at the core of the family's Toryism. The first was concern over Nonconformity. The Frewens, as High Churchmen, felt that Dissenters ought to be proscribed, and that the toleration they had received in 1689 was ill-advised at best, and woefully destructive at worst, for they threatened the state and society as well as the Church.

The Frewens' fear of Dissent may have been heightened by agitation of Nonconformists in or near their own parishes. John Frewen certainly had problems with them. In 1708 he wrote to the SPCK, complaining that a pamphlet defending and encouraging Dissent was being 'with great Industry dispers'd' among the people in his parish with deleterious effects.[5] It is not surprising, therefore, to find in John Frewen's papers a series of notes carefully taken from books, which would arm him against the principles of the Dissenters in order to keep his parishioners from being contaminated, and, if possible, to convince schismatics to conform. These he summarized in his notes for ready reference. His choice of books is instructive. Though he was part of the post-Toleration Act generation and attended the Whiggish Merton College, Oxford,[6] the books to which he made recourse were written well before his time and, though temperate, granted nothing to the justice of the Dissenting cause. The notes he entitled 'London Divines Cases: for communion with the Church of England',[7] were taken from a tract by Robert Grove, bishop of Chichester, which was written in the wake of the Exclusion crisis after renewed attacks on the established Church by Dissenters.[8] This work reiterated the Laudian defence that it was lawful for the Church of England to command practices such as wearing the surplice, signing the cross in baptism and kneeling at the sacrament, because they were things 'indifferent', in no way destructive of faith. Parishioners had no right to balk at these practices or to separate from the Church because of them – doing so demonstrated sheer obstinacy and rebellion against legitimate authority.[9]

In complete sympathy with this temperate but unyielding approach, John Frewen contended with his people over the practice of kneeling at communion, insisting that a truly worshipful Christian would kneel because his bodily posture manifested the disposition of his heart, 'so that he who truly bows his soul to God cant forbear at the same time to bow his knees to him also and he who does not is much to be suspected not to

[4] See below. [5] SPCK, Abstract Letter Book, CR1/1: 1327, 1480.

[6] W. R. Ward, *Georgian Oxford* (Oxford, 1958), pp. 39, 40.

[7] ESRO, FRE 519, fos. 56–60, 103.

[8] [Robert Grove], *A Perswasive to Communion with the Church of England* (1683). For background to the attacks, see William Nichols, *A Defence of the Doctrine and Discipline of the Church of England* (1715), pp. 89–90. [9] [Grove], *Perswasive*, pp. 13, 26.

entertain reverential thoughts and affections towards God'.[10] Thus he accused the Dissenters – and those who sympathized with their practices – of impiety. To Frewen, Nonconformists were not conscientious but recalcitrant. He would not give in to their impertinence; they would have to submit, or be ostracized.

Other Frewens feared Dissent too and made it a key political issue as late as 1741. When in that year, Lord Middlesex, the Duke of Dorset's son, stood for Knight of the Shire in Sussex, Thomas Frewen of Brickwall and Thankful, his cousin, opposed him, and thought all clergy ought to oppose him, because he had voted for repeal of the Test Act. As far as they were concerned, the Church was still 'in danger' from Dissent, and the clergy who voted for him were merely unprincipled sycophants who were selling out their religion. After the opposition against Middlesex collapsed, Thomas wrote to Thankful:

> I can scarce refrain from Tears to see our native Land in such bondage, and in so dangerous Hands. I think the clergy who were such strenuous Advocates for him [Lord Middlesex], can scarce be reckon'd friends to that Rubrick they have subscribed, For if repealing the Test Act, be not undermining our church & its very foundation; I desire them to tell me what is?[11]

Though there appears to be little direct evidence to confirm it, Thomas Frewen may have been alarmed by the large numbers of Dissenters who congregated in the nearby borough of Rye. He was certainly acquainted with some neighbours who were Nonconformists – especially the Jeakes family – and was disturbed by their activities.

The Frewens simply could not understand the impulse to give Dissenters not only freedom from persecution, but rights as well. They were for withholding all benefits from them. Thomas Frewen of Brickwall, in fact, encouraged the Reverend Thankful to forbear giving alms to any 'who dont frequent the communion of our excellent Church'.[12] Nevertheless, the Frewens thought of themselves as charitable, and even preached up the duty of charity and benevolence as hallmarks of the Christian faith. Interestingly, Thomas Frewen, John's son and successor at Sapcote, could even use the 'Latitudinarian' language of charity and moderation, making it sound as if he unquestionably favoured toleration of and charity towards

[10] ESRO, FRE 687.

[11] ESRO, FRE 1302. Frewen may have been too critical of the clergy here. Evidence is sketchy, but the fragments of information that have survived for that election demonstrate that many of the clergy opposed Middlesex. It is true that a fair number were campaigning for him (see the letters to the Duke of Dorset in the Kent Archives Office, Sackville of Knole papers, C150), but the records of the Duke of Newcastle show that as many as half of the clergy opposed him. See BL, Add. MS 33085, fos. 437–8. What might have galled Frewen is that his own kinsman, John Frewen, rector of Guestling, was on Middlesex's side.

[12] ESRO, FRE 1302.

Nonconformists. In a sermon on loving God and our neighbour, Thomas preached that love and charity were integral to Christianity and were to be demonstrated by all true Christians. Loving one's neighbour and being charitable were, therefore, essential duties, to be extended to 'every man of whatever County, or Calling, Sect or Interest'.[13] Though he invoked the story of the Good Samaritan (the Jews and Samaritans were in some ways a good parallel to the Anglicans and Nonconformists) to prove his point, he remained hostile to the Dissenters. Despite his moderate and charitable rhetoric, he could not, on the practical level, accept Nonconformists. He still felt that they were stubborn and obstinate and only worshipped separately out of motives of perversity and rebellion. They would be called to account for their recalcitrance. In his lectures on the Catechism, he maintained that such schismatics

> will have a sad and fearful account to give of themselves at the day of retribution: and it were to be wished that all those concerned would be so wise as to think seriously what they are about and whither this wrong road will carry 'em before its too late and the night comes upon 'em, the night of Death, wherein they cannot work any ammendment tho ever so desirous of doing it.[14]

In another sermon, in fact, he deprecated 'charity and moderation' if by that was meant 'indifference to all religions and all communions'. In his mind, such indifference was 'deservedly odious'. As High Churchmen earlier in the century had pointed out, it was not charitable: rather, it was perilous because it tended to undermine true faith.[15] Thus, though he preached charity and used language that sounded moderate and benevolent towards Dissenters, he was not prepared to countenance any of their stubborn practices. This should give us pause about uncritically characterizing the age as one of moderation simply because the preachers used the language of charity. Thomas Frewen's charity was not moderation, however it may have sounded.

The Frewens' fear of Dissent contributed to the perpetuation of their High Church/Tory perspective until late in the eighteenth century. Another critical issue for them was the succession of the Crown. There were no Frewens in orders at the time of the Revolution, but both Thankful and Stephen were ordained within the next ten years. Whether or not they went through any struggles over subscription to the oaths before taking orders is uncertain. Some pamphlets in the Frewen archives, however, indicate that

[13] ESRO, FRE 706.

[14] ESRO, FRE 709, fos. 5, 6. Though Sapcote itself seems to have had little in the way of Dissenting activity, several neighbouring parishes displayed continuing Nonconformist vigour. See Leicestershire RO, QS44/1/1–2 and QS44/2/9, 11, 13, 23, 36.

[15] ESRO, FRE 708; see, for example, *The Distinction of High-Church and Low-Church Distinctly Consider'd* (1705).

some members of the family were thinking through these issues carefully.[16]

What is clear, is that the majority of them were not happy with the Hanoverian accession. There are hints of their disapproval at the time of the succession and of continuing opposition to the Hanoverians. All of the Sussex Frewens, for instance, demonstrated their solidarity with the one parish priest in the Chichester diocese who refused the oaths to King George I when they subscribed to his publications to support himself and his family.[17]

John Frewen found himself obligated to preach a thanksgiving sermon for the accession of George I, surely a task he did not relish. He preached the sermon, but its tone is markedly cooler than that of a thanksgiving sermon he preached some years earlier, commemorating some occasion in the reign of Queen Anne.[18] The earlier message was imbued with joy and delight, as he rhapsodized over the blessings of the reign and praised God for his bountiful goodness in granting such success to the nation. Under Anne's benevolent and enlightened leadership, he said, God had 'constantly showered down his blessings and deliverance upon us'. Indeed, Frewen was well-nigh ecstatic in his paean to Queen Anne and her care and concern for the Church and people of England. This jubilance was remarkable for a man who was characterized by a descendant as 'very grave, never having been seen to laugh except once when his youngest daughter pinched the cat's tail'.[19]

His 'thanksgiving' sermon for the accession of George I, on the other hand, has more of a tone of lamentation than jubilation. He began by observing his obligation to preach such a sermon:

We are this day *calld upon by authority* to give thanks to Almighty God for bringing his Majesty to a peaceful and quiet possession of the throne, and not only in *obedience* to that *authority*, but *in conformity* to our engagements to the succession

[16] E.g. *A Letter Written to a Gentleman in the Country about the LATE Northern Invasion* (1708), which argues that one need only accept that the succession was legal in order sincerely to take the Oath of Abjuration.

[17] Richard Russel was one of a very few Hanoverian Nonjurors. His translation of Pasquier Quesnel's *Moral Reflections on the New Testament* (1719) was printed by subscription, and it is clear that much of the support was political in nature. The vast majority of subscriptions came from Sussex – from those who knew Russel – and though some notable Whigs subscribed, the bulk of the names are those of Tories. Thankful, Stephen and Thomas Frewen of Brickwall all subscribed.

[18] The occasion is not clear. All Frewen said of it in the sermon was that 'we are mett by public order to commemorate with thankfulness to God the blessing we have received'. In the homily he said he would 'recount the many great deliverances that God has wrought for us in the severall days of our distress and the many amazing successes that he has blessed us with ... for many generations ... against our enemys abroad [and] the disturbers of our peace at home'. It is conceivable that this was a 5 November sermon, in which he applied the theme of deliverance to the Stuarts (at the Restoration) as well as to Queen Anne's reign. ESRO, FRE 687.

[19] ESRO, FRE 826: notes on family history by Thomas Frewen IV of Brickwall.

in the Hanover line we are *obliged* to give this our public approbation, by offering up the suitable prayers and praises which are injoined.[20]

Since they had already offered the correct prayers, he said, 'I dont know better how to answer the design in the remaining part of the day than by saying before you some considerations to prevent our doing it in an indecent and undutiful manner.' There were no exclamations of joy here, no cries of exultation, and little sense of hopeful expectation for the future. Instead there was only the admonition to his parishioners, which occupied most of the rest of the sermon, not to become debauched in revelry. He had, it should be noted, made the same admonition in the previous sermon, but only as a footnote appended to his discourse: here it dominated the message, as if there was nothing else he could think of to say. Although Frewen fulfilled his official obligation in preaching on this day, he seemed to deny the spirit of it, since there was very little genuine gratitude expressed.

The Frewens also demonstrated their sympathies in the associations they maintained. Both John and his son Thomas were well acquainted with Francis Atterbury, the bishop of Rochester, who was ultimately charged with treason and exiled. Apparently they both knew him personally and counted themselves his friends. Atterbury himself presented a copy of a volume of his printed sermons to John Frewen in 1708 (the book is autographed by the author). Furthermore, Thomas was personally acquainted with Alexander Pope and Jonathan Swift, and he and his cousin Laton dined with them on at least one occasion. This familiarity is most likely the means by which Thomas was able to procure several letters which demonstrate Jacobite sympathy. In his papers are a couple of epistles written by Francis Atterbury in exile, as well as a curious letter purporting to be an Englishman's favourable account of his encounter with the Young Pretender in Rome.[21] The fate of Atterbury must have been very important to Frewen, since he copied these letters in his own hand. The missives of Atterbury, written to his son and his friend Alexander Pope, display the disillusionment and heartache experienced by the exiled Bishop. Some of these sentiments seem to be mirrored in Thomas Frewen's thinking. Most poignant of these is Atterbury's feeling that

My country to me at this distance seems a strange sight, I know not how it appears to you who are in the midst of the Sun, & yourself a part of it . . . I do & must love my country with all its faults and blemishes, even that part of the constitution which wounded me unjustly, & itself through my side, will ever be dear to me.[22]

This melancholy, this mournful sense of affection for a country – indeed a

[20] ESRO, FRE 687: sermon 20 Jan. 1715. My emphasis.

[21] ESRO, FRE 6774. There is a copy of this letter about the Pretender in Archbishop Wake's papers. The letter in Wake's collection is dated 6 May 1721. Christ Church, Oxford, Arch.W.Epist. 22, fo. 18.

[22] ESRO, FRE 6774.

world – which was tumbling out of control can also be found in the Frewens' discourse. In fact, this lamentation was probably the most active expression of their Jacobitism. The sense of unfulfilled and unfulfillable hopes and dreams probably contributed to the melancholic otherworldly tone of the Frewens' sermons. In one, for example, Thomas Frewen explained that it was only right that we should look towards eternity for our hope because everything here is transitory. With an air of wistfulness, he pointed out that

> There's no man that lives any considerable time in the world but must see a great many things which he would not; his own miseries & the calamities of others, public confusions & disorders, wars abroad and factions at home, besides the loss of his nearest and dearest friends & relations; so that upon summing up the account he will find that scarce anything now is as it was 40 or 50 years ago . . . which is abundantly sufficient to convince him that the world passeth away.[23]

He may well have been thinking of Francis Atterbury in his reference to friends lost. Certainly his frustration with the political and religious direction of the country led to his identification with the Scripture upon which the sermon was based – 'the world passes away' (I John 2.17). Further, his choice of '40 or 50 years ago' would seem to be anything but arbitrary: since the sermon was written in the mid-1730s, he appears to be implying that nothing was the same as it had been before the Revolution. Everything was downhill from that point, and the only hope for men was to do the will of God and to 'sit as loose as they can from the things of this world', so that they could 'secure an estate of eternal happiness'.

In this way the sadness and disappointments of this world might be circumvented. It was no sacrifice to mortify the pleasures of this life, since such things would only bring heartache. It was better not to place one's hopes on anything earthly – politics, people or pleasures – than to have those hopes dashed. Quoting the apostle Paul, he noted poignantly that 'if in this life only we have hope, we are of all men most miserable'.[24]

This sense of the inevitability of disappointment and futility appears to have led the Frewens to a grudging acceptance of the affairs of this world, which may explain their resigned inaction in later years. They remained High Churchmen and probably Jacobites, but they were by no means eager to participate in the '45. They seemed genuinely frightened about the prospect of the Young Pretender's victory, despite the fact that their sympathies had been clearly with the Stuart family. In March of 1746, Thomas Frewen of Brickwall wrote to his cousin Laton in Yorkshire that

> I guess the Rebels alarm'd ye a good deal in their march tho' it was southward, but hope in a little while to hear all their daring enterprizes be at an end. To shew our affection and zeal for the present Establishment, our Sussex Gentry join'd in an

[23] ESRO, FRE 708. [24] ESRO, FRE 708: sermon on I John 2.17.

Association; for raising a Regiment of 1200 men to defend the Country instead of raising the Militia. I contributed a small matter towards the expence, but the less as I was to have no command amongst them.[25]

Despite the rhetoric of support and 'affection' for the establishment, Thomas Frewen was very late to contribute his share to the cause. The Association was formed 11 October 1745, and Frewen's name does not appear on the subscription lists at any time in that month, though other prominent Tories embraced the opportunity immediately.[26] It may, in fact, have been that Frewen was not appointed a deputy lieutenant because his temporizing prompted doubts about his loyalty.[27] In any case, the Frewens, unlike some other Tories, continued even after the '45 to complain against the administration, though when push came to shove, the actual invasion of the Young Pretender had posed more risks than they were prepared to countenance. It seemed better to put up with the current *de facto* king, than to sponsor the uncertainties of a new Stuart monarch.

Though the Frewens remained diehard Tories, they had many associations with people whose politics they opposed, even though they considered them 'enemies' on the battlefield of an election. When friends and associates became Whigs or developed Whig associations, the Frewens did not automatically cut off relations. In fact, rather than making politics and churchmanship occasions for conflict as they were in some places,[28] the High Tory Frewens sought to work with Whigs toward common goals (or, at least, sought – frequently successfully – to get Whigs to work with them). One illustration of this is the family's connexions with George Barnesley. Barnesley was known as a diligent clergyman,[29] and he established

[25] ESRO, FRE 1323.

[26] BL, Add. MS 33085, fos. 459–64.

[27] The 'Lewes Association' brought Whigs and Tories together in a new way. They had been working together in the administration of the county all along (see P. J. Le Fevre, 'Justices and Administration: The Political Development of Sussex 1660–1714', PhD dissertation, CNAA (Brighton Polytechnic), 1989), but Tories had been proscribed on the national scene. Because of the way they had rallied to the cause in the '45, many prominent Tories, who as recently as 1741 had been fighting the Newcastle coalition tooth and nail in elections, were made deputy lieutenants for the county. Among them were Thomas Sergison, Sir Cecil Bishop and John Fuller, all of whom had been Tory candidates. See list of deputy lieutenants for Sussex, BL, Add. MS 33085, fo. 467. But Frewen was not among them. It is not at all unlikely that Frewen had been secretly hoping for the Pretender's victory and only joined the Association when all hope was lost. All the county's gentry ultimately joined, even known Jacobites, so his entry is not necessarily proof of his support for their intentions. Further, the letter to his cousin may have been a ruse, since it was known that letters were frequently intercepted and scrutinized for evidence of treason. See Paul S. Fritz, 'The Anti-Jacobite Intelligence System of the English Ministers, 1715–45', *HJ*, 16 (1973), 265–90.

[28] See John Trifitt, 'Believing and Belonging. Church Behaviour in Plymouth and Dartmouth 1710–30', in *Parish, Church and People*, ed. S. J. Wright (1988), pp. 179–202.

[29] In his later years he canvassed collections for the SPG, was a corresponding member of the SPCK, was involved with helping to start charity schools and when he died he left large

friendships with both Whigs and Tories. He was rector of the Frewen family living of Northiam from 1677 to 1692, where he undoubtedly earned their appreciation and affection. But he also gained powerful friends among the Whigs – especially Thomas Bowers, friend of and chaplain to the Duke of Newcastle, and ultimately bishop of Chichester.[30] Barnesley, therefore, was able to act as a mediator between parties.[31] The Frewens deliberately solicited his help in starting a charity school in Northiam, largely because they felt he could enlist the support of Whigs for the project.[32] In death, too, Barnesley brought Low and High Churchmen together: he chose the Tory Stephen Frewen and the Whig Thomas Bowers to be among the executors of his will.[33]

Though the Frewens were Tories, their appreciation of a man was not contingent on his politics. When a new Whig bishop, Matthias Mawson, was appointed to the see of Chichester in 1740, Thomas Frewen and his cousin Thankful both expressed appreciation of and unfeigned admiration for him. His politics did not alter their assessment. As Thomas wrote to Thankful: 'I am vastly pleas'd with your account of our present Bishop, and wish him long to fill that station with so much deserv'd applause.'[34] In this case the piety, orthodoxy and diligence of the man mattered more than his politics, for Mawson was very much a Newcastle man, as were all the bishops of Chichester from the time of Thomas Bowers's appointment in 1722 until the end of the century. By the same token, the Frewens seemed unhappy with Thomas Herring's promotion to the archbishopric of York, not because he was a Whig appointee, but because his orthodoxy was suspect since he 'used to say in the pulpit that our saviour was a good man; & better than the philosophers'.[35]

Ties of kinship, too, were much stronger than ties of politics. The Frewen family was closely allied to the Ashe family and maintained an interest in the nearby parish of Salehurst, where Simeon Ashe was the rector from 1690 to 1727.[36] Undoubtedly the families were knit together in sympathy as well as blood: Simeon voted Tory in every election that occurred before his death. Sometime after his demise the Frewens procured the right of

sums of money to the SPG, the Corporation of the Sons of the Clergy and a charity school. LPL, SPG Papers, VII, fos. 123, 137, 201; SPCK, Abstract Letter Book, CR1/3: 2949; 5:3905 and *passim*; PRO, Prob 11/601/26.

[30] SPCK, Abstract Letter Book, CR1/3: 2949, demonstrates a close connexion between them.

[31] There seems to be no way of determining Barnesley's politics since he does not appear to have voted in Sussex elections.

[32] ESRO, FRE 1271, 1272. Anthony Springett, rector of Plumpton in Sussex, also seems to have succeeded in uniting Whig and Tory in the creation of charity schools. He brought such disparate political personalities as the Whig Pelhams, the Tory Henry Campion and several clergymen on both sides into a common cause. See his will, PRO, Prob 11/675/44.

[33] PRO, Prob 11/601/26.

[34] ESRO, FRE 1294.

[35] ESRO, FRE 1299.

[36] Ashe married Winifred, the daughter of the Rev. Thomas Frewen of Northiam (d. 1677). See genealogy in Heather M. Warne, *A Catalogue of the Frewen Archives* (East Sussex RO Handbook no. 5, 1972).

patronage to Salehurst. In 1731 they presented William Jenkin to that living, undoubtedly because he had married into the Frewen–Ashe family alliance.[37] At that time, Jenkin was already a devoted Whig. Not only did he vote Whig in 1734, but he actively courted the favour of the Duke of Newcastle and his allies. In fact, Jenkin was probably already chaplain to Newcastle in 1731 when Frewen appointed him to his new living. This is remarkable given the antipathy that Frewen could voice towards Jenkin's other patron, the Duke – the 'Great Man', as he sarcastically called him.[38] Furthermore, Jenkin energetically campaigned for the Whigs in 1740 while his kinsman, the patron of Salehurst, earnestly solicited for the opposition.[39] They may not have been very close in ideology, but that did not keep them from favouring one another's interests (at least, non-political interests).

Even closer to home was the defection of Thankful Frewen's son, John, from the Tory ranks. Unfortunately, none of his correspondence or memoranda survive to inform us of his thoughts and feelings. It may be that he was persuaded by Sir William Ashburnham, who later presented him to the vicarage of Guestling, but his motives are by no means certain. There must have been much concern among the Frewens regarding John's departure from family politics, for at the very time they were campaigning zealously for the Tory candidates, he was canvassing for 'the enemy'.[40] John Frewen had become, in fact, one of those blind clergymen who, in Thomas Frewen's mind, were endangering the Church because they supported Lord Middlesex.[41] Nevertheless, this fundamental political difference does not seem to have disrupted familial harmony and goodwill, since Thomas Frewen considered John a 'good Friend'. He was known to all the branches of the family – in Sussex, Leicestershire and Yorkshire – as a pious man, one who was 'near and dear' to them.[42]

In politics, then, the Frewens (with the exceptions of John Frewen of Guestling and William Jenkin) were Tories and probably 'sentimental' Jacobites.[43] They opposed the Whig oligarchy and fought against any

[37] He married Palacia, daughter of Simeon Ashe, in January of 1718. After his death, Palacia married Edward Frewen, DD, of Robertsbridge. BL, Add. MS 39326, fo. 192; Warne, *Frewen Archives*. [38] ESRO, FRE 1335.

[39] Interestingly, they are both mentioned by Robert Burnett, the Duke's primary agent in Sussex, in the same letter – Jenkin with Newcastle's forces, and Frewen against. BL, Add. MS 32694, fos. 511–12.

[40] He appeared at the Whig show of solidarity in a meeting at Horsham at the beginning of the campaign of 1740. This indicates that his sympathies for the Whig cause were much warmer than mere acquiescence. BL, Add. MS 33085, fos. 412–13.

[41] BL, Add. MS 33085, fos. 437–8. [42] ESRO, FRE 1299.

[43] Paul Monod cautions against the use of the term 'sentimental Tory', since it tends to evoke a sense of less than serious attachment, as was the common view in the nineteenth century. That is not the intention here. The Frewens were seriously devoted to their beliefs, even if they were not always translated into action. See Monod, *Jacobitism and the English People 1688–1788* (Cambridge, 1989), p. 7.

further relief for Dissenters, but when the moment of decision came in 1745, they preferred to be resigned and wistful, rather than to gamble on a military venture to restore the Stuarts. They lived in a Whig world, and, though they deplored Whiggery and all it stood for, they coped with its existence and even befriended its proponents.

IV

Theologically, the Frewens followed the example of their Archbishop patriarch and remained true to the Laudian tradition, as they interpreted it, throughout most of the eighteenth century. Preserved among John Frewen's papers are extensive handwritten notes on works such as *Laud's Conference with Fisher* and Peter Heylin's *Cyprianus Anglicus*, a Restoration defence of, and paean to, Archbishop Laud.[44] These were important writings to him, which he carefully indexed for easy reference, and they laid a foundation for his theology and practice.

It has already been noted, in connexion with John Frewen's struggle with Dissenters, that he was concerned to preserve the practice of kneeling at communion. This is indicative of the high value that he ascribed to communion, which was for him a 'holy mistery', a 'solemn ordinance that Christ has appointed for the conveying his grace to us and enabling us to overcome our sins and grow dayly in vertue and goodness'. For this reason he constantly pleaded with his parishioners to communicate often. He seems to have had some success, judging by a farewell sermon to one of his early congregations, in which he commented that he had often spoken on this topic 'and by God's blessing with good effect upon many'.[45]

John's son, Thomas, shared his father's sacramentalism. He too called communion a 'holy mystery' and urged his flock to attend with all possible frequency. He was dismayed when they held back, and warned them that their very souls were at stake, since the Lord's Supper was a much-needed agency of grace, which it was perilous to neglect.[46]

Thomas Frewen of Brickwall reflected the same high view of and concern for the sacrament. Discovering that, while he was away in Leicestershire, his servants were absenting themselves from the Lord's Table, he wrote to Thankful that he could not 'be satisfyd if they dont make the dutys to God and religion consistent with their service to me. I must beg you to instruct them before Xmass in their obligations to it, and I expect them to communicate as Christians, if they expect to continue in my family.'[47]

With their emphasis on the importance of communion and their exhortations to partake frequently, one might imagine that the Frewens would

[44] ESRO, FRE 687. [45] ESRO, FRE 687.
[46] ESRO, FRE 706. [47] ESRO, FRE 1292.

have offered it monthly, if not even more frequently. But they did not: just like the majority of other Georgian clergymen, they made it a quarterly practice.[48] Evidently a parson's decision to offer the Lord's Supper quarterly rather than monthly was not determined by his churchmanship. Nor was the prevalence of quarterly communion necessarily symptomatic of laxity of religious fervour. It was not even an indicator of a decrease in sacramentalism (at least from the perspective of the parsons). Rather, the decision about how frequently to offer it seems to have been made more from the practical considerations of who would come and how it was to be paid for. Small parishes did not usually find it feasible to sponsor more frequent communions. In large population centres, on the other hand, it was much easier, and in Sussex it was such parishes that managed to offer the Lord's Supper monthly.[49]

These tendencies can be illustrated by the example of the Frewens. Thankful Frewen, the rector of Northiam, had been in the practice of offering communion three times a year when his cousin, Thomas Frewen of Brickwall, who also served many years as churchwarden, wrote to him from Cold Overton and asked him if he could administer the 'Blessed Sacrament on the Sunday after Michaelmas day, which if you calculate right, will bring it to once every Quarter'. Thomas added that quarterly communion was what he was used to both in Cold Overton and Shermanbury, where he had been tutored by the rector, John Bear, who was also a High Churchman. He thought that 'the size of the parish w[ould] bear it'. Thereupon Thankful obliged his cousin and Northiam henceforth observed communion four times a year.[50] Thus the Frewens, and perhaps many other Georgian clergymen, could be strongly sacramental even though they offered communion only three or four times a year.

Baptism too was a holy occasion in which God touched humans in a special way. In his catechetical lectures, Thomas Frewen spoke of baptism as the regenerating sacrament. In baptism, he said, children were 'born again of water and of the Holy Spirit and so made Christians'. In this he was in the mainstream of eighteenth-century religious thought, since the majority of the divines of the age believed in baptismal regeneration.[51] This in itself should give pause to any who might assert that the Church was losing its emphasis on the sacraments. If it is true that rationalism was

48 Sykes, *Church and State*, pp. 250–2. Evidence for the frequency of communion in Sapcote comes from the churchwardens' accounts. During John Frewen's tenure there were three disbursements a year for bread and wine; during his son Thomas's there were four. Leicestershire RO, DE 933/25. I am indebted to Catherine Patterson for this information.

49 As is evident in Bishop Bowers's visitation of 1724. West Sussex RO, EpI/26/3.

50 ESRO, FRE 1291, 1292.

51 C. John Sommerville, *Popular Religion in Restoration England* (Gainesville, 1977), pp. 94–5.

predominant in this age, then it existed alongside the strong pull of sacramentalism, at least in the rite of baptism, and perhaps in that of communion as well. Grace came through the mystery of baptism before it ever reached men's ears in logical, closely reasoned sermons. Men might respond to a benevolent God when his truths were communicated through rational discourses, but they had first to experience his grace in a sacrament.

Furthermore, the Frewens could be just as rationalistic as those often termed 'Latitudinarian', despite their sacramentalism and emphasis on mystery in their religion. Though their sermons were usually steeped in Scripture and frequently emotive as well, they could appeal to their audience in the same terms as those supposedly rationalistic preachers. As we have already seen in their preaching on charity, they could defy the boundaries of Latitudinarianism, as defined by some historians.[52] They could slip in and out of rationalistic 'moods', and yet maintain their High Anglican theology.

This can be illustrated by the striking differences between two sermons preached by Thomas Frewen in roughly the same period. One is a rationalistic discourse, full of rhetoric concerning the benevolence of God and the 'reasonableness' of religion. It was based on the foundation of natural religion, using language often associated with Latitudinarian homiletics:

> wherever we turn our eyes we may find repeated instances of the Divine Bounty; ever the most minute Being partakes of its influence, for Providence, taking in a large circle, extends itself to the utmost bounds of the world, & the divine benevolence is everywhere manifested to an enquiring eye; These instances of divine profusion when made the subjects of our religious reflections of reasonable and intelligent nature are to be considered as so many intimations from the Fountain of Light.[53]

This was the introduction to a homily in which he encouraged his hearers to do good to one another and practise the Golden Rule. But another sermon containing the very same injunction began only with biblical theology – with an explanation of the background of the text. In this discourse Frewen likewise made his appeal on the basis of the goodness of God and his glory and majesty, but the tone was markedly different. Here he used biblical allusions to make the same point; he concentrated on the attributes of God revealed in Scripture rather than those which come from the light of nature, which were his focus in the previous sermon. It appears, therefore, that the 'Latitudinarian mood' was, at least for Thomas Frewen, just that – a mood that fitted one occasion but not another. The same theology could be expressed in wholly different ways, and the use of rational language by a

[52] L. P. Curtis, for example, defines the 'Latitudinarian mood' as one of 'moderation, sweetness of disposition, and reasonableness'. *Anglican Moods of the Eighteenth Century* (New Haven, 1966), p. 6.

[53] ESRO, FRE 706.

preacher did not necessitate his purging mystery from his religion, or accommodating his beliefs to the point that he was nearly a Deist.

The Frewens maintained a high view of worship as well. God was to be honoured and venerated by attendance at divine service, and so they continued to hold services twice every Lord's day (though only one sermon a day, this in accordance with the Laudian perspective that it was not proper to over 'sermonize' the people[54]) and on all holy days, though they were disgusted by the lack of attendance at the latter. Furthermore, the Frewens complained, when their parishioners did come to church, they were not respectful enough of the divine presence in worship. Either they came late and bumptiously disrupted the service,[55] or they did not pay due respect to the 'holy utensils' of worship.[56] For the Frewens, worship was 'holy awe'. Much more than a civic or social gathering, it was a time when God actually deigned to visit with men, and his presence could be felt in the sacraments, in the prayers and in the sermon. Worship was to be performed in the 'beauty of holiness'.

But in their role as spiritual guides, the Frewens often felt that they had failed, just as they had in the political arena. They all bewailed the lack of respect offered to the office of priest in general, and to themselves in particular.[57] They pleaded for more respect for those in the ministry. This plea was obviously to some extent a highly personal desire for status and esteem, but it was much more than that: it also reflected a firmly entrenched view that society was by nature and right deferential. The ideals of divine right monarchy and apostolic succession also had ramifications for pastoral authority, and, in the minds of the Frewens, all of them were challenged in eighteenth-century society. Disrespect for country parsons was only a symptom of a larger problem: the chipping away at a divinely ordered society.

All this disappointed and disillusioned the Frewens. Thankful Frewen, at the end of his life, felt despondent over his inability to halt the slide of society into disrepair and ultimate ruin. His efforts to loosen the Whig stranglehold on the Court and Parliament had been frustrated, and his efforts in Church and society had failed to produce the results he desired. He was, accordingly, downcast. Thomas Frewen of Brickwall tried to buoy his spirits by assuring him that not only was he 'one of the best Christians this age' had produced and worthy of imitation, but that he had also created an extraordinarily 'well regulated congregation'.[58] It is doubtful, however, that this praise had its intended effect: Thankful, perhaps even more than

[54] Peter Heylin, *Cyprianus Anglicus* (1668), p. 9; cf. John Frewen's notes, ESRO, FRE 687.
[55] ESRO, FRE 687. [56] ESRO, FRE 706.
[57] ESRO, FRE 709. [58] ESRO, FRE 1293, 1296.

John or Thomas, died with faith in God intact, but faith in this world crushed.

V

This study is a vignette, a portrait of one High Church dynasty, but it is suggestive of the mood and bearing of a large clerical group. The case of the Frewens throws light on the clerical mentalities of the age, and especially those of High Churchmen. They represent an entire class of Georgian parsons about whom we know relatively little.

The Frewens persevered in their High Church ideals for several reasons. First, they were indebted to the heritage of their seventeenth-century patriarch, Archbishop Accepted Frewen. The force of this legacy should not be underestimated. The prelate was a hero to the Georgian Frewens, and his churchmanship and politics were virtually sacrosanct; through him Laudian principles were transmitted well into the eighteenth century.

Secondly, the threat of Nonconformity remained real to the Frewens. Whether this was due to unusual activity of Dissenters in the localities in which the Frewens lived and worked, or whether it was due to their persistent fears for the Church's well-being, is uncertain. Yet they, unlike many other eighteenth-century Churchmen, remained watchful and vigilant even when the threat of Nonconformity to Anglicanism had diminished to insignificance.

Thirdly, the Frewen family was close knit, and they were able to impart to each other beliefs and ideals which lasted for generations. The Frewens were able to establish a regular network of support among their kin which toughened their resistance to change and reinforced their collective perspective on the decay of church and state.

Fourthly, they were able to avoid the Whig patronage machine. The livings of Northiam and Sapcote were controlled by family members who preferred only those who suited their political and religious sympathies. It may be significant that when a Frewen changed his political orientation, he also accepted the patronage of one of the Whig elite, thereby reaching out beyond the closely guarded nexus of his fellow family members.[59]

John Frewen's 'defection' indicates another salient point: despite his

[59] But it must be stressed that this was only one element in the matrix out of which parsons formed their opinions. Patronage as a force for political change has been overemphasized by many historians, to the point that it is frequently depicted as the over-riding or only consideration for clergymen. S. W. Baskerville, 'The Political Behaviour of the Cheshire Clergy', *Northern History*, 23 (1987), 74–97; Paul Langford, 'Convocation and the Tory Clergy, 1717–61', in *The Jacobite Challenge*, ed. Eveline Cruickshanks and Jeremy Black (Edinburgh, 1988), pp. 107–22.

change of loyalties, he does not seem to have become an outcast – he was still beloved, respected and supported by the family. Furthermore, the Frewens also were able to work with Whigs in the local and diocesan context, and, what is more remarkable, respect them. Neither Church nor society was disrupted by their churchmanship or political views. Their views remained distinct – they did not lose zeal for their cause – but that did not keep them from associating with gentry, magistrates, friends or relatives who opposed their position and even campaigned against them. Though their closest friends were usually those with whom they saw eye to eye, they did not let politics destroy relationships.

The Frewens' theology and churchmanship also remained traditional. Rationalism was not allowed to destroy the 'beauty of holiness', even if it was present in their thinking. Neither was their sacramentalism diminished by relatively few celebrations of communion. Nothing like a revolution occurred in the thinking and practice of the Frewens; to all intents and purposes they were self-consciously carrying on the tradition of their Restoration forbears, with little if any divergence.

Though this might be easier said of Tory High Churchmen than Whig Low Churchmen, it is probable that the outlook of a great many clergymen of the age did not differ vastly from that of the Frewens. There was undoubtedly more sacramentalism, more mystery and less moralism than has hitherto been recognized. At the very least, the evidence for a religious establishment dominated by rationalism and moralism has been overstated because the sources are misleading: the frequency of celebrations of communion in a parish church cannot prove much about the sacramental views of the parson, nor can 'rationalistic' sermons prove the obliteration of the presence of mystery in the religious sensibility of the preacher or hearer. The likelihood is that the majority of parochial clergymen in early Georgian England were very close to the Frewens in piety and churchmanship, even if they adopted Whig politics. They were traditionalists trying to keep their religious foundations secure amidst the shifting sands of government and society.

For the Frewens, the Collect in the Book of Common Prayer for the fourth Sunday after Easter must have had particular relevance. They could wholeheartedly pray that 'among the sundry and manifold changes of the world, our hearts may surely ... be fixed [in heaven], where true joys are to be found'. They found this world a disappointing place. Though they stood firm for the principles of Christianity as they understood them, they were constantly undermined. They felt as if they stood as the last bastions of religion and truth in the midst of a rapidly disintegrating society. All around them they saw the casualties of unwanted change – faulty morality, doctrine and politics – and yet they were powerless to repel the assaults which were demolishing everything God had ordained. But there was still a world to come where God's laws reigned supreme, and it was to this world that they increasingly repaired for sustenance and succour. They breathed the heady air of heaven in order to survive amidst the pollution on earth.

15 'Papist traitors' and 'Presbyterian rogues': religious identities in eighteenth-century Lancashire

Jan Albers

On Sunday 19 January 1690, the Reverend Henry Newcome, Senior, grand old man of Manchester Presbyterianism, found himself 'much disturbed by the rabble throwing snowballs'. 'But alas,' he wrote in his diary, 'it is but what these late times has bred them to. No matter how profane they be, if they be not Presbyterians.' He rested secure, however, in the protection he felt under the new regime, finding 'it is a mercy that they have not a present power to disturb us, though we cannot restrain them'. By 'disturb', Newcome seems to have meant physical violence, but he could not prevent the verbal abuse of his neighbours. Later that spring he recorded an incident in which 'A poor miller at Knotmill, as I was coming home, cursed me, and bade the devil go with all Presbyterians.'[1]

Eighteenth-century England has generally been regarded as a society that was particularly tolerant of religious diversity. The Revolution settlement had retained the state Church and denied full political participation to all; but in law or in practice most English men and women of the period had far more freedom of worship than their contemporaries on the Continent. The Civil War seems to have slaked the English thirst for religious blood-letting, and in the eighteenth century most religious violence was focused on the destruction of property rather than people.

Yet in researching the social and political history of the period, it is difficult to ignore the strength, persistence and ubiquity of religious animosities. Religious stereotyping was one of the rhetorical foundations of Georgian discourse, and the popular shorthand of the street. It can be found everywhere – in government documents, newspapers, sermons, letters, diaries, novels. Historians have had difficulty in dealing with this material. They have tended to minimize its importance in eighteenth-century culture, both because it does not conform to the traditional view of

I would like to thank my colleagues from the Conference on the Functioning of the Church of England and the History Work-in-Progress seminar at the University of Sussex for their helpful comments on this essay, with special appreciation to Paul Monod, Stephen Taylor, William Lamont and Ellen Oxfeld.

[1] *The Autobiography of Henry Newcome*, ed. Richard Parkinson (Chetham Society, 2, 1852), p. 271.

this period as an 'age of reason', and because of the rudimentary state of our conceptions of popular religiosity.

The key to understanding the significance of religion for individuals in this society may lie in a cultural analysis of denominational and sectarian religious identities. The word 'identity' has an etymology going back at least as far as the late sixteenth century, although in a religious context eighteenth-century contemporaries more often used value-laden terms like 'right religion' to describe themselves and 'sect' (if not 'creatures of the papist anti-christ') to describe their enemies.[2] For this reason, 'identity' is useful as a neutral term for describing the ways in which any religious community achieved a sense of 'oneness' internally and of common purpose in relation to other religious groups.

The purpose of this essay is to examine the creation, promulgation and content of religious identities – and the concomitant use of religious stereotypes – in the particularly heterodox county of Lancashire. Lancashire was not a 'typical' county, for it had more Roman Catholics than any other, and one of England's most populous Dissenting communities, along with a healthy Church of England.[3] The proximity of large numbers of people of different religions may have fostered stronger sectarian feelings here than in some parts of the country, but it should be remembered that proximity also means familiarity, which can have a dampening effect on conflict in some circumstances.

Conflict tends to generate historical records, so that it is often easier to analyse interdenominational relations than to understand the sense of identity created within a religious community. Clifford Geertz has described the way in which religious belief and practice 'render a group's ethos intellectually reasonable by showing it represents a way of life ideally adapted to the actual state of affairs the world view describes, while the world view is rendered emotionally convincing by being presented as an image of an actual state of affairs peculiarly well-arranged to accommodate such a way of life'.[4] Within a given religious system, identity and reality are mutually reinforcing and give the appearance of creating a sensible universe. However, when differing religious systems confront one another, one person's ethos is refracted as another's stereotype. The cornerstone of sectarian conflict is the stereotype – the tendency to reduce those of differing views into a simple archetype which seems to explain everything

[2] The Oxford English Dictionary's earliest definition of 'identity' dates to 1570 and reads 'The quality or condition of being the same; absolute or essential sameness; oneness.' See also the definitions of 'religion' and 'sect'.

[3] For a more detailed study of Lancashire religion, see my 'Seeds of Contention: Society, Politics and the Church of England in Lancashire, 1689–1790', PhD dissertation, Yale University, 1988.

[4] Clifford Geertz, *The Interpretation of Cultures* (New York, 1973), p. 90.

important about them. The sources for recovering such attitudes are numerous, and can probably best be divided into the public and the private. The public sources include newspapers, broadsides, sermons and the ephemera of electioneering.[5] They were generally written for overt propaganda purposes, and provide a clear sense of governmental initiatives and changes in rhetorical usages over time. The main private source for examining religious attitudes is the diary, with which Lancashire is particularly well supplied in this period.[6] Religious tensions were a common preoccupation for the Lancashire diarists, and show both the personal expression and the persistence of public attitudes toward other denominational groups.

The ubiquity of religious identifications does not mean that the men and women of eighteenth-century Lancashire were uniformly pious or devout. Neither is it meant to imply a variation of J. C. D. Clark's view of the period in which religious identity is rooted in elite theology which may or may not have been understood by a large proportion of the population.[7] A broad cultural definition of religious identity, encompassing theology, social and economic values, family and community networks and political predispositions is both more useful and more accurate. A cultural understanding of religious identity does not *preclude* theological awareness or active piety, but does not *base* itself upon them. Within any religious identity, whether Anglican, Methodist, Roman Catholic or the various forms of Dissent,

[5] Particularly useful sources of this type for Lancashire include the *Manchester Weekly Journal*, the *Manchester Mercury and Harrop's General Advertiser*, the *Preston Weekly Journal* and the widely read *Adams' Weekly Courant* from Chester. The broadside collections of the Chetham Library and the Manchester Central Library are excellent. The many sermons published by Lancashire clergymen of the period can be found in the BL, the Liverpool and Manchester Central Libraries and the Chetham Library. Electioneering material is available at the Lancashire RO in Preston.

[6] For Anglicans, see *Social Life and National Movements in the 17th Century (1688–89–90). Diary of Thomas Bellingham, an Officer under William III*, ed. Anthony Hewitson (Preston, 1908); *The Diary and Letter Book of the Rev. Thomas Brockbank, 1671–1709*, ed. Richard Trappes-Lomax (Chetham Society, 2nd ser., 89, Manchester, 1930); the Diary of the Rev. Henry Newcome, rector of Middleton (1791–1814), Manchester Central Library, MSS 922/3/N21 (not to be confused with his father, the Presbyterian of the same name, cited above, n. 1) and Diary Extracts from the Rev. Turner Standish, Chetham Library, Raines MSS, vol. XXIII. For a Nonjuror, see *The Private Journal and Literary Remains of John Byrom*, ed. Richard Parkinson (Chetham Society, 32, 34, 40, 44, 1854–7). For a Methodist (later an Independent), see the Diary of John Bennet, JRL, Methodist Archives. Presbyterian diaries include Newcome, *père*, and *The Diary of Richard Kay, 1716–51 of Baldingstone near Bury: A Lancashire Doctor*, ed. Frank Brockbank and F. Kenworthy (Chetham Society, 3rd ser., 16, Manchester, 1968). The Quakers are represented by *The Autobiography of William Stout of Lancaster, 1665–1752*, ed. J. D. Marshall (Chetham Society, 3rd ser., 14, Manchester, 1967). Two excellent Roman Catholic diaries have been published: *The Tyldesley Diary. Personal Records of Thomas Tyldesley ... 1712–13–14*, ed. Joseph Gillow and Anthony Hewitson (Preston, 1873) and *The Great Diurnal of Nicholas Blundell of Little Crosby, Lancashire*, ed. Frank Tyrer (Record Society of Lancashire and Cheshire, 110, 112, 114, 1968–72).

[7] Clark, *English Society*, chs. 4 and 5, *passim*.

there were enormous variations in theological understanding and experience. And just as our historical sophistication has grown in recognizing differences among individuals who were involved in riots, the same care must be taken when we examine religious groups. The most important thing to remember is that we are dealing with 'identity' – with something so fundamental that it coloured most aspects of an individual's world. In eighteenth-century England, religion, like gender or socio-economic status, was an identity, and so determined a particular world-view. One of the chief advantages of this approach is that it removes us from the trap of rating everything with religious content on some sort of 'piety' scale, so that the main question is always 'But how devout *were* they?' This has led to a number of distortions and a general diminution of the role of religion in eighteenth-century culture.

One of the clearest ways of investigating the meaning of religious identity in this period is through the analysis of stereotypes. In the eighteenth century, as in our own, stereotypes tended to contain a grain of truth. However, stereotypes are caricature, purposely presenting a flat and uncomplimentary view of something far more complex, in order to render it ridiculous and contemptible. What stereotypes were assigned to different religious identities in eighteenth-century Lancashire, and did such stereotypes tend to change over time? How all-encompassing *were* such stereotypes – in other words, were they restricted to certain areas of experience or did they touch all areas? Finally, what conditions produced religious stereotyping, and did those conditions also tend to lead to overt displays of bigotry or violence?

The political and social culture of eighteenth-century Lancashire was often expressed in the language of religious stereotypes, many of which will be familiar to anyone who has done research in English history in this period. The county's Anglican community was sharply divided into High and Low Church camps, especially before the 1750s, with popular stereotypes more commonly depicting High Churchmen. The Churchmen were usually portrayed as grasping, worldly bigots, intolerant of other denominations and tinged with Jacobitism or crypto-Catholicism. Henry Newcome, Senior, the Presbyterian, worried as the Revolution settlement was being debated in 1689 that 'Much struggling we are likely to have with the churchmen, who would unravel all, rather than not rule to persecute.' The aftermaths of the Jacobite rebellions produced an avalanche of similar Whig and Dissenting rhetoric equating High Churchmanship with Jacobitism. As one Whig wrote in *Manchester Vindicated*: 'Has not that old High-Church Maxim, that it is better to be a *Papist* than a *Presbyterian*, and better a *Presbyterian* than a *Whig*, been industriously propagated; that is that it is better to be a Bigot and a Persecutor, than a friend to Liberty, Truth, and King *George*?'[8]

While the Whig and Low Church stereotypes of High Churchmen focused on their purported Jacobitism, Dissenters were also preoccupied with their worldliness and rapacity. Quakers often accused them of being 'worshippers of Baal and Dagon' for their collection of tithes, while others found Anglican ceremonies offensive.[9]

The High Church stereotype was strikingly consistent and persistent. When religious animosities were again at their height in 1790 during the campaign for the repeal of the Test and Corporation Acts, the Whig and Dissenting propaganda against the Anglican anti-repealers revived the stereotypical High Churchman in a form that was now anachronistic, but would have been totally recognizable in 1715. One repeal broadside, for example, spoke in the 'voice' of a High Churchman:

> Ah! Mr. B[oroughreev]e! had you seen us in those Days . . . throwing our Wigs into the Fire, and drinking success to the Old Cause on our bare Knees! – or on the tenth of June parading the Streets with our Plaid Waistcoats, and White Roses! . . . you would have been charmed with our Selection of Tunes – '*Over the Water to Charley*' – '*The 29th of May*' – '*The King shall enjoy his own again*' – and many others equally expressive of our strong Attachment to the *House of Brunswick*.[10]

The county had many Low Churchmen, whose image was closely bound to that of their Presbyterian allies in the imaginations of their enemies. There is little evidence of a Low Church stereotype that differed markedly from that of the Dissenting elite. Accusing Whigs of Presbyterianism was most effective through being both simple and extreme. As their Jacobite enemies wrote of 'our Modern Manchester Whigs' in 1749: 'Their *Sectarian* Heterodoxy proves them determin'd Enemies to our Ecclesiastical Establishment, and their State Principles are manifestly the same with those, which once ruin'd our Constitution and brought the best of Kings to the Block.'[11] In this quotation, Whigs and Presbyterians are identical, both guilty of killing Charles I, embracing a heterodox theology and putting the Church in danger. Many High Churchmen had a difficult time believing that a genuine Low Church position was possible, preferring to think that Low Churchmen were crypto-Presbyterians who had conformed to the Church for their own gain. During times of severe party conflict, denominational distinctions became blurred within each party as well. As one

[8] *Autobiography of Newcome*, ed. Parkinson, p. 269; [John Byrom and Robert Thyer], *Manchester Vindicated* (Chester, 1749), p. 73.

[9] Gabriel Dutton, quoted in Robert Halley, *Lancashire: Its Puritanism and Nonconformity* (2 vols., Manchester, 1869), II, 331–2.

[10] Manchester Central Library, Broadsides Collection, f1790/13.

[11] [Byrom and Thyer], *Manchester Vindicated*, p. viii.

Presbyterian wrote in 1746, 'Party Matters run very high, our high Church Men (or Jacobites, alias Papists) oppose the low Church or Presbyterians very much.'[12] This melding of Low Churchmanship with Presbyterianism was particularly useful to the Tories after 1714, when the Whigs held all the cards. Disgruntled Tories and Roman Catholics could rail against the Presbyterians – meaning all Whigs – and then retreat to the somewhat protected position of saying that they had only meant to refer to the Dissenters. It was more practical to hurl their mud at the Presbyterians and hope that much of it would stick to their Anglican associates.[13]

The stereotypes that developed about the Presbyterians possessed remarkable resiliency. Anti-Presbyterian attitudes must not be confused with anti-Dissenting attitudes in general, because the Presbyterians attracted far more vitriolic reactions than all other Dissenting denominations put together. The reason for this is that the most elaborate stereotypes are produced under a perceived threat, and as the wealthiest, most influential and most articulately vocal denomination, Presbyterians posed the greatest challenge to Anglicans and poorer Dissenters alike. Added to this was their connexion in the popular mind with the execution of Charles I and the years of Cromwellian rule.

Presbyterians came in for a great deal of abuse on the streets – the anecdote which began this essay being but one example of many hundreds recorded in Lancashire in this period. The most common form this took was yells of 'Down with the Rump', but Presbyterians were also taunted for their religious gravity and a perceived air of snobbishness. When a new Presbyterian meeting-house was built in Rochdale, it was promptly dubbed the 'Amen Corner' by derisive Churchmen. In 1745 a group of Jacobites at Failsworth taunted a Presbyterian boy, telling him 'that he wore his breeches-knees out with praying for King George'.[14]

The most surprising thing about stereotypes dealing with Presbyterians is that they came from other denominations of Dissenters almost as often as from Anglicans. Priestley himself wrote in 1771 that 'Dissenters, as such, have nothing in common but a Dissent from the Established Church, and it by no means follows that they, therefore, agree in anything else.'[15] The Dissenting stereotype of Presbyterians did not include political elements –

[12] *Diary of Richard Kay*, ed. Brockbank and Kenworthy, p. 116.

[13] This phenomenon can be seen at work in the fight over a proposal to build a workhouse in Manchester in 1731 and in the High Church Bishop Gastrell's long-running feud with the Low Church Samuel Peploe when the latter was Warden of the Collegiate Church in Manchester. See Albers, 'Seeds of Contention', pp. 342, 420–1.

[14] Henry Fishwick, *The History of the Parish of Rochdale in the County of Lancaster* (Rochdale, 1889), p. 251; Alexander Gordon, *Historical Account of Dob Lane Chapel, Failsworth, and its Schools* (Manchester, 1904), p. 33.

[15] Quoted in John Seed, 'Gentleman Dissenters: The Social and Political Meanings of Rational Dissent in the 1770s and 1780s', *HJ*, 28 (1985), 299–325.

calling them 'King Killers' or 'Oliverian rogues' – but accused them of being denominationally separatist, snobbish and socially intolerant. As the Quaker, Richard Gledhill, wrote in an open letter to the Presbyterians:

You say . . . that it is not possible for any man to come forth to declare ye Gospell of God our saviour, except they be well furnished & taught ye tongues of Greek & Hebrew . . . I Answer that your Knowledge in this is very much below God, for it is but of man, & is earthly, & ariseth out of ye bottomless pit, & it is that beastly dragon that makes war with ye lamb.[16]

The most bitter denunciations of the Presbyterians by other Dissenters came on the issue of snobbery, and was felt most acutely by the Baptists and the Quakers. As William Mitchell, the Baptist evangelist, wrote to a friend: 'We have the communion with the Independents, Baptists and Congregational. As for the Presbyterians, we have little communion with them in the Way of the Gospel. They think it below them to have communion or exercises with us (for all that I know).'[17] Mitchell's letter makes it clear that the notion of a 'Dissenting community' is often more apparent in retrospect than it was to contemporaries.

The only new element added to anti-Presbyterian mythology came after 1750, as most of the county's Presbyterians embraced Unitarianism. Both Anglicans and other Dissenters believed that the Unitarians were simply not Christians. This theme was stressed by the Anglican repealers in 1790. As one wag wrote in a poem on the Unitarians supporting repeal:

Ye deluded poor Whigs, why can't you be easy,
These Fellows that talk so, will drive you all crazy;
Such religious Supports, will your Cause give a fall,
As they op'nly profess no Religion at all.[18]

Those who remained loyal to Old Dissent felt this even more acutely. One Congregationalist told a Unitarian what he thought of his religion, 'That it has no more foundation in Divine Revelation, than *Mahomet's*; and that persons of your sentiments have no more right to the name of *Christian*, than his disciples.'[19]

Other Dissenting denominations inspired fewer and less elaborate stereotypes than the Presbyterians. If Baptists and Quakers felt that others looked down on them, their feelings were not totally groundless. When John Hirst, a warehouseman in Manchester, told his wealthy Methodist employer, Mr Booth, that he was planning to become a Baptist in 1767, his biographer described the reaction: 'Mr. Booth could scarcely bear the idea

[16] Manchester Central Library, Quakers, 1686–1705, MSS L1/43, p. 1: 'A Letter of Richard Gledhill's to ye Presbyterians'.
[17] Quoted in W. T. Whitley, *Baptists of North-West England, 1649–1913* (1913), p. 75.
[18] Manchester Central Library, Broadsides Collection, f1790/1/G.
[19] Ibid., f1790/2/B.

of his leaving the Methodists, much less of his uniting with the despised Baptists. He considered the Independents as more reputable than the Baptists and in process of time consented to his joining them.'[20] The Lancashire Quakers were often vilified both for their poverty and their principles, a common criticism being their 'pretension to infallibility by their inward light'.[21] The Independents were generally considered to be socially superior to the Baptists and Quakers, although in the late eighteenth century it was said by Anglicans that they 'are extremely rigid and puritanical in their outward deportment; but they do not breathe all the *sweetness* of piety, nor are their annals untainted with instances of intolerance and persecution'.[22]

The sectarian conflicts that arose among diverse denominations of Protestants could be fierce, but their most horrific visions were saved for the Roman Catholics. Anti-Catholicism had been firmly rooted in English culture for so long by the eighteenth century that the Catholic stereotype was particularly elaborate. Roman Catholicism was a corruption of early Christianity, controlled by the popish Anti-Christ, who kept his flock obedient through the inculcation of superstition and idol-worship. In the political sphere, the Catholics wished to replace the rights of free-born Englishmen with unquestioning obedience to an arbitrary monarchy. Catholicism tapped a primal wellspring of fear of foreign intrigue, French or Romish domination, loss of liberty and monarchical tyranny – all of which had been proved from the Reformation to Bloody Mary and Foxe's Martyrs; from the Gunpowder Plot to the Civil War; from the Glorious Revolution to the '15 and the '45.[23]

The papist bogeyman gripped the Lancastrian folk mentality with more ferocity than the local fear of boggarts. The Presbyterian, Richard Kay, often ended his diary entries by asking God to 'preserve us from Popish Slavery and vain Idolatry'.[24] The pastor of Cross Street Chapel in Manchester, Joseph Mottershead, delighted his audience with the horrifying spectre of Catholics kneeling down to worship 'The Tooth of St. *Christopher*, the Hair of St. *Peter's* Beard.'[25] The stereotypical Roman Catholic was a wolf in sheep's clothing, wanting only opportunity to devour English Protestants. As an anonymous correspondent in a local newspaper wrote in the late 1740s:

[20] James Hargreaves, *The Life and Memoir of the Late Rev. John Hirst, Forty Two Years Pastor of the Baptist Church, Bacup* (Rochdale, 1816), p. 73.

[21] Edward Owen, *The Necessity of Water-Baptism* (Liverpool, 1763?), p. 5.

[22] John Bennett, *Letters to a Young Lady* (Warrington, 1789), p. 109.

[23] For a detailed analysis of anti-Catholicism, see Colin Mark Haydon, 'Anti-Catholicism in Eighteenth-Century England, *c.*1714–*c.*1780', DPhil dissertation, University of Oxford, 1985.

[24] *Diary of Richard Kay*, ed. Brockbank and Kenworthy, p. 101.

[25] Joseph Mottershead, *A Thanksgiving Sermon: Preach'd at Manchester, November 14, 1718* (1719), p. 16.

My Friends, be prepar'd against the impudent Denials of Popish Emissaries; for they are their greatest Strength ... Particularly beware of such as pretend to be Protestants, and plead the Cause of Popery. The two Religions are as opposite as Light and Darkness, Truth and Falsehood; and as long as *Guy Fawks* and his dark Lathorn stand conspicuous in your Common Prayer Books, never be persuaded that Popery can be a *harmless* Religion.[26]

The popular stereotype of Roman Catholics did not change very much over the course of the eighteenth century, although references to it diminished in frequency as the threat of Jacobitism retreated after the '45. As late as 1789, the Anglican John Bennett described Catholicism in his *Letters to a Young Lady* in the following vein: 'This religion, which has subsisted for such a length of time, and covered so considerable a part of the world, is little else but a system of *political tyranny*, established by the clergy, over the *consciences* and *fortunes* of men, merely to enrich and aggrandize *themselves*.'[27] The assumption that Catholicism was intrinsically wily and despotic was unchanged, but the level of vituperation declined as English Protestants became more secure in their own political supremacy.

The group whose stereotype probably changed the most over the course of the eighteenth century was the Methodists. John Wesley's colleague, John Bennet (an early Methodist who later became an Independent), described many stories of persecution as a young preacher in the 1740s. On 2 March 1747, as he walked to Davyhulme, 'a Man step't out of his House in a great Rage Calling me a Hedge hogg', an insult to his itineracy. Because they travelled widely and often attracted women to their meetings, early Methodists were frequently accused of immorality. On one occasion, a Presbyterian pastor shocked Bennet by mentioning a woman and then telling his friends 'he supposed the Methodist Parson's had *riden* her &c O Scandalous Expression!'[28] This is not an obscure example, as the Presbyterians were particularly virulent in their hatred of Methodism in Lancashire. Along with the Anglicans, they were horrified by the enthusiasm and emotionalism of the movement. However, increasing respectability and greater familiarity brought a measure of acceptance for the Methodists by the late eighteenth century. As the Anglican John Bennett wrote in 1789, 'They had *originally* a great share of *enthusiasm*. But it is greatly softened by the indulgence, they have received, and mellowed down by time. They are no longer a new; they are no longer, a *persecuted* sect.'[29]

The sources used so far to describe religious stereotypes in eighteenth-century Lancashire have, necessarily, been biased toward the middling and

[26] [Byrom and Thyer], *Manchester Vindicated*, p. 314.

[27] Bennett, *Letters*, pp. 101–2.

[28] JRL, Bennet Diary (unpaginated), 2 Mar. 1747; 2 Oct. 1748. This John Bennet should not be confused with the Anglican John Bennett quoted previously.

[29] Bennett, *Letters*, p. 112.

upper classes because they described these things articulately, in writing. It should not be assumed from this that religious stereotypes were only created or perpetuated by the elite, or that they merely 'trickled down' to the masses. Social attitudes are not confined by the forces of gravity, so that stereotypes could also 'trickle up' from popular attitudes formed quite independently during the experience of coming into contact with people of different religious persuasions or, perhaps more virulently, from not having such contacts. For this reason, those who have posed questions about whether wealthy persons were funding or promoting a religious riot, for example, have too often ascribed popular participation to financial motives, when it is more likely that the elite knew who among their poorer acquaintance would share a commonality of interest in such matters. Many other instances of religious conflict had no elite involvement. The 'people', whether artisans, labourers or shopkeepers, were perfectly capable of acting out of their own sense of denominational imperative. The most important thing to recognize is that within each religious ideology there were communal stereotypes about other groups, and that these stereotypes transcended internal socio-economic divisions.

The emotions and observations that produced religious stereotypes could lead to various forms of verbal abuse, collective action and violence – and this was periodically the case in eighteenth-century Lancashire. Examples of name calling and other verbal abuse are recorded in every decade of the period. It was perhaps most remarkable that physical violence happened so seldom. People could live quite harmoniously with neighbours who embraced a different religious identity while still harbouring a stereotypical view of them that rendered them inferior, uncomfortably different, as somehow 'the *other*' (a phenomenon still widely prevalent in race relations today, for example).

So what was necessary to make people act upon their sectarian anxieties? In reviewing the incidence of overt religious violence in Lancashire from the Glorious Revolution to 1790, the common thread is always a heightened sense of social, political or religious threat. It is not surprising that such a sense of threat most often involved those denominations about whom the most elaborate stereotypes had developed – High Churchmen, Presbyterians and Roman Catholics. However, it must also be noted that even in periods of widespread pressure, outbursts of violence tended to be localized and dependent upon tensions that set off triggers in specific neighbourhoods.

Sectarian strife was most heated in Lancashire at four periods: the aftermath of the Glorious Revolution, the Jacobite rebellions of 1715 and 1745, and the campaign for the repeal of the Test and Corporation Acts in the late 1780s. In each of these tense epochs, the religious stereotypes described above were hauled out and promulgated with a vengeance.

The Glorious Revolution provoked a number of minor incidents of anti-Presbyterianism from disgruntled supporters of James II, such as the one mentioned at the beginning of this essay. However, given that there had been a widely supported transfer of power at the national level, such outbursts were necessarily circumspect. The greater focus of animosities was the Roman Catholic community, particularly in the deeply divided town of Preston. Preston contained the townhouses of a number of prominent Anglican and Roman Catholic gentry, the Church of England was dominated by Low Churchmen, and in the aftermath of the Revolution it was home to a regiment of William III's army, who had been sent to keep the peace in a strongly Catholic part of the country. In 1689 two Catholic chapels in the area were destroyed. The army itself dismantled the chapel in Preston, one officer recording in his diary, 'Ye soldiers unslated the Popish Chappell' on 18 July 1689. This action by the military seems to have sent the message that such demonstrations would be winked at, should anyone care to undertake them. A mob soon descended on the chapel at Goosnargh and levelled the building.[30] A similar incident occurred in the same year at Wigan, a parish that formed the dividing line between the strongly Roman Catholic West Derby hundred and the Low Church and Presbyterian Salford hundred. The town was home to a relatively recent – and very successful – Catholic mission and school, both of which were razed by a mob. They were not to be rebuilt until 1740.[31]

Not all sectarian conflict involved the destruction of meeting-houses. Elections often provided venues for the reinforcement of denominational identities. In the volatile Liverpool elections of 1710, held in the divided atmosphere following the Sacheverell verdict, a huge crowd gathered at the poll, many fights broke out and cudgels were used on the mobs. The Whig crowd was screaming 'No Doctor Sacheverell, no Prince of Wales, No King of France, no Papist!' while their Tory counterparts yelled 'A Church! a Church! no Whigs! no Palatines! no roasting of Parsons! no shovel-board players!'[32] It would be difficult to find a better example of the stereotypical shorthand of the streets, with the Low Churchmen raising images of High Church fanaticism, Jacobitism and crypto-Catholicism, while the High Churchmen touched on the Church in danger, Presbyterianism and invasion by foreign refugees. The cries of the crowd also show the seemingly indissoluble links between religion and politics in the popular imagination.

The dramatic meeting-house riots of 1715 have been described elsewhere, and would take too long to examine in detail here.[33] They took place in the

[30] *Bellingham*, ed. Hewitson, p. 73; *The Victoria History of the County of Lancaster*, ed. William Farrer and J. Brownell (8 vols., 1907–14), VII, 205 and n. 222.

[31] *VCH*, IV, 78 and n. 127.

[32] J. A. Picton, *Memorials of Liverpool* (2 vols., 1875), I, 216.

[33] For more on the meeting-house riots of 1714 and 1715, see John Stevenson, *Popular Disturbances in England 1700–1870* (1979), pp. 20–3; Nicholas Rogers, 'Riot and Popular

context of a national outburst of anti-Presbyterian feeling in the wake of the accession of George I. Out of forty meeting-houses destroyed in England, eight were in Lancashire. Their 'Mob Captain' was a blacksmith named Thomas Syddall, who at some points was leading several hundred men and women, and their chants included 'The Church in danger!', 'Down with the Dissenters!', 'Down with the Rump!', 'God save King James the Third!', 'No King but a Stuart!' and 'Church and King!' As the rioters made their way across south-east Lancashire, every chapel they attacked was Presbyterian, although they passed by chapels belonging to most other Dissenting denominations. Most of the rioters were textile workers and artisans, but it would be difficult to give a purely economic explanation for these riots, because, apart from the wealthy Cross Street Chapel in Manchester, the rural Presbyterian congregations mainly consisted of weavers and artisans as well. The mob knew it had the protection of the Lancashire magistracy, an overwhelmingly Tory body in the summer of 1715. The JPs made no move to stop the attacks, and one justice was said to have given the group directions as they moved through the countryside.[34]

The mid-eighteenth century also saw a number of violent confrontations. Many Methodist preachers and meeting places were attacked in the 1740s and 50s, the perpetrators most often being Anglicans and Presbyterians.[35] In 1752 the Tory newspaper, *Adams' Weekly Courant* (widely read in southern Lancashire), revelled in the purported evils of Methodism:

> The wives of the industrious Manufacturers are tempted to purloyn and carry off, not only Money and Goods, but even the very House-Provisions to these ravening *Wolves* in *Sheep's Clothing*; several well-meaning young Maidens have been seduced and debauched by these lewd Hypocrites, and by their Means various Destresses and inconceivable Miseries have been heaped upon a number of Families . . . When this *religious Folly* and *Wrongheadedness*, have taken Root, they produce Fits of *Enthusiasm* which in their Jargon, are called, *the Workings of the Spirit to Regeneration*, and some have been so outrageous in these Hours of *Despair* that no Confinement less than *Bedlam* could restrain them.[36]

However, the factor that made Methodist-bashing so attractive was that the Methodists had very few highly placed protectors in some parts of the county. When the preacher, John Bennet, tried to bail a fellow Methodist, John Jane, out of Preston gaol in 1748, he first took up the case with the Presbyterian, Sir Henry Hoghton, probably out of a belief that the latter

Jacobitism in Early Hanoverian England', in *Ideology and Conspiracy*, ed. Eveline Cruickshanks (Edinburgh, 1982), pp. 70–85; Paul Monod, *Jacobitism and the English People 1688–1788* (Cambridge, 1989), pp. 173–94.

[34] *Flying Post*, 3660, 18–21 June 1715, and 3667, 5–7 July 1715; *Palatine Notebook*, 20 (Manchester, 1882), pp. 240–3; Albers, 'Seeds of Contention', pp. 405–13.

[35] Albers, 'Seeds of Contention', pp. 569–85.

[36] *Adams' Weekly Courant*, 3 Mar. 1752, p. 1.

would be supportive in a case of religious persecution. The reception Bennet received was far from friendly: Hoghton 'fumed & raged exceedingly – He said we wou'd all turn Quakers in a little Time, talking of ye Sp[iri]t. He wo'd encourage no such Works – We said we were liable to be prosecuted only the Desenting Ministers had favoured us &c.'[37] It was easy to harass Methodists with impunity in the early years because no one cared enough to stop it. For Anglicans, the Methodist 'threat' centred upon the movement's enthusiasm and a perceived challenge to Church and familial authority, while Presbyterians were suspicious of its emotionalism and High Churchmanship.

The Jacobite rebellion of 1745 and its aftermath led to a revival of religious stereotyping and renewed confrontation. While the '15 had produced little overt anti-Catholic violence – probably because there was an unclear sense of the safety of engaging in it after the meeting-house riots and the passage of the Riot Act – the '45 was another story. After defeating the rebels, Whig mobs destroyed a Catholic chapel and house in Liverpool, and Catholic missions in Ormskirk and Woodplumpton. In all three places, the Catholics were unprotected in pockets of Low Church strength. The political polarization caused by the '45 continued until at least 1750. In this period, there are many examples of Presbyterians being harassed in High Church areas as well. In Manchester in 1751, *The True British Courant or, the Preston Journal* reported that gangs of young toughs had 'in dark Nights, gone about the Streets, crying D--n with the R-mp, and even Themselves breaking the Windows of such, as would be accounted *burning and shining* Lights of Loyalty'.[38]

In the reign of George III, religious stereotypes were frequently revived, but sectarian conflict rarely escalated into violence. The volatile Preston election of 1768 led to the destruction of two Roman Catholic chapels.[39] However, while interdenominational mistrust remained, the sense of threat seems to have been greatly reduced under the new monarch due to the decline of older Whig and Tory party alignments.[40] To what extent, then, had the Whig and Tory parties been promoting sectarian conflict? As the evidence already cited in this essay suggests, both parties had promulgated negative denominational identifications during times of conflict, particularly through sermons, broadsheets and electioneering. However, by the

[37] JRL, Bennet Diary, 29 July 1748.

[38] *The True British Courant or, the Preston Journal*, 1–8 Feb. 1751, p. 3; *VCH*, IV, 51 and n. 897; *Gentleman's Magazine*, 15 (Nov. 1745), 613–14; Albers, 'Seeds of Contention', pp. 427–8, 546–9.

[39] Winifred Procter, 'Electioneering in Lancashire before the Secret Ballot: The Preston Election of 1768', *Transactions of the Historic Society of Lancashire and Cheshire*, 111 (1960), 105; Joseph Gillow, *A Literary and Biographical History, or Bibliographical Dictionary of the English Catholics* (5 vols., 1885–1902), II, 145–6; *VCH*, VII, 291.

[40] Albers, 'Seeds of Contention', pp. 500–1, 441.

eighteenth century the evidence from diaries suggests that the parties had to do very little to create such stereotypes, for they played upon earlier politico-religious divisions stretching back at least to the Civil War.

This is not to say that nothing changed over the course of the century. After the Hanoverian accession, the Whig government quickly realized that popular Toryism posed a threat that could best be countered by a dampening of sectarian conflict. Peace would muzzle the Tories more effectively than any amount of anti-High Church propagandizing. The early modern abhorrence of party and faction was not enough to stop it from splitting English society and politics in two through the reign of Queen Anne; but, as Stephen Taylor's work on the Duke of Newcastle's ecclesiastical patronage has shown, the Whigs succeeded in dampening conflict within the Church of England through injunctions urging an end to party conflict and the selective preferment of a complement of very loyal High Churchmen.[41] The Whigs managed to create a great deal of harmony at the top of the Church, but they had far more trouble spreading this message in the localities. As the evidence already presented suggests, English sectarian divisions ran very deep in Lancashire, and were widely exploited after the Jacobite rebellion of 1745. Clerical cries for the setting aside of sectarian and intra-Anglican animosities may have begun in London under George I, but did not appear in Lancashire until the 1750s. A sermon by the Whig rector of St Ann's, Manchester, Abel Ward, delivered in 1756, expressed the new anti-party initiative in the north: '*live peaceably with All Men* . . . a Lesson – This – both to the Party-Zealot, and the Bigot in Religion; and [call] upon them to lay aside Enmity, and Persecution, and desist from that Hatred, and furious Warmth, which is absurd in itself, and inconsistent with the Character either of Man or Christian'.[42] The Whig policy of eliminating sectarian divisions was finally spreading to the provinces – only forty years late. The reason such a message took so long to arrive in the north-west probably has more to do with the vigour of Lancashire Toryism, the heterogeneous religious make-up of the region and the frightening local animosities raised by the '45 than the final success of governmental policy. The sectarian conflict that emerged during the rebellion finally scared the Lancashire elite into a harmony that had held little appeal in earlier decades.[43]

[41] Stephen Taylor, 'Church and State in England in the Mid-Eighteenth Century: The Newcastle Years 1742–62', PhD dissertation, University of Cambridge, 1987, pp. 93–105.

[42] Abel Ward, *An Assize Sermon Preached in the Cathedral Church at Chester . . . 1756* (Manchester, 1756?), p. 19.

[43] This discussion is not meant to imply that all of Lancashire's Tories were active or sympathizing Jacobites – they were not. The High Church clergy were loyal to the government, apart from a few Jacobites in Manchester, while the Tory gentry were divided. It is in the nature of sectarian conflict to exaggerate the political sins of one's enemies. The '45 not only destroyed Jacobitism in Lancashire, its attendant prejudices also managed severely to undermine the vestiges of traditional Toryism in the county.

The first two decades of the reign of George III were an era of unprecedented denominational harmony in the north-west, as the Anglican and Dissenting clergy turned their attention from politics to philanthropy. The late 1780s provide a striking example of the weakness of public policy in the face of popular prejudice. Sectarian divisions re-emerged in full force in 1787 with the campaign to repeal the Test and Corporation Acts, as some old stereotypes were revived with a virulence that may have even surprised the participants. While the political structure of England had undergone enormous changes since the mid-century, underlying tensions were again expressed through appeals to old stereotypes. The Churchmen announced a public meeting to organize against the repealers with a handbill asking fellow Anglicans to 'Remember, who trampled upon, and made Shipwreck, of both Church and State, in the last Century, and guard against the Repetition of the like dreadful Scene.'[44] They also churned out doggerel on the threat repeal posed to church and state:

Let us by begging once destroy
That barrier of the Test;
Then soon, with PRIESTLEY's gunpowder,
We'll blow up all the rest –
* * *
When once the hop'd-for breach is made,
We'll do whate'er we chuse;
The Church's-doors shall open stand,
To Papists, Turks, and Jews –[45]

The repealers responded to such efforts by publishing a mock advertisement asking for a poet, applicants to send specimens of their work to 'my Lord Hurdy-Gurdy, at Highflyer House; the Rev. Dr. Pluralist, at Ingratitude Hall; or to the Chairman of the "Down with the Rump" Committee, at the Pretender's Head, in Jacobite Alley'.[46]

Lancashire was in a state of great tension over repeal from 1787 until the Dissenters' defeat in 1790, with the examples quoted being typical of the rhetoric employed by both sides.[47] The old stereotypes were revived – Dissenters as king-killing, Oliverian rogues and High Churchmen as intolerant crypto-Jacobites – suggesting that popular conceptions of politico-religious divisions retained a good measure of their appeal. Beneath the surface, however, a change of tone had taken place. While the language was

[44] Manchester Central Library, Broadsides Collection, f1790/1/A: 'To the MEMBERS of the CHURCH of ENGLAND'.

[45] Chetham Library, Broadsides Collection, p. 43. [46] Ibid., p. 107.

[47] Detailed accounts of the repeal campaign can be found in Albert Goodwin, *The Friends of Liberty* (1979), ch. 3; G. M. Ditchfield, 'The Campaign in Lancashire and Cheshire for the Repeal of the Test and Corporation Acts, 1787–90', *Transactions of the Historic Society of Lancashire and Cheshire*, 126 (1979), 109–38; Albers, 'Seeds of Contention', pp. 459–70.

similar, and sincere in its political purpose, it was far more exaggerated, and more satirical, than it would ever have been during the earlier 'rage of party'. The party rhetoric of that age may have been comforting, for it described a simpler political universe where the lines of demarcation were clear and both patrons and people could unite to play the game. Yet it now took a distinctly religious issue in politics to revive earlier divisions, and even with that the element of caricature had become more pronounced.

In the late 1780s, tempers flared but no one was physically injured and property was not destroyed. Sectarian conflict had become more polite, as it had become more rhetorically florid. As earlier examples have shown, this was a change from earlier in the century, when religious stereotyping had a tendency to explode into physical violence in Lancashire. However, it must be remembered that overt action against people of other denominations was relatively rare. Three conditions seem to have been necessary for such antipathies to lead people to take to the streets. First, a 'language' of assumptions about the character and motivations of a perceived denominational enemy; secondly, an exacerbated sense of threat perceived to be emanating from that group; and finally, the belief that it was possible to move against another group with relative impunity because one would receive protection. The importance of the third point cannot be overstressed, because people rarely received more than a token punishment for sectarian violence.[48]

This essay has dealt with the projection of stereotypical religious identities on to other groups, but it should also be remembered that these stereotypes simultaneously reinforced a sense of identity *within* the group. Thinking of 'them' reinforces a sense of identity as 'us'. This is an important part of why stereotypes are revived and elaborated in times of stress. Stereotypes also serve the important function of objectification of the subjects – reducing them to caricatures whose thoughts and feelings are far less real than our own. The irony of this is that the process is so subconscious that people rarely recognize themselves as bigots. Our own position is always eminently reasonable. As the Anglican John Bennett told his young lady friend in 1789, '[The Church of England's] piety has a rational, sedate, composed air, and is uniformly grave and decent without pretending to the flights, the fervours and the visions of some, *modern* fanaticks.'[49]

[48] The most extraordinary example of this comes from Manchester on May 28, 1715 – George I's birthday – when a group of Hanoverian loyalists was holding a bonfire in the new King's honour. The gathering was violently dispersed by a Jacobite mob. When the Whigs asked for indictments against their persecutors, they found *themselves* charged with 'disturbing subjects of the King's Anglican Church with a bonfire'. *Flying Post*, 3660, 18–21 June 1715; PRO, PL 28/1, p. 236; L. K. J. Glassey, *Politics and the Appointment of Justices of the Peace 1675–1720* (Oxford, 1979), pp. 290–2; Albers, 'Seeds of Contention', pp. 405–6.

[49] Bennett, *Letters*, p. 140.

Religious stereotypes remained enormously powerful tools for the transmission and reinforcement of religious identities throughout the eighteenth century. They operated as a type of shorthand, providing an all-encompassing version of the character of one's opponents: their motivations, style of life, view of God, vision of history and social and political ideologies. As a fundamental form of identification, religion could cut across the social scale vertically – joining rich and poor Presbyterians and Roman Catholics, as well as Anglicans, in a common world-view and a communal sense of purpose. This verticality helped to make the espousal of a religious identity attractive to labourers and artisans *as well* as the upper and middling sorts, because it gave them access to, and the protection of, those in power. This relationship was not simply hegemonic, for there is a great deal of evidence that many of the 'people' took what they wanted from a given religious identity without necessarily allowing the imposition of those aspects they did *not* want.[50] A religion was a culture and a cosmology as well as a theology, available for the individual to adapt in whatever ways and to whatever degree he or she saw fit. For some this involved a fundamentally spiritual experience expressed in church attendance and formal piety; for others throughout the social scale the identification was essentially cultural, operating more like a modern ethnic identification. Fundamental to Christian thought is the idea that all people are equal in the sight of God, and this in itself helped to make religious identity inclusive in a way politics alone could not yet be. Eighteenth-century stereotypes may have been closely allied to party politics, but in the end they were more resilient, outlasting party by many decades in the popular imagination.

What does the evidence presented here reveal about eighteenth-century England as a religiously tolerant society? The ubiquity of sectarian tensions and religious violence does not, in fact, refute this elemental tenet of English historiography. Religious bigotry was an unpleasant fact of life and led to occasional outbreaks of violence, but the destruction of a meeting-house, or the taunts and intimidations of a mob, were hardly the rack, the stake or the Inquisition. In granting toleration, the English government sent the message that excesses of religious violence were considered too disruptive of social and political harmony to be allowed. It did not lessen the power of religious identities, eliminate the sense of interdenominational threat or cause all men to live as brothers, but it does seem to have made the English more tolerant.

[50] Popular reluctance to take communion, for example.

16 Church parties in the pre-Tractarian Church of England 1750–1833: the 'Orthodox' – some problems of definition and identity

Peter Nockles

'It has been the fate of the Church of England from the beginning to be divided into parties', observed J. B. Marsden in 1856.[1] This was a view which squared uneasily with the assumption of many mid-nineteenth-century Churchmen and some later historians that party division within the Church of England was but one of the unwelcome legacies of the Oxford Movement after 1833. Moreover, the very idea of church parties and party spirit was widely portrayed as an unmitigated evil, redolent of sectarianism. However, long before Tractarianism's rise the assumed evil of party distinctions had become a subject of comment and concern. For instance, Richard Whately devoted the whole of his Bampton Lectures at Oxford in 1822 to warning against the consequences.[2]

Whately's strictures on party feeling were based on the reality of contemporary divisions within the pre-Tractarian Church of England which could not only be traced back to the Reformation settlement itself but also had had a continuous existence since that era. Certainly, these divisions appeared to be more pronounced at some times than at others. For instance, the history of the Church of England during Queen Anne's reign notoriously was one dominated by party strife. In the subsequent Georgian epoch of supposed 'moderation' and somnolence, such divisions seem somewhat smothered. Nonetheless, party differences even then were not eradicated, and in the last decades of the century were reactivated.

Yet, to accept the validity of church party divisions prior to the age of Tractarianism is not to assume that the basis or scope of such divisions were the same before and after 1833. Neat categorizations and labels ought to be curbed, if not avoided.[3] This warning is particularly applicable to the pre-Tractarian era. Of all the many labels descriptive of church party, none has suffered more from over-usage and misapplication than that of 'High Church'. To form a clearer perspective one needs to go behind certain

1 J. B. Marsden, *History of Christian Churches and Sects* (2 vols., 1856), I, 322–3.

2 R. Whately, *The Use and Abuse of Party-Feeling in Matters of Religion* (Oxford, 1822).

3 G. Best, 'Church Parties and Charities: The Experience of Three American Visitors to England, 1823–4', *EHR*, 78 (1963), 262.

presuppositions engendered by the Oxford Movement. For, as J. C. D. Clark has rightly noted, 'the Victorian conception of High Church was one largely drawn from the Oxford Movement'; 'applied to the world before 1832, few enough men would be found to fit it'.[4] The emergence of more self-conscious and self-contained church parties after 1833 has led followers and historians of the later rival parties of Tractarians and Evangelicals, to project back the depth and intensity of their own disputes to an earlier, seemingly more harmonious period in the internal history of the Church of England.[5] Nonetheless, labels such as 'High Church' did retain a certain validity and relevance in the pre-1833 era, though the need for clarification and stricter definition remains. It is our aim in this essay to seek to provide such a focus.

The question of party in the Church of England has been the subject of much historical analysis recently. Some historians have questioned the theological validity of party labels altogether prior to the Tractarian era.[6] However, as we shall see, the evidence suggests that there was a genuinely theological basis and content to the gradations of 'High' and 'Low'. The term 'High Church' was used to denote a religious tradition that had several common facets or constituent elements, political, ecclesiological, liturgical, spiritual and sacramental. Not all these elements would always be held together or be given the same respective emphasis by different adherents, though there was enough of a consensus for a definition to be attempted. What is required is simply for the term 'High Church' to be rescued from the misappropriation and glosses of much post-Tractarian historiography.

It has been rightly suggested by David Newsome that the term 'High Church' ought to be 'understood as a loose and general description covering a conglomeration of various groups which differed greatly in their interpretation of the needs of the church'.[7] The following definition could serve as applicable to the period. A High Churchman in the Church of

[4] J. C. D. Clark, *Revolution and Rebellion* (Cambridge, 1986), p. 109. I have developed this argument elsewhere. See P. B. Nockles, 'Continuity and Change in Anglican High Churchmanship in Britain, 1792–1850', DPhil dissertation, University of Oxford, 1982, esp. Intro. This dissertation is to be published in revised form by Cambridge University Press. For a late nineteenth-century recognition of the enormous gulf separating Victorian from Georgian understandings of the term 'High Church', see, A. H. Hore, *History of the Church of England* (1886), pp. 418, 462. In his article on 'Church Parties' in 1853 William Conybeare distinguished a 'normal type' of High Church from a Tractarian or 'exaggerated type'. See W. J. Conybeare, *Essays Ecclesiastic and Social* (1855), p. 158.

[5] Cf. W. Ervine, 'Doctrine and Diplomacy: Some Aspects of the Life and Thought of the Anglican Evangelical Clergy, 1797 to 1837', PhD dissertation, University of Cambridge, 1979, p. 134; S. Taylor, 'Church and State in England in the Mid-Eighteenth Century: The Newcastle Years 1742–62', PhD dissertation, University of Cambridge, 1987, p. 215.

[6] E.g., M. Evershed, 'Party and Patronage in the Church of England, 1800–1945', DPhil dissertation, University of Oxford, 1985, p. 10.

[7] D. Newsome, *The Parting of Friends* (1966), p. 318.

England tended to uphold in some form the doctrine of apostolical succession which was the basis of his strong attachment to the catholicity and apostolicity of the Church of England as a branch of the universal catholic church, within which he did not include those reformed bodies which had wilfully abandoned episcopacy, so that a distinction was made between Nonconformist congregations and continental Protestant churches. He believed in the supremacy of Scripture and set varying degrees of value on the testimony of authoritative tradition, but generally insisted that the Bible needed to be interpreted in the light of such authoritative standards as the Prayer Book, the Catechism and the Creeds. He tended to value the writings of the early Fathers, especially as witnesses to scriptural truth when a catholic consent of them could be established. He laid emphasis on the doctrine of sacramental grace, both in the eucharist and baptism, while tending to eschew the principle of *ex opere operato*. He tended to cultivate a practical spirituality which many emphasized as based on sacramental grace and nourished by acts of self-denial, rather than on any subjective conversion experience or unruly manifestations of the Holy Spirit. He invariably stressed the importance of a religious establishment but insisted on the duty of the state as a divinely ordained rather than merely secular entity, to protect and promote the interests of the Church. Of course, some of these features of our definition would be held more explicitly and unequivocally by some more than by others to whom the term 'High Church' might be applied, while many might prove to be beyond categorization. The best model is that preferred by Gerald Parsons and Paul Avis. They both admit that church parties did exist in the pre-Tractarian Church of England, but insist that they formed part of a broadly based theological consensus which the Tractarians destroyed, and which according to Avis 'may be likened to a series of mutually overlapping circles'.[8]

Many scholars date the origin of the term 'High Church' to the later part of the seventeenth century.[9] Henry Sacheverell traced usage of the term back as early as the 1650s when Richard Baxter apparently first applied it as a label of reproach against Richard Hooker.[10] In the eighteenth century, certain pejorative connotations became attached to the term. Under Queen Anne the term 'High Church' came to be defined in almost exclusively political terms, becoming synonymous with 'Tory'. Moreover, Whig and

[8] P. Avis, *Anglicanism and the Christian Church* (Edinburgh, 1988), pp. 77–96; G. Parsons, 'Introduction', in *Religion in Victorian Britain*, ed. G. Parsons (4 vols., Manchester, 1988), I, 32.

[9] G. Every, *The High Church Party 1688–1718* (1956), p. 1; W. R. Fryer, 'The "High Churchmen" of the Earlier Seventeenth Century', *Renaissance and Modern Studies*, 5 (1961), 112; *Anglicanism*, ed. P. E. Moore and F. L. Cross (1935), pp. 23–52.

[10] H. Sacheverell, *The Character of a Low-Churchman* (1702), p. 27; *Reliquiae Baxterianae*, ed. M. Sylvester (1696), Part ii, p. 387.

Dissenting pamphleteers encouraged this trend by seeking to make political capital from the residual Jacobite associations of some High Churchmen.[11] The theological and sacramental aspect of the religious tradition of High Churchmanship which had been prominent in the Laudian era was increasingly given less attention by critics. According to James Brewster in a survey of church parties published in 1802, during the eighteenth century 'the characteristic terms of High Church and Low Church became imperceptibly changed into Court and Country-party'.[12] Moreover, Protestant 'Rational Dissenters' such as Samuel Heywood took political advantage of admissions once made by William Warburton that the *jure divino* theological basis of High Church claims had been undermined fatally at the Revolution in 1688, to argue that any residual adherence to High Church tenets in a doctrinal sense was illogical and no longer tenable.[13]

It was Samuel Horsley in a well-known episcopal charge delivered in 1790 when bishop of St David's who made one of the most famous definitions of 'High Church' in a positive, theological sense. In conscious repudiation of what he regarded as the pejoratively political connotations of the term, Horsley defined 'High Church' as denoting an attachment to the Church of England on purely doctrinal grounds and a conviction in favour of its divine authority and spiritual independence. Disdaining any baser signification of the term, Horsley denounced the 'idle terror of a nickname, artfully applied, in violation of the true meaning of the word, to entrap the judgment of the many, and bring the discredit of a folly long since eradicated upon principles which have no connexion with it'.[14] In his influential *Guide to the Church* published in 1798, Archdeacon Daubeny similarly defined 'High Church' simply as 'a decided and principled attachment to the Apostolic government of the Church'.[15]

In 1802, James Brewster maintained that since 1760 there had been not only a revival of High Church principles thus defined but that there was a renewed theological basis to dormant differences between 'High' and 'Low'.[16] These residual differences partly were reactivated by the perceived need among Churchmen to respond to the so-called Feathers Tavern

[11] *High Church Politics* (1710), p. 16; *The High Church Mask Pulled Off* (1710), p. 10; *The Criteria or Touchstone, by which to Judge the Principles of High and Low-Church* (1710), p. 5. For some later examples of the genre, see, [S. Heywood], *High Church Politics* (1792), esp. ch. 3; *High Church Claims Exposed* (1808), pp. 71–2.

[12] J. Brewster, *A Secular Essay* (1802), p. 89.

[13] [Heywood], *High Church Politics*, pp. 6–7.

[14] *Charges of Samuel Horsley* (Dundee, 1813), pp. 40–1.

[15] C. Daubeny, *A Guide to the Church* (1798; 2nd edn, 2 vols., 1804), I, xliv; idem, *Appendix to the Guide to the Church* (1804), pp. 431–2. For other examples of an equation of the term with *jure divino* notions of episcopacy and church authority, see T. Le Mesurier, *The Nature and Guilt of Schism* (Oxford, 1808), p. 437; cf. T. Belsham, *The Present State of Religious Parties* (1818), pp. 9–13.

[16] Brewster, *Secular Essay*, p. 245.

petition in favour of a relaxation of the terms of subscription to the Thirty-Nine Articles. Recent scholarship has corroborated this view. For instance, at the local level of provincial politics, James Bradley has demonstrated the extent to which after 1760, 'it was Low Church and Dissent versus High Church and Tory that went to the heart of much party conflict'. He makes clear that there was more than a political dimension to the divide between 'High' and 'Low' even in the constituencies, observing that 'religious animosities, expressed in the old party terminology, burst on the scene with . . . force over the Subscription controversy in the early 1770s'.[17]

Yet, while pre-Tractarian High Churchmen might fairly protest that there was a real theological and sacramental meaning to the term 'High Church', the relentless propagation of a pejorative signification by opponents of the Church of England ensured that late eighteenth-century Churchmen would come to prefer the label 'Orthodox' to that of 'High Church'. As a label, 'Orthodox' appeared less redolent of a particular faction, subdivision or party within the Church. Moreover, it had an impressive historical lineage, apparently being first coined by William Laud in the 1620s as a label descriptive of those clergy who were not 'Puritan'.[18] As such, the term had theological connotations but denoted a wide spectrum of theological opinion. This defining characteristic of being anti-Puritan prefigured later eighteenth-century connotations as applying to a Churchman who was non- or anti-Evangelical, regardless of the fairness of the implied equation between 'Puritan' and 'Evangelical'.

Some modern historians have taken up the theological usage of the label, 'Orthodox', and used it interchangeably with 'High Church'.[19] For some, the term implied Trinitarianism only, and in this sense was deemed to be meaningful when used in contradiction to Socinianism or Unitarianism. As G. M. Ditchfield puts it, 'the term "orthodoxy" without qualification referred to one's position on this question'.[20] J. C. D. Clark also emphasizes the primarily Trinitarian connotations of the label. However, Clark also relates the term to a comprehensive set of political and philosophical values

[17] J. Bradley, *Religion, Revolution and English Radicalism* (Cambridge, 1990), p. 112. For similar arguments applied on the intellectual level, see, B. W. Young, '"Orthodoxy Assail'd": An Historical Examination of some Metaphysical and Theological Debates in England from Locke to Burke', DPhil dissertation, University of Oxford, 1990, p. 127; A. M. C. Waterman, 'A Cambridge "Via Media" in Late Georgian Anglicanism', *JEH*, 42 (1991), 422–3. For an example of a revived theological definition of 'Low Church' in the 1790s, see J. Milner, *The History and Survey of the Antiquities of Winchester* (1798; 3rd edn, 2 vols., 1839), II, 46.

[18] P. Collinson, *The Religion of Protestants* (Oxford, 1982), p. 81.

[19] J. M. Turner, *Conflict and Conciliation* (1985), pp. 110–11; A. M. C. Waterman, *Revolution, Economics and Religion. Christian Political Economy 1798–1833* (Cambridge, 1991), p. 196.

[20] G. M. Ditchfield, 'Anti-Trinitarianism and Toleration in Late Eighteenth-Century British Politics: The Unitarian Petition of 1792', *JEH*, 42 (1991), 39.

regarding the family, society, monarchy and kingship, the nature of political obligation and the basis of social order; a set of values which he encapsulates in the phrase 'orthodox political theology'. Clark has done much to restore focus on the religious basis and framework of the political dimension of the 'Orthodox' tradition in the Church of England and its continued relevance and vitality in the eighteenth century[21] – themes long neglected or misunderstood by secular historians. Yet, for all his exploration of the religious underpinnings of these political ideals, the primarily political orientation of Clark's discussion of eighteenth-century 'Orthodoxy' leads him to give less than due consideration to its theological content, apart from the question of Trinitarianism. In his refinement of Clark's study, Robert Hole points to this limitation[22] but his own terms of reference remain no less 'political'. At one level, Clark's argument that Anglican Evangelicalism and even Methodism represented just another 'new branch' of 'Orthodox' churchmanship is valid, precisely because many Evangelicals accepted both the 'political theology' and Trinitarianism that were two of its defining characteristics. However, at the same time an exclusive preoccupation with the political dimension of 'Orthodoxy' tends to divest the term of any of those distinctively ecclesiastical, sacramental and liturgical preferences which ultimately made the 'Orthodox' a separate theological party within the Church of England.[23] For while Orthodox Churchmanship was bound up with and infused by political Toryism and loyalism, it was not a mere appendage of it. Certainly, Clark's insistence that High Churchmanship was 'defined primarily in political rather than sacramental terms' is less valid at the end of the eighteenth century than at the beginning.[24]

Others have defined 'Orthodox' in a very narrow, restricted sense, drawing a too rigid distinction between 'Orthodox' on the one hand and 'High Church' on the other, in a way which few contemporaries would have understood.[25] In contrast, the best model would seem to be one that recognized a relatively broad Orthodox spectrum on the lines suggested by Newsome and Avis, within which it can be acknowledged that some were more 'High Church' than others on particular points of doctrine and practice. Such a model would allow for the clear differences of theological

[21] Clark, *English Society*, pp. 216–35.

[22] R. Hole, *Pulpits, Politics and Public Order in England 1760–1832* (Cambridge, 1989), pp. 266–7. [23] Clark, *English Society*, p. 235.

[24] Ibid., p. 243. See P. B. Nockles, 'The Oxford Movement: Historical Background, 1780–1833', in *Tradition Renewed*, ed. D. G. Rowell (1986), pp. 24–42.

[25] N. Murray, 'The Influence of the French Revolution on the Church of England and its Rivals, 1789–1802', DPhil dissertation, University of Oxford, 1975, p. 71; R. Braine, 'The Life and Writings of Herbert Marsh (1757–1839)', PhD dissertation, University of Cambridge, 1989, pp. 1–2.

emphasis within the spectrum that can be delineated, as for example between Bishop Marsh and Archdeacon Daubeny.[26] Such differences mattered much less prior to 1833 than subsequently. In the context of the pre-Tractarian Church of England, what counted was that a wide spectrum of divines could feel that they were basically allies united in defence of the cause of orthodoxy against the Church of England's Dissenting and Unitarian opponents.

The leading group within the pre-Tractarian High Church party was the so-called 'Hackney Phalanx' whose name derived from the place where one of its leaders, Archdeacon John James Watson, was rector, and where the Archdeacon's younger brother, the layman Joshua Watson, also resided. The rector of South Hackney was Henry Handley Norris, a close friend of the Watsons and the other leading figure in the 'Phalanx'.[27] Yet, the essential fluidity as well as convergence of different religious parties within the pre-Tractarian Church of England is revealed by the important links between the 'Phalanx' and that group of Oxford 'liberal' Churchmen known as the Oriel Noetics which Pietro Corsi and Richard Brent have unravelled.[28] Significantly, the leading theological spokesman of the 'Phalanx', William Van Mildert, had close 'Noetic' contacts. Even that future *bête noire* of the Tractarians, Renn Dickson Hampden, had remarkably close ties with the Orthodox party. Not only did he actually edit for a time the Orthodox journal, the *Christian Remembrancer*, but he was also a curate to H. H. Norris himself at Hackney. Though Baden Powell emerged as an advanced liberal in the 1830s, his authorship of several articles in the High Church *British Critic* as well as the *Christian Remembrancer* between 1823 and 1826 is significant, as is his favourable notice of Van Mildert's influential edition of the works of that great exponent of eighteenth-century Orthodoxy, Daniel Waterland.[29] What one can fairly conclude is that the less rigid and theologically precise nature of pre-Tractarian High Churchmanship compared to that of the post-1833 era meant that many such divines could feel that what for them at that time were relatively minor differences of emphasis upon collateral points, as for instance between Daubeny and Marsh on the subject of Tradition, did not impair the substance of Orthodox apologetic. The Orthodox position was bounded by

[26] See E. A. Varley, *The Last of the Prince Bishops. William Van Mildert and the High Church Movement of the Early Nineteenth Century* (Cambridge, 1992), p. 58.

[27] The best account of the Hackney Phalanx is by E. Churton, *Memoir of Joshua Watson* (2 vols., 1861). See also A. Webster, *Joshua Watson* (1954); P. Corsi, *Science and Religion. Baden Powell and the Anglican Debate 1800–60* (Cambridge, 1988), pp. 9–20. On the composition of the Hackney Phalanx, see C. Dewey, *The Passing of Barchester* (1991), 'Appendix', pp. 149–68.

[28] Corsi, *Science and Religion*, ch. 2; R. Brent, *Liberal Anglican Politics. Whiggery, Religion and Reform* (Oxford, 1987), pp. 148–9.

[29] Corsi, *Science and Religion*, p. 22.

parameters and there was unity on certain essentials of the faith, but otherwise there was no one, monolithic viewpoint. On the contrary, a certain eclecticism was common and this was reflected in the reading lists and *catenae* of divines drawn up by young Churchmen of the rising generation as worthy of perusal. It was precisely such eclecticism that dismayed Newman the Tractarian when he set about trying to systematize Anglican divinity when constructing his *via media* in the 1830s.[30]

The apparent vagueness and even contradictions to which the term 'Orthodox' could be put led Corsi to conclude that it is impossible to provide a clear-cut definition.[31] It would seem then that the label 'Orthodox' has as many potential drawbacks and as much ambivalence as that of 'High Church'. Nonetheless, the fact that so many Churchmen in the pre-Tractarian era used the term and sought to define it as precisely as possible renders it an appropriate label descriptive of a religious party within the Church of England. As early as the mid-eighteenth century the ultra-Latitudinarian Archdeacon Blackburne claimed that the label was being appropriated by contemporary High Churchmen.[32] This 'High Church' sense of the term gained ground.[33] However, the most persuasive contemporary source for the validity of church party divisions, and in particular for the wide currency of the term 'Orthodox', comes from the little-known writings of Johnson Grant. In the fourth volume of his *Summary History of the English Church* (1811–25) Grant used the term 'Orthodox' as essentially synonymous with 'High Church'. He divided the contemporary Church of England into four distinct, albeit not always mutually exclusive, groupings or parties – the Orthodox, the Latitudinarian, the Evangelical and the Secular. Here he was merely adopting the categories drawn up by a contemporary Evangelical author, J. W. Middelton, of a work entitled *An Ecclesiastical Memoir of the First Four Decades of the Reign of George the Third*, published in 1822.[34] Grant and Middelton belonged to different poles of the current ecclesiastical spectrum, yet largely agreed in their delineation of the theological standpoint of contemporary church parties.

[30] See, P. B. Nockles, 'Oxford, Tract 90, and the Bishops', in *John Henry Newman*, ed. D. Nicholls and F. Kerr (Bristol, 1991), pp. 38–40; Waterman, '"Via Media"', pp. 429–36.

[31] Corsi, *Science and Religion*, p. 19.

[32] Francis Blackburne, *Works, Theological and Miscellaneous* (7 vols., Cambridge, 1805), I, xxxiii.

[33] The title of a new Church of England review established in 1801, the *Orthodox Churchman's Magazine*, represented a conscious appropriation of the label by members of the High Church party. For the new review's own definition of the term, see *Orthodox Churchman's Magazine*, 5 (Nov. 1803), 301; cf. J. A. Park, *Memoirs of the Late William Stevens Esq.* (1812), pp. 20–1. Similarly, in 1817, one writer described the Caroline Divines as the 'ORTHODOX DIVINES'. R. Warner, *Old Church of England Principles* (Bath, 1817), p. vi.

[34] J. Grant, *A Summary History of the English Church* (4 vols., 1811–25), IV, 29. I am indebted to Mr Christopher Zealley for drawing my attention to this neglected source. See also J. W. Middelton, *An Ecclesiastical Memoir* (1822), p. 20.

Middelton's use of party labels in turn drew upon a very similar earlier categorization made by the Evangelical opponent of Daubeny, John Overton, as early as 1801 in his *True Churchman Ascertained.* Significantly, when Overton was criticized for using the labels 'Orthodox' and 'Evangelical' as the major terms of theological distinction in the Church,[35] he insisted that at the time they were very widely used as 'terms of distinction' and had 'use to a theologian'.[36]

One apparent source of difference that distinguished the two parties in the pre-Tractarian era was that perennial dispute over the relative merits of Arminianism and Calvinism which centred on rival interpretations of the seventeenth of the Thirty-Nine Articles, relating to the subjects of election and free will. A common ingredient of anti-Evangelical polemic from the Orthodox was that Evangelicals, while claiming to be the 'True Churchmen', were really Calvinists whose views in favour of predestination were potentially subversive of actual Church of England doctrine and practice.[37] The vigour of this debate in the 1800s and 1810s led some contemporaries to conclude that the only truly valid theological division in the Church at the time was between Arminian and Calvinist.[38] However, it needs to be emphasized that there was no automatic correlation between 'Orthodox' and 'Arminian' on the one hand, or 'Evangelical' and 'Calvinist' on the other: Arminian was even less satisfactory as shorthand for High Church, than was Calvinist for Low Church. Historically the Arminian ranks had contained many who could more properly be described as Latitudinarian or 'secular', holding lower views of both church order and the sacraments than many moderate Calvinists.[39] The Orthodox of the early nineteenth century, unlike their forebears of two centuries earlier, may have been invariably Arminian or at least anti-Calvinist, but this was by no means the exclusive ground of their High Churchmanship. In fact, Johnson Grant was able to distinguish two quite distinctive strands of response to Evangelicalism from within the Orthodox ranks, which bear out the distinction we noted above. He differentiated between 'the Arminian school', represented by such figures as Pretyman-Tomline, Marsh, Dean Kipling and Archdeacon Warner, and the more unreservedly High Church variant represented by Horsley, Daubeny and the Hackney Phalanx.[40] Of course there was overlap between the two, but, in general, the former group was more exclusively concerned with what it regarded as the 'refutation of

[35] E. Pearson, *Remarks on the Controversy . . . between the Arminian and Calvinist Ministers of the Church of England* (York, 1805), p. 24.
[36] J. Overton, *Four Letters to the Editor of the 'Christian Observer'* (York, 1805), p. 24.
[37] *Orthodox Churchman's Magazine*, 5 (1803), 183; 12 (1807), 72.
[38] Pearson, *Remarks*, pp. 6–7.
[39] H. C. Grove, *The Teaching of the Anglican Divines* (1858), pp. 6–7.
[40] Grant, *History*, IV, 99.

Calvinism', while the latter, at least in the case of Horsley, was more ready to leave the Arminian–Calvinist debate as an open question, as long as supposed Evangelical 'irregularities' over church order were corrected. It was a difference of approach which dismayed the Marsh–Tomline school, while in no way leading to a breach.

At the real root of the distinction between Orthodox and Evangelical Churchmen in the pre-Tractarian Church of England was a difference not so much over predestination and free will – there were many Evangelicals such as J. B. Sumner who were Arminian on these questions and claimed to be 'above party' – but over the relative priorities each accorded to various paths to grace and holiness in the general economy of salvation. In crude Evangelical parlance, the Orthodox were often faulted for not preaching the 'whole Gospel' or 'the peculiar doctrines of Christianity'.[41] For their part, the Orthodox sometimes faulted Evangelicals for preaching but a 'mutilated sketch'[42] of what they regarded as the true Gospel. Doctrinal differences comprised such doctrines as that of original sin, justification by faith and its relation to works and sanctification, the nature of repentance, and whether or not there was a need for a conversion experience and an indwelling of the Holy Spirit on the part of a true believer. Yet, it was not these particular doctrines *per se* but the Evangelical interpretation or gloss of them which the Orthodox tended to dispute. The Orthodox did not deny justification by faith but only what they considered the Evangelical understanding of the doctrine and some of the consequences that flowed from that understanding.[43] Thus, the Orthodox felt that Evangelicals undervalued or denied baptismal regeneration in particular, while, in general, the Evangelical stress on the value of a conversion experience ideally accompanied by powerful manifestations of the Holy Spirit was deemed ultimately to be subversive of the efficacy of sacramental grace.[44] In turn, Evangelicals reproved in equal measure the Orthodox such as Daubeny and Latitudinarians such as Hey for appearing to hold that there were two justifications, the first linked directly to baptism and the second to the final judgement.[45] In Evangelical eyes, the connecting of justification with baptism had potential Pelagian overtones. Nonetheless, the more moderate Evangelicals drew back from including the Orthodox in the general charge of Pelagianism which they made against Latitudinarian divines. As J. W. Middelton candidly allowed, the Orthodox 'upheld the Trinity against Arians; the

[41] *A Call to Unanimity in the Established Church* (1816), pp. 7–8.

[42] C. Daubeny, *A Vindication . . . of Bishop Bull* (1827), p. 2; R. Mant, *An Appeal to the Gospel* (Oxford, 1812).

[43] Grant, *History*, IV, 35.

[44] R. Laurence, *The Doctrine of the Church of England* (Oxford, 1816), pp. 28–9.

[45] J. Overton, *The True Churchman Ascertained* (York, 1801), p. 179. For the churchmanship of John Hey, Norrisian Professor at Cambridge, 1780–94, see Waterman, '"Via Media"', pp. 429–32.

Atonement against the Socinian; and the depravity of our common nature against the Pelagian'. For Middelton, the only limitations of Orthodox apologetic were that 'in stating the plan of salvation, they were not always sufficiently clear in representing repentance and faith as the conditions of the christian covenant, and obedience as the fruit or evidence of justifying faith'.[46] Misunderstandings and a certain caricaturing of each other's positions can be said to have occurred on both sides, with the Orthodox Richard Mant in particular offending Evangelical sensibilities with the vigour of his assault in the 1810s. Yet, in reality, the two sides often were closer to one another than could have seemed possible when viewed from a later, post-Tractarian context. For instance, in the pre-Tractarian era, many Evangelicals such as J. B. Sumner, in his treatise *Apostolical Preaching* in 1815, did uphold a version of baptismal regeneration. Moreover, even on the subject of eucharistic doctrine, a source of bitter strife after 1833, prior to Tractarianism something of a consensus united Orthodox and Evangelical. While some of the Orthodox adhered to the so-called 'Virtualist' interpretation that had been upheld by the Nonjurors – the most 'High Church' position in a sacramental sense – most were at one with Evangelicals in taking the so-called 'Receptionist' view as expounded by Hooker and Daniel Waterland. Receptionism entailed an acceptance of the doctrine of the Real Presence but in a strictly spiritual or 'heavenly' sense. The many Evangelicals who took this view were thereby repudiating the 'Low Church' Zwinglian idea of the eucharist as a bare memorial of Our Lord's passion which was propagated by Hoadly, Blackburne and other Latitudinarian divines.

The real thrust of the perennial Evangelical critique of contemporary preaching for its neglect of doctrinal matter and for extolling the 'all-sufficiency of mere morality' was directed not so much at the Orthodox *per se* but at the Latitudinarian and 'secular' parties in the Church of England. Though some Evangelicals placed the Orthodox in the category of divines who were 'unspiritual', others such as Middelton were more generous and distinguished the Orthodox from 'Paley and his school'.[47] One of the Orthodox whom Middelton eminently had in mind was Samuel Horsley. For all his rigid High Churchmanship, he was a particular favourite among Evangelicals and his episcopal charges in the 1790s and 1800s earned for him a degree of Evangelical respect. Horsley's openness and neutrality over the Calvinist–Arminian controversy distinguished him from Orthodox

[46] Middelton, *Memoir*, pp. 32–3.

[47] Ibid., p. 31. For pre-Tractarian High Church deference to 'Paley and his school', see Waterman, '"Via Media"', pp. 432–4. Paley himself insisted that he 'was of every party, and friends with men of all parties'. *The Works of William Paley*, ed. E. Paley (7 vols., 1825), I, 72.

divines such as Daubeny, Mant, Marsh and Tomline. Moreover, while Horsley the High Churchman might rebuke Methodism's 'disorderly zeal for the propagation of the truth', he pointedly refrained from regarding it as heterodox. Above all, he impressed Evangelicals with his view that 'an over-abundant zeal to check the frenzy of the Methodists first introduced that unscriptural language which confounds' religion and morality.[48] Such sentiments led Middelton to hail Horsley's charge of 1790 as having 'caused a greater sensation among the friends of religion, than had been produced by any similar event since the best age of the English Church'. Such was Horsley's stature in Middelton's eyes that he called him the 'Gregory Nazianzen of the English Church'.[49]

The portion of the Orthodox to whom Middelton's praise was especially directed was that of the so-called Hutchinsonians such as William Jones of Nayland, George Berkeley, Junior, George Watson, Nathaniel Wetherell and Samuel Glase, of an earlier date. The Hutchinsonians were a coterie of divines who followed the anti-Newtonian philosophical theories of the eccentric Hebraist, John Hutchinson, who died in 1727.[50] They first emerged at Oxford in the 1740s and 1750s and the Oxford link, symbolized by several of their number such as Horne and Wetherell holding high university office, was such that Edward Churton later asserted that they had as much claim to be an 'Oxford Movement' as had the later Tractarians.[51] In contrast to the Marsh–Tomline school, the Hutchinsonians combined with their 'High Church' notions on 'political theology', church authority and the sacraments, a certain mysticism, a vigorous anti-rationalism and a fervent spirituality that had affinities with that of the leaders of the Evangelical Revival.[52] Although the warmth of their early relations with Evangelicals cooled in the 1760s,[53] the Hutchinsonian High Churchmen continued to make common cause with Evangelicals in the campaign against mere moralism and ethical priorities in popular preaching.

Yet, it would be wrong to define High Churchmanship by the criteria of Hutchinsonianism alone. For as Stephen Taylor rightly argues, this would

48 Middelton, *Memoir*, p. 324.

49 Ibid., p. 328; 'Observations on Bishop Horsley's Charge' (1806), in *Miscellaneous Papers* (Hull, 1827), pp. 59–65.

50 For accounts of Hutchinsonianism, see Churton, *Watson*, I, 39ff; R. Spearman, *Life of John Hutchinson* (1765), pp. i–xiv; G. Horne, *An Apology for Certain Gentlemen in the University of Oxford* (Oxford, 1756).

51 Pusey House, Oxford, Pusey MSS: E. Churton to W. Gresley, 21 May 1846.

52 D. W. Bebbington, *Evangelicalism in Modern Britain* (1989), p. 57; A. S. Wood, *Thomas Haweis* (1957), pp. 46–7; G. H. Tavard, *The Seventeenth-Century Tradition* (Leiden, 1978), pp. 254–5. Even as late as 1833, the *Christian Observer* could devote an article to a defence of Hutchinsonianism. See *Christian Observer*, 35 (1833), 219–21; E. Sidney, *The Life of Sir Richard Hill* (1839), pp. 129–30.

53 W. Jones, *Memoir of . . . George Horne* (1795), p. 65.

mean excluding such eighteenth-century divines as Gibson, Sherlock and Secker all of whom were vigorous defenders of the rights of the Church and of episcopacy.[54] It would also mean excluding Horsley himself who opposed Hutchinsonian theories. In truth, the Hutchinsonians formed but one part of the Orthodox spectrum. Moreover, as the example of Horsley shows, within that spectrum they were not alone in evincing a spiritual temper distinct from that of Latitudinarians and more akin to that of Evangelicals. In fact, it had been a non-Hutchinsonian Orthodox, Archbishop Secker, who had been the first to lament the 'want of Evangelical preaching' in his day, becoming, in consequence, a particular favourite of Evangelicals.[55] Like them, he opposed 'the moral-philosophy preaching' characteristic of the Latitudinarian tradition. Johnson Grant admitted that the Orthodox were at one with the Latitudinarians in repudiating inward feelings of the Spirit as tests or criteria of faith, yet he nonetheless conceded that the Orthodox allowed inward feelings, which could be cultivated, an important place in the devotional life. Many divines of what he called the anti-Methodist 'Warburtonian school' such as Joseph Trapp had, he considered, sadly failed 'to distinguish between the fancies of the visionary, and that inward witness which is the blessed privilege of those who truly believe'.[56] Grant was also frankly critical of some Orthodox divinity of the Marsh–Tomline variant emanating from the anti-Calvinist controversy of the 1800s for being 'blind to the promotion of spiritual religion',[57] but commended George Nott's Bampton Lectures of 1802 for allowing spiritual 'influence its due extent, both in the understanding and on the will'.[58] Even Archdeacon Daubeny could refer positively to the religious witness of moderate Evangelicals such as William Wilberforce and Hannah More despite his sometimes keen strictures on their theological system.[59] In the preface to his *Guide to the Church*, Daubeny stressed that both he and Wilberforce 'look to the same Cross as our only hope and title to salvation'. He expressed the hope that Wilberforce might 'become the blessed instrument in God's hand of raising the dead to life, by bringing back the soul of Christianity to that body from which it has long since disappeared'.[60] Such

[54] Taylor, 'Church and State', p. 216.

[55] As John Overton put it, 'few men, it may be presumed, have worn the Mitre with more lustre than Archbishop Secker'. Overton, *The True Churchman Ascertained*, p. 36. For Overton, Secker was an 'Evangelical Divine'. Yet, Secker was often compared by contemporary Latitudinarian critics to Archbishop Laud. E.g., [F. Blackburne], *Memoirs of Thomas Hollis* (2 vols., 1780), I, 227.

[56] Grant, *History*, IV, 35; Middelton, *Memoir*, p. 30.

[57] Grant, *History*, IV, 160. [58] Ibid., p. 565.

[59] For Daubeny's strictures on Wilberforce's *Practical View*, see ESRO, Locker–Lampson Papers, B/5/20: C. Daubeny to J. Boucher, 3 Mar. 1801. For Daubeny's criticisms of Hannah More's theology, see ESRO, Locker–Lampson Papers, B/5/15: Daubeny to Boucher, 16 Apr. 1800. [60] Daubeny, *Guide to the Church*, pp. v-vi.

candid eirenicism, often obscured by the public face of the party conflict in which the Orthodox and Evangelicals later would become increasingly engaged, was a reflection of the degree of cross-fertilization and overlap that pertained in an earlier period. One could cite numerous examples of Churchmen of the 1790s, 1800s and 1810s, such as G. S. Faber and bishops such as Shute Barrington, Beilby Porteus, Thomas Burgess and George Huntingford, who cannot readily be categorized in an exclusive way. Such Churchmen could be claimed by the Evangelical and Orthodox parties alike. As Gladstone later argued, in some ways they represented something of a synthesis of elements of the two.[61]

There were also other theological ingredients in the pre-Tractarian church party consensus. Though issues of church order could be a divisive force – as in the Bible Society controversy – questions of church authority and even apostolical succession did not generally prove to be the major sources of conflict between High Churchmen and Evangelicals in the pre-Tractarian era that they were to become after 1833. Later Tractarians tended to assume that Evangelicals must be the natural allies of the Latitudinarians on matters of church polity and order, even if the two parties might widely differ in their respective notions of the nature of faith and salvation; a misconception that perhaps might be ascribed to the fact that Tractarians such as Newman tended to base their view of Evangelicalism in the 1830s on the extreme and unrepresentative element of the party in Oxford associated with H. B. Bulteel.[62] The term 'Low Church' was not levelled at Evangelicals, but strictly confined to the older Latitudinarian party associated with Hoadly.[63] If there was an epithet that some Evangelicals could accept, it was not 'Low Church' but 'moderate'.[64] For instance, in response to the *Christian Observer*'s application of 'High Church' to label his Bampton Lectures in 1807, Thomas Le Mesurier retorted that he would never have considered tarnishing Evangelicals with the label 'Low Church', which, 'as every one knows, has for many years disappeared; it did not flourish greatly even in the days of Hoadly, and seems to have expired with Archdeacon Blackburne'.[65]

[61] W. E. Gladstone, *Gleanings of Past Years* (7 vols., 1879), VII, 216; cf. B. Hilton, *The Age of Atonement* (Cambridge, 1988), pp. 26–31.

[62] G. Carter, 'Evangelical Seceders from the Church of England, *c.*1800–50', DPhil dissertation, University of Oxford, 1990, pp. 385–7.

[63] J. Gascoigne, 'Anglican Latitudinarianism and Political Radicalism in the Late Eighteenth Century', *History*, 71 (1986), 24.

[64] *Christian Observer*, 3 (Nov. 1804), 680; 6 (Oct. 1807), 677. I am grateful to Dr Grayson Carter for this reference.

[65] Le Mesurier, *Schism*, p. 431. In 1799, the High Churchman Jonathan Boucher could maintain that 'Hoadlyite' principles had 'now sunk into very general dis-esteem'. *Anti-Jacobin Review*, 4 (Nov. 1799), 253. Significantly, even that so-called 'Latitudinarian', Richard Watson, could insist in 1785, that he had 'no regard for Latitudinarian principles'. *A Collection of Theological Tracts*, ed. R. Watson (6 vols., Cambridge, 1785), I, xvi.

Prior to the rise of Tractarianism, Evangelicals could be as anti-'Low Church' in the above sense as any High Churchman. For instance, in 1820, the Evangelical Daniel Wilson insisted that a firm belief in 'the authority and purity of our national church' by which he included episcopal order and valid ministry, was a view common to both Evangelical and Orthodox alike.[66] Sometimes it is true that exception was taken to the full *jure divino* episcopal edifice erected by divines of the Daubeny school,[67] but it is noteworthy that the writings of Jones of Nayland, which the *Christian Observer* commended as worthy of instruction in 1804, were precisely those on the constitution of the Church. Moreover, even the bitter controversy involving Daubeny on the one hand and Overton and Sir Richard Hill on the other between 1798 and 1805 focused much more on issues such as grace, free will and justification than on church order and authority. Again, comparisons with the Tractarian era are instructive. The *Christian Observer* of the 1800s actually had sought to mediate and appear even-handed in this controversy. Its successor of the 1830s was notably more partisan and antipathetic to the appearance of High Church claims. The controversy of the 1800s had been mainly confined to but a small portion of the whole range of doctrines in dispute in the 1830s. Above all, the difference in position which Evangelicals and especially the *Christian Observer* itself took up in the respective controversies is significant. For all Daubeny's taunts, not only the *Christian Observer* but even Overton and Hill had been eager not to get drawn into a debate over church polity and authority which was considered quite peripheral, if not irrelevant, to Evangelical objections to what Overton called 'Daubenism'.[68] Prior to 1833, one can even find examples of Evangelicals themselves being awarded the soubriquet of 'High Church'. For instance, in 1827, a visiting American Churchman described some Anglican Evangelicals such as Bishop Ryder as 'High Churchmen'.[69] It was only from the 1840s onwards that Evangelicals came to acquire the label 'Low Church', and then mainly from Tractarian opponents, though it must be said that by that date they did not appear always to resent it; one of its earliest uses in this sense dates from 1835, when an Evangelical pamphleteer appeared proud to describe himself by this title.[70]

[66] Quoted in J. Bateman, *Life of Daniel Wilson* (2 vols., 1860), I, 205–6.

[67] R. Hill, *Reformation-Truth Restored* (1800), pp. 15–20; Middelton, *Memoir*, pp. 31–2.

[68] Overton, *Four Letters*, p. 49; R. Hill, *An Apology for Brotherly Love* (1798), p. 190.

[69] *An Address to Protestant Episcopalians* (New York, 1827), pp. 1, 3–4.

[70] *An Address to the . . . Archbishops and Bishops . . . on the Internal Discipline of the Church of England* (1835). An early example of an Evangelical being called a 'Low Churchman' was W. F. Hook's designation of Charles Sumner as one in 1826. W. R. Stephens, *The Life and Letters of Walter Farquhar Hook* (2 vols., 1878), I, 109. For discussion of the historical distinction between 'Evangelical' and 'Low Church' and the later, apparent fusion of the two, see, P. Toon, *Evangelical Theology 1833–56* (1979), pp. 207–9.

When compared to the well-known, often bitter polarization within the Church of England which the Oxford Movement, and the reaction to it, helped engender during the later 1830s and 1840s, the pre-Tractarian era indeed appears to exemplify a Church that was characterized by relative internal harmony in spite of some latent theological differences. Even the undoubtedly warm disputes between Arminian and Calvinist Churchmen over the Seventeenth Article, and between Orthodox and Evangelical over baptismal regeneration as well as the merits or otherwise of the Bible Society, apparently did little to destroy this harmony. The exceptions seemed to prove the rule. For instance, Bishop Marsh stirred up bitter controversy by drawing up his notorious eighty-seven questions for ordination candidates, which were clearly designed to identify and weed out Calvinists. Yet, in the 1820s, the drastic polarization and turmoil that were to characterize reactions to the Gorham Judgement in 1850[71] were averted. Above all, in the 1820s the episcopal bench, which was broadly identified with the Orthodox school of churchmanship, managed to restrain any overt centrifugal pressures, whatever private misgivings individual bishops may have had about Marsh's method of proceeding. Significantly, some Orthodox Churchmen looking back with nostalgia to this period from the very different vantage-point of the 1850s drew an interesting parallel between the way in which the two theological disputes, involving Marsh in 1821 and Phillpotts in 1850,[72] were resolved.

In the pre-Tractarian era, the rival party allegiances of Orthodox and Evangelical were reflected in rival organizational loyalties: in the case of the Orthodox, the SPCK, in the case of Evangelicals, the CMS. Yet, the pre-Tractarian Church of England, while encompassing different parties, was not riddled with the 'mutual suspicion, and an apartheid of personalities, theological colleges, journals and publishing imprints' which characterized the post-Tractarian Church.[73] On occasions, the Orthodox and Evangelicals could act together in the closest harmony. Joanna Innes has shown how both Claphamite Evangelicals and the High Churchmen of Hackney could co-operate in the Proclamation Society in the 1800s. She suggests that the common social and cultural backgrounds of both sets of rival metropolitan Churchmen was not without significance here.[74]

Was the relative openness of pre-Tractarian High Churchmen to alliances and co-operation with moderate Evangelical as well as moderate 'liberal' Churchmen fortuitous, the mere accidental result of the family or

[71] *The Thirty Years Conflict in the Church of England* (1855), p. iii.

[72] *Quarterly Review*, 101 (Apr. 1857), 552; cf. *Edinburgh Review*, 92 (1850), 266.

[73] Avis, *Anglicanism*, p. 86.

[74] J. Innes, 'Politics and Morals. The Reformation of Manners Movement in Later Eighteenth-Century England', in *The Transformation of Political Culture*, ed. E. Hellmuth (Oxford, 1990), pp. 102–3.

patronage networks recently explored by Clive Dewey? Or did it signify something deeper; a blurring of the theological edges, a lack of ideological coherence on the part of High Churchmanship prior to 1833? Corsi suggests both explanations,[75] while the present author suggests elsewhere that the old High Churchmen adhered more faithfully to the more liberal theological method of appealing to Scripture and reason as well as Tradition characteristic of the Caroline Divines, than did Newman and the Tractarians.[76] Moreover, this method also characterized the theological approach of the Oriel Noetics. It was only from a later Tractarian perspective that the connexion of R. D. Hampden with High Churchmen in the 1820s could appear embarrassing and puzzling. Such linkages reveal the complexity of pre-Tractarian High Church alignments before party positions had solidified into mutual exclusion.

Prior to 1833, common ground uniting not only High Churchmen and Noetics but also Evangelicals was provided by the overarching importance attached to the constitution in church and state. As J. C. D. Clark demonstrates, the rationale for establishment in the 1820s continued to have a religious rather than a secular basis.[77] Lord Eldon's aphorism that the purpose of establishment was to make the state religious and not the Church secular summed up a widespread viewpoint. The Hutchinsonians and Hackney school appealed to patristic testimony in favour of the divine sanction of establishment no less than in favour of episcopacy.[78] Similarly, for Evangelicals, scriptural testimony rather than utilitarian considerations was the paramount staple of argument. It was because the 'Protestant Constitution' represented a religious as well as political standard that it was the Orthodox in the Oxford of the 1820s who were in the forefront of the opposition to Catholic Emancipation. Moreover, when the University of Oxford rejected Sir Robert Peel as its MP in 1829 after his *volte-face* over Emancipation, it was to Sir Robert Inglis, a Tory but reputedly a doctrinal Evangelical, to whom the Orthodox majority eagerly turned.[79] Here was apparent confirmation that consistency in constitutional principles could

[75] Corsi, *Science and Religion*, pp. 22, 24, 34–5; cf. Dewey, *Passing of Barchester*, chs. 8–9.

[76] Avis, *Anglicanism*, pp. 276–8; S.W. Sykes, 'Newman, Anglicanism and the Fundamentals', in *Newman after a Hundred Years*, ed. I. Ker and A. G. Hill (1990), pp. 363, 365–6; Varley, *Van Mildert*, pp. 60–1; Nockles, 'Oxford, Tract 90, and the Bishops', pp. 39–40.

[77] Clark, *English Society*, pp. 387–93. Robert Hole exaggerates the degree to which the ideological *raison d'être* of the confessional state was undermined prior to the final removal of the legislative props underpinning it between 1828 and 1833. *Pulpits, Politics and Public Order*, p. 267.

[78] See G. Horne, 'A charge intended to have been delivered to the clergy of Norwich' (1792), in *The Works of George Horne*, ed. W. Jones (2nd edn, 4 vols., 1818), IV, 528–9.

[79] On Inglis's Evangelical credentials, see J. Wolffe, *The Protestant Crusade in Great Britain 1829–60* (Oxford, 1991), p. 68 n. 14.

offset doctrinal differences, and that 'the confessional state was not the property of one piety alone'.[80] Thus, while theological differences did distinguish church parties, prior to 1829 the Protestant constitution acted as a ballast and guarantor of a certain internal cohesion within the Church of England.

For Orthodox Churchmen living into the troubled era of the Oxford Movement, the apparent loss of an earlier relative internal harmony was a cause for lament. Whereas as late as the 1820s the Orthodox seemed to be centre-stage in the counsels of church and state, by the 1840s they felt themselves becoming marginalized by rival extremes within the Church. Henry Rose later argued that an Orthodox revival which his more famous brother, Hugh James Rose, first launched from Cambridge in the 1820s had been designed to strengthen internal unity. In contrast, the Oxford Movement became a source of division.[81] Moreover, the Orthodox continued to maintain that they had never been party men in the way that Evangelicals had been and the Tractarians would become. It was an attitude well illustrated by a telling comment of Joshua Watson: 'Alas! I fear that schools and parties will ever be the same, whether led by a Newman or a Simeon.'[82]

Nonetheless, real conflict and division did coexist alongside the relative internal harmony characteristic of the pre-Tractarian Church of England. The reaction to the French Revolution initially helped bolster a revival of High Church principles as well as cement Evangelical and Orthodox into a common political bond. Yet this bond was fragile. The anti-Jacobin mania that took hold of some of the Orthodox led many to look with increasing alarm on the irregularity of some Evangelicals which seemed not only destructive of church order but also potentially politically subversive.[83] This attitude was exemplified by John Randolph, who complained in 1802 of Evangelicals, 'that while they bring everything within private suggestion, they encourage in Religion the very principle, which in Politics has proved so fatal to the peace and good government of states; being no other than giving the reins to private opinion, in opposition to public authority'.[84]

In the 1790s, there was a manifestly apocalyptic quality not only to

[80] J. C. D. Clark, 'England's Ancien Regime as a Confessional State', *Albion*, 21 (1989), 461 n. 42.

[81] [H.J. Rose], 'Ecclesiastical History from A.D. 1700 to A.D. 1858. The Church of England', section ii, 'From A.D. 1815 to A.D. 1858' in *Encyclopaedia Metropolitana* (1858), XL, 379. I am indebted to Mr Christopher Zealley for this reference. See also J. W. Burgon, 'Hugh James Rose', in *Lives of Twelve Good Men* (2 vols., 1888), pp. 116–283.

[82] Marychurch, Torquay (private), M. Watson, MS 'Reminiscences', fo. 105 [25 Feb. 1843].

[83] S. Gilley, 'John Keble and the Victorian Churching of Romanticism', in *An Infinite Variety*, ed. J. R. Watson (1983), p. 228.

[84] J. Randolph, *A Charge Delivered to the Clergy of the Diocese of Oxford* (Oxford, 1802), p. 11.

Evangelical but even to some High Church rhetoric, as in the case of Jones of Nayland's and Horsley's sermons.[85] However, a consequence of the excesses of popular millenarianism in the era of the French Revolution was that appeals to the imagination and emotions among many of the Orthodox became increasingly suspect, thereby enhancing any tendencies towards a 'high and dry' mentality. Even some of the Hackney Phalanx were not immune from this trend.[86] In turn, this began to foster a narrower, harsh edge and tone to the High Churchmanship of even some of the 'Phalanx' after about 1805 which contrasts with the relative openness and warmth of their 'Hutchinsonian' forebears in the second half of the previous century. Relations between some of the Orthodox and Evangelicals began to become less cordial. Apart from some notable exceptions, such as Bishop Jebb, Alexander Knox and Oxford's leading High Churchman, Charles Ogilvie,[87] the striking eirenicism towards Evangelicalism and even Calvinism that had been displayed by such figures as Horne and Horsley was abandoned. Indeed it was precisely here that the loss of Horsley who died in 1806 was to be most keenly felt. Elizabeth Varley has suggested that the tenor and character of the Orthodox party thereafter suffered as a consequence, for Horsley was a great reconciler as well as a stout defender of High Church principles.[88] His real hope had been to encourage a realignment of High Church episcopal claims and sacramental theology on the one hand, with a doctrinal 'Evangelicalism' that could embrace even moderate Calvinism on the other: an essentially pre-Laudian alliance that had characterized early seventeenth-century divines of the school of Ussher, Davenant, Carleton, Jackson and Hall, but which at least since 1662 had scarcely again been realized. Horsley was a firm advocate of apostolical succession[89] and had a preference for the more 'catholic' 1549 Prayer Book;[90] in such ways he was a true forebear of Tractarianism. At the same time, Horsley's eirenic and sympathetic understanding of the distinctive emphases of Evangelical and Methodist spirituality, while arguably later to

[85] W. H. Oliver, *Prophets and Millenialists* (Auckland, 1978), pp. 50–1; Hole, *Pulpits, Politics and Public Order*, pp. 170–2.

[86] Gilley, 'Keble', p. 229. In this context, the gradual abandonment of Hutchinsonianism by the leaders of the Hackney Phalanx may be significant. Corsi, *Science and Religion*, p. 76.

[87] *Thirty Years Correspondence between John Jebb and Alexander Knox*, ed. C. Forster (2nd edn, 1836), pp. 539–40; A. Knox, 'On the Situation and Prospects of the Established Church' (1816), in *Remains of Alexander Knox* (2 vols., 1834), I, 58; Bodl., MS Eng. Lett. d. 124, fos. 103–4: H. More to C. A. Ogilvie, 2 Apr. 1816.

[88] Varley, *Van Mildert*, p. 63; F. C. Mather, *High Church Prophet. Bishop Samuel Horsley (1733–1806) and the Caroline Tradition in the Late Georgian Church* (Oxford, 1992).

[89] *Speeches in Parliament of Samuel Horsley* (2 vols., 1813), II, 156–9.

[90] Horsley 'long lamented the alterations that were made in 1552, to humour those who, we find in experience, never will be satisfied'. Quoted in *Christian Remembrancer*, 7 (Jan. 1844), 73.

be shared by Pusey, was yet sadly lacking as a guiding principle in the era of the Gorham controversy.

Significantly, some Orthodox Churchmen became increasingly out of tune with Horsley's attitude of openness towards and solidarity with Evangelicals.[91] An example of a narrower attitude is provided by Thomas Sikes in a private, ill-tempered quarrel with the eirenic and mild-mannered Beilby Porteus, bishop of London, in 1806. Sikes sharply criticized Porteus for his patronage of the Bible Society and was only with difficulty dissuaded from publishing his critique. A manuscript record of the exchanges between the two reveals Sikes to have been obsessed with the bogey of a 'Puritan' conspiracy and a recurrence of the events of 1649. Sikes was not conciliated by Porteus's reminder as to the number of High Churchmen, many associated with the Hackney Phalanx, whom he had promoted in the diocese, nor even his assurance of his own anti-Calvinism. As Sikes sternly recorded, the Bishop 'is hostile to Calvinism as an opinion, but dreads it not, as that which once pulled down our church and state'.[92] Indeed, a sweeping characterization of Evangelicals as direct descendants of seventeenth-century Puritans became an increasing commonplace of 'Arminian' Orthodox apologetic from the 1800s onwards; a charge made regardless of the historical fact that the original episcopal-inspired opposition to historic Puritanism had emanated from divines who were themselves manifestly Calvinist.[93]

When the eirenic High Churchman, John Jebb, visited his Hackney friends and apparent allies in 1820 he was struck by what he perceived as their narrowness and rigidity.[94] In fact, some of the private correspondence of various members of the 'Phalanx' reveals an ever-growing sensitivity to a perceived political threat posed by Evangelical organizations. These anxieties were greatly accentuated by the 'Western Schism' of a group of Evangelicals. In 1817 the seceders and the Evangelical-inspired Bath Church Missionary Society were assailed by the Orthodox Churchman Richard Warner. Together with Josiah Thomas, archdeacon of Bath,

[91] T. Kipling, *The Articles of the Church of England* (1802), pp. 69–71.

[92] 'March 3, 1806' Manuscript 'Minutes of a Conversation with Bishop Porteus on his own invitation, occasioned by the suppression of the foregoing Pamphlet' [in Thomas Sikes's hand], Appended to [T. Sikes], *An Humble Remonstrance to the Lord Bishop of London* (1806).

[93] A. H. Kenney, *Principles and Practices of Pretended Reformers* (1819), p. 412. Evangelicals complained that the confounding of Calvinists with Puritans represented a gross historical fallacy deriving from partisan High Church writers such as Peter Heylin and Jeremy Collier. See *Christian Observer*, 3 (July 1804), 429; G. S. Faber, *Thoughts on the Calvinistic and Arminian Controversy* (1804), p. 42.

[94] Bodl., MS Eng. Lett. d. 123, fo. 141: J. Jebb to C. A. Ogilvie, 16 June 1820; *Thirty Years Correspondence*, ed. Forster, II, 4.

Warner called for the disbandment of the Society by direct episcopal intervention.[95] In fact, the language of some of the Orthodox against Evangelicals over this episode bordered on the warlike, and some did come close to supporting a policy, in general not taken up, of seeking to drive Evangelicals out of the Church of England.[96] Here at least were some similarities to the later Gorham affair, with the notable difference that ecclesiastical politics rather than doctrine was at stake in 1817. Evangelicals were even accused of making 'religion a cloak for ambition; and under a pretence of inculcating the pure and undefiled doctrines of Christ, they seek only the advancement of their fortune, and the increase of their power'.[97] Of course, this was language which later Tractarian opponents of Evangelicalism would hardly have resorted to. Evangelicalism might have been assailed by Tractarians as doctrinal heresy as in the Gorham affair but not as a political conspiracy with the good faith of its adherents malignantly traduced. The contrast shows that the apparently greater doctrinal fluidity and indistinctness of the pre-Tractarian Church of England was not always accompanied by a greater genuine charity or sense of fair dealing in controversial debate. It was a contrast generously conceded by the sternest Evangelical critics of the Tractarians.

For a time, in the wake of the Bath CMS affair, faction and discord within the Church did seem poised to overturn any residual harmony between the rival parties even if a fragile doctrinal consensus remained largely unimpaired. Any preferment granted to Evangelicals appeared to be perceived by some of the Orthodox as a direct challenge to their own standing. For instance, Bishop Marsh interpreted the preferment of the Evangelical Daniel Wilson to a prebend at Rochester in 1824 as an immediate sign 'that the principles, which overturned the Established Church in the time of Charles I have now gained so complete an ascendancy, that further resistance is useless'.[98] For their part, some Evangelicals were already beginning to indulge in the harsher invective against the Orthodox on theological grounds that would become commonplace in the era of the Oxford Movement: thus, in 1817 the *Christian Observer* complained that 'some of the worst errors of popery' were being advocated by dignitaries of the Church of England.[99] Indeed, party strife had become

[95] Bodl., MS Eng. Lett. c. 789, fos. 89, 85: J. Thomas to H. H. Norris, 22 Dec. 1817, J. H. Spry to H. H. Norris, 12 Dec. 1817; *A Second Protest against the Church Missionary Society* (Bath, 1818).

[96] R. Warner, *A Letter to the ... Bishop of Gloucester* (1818), p. 14.

[97] *A Defence of the Protest of Archdeacon Thomas* (Bristol [1818]), p. 4; W. B. Whithead, *A Letter to Daniel Wilson* (Bath, 1818), p. 31; *Orthodox Churchman's Magazine*, 5 (Sept. 1803), 182.

[98] Bodl., MS Eng. Lett. c. 789, fos. 126, 106: H. Marsh to H. H. Norris, 31 July 1824, W. Johnson to H. H. Norris, 27 Nov. 1822.

[99] *Christian Observer*, 16 (1817), vi.

such that the elder Rennell could liken the state of religious parties in the Church in 1817 to the description of Roman politics given by Bolingbroke in his *Patriot King*.[100]

Thus, relations between the Orthodox and Evangelicals had begun to sour long before the rise of Tractarianism. There were also tensions in the relationship between the Hackney Phalanx and the Oriel Noetics. If there did appear to be a blurring of theological differences between 'High Church' and 'liberal' Churchmen in the 1820s, this can partly be explained by recognizing that Noetics such as Baden Powell and Hampden, still less the moderate High Church or Orthodox, Copleston and Hawkins, were not the theological liberals[101] that the former at least came to be regarded as in the 1830s. Polarization took place in the 1830s and an earlier doctrinal consensus was destroyed, but, as Corsi acknowledges, this was not a one-sided process. For if the future Tractarians moved in one direction after the cathartic experience of the Peel election in 1829, some of the Noetics moved no less far in another. After 1829, according to Henry Wilberforce, there was widely attributed to the influence of Richard Whately 'a whole new turn to what had formerly been called the Oriel school, a turn towards rationalism'.[102] The operative word here is 'new'. Yet, there had already been private rumblings of discontent at the direction of Noetic philosophizing among the Hackney Phalanx from a somewhat earlier date. Thus, by 1829 John Hume Spry was declaring, 'I am sick of Oriel, and its writers'. The publications of Whately containing 'his sophistical attempts to destroy the Christian Priesthood' were singled out for censure. Significantly, Spry condemned Whately 'as the leader, and mouthpiece, and indefatigable supporter of a party in the Church, which promises to do more harm to her doctrine and discipline than all the Calvinism, or Dissent, or Evangelism of the last century had effected'.[103] It is in this climate that the rise of Tractarianism and the initial welcome given it by the Orthodox needs to be understood.

The argument that Tractarianism provoked party strife from the mid-1830s and destroyed residual elements of an earlier doctrinal consensus can be broadly accepted but requires qualification. The underlying trend towards greater internal party division and religious pluralism has been shown to have been discernible for at least twenty years prior to 1833. Yet clear differences separate the climate of the Church of England before and after the rise of Tractarianism. Prior to 1833, it was often personality and

[100] Bodl., MS Eng. Lett. c. 789, fo. 83: T. Rennell (Sen.) to H. H. Norris, 8 Nov. 1817.

[101] See P. B. Nockles, 'An Academic Counter-Revolution: Newman and Tractarian Oxford's Idea of a University', *History of Universities*, 10 (1991), 50 nn. 44, 48, 131.

[102] [H. Wilberforce], 'Dr Hampden and Anglicanism', in *Dublin Review*, 17 (July 1871), 72–3.

[103] Bodl., MS Eng. Lett. c. 789, fos. 200–1: J. H. Spry to H. H. Norris, 10 Dec. 1829.

social connexions as much as 'party' allegiance to a set of distinct doctrinal principles that dictated the attitude a particular Churchman might adopt on a question, as in the case of the patronage of the Bible Society by the non-Evangelical Bishops Burgess and Porteus. Even the Hackney Phalanx itself owed its sense of party cohesion more to the ties of location, family and friendship than to any absolute theological unanimity. Certainly, personality rather than party label often determined whether an Orthodox Churchman adopted an eirenic or a confrontational stance in dealings with Evangelical brethren. Sometimes, it was individuals whose High Churchmanship in the sacramental sense was the most advanced such as Bishop Jebb or his friend Alexander Knox who could be the most eirenic towards Evangelicals, while Orthodox Churchmen of the so-called 'high and dry' variant, often notorious for the vigour of their anti-Calvinism, could be the most confrontational and intolerant. Thus, while party concerns were important, they could always be offset by pastoral concerns or the vagaries of temperament.

After 1833 the Tractarians highlighted in a provocative way theological issues that had often lain dormant. They thereby forced Churchmen to take sides, and not only to adopt a more rigidly dogmatic position, but also to face up to the implications of doctrines hitherto largely taken for granted. It was a process well portrayed by a perceptive writer in the *Quarterly Review* in 1858, who made clear that while the divisions between High Church and Low Church were by no means the product of the Oxford Movement, yet prior to 1833 they had tended to be 'a matter of feeling much more than of reasoning'. The writer argued that Tractarianism solidified pre-existing party divisions, but at the same time encouraged many who had been hitherto High Church 'in sentiment' or on primarily constitutional grounds to embrace a more theologically systematic and sacramental form of High Churchmanship.[104] It could be maintained that the crucial figure of Henry Phillpotts whose active ecclesiastical career spanned the period from the early 1800s till the late 1860s represented an example of this trend. One can discern an evolution in the character of Phillpotts's High Churchmanship. Phillpotts, the Protestant constitutionalist assailant of Roman Catholic political claims in the 1820s, could in his *Letters to Charles Butler* dismiss the 1549 Prayer Book which was a favourite of many old High Churchmen as well as the early Tractarians as 'an order composed by Cranmer, for which we are no more responsible than for any thing in your missal'.[105] As late as 1833, Phillpotts could find no ground of theological fault with Methodism.[106] Yet, in 1850 Phillpotts the sacerdotalist combatant in the

[104] *Quarterly Review*, 104 (July 1858), 155.
[105] H. Phillpotts, *Letters to Charles Butler* (1825), pp. 207–8.
[106] Idem, *A Charge to the Clergy of Exeter* (London, 1833), p. 69.

Gorham controversy struck a somewhat different note. Newman noted the apparent change, as did Phillpotts's Evangelical critics in the Gorham affair. One writer later even described Phillpotts 'as a renegade from political Protestantism to the side of the reaction Romewards'.[107] In reality, the differences between the earlier and later Phillpotts represented development and modification, a new tone in response to altered circumstances rather than any sudden *volte-face*. Elements of ideological continuity persisted. In no meaningful sense can the later Phillpotts be described as a 'Tractarian'.[108] In a similar way, a distinction can be drawn even between the pre-Tractarian and Tractarian John Keble. Of course, prior to 1833, politically and ecclesiastically Keble was a High Churchman, but it was only after 1833 that aspects of his hierarchical and sacramental theology were developed; a development which, as the present author has explained elsewhere, represented a divergence from the older High Churchmanship.[109]

Yet, it is possible to exaggerate the intensity of post-Tractarian church party divisions, as some later writers pointed out.[110] For instance, the Hampden controversy in 1836 showed that an alliance between High Churchmen and Evangelicals could still be reactivated even in the Tractarian era to meet a particular danger from another quarter. Some recent scholarship has also qualified the perception of the post-1833 era as one of unrelieved party warfare in other ways. H. C. G. Matthew has demonstrated how the theological disputes that divided the Church in the 1840s were offset by Churchmen of various parties coming together on the principle of 'union of action'.[111] Similarly, at the administrative level, Arthur Burns has shown how an Orthodox-inspired revival of various diocesan structures acted as a brake upon centrifugal forces.[112]

It was partly altered political circumstances that provided the conditions for the theological polarization that attended the rise of Tractarianism. If the external political and military threat from France between 1789 and 1815 helped foster a degree of unity in Church as well as state, the logic of political development after 1828 was to engender division in matters

[107] J. B. Heard, *National Christianity or Caesarism or Clericalism* (1877), pp. 231–2. See *Letters and Correspondence of John Henry Newman*, ed. A. Mozley (2 vols., 1891), I, 222.

[108] J. A. Thurmer, 'Henry of Exeter and the Later Tractarians', *Southern History*, 5 (1983), 210–12. I have benefited here from discussions with Dr David Maskell and Dr Grayson Carter.

[109] Nockles, 'Continuity and Change', esp. Conclusion.

[110] A. W. Haddan, 'On Party Spirit in the English Church' [*Guardian*, 10 April 1861], in *Remains of Arthur West Haddan*, ed. A. P. Forbes (Oxford, 1876), pp. 478–9; E.H. Browne, *The Position and Parties of the English Church* (1875), pp. 58–9.

[111] H. C. G. Matthew, 'Noetics, Tractarians, and the Reform of the University of Oxford in the Nineteenth Century', *History of Universities*, 9 (1990), 200.

[112] A. Burns, 'The Diocesan Revival in the Church of England, *c*.1825–65', DPhil dissertation, University of Oxford, 1990, p. 315.

ecclesiastical. In 1833, there was a new enemy which the pre-Tractarian Church of England had not had to face – a Whig government, bent on state interference in the Church's spiritual affairs. In itself, this helped shape the ensuing controversy in new ways. For once the *ancien régime* in church and state had been overturned, it was that much easier for Churchmen to transcend party politics and for certain intrinsic elements of High Churchmanship to reveal themselves more fully. It was in this way that prominent Protestant High Churchmen such as Henry Phillpotts gave the appearance of abandoning the old political or constitutional ground of their churchmanship after about 1830 in a way parallel to but separate from the line propagated by the Tractarians from 1833 onwards. As J. B. Heard, a Nonconformist writer put it, royal support was 'seen to fail', so Phillpotts 'and others of his school began to look out for a fresh support for the tottering Church Establishment. They sought it in Church principles, and where they sought for it they found it.'[113] There is a certain truth in this, though the writer overlooked the extent to which Phillpotts and others of his school could combine *jure divino* church principles alongside their Protestant constitutionalism. Nonetheless, the former were given a more exclusive prominence and took on a new significance once the previous political props of church defence proved to be inadequate. Theological development ensued and differences, which had hitherto been latent, came to the surface. Thus, while initial unity was fostered by a rallying to the cry of 'the Church in danger' in the period from 1829 till 1833, before long this gave way to a theological disintegration that matched the political disintegration. For while many who could be classed as 'Orthodox' warmly supported the Tractarians and stressed the undoubted lines of theological continuity with the tradition which they represented, others of the same school, such as Godfrey Faussett who was regarded as an extreme High Churchman in the 1820s, often citing the same authorities, made some of the telling and damaging critiques of Tractarianism. Indeed, some divines under the 'Orthodox' umbrella appealed to the High Church school of Jones of Nayland, Archdeacon Daubeny and Bishops Mant and Van Mildert in their very repudiation of Tractarian claims.[114]

The pre-Tractarian Church of England might be presented as something of a calm before the storm, with differences held in check. Yet, the calm was uneasy. The Tractarians sharpened a sense of party identity in the Church of England but they did not create it. The forces unleashed by the whirlwind of Tractarianism completed a process that had already begun. 1833 did represent something of a landmark, not least because Tractarianism in time

[113] Heard, *National Christianity*, p. 232.

[114] [G. Townsend], *A Few Remarks on the Idolatrous Tendency of Some Parts of the Oxford Tracts* (1839), p. 8.

came to diverge in theologically significant ways from the older 'Orthodox' tradition. Nonetheless, the ultimate significance of 1833 can and has been exaggerated. Tractarian historiography has ensured that the real continuity and vitality of the tradition upheld by the 'Orthodox' over the preceding seventy-five years, in spite of variations, weaknesses and even apparent contradictions, has been for too long overlooked or underestimated. Mark Pattison's pertinent complaint in 1860 against the High Churchman of the day, that in 'constructing his "Catenae Patrum" he closes his list with Waterland or Brett, and leaps at once to 1833', remains a valid criticism. For, as Pattison reminded Victorian High Churchmen, 'the history of a party may be written on the theory of periodical occultation; but he who wishes to trace the descent of religious thought, and the practical working of religious ideas, must follow these through all the phases they have actually assumed'.[115]

[115] M. Pattison, 'Tendencies of Religious Thought in England, 1688–1750', in *Essays and Reviews* (1860), p. 255.

Index